To Joan, who understands;
and Anne, and the Luck of the Irish;
and Herb, who is always there

A Time of Paradox
America since 1890

GLEN JEANSONNE

WITH DAVID LUHRSSEN

ROWMAN & LITTLEFIELD PUBLISHERS, INC.
Lanham • Boulder • New York • Toronto • Oxford

ROWMAN & LITTLEFIELD PUBLISHERS, INC.

Acquiring Editor: Laura Roberts Gottlieb
Developmental Editor: Ann Grogg
Production Editor: Terry Fischer
Photo Editor: Andrew Boney
Typesetter: Andrea Reider

Published in the United States of America
by Rowman & Littlefield Publishers, Inc.
A wholly owned subsidary of The Rowman & Littlefield Publishing Group, Inc.
4501 Forbes Boulevard, Suite 200, Lanham, Maryland 20706
www.rowmanlittlefield.com

PO Box 317
Oxford
OX2 9RU, UK

British Library Cataloguing in Publication Information Available

Library of Congress Cataloging-in-Publication Data

Jeansonne, Glen, 1946–
  A time of paradox : America since 1890 / Glen Jeansonne with
David Luhrssen.
    p. cm.
  Includes bibliographical references and index.
  ISBN 0-7425-3376-X (cloth : alk. paper) —
  ISBN 0-7425-3377-8 (pbk. : alk. paper)
    1. United States—History—20th century. 2. United States—History—
20th century—Biography. 3. United States—Civilization—20th century.
I. Luhrssen, David. II. Title.
E741.J43 2005
973.91—dc22   2005029323

Printed in the United States of America

♾™ The paper used in this publication meets the minimum requirements of
American National Standard for Information Sciences—Permanence of Paper
for Printed Library Materials, ANSI/NISO Z39.48-1992.

Contents

PART II
An Era of Trial and Triumph, 1920–1945

PART III
An Era of Uncertainty, 1945–1968

PART IV
An Era of Diversity, since 1969

Preface

THE HISTORY OF *A Time of Paradox* is a story of my own intellectual journey. The research consumed ten years and the writing went through five drafts under nine editors at three publishers. The actual writing of the final version, however, took only a few months.

The trouble with the book all along was that it lacked a message, and, because the message was not in me, I could not put it into the book. I could not have written it at any time other than when I did. To her credit, Laura Roberts Gottlieb of Rowman & Littlefield, the last in a long line of editors, let me write the kind of book I had wanted to write all along. The original idea, developed by me and Bruce Borland of HarperCollins, was for a book that could be used as a textbook that would anticipate a new breaking point in the American history survey course, but would also appeal to a trade audience. It is deliberately more personal, speculative, and provocative than most textbooks, yet it includes the essential facts and is organized so that it can be used, either as a twentieth-century textbook, or in a survey course. It will also be published in two volumes, 1890–1945 and 1945–present.

A Time of Paradox has both a theme and a message. The theme is self-evident: The period covered was a time of contradiction and irony, in other words, paradox, similar to the time Charles Dickens described as a glass half-empty and half-full. Like the time of Dickens it was a combination of euphoria, tragedy, reason, and chaos. Who would have imagined that a man in a wheelchair would be elected president; that his successor would engineer the biggest political upset of the twentieth century; that when a tenth planet was discovered in our solar system it was not even front-page news in many of the nation's newspapers—the bigger irony being that the local always appeared more important than the cosmic. In another significant paradox, in the twentieth century as at Valley Forge in the eighteenth century, World War II was both America's darkest moment and its finest hour. In the Time of Paradox the human condition never seemed more poignant; much was accomplished and much was lost. We created the capacity to destroy our world in a thermonuclear holocaust and resisted the temptation. This is the epoch's greatest accomplishment.

I employ the word "paradox" in a metaphorical rather than in a literal sense. It is not a dictionary definition but can mean, in this context, irony, contradiction, a thing that seems to be what it is not, an unlikely event, or an oxymoron.

The message of *A Time of Paradox* is not quite so obvious. It is subtler and potentially more important, yet it cannot be summed up in a byte and might resonate differently with individual readers. It is expressed most clearly in the prologue and the epilogue and, to a lesser extent, in the prologues to the individual eras and the conclusions to the chapters within those eras.

Whether one reads *A Time of Paradox* as a scholar, a student, or a general reader, I hope it brings them pleasure as well as knowledge. The facts might be forgotten within a few years or submerged in the subconscious. The message in the metaphors might stick longer. Further, I have proceeded on the premise that history is a story about people much like ourselves and that when we read or write it we hold up a mirror to ourselves. People feel as well as think and *A Time of Paradox* is meant to appeal to feelings as well as to the intellect. The residue of the feelings will probably outlast the residue of the facts.

In addition, I believe the best guide to understanding history lies not in elaborate paradigms but in experience and common sense. There are definite patterns in history, but their origins and the way they emerge results from a mixture of factors, some obvious, some obscure, and some beyond human understanding. Though I believe things happen for a reason—otherwise there would be little point in studying or remembering them—I do not claim to know each specific reason. At best, I am an experienced guesser. Scholars should be careful about assuming that we are wiser than others. I have worked with fellow Ph.D.'s my entire career, yet I suspect there are beggars on the streets of Calcutta with a potentially higher I.Q. than anyone at my university.

Another premise is that everything is connected. Thus I have tried to incorporate many varieties of history without purporting to be an expert in all of them. But appreciation of history requires not only an appreciation of its diversity but an understanding of how that diversity is connected. Albert Einstein believed that imagination was more important than knowledge in the study of physics. That is true in the study of history as well.

After all, history tells us only the story of paths chosen. We do not know the results of where those not chosen might have led.

In analyzing the characters in our history books, I believe it is important to strike a balance between imposing the standards of our time on them, and viewing them in terms of what they knew at their time, and the realistic options they had. One supposes, for example, that General George Armstrong Custer might have reacted differently at Little Bighorn had he known of the Indians over the hill.

The organization of *A Time of Paradox* is related to its philosophical underpinnings and designed to facilitate its use as a teaching tool, and as an escort through the past. The book is divided into four Eras, each with a theme: An Era of Awakening, An Era of Trial and Triumph, An Era of Uncertainty, and An Era of Diversity. Each era is divided into six chapters which cover topically, within a rough chronological framework, the events of that era. The chapter themes tie in to the theme of the Era, which in turn is connected to the overall theme of *A Time of Paradox*. Every Era includes three brief biographical profiles which illustrate some subtheme of the period. The individuals are not selected for their significance, nor are they necessarily representative. In fact, most are secondary figures. Rather, they are chosen because of their illustration of the diversity of the era and the overall theme of paradox, as well as for their human interest.

The book includes a Prologue and an Epilogue, which are the most important elements. Anyone wanting an overview might read these first. In addition, there is a separate Prologue introducing each Era which provides an interpretive overview. There is a Time Line for each era and a selective list of readings. Originally intended as a twentieth-century book, *A Time of Paradox* has been extended in both directions. It includes an introductory chapter on the 1890s—the point at which the frontier of unsettled land in the West is said to have closed—and a postlude on evolving events of the twenty-first century.

In retrospect, what impresses me most about the Time of Paradox is its evolution in the direction of diversity and its acceleration in the velocity of change. Few periods, for example, pack into just over a generation, the events of the Era of Trial and Triumph: two world wars, a decade of prosperity, and a world depression. The interconnections mentioned earlier include not only the interconnections of events to one another, but the interconnections of America to other nations, perhaps, we will find, to other worlds. More important are the connections between individuals. All of these connections were necessary to arrive at the point we now stand.

We are mortal, in a narrow sense, yet each of us leaves behind an imprint on the planet earth. King Arthur is supposed to have told his aspiring Knights that before he gave them a sword they must become a poet. The world needs poets and students, spiritual warriors and military warriors, scholars, and plumbers. It would not work if we were one kind. I am proud to be a historian and consider it important. Yet I have never been summoned in the middle of the night to fix a history book that had suddenly burst open.

Acknowledgments

I EMBARK UPON the prospect of thanking those who contributed to *A Time of Paradox* with trepidation. Because the genesis of the book is distant, and my memory is fallible, I might omit someone who rendered me valuable service. On the other hand, the help of some might be so subtle they may be surprised to be mentioned.

Bruce Borland, formally of HarperCollins, was crucial in accepting my idea for the book and more than any single editor believed in its trade potential. Mary Carpenter was largely responsible for bringing the book to Rowman and Littlefield. Laura Roberts Gottlieb of Rowman and Littlefield, the book's final editor, exercised patience and coaxed out of me the best I could do.

Dozens of referees read portions of the manuscript. However, only Ronald Snyder read the entire manuscript and he wrote the most complete and thoughtful analysis. Of the readers who signed their reports, the most helpful were Leo Ribuffo, who, as usual, was intellectually honest, and Kari Frederickson, a former student, now an established historian.

David Luhrssen worked closely with me, especially in the book's final stages. He did the research and wrote the first draft of two of the chapters on cultural history in the Era of Diversity. In addition, he helped with photograph selection, captions, and indexed the manuscript. I turned to Herbert M. Levine whenever I encountered a problem. An old teacher, colleague, and friend, Herb helped with photo and map research. He used his computer skills and strategic location near the Library of Congress to iron out numerous difficulties. I am grateful for the assistance of Michael Gauger, although he did not agree with the final version of the book.

I had a superb copy editor, Ann Grogg, who edited my previous book, *Transformation and Reaction*. Like most writers I incline to believe that the best strategy to altering my prose is benign neglect. Yet Ann improved it, while adhering to the principle: "If it ain't broke, don't fix it." Ann's husband Bob, who fact-checked, is one of the most meticulous historians I know. Meredith Vnuk checked facts and updated, as did Nick Katers, and Sarah Lager. Stacey Smith aided with photographic research, as did Mary Manion. Jacqueline Kelnhofer was my chief proofreader. Other proofreaders included David Luhrssen, Lori Lasky, and Joan Hoss.

I owe major personal and professional debts to Joan Hoss. She literally lived with the book, typed the final manuscript, and prepared it for submission while I was away researching my next book on Herbert Hoover. Joan and John Kiekhaefer were my chief computer gurus. Though she is not a historian, Joan understands the book's underlying message better than anyone who has read it.

Greg Hoag is a wonderful teacher of non-academic truths and Sarah Sullivan, my personal trainer, kept my body intact. Milton Bates advised me on many aspects of the manuscript, including style, content, and publishing strategy, from its inception.

Some of my colleagues lent key support. Neal Pease, Jeffrey Merrick, Joe Rodriguez, and especially Lex Renda helped adjust my teaching schedule to my biorhythms. Among colleagues or former colleagues who suggested sources in their areas of expertise are Michael Gordon, Mark Bradley, Bruce Fetter, Victor Greene, David Hoeveler, and David Healy. No persons in the department were more essential to the book's completion than Louise Whitaker, Anita Cathey, and Teena Rawls.

The past and current directors of the Golda Meir Library provided access to its resources and all have been personal friends: Bill Roselle, Peter Watson-Boone, and Ewa Barczyk. My most important friend who navigated me through the labyrinths of library research is Ahmad Kramah, whose knowledge of recent American history is exceeded only by his generosity. Two of my colleagues on the University Library Committee, Winston Van Horne, and Mordecai Lee, have been particularly supportive.

There are several historians from whose work I have profited, some of whom are personal friends: Thomas C. Reeves, John Milton Cooper, William B. Pemberton, David Fromkin, James MacGregor Burns, Michael Beschloss, Dennis Dickerson, James W. Cortada, Thomas Schoonover, John Ehrman, and the late Stephen Ambrose.

I want to acknowledge some of the major influences in my life: my late father, Ryan J. Jeansonne, who knew the New Deal firsthand; the late William Ivy Hair, who steered me through the shoals of graduate school and onto the dry land of an academic career; and Amos E. Simpson, a former teacher and mentor.

For providing the supportive environment that everyone needs, professionally and personally, I would like to thank Helena Pycior, Kathy Callahan, Vann Mobley, Patrick Steele, Stephen A. Webre, Edward F. Haas, Mathé Allain, Bill Pederson, Paul George, Dan Kohl, Michael Wynne, Eddie Lager, Richard Osborne, Irv Becker, Richard Pierce, Carl Brasseaux, William Warren Rogers, Lynnell Ransome, Bob and Bonnie Bruch, Michael Seeley, Sharon Pace and Anne Shannon.

For inspiration, I had Leah and Hannah Jeansonne.

A Time of Paradox:
America since 1890

> I see this too under the sun: the race does not go to the swift, nor the battle to the strong; there is no bread for the wise, wealth for the intelligent, nor favour for the learned; all are subject to time and mischance.
>
> —Ecclesiastes 9:11

NEAR THE conclusion of the 1787 Constitutional Convention, Benjamin Franklin looked at a carving of the sun and asked whether it was a rising sun or a setting sun. The same question, he observed, could be asked of the nation the delegates were creating: Was the American experiment with democracy a rising sun or a setting sun?

After 1890, the answer would not come easily. The United States emerged from the nineteenth century in the pack of developing nations and proceeded to create the world's dominant civilization, one that offered second chances and second helpings. America helped unlock the mysteries of the atom, of space, of the human mind, and the nation reacted to crises courageously. As the twentieth century ended, Americans reflected on their successes and failures and hoped they would be able to keep their democracy in its place in the cosmos, for the twenty-first century posed a host of new dilemmas, complex and persistent. America could not solve the problem that has haunted every civilization: how to progress without creating new perils. The storehouse of human knowledge expanded exponentially, but human wisdom lagged. The country was fraught with prejudice, inequity, greed, violence, and ignorance. Periods of pleasure, riches, and intoxication mixed with periods of pain, shortages, and bitterness. By the standards of world civilizations, the United States is still an adolescent; it would be surprising if it did not make mistakes while growing up.

Because of its size, might, and accomplishments, the country generated high expectations. It could not fulfill completely the hopes of its own people and of the planet, and it could not decline to address them. Its democratic capitalism won the test of time against the communist Soviet Union, a competition that shaped much of the last half century. Underproduction and repression were vices of the Soviet system. But American capitalism produced to the point of exceeding consumption, requiring infinite expansion for sustained prosperity, and generated its own hardships, mainly against the workers on whom the economy depended. Democracy and capitalism outlasted communism, yet they are methods, not magic.

Although capitalism worked, American reformers recognized that it did so unevenly, unpredictably, and sometimes unfairly. It offered a taste of opportunity, often increasing the appetite without satisfying the hunger. Poverty persisted. Government intervened to help the needy, a major theme of the century, although the necessity and effectiveness of such intervention remain subjects of debate.

Equally troubling were racism, anti-Semitism, and sexism. African-Americans, Jews, immigrants, and other minorities faced economic, political, and cultural discrimination, as did women. By the end of the century, righteous indignation and a passion for justice had helped gain ground for these groups, yet they had also encountered a backlash.

In suppressing tyrants around the world, American power seemed providential, but Americans could not always agree on a definition of tyranny or on the extent of their responsibility to eliminate it. Many times the United States was the only nation sufficiently powerful to remove oppressors. Some still condemned the United States for trampling small republics, particularly in Latin America, that appeared to be annoyances rather than threats to the national interest. And sometimes military intervention ended in a stalemate that cost the nation more than it achieved.

Another destabilizing force—perhaps the most disruptive—was not economics, politics, or war, but sexuality, the oldest frontier of human experience. Sexual experimentation, contraception, and changing gender and family relations clashed with traditional social and religious doctrines over issues involving social welfare, civil liberties, drug use, images in the mass media, and community values. Moral questions arising from sex, such as abortion, could not be compromised.

Even the scientific and technological achievements of twentieth-century America were parts of the mosaic of paradox. From the eras of inventors and tinkerers such as Thomas A. Edison and Henry Ford, the United States evolved into a land of gargantuan collaborative scientific efforts, often financed by the government, that led to breakthroughs in industry, medicine, physics, chemistry, mathematics, and communication. If the accomplishments are beyond the comprehension of many, there is no doubt about the benefits. Easier to appreciate are the automobile, the television, the radio, the computer, and various appliances that make life more comfortable and enjoyable. But again, these conveniences came at a price, such as greater demands on finite energy resources, pollution, and a loss of jobs.

The ends of centuries and millennia and the beginnings of new ones are occasions of mixed feelings, of optimism about the potential for good amid fears of what the dark side of humanity will yield. This was especially true at the dawn of the twenty-first century, when much of the peace of mind that the United States felt at the start of the twentieth had been lost. Life was less laborious, but more stressful. Natural resources had been plundered, and the scourges of war, terrorism, and hatred shadowed a nervous world. Americans excelled at going places swiftly, although there was no consensus on where they were headed. Hope and fear were inseparable companions. Having survived the twentieth century, conquering obstacles, and sustaining setbacks, the challenge for the twenty-first century is to survive and solve the conflicts and issues inherited from the twentieth century, and to move beyond them. Paradoxically, while moving on to new challenges, Americans must hold on to the values that nourish us, while adapting them to inevitable changes.

The 1890s:
Bridge to the
Twentieth Century

A MERICANS TRAVELED a narrow path to the twentieth century that widened into a highway as the century progressed and the velocity of change accelerated. When they traversed the bridge of the 1890s into the new century, they found not a paradise but a paradox. The prelude was filled with surprise and disappointment and ended with a roar and new responsibilities.

The End of the Century

The gala that previewed the twentieth century was the World's Columbian Exposition held at Chicago in 1893. There were new inventions galore, including a fabulous White City aglow with tens of thousands of lights when the sun set. Visitors rode the world's first Ferris wheel and watched magicians and the belly dancer "Little Egypt" perform her gyrations. The historian Frederick Jackson Turner warned that the American frontier was closed. The 1890 census, he said, revealed that there was no longer a continuous westward moving line of settlement. The frontier, with the abundance of free land, shaped the American character and Americans would be a different people without it, he forecast.

The decade was stressful, with industrialization, labor turmoil, massive immigration, and business consolidation. Some of America's political leaders straddled the centuries. Theodore Roosevelt, for example, blended the old and the new. He was at home in the city and on the open range, thirsting for adventure as America awakened to world power. William Jennings

THE GREAT WHITE CITY
Columbian Exposition in Chicago, 1893.
(Library of Congress)

Bryan championed rural interests, ran for president three times, and also was involved in the debates over world power.

The debate over world power was accompanied by a debate over economic power. Many of the industrial moguls overlapped the centuries, and they saw themselves hailed as industrial statesmen and condemned as "robber barons" who gouged the public and exploited labor. Partly, their status went up or down with the economy and the economy was, for the most part, an engine of prosperity, yet the Panic of 1893 inaugurated the most catastrophic depression to date. Politicians, too, saw their fates rise and fall as they tried to ride the winds of change. Political power shifted to states, regions, and cities, as well as ethnic concentrations. Yesterday's city boss was today's villain. Reform began below and crested just after the turn of the century when an assassin's bullet introduced an Era of Awakening.

From Farm to Factory

Between the Civil War and the turn of the century, everything—good and bad—grew. First was the economy. Second was the city. From a nation of billowing fields, America became a land of belching smokestacks. In the 1890s, for the first time, the value of industrial goods eclipsed the value of agricultural products. By 1890, 51.7 percent of the labor force worked outside agriculture, and by 1894, American industry was producing twice as much as British industry. Industry not only grew, but its range of products became broadened. By 1900 the chief industries, in order of value, were slaughtering and meatpacking, flour milling, lumbering, iron and steel, and machine-shop products. American agriculture, the chief exports, dominated world markets, and total exports exceeded imports.

Innovations in technology drove industrial production. Moreover, there were improvements in business management, in more efficient use of labor, and in industrial organization, as well as revolutions in transportation and communication. Especially important was the mass of relatively prosperous consumers on which industry thrived. The vast empire of the British, by contrast, had greater numbers but less purchasing power.

The stories of some of the industrial titans, whether one admired or loathed them, are the stuff of fantasy fiction. Within their stories are imbedded some of the paradoxes of the age. Andrew Carnegie, a poor immigrant from Scotland, is an archetypal example. Beginning as a telegrapher for the Pennsylvania Railroad, by age twenty-four, Carnegie became superintendent of its western division. Meanwhile, he invested his savings, surviving the downturn of 1873, and concentrated his money in the steel industry. Employing new technology he created a steel monopoly that also controlled iron mines and railroads. A ruthless businessman, he undersold rivals, bankrupting them. In 1901 he sold his empire to the United States Steel Corporation for $250 million, making him one of the richest men in the world. Carnegie spent the rest of his life as a philanthropist, endowing libraries, universities, charitable trusts, foundations, and Carnegie Hall in New York City. Some felt the gifts were tainted because of Carnegie's merciless business tactics. Figures such as Carnegie, hard-fisted at times, softhearted at others, are among the paradoxes of the era.

Similar to Carnegie, only richer and more ruthless, John D. Rockefeller did for oil what Carnegie did for steel. Ironically, he retired before widespread use of automobiles created an even greater demand for his product (used largely for lighting and medicine during his time). Like Carnegie, Rockefeller created a vertical monopoly including pipelines, refineries, and oilfields, forcing railroads to pay him rebates for his business. By 1880 Rockefeller's Standard Oil controlled 90 percent of the American oil industry. Staying just within the law, company attorneys devised a form of organization whereby stockholders held shares not in tangible assets, but in a trust composed of the assets of other companies. By 1897 Rockefeller largely retired from managing the company and devoted much of his time to philanthropy. Before his death in 1937, he gave away an estimated $550 million, establishing the Rockefeller Foundation and the General Education Board and endowing the University of Chicago.

For all the good works done with their money, the industrialists had more power than is healthy in a democracy. They wielded it to crush strikes—including the Homestead strike at a Carnegie Steel mill in 1892, a violent 1892 silver mine strike at Coeur d'Alene, Idaho, and the 1894 strike at the Pullman Palace Car Company near Chicago. Carnegie was not involved in the Homestead strike, having retired and left management of the mill to Henry Clay Frick; nevertheless, it tarnished his reputation. When contract negotiations deadlocked, Frick locked out the workers, hiring replacements and guards to protect the new employees. The strikers threatened the guards, and in response Frick employed some three hundred Pinkerton detectives, who engaged in a gun battle with the strikers, in which seven men died. After the detectives surrendered, the governor dispatched the militia to preserve order. Much of the public seemed to sympathize with the strikers until an anarchist not connected with the strike attempted to kill Frick, but Frick recovered from his wounds, and the strike was settled on company terms.

The Pullman strike occurred in the wake of the Panic of 1893. George Pullman, whose company manufactured railroad sleeping cars, slashed wages and laid off workers, claiming that the company's solvency depended on the cuts. Laborers complained that he refused to reduce rents and prices at his company town. Pullman would not negotiate with the American Railway Union, so Eugene V. Debs, president of the union, organized a strike against all lines handling Pullman cars. U.S. Attorney General Richard Olney obtained an injunction against the strike on the grounds that delay of the trains interfered with delivery of the mail. The union refused to obey the order, federal troops were sent in, and riots ensued, leaving thirteen dead, fifty-three wounded seriously, and seven hundred freight cars burned. The strike was lost and Debs served six months in prison for defying the injunction. The Supreme Court upheld his sentence and the use of injunctions against strikes, a practice that Congress did not outlaw until 1932.

Companies in the sugar, whiskey, copper, and lead industries abused their power by copying Rockefeller and forming trusts. As the public came to fear the trusts because of their unscrupulous conduct, huge profits, and monopolies, lawmakers investigated, condemned the trusts, and, on the federal level, passed the 1890 Sherman Antitrust Act to ban them. But there were few prosecutions under the vague law. Standard Oil circumvented it by reorganizing as a holding company, a corporation that held a controlling share of at least one other firm; and the Supreme Court adopted a probusiness interpretation of the act. Corporate combinations grew, and by 1900, large companies accounted for almost two-fifths of all manufacturing capital.

The Rise of the Cities

In the 1890s the growth of cities accelerated. Soon they displaced the towns and farms that had dominated American life for much of the nation's history. In the twentieth century, the story of America would be largely the story of its cities. Urbanization made America, and Americans, more diverse and complex, fusing trends involving immigration, industrial centralization, and internal migration, especially of minorities. The sources of immigration shifted from the British Isles, Germany, and the Low Countries to the east and south: Italy, Poland, Russia, and Austria-Hungary.

Catholics, Jews, and Orthodox Christians, speaking a variety of languages, mixed with the largely Protestant, English-speaking population. Land and jobs remained the major attractions of America, but because of the declining availability of cheap land in the West, many settled in cities in the East and Midwest. There they formed enclaves, crowded into tenements, and filled the demand for unskilled workers in low-paying and often dangerous factory jobs. Native workers claimed the newcomers competed for jobs and depressed wages. Others feared that the mix of languages, religions, and ethnic loyalties could not be assimilated or absorbed into American life. Barricades to immigration were erected. In 1882, for instance, Chinese immigration was prohibited for ten years, and later made permanent. That same year, paupers and the insane were barred entry. In 1897 Congress passed a bill requiring that immigrants be literate in some language, but President Grover Cleveland vetoed it.

In the late nineteenth century, cities grew up and out, revolutionized by the elevator, the skyscraper, the trolley, the elevated train, and the subway. Streets began to be paved, especially after the advent of the automobile; telephone, trolley, and telegraph lines began to be placed underground. Electricity changed the rotation and rhythm between work in the daytime and sleep at night. Specialization by space separated work from residence and recreation, and neighborhoods divided by class, race, and ethnicity. The success of the White City at the World's Columbian Exposition popularized the idea of urban planning. Cities centralized culture, attracting artists, writers, and intellectuals. Urban schools provided a greater variety of courses and better-educated teachers. Athletics took root in the cities: professional baseball, the invention of basketball, a bicycle craze, and women played tennis and golf. Sports contributed identity to cities.

The alter ego of city excitement was city vice. Immigrants were packed into slum tenements and were vulnerable to fire, disease, and crime, a condition that Jacob Riis documented in *How the Other Half Lives* (1890). Venal bosses who dominated urban politics contributed to the exploitation of immigrants, gaining support by providing jobs, food, clothing, housing, and fuel. If the power to give lay with the bosses, so did the power to take. In exchange for bribes, they protected criminals and steered public business to profiteers.

Cultural Independence

For much of its history, the United States was an importer of culture, including literature, and the products of its writers were considered inferior to European artists. Some American intellectuals not only imitated Europe but preferred to live there. Yet, by the dawn of the twentieth century, Henry James and other major writers emerged to embellish America's reputation. James wrote his best-known novel, *The Portrait of a Lady*, in England in 1881. His theme, the encounter of American innocence and European sophistication, was viewed through the lens of female characters. James's novels were hardly representative of life in the United States, yet they were more realistic than those of earlier novelists.

William Dean Howells owed his reputation more to his influence as an editor than to his fiction. From the 1870s through the 1920s he was the impresario of American literature, setting standards of taste, encouraging new authors, writing criticism, and creating. He wrote more than four hundred book reviews, numerous critical essays, and about a book a year. A socialist, Howells portrayed the venality of business, the exploitation of workers, and the corruption of politics. He supported literary realism and provided continuity to a culture fragmented by divisions between East and West, cosmopolitanism and nationalism, elite taste and popular taste. By the 1900s, however, naturalist writers were angered by his insistence that, although realism required a faithful description of life, the view that the universe was amoral had grown excessive. The naturalists who began their careers in the 1890s were cynical; they believed that realists failed to appreciate the bleakness of nature and society. Of the naturalists, Stephen Crane soared highest and crashed most dramatically. He explored the life of a prostitute victimized by poverty in *Maggie: A Girl of the Streets* (1893) and stripped romanticism from war in *The Red Badge of Courage* (1895).

Regional, or local color, writers helped satisfy publishers' vast demand for short fiction and preserved regional language and folkways in danger of being submerged by a coming tidal wave of a homogeneous culture.

Among the more complex regionalists was Kate Chopin, who explored Louisiana's Cajun and Creole societies and the emergence of women. Her novel *The Awakening* (1899), a serious treatment of sex and gender in middle-class life, was labeled prurient. The incendiary issue of race informed the fiction of George Washington Cable, who wrote magazine stories about the racially mixed Creole society. After writing *The Grandissimes* (1888), which examined conflicts of race and status, he was ostracized in Louisiana and moved to New England. Charles W. Chesnutt, a free black who was born in Ohio and lived in the South, wrote about the African American experience in southern settings. The racial violence of *The Marrow of Tradition* (1901) repelled Howells, though, and the loss of the critic's endorsement set back Chesnutt's career.

Among late nineteenth-century poets, Walt Whitman and Emily Dickinson, are preeminent. Rugged and egotistical, Whitman called himself "the bard of democracy." His reputation rests upon a single volume, *Leaves of Grass* (published in six editions between 1855 and 1892). The collection drew a line of demarcation between poetic romanticism and realism and marked the shift from the New England aristocracy to the ordinary people. Dickinson was almost too sensitive and not until after her death was her greatness recognized. Proving that one need not be traveled or worldly to become an eminent poet, because what matters lies inside, Dickinson was a recluse who traveled outside her state of Massachusetts only once and, in the last fifteen years of her life, remained in the house in which she was born. She refused visitors and letters because they were too stimulating. Yet she poured her passion and pain into poetry; her gifts were imagination and originality. As with other poets, writing was therapy. For Dickinson, it was salvation. Nearly all of her 1,775 poems were published after her death, with public interest piqued by the publication of three thin volumes in 1890, 1891, and 1896. Dickinson is considered America's finest female poet.

Politics in Hard Times

At the national level, politics were fought chiefly about monetary issues. Republicans supported business and a more active role for the federal government. Democrats espoused states' rights and lower tariffs more favorable to consumers. Strong in the Midwest and the East, Republicans dominated northern states, as Democrats dominated the South. Democrats had just one president between the end of the Civil War and the turn of the century, Grover Cleveland, elected in 1884, defeated in 1888, and reelected in 1892. Another constant was disenfranchisement of African Americans.

For two decades after the Civil War, black men had voted in large numbers in the southern states. In the late 1880s and 1890s, they were disenfranchised by poll taxes, property requirements, and literacy tests. Congress tried to compel Southern whites to permit black voting in 1890, debating a bill to provide federal protection for voters. Soundly defeated, the measure was the last serious attempt to protect black voters in the South until passage of the Civil Rights Act of 1957. African Americans were segregated in schools, restaurants, railroads, and public facilities. In 1896 the Supreme Court sanctioned segregation, ruling in *Plessy v. Ferguson* that separate accommodations for whites and blacks were permissible so long as they were roughly equal. White lynch mobs were another menace.

In 1890 Congress passed not only the Sherman Antitrust Act, but two other significant economic laws: the McKinley Tariff and the Sherman Silver Purchase Act. The tariff, sponsored by Ohio Representative William McKinley, was the highest to that time. Its protectionist rates, favored by domestic manufacturers, reduced competition from imports. The silver act required the Treasury to increase silver purchases and issue silver-backed currency. Silver-backed currency benefited debtors by enhancing the money supply and producing inflation, aided farmers by raising prices for their products, and enriched western silver miners. Eastern Republicans supported a gold standard and voted for silver purchases in return for their western colleagues' votes for the tariff. Two years later, the presidential election was a rematch between Cleveland and Benjamin Harrison. Republicans advocated a bimetallic currency standard of gold and silver, high tariffs, and construction of an isthmian canal linking the Atlantic and Pacific oceans. Democrats denounced the McKinley Tariff and Cleveland supported civil service reform and gold-backed currency. But there was a third faction in the election: the Populist, or People's Party, a movement of agrarian insurgents.

Their ranks swelled by hard times, the Populists declared in their platform, "We meet in the midst of a nation brought to the verge of moral, political, and material ruin. The fruits of the toil of millions are boldly stolen to build up colossal fortunes for the few." The platform advocated unlimited coinage of silver; the initiative and referendum, devices that allowed voters to enact legislation; the election of senators by popular vote; a graduated income tax; government ownership of transportation and communication facilities; and government-sponsored loans and crop storage facilities for farmers. James B. Weaver, a former Union Army general, and James G. Field, a former Confederate general, were nominated for president and vice president, respectively.

The Populists spoke for the rural poor who felt victimized by the industrial and agricultural revolutions. In the late nineteenth century, farmers increased production by introducing machinery, employing innovative methods of cultivation, and bringing millions of fertile acres in the West under cultivation. The most productive farmers in the world, their harvest exceeded demand and caused prices to plummet. Farmers paid dearly to get their products to market because railroads charged them exorbitantly. Banks extorted unreasonably high interest rates. Compounding their plight were cultural isolation, lack of access to city conveniences, and a decline in status. Once viewed as the backbone of democracy, farmers were now stereotyped as crude and ignorant. Some Populists blamed Jews and other scapegoats for their problems. Yet their movement addressed valid grievances, and many of their reform proposals later became law. Their most enduring legacy was their idea that the government was responsible for reforming the economy.

Farmers had created fraternal groups that became political ones, beginning with the Grange in 1867 and continuing with the Farmers' Alliances, the forerunners of the Populist Party. In 1890 the party was born at a convention in Topeka, Kansas, and some Populist candidates won election to Congress. The farmers who organized heeded Mary Lease of Kansas, who urged them to "raise less corn and more hell!" But not enough hell was raised in the 1892 presidential election, in which Cleveland polled 5.5 million popular votes and 277 electoral votes to Harrison's 5.18 million and 145. The Populist ticket won more than 1 million popular votes and 22 electoral votes, carrying Kansas, Colorado, Idaho, and Nevada. The elections were the first in which the Australian, or secret, ballot printed by the government rather than by the parties, was used nationally.

Shortly after Cleveland's inauguration, the Panic of 1893 struck, the stock market collapsed, and the nation plunged into depression. By the end of the year, some five hundred banks and almost sixteen thousand businesses failed. Railroad construction declined, consumer sales fell, and unemployment reached about 20 percent. In 1894 Jacob Coxey, in a widely imitated demonstration, led a march of unemployed workers called "Coxey's Army" on Washington. He wanted to protest the administration's refusal to inflate the currency in order to create jobs. The economy rebounded in 1895, only to bottom out the next year.

Cleveland blamed the Sherman Silver Purchase Act and bimetallism; he believed restoration of the gold standard was essential. Populists continued to argue that gold was the problem, not the solution. Cleveland persuaded Congress to repeal the act, but the drain of gold from the Treasury continued. When the reserves fell below $100 million, the level that economists considered essential to maintaining the standard, Cleveland floated four bond issues. These increased gold reserves, yet they were costly to the government and reaped lucrative profits for rich investment bankers such as J. P. Morgan. Moreover, they failed to end the depression. Cleveland also failed to provide the meaningful tariff reform he had promised in his campaign. The Wilson-Gorman Tariff enacted only marginal reductions; it was amended more than six hundred times in the Senate, mostly to protect special interests. The one progressive feature of the legislation, a small income tax, was rejected by the Supreme Court in 1895.

The economic dislocation cost the Democrats control of both the House and Senate in 1894. Southerners and westerners who sympathized with Populist demands for inflation rejected Cleveland. In 1896, the silver Democrats gained the upper hand and nominated William Jennings Bryan, who roused the convention with his speech in defense of the silver standard. At thirty-six, the Nebraskan was the youngest major party nominee in history. His nomination on a silver platform preempted the chief issue of the Populists, whose only realistic chance for victory was to endorse Bryan, though that would sacrifice their overall program in pursuit of a single plank. Nonetheless, they nominated Bryan.

Bryan was one of the more famous politicians never elected president. A great orator, if not a great intellect, he was an economic liberal and a religious fundamentalist. He considered becoming a minister before turning to law and politics. Moving from his native state of Illinois in 1887 in pursuit of a career, he was elected to Congress from Nebraska in 1890 and 1892. Defeated in his bid for the Senate in 1894, he became a journalist for a prosilver newspaper. In many respects, Bryan was a symbol of America about to enter the century of paradox, an amalgam of consistency and contradiction, of principle and pragmatism, confident in his faith, yet confused and appalled by some of the developments of his time. To oppose him, the Republicans nominated McKinley and endorsed the gold standard, the protective tariff, and the Monroe Doctrine forbidding encroachment in the Americas. McKinley, an ex-major in the Union Army, served as governor of Ohio and as a congressman. He won the nomination with the aid of his patron, millionaire Cleveland businessman Mark Hanna.

With Bryan popular in the South and West and McKinley commanding the East, the Midwest became the battleground. Bryan found it difficult to attract workers on fixed incomes who would not gain from inflation; their weekly wages, in a relative sense, would be worth less. Thus, workers and the urban poor were unwilling to join the rural poor and indebted

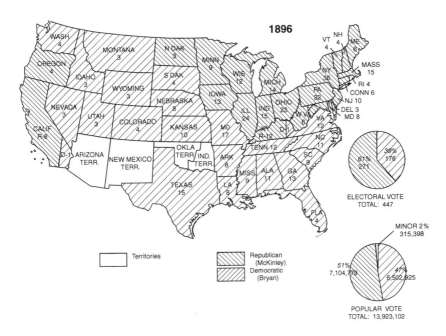

Election of 1896

farmers. Besides the currency issue, the election presented voters with a choice foreshadowing the cultural wars of the twentieth century. McKinley represented stability and the rising industrial nation, while Bryan represented a way of life based on rural values.

McKinley's lavishly financed campaign spent $3–$5 million. Directed by Hanna, it was the best-organized campaign to that point in American history. The candidate remained at his home in Canton, Ohio, where he spoke to visiting delegations while spokesmen saturated the Midwest with literature. They touted McKinley as "the advance agent of prosperity" and ridiculed Bryan as a country buffoon. Bryan, whose campaign spent just $25,000, made six hundred speeches to some 5 million people. In one of the watershed presidential elections of American history, McKinley polled 7.1 million votes to Bryan's 6.5 million and won in the Electoral College by 271 votes to 176.

True to the predictions of McKinley's partisans, his term heralded the return of prosperity, though it was not because of the president. McKinley supported, and Congress passed, the 1897 Dingley Tariff that increased duties. Congress also increased taxes on estates, corporations, tobacco, alcohol, and some luxury items. In addition, in 1900 lawmakers passed the Gold Standard Act, providing for currency backed solely by gold. Predating those moves, gold discoveries in Alaska, Australia, and South Africa and the introduction of new mining technology enabled world gold production to more than double between 1891 and 1896. The abundance spurred inflation, and by 1898, farm prosperity returned. Prosperity, ironically, nailed the coffin shut on the Populist Party. Farm-based protest would arise in the twentieth century as the economy collapsed in the greater depression of the 1930s.

Expansion and War with Spain

Of the events that initiated the Era of Awakening, the most important was the Spanish-American War that ended the nineteenth century. The war was vital in the shift from the old style of American diplomacy to the new. Before the 1890s, policy makers were often isolationist; their conduct of foreign policy was reactive; they gave little specific guidance to diplomats abroad; and the army and navy were not prepared for international warfare. But during the 1890s, the United States embarked upon a more aggressive and activist role in foreign affairs. Several factors inspired the change: the depression, which stimulated an unprecedented interest in foreign trade and new markets overseas, and the maturing of a post–Civil War generation that did not share its predecessor's distaste for military adventure. Also contributing to the awakening were greater knowledge of and contact with other countries through missionaries and journalists, and Alfred Thayer Mahan, whose *The Influence of Sea Power upon History, 1660–1783* (1890) prodded officials to modernize the navy.

Under Harrison and Cleveland, the United States had become increasingly involved in hemispheric affairs. The Harrison administration secured a three-part protectorate of the Samoan Islands, where America, Germany, and Britain wanted Pacific coaling stations, and stopped Canadian fishermen from slaughtering seals. Diplomacy settled a dispute with Italy over the lynching of eleven Italians in New Orleans, and preserved peace with Chile after two American sailors died in a brawl in Valparaiso. Cleveland compelled Britain to accept an American commission's settlement of a dispute between London and Venezuela over British Guiana's border, but he opposed Harrison's plan to annex Hawaii.

Cuba, just one hundred miles off the tip of Florida, was tied to the United States strategically, commercially, and emotionally. To many Americans, Spain's rule of the island seemed a violation of the Monroe

Doctrine, and Cubans rebelled for independence in the Ten Years War (1868–1878) and in 1899. Cuban exiles in New York helped finance the 1899 insurrection and furnished propaganda to provoke American involvement. William Randolph Hearst's *New York Journal* and Joseph Pulitzer's *New York World*, locked in a circulation war, exaggerated Spanish cruelty. Americans were particularly angered when Governor General Valeriano Weyler, soon to be known in the United States as "Butcher" Weyler, forced Cubans to move from the countryside to enclaves guarded by Spanish troops. Anyone outside the hamlets might be shot.

American outrage did not lead directly to war. The business community, still recovering from the depression, was not enthusiastic, and Cleveland announced that the United States would be neutral. Yet in 1896, both major party platforms called for Cuban freedom. McKinley sought Cuban autonomy within the Spanish Empire and humane rule of the island, preferring to pursue his goals through private negotiations. Much of the pressure for intervention arose in Congress and heated toward the boiling point, particularly after two incidents in February 1898. First, the Spanish minister in Washington, Depuy de Lome, wrote to a friend in Havana that McKinley was weak, cowardly, and opportunistic. A rebel sympathizer who noticed de Lome's return address opened the letter and sent it to insurgent supporters in New York, who published it in the *Journal* on February 9. In the United States, de Lome's letter was considered an insult indicating that Spain was not negotiating in good faith. Next, the battleship *Maine*, which McKinley had dispatched to Havana as a goodwill gesture and to evacuate Americans, exploded and sank on February 15, killing 260 sailors. Blaming the blast on a Spanish-laid mine, war became almost certain. (In 1976, after a thorough review of the evidence, investigators concluded that a fire in a coal-storage bunker triggered an ammunition explosion on the ship. Twenty-two years later, however, a *National Geographic* study found evidence suggesting that a mine could not be ruled out as a cause.)

Cubans rioted for independence, and the Hearst press carried the headline "Remember the *Maine* and To Hell with Spain!" Assistant Navy Secretary Theodore Roosevelt, eager for war, ordered the Hong Kong based Pacific squadron under Commodore George Dewey to prepare to attack the Philippines, a Spanish colony. Spain offered to arbitrate the *Maine* episode, accept American relief aid for the Cubans, and consider granting the island autonomy, but refused to accept American mediation over Cuba's status in the Spanish Empire. When the United States upped the ante by insisting on independence for Cuba, the Spanish refused, preferring war to diplomatic surrender. Finally, on April 11, McKinley delivered

THE ROUGH RIDERS
Theodore Roosevelt (Center) in the Spanish-American War.
(Library of Congress)

a war message to Congress. The House and Senate adopted a joint resolution recognizing Cuban independence and approving force to dislodge Spain. The upper chamber attached an amendment by Colorado's Henry M. Teller, stating that the United States would liberate Cuba rather than annex it. In response, Spain declared war and Congress followed.

The war lasted slightly more than three months and appeared to confirm Mahan's theories about naval power. On May 1 at Manila Bay in the Philippines, Dewey destroyed his opponent and lost just one American life. Striking another decisive blow, the Atlantic fleet trapped the Spanish ships in Santiago harbor and sank them with almost no U.S. casualties on July 3. Four days later, in the afterglow of triumph, McKinley signed a joint resolution of Congress to annex Hawaii, which became an American territory.

On the ground, logistical problems and inexperienced leadership plagued the American effort, but the ineptitude of the Spanish generals compensated. Combat focused on the city of Santiago, where the Americans placed 17,000 Spanish troops under siege. On July 1 the Army took El Caney and San Juan Hill, gaining control of the high ground around Santiago and preventing the Spanish from escaping. The most glorified hero of the ground war was Roosevelt, who resigned his post to organize a volunteer cavalry unit, the Rough Riders, that included cowboys and Ivy League students. A contingent of black soldiers, like the Rough Riders, stormed up San Juan Hill.

Victory followed in the Philippines and Puerto Rico, and on July 17, Santiago surrendered, virtually ending the combat. The war stopped on August 1 when Spain surrendered. Cuba became independent; Puerto Rico became an American territory; and American troops occupied the Philippines pending a decision on their fate. Some 5,462 Americans had died in Cuba, only 379 in battle. Disease killed most, spread by unsanitary conditions in army camps, impure food, insects, and sweaty dress inappropriate to the tropics.

Making the peace proved more difficult than winning the war. Many Americans, opposing imperialism, wanted to liberate the Philippines. Bolstering their arguments, Emilio Aguinaldo, whose rebel forces helped American troops seize the islands, resisted U.S. control. McKinley believed that failure to accept the Philippines might mean their takeover by Japan or Germany, and that the islands were unprepared for independence. Congressional Democrats did not want to accept the islands as a colony, yet some changed their minds after Bryan, who wanted to make imperialism an issue in the 1900 presidential election, endorsed the treaty. On February 6, 1899, the Senate approved the treaty 57 to 27, just one vote more than the required two-thirds majority.

Even without the Philippines, the United States was destined to be a Pacific power because of its long western coastline, but acquisition of the islands gave the country a more tangible stake in the area. Many Americans embraced world power enthusiastically, as if invigorated by a rousing Sousa musical march. Others accepted it soberly, realizing that if their nation were to call the tune, they would have to pay the piper.

An Era of Awakening, 1900–1919

Prologue

AS THE TWENTIETH century dawned, America awakened to the world, seeking to seize the new century and possess it, with its industrial and military might, its innovative culture, and its spirit of adventure. Perhaps the optimism was exaggerated for a nation so young, yet it was unquenchable, soon to be stimulated by a new president whose energy and charisma were electric. If Thomas Edison had wired Theodore Roosevelt, it might have lighted a city.

Entering the Era of Awakening, Senator Albert J. Beveridge proclaimed: "The twentieth century will be American. American thought will dominate it. American progress will give it color and direction. American deeds will make it illustrious."

At the dawn of the century, the United States was primitive in many respects. Automobiles were rare; paved highways did not exist, nor did aviation. Women could vote in only four states; African Americans, who could not vote at all in most places, endured poverty, racism, and discrimination. But there were reasons for ebullience, due to the realization that the country's size, location, population, and natural and human resources would guarantee it a major place in the world. In 1900 the nation consisted of forty-five states, 76 million people, and thirty-eight cities of more than 100,000 inhabitants. The third largest country in the world in land area behind Russia and Canada, the United States boasted the most dynamic economy. It had the most productive farms, the most miles of railroads, the greatest steel production, the highest per capita income.

Furthermore, the progressive movement was overhauling the engine of democracy for a dash at the future. Over the next two decades, four amendments would be added to the Constitution, providing for the popular election of senators, a federal income tax, woman suffrage, and prohibition of alcohol. A host of other reforms were enacted on the federal, state, and local

RIDING INTO THE FUTURE
Carriages fill New York City's 5th Avenue, 1900.
(National Archives)

levels. And under Theodore Roosevelt and Woodrow Wilson, the presidency experienced a renaissance. Seldom have two luminaries so ignited the public mind within a single generation. The most significant chief executives between the end of the Civil War and the start of the New Deal, they contrasted in styles and temperaments and exploited each other as a foil. Each possessed an iron will that would not permit him to give up (although fate might have been kinder to them if sometimes they had given up).

Roosevelt, who took office in 1901, awakened the country like a fire bell in the night. He thrilled, confounded, and polarized Americans. The first to recognize and exploit the press, he created a mystique around his job and curiosity about him and the first family. With TR work and play, joy and conviction, commitment and passion were fused. In the three-ring circus of American politics, Roosevelt was the uncaged lion in the center ring, and when he roared the world applauded.

Where Roosevelt was fire, Wilson was ice. Roosevelt's rhetoric was inflamed by the power of his delivery, but Wilson's was inspired by the magic of his ideas. Roosevelt was an evangelist who proselytized from the "bully pulpit" that the presidency offered him; Wilson, a former professor and university president, led by wit and collegiality. Much of what Roosevelt did was more show than substance, and the opposite was true with Wilson. Independently, they were incomplete; combined, they would have made a consummate statesman. TR opened the era with an explosion of vigor and passed the torch to a successor under whom it dimmed. The flame blazed anew under Wilson, only to die at the epoch's end, almost simultaneously with Roosevelt's death and Wilson's political defeat.

Roosevelt brought the United States into a greater involvement in world affairs, an engagement that, under Wilson, led the country into World War I. The influx of American manpower and logistical aid broke the deadlock, a more impressive achievement than the easy victory over the decrepit Spanish Empire that antedated the century. But Wilson did not realize his dreams of a "world made safe for democracy" by American military sacrifice, and of a League of Nations. He ruined his health in a fruitless effort to persuade the Senate to consent to the Versailles Treaty—a tragedy for him and for the nation. He would, however, leave an enduring dream.

A third remarkable political personality, William Jennings Bryan, lacked the intellectual virtuosity of Roosevelt and Wilson, yet was loved more. Humble, genial, charismatic, intellectually honest, a spellbinding orator, Bryan had intangible qualities that were more enduring than his tangible accomplishments (which were considerable). Combining beliefs that were economically and politically progressive, while socially and theologically conservative, he was a transitional figure, a paradoxical politician with one foot in the nineteenth century and the other in the twentieth. He was simultaneously ahead of his times and behind them.

The major political issues of the era stemmed from the question of where personal responsibility ended and where the responsibility of the state began. Were the interests of individuals and the nation the same? Was the state its citizens' keeper? Could the United States be the world's keeper, as Wilson hoped? What role should the government play in regulating capitalism? How much should the government be doing on behalf of labor? How large and powerful should the government be relative to the private sector? How powerful should the president be? What responsibilities were best handled by the federal government, and what were best handled by the states? How should the United States respond to the economic and ideological challenges posed by the Bolshevik Revolution that brought communism to Russia?

Like politics, gender and race relations were in flux during the Era of Awakening. Women joined the cause of reform to uplift the poor, to apply ethical standards to politics, and to preserve world peace. African Americans joined the National Association for the Advancement of Colored People (NAACP) to advance their claims to political rights. Intellectuals fretted about the place of women and minorities in society, as well as tensions generated by rising expectations and persistent inequality, the anonymity of urban life, and the low standards of popular taste. The country and its citizens were the subjects of psychoanalytic interpretations. Among intellectuals the consensus appeared to be that the nation, like the Liberty Bell, was flawed and cracked and that as the nation aged, the crack widened.

The calm, dignified President William McKinley, it seemed, would lead a comfortable transition to the new century. But the future arrived in a rush with the assassin's bullet that felled him in 1901.

Time Line

An Era of Awakening, 1900–1919

March 20, 1900 Open Door in China declared approved.

September 6, 1901 Anarchist shoots President William McKinley, who dies September 14. Vice President Theodore Roosevelt succeeds him.

July 15, 1903 Henry Ford sells first car.

November 18, 1903 United States signs treaty to acquire Panama Canal zone.

December 17, 1903 Orville and Wilbur Wright make first airplane flight.

December 6, 1904 Roosevelt announces Roosevelt Corollary to Monroe Doctrine.

February 12, 1909 National Association for the Advancement of Colored People founded.

November 5, 1912 Democrat Woodrow Wilson defeats Republican incumbent William Howard Taft and Progressive candidate Theodore Roosevelt in presidential election.

February 25, 1913 Sixteenth Amendment authorizing a federal income tax ratified.

May 31, 1913 Seventeenth Amendment providing for direct election of senators ratified.

December 23, 1913 Wilson signs Federal Reserve Act.

April 6, 1917 United States enters World War I.

January 8, 1918 Wilson outlines "Fourteen Points" for peace terms.

March 11, 1918 First U.S. case of influenza that would kill more people than World War I, including 686,000 in America.

November 11, 1918 Armistice ends World War I.

January 29, 1919 Eighteenth Amendment, Prohibition, ratified.

November 19, 1919 Senate rejects Treaty of Versailles.

CHAPTER ONE

TR, Taft, and the Progressive Impulse

THE 1900 presidential election saw William McKinley once again defeat William Jennings Bryan for the presidency. The new vice president was Theodore Roosevelt, the hero of the Rough Riders of the Spanish-American War. TR replaced Vice President Garret A. Hobart, who had died before the campaign. During the campaign, Roosevelt opened the Era of Awakening with a jolt. Vibrant, ambitious, he had a child's delight in politics. With Roosevelt and Bryan jousting on the stump, and McKinley remaining in the White House above the fray, the Republican ticket trounced the Democrats, gaining more than 7.2 million popular votes and 292 electoral votes to the Democrats' 6.35 million and 155. Bryan not only failed to expand his southern and western base; he lost his home state of Nebraska.

Six months later, McKinley traveled to Buffalo, New York, for the Pan-American Exposition, a celebration of hemispheric scientific and artistic progress. At a public reception, Leon Czolgosz, an anarchist angered over the president's taking of the Philippines, shot McKinley twice. Eight days later, one of the bullets killed him. Mark Hanna, McKinley's patron, exclaimed: "My God, that damned cowboy is in the White House!"

Theodore Roosevelt

A cowboy Roosevelt was—and much more. He was also a conservationist; a zoologist; a hunter; an athlete; an amateur historian; an author who would write thirty-six books remarkable for their intellectual range and quality; and an assistant navy secretary. He spent time as a federal civil service commissioner; a police commissioner; and a state legislator, as well as an acclaimed war veteran and governor. The youngest man ever to assume

STRIKING AT THE PRESIDENCY
A depiction of the assassination of William McKinley
at the Pan-American Exposition, 1901.
(Library of Congress)

the office of president, at forty-two, he was to institutionalize the strong presidency and become one of the greatest men ever to occupy the White House. Reflecting the Time of Paradox, he had a zest for living but was burdened with great sorrow; he would leave the country a great deal but he felt that he had not left enough.

Born in Manhattan to Martha "Mittie" and Theodore Sr., a noted philanthropist, this exceptional American was a sickly child, suffering from asthma, nervousness, stomach problems, a skinny body and eyes requiring thick spectacles. Roosevelt overcame his physical obstacles and anxiety, however, with a regimen of discipline, boxing, weight lifting, hiking, swimming, rowing, and tennis. He improved his mind, reading prodigiously, killing and stuffing birds and animals, collecting and cataloging plant specimens, and aspiring to a career in zoology. Military service also figured in Roosevelt's plans. His mother came from a wealthy southern family, and because her relatives fought for the Confederacy in the Civil War, her husband did not serve in the Union Army, hiring a substitute. Young Theodore considered this a stain on his family's record and yearned for action.

In 1876 Roosevelt entered Harvard University, where he boxed, wrestled, wrote two pamphlets on the birds of New York, and graduated with honors. Over the next few years, his personal life reached other turning points. First, halfway through his college studies, his father died and left Roosevelt $125,000, making it unnecessary for him to earn a living. Next, Roosevelt's interests shifted from zoology to the humanities. Finally, after planning to marry his childhood sweetheart, Edith Carow, Roosevelt was introduced to the beautiful Alice Hathaway Lee by a classmate, fell in love, and asked Alice to marry him. After some hesitation, she accepted, and in 1880 they wed.

Roosevelt built a large home on Long Island, began to study law at Columbia University, and started to work on the first of ten books he was to write before entering the White House. When he was just twenty-three, he published the well-received *Naval War of 1812*, which argued that the United States nearly lost the war because it had not built a powerful navy. He also entered politics as a Republican state assemblyman. His naiveté and uninhibited campaign style made party regulars wince, yet his incandescent energy impressed them. In office, the aggressive Roosevelt attacked boss rule, patronage politics, and special interests. He appeared to strike a balance between independence and party loyalty. Critics thought the Harvard boy with a squeaky voice was effeminate, a notion Roosevelt shattered by punching a Democratic colleague.

But in February 1884, Roosevelt's life grew dark. Two days after Alice gave birth to a girl, his mother died of typhoid fever. Hours later, his wife succumbed to kidney failure. He named his daughter after her mother and wrote of his wife in his diary, "And when my heart's dearest died, the light went from my life forever." It was too painful for Roosevelt to mention his wife Alice afterward; he never wrote about her, nor did he speak of her to his daughter. Followed by what he called "black despair," he left the baby with his sister, Bamie, and headed for the Dakota Badlands, where he became a rancher and cowboy. His brief sojourn was one of the formative experiences of his life. He rode the range, camped, hunted, pursued outlaws, and won the admiration of fellow cowboys. No political opponent would ever again credibly charge that Roosevelt was an effete intellectual. The austere surroundings, the arduous physical work, and the long hours toughened Roosevelt's body and healed his soul. Ranching in Dakota territory also inspired him to write the four-volume *Winning of the West*, one of the most popular histories of its time.

Returning east in the fall of 1884, Roosevelt resumed his relationship with Edith Carow. The couple became secretly engaged and married quietly in 1886. Shortly before the wedding, TR ran for office and finished third in a three-man race for New York mayor. In 1889, though, he went to Washington to serve as a civil service commissioner under Benjamin

Harrison. Roosevelt was a controversial commissioner, exposing corruption in the administration that appointed him.

Six years later he resigned to accept appointment as a New York police commissioner. Again, Roosevelt was incorrigible. He roamed the city in the early morning, seeking crime and corruption and observing the underside of life among the impoverished. Often reporters, such as Jacob Riis, accompanied Roosevelt, and the press helped build his legend. Perhaps worst of all, as far as his bosses were concerned, he fired the police chief and enforced Sunday closing laws against taverns, making him a political liability for the Republican mayor.

His support of McKinley's candidacy earned Roosevelt another tour of duty in Washington in 1897, this time as assistant navy secretary. He was determined to see the nation build a superior navy, necessary for a great country. A potent fleet was needed for the United States to approach the level of the British, Germans, and Japanese. War was noble and romantic, TR thought, and the country needed one. Hence when the sinking of the *Maine* heightened tension with Spain, Roosevelt urged McKinley to drive the Spaniards from the New World. When war arrived, Roosevelt could not wait to dive into it. Resigning his post, he was commissioned a lieutenant colonel and authorized to assemble the Rough Riders. From some twenty thousand applicants, including cowboys, Indians, Ivy League scholars, and football, tennis, and polo players, he selected one thousand who embodied his ideal of masculinity, trained them, and transported them to Cuba. In what he described as his "crowded hour," Roosevelt showed courage under fire and inspired his troops. He said it was the most important event in his life.

Victory on the battlefield helped lead to victory in politics. Roosevelt ran for governor of New York in 1898 at political boss Thomas Platt's request. He agreed to consult with Platt on patronage. As a campaigner, the Rough Rider was more show than substance, but the show was important. Roosevelt won narrowly and once more proved willing to work with reformers and bosses. He obtained passage of a civil service law, a raise for teachers, a tax on utilities, an eight-hour day for state employees, and a ban on racial segregation in schools. He supported unions, only to anger them when he called out the National Guard to keep order. Platt, too, grew disillusioned, fearing Roosevelt as a rival for control of patronage. Thus Platt engineered placing his rival on the McKinley ticket in the presidential contest of 1900.

The Spirit of Reform

Roosevelt became president when the progressive impulse was beginning to inspire measures to alleviate the social problems of expanding capitalism. Spanning the early decades of the 1900s, progressivism was a spirit of reform among intellectuals and local reformers that percolated to the federal government. Unlike farm-based populism, progressivism took root in cities and towns. Progressives wanted to save capitalism, not destroy it, and they advocated moderate change. Much hardship, progressives believed, arose from social ills, and reformers, with the help of social scientists, might improve society. "Those who have studied the causes of poverty and social evils have discovered that nine-tenths of the world's misery is preventable," Toledo Mayor Samuel Jones said.

Progressivism overlapped with the feminist movement, which strived to enact reforms related to women, children, families, and politics. Foremost among their objectives was woman suffrage, a cause that united most women. Other aims were the abolition of child labor, the establishment of juvenile courts, mandatory school attendance, limits on hours for working women, prohibition of alcohol, and the direct election of senators by voters instead of by legislatures. Because of respect for motherhood, women were considered uniquely qualified as advocates of reforms affecting families. Perhaps the most eminent progressive woman's leader was Jane Addams, a social worker who established Hull House in Chicago, one of many settlement houses providing social services to the underprivileged. One of Hull House's residents was Florence Kelley, leader of the National Consumers' League, which lobbied for protective labor laws that would limit what employers could require of women and children. Chicago was also the birthplace of the General Federation of Women's Clubs. Started in 1890 with ten thousand members, it grew to more than 1 million by 1910 and provided a voice for progressive reform.

Some women and other reformers, were motivated in part by the Social Gospel, a link between political progressivism and liberal Protestantism. Frequently called Christian Socialism, the Social Gospel emphasized the duty of the able, the wealthy, and the state to help the masses. This creed clashed with Social Darwinism, the application of Charles Darwin's theories of evolution in nature to human society. Social Darwinists held that the survival of the fittest in the marketplace led to progress, an idea that rationalized the status quo and opposed government attempts to regulate business or uplift the poor.

Progressives gave the first serious attention to urban poverty. Crowded, tenements were breeding grounds for crime, disease, and alcoholism. Social scientists, reporters, and politicians questioned the assumption that the poor were victims of their own flaws, suggesting they might be victims of society's flaws. Private charity, offering services rather than money, had long served the poor. Now people asserted that government should deal with poverty. This idea was championed among organizations such as the Socialist Party and by moderate reformers, including Roosevelt. The wealthy ignored the poor at the risk of revolutionary upheavals that might abolish capitalism, TR believed.

Urban vice often was connected with machine politics and bosses. The bosses of Democratic machines on the East Coast and Midwest often proved too formidable for the reformers, however. Their constituents were loyal because the machines provided rudimentary services and interceded with authorities. Held in a relationship of dependency, city dwellers considered bosses their friends, and opposed attempts to end boss rule. But there was no denying the extent of corruption, as journalist Lincoln Steffens documented in his 1904 book *The Shame of the Cities*. In nearly every city he studied, Steffens found bosses who took bribes for favoring businesses in granting utility franchises, contracts for public services, and construction of municipal buildings; these businesses, in turn, charged exorbitant prices. Bosses also stole from the public by padding city payrolls with "deadhead" employees who did little for their paychecks.

Steffens's revelations provoked some cities to invent forms of government that applied business efficiencies to government and removed administration from politics. Galveston, Texas, introduced the commission government, whereby each elected commissioner was responsible for a specific facet of government. By 1912 some two hundred cities and towns had adopted this approach. Other communities hired professional managers to run municipal affairs. The mayor-council system did not disappear. Many progressives used it to improve their cities, to bring politics closer to the people. Samuel Jones had rented an empty factory and hired unemployed workers to run it according to the Golden Rule, a principle that he tried to apply to politics by establishing an eight-hour day for city employees and reforming the police. Mayor Tom Johnson, who made Cleveland a model city, introduced public ownership of utilities, reduced trolley fares, humanized prisons, and created parks, playgrounds, and public baths. He demonstrated not only the potential of municipal reform but also the difficulty of sustaining it, because some of his improvements were abolished after his term ended.

From the cities, Progressivism leaped to the states. Most impressive were the reforms created by governors such as Robert M. "Fighting Bob" La Follette of Wisconsin. La Follette served three terms in the U.S. House of Representatives as a Republican Party regular before his defeat in 1890. Rebelling against the party bosses, he welded a coalition of insurgent followers and won the governorship on his third attempt, in 1900. Under La Follette, Wisconsin embarked on reforms that he said made the state a "lab-

THE FIGHTING
REFORMER
Wisconsin's Robert M.
La Follette.
(Library of Congress)

oratory of democracy." "Fighting Bob" tightened regulation of corporations, taxed railroads on the full value of their assets, taxed inheritances,
compensated injured workers, required primary elections for state offices,
and conserved water and forest resources. Also, La Follette was one of the
first politicians to use university professors to help draft legislation to alleviate social problems, a process he called the "Wisconsin Idea." From the governor's mansion, La Follette moved to the U.S. Senate in 1906 where he
served until his death in 1925. La Follette was a more radical reformer than
Roosevelt, whom he considered overly cautious. TR dismissed La Follette
as an impractical, uncompromising idealist.

The Midwest produced the most progressive governors, including
La Follette and Albert B. Cummins of Iowa. The Northeast boasted Charles
Evans Hughes of New York; on the West Coast there was Hiram Johnson of
California. In the South, James K. Vardaman of Mississippi was a rabid seg-
regationist, yet he ended the convict lease system, regulated corporations,

improved social welfare and educational services, and helped pass the nation's first direct primary law, whereby candidates were nominated directly by primaries rather than by conventions. One of the ironies of progressivism was its coexistence with white racism in the South. Moreover, some progressives nationwide supported immigration restrictions on the grounds that immigrants were the offspring of inferior races, an idea based on the pseudo science of eugenics, the ranking of races by intelligence. Eugenecists also advocated "scientific" breeding of humans to produce a superior race. It led to sterilization of criminals and of the mentally handicapped in some states.

Invigorating the Presidency

Roosevelt's robust approach to politics gave some the impression that he was more liberal than he was. In fact, Roosevelt's chief motive for reforming capitalism was to preserve it. Before he could move the nation forward, he must educate the people by exhortation. A rousing orator, he described the office as a "bully pulpit" from which he could do so, though he moved ahead of public opinion. Despite his aristocratic background, he seemed closer to the people than his predecessors.

Roosevelt strengthened the presidency by challenging the supremacy of business. When he became president, huge business combinations—the trusts pioneered by Standard Oil—were beginning to dominate markets, and despite the Sherman Antitrust Act, they seemed to be immune from government regulation. Roosevelt startled the nation in 1902 by filing suit against one of the largest, the Northern Securities Company, a combination of three major railroads, and compelling it to dissolve. One of the company's magnates, investment banker J. P. Morgan, considering himself an equal of the president, wanted the two to settle the affair privately. Roosevelt achieved his purpose of demonstrating that the authority of government surpassed that of business. The administration filed forty-three additional antitrust suits during Roosevelt's tenure, earning him a reputation as a "trustbuster." Later, Roosevelt somewhat relented, concluding that size alone was an insufficient reason to attack business combinations; only those that violated the public interest need be broken up.

Although some considered Roosevelt an enemy of business, an assumption that was misleading, it did not follow that he always sided with labor. A 1902 coal strike in Pennsylvania, which dragged on and threatened to deny part of the country coal during the winter, was settled by intimidation. When the sides could not agree, the president prepared the army to take over the mines, denying wages to the miners and profits to the owners. Under this splash of cold reality, both sides relented and the strike was settled by a mediation commission appointed by the president. The commission granted the miners a 10 percent wage increase but denied the union recognition. Roosevelt believed he had given both sides a "Square Deal," a phrase that became associated with his administration.

Advancing on all fronts, Roosevelt tightened business regulation in 1903 by helping engineer the Elkins Act that prohibited railroads from paying secret rebates to large shippers in return for their business. The president proposed, and ushered through Congress, a bill creating a Department of Commerce and Labor. The measure included a Bureau of Corporations armed with subpoena power to investigate interstate business and expose illegal activities.

Other successes came in conservation. Roosevelt was the first president to focus public attention on natural resources. Emphasizing the overdevelopment of grazing, lumber, and water projects on public lands in the West, he withdrew about 120–160 million acres from development, increasing reserves by nearly one-half during his first term. Additionally, he supported the Newlands Reclamation Act of 1902, which set aside almost the entire

THE PRESIDENT AND THE ENVIRONMENTALIST Theodore Roosevelt and conservation pioneer John Muir on Glacier Point, Yosemite Valley, circa 1906.
(Library of Congress)

proceeds from western land sales for construction and maintenance of irrigation projects in arid regions.

A ringmaster in the arena of governing, Roosevelt craved, and attracted, attention. He was the first president to hold press conferences, the first to be known by his initials, and the first to allow the press to cover the life of the first family. Family picnics and beeline hikes were the subjects of stories and Edith distributed family photos. Preferring simplicity, Roosevelt changed the name of the first family's residence from the Executive Mansion to the White House.

In 1904 Roosevelt became president in his own right by defeating the Democratic nominee, Judge Alton B. Parker, an obscure conservative from New York. William Jennings Bryan, a liberal who had lost twice, withdrew from consideration, stating that it was time for the party to try a conservative. Although Parker was an ineffective campaigner, one charge did strike the president in a vulnerable spot. He pointed out that the very corporations Roosevelt was boasting of taming had contributed to his campaign to protect themselves from antitrust prosecutions. Still, Roosevelt rolled over the Democrats, winning more than 7.6 million votes (57 percent) and 336 electoral votes to the Democrats' more than 5 million and 140.

As much as he loved power, Roosevelt revered tradition. He believed that he should preserve the two-term precedent set by George Washington and that his completion of McKinley's term represented nearly a full term. He did not want to appear power hungry. Thus, on the evening of his reelection, he announced he would not be a candidate for another term. He hoped this promise would remove political expediency from his policy making and allow him to do the right thing for the country. Yet expediency is the currency of politics, and the promise weakened TR politically. Further, he did love power and would leave the presidency still a young man, bored, with unfinished business, and an ego that would not allow any successor to fill his shoes.

Raking the Muck

In his second administration, TR resumed his reform agenda. In his first term he had concentrated largely on dismantling the trusts. Now he turned his attention to the railroads, considering strengthened transportation regulation and enhanced powers for the Interstate Commerce Commission (ICC) top priorities. TR thought about tariff reductions as well, yet believed they would divide the GOP. Consequently, he dodged the tariff issue, leaving it to his successor. But in collaboration with the president, Republican Representative William P. Hepburn of Iowa drafted a bill allowing the ICC to fix maximum railroad rates, audit railroad records, and require uniform bookkeeping methods. It could also regulate pipelines, terminals, and sleeping cars, and force railroads to sell steamship and coal properties to eliminate transportation monopolies. After the House adopted the measure, Roosevelt compromised to win Senate consent, amending the bill to give courts more discretion in determining rate changes. La Follette broke with him, claiming that the weakened bill betrayed the cause of reform. However altered, the law was the most significant regulatory measure enacted during Roosevelt's presidency.

Investigative journalists fed the demands for reform, exposing railroad practices, political corruption, adulterated drugs, and impure meat. Even though the journalists' aims resembled Roosevelt's, he denounced them as "muckrakers" after a character in Paul Bunyon's *Pilgrim's Progress* who would only look down and rake muck rather than look up to contemplate nobler matters. During the Senate debate over the Hepburn Act, TR condemned David Graham Phillips's book *The Treason of the Senate* (1906) as excessive in its criticism. Yet, although the influence of journalistic exposes declined after 1906, Roosevelt continued to seize upon the issues they raised. He introduced bills to regulate food and drugs and require meat inspections, the latter aided by Upton Sinclair's muckraking novel *The Jungle* (1906). The book tells the story of exploited workers at a meatpacking plant, where tubercular beef and poisoned rats are ground up into meat and workers who fall into the vats emerge as lard. Roosevelt signed the Meat Inspection Act and the Pure Food and Drug Act on the same day in 1906. The first law established standards and federal inspection for the slaughtering, processing, and labeling of meat. The second created the Food and Drug Administration with authority to test and approve drugs before they could be sold and to remove impure or fraudulently labeled drugs from interstate commerce. With the Hepburn Act, these measures constituted the high tide of TR's domestic reforms.

When it came to conservation, Roosevelt used executive orders to create national forests, monuments, parks, and wildlife reserves. This aggressive use of power irritated Congress. If Roosevelt annoyed some, he engaged the press and the public. On a hunting trip he refused to shoot a bear cub, and manufacturers created a toy "Teddy bear"; it became a favorite with children. Only the catastrophe of the 1906 earthquake and fires that devastated San Francisco could push Roosevelt off the front page momentarily.

Through much of Roosevelt's tenure, the nation was prosperous: the gross national product (the value of all goods and services produced in the country), income, and consumption grew. Farmers enjoyed one of their most prosperous decades in history, but in October 1907 a banking panic struck New York. Two financiers attempted to corner the copper market, and, when their scheme failed, investors began a run on companies that had financed it. The stock market tumbled, interest rates soared, and the unsound banking system was unable to control the crash born of reckless speculation.

Banker J. P. Morgan stepped in, helping pool funds of strong banks to sustain unsound ones in order to avert a total collapse. Treasury Secretary George Cortelyou issued $150 million in government bonds and certificates at favorable rates; by purchasing them, banks could bolster their collateral, shore up investor confidence, and avoid panic withdrawals. Morgan also acted to avert panic among brokerage firms by arranging the United States Steel Corporation's purchase of the Tennessee Coal and Iron Company. Roosevelt accepted the deal despite concerns over antitrust violations. The economy soon recovered, but the president's reputation among congressional Republicans never rebounded. As conservatives, they blamed his anti-big business rhetoric for the depression.

The courts too, slowed Roosevelt's pace of reform. The Supreme Court was a special source of bitterness, even though TR had appointed three justices, including Oliver Wendell Holmes Jr., who would be one of the greatest in history. In *Lochner v. New York* (1905), a ruling that infuriated TR, the court nullified a New York state law limiting bakers to ten working hours per day on the ground that the statute interfered with the freedom of contract. Yet three years later, in *Muller v. Oregon*, the court upheld an Oregon law that limited women laundry workers to ten hours per day. The justices accepted attorney Louis Brandeis's presentation of sociological and scientific data in favor of protective legislation for women.

TR and Taft: From Friends to Foes

In his final years as president, Roosevelt grew frustrated by his promise not to run again. He had been a good chief executive, he knew, but he felt he had fallen short of greatness because fate had not presented the opportunity to overcome a major crisis. Roosevelt, nonetheless, would not break his promise against running. Wishing to leave the nation a capable replacement, he turned to his close friend William Howard Taft.

Genial, intelligent, and humane, Taft had impressive administrative credentials. He had served as solicitor general, governor general of the Philippines, and secretary of war. He was, moreover, loyal to Roosevelt and a moderate progressive. Yet Taft had never run for office and hated campaigning. He did not like public speaking and lacked Roosevelt's fire; the public considered him bland in contrast to TR. But Roosevelt promoted Taft and the Ohioan easily won the Republican nomination. Then he

IN THE COMPANY
OF MILLIONAIRES
William Howard Taft
on the golf course.
(Library of Congress)

defeated Bryan, running futilely for the third time. Taft's victory was immense for a novice. He collected almost 7.7 million popular votes and 321 electoral votes to the Nebraskan's 6.4 million and 162.

Roosevelt sailed to Africa for a big-game safari, leaving Taft to run the country. Still, TR feared his successor was malleable and might be molded by stronger men while the Rough Rider was slaughtering lions. As Roosevelt feared, Taft moved to the right. Still, it would be wrong to conclude that Taft was not a progressive; his biggest flaw was that he was not Roosevelt. He lacked confidence and Roosevelt's aggressive spirit. A huge man, who overate and appeared passive, he was more suited for the judiciary. He could stand on principle, yet be indecisive. He did not like making political deals and failed to bedazzle the press. His only outdoor activity was golf, which he sometimes played in the company of millionaires. Most embarrassing, the obese president once got stuck in the White House bathtub and needed the Secret Service to pry him out.

Taft addressed the tariff issue and found out why TR had avoided it. It split the party. In 1909 he summoned a special session of Congress that produced a House bill with moderate cuts. Yet Senator Nelson Aldrich added nearly 850 special interest amendments. The resulting law did lower tariffs to an average of 38 percent from 57 percent in 1897, though a reciprocal rate provision allowed the president to raise or lower rates consistent with acts of other nations. The president alienated progressives by siding with their foe, arch-conservative House Speaker Joseph Cannon, in a power struggle. Congress also adopted the Sixteenth Amendment, allowing an income tax, which was ratified in 1913. Taft's record on these issues appeared more conservative to Roosevelt than it actually was. The Republicans were splintering, nonetheless, and Taft was unable to enforce party unity.

In 1910 the president entered another crossfire, this one between Interior Secretary Richard A. Ballinger and Chief Forester Gifford Pinchot. With Taft's approval, Ballinger sold millions of public acres that Pinchot had closed under TR's administration. Striking back, Pinchot accused Ballinger of facilitating the sale of public coal deposits in Alaska to a banking syndicate that included J. P. Morgan. Finding no basis for the charge, Taft ordered Pinchot to desist. Pinchot persisted and Taft fired him for insubordination. A congressional panel exonerated Ballinger, but that did not end the affair. Pinchot went to Italy to tell TR, just emerged from Africa, that Taft had betrayed the cause of conservation. In truth, Taft was committed to conservation and in a single term removed nearly as many acres from development as had Roosevelt in nearly two terms.

Even when Taft, identified with corporate interests, tried to regulate businesses, he fell short. In 1910 he engineered passage of the Mann-Elkins Act prohibiting railroads from charging more for short hauls than long hauls, a discriminatory practice used to gouge small shippers. Yet progressives considered the bill weak. Taft was more active than Roosevelt in filing antitrust suits, instigating more in four years than TR had in seven. Still, he angered TR in October 1911, when the Justice Department sued United States Steel over the acquisition of the Tennessee Coal and Iron Company. The suit made Roosevelt look dishonest or inept, perhaps duped by clever monopolists in his approval of the merger. TR complained that Taft had not objected to the deal at the time.

"We Stand at Armageddon"

In June 1910 Roosevelt returned from Europe to a hero's welcome in New York. Two months later, he delivered a series of speeches in support of progressive GOP congressional candidates in the fall elections. Using rhetoric that appalled Taft, TR declared that the rights of workers superseded the rights of capital and outlined reforms more leftist than any he had supported, including public review of state judges' decisions. Taft, believing the judiciary sacrosanct, thought Roosevelt had become power mad, yet neither could claim satisfaction in the election results. Roosevelt's progressives defeated Taft's conservatives in the primaries, yet lost to Democrats in the general election.

In February 1912, Roosevelt broke with Taft, entering the campaign for the Republican presidential nomination. He won most of the primaries (yet there were only a handful of primaries at that time), but Taft ingratiated himself with the party bosses and won the nomination. Roosevelt supporters walked out after being denied disputed delegates, muttering "Thou shalt not steal." The next day Roosevelt urged his followers to back him as a third party candidate in a speech with biblical gravity, concluding, "We stand at Armageddon and we battle for the Lord." Seven weeks later the new Progressive Party nominated its hero, singing "Onward, Christian Soldiers" and "The Battle Hymn of the Republic." Roosevelt said he felt as strong as a bull moose and the party acquired a nickname: "the Bull Moose Party." The party nominated Hiram Johnson for vice president.

TR hoped the Democrats would nominate a conservative, yet they turned instead to New Jersey's progressive governor, Woodrow Wilson. A political scientist, the president of Princeton before his election as governor, Wilson excelled Roosevelt in cold eloquence if not in demonstrative display. Wilson urged regulation of business by controlled marketplace competition, a program he called the "New Freedom." Roosevelt stuck to tougher direct government regulation, a plan known as the "New Nationalism." In truth, the differences were chiefly semantic. Yet the dialogue started one of the fundamental debates of the Time of Paradox, an argument over the degree to which the federal government should intervene in the economy.

In Milwaukee, on October 14, a would-be assassin wounded Roosevelt, who declined medical help and completed his speech. In fact, the Rough Rider seemed to enjoy the suspense. TR won his battle with mortality, but he, like Taft, realized he had little chance to win the election. The Republican fratricide had wrecked the party and carved a canyon between one of the closest political friendships of the era. A reporter found Taft sobbing, head in hands, on his campaign train, "Roosevelt was my closest friend." More than an election had been lost. Roosevelt wandered in the political wilderness, an outsider to the party he had helped rejuvenate, for the rest of his life. In time he resumed his friendship with Taft but became a shrill critic of Wilson.

Wilson's victory was a watershed, yet it was unclear whether voters had rejected the Republican party in favor of the Democrats or simply, exasperated, asked, "Which Republican party?" Wilson polled almost 6.3 million votes and won with just 43 percent of the popular vote in the three-way race. Roosevelt won 4.1 million popular votes and Taft drew 3.5 million. In the Electoral College, however, it was a Democratic landslide: Wilson, 435; Roosevelt, 88; and Taft, 8. Socialist Party candidate Eugene V. Debs received 900,000 votes, almost 6 percent.

Taft took the defeat much better than Roosevelt. He had never wanted to be president, preferring a place on the Supreme Court. Taft was neither

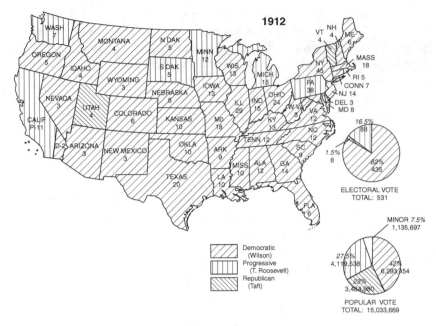

Election of 1912

a great nor an incompetent president. Temperamentally, he lacked the imagination and vision to inspire the masses, and he followed a man who excelled at leadership. Yet his accomplishments are sometimes underestimated. By no means dull or unintelligent, he left as his legacy the Mann-Elkins Act, conservationist activities, trustbusting, and the income tax amendment which Taft submitted in 1909 and the states ratified in 1913. The income tax levy started at 1 percent on incomes over $3,000 for single people and over $4,000 for married people, peaking at 6 percent on incomes over $500,000. Under his administration, Congress passed a constitutional amendment that placed the election of U.S. senators in the hands of the people (rather than state legislatures); it was ratified as the Seventeenth Amendment in 1913. Legislation also created postal savings banks as an alternative to commercial banks, a Federal Children's Bureau to supervise child welfare matters, and a commission to investigate labor conditions; established a Commerce Department separate from the Labor Department; and limited work on federal projects to eight hours a day. Moreover, as president, Taft appointed 45 percent of the federal judiciary, including six justices to the Supreme Court, the tribunal to which he aspired. In 1921 President Warren G. Harding made Taft chief justice and gave him a place in history as the only man to lead the high court and serve as president.

CHAPTER TWO

America Looks Outward, 1900–1912

A S THE NINETEENTH century ended, America had dived into the treacherous waters of international diplomacy. The century ended with a splash. The coldness of the water was invigorating and sobering. It was to be an Era of Awakening.

Theodore Roosevelt was fond of citing a west African proverb, "Speak softly and carry a big stick, you will go far." In reality, the proverb described TR's policies in reverse. He bellowed yet rarely inflicted force. He initiated no combat by American troops during his presidency. The only place where Americans died in battle was in the Philippines, where fighting began before he took office. But if Roosevelt was restrained in the use of force, he was not reluctant to threaten it. He took pride in presiding over a buildup of the navy from fifth largest on the planet to second, behind Britain's. Roosevelt welcomed the opportunity to be at the center of action. An assertive foreign policy, he believed, would help provide Americans with a sense of purpose and define their place in the world. His romance with war aside, he did not desire it while president, but sought a Pax Americana or, perhaps, a Pax Roosevelt.

The Roosevelt Corollary

Roosevelt's foremost concern was the Western Hemisphere. After the Cuban Revolution, the United States insisted on an amendment to the new Cuban constitution making it a virtual protectorate of the United States. The United States used the Platt Amendment in 1906, dispatching troops to maintain order on the island, where they remained until 1909.

Roosevelt was annoyed by European nations' attempts to employ their military to collect debts from Latin American countries. He particularly

VISIONS OF AMERICAN POWER
President Theodore Roosevelt speaking in South Lawrence,
Massachusetts, circa 1902.
(Library of Congress)

disliked Germany. TR believed Kaiser Wilhelm II was the most aggressive imperialist in the world. Early in his presidency, Venezuela refused to pay more than $70 million it owed to Germany. The European powers, joined by Venezuela's other creditors, Britain and Italy, hoped to compel payment by declaring a blockade of the coast in November 1902. The coalition sank Venezuelan vessels and the Germans landed troops. Roosevelt became involved when the Venezuelan dictator, who initially refused to negotiate, asked him to arbitrate. The president proposed that the claims be submitted to the International Court of Justice at The Hague. The coalition agreed, but maintained the blockade as the court deliberated. In 1904 the tribunal ruled in favor of the creditors.

The bankrupt Dominican Republic was another source of turmoil. To keep Germany and fellow creditors from collecting debts there, and to establish a rationale for American intervention in other Caribbean crises, the president and Secretary of State John Hay devised the Roosevelt Corollary to the Monroe Doctrine. The corollary, announced by TR in December 1904, declared that the United States would police the hemisphere to rectify "chronic wrongdoing" in Latin America. Under the corollary, from 1905 to 1907, U.S. Marines occupied the Dominican Republic, supervised customs collections, and used them to pay off debts.

Roosevelt and the Panama Canal

Of Roosevelt's foreign initiatives, the boldest and most controversial was his virtual seizure of a zone in Panama to construct an interoceanic canal. Americans had dreamed of a canal that would eliminate the voyage around South America. Plans were set in motion in 1850, when the United States and Britain signed the Clayton-Bulwer Treaty providing for joint construction. Fifty-two years later, in the 1902 Hay-Pauncefote pact, Britain yielded its rights to joint construction and was promised equal access and equal tolls. At the time Roosevelt became president, the canal remained just an idea. As a champion of a strong navy with an interest in the Pacific, he was in a hurry to build a canal.

Two options were proposed: a sea-level canal through Nicaragua, and a canal through Panama requiring locks. For the second, the United States had to buy the rights from a French company whose ten-year attempt to construct a canal ended unsuccessfully in 1889. The bankrupt company demanded $109 million for the rights, which were to expire in September 1904. On the recommendation of a government commission, the House voted for the cheaper Nicaraguan route. Nevertheless, the company prodded the Senate into endorsing the Panama route, publicizing a volcanic eruption in a Nicaraguan lake through which the canal was to be built and reducing its price for its rights to $40 million.

In 1902 Congress directed TR to accept the company's offer and to negotiate terms for operating the canal with Colombia, of which Panama was a province. The 1903 Hay-Herran Treaty met these aims. It guaranteed the company $40 million and Colombia $10 million plus $250,000 annually for a ninety-nine-year renewable lease on a six-mile-wide canal zone. The U.S. Senate approved the arrangement but the Colombian Senate deferred action, hoping for a better deal after the company's rights expired. Outraged, Roosevelt considered the rejection a national insult. He offered Colombia the treaty on a take-it-or-leave-it basis and exhibited a contempt for the South Americans bordering on racism. Then a representative of the French company, Philippe Bunau-Varilla, traveled to Washington to tell him a revolution was brewing in Panama and asked how America would respond. TR was noncommittal but did not discourage the uprising.

Panamanian business interests supported revolution, afraid that Colombia's repudiation of the treaty might persuade the United States to turn to Nicaragua. Moreover, if Panama became independent it might receive the money to be paid to Colombia. Panama had a long revolutionary tradition, including numerous rebellions against Colombia. A nearly bloodless revolution occurred on November 3, 1903. Bunau-Varilla, author of a declaration of independence and constitution for the new country, had bribed Colombian soldiers in Panama not to suppress the revolt. An American gunboat offshore intimidated Colombia from landing soldiers.

Events raced to a climax. On November 6 the United States diplomatically recognized the Republic of Panama. A week later Secretary of State John Hay accepted a visit from Bunau-Varilla, and the Hay–Bunau-Varilla Treaty was negotiated. In exchange for a ten-mile-wide canal zone, the company received $40 million and Panama received essentially the same financial terms that Colombia would have received. Both countries consented to the treaty early in 1904 and construction began in midyear. In the United States the canal was wildly popular and embellished TR's glamour at election time. In Latin America, Roosevelt's tactics were resented. Still, he never expressed regret for bullying smaller nations in the hemisphere. Not until 1921 did the United States pay an indemnity to Columbia for helping strip it of a province.

One of the great engineering feats of the first half of the twentieth century, construction of the canal took ten years and cost more than $365 million. The project also led to a medical breakthrough when Colonel William C. Gorgas developed methods to eradicate the mosquito carrying yellow fever, which had decimated construction workers. Although it did not open until August 1914, years after he left the White House, the Panama Canal always has been identified with Theodore Roosevelt. "I took the canal zone, and let Congress debate, and while the debate goes on, the canal does also," he boasted.

TR believed Central American stability was essential to the security of the canal, but he preferred not to intervene militarily in the region. The outbreak of several wars made some action imperative, though, so the U.S. summoned a Central American peace conference to meet in the fall of 1908 in Washington. The Central American nations reached eight agreements designed to preserve the peace.

LINKING THE ATLANTIC AND PACIFIC OCEANS
The Panama Canal under construction.
(Library of Congress)

America as a Pacific Power

The United States sent missionaries to China, tried to develop trade there, and wanted to prevent Japan from conquering its larger, weaker neighbor. Because the major European nations and Japan had carved out spheres of influence in which they monopolized trade, the United States sought to maintain an "Open Door" in which nations shared trade in areas they dominated. America also owned Hawaii and occupied the Philippines, which it developed economically, although the Filipinos wanted independence and fought a costly war against America to obtain it. Competition between Russia and Japan in the Far East provoked the Russo-Japanese War. It began when the Japanese, in a surprise attack, sank the Russian fleet at Port Arthur in February 1904. Japan gained the upper hand in the war, yet Roosevelt preferred a compromise peace that would prevent either nation from becoming overly powerful. When the Japanese asked Roosevelt to mediate the war, he agreed, and Russia, experiencing internal turmoil, agreed as well. The parties met in August 1905 in Portsmouth, New Hampshire, where, after much frustrating haggling, the combatants reached terms. Russia accepted Japanese domination of Korea, and Roosevelt received the Nobel Peace Prize for his efforts.

Japanese pride and American prejudice clashed in California. In 1906, San Francisco officials segregated Asian children in public schools. Roosevelt informed the Japanese that he opposed the system, yet he was worried about alienating voters in California, who wanted to curtail Japanese immigration. An informal "Gentlemen's Agreement" was worked out. The Japanese voluntarily restricted immigration and the segregated system was ended.

Roosevelt feared that perhaps he had spoken too softly to the Japanese and not brandished a big enough stick. To impress them, and other nations, he dispatched all of America's battleships, painted gleaming white, on a global tour. Though billed as a goodwill tour, Roosevelt intended to intimidate. In fact, it heightened the naval arms race. Nonetheless, in 1908 Japan and America concluded the Root-Takahira Agreement whereby the United States recognized Japan's interest in Manchuria, and both countries agreed to observe China's territorial integrity and the Pacific status quo. When Congress threatened to withhold funds from the fleet, which Roosevelt high-handedly had dispatched without congressional approval, Roosevelt countered that he would leave the fleet, penniless, in the distant East. The funds flowed and the fleet returned on February 22, 1909, providing a going away party for the former president as he set out for Africa.

European Diplomacy

The United States shared the longest undefended border in the world with Canada, a British dominion. In the twentieth century Britain became America's closest informal ally. Yet, good neighbors occasionally quarrel. In 1902 Canada claimed lands in Alaska that cut off gold mines from the sea. The issue was settled in favor of the United States by a trilateral commission including representatives from the United States, Britain, and Canada. The British voted with the United States, feeling that friendly relations with America outweighed the interests of their own dominion.

Britain was willing to forsake ambitions in the Western Hemisphere and sought American support for its interests in the Middle East, Africa, and Asia. Britain also agreed with Roosevelt that Germany was the chief menace to world peace and that Wilhelm's designs in North Africa had to be stopped. The issues arose in the early 1900s when Wilhelm, resenting French domination of Morocco, part of the Ottoman Empire, implied that he might use force to prevent the establishment of a French protectorate. Asked by the kaiser to mediate, Roosevelt induced the French to participate in a conference in January 1906 at Algeciras, Spain, assuring the French that the Americans would support them on substantive issues and try to contain Wilhelm. The agreement reached in April effectively left France in control of Morocco, but not in an official sense. It affirmed Moroccan independence, guaranteed free trade, and provided for a police force trained by France and Spain to maintain order. TR's mediation added to his international stature.

Taft's Foreign Policy

In foreign affairs, William Howard Taft lacked his predecessor's glamour and finesse. He was neither as imaginative nor as aggressive as the Rough Rider and less ambitious about America's place in the world. It was time to consolidate TR's achievements rather than expand them, Taft believed. In China and Latin America he tried to substitute Dollar Diplomacy for Big Stick Diplomacy. America would influence world events through trade and loans rather than by rhetoric or intimidation. Taft was not notably successful in his tactics.

Taft was stymied in his efforts to conduct Dollar Diplomacy in Latin America, where the policy was perceived as patronizing. In Honduras, his minister helped reorganize the finances of that nation, which defaulted on its debts and could pay but a few cents on a dollar. When even that amount proved beyond the Hondurans, Secretary of State Philander Chase Knox negotiated a 1911 agreement providing for U.S. banks to take over the supervision of payments, using customs collections, but the senates of both countries rejected the pact. Knox also met with failure when Costa Rica and Guatemala rebuffed his attempts to supervise their finances and customs collections. No such obstacles presented themselves in Haiti, where the United States refunded the debt of the crumbling government, and in the Dominican Republic, where Taft sent Marines to force the resignation of the president and supervise an election after a revolution began. The Marines departed in December 1912, although Taft's successor, Woodrow Wilson, sent gunboats to the coast in September 1913 when another revolution loomed.

Affairs in Nicaragua proved tangled. Taft and Knox were concerned about dictator Jose Santos Zelaya, an American adversary who, it was said, was going to lease another country rights to build an isthmian canal that would compete with the Panama Canal. In 1909 American businessmen, with the aid of U.S. diplomats and Marines, helped engineer Zelaya's overthrow.

ADVOCATING DOLLAR
DIPLOMACY
William H. Taft in the
White House.
(Library of Congress)

The following year a pro-American president, Adolfo Diaz, was installed. American dominance was reinforced when Knox and the Nicaraguan minister to Washington forged a deal giving the United States the right to intervene to prevent the collapse of the government. Despite an American decision to refund the debt, Nicaragua defaulted on loans to European bankers in October 1911, and two months later American bankers took over the customs houses to satisfy the obligations. The Senate had rebuffed the agreement, but the United States continued its protectorate. In 1912 Taft sent Marines to keep Zelaya from overthrowing Diaz; the forces, although reduced, remained almost continuously until 1933.

American-Mexican relations were turbulent during Taft's tenure and into the administration of his successor, Wilson. The chief issues were American control of much of Mexico's natural resources, especially oil, and the domination of education by the Catholic Church. Porfirio Diaz had long permitted American exploitation of his country's resources, yet was overthrown in 1911 when a leftist, Francisco Madero, seized power. Madero did not move rapidly enough to satisfy his supporters and was overthrown and murdered by Victoriano Huerta in February 1913. Taft left the choice of whether to recognize Madero's regime to Wilson.

Meanwhile, hearing rumors that a Japanese company was trying to obtain strategic territory in Mexico, Senator Henry Cabot Lodge obtained Senate approval of the Lodge Corollary to the Monroe Doctrine, barring foreign nations and corporations from gaining strategic sites in the Western Hemisphere.

In China, Taft tried to replace British and Japanese capital with American capital for railroad construction and other internal improvements. In Manchuria, American bankers were reluctant to invest in a risky railroad venture and yielded to the Japanese and the Russians. In a 1911 revolution, Dr. Sun Yat-Sen overthrew the Chinese monarchy and set about unifying China under a republican form of government. By now, American bankers were weary of being prodded by the president to risk loans in unstable regions. Taft decided to cease urging them.

The president placed great faith in legal agreements among nations and wanted to improve arbitration treaties negotiated during TR's tenure. Yet TR and Senator Lodge opposed his efforts, and the treaties remained ineffectual. Taft also encountered trouble with Britain over tolls paid by the two countries for use of the Panama Canal. In 1912 Congress passed legislation exempting from tolls American vessels using the canal to navigate between the East and West coasts. Britain complained that the law violated the Hay-Pauncefote Treaty guaranteeing equal tolls and demanded arbitration. The issue was not settled until 1914.

More successfully, Taft submitted a dispute over fishing off the Newfoundland coast involving the United States, Canada, and Britain to The Hague Tribunal, whose settlement satisfied all parties. He also worked to improve trade relations with Canada, complicated since passage of the Payne-Aldrich Tariff of 1909. Taft negotiated an agreement in 1911 to open Canadian markets to American goods and to reduce the price of Canadian goods to American consumers. The Senate accepted the deal, only to see the Canadian Parliament reject it after Conservatives, opponents of trade reciprocity, scored an election victory over Liberals.

Overall, Taft's diplomacy, although more cautious than TR's, was not exactly the eye of the storm. Rather it rode on breezes between the tempest of Roosevelt and the tornado that would blow in with Wilson.

CHAPTER THREE

Nations within: The Experiences of Immigrants, Minorities, and Workers

> Do I contradict myself? Very well, then, I contradict myself (I am large—I contain multitudes).
>
> —Walt Whitman, "Song of Myself" (1855), *Leaves of Grass*

RIPE WITH opportunity, riven by canyons of despair, the city offered the bleak and the bright images of the Time of Paradox. With the promise of jobs, capital, housing, modern plumbing, public transportation, and cultural amenities, the city beckoned immigrants and minorities. Surges of newcomers boosted urban economies, yet necessitated greater services, straining resources. Neighborhoods divided by class, race, and ethnicity; the rich and the privileged found spaces where they could live in seclusion from the poor.

Reform in the City

Reformers grappled with urban problems, including poverty. Progressives focused on the social causes of privation. Government began to furnish some poor relief in the form of money. One example was the "mothers' assistance" programs implemented in some states in the 1910s to allow women to remain at home and care for their children instead of getting jobs. A related problem, a poor living environment, was another target of reformers, who improved tenements in cities.

Crime was attacked. To end police corruption and brutality, reformers increased qualifications and training for officers. Fingerprinting tracked and identified lawbreakers. Locally, vice commissions and special courts attempted to eradicate prostitution. At the national level, Congress passed laws prohibiting the importation of prostitutes, authorizing the deportation of immigrant prostitutes, and outlawing the transportation of women across state lines for immoral purposes. Drugs—morphine, heroin, and cocaine—had been sold legally in the nineteenth century. Reaction set in by 1900, when Coca-Cola removed cocaine from its beverage after it was learned the drug could cause hyperactivity and paranoia. Despite the U.S. approval of the 1912 Hague Opium Treaty curtailing international trade of opium and cocaine, the federal government did little to control narcotic sales until 1919, although there were some state and local restrictions.

Immigrants

Cities attracted more residents who made up a greater share of the national population. From 1900 to 1910 more than 8 million immigrants settled in the United States, the greatest number in any decade before or since. In 1907, the record year, 1,285,349 arrived. Immigrants constituted more than 10 percent of the population and more than one-third the population of the twelve largest cities. By 1910 New York had more Italians than Naples, more Germans than Hamburg, twice as many Irish as Dublin, and more Jews than all of Western Europe.

Looking to America for democracy, religious freedom, and economic opportunity, the immigrants, most of them Catholics, found their best hope of employment in factories. Without immigrant workers, the industrial revolution of the late nineteenth and early twentieth centuries would have been impossible despite technology. Immigrants contributed skills, muscle, and a work ethic, taking dangerous, low-paying jobs in mines, mills, construction, canning, and meatpacking. Sixty to eighty percent of immigrants, excluding Jews, came to America to make money and take it back to their native lands.

Jews, while retaining their ancient cultural identity, were one of the most successful immigrant groups. Most immigrated from Russia and Eastern Europe, constituting more than half the immigrants from Russia between 1900 and 1920. About 45 percent lived in New York City, where they constituted one-quarter of the population. Many worked in the garment district, cigar factories, and printing plants. Some 75 percent of the first generation of Jewish immigrants' children rose to the middle class, the highest ratio of any group. Some Jews became socialists and leaders in the radical labor movement. Jews also thirsted for education. A higher percentage of Eastern European Jews obtained college educations than any other immigrant group during the Progressive Era.

THE CHANGING FACE OF AMERICA
Immigrants landing at Ellis Island, 1912.
(Library of Congress)

Some groups, such as Italians, French Canadians, and Mexicans, placed greater emphasis on family loyalty and proximity. Helping the family earn an income and taking care of children was more important than learning English or going away to college. Cultural assimilation was discouraged. Mexicans moved north in large numbers early in the new century to work in the irrigated fields of the Southwest; others fled the Mexican Revolution of 1910. Before 1924 there were no border guards and no laws prohibited immigration from the Western Hemisphere. By 1925, Los Angeles had a larger Spanish-speaking population than any North American city except Mexico City. Other immigrants included Filipinos and some 450,000 from the Middle East.

Immigrants changed, and were changed, by America. They intermarried and introduced new lifestyles, talents, and religious observances. Partly because they differed from the dominant Nordic Protestant culture, some feared them and considered them economic competitors. Discrimination, born of exploitation and a distaste of differences, was often their lot. Some believed the newcomers, especially Jews and Catholics, conspired to overthrow the government and monopolize the economy. In 1915, Leo Frank, a Georgia Jewish factory owner convicted of murdering a young Caucasian girl on dubious evidence, was dragged from his jail cell and lynched. Racial and religious prejudice were not the only elements in discrimination against foreigners. Some feared foreign ideologies, such as communism, socialism, and anarchism, and believed America could be saved by cleansing the nation of immigrants carrying the infection of such beliefs.

Women's Suffrage and New Possibilities

The twentieth century was a time of accelerated feminist consciousness that had germinated since the abolitionist crusade. Feminism, a movement for women's equality, made substantial progress during the Progressive Era, winning the vote in some states and accomplishing its chief objective in 1920, a constitutional amendment giving women the vote across the nation. The White House was of little help for much of the period. Roosevelt, for example, said, "Personally I believe in women's suffrage, but I am not an enthusiastic advocate of it because I do not consider it a very important matter." Feminists grew more militant, staging marches and protests and starting to break out of their narrow organizational base of upper-middle-class, educated white women. Also on the feminist agenda were equal educational opportunities and property rights, access to the professions, and liberalized divorce laws.

Women gained opportunities in education and employment and dominated new fields such as social work. Jane Addams, Florence Kelley, Lillian Wald, and Julia Lathrop pioneered in serving the urban poor. Lathrop, appointed to head the Children's Bureau in 1910, became the first woman to head a federal agency. Women entered the workforce in large numbers as stenographers, typists, and salesclerks. Women's image changed. Charles Dana Gibson created the prototypical "Gibson Girl" in his sketches, especially for magazine covers. The Gibson Girl was young, thin, and uninhibited and flaunted her sexuality by smoking, drinking, and wearing casual clothes. The sexual revolution advanced on other fronts as city environments made chaperoned dates more difficult to arrange and prostitutes available. Margaret Sanger, a New York nurse, promoted birth control, even though it was illegal in some states, and her activities got her arrested. Also, women began talking more frankly about sex, often in mixed company. The pressure for an explosion of sexuality in American culture gathered momentum throughout the era, which was an era of awakening for sexual change.

An Expanding Economy

The first two decades of the twentieth century were dominated by prosperity, interrupted by brief recessions that began in 1907 and 1914. Good times spared the era some of the turmoil and demand for radical change of the 1890s. Most people accepted the need for some government regulation of corporations. Total production nearly doubled between 1900 and 1910, then tripled by 1920. Farm prosperity complemented business and industrial prosperity. Pockets of poverty nonetheless persisted, especially in the South and the West, among rural people, minorities, and debtors. Railroad expansion slowed with the increasing competition from automobiles. Car registration climbed from 8,000 in 1900 to 458,000 ten years later. Power shifted from magnates such as John D. Rockefeller and Andrew Carnegie to investment bankers such as J. P. Morgan. Capital, not tangible national resources, was the lifeblood of capitalism. Expansion was the key to capitalism's success. In 1901 Morgan helped organize the world's largest corporation, United States Steel, capitalized at $1.4 billion. Like Rockefeller and Carnegie, Morgan was a ruthless business competitor and a philanthropist. He left much of his vast art collection to New York's Metropolitan Museum of Art.

The economy had a place for entrepreneurs such as Henry Ford, producer of the first practical mass-produced car. After building his first car in 1896, he applied the first movable assembly line to the automobile industry and introduced the Model T in 1908. Ford changed America fundamentally, as did the Wright brothers, Orville and Wilbur, inventors of the first practical heavier-than-air manned aircraft. Financing their work with profits from their bicycle company, they made their initial flight on December 17, 1903, at Kitty Hawk, North Carolina. By the close of 1905, they founded a company to build and sell airplanes and license European manufacturers. Glenn Hammond Curtiss, a motorcycle builder, also emerged as a major figure in aviation. In 1909 he won a race in France with a plane that averaged forty-seven miles per hour. By midcentury the leading producers of airliners were Boeing, McDonald Douglas, and Lockheed.

Growth of Organized Labor

Organized labor awakened to new leadership during the era. Its ranks swelled by immigrants and city workers, the number of union workers stood at 1.4 million by 1901, of which 1 million belonged to the American Federation of Labor (AFL). Just three years later, the AFL's membership had doubled. The efforts of Samuel Gompers, the president and cofounder, were largely responsible for the increase. A Jewish immigrant from London, Gompers became a cigar maker and organizer for the Cigar Makers International. As leader of the AFL, he pursued a pragmatic program: higher wages, shorter hours, and better working conditions. He collaborated with Marxists, yet was not a socialist and opposed violent strikes.

Gompers believed in a strong central organization that admitted unions based on the skills, or crafts, of their workers. He opposed the idea of industrial unions whereby all workers who made a single product belonged to the same union. He supported immigration restrictions, though an immigrant himself, on the grounds they depressed wages, and opposed the eight-hour day. Gompers supported Woodrow Wilson for president in 1912 and 1916, gaining influence within the councils of government. By 1900, the AFL had no durable rival. A small, temporary challenge emerged in the Western Federation of Miners. After several unsuccessful strikes among Colorado miners from 1903 to 1905, they created the stronger Industrial Workers of the World (IWW), led by William "Big Bill" Haywood. The IWW practiced class warfare, sabotage, and violence, claiming the AFL was insufficiently militant. The "Wobblies," as they were known, hoped to organize smaller industrial unions into "one big union" and stage a general strike to destroy capitalism.

The American Socialist Party, led by Eugene V. Debs, was more militant than the AFL, and, like the IWW, hoped to overturn capitalism. However, the Socialist Party expelled Haywood because he espoused violence, counter to its ideology. Unlike the AFL in another way, the Socialist Party ran candidates for office. Debs ran for president five times from 1900 to 1920. In 1910 the party elected its first big city mayor, Victor Berger of Milwaukee.

Women, too, were prominent in the ranks of radical labor, the most colorful of whom was Mary Harris "Mother" Jones. A heroine to miners, Jones was a participant in every major coal strike of her time. Belying her grandmotherly looks, she was militant, witty, tough—urging wives of miners to disrupt strikebreakers by parading through the mountains banging tin pans. During the second wave of feminism a radical magazine was named *Mother Jones* in her honor.

Elizabeth Gurley Flynn had a long career as a revolutionary and organizer for the IWW and the Communist Party. In the first two decades of the century, her celebrity was comparable to a movie star's. A charismatic orator, she welcomed court trials as forums to attract public sympathy for labor. Flynn was elected chair of the IWW in 1906 while Haywood lectured in Europe to celebrate his acquittal on charges of murdering the Idaho governor, who had called out the National Guard to suppress a strike.

Emma Goldman, a labor radical, anarchist, peace activist, and birth-control advocate, was an early backer of the Bolshevik Revolution. She helped her lover, Alexander Berkman, plot to assassinate Henry Clay Frick during the Homestead strike. Goldman also spent prison terms for urging workers to steal to eat, for espousing birth control, for distributing contraceptives, and for organizing a campaign against conscription during World War I. In 1919 Goldman and other radicals were deported to the Soviet Union. There, she became disillusioned with regimented rule and wrote one of the early internal critiques of the Soviet State. Leaving the U.S.S.R., she spent the rest of her life in Europe and Canada.

Less notorious than Goldman, but influential as a labor organizer, was Rose Schneiderman, a Jewish immigrant from Poland. One of the most effective labor orators, she helped organize successful strikes of New York shirtwaist makers (tailors) in 1909 and 1910. Those workers became martyrs for reform in 1911, when a fire at the Triangle Shirtwaist Factory killed 146 women. The owners had locked the fire escape doors to prevent union organizers from entering and employees from taking breaks. The building was a deadly trap for those who worked for a pittance in dangerously crowded conditions. Schneiderman encountered opposition in the New York Women's Trade Union League (NYWTUL), in part due to her efforts to organize immigrants, especially Jews. Resigning in protest, she joined the International Ladies Garment Workers Union, became frustrated with its lack of support for her efforts, and returned to the NYWTUL as president. In the meantime, Schneiderman had become convinced that suffrage was critical to women's progress and that the movement had to reach beyond its elitist roots to working-class women. She helped found the Wage Earner's League for Woman Suffrage, the first suffrage organization made up largely of industrial women workers, in 1911. Her advocacy was rewarded in 1917, when New York women won the vote. Many of Schneiderman's attempts to obtain safer work conditions, higher wages, and union recognition succeeded as well.

Crystal Eastman's investigations of labor conditions in New York led her to write *Work Accidents and the Law* (1910), a study in the new field of worker's compensation law. She helped draft such a law for New York State. During Wilson's presidency, Eastman served as an attorney for the U.S. Commission on Industrial Relations. Radicalized by her failure to obtain women's suffrage in Wisconsin, she joined Alice Paul in helping found the Congressional Union, a forerunner of the militant National Woman's Party. She also worked against militarism and war and was instrumental in creating the Women's Peace Party. Renamed the Women's International League for Peace and Freedom in 1921, it became the longest-lasting women's peace organization. Finally, Eastman helped form the National Civil Liberties Union, an early version of the American Civil Liberties Union, to protect the rights of conscientious objectors and defend freedom of speech.

Labor was caught in a paradox: militance sometimes gained concessions, yet it also frightened away recruits. By World War I, the IWW had only 60,000–100,000 members. The conviction of two radical union leaders in a bomb blast that destroyed the Los Angeles Times building and killed twenty nonunion men was a stigma for the IWW cause. Another setback came when a firm of hatters in Danbury, Connecticut, sued the hatters' union for $240,000 for a boycott under the Sherman Act. The United States Supreme Court upheld the judgment, saying the boycott was an illegal combination in restraint of trade. The IWW received a mixed decision in 1912, when tens of thousands of textile workers in Lawrence, Massachusetts, struck to protest wage cuts. With the AFL standing aloof, the Wobblies sent Haywood, Flynn, Mother Jones, and Sanger. Within six weeks the company yielded to many of the strikers' demands for higher pay, shorter hours, overtime, and no discrimination against strikers. Victory for the workers nonetheless proved temporary; the owners reversed most of their concessions within a year. Soon textile workers struck again, at Paterson, New Jersey, and Haywood and the Wobblies intervened again, but the strike was broken by May 1913.

Another strike in 1913 occurred at the Rockefeller family mines in Ludlow, Colorado. The state militia was summoned and several miners were killed in a skirmish known as the "Ludlow Massacre." Despite exhortations by Goldman, the exhausted strikers gave up. A commission investigating the strike caught John D. Rockefeller in a lie and tarnished his image. Though he claimed no knowledge of atrocious conditions in the mines, correspondence proved that he had known. Still, the Wobblies lost most. Their fiery rhetoric produced few tangible gains, and members defected to more pragmatic unions. Haywood was convicted of organizing strikes during wartime under the Sedition and Espionage Acts and fled to the Soviet Union to escape imprisonment. Like Goldman, he became disillusioned with Soviet communism, declined into alcoholism, and died in 1928. Yet, he was still revered in the U.S.S.R. and in some radical circles in America. His ashes were divided: some were buried within the Kremlin Walls and some in a Chicago cemetery.

Progressive Era presidents clearly disliked radical labor unions and placed a premium on maintaining order. Theodore Roosevelt supported union objectives such as the eight-hour day for federal workers and the elimination of convict labor. William Howard Taft shared some of TR's views, yet inclined in the direction of capital and, unlike Roosevelt, never invoked presidential power to settle strikes. At Taft's request, Congress created the Industrial Relations Commission to investigate working conditions, yet refused to confirm some of Taft's conservative nominees. Woodrow Wilson replaced some of Taft's selections with liberals and reappointed others. The commission's report to Wilson in 1915 confirmed the existence of harsh conditions, yet differed over remedial measures. Because he had benefited from AFL support in 1912, Wilson became the first president to recognize labor as a legitimate interest group, and he met often with Gompers. Union leaders were gratified by the president's appointment of liberals Louis D. Brandeis and John Hessin Clarke to the Supreme Court and by prolabor laws enacted during his administration.

Most critical was the Clayton Antitrust Act of 1914, decreeing that unions were not to be considered combinations in restraint of trade. Gompers compared the law with the ancient English charter, the Magna Carta, which defined the rights of Englishmen, but courts limited its impact. The La Follette Seaman's Act of 1915 limited penalties that could be imposed upon seamen under contract and set federal standards for living and working conditions aboard ships. The Adamson Act of 1916 gave railroad workers the eight-hour day. States joined the progressive parade by enacting a host of reform laws. These included child labor restrictions, compulsory school attendance, limits on the number of hours women could be required to work, and worker's compensation.

World War I stimulated the economy and strengthened the hand of labor. Strikes increased, despite a federal ban and Gompers's order forbidding AFL members to participate. Workers sought to keep pace with the rising cost of living and exploit the high demand for labor. The government, interested in maximizing production for the war effort, tightened its control over industry, allowing generous profits that facilitated higher wages. Profits and productivity, however, rose more rapidly than wages, and most unions did not win mandatory recognition by their employers.

Progress and Problems for African Americans and Native Americans

The progressive movement was nearly oblivious to the problems of minorities, as were most labor unions. African Americans, for example, benefited little from government regulations of working conditions or improvements in union contracts. Indeed, sometimes employers hired them as strike breakers. About three-quarters of African Americans lived in the rural South in 1900. They were less an urban people than were white Americans during the Era of Awakening; a majority did not live in cities until 1950. Yet blacks began voting with their feet during the first two decades of the century—two hundred thousand in the first decade, three hundred thousand in the second—moving to northern cities to escape segregation and find employment. One of the defining movements of the twentieth century, this Great Migration peaked during World War I when European immigration declined drastically and war industries needed workers. Before the migration, northern cities had relatively modest black populations dispersed in small neighborhoods, where their presence was largely unnoticed. Then population growth led to the emergence of densely settled black neighborhoods because African Americans desired community, but also because of white animosity.

Harsher than white immigrant enclaves, black ghettos had a grip on their inhabitants that lasted generations. Inside the ghetto, blacks developed an infrastructure of businesses, newspapers, churches, social clubs, and fraternal organizations. A diversity of religions flourished, yet religion remained one of the stabilizing forces of the community. Secular groups such as the Negro Improvement Association, the Urban League, and the National Association for the Advancement of Colored People (NAACP), recruiting some of their members through the churches, helped bind the community politically, socially, and economically.

Black leaders attained national prominence, including Booker T. Washington, who spanned the nineteenth and twentieth centuries. Born to a slave, he became principal in 1881 at what evolved into Tuskegee Institute in Alabama, an industrial school for blacks. From an initial legislative appropriation of $2,000, he built a college of 2,500 students and eleven buildings by his death in 1915. His autobiography, *Up from Slavery* (1901), is a classic success story of a self-made man. Humble and folksy, Washington appeared nonthreatening to white people and became a conduit for northern philanthropists who wanted to subsidize black education. Roosevelt and Taft consulted him on federal patronage, and TR invited him to dine at the White House in 1901. The meal left a bad taste in the mouths of southern politicians who condemned TR after the story of Washington's visit appeared in newspapers. Never again did the president extend a similar invitation to a black person.

A polished speaker, Washington attracted attention with his "Atlanta Compromise" talk of 1895, in which he temporarily accepted social inequality as the price of economic advancement. He wanted to train students to meet the demands of the job market. "The opportunity to earn a dollar in a factory just now is worth infinitely more than the opportunity to spend a dollar in an opera house," he declared. The speech and his mild-mannered

FOSTERING
BLACK PRIDE
Scholar and activist
W.E.B. Du Bois.
(Library of Congress)

public persona concealed Washington's behind-the-scenes work as a power broker who attacked segregation by encouraging lawsuits and writing anonymous letters to newspapers.

W.E.B. Du Bois, a brilliant intellectual, clashed with Washington, whom he considered submissive to rich, powerful whites. Du Bois wanted change not by compromise with white racists, but seized by a black elite educated to lead. Change was to come in all areas at once, including social equality. More militant than Washington, Du Bois was feared as a revolutionary by some whites. The first African American to receive a Harvard Ph.D., Du Bois was a prolific and highly acclaimed writer in black studies. His first major book, *The Souls of Black Folk* (1903), urged black people to be proud of themselves and their heritage. From academia, Du Bois moved to activism. He was a leader in an early civil rights organization, the Niagara Movement, and a founder of the NAACP. After leaving his professorship at Atlanta University in 1910, he edited the NAACP journal, *The Crisis,* for the next quarter century. By 1919, *The Crisis* was reaching 100,000 readers.

Better known to the general public than Du Bois or Washington was Jack Johnson, the world heavyweight boxing champion. Near-invincible, he frustrated white people by demolishing many a "white hope"—and marrying a white woman. Johnson was one of the first African Americans in a highly publicized field to hold the spotlight for years. Other blacks achieved scholarly and literary recognition. Carter Woodson, the only black person born of a slave to receive a Ph.D. in history, from Harvard, pioneered in social history. Devoting his life to the study of African Americans, he depicted them as major participants, not victims. Black journalists, with William Monroe Trotter and Ida Barnett Wells in the vanguard, crusaded for racial equality and against lynching, the vigilante violence used against black men.

Race riots broke out across the nation, the most serious of the southern violence occurring in Atlanta in 1906. White people attacked blacks after newspapers reported that black men had assaulted white women. Blacks retaliated, and looting and arson followed, turmoil that killed eleven blacks and injured sixty. Two riots erupted out in Springfield, Illinois, the home of the Great Emancipator, Abraham Lincoln, during the first decade of the century. In 1919 more than twenty riots scarred the country, the worst in Chicago, where fifteen white people and three black people died in thirteen days.

Race flared intermittently as a national political problem during the Roosevelt administration. TR appointed William D. Crum, a black Republican, as collector of customs in Charleston, South Carolina, angering whites. A bitter debate ensued over confirmation and the Senate did not approve the nomination until 1905. Another controversy arose when the African American postmistress in Indianola, Mississippi, who had served since the 1880s, resigned under pressure from white people. The Post Office refused to accept her resignation, and during the impasse the Indianola branch was closed for months, finally reopening under a white postmaster. Roosevelt appointed fewer African Americans to patronage positions than previous GOP presidents and tried to court southern whites by ignoring black political interests. TR and his successor expediently thought that the GOP, as the party of Lincoln, could take black votes for granted. Roosevelt avoided public race baiting. He believed African Americans could be uplifted by education. Nonetheless, he shared the belief, common in his time, that they were genetically inferior to white people and that social reforms could never make the races intellectually comparable.

The most controversial racial dispute involving TR occurred in 1906. White residents of Brownsville, Texas, accused black soldiers from a nearby army base of shooting up the town, killing one white man and wounding a white police officer. None of the men in a battalion of all-black 25th Infantry Regiment would admit to guilt or identify guilty parties. Roosevelt had every battalion member dishonorably discharged and barred them from federal employment. His action inspired protests in the North and among blacks and some white Republicans. Ultimately the president admitted that he did not have the authority to prevent future employment and allowed reenlistment for those who swore they had not participated in or witnessed the incident. In 1972 the army changed the discharges to honorable ones.

Taft, who was secretary of war when the dishonorable discharges were issued, shared the belief in genetic inferiority of African Americans. He told a southern audience during the 1908 presidential campaign that he did not object to their disenfranchisement because the votes of the illiterates debased elections. Such questions, he believed, were best handled by state and local governments.

Wilson probably shared the beliefs of Roosevelt and Taft about black inferiority. He was not a crusader for civil rights, yet he was chiefly neutral on the subject. It simply was not a priority for him, and he dealt with most racial issues as matters of political expediency. For example, he helped individual African Americans, yet allowed his Treasury secretary and postmaster general to segregate their departments to appease congressmen.

Dealing with Native Americans, Roosevelt, Taft, and Wilson were assimilationists. Indians could learn to compete in the capitalist order by leaving their reservations and obtaining an education. TR wanted Indians to rise or fall on their own, separated from their tribal connections. Indian problems would disappear along with tribal cultures, he believed. Reflecting his intentions, the Burke Act of 1906 allowed Indians to sell land granted to them individually, so they could move to cities and take jobs or start businesses. Under this "Americanization" drive, rooted in the 1870s, some Indians prospered, but for the great majority, the program was ruinous. White people eager to exploit natural resources such as timber, oil, and minerals cheated Indians of their lands, cut their important tribal ties, and sent their standard of living spiraling further downward. By the end of Wilson's second term, Native Americans had lost two-thirds of their land and most of them were destitute, ravaged physically by alcoholism and other diseases. What was for white Americans an Era of Awakening was for Indians an epoch of misery.

CHAPTER FOUR

A Culture Awakening, 1900–1919

A S THE ERA OF Awakening jarred politics, the economy, and foreign policy, so did it stimulate culture. Cultural blossoming, initially, was less important in producing art and entertainment than consuming it. In popular culture, America offered the most lucrative mass markets in the world. When Americans turned to the fine arts, they preferred the work of Europeans. But the culture reflected social changes as well. The federal government assisted by allowing income tax deductions for contributions to the arts, which over time contributed more to artistic development than the direct subsidies of European governments. Under these conditions, it was likely that good art would emerge, and some did.

Americans began to export culture, including technology, political criticism, and science. Their research universities acquired resources and status. A U. S. resident who told a Frenchman that he reveled in the coffee shops of Paris was surprised when the Frenchman replied that he was more interested in the skyscrapers of New York. If the budding culture demonstrated that America was becoming more sophisticated, it also showed how the country was losing its innocence before World War I. Cultural criticism helped Americans understand there was a dark side to their nation—even before the war drove the point home.

Reading for the Masses

Before there can be art, there must be a demand for it. For writers, the way was paved in the 1900s and 1910s, a period of mass readership in which people devoured pulp and serious literature (mostly the former), magazines, newspapers, and specialized journals. The popular book market had been established earlier, as volumes written, printed, and published by

Americans began to outsell those of Europeans by the mid-1890s. Public schools produced an audience of readers. Developments in printing technology, including the linotype machine, rotary press, and cheap pulp paper, along with a national distribution system by rail, aided mass publishing. These improvements helped reduce magazine prices, making the publications affordable for a wide public and appealing to advertisers.

Readers found fiction and poetry, once sources of cultural continuity, converted into sources of rebellion, much like muckrakers altered journalism. Writers applauded revolution in foreign lands and called for it in their own. Novels described graphic sex, violence, and the seamy aspects of capitalism. Authors presented female characters who had sexual appetites, who were not gratified in traditional marriages, and who disliked being treated as porcelain dolls in high society. Poets evoked sadness and bleakness.

In the late nineteenth century, realism supplanted romanticism in fiction, and early in the twentieth, naturalist authors emerged to depict a harsher reality. Naturalists thought that realists underestimated the caprices in the universe that cast humans into tempests as mere objects, not as actors. Taking their cues from some of the intellectual trends that Sigmund Freud, Karl Marx, Charles Darwin, and Friedrich Nietzsche popularized, they described a world that was more turbulent than the world of the realists. To some degree, though, the naturalists mellowed with age, the women more gracefully than the men. Most concluded that the inhospitable environments that frustrated them in youth were not so bad after all, and that the ideals they pursued elsewhere were not as sublime; one could not escape one's roots, and one should not try to do so. Never completely recovering from bitterness, some naturalists nevertheless learned to place their suffering in context. They cultivated irony and concluded that the most mundane values are the most human, a lesson as important as the message that humans inhabit a world that is frequently impersonal and cruel.

Jack London's tales were widely read for their apparent romanticism when, in truth, he wanted to show the Darwinian struggle in nature that spun beyond human control. His stories of miners and animals in the Yukon, where he tried to strike it rich in the gold rush of 1897–1898, have been his most enduring works, including *The Call of the Wild* (1903), *The Sea Wolf* (1904), and *White Fang* (1906). A fine craftsman with a vivid narrative style, London was one of the better-known and higher-paid writers in America from 1900 to 1910. Then, burned out physically and emotionally, he died of a drug overdose in 1916.

Some considered Theodore Dreiser crude and immoral, and critics called his prose ponderous and his storytelling skills mediocre. But he became the most influential naturalist, writing prolifically and, as an edi-

HEEDING THE CALL OF THE WILD
Best-selling author Jack London.
(Library of Congress)

tor, mentoring younger authors and persuading publishers to take a chance on experimental fiction. From his often-unhappy life he created a literature that was sober, profound, complex, and interesting. The sexuality and profanity in his first novel, *Sister Carrie* (1900), offended many, and his publisher did not promote the book, a reception that plunged him into depression and a nervous breakdown. In 1911, he published his best novel, *Jennie Gerhardt*, whose protagonist is a sexually active female. *The Financier* (1912) and *The Titan* (1914) chronicled the activity of Frank Cowperwood, a renegade businessman with a powerful sexual appetite.

The life and novels of Henry James were more restrained. Considering writing a way of life, not just a profession, James became a literary master in the grand European fashion. Over a career that stretched from the 1870s to his death in 1916, he proved one of the most productive and influential novelists in American literature. Born into a wealthy, socially eminent family, he spent much of his life in Britain, which informed his focus on American and European aristocrats and the clash of American innocence and European sophistication. In his mature phase, James wrote complex novels demanding intense attention, *The Wings of the Dove* (1902), *The Ambassadors* (1903), and *The Golden Bowl* (1904) among them. His complexity and elitism prevented most of his works from achieving best-seller status, but as tastes became more seasoned, appreciation grew.

Sherwood Anderson, whose forte was the short story, or novella, helped establish the genre of fiction critical of the small town Midwest. His first noteworthy novel, *Windy McPherson's Son* (1916), is the story of a man who leaves his Ohio home to earn a fortune in Chicago at the cost of his principles. *Winesburg, Ohio* (1919), the collection of short stories for which he is best known, includes common characters. Anderson's tone was somber and his character portraits were stark. His realism struck a chord with readers. He discussed sex candidly and described realistic female characters.

Among the celebrated women naturalist writers, those whose reputations have endured include the regionalists Edith Wharton (the East), Willa Cather (the Great Plains), Ellen Glasgow (the South), and Gertrude Atherton (the Far West); except for Atherton, all were recognized with Pulitzer Prizes. Wharton, member of a rich New York family, was tied to an unhappy marriage at twenty-three and began to write to overcome her boredom, pain, and mental illnesses. She painted vivid word portraits of female characters in the decaying aristocracy of New York and New England and was an astute observer of suffering. Her most critically acclaimed novel, *Ethan Frome* (1911), tells of a doomed love affair in a New England village. Cather, a Nebraska native, wrote short stories and poems focusing on the frontier. *The Troll Garden* (1905), a book of short stories, made her a major author, and subsequently she accepted the editorship of *McClure's*, one of the most prestigious magazines of the time. Three years later in 1911, Cather suffered a nervous breakdown owing to the tension between remunerative journalism and the creative writing that she loved. Turning to fiction, she found redemptive qualities in the barren landscape and common people of her frontier home, writing works such as *O Pioneers!* (1913), which depicted the power of the land, the conflict of urban and rural lifestyles, the attempt to break from the land, and the urge to return.

Glasgow also found value in the homeland she once desired to flee, describing the stresses of the changing order in the New South; her second novel, *The Battle-Ground* (1902), was a best seller. Atherton's early books were considered too shocking for proper society. She left California for Paris, where she wrote her first novel about the Golden State, *Los Cerritos* (1890); although not critically praised in the United States, it was popular in Europe for its quaint descriptions of the state. Atherton finished two books in London after researching them in California, then returned to the state permanently and produced the highly popular *Senator North* (1900) and her most successful book, *The Conqueror* (1902), a fictionalized life of Alexander Hamilton. Her popularity faded after the 1910s, as her once racy novels appeared tame.

As in fiction, the mood in poetry was pessimism. Founding "little magazines" started to offer them opportunities, poets clustered in Greenwich Village, although some of the better ones were temporary or permanent expatriates in Europe. Of the four major poets of the era, Ezra Pound and T. S. Eliot spent their careers in Europe, honing erudite, epic works; and the more popular Robert Frost and Carl Sandburg were quintessentially American regionalists.

Living in London, too esoteric to be popular, Eliot tirelessly experimented with poetic forms and read extensively in the classics. He attempted to fuse language and images, creating complex poetry of enduring quality, notably "The Love Song of J. Alfred Prufrock" (1917) and the despairing work for which he is best known, "The Waste Land" (1922). Pound's poetry was even more complex and erudite than Eliot's. A perfectionist, he mentored young poets, emphasizing the significance of non-Western culture. Pound's major work, *The Cantos*, was compiled and polished between 1917 and 1968.

Frost published his first collection of poems, *A Boy's Will* (1913), and *North of Boston* (1914) in England, where he found a better reception for his work initially. Returning to the United States, he became known as the poet of rural New England, attracting the public because his plainspoken words were moving, witty, and humorous in a framework of conventional rhyme and meter, in such works as "After Apple-Picking" (1914) and "Stopping by Woods on a Snowy Evening" (1923). Yet Frost's poetry and personality were more melancholic than they seemed and his work, honored with four Pulitzer Prizes in the 1920s, 1930s and 1940s, evokes nostalgia. In 1961 he recited poetry at John Fitzgerald Kennedy's presidential inauguration.

What Frost was to New England, Sandburg was to the Midwest. A populist and socialist, he cultivated an image as the poet of the common person, epitomizing the down-to-earth simplicity of the midwestern worker and of the heartland's industrial metropolis, Chicago. *Chicago Poems* (1916) marked him as a major poet. Another poet of Illinois, Vachel Lindsay, toured the country reciting rhythmic poetry for food and lodging. His poems, among them "General William Booth Enters into Heaven" (1913) and "The Congo" (1914), were to be chanted and acted out. Edgar Lee Masters, also of the Land of Lincoln, produced a best seller, *The*

Spoon River Anthology (1915), a series of elegiac poems written after a visit to a cemetery. The poems describe shadows in the lives of small town residents, including murders, suicides, and infidelity.

Edwin Arlington Robinson sounded a similarly grim note in his character portraits of fictional New Englanders. President Theodore Roosevelt, an admirer, offered him a clerkship in the New York customs office so Robinson could support his family and write poetry. Winning awards and honorary degrees, he was recognized as one of the most celebrated American poets. Amy Lowell, too, achieved distinction, publishing several collections and numerous poems in magazines, in addition to a biography of the English poet John Keats. She was a fine member of a talented, eclectic group that worked in several genres, and dared to be original.

The Promise of Politics, History, and Philosophy

Writing on politics was of high quality during the era, thanks to Herbert Croly and Walter Lippmann, who helped launch the respected magazine *New Republic* in 1914. Earlier, Croly's *Promise of American Life* (1909) outlined the basis for Roosevelt's view of how government ought to work. TR even appropriated Croly's term "New Nationalism" for his 1912 presidential campaign. Croly and Lippmann were friends of Roosevelt, but they broke with the Rough Rider over his eagerness to enter World War I. Lippmann, the most distinguished commentator on politics and foreign policy in the century, was a prolific author of books, articles, and newspaper columns. His first book, *A Preface to Politics* (1913), pessimistically argued that Americans made political decisions due to emotion, not logic. He followed with *Drift and Mastery* (1914), urging that an educated political elite should lead.

In the historical profession, Charles A. Beard defied the genteel tradition, asserting in *An Economic Interpretation of the Constitution of the United States* (1913) that financial interests motivated the founding fathers in drafting the Constitution. The first historian to devote attention to the relationship between politics and economics, Beard polarized academia by injecting class conflict into views of American history and stripping some of the romanticism from the founding fathers. In 1917 he resigned his professorship at Columbia University to protest the refusal of the school administration to renew the contracts of colleagues who had opposed World War I (he supported the war effort). Thereafter, Beard was unaffiliated with any academic institution, but books, some written with his wife, Mary, continued to flow from his typewriter, involving him in a long series of professional and political debates. Mary Beard's pioneering efforts in women's history were also the subject of debate.

Henry Adams, whose great-grandfather was the second American president and whose grandfather was the sixth president, used the *North American Review*, which he edited, to crusade against political corruption and economic abuse. Adams found the Era of Awakening a jarring time, an alarm that many intellectuals shared, as his most influential book, *The Education of Henry Adams* (1907), indicated. Technology would drive the century, he predicted, and men of his generation were unprepared for it, having received classical educations at the best schools. First printed in a small, private edition, the book did not become available to the public until 1918, after Adams's death, and the next year it won a Pulitzer Prize.

Whereas Adams feared that education could not address the problems of the unfolding century, John Dewey proposed changes to improve education. The teacher, psychologist, and philosopher was largely responsible for the proliferation of progressive education in elementary and secondary schools during the period. At the University of Chicago, he directed the laboratory school that experimented with teaching methods, deemphasizing memorization and discipline in favor of imagination. In psychology Dewey introduced the idea of functionalism, holding that intelligence is constantly changing as a result of interaction between individuals and their environment.

The emergence of Dewey's progressive education coincided with an enrollment boom in schools. Only 4.5 percent of children ages fifteen to nineteen were enrolled in secondary schools in 1890, but 41.6 percent were attending by 1930. A kindergarten movement that began in the early 1900s got children into school when they were young, and attendance laws kept them there longer. Other school reforms rose from political progressivism. Progressives tried to apply the scientific methods of the social sciences to education and to make teaching a profession by offering college degrees in education. A division of labor evolved between teachers and administrators. In the South, progressive education, paradoxically, coexisted with segregated schools.

More people sought a college education. Undergraduate enrollment rose from 1.8 percent of the college age population in 1890 to 4.7 percent in 1920; college ranks doubled by World War I. Income, race, religion, and gender limited opportunities to attend college. Women continued to enroll in the elite women's colleges founded after the Civil War, yet most matriculated at coeducational land grant universities in the Midwest and Southwest. Female college graduates wed in lower percentages than noncollege women, married later, and had fewer children. Some women made careers in academia, constituting one-fifth of college faculty by 1910.

Dewey's concepts were less important in higher education, a field that came to involve more graduate study and specialized research. Departing from its Protestant orientation, it became overwhelmingly secular. Scholars began to write mainly for other academics. Graduate study likewise encouraged specialization. Basic curricula included classes in sociology, social work, political science, and natural science.

Those fortunate enough to win admission to Harvard at the right time could study under William James, older brother of the novelist Henry James and a professor for decades until his retirement in the 1900s. A medical doctor and a teacher of philosophy, psychology, physiology, and anatomy, he was also interested in religion, psychic phenomena, psychotherapy, and education. *Principles of Psychology* (1890), James's major work in the field, became a widely used text for its concrete examples and humorous, colloquial, and metaphorical style. His most popular work, *The Varieties of Religious Experience* (1902), included studies of people whose lives were changed by mystical experiences. His chief contribution to philosophy was *Pragmatism* (1907), in which he introduced the idea that truth comes from daily experience, not from universal laws or theories. One had to "live today by what truth he can get, be ready tomorrow to call it a falsehood," James said.

Realms of Religious Belief

At the grass roots, affiliation with religious groups increased; by 1900 some 35.7 percent of Americans belonged to churches or synagogues, up from 15.5 percent in 1850. Religions that embraced urban values—Catholicism, Judaism, Quakerism, and Unitarianism—thrived naturally in cities; mainline Protestant denominations began to retreat to the outskirts of cities and retained their rural preponderance. Numerically the leading churches were, in order, Catholic, Methodist, Baptist, and Presbyterian. Among immigrants—Italians, Poles, Hungarians, Austrians, and Mexicans—the vast majority were Catholics, who founded schools and recreational organizations as options to public schools whose students were heavily Protestant.

Immigrant Jews adjusted to their new land, in part, by creating a big city network of cultural and philanthropic organizations, including the Young Men's Hebrew Associations and B'nai B'rith, and the branches of Reform Judaism and Conservative Judaism. Reform Jews rejected the idea that all Jews were exiles awaiting return to Israel, and used English prayers and organ music in services. Conservative Jews, choosing a middle ground between the changes of liberal Reform congregations and Orthodox synagogues, adapted to American culture but kept elements of ritual. They were especially involved in raising money to realize the Zionist goal of creating a Jewish state in Palestine. Other Jewish fund-raising was directed toward fighting anti-Semitism.

Much of the growth in religious membership, particularly in Christian denominations, was the result of loosened requirements for adherents. This was encouraged by evaluating preachers by the number of their recruits. The practice not only alienated traditionalists but left religious institutions less stringent in enforcing behavior. Families, churches, and synagogues passed on moral responsibility to government and secular officials. In foreign affairs religion retained an ambiguous role, a justification for dominance and a rationale for humanitarianism. William McKinley and Theodore Roosevelt cited Christianity to explain intervention and expansion overseas. Woodrow Wilson invoked religion in an effort to validate neutrality in World War I, then to justify the American entry into war, and, finally, membership in the League of Nations.

Challenges to religion also came from science, politics, and philosophy. The ideas of Charles Darwin, Sigmund Freud, and Karl Marx were controversial, especially Darwin's theory of evolution, for it contradicted the biblical story of creation. Modernists believed that the Bible could be reconciled with Darwin, that one umbrella could cover both religion and science, yet fundamentalists claimed that the umbrella favored science. To modernists, fundamentalists who interpreted the Scriptures literally were simpletons; to fundamentalists, modernists were at best lukewarm Christians. "Fundamentalism" had not been used frequently to define a set of religious beliefs until 1909, when a group of Protestants formed the World's Christian Fundamentalist League. The movement crystallized, in part, because women, immigrants, and changing sexual standards diluted tradition.

Protestants were divided over the concept of millennialism. Premillennialists, most of whom were religious conservatives, said the Second Coming of Jesus Christ would precede the thousand years of peace and bounty predicted in the Book of Revelation. Human attempts to reform the world were futile because redemption had to await the return of the messiah. One facet of premillennialism was dispensationalism, a doctrine that divided history into periods, ending with the Second Coming. Modernists were skeptical of premillennialism and dispensationalism, perceiving them as disincentives to engage in God's work on earth, that is, to improve the world. Critics responded that the modernists' Social Gospel elevated ephemeral concerns over eternal truths. Catholics had their own disputes, debating whether scientific theories and progress were compatible with church custom. Were the pronouncements of popes open to change by subsequent generations, priests, and theologians? Finally, could the laity interpret Scripture? Among Jews, the major question concerned the extent of assimilation permissible, evidenced in the split between Reform and Conservative Judaism.

Ash Cans and Architects

Around 1900 American painting threw a gauntlet at gentility with the advent of a group known as the Ash Can school because its disciples depicted tenements, dirty laundry, and trash cans on city streets, hoping to capture the vital and robust instead of the dainty. Some of its painters, especially the Ash Can leader, Robert Henri, and George Luks, were attracted to athletics. Luks's paintings of prizefighters became famous. Victorian sensibilities got another jolt from the New York Armory Show of 1913, which exposed some three hundred thousand visitors to the most recent European abstract art. Creating sensations at subsequent stops in Boston and Chicago, the exhibition shocked provincial Americans and propelled the transition from representational art to abstract art that projected the painter's feelings onto canvas. It took a long time before abstract art reached beyond the avant garde, but since 1913 modernism has dominated American painting.

Alfred Stieglitz promoted photography as a fine art, persuading museums to stage exhibits and maintain permanent collections. He gained recognition with a group self-styled the "Photo Secessionists." Stieglitz emphasized "straight" photos as opposed to doctored ones. Not surprisingly, the group took photos like those of the amateurs, only better, revealing trained eyes, discipline, and timing. Stieglitz's protégé, Edward Steichen, tested all facets of photography, including color. He became a brilliant portrait photographer and a pioneer of aerial photography. Another trailblazer, the documentary photographer Paul Strand, employed series of photos without captions to tell a story.

In architecture, the most pronounced trend was eclecticism. The Beaux Arts style, which sacrificed function to embellishment and comfort to decoration, reigned until the 1930s, but the midwestern practitioners Louis W. Sullivan and Frank Lloyd Wright were more significant. With his lean and spare designs, Sullivan broke with Beaux Arts and purportedly coined the phrase "Form follows function." He thought a building should reflect its purpose, originate in the architect's imagination, and be constructed from the inside out. Sullivan also helped popularize the building of skyscrapers, made possible by steel frames that supported walls hung like curtains. These tall office buildings materialized from the enterprise of architects, engineers, and businessmen rebuilding downtown Chicago after the devastating fire of 1871.

Wright surpassed his teacher Sullivan, becoming the most renowned—and likely the most controversial—American architect ever, designing more than eight hundred buildings, of which four hundred were constructed.

Even more than Sullivan's designs, Wright's welled up within him and over-flowed to become reality. He combined imagination with technical competence and the vision to integrate structures into their natural settings. Wright synthesized the functional and ornamental prairie school house, whose long, low, horizontal lines harmonized with the landscape.

Innovations in Music

The major American musical style, jazz, emerged after World War I, although its roots, ragtime and the blues, appeared during the Era of Awakening. A mix of West African syncopated rhythms and the refinements of American slaves, ragtime spread among southern blacks who listened to touring minstrels and "professors" of music, often pianists, who entertained customers in houses of prostitution (practically the only places where they could find work) in New Orleans and Memphis. In the 1890s it moved up the Mississippi River and became a national obsession, but began to wane

LEADING THE WAY FOR RAGTIME
The fascinating lure of ragtime dance.
(Library of Congress)

by wartime. Scott Joplin, the top ragtime composer and performer, made his mark in 1899 with "Maple Leaf Rag," the first piece of American-composed sheet music to sell 2 million copies. He failed to realize fully his dream of merging ragtime with classical music and died at age forty-eight, insufficiently mourned for decades. Still, the form that Joplin helped create began the century on an upbeat tempo, spawned hundreds of compositions, and made possible a big mainstream hit, "Alexander's Ragtime Band," a 1911 work by white composer Irving Berlin. Berlin, the most accomplished popular composer in American history, published more than fifteen hundred songs, including "God Bless America," "White Christmas," and "Easter Parade," for Broadway, musical revues, and motion pictures. He was the king of Tin Pan Alley, the legendary mecca of popular melodic music in New York, a section of restaurants, clubs, ballrooms, and composing studios where the banging of tinny upright pianos sounded like a person striking pans.

Blues also entered the musical mainstream after whites popularized it. Originating from spirituals and work songs, blues preserved the memory of slavery and injustice, not to deny them, but to transcend them. W. C. Handy, a white coronetist, was instrumental in promoting blues and moving them north. His 1914 hit, "St. Louis Blues," provided a bridge to jazz.

Serious music continued to operate in the shadow of Europe, a supplier of symphonies, operas, instrumentalists, and conductors to the United States. Charles Ives tried to create a truly American symphony imbued with the spirit of his native New England, composing music that was original, if difficult to perform or appreciate. His most productive period occurred before he suffered a serious heart attack in 1918, yet in 1947, long after his retirement from writing music, Ives received a Pulitzer Prize for his Third Symphony, composed during 1901–1904.

But Europe did not dominate popular dance. Here the United States led, and popular dance enjoyed a considerable following throughout the twentieth century. Before 1900, many dances started in rural areas and then came to cities, a path reversed in the century. Once again blacks were in the forefront, initiating a series of fads incorporating aspects of African dances mimicking animal movements, among them the Turkey Trot, the Kangaroo Hop, and the Grizzly Bear.

Another pioneer, Ruth St. Denis, introduced a form of artistic dance derived from the French Delsarte form that blended rhythmic gymnastics with gestures conveying intense emotions. She helped to found the Denishawn school to teach her interpretive style, which integrated the spiritual and the exotic. St. Denis, however, did not make as much of an impression as did Isadora Duncan, a designer of solo performances who forged a genre of modern dance distinct from ballet. Duncan also conceived a system for training children to dance in a natural style.

Stage and Screen

Theater, particularly melodrama and musical comedy, flourished between 1890 and 1910. Few serious dramatists enjoyed wide recognition, although works of William Shakespeare, Henrik Ibsen, George Bernard Shaw, and August Strindberg had audiences in America. Drama centered on Broadway, but in 1915 the Washington Square Players were founded in New York to perform experimental drama, followed the next year by the Provincetown (Massachusetts) Players, organized to stage less slickly commercial plays, including ones by their own members, such as Eugene O'Neill.

In melodrama, the master was William Clyde Fitch, producer of numerous Broadway hits before his death in 1909 at forty-four. Fitch showcased the royal family of American stage, Ethel, John, and Lionel Barrymore. Fitch's plays were comedies of manners stemming from superficial episodes in the lives of the upper class, performed with exaggerated gestures. Musical comedies were another Broadway staple, a derivation of the European operetta, or comic opera, and the musical revue. *The Ziegfeld Follies*, a production that ran from 1907 to 1932, was the most lavish. It relied on lively songs, dance, jokes, flashy costumes, and beautiful women. Equally invigorating, singer, dancer, songwriter, playwright, and promoter George M. Cohan brought excitement to Broadway for two decades. "Mr. Broadway" wrote the songs "Give My Regards to Broadway" and "Over There" and produced shows bubbling with patriotism.

Vaudeville shows began in New York cabarets and toured the nation from the late 1800s to the Great Depression. Comedians, acrobats, jugglers, dancers, singers, musicians, ventriloquists, magicians, and animal acts performed for family audiences in "palaces" in towns and cities. The fame of many of the artists outlasted vaudeville: singer and comedian Eddie Cantor, magician and escape artist Harry Houdini, cowboy humorist Will Rogers, and comics W. C. Fields, the Marx brothers, and Fanny Brice.

Technology contributed new forms of urban entertainment, starting with the "talking machine," or phonograph, that Thomas Edison and others devised. Edison developed the first machines for business and abandoned the effort when he found no market. He resumed research after competitors found a market for phonographs to play music for saloon customers who deposited a nickel in a slot. Later, "penny arcades" were established, housing machines that dispensed gum, candy, and patent medicine, as well as music. Traveling lecturers carried "concert horns" with recorded entertainment to attract crowds.

★ JIM THORPE: VICTORY AND DEFEAT ★

None of the strong men of history could have competed successfully with him.
They had great strength, we may infer, but they lacked his speed, his agility, his skill.
A wonder, a marvel, is the only way to describe him.
—JAMES E. SULLIVAN, AMATEUR ATHLETIC UNION PRESIDENT

A STAR ATHLETE
Champion Jim Thorpe
in the uniform of the
Carlisle Indian School
football team, 1909.
(National Archives)

COACH GLENN "Pop" Warner had had enough of the young man who was begging to play football. He was Warner's top track athlete, too valuable for a contact sport that might injure him. Finally, the coach handed him a ball and told him to give the defense some tackling practice. Jim Thorpe did no such thing; he ran around, past, and through them, not once but twice. "Nobody is going to tackle Jim," he said, flipping the ball to an astonished Warner.

With that display, Thorpe won a place on the team at Carlisle Indian School in Pennsylvania and went on to amazing performances. In 1911 he kicked four field goals and ran for a touchdown, giving his unheralded squad all of its points in a stunning 18-15 victory over powerful Harvard. In 1912 he returned kickoffs ninety and ninety-five yards for touchdowns on successive plays (the first was nullified by a penalty) in a 27-6 victory over an Army team led by Cadet Dwight D. Eisenhower. College football, however, was only one game in which Thorpe excelled. He was an Olympic track champion; he played hockey, professional football, and baseball; he golfed, swam, bowled, and wrestled—a record of remarkable versatility. Sportswriters recognized his achievements in 1950, naming Thorpe the greatest athlete and the greatest football player of the half century.

Thorpe's most memorable triumph came at the 1912 Olympic track and field competition in Stockholm, Sweden. He won the pentathlon, finishing first in four of the five events, then easily won the ten-event decathlon even though he had never competed in it. "Sir, you are the greatest athlete in the world," Swedish King Gustav V said. Thorpe meekly replied, "Thanks, King."

Alas, the glory soon disappeared. In 1913, after investigating reports that Thorpe played semiprofessional baseball in 1909 and 1910, the Amateur Athletic Union declared him a professional and ruled that he had been ineligible to compete at Stockholm. His feats were purged from the record books and he was ordered to return his Olympic medals and trophies. Thorpe had played professionally, but without realizing that he was jeopardizing his amateur standing. Moreover, as his defenders pointed out, the AAU did not challenge his eligibility within the time limits allowed by Olympic rules. It was a setback from which Thorpe never recovered. "Rules are like steam rollers," he wrote. "There is nothing they won't do to flatten the man who stands in their way."

The years after sports were difficult: Thorpe worked at several jobs without much success, he was troubled by poverty and alcoholism, and he lost much of his once-formidable physique. He went to his grave in 1953, without the vindication he sought. It took nearly forty years for the campaign on his behalf to bear fruit, but in 1982 the International Olympic Committee decided to lift the ban against Thorpe, reinstate his records, and present new medals to his children. Two years later, his grandson, Bill Jr., honored his memory by running in the first leg of the relay that carried the Olympic torch to the Los Angeles games.

Sources: Perhaps the best extended treatment of Jim Thorpe's life is Robert W. Wheeler, *Jim Thorpe: World's Greatest Athlete* (1975). For helpful short essays on Thorpe's life, see Robert Lipsyte and Peter Levine, *Idols of the Game: A Sporting History of the American Century* (1995); Associated Press sports staff, *The Sports Immortals* (1972); *Dictionary of American Biography, Supplement Five* (1977); and David Wallechinsky, *The Complete Book of the Olympics* (1984). Jack Newcombe, *The Best of the Athletic Boys: The White Man's Impact on Jim Thorpe* (1975), is also useful.

The greatest potential lay in the silent motion pictures introduced in the late nineteenth century and perfected in the twentieth. Again, Edison and his associates contributed to the progress of this medium, although Edison did not perfect it. Early movies using the kinetoscope were peep shows watched by one customer at a time. Next came the vitascope, projecting short films on a screen for a larger audience. This device gave way to nickelodeons, where people could see movies for a nickel and hear organ accompaniment. Some four thousand to five thousand nickelodeons were operating nationwide by 1907, but the market became saturated. One director, D. W. Griffith, grew tired of making short films. Determined to direct an epic, he adapted for the screen southern writer Thomas Dixon's novel of the Civil War and Reconstruction, *The Clansman*. The extravaganza glamorized the Ku Klux Klan and showcased racial stereotypes. At the time, though, *Birth of a Nation* (1915) was a financial and aesthetic triumph. Using multiple cameras that swept a broad field and showing hundreds of actors in battle scenes, Griffith demonstrated the power and potential of the young medium.

Competition in the once-chaotic industry was rationalized before and during World War I. Hollywood, California, possessing favorable weather and topography, became the center of the business. Stars such as the comic genius Charlie Chaplin, the demure Mary Pickford, and the heartthrobs

Theda Bara, Greta Garbo, Lillian Gish, Gloria Swanson, Rudolph Valentino, and John Barrymore commanded huge salaries. Genres of films arose, such as Westerns, romances, comedies, and adventures. Amid outrage over cinematic values, a code was enacted, limiting passionate embraces and sexual innuendo, and ensuring that good would prevail over evil. The code, of course, only temporarily slowed the tides of sexuality and violence that resisted attempts to ban them. African Americans presumably ran little if almost no risk of being corrupted by immoral portrayals, for they were not permitted to attend many theaters. When they could enter the establishments, they sat in segregated sections and watched white performers sing as blackface minstrels. Other racial and ethnic stereotypes, such as the penurious Jew, appeared on stage and screen.

Spectator Sports

Athletic competition was a frontier of entertainment, giving people liberty to participate in physical activity or to experience it as spectators. Initially recreation focused on hunting, fishing, and swimming. But as the economy grew centralized and urbanized, the organization of time became essential, and the spontaneity of rural activity diminished. In cities there was not much space for doing sports, but there were large audiences ready to watch them.

Parents and religious leaders who once considered sports unwholesome now deemed it character building, a cornerstone of Christian education. Teams were sponsored by the Young Men's Christian Association (YMCA) and the Young Women's Christian Association (YWCA). Americans loved sports heroes and contests because winners and losers were clearly defined, more clearly than in the increasingly complex industrial world.

By 1900 baseball was so popular that it was called the national pastime. The National League, established in 1876, appealed to the middle class by charging 50-cent admission to games, prohibiting alcohol sales in ballparks, and avoiding Sunday play. The American League, created in 1901, appealed to immigrants and the working class by charging 25 cents and allowing alcohol sales and Sunday games. Owners controlled the professional game by reserving the power to grant franchises. Players were contractually bound to their teams unless released or traded. Rival leagues for white players occasionally surfaced, signing a few marquee players from the major leagues before being driven out of business. African Americans, to whom the major leagues were closed, formed their own touring teams, the springboard for the Negro Leagues organized in the 1920s.

The so-called dead ball of this age made for low-scoring games featuring pitching and defense. Dead baseballs did not mean deadly dull play, as the period had many exciting players. The greatest was Ty Cobb, a master of offense and defense who compiled a .367 lifetime batting average and set records for stolen bases and hits that stood for decades. All the fame that the game gained because of Cobb and others was seriously threatened because of the "Black Sox" scandal. Eight Chicago White Sox players were accused of taking $80,000 in bribes from gamblers to deliberately lose the 1919 World Series to the underdog Cincinnati Reds. Seven were acquitted in court, and charges against the eighth were dismissed for lack of evidence. But Kenesaw Mountain Landis, the autocrat whom owners brought in as commissioner to handle the matter, banned all eight from the Major Leagues for life.

Although baseball dominated professional sports, the big men on college campuses were the football stars. By the end of the nineteenth century, football had become the most popular collegiate sport, a defining element in campus life and a major revenue producer from ticket sales and alumni donations. Professors and university administrators objected to the detrimental by-products: a win-at-all-costs mentality, an emphasis on athletic victories over academic objectives, the use of "ringers" on teams, and the violence of the game that resulted in injuries and even deaths. To rescue the sport, Roosevelt summoned leading football powers to a 1905 White House conference to "persuade them to play football honestly." From the meeting came rules that made the game safer, more credible, and more exciting, measures championed by Walter Camp of Yale University, the greatest coach of the period. Camp's rules helped keep college football far more popular than professional football, whose foundation was shaky. The inception of the American Professional Football Association, the forerunner of the National Football League, in 1920 stabilized the ranks somewhat, but the league would not truly capture public attention until the mid-1920s.

A third major sport, basketball, proved easily adaptable to urban and rural environments, middle classes and lower classes, men and women, amateurs and professionals. Seeking a safe, indoor alternative to football during the winter, James Naismith invented the game in 1891, nailing peach baskets to the gymnasium balconies at the YMCA training school in Springfield, Massachusetts. Basketball quickly pervaded city playgrounds, settlement houses, YMCAs, YWCAs, and schools.

Culture in the era was memorable for the variety of its offerings, the innovations and quality of artists, and the curiosity and open pocketbooks of its admirers. There were, nonetheless, limitations, as Americans were still largely conventional and imitative, more important as collectors and consumers than as creators. The period was one of rebellion, not quite revolution. That would come after 1919.

CHAPTER FIVE

Wilson, Reform, and the Coming of War

L IKE THEODORE Roosevelt, Woodrow Wilson brought intellect and emotion to the White House, swaying Americans with his eloquence and profound thought, and urging them to be the world's peacemaker, with him as peacemaker-in-chief. He was pious, yet competitive, a reluctant, yet spirited, combatant Historian. John Cooper, in his comparative biography of the two presidents, *The Warrior and the Priest*, leaves appropriate ambiguity as to which was the warrior and which was the priest. Like characters in a Shakespeare play they shared greatness and flaws. From a seemingly auspicious destiny, they both ended badly, surely a paradox.

Woodrow Wilson

A southerner, born in Virginia and raised in Georgia and South Carolina, Wilson was shaped by the Presbyterian faith of his father, a love of scholarship, and an ambition to become a great orator. Honing his oratorical gifts from solitary tree stumps, tempering his competitive streak to accommodate his frail body, and developing the patience of a scholar, he briefly practiced law, earned a Ph.D. in political science in 1886, and launched an academic career that brought him fame. Teaching at elite schools— Bryn Mawr, Wesleyan, and Princeton, he wrote well-received scholarly monographs such as *Congressional Government: A Study in American Politics* (1885) and a five-volume popular study, *A History of the American People* (1902). In 1902 Wilson became president of Princeton. After early success, he suffered frustrating defeats in academic politics and turned to a career in a presumably less frustrating field—state and national politics. He was invited to run for governor of New Jersey in 1910. Some of his backers doubted that he lacked the internal fortitude. "After dealing with university men, the men I am striving with appear as amateurs," said Wilson.

Wilson won the election comfortably and enacted a progressive agenda in his first term. The legislature passed laws for party primaries, limits on campaign spending, a worker's compensation law, a state board to regulate utilities, and authorized for commission forms of local government. Elected to a second term, Wilson did not equal the achievements of his first term, but spent much time campaigning for president. The initial leader at the convention, House Speaker Champ Clark, with Alabama Representative Oscar W. Underwood in the race, could not muster the necessary two-thirds majority. Finally, Wilson prevailed, thanks to the support of William Jennings Bryan. Wilson was a compromise choice who appealed to his party's regional loyalties and was satisfactory to the rural and urban factions. In the general election, he was the strongest candidate in a field that included the shrill Theodore Roosevelt and the phlegmatic William Howard Taft. Ironically, the race featured three of the finest intellects ever to challenge one another.

Domestic Reform under Wilson

Wilson, like TR, used the forum of the presidency to educate not only the public but Congress. He delivered his State of the Union messages to Congress in person, breaking Jefferson's tradition of sending them in writing. In his first congressional session, Wilson helped enact a more comprehensive program of domestic reform than any previous president. The former academic went on to compile one of the most impressive records of domestic legislation of any chief executive.

Almost immediately, Wilson summoned Congress into special session and fulfilled his campaign promise to lower the tariff. The Underwood Tariff, signed by Wilson in 1913, reduced duties by almost 33 percent. Wilson's most enduring achievement was currency reform. The country badly needed more paper currency in circulation to support the expanding economy. Currency should, Wilson believed, be expanded or reduced to counteract trends in the economy that led to boom and bust cycles, such as the Panics of 1893 and 1907. Because conservatives favored private control and progressives wanted strong federal authority, the Federal Reserve Act of 1913 provided for a mix. It created a Federal Reserve Board of seven members, appointed by the president, and twelve regional federal reserve banks. The system was empowered to regulate the currency supply by raising or lowering the rate that it charged private banks to borrow from it or by buying or selling government bonds on the open market. In addition, the system issued new currency, Federal Reserve notes.

FROM ACADEMIA
TO THE WHITE
HOUSE
Woodrow Wilson
pushes for reform.
(Library of Congress)

To improve business regulation, Wilson submitted to Congress a pair of proposals adopted in 1914 as the Federal Trade Commission Act and the Clayton Antitrust Act. Superseding the weaker Bureau of Corporations, the new commission was authorized to collect data on monopolies, publish information to expose unfair practices, provide statistics for economic planning, issue injunctions, and file lawsuits to end practices restraining trade. The Clayton Act exempted labor boycotts and strikes from prosecution under the Sherman Act (although court interpretations would undermine the value of the law to unions) and prohibited firms from conspiring in price agreements that restricted trade. In supporting the laws, Wilson moved toward TR's advocacy of regulating, rather than busting trusts, but he did not fully accept TR's premise of the New Nationalism that espoused regulated monopoly. Wilson believed monopoly would crush competition and discourage entrepreneurs from starting businesses. Attorney General James McReynolds, a future Supreme Court justice, filed lawsuits to dismantle corporations that controlled more than 50 percent of the production, raw materials, and distribution of a commodity. The government won 70 percent of the cases, including suits against United States Steel, International Harvester,

Quaker Oats, National Cash Register, and the American Can Company. These companies were not "bad" monopolies in terms of conduct; their size induced the administration to dismantle them.

When it came to aid for farmers, Wilson was hesitant, but Bryan's partisans in the West and South insisted on assistance. Two noteworthy bills were passed in 1914. The Smith-Lever Act provided federal funds for experimental farming methods to increase production. The Cotton Futures Act limited speculation and required grading and labeling of cotton according to federal standards.

Personal tragedy struck Wilson on August 6, 1914, when his wife died of kidney disease. Throughout most of her months in the White House, Ellen Wilson was seriously ill and taxed by the stress of serving as first lady. Shortly before her death, Congress paid her tribute, passing a housing and slum clearance bill for which she had campaigned and naming it for her. In promoting legislation, Ellen Wilson set a precedent for her successors. Seven months after her death, in March 1915, Wilson met Edith Bolling Galt, an attractive widow, and they fell in love. Courting in the glare of White House cameras, though less newsworthy because of the war in Europe, the couple wed in December 1915.

Despite Wilson's legislative achievements, the 1914 congressional elections were a disaster for the Democrats, shrinking their majorities to narrow margins in both houses. Wilson began to tilt from the New Freedom to the New Nationalism, to measures that would not match those of 1913 and 1914 but still would be impressive. He helped create a Tariff Commission to recommend rate changes; a Shipping Commission to regulate and stimulate the dormant merchant marine industry; a prohibition on child labor in interstate commerce. In addition, Congress passed laws providing worker's compensation for federal employees; higher income and inheritance taxes on the wealthy; and the Adamson Act mandating an eight-hour day for railroad workers. Wilson also made his most important appointment, selecting his adviser, Louis Brandeis, for the Supreme Court. The first Jew to serve on the tribunal, Brandeis became one of the most distinguished justices ever.

Although Wilson is usually remembered for his foreign policy, his legacy in domestic matters deserves recognition. He and Theodore Roosevelt posed questions that would be debated for a century: At what points did the interest of the state and the interest of the individual clash? At what points did they complement each other? No one doubted the needs for self-interest, toward which Wilson shaded, and national interest, toward which TR shaded, but doubt persisted over the blend that carried the best hope for happiness. The two presidents offered vision, not a solution. The desire for both freedom and security is as old as humanity, and as evasive as the phantom of ultimate wisdom.

Wilson and the World

Just before becoming president, Wilson confided to a Princeton friend, "It would be an irony of fate if my administration had to deal with foreign problems, for all my preparation has been in domestic matters." In fact, Wilson was interested in foreign policy, but it was not his academic specialty. His only political experience was on the state level.

Latin America tested Wilson's resolve. Like his secretary of state, Bryan, he believed dark-skinned people were inferior. The administration established protectorates in Haiti and the Dominican Republic and continued Taft's protectorate in Nicaragua. Haiti was in tumult. A mob seized the president and the commander of the army and hacked them to death. A period of French military intervention and British occupation caused Wilson to send four hundred Marines in July 1915. Under a 1915 treaty, drafted chiefly by Americans, they remained in the country nineteen years, an occupation that some 3,250 Haitians died resisting. Under a constitution that also was drawn up mainly by Americans and adopted by Haiti in 1918, the United States managed the country's finances, elections, and internal improvements for a decade.

In the Dominican Republic, conditions were deteriorating at the end of the Taft administration. The assassination of the president in 1911 created a power vacuum that was not filled until Juan Isidro Jimenez won a U.S.-supervised election in December 1914. But Jimenez, caught between factions, resigned in May 1916, and America stepped in, taking charge of the government to prevent a civil war.

The administration attempted to improve its standing in Latin America succeeding in Puerto Rico because of the Jones Act of 1917, also known as the Organic Act. This law made the island a U.S. territory and gave its residents American citizenship and nearly all rights guaranteed in the U.S. Constitution. Many Puerto Ricans came to America in search of economic opportunity. The upper house of the legislature was made elective, as the lower house had been, and revenues that the United States helped collect were earmarked for the island treasury.

Relations with Mexico were turbulent. A 1911 revolution overthrew longtime dictator Porfirio Diaz, who was succeeded by Francisco Madero, overthrown in turn by one of Diaz's generals, Victoriano Huerta. Wilson encouraged General Venustiano Carranza, another aspirant to the presidency, refusing to recognize Huerta because he had seized power illegally. Meanwhile, the U.S. president pursued a policy of "watchful waiting." Relations with Huerta deteriorated further when American Marines clashed with Huerta's troops at Tampico Bay. The skirmish provoked resentment against Americans by all Mexican factions.

The Mexican president's seat seemed the object of a game of musical chairs. Carranza assumed power but split with one of his generals, Pancho Villa. The United States initially favored Villa, believing him pro-American. The administration switched sides, however, after Carranza's troops routed Villa, who retreated toward the United States. Feeling Carranza had popular support; America gave de facto recognition to his regime on October 19, 1915. This act alienated Villa. He looted a train and killed American passengers. In March 1916, he attacked towns in New Mexico and Texas, murdering Americans. Wilson federalized 100,000 troops from the Texas National Guard to protect the border. The president also assigned 12,000 soldiers under General John J. "Black Jack" Pershing (so called because he had commanded a regiment of black cavalrymen) to invade Mexico and capture Villa. The incursion failed, embarrassing the United States and angering Carranza, whose men fought with Pershing's. A joint commission stabilized the situation. Finally, in January 1917, Wilson, concerned about war with Germany, began withdrawing U.S. troops from Mexico. On March 11, Carranza was confirmed as president, and two days later Washington recognized his government.

If Wilson was tempted to intervene again, World War I smothered it. Villa died fighting Mexican troops. In 1919 Carranza codified anti-foreign practices. Foreigners were denied a dominant place in Mexican affairs, Mexican natural resources were to be controlled by Mexicans, and Mexico rejected the Monroe Doctrine.

Secondary to the focus on Latin America and Europe, involvement in the Pacific under Wilson focused on China, Japan, and the Philippines. On May 2, 1913, the United States became the first major nation to recognize the new republic of China. But America's belief in its mission to Christianize and Westernize China and to preserve Chinese territorial integrity brought conflict with Tokyo. Japan considered its huge, weak neighbor ripe for economic penetration.

To a lesser extent, Japan coveted the Philippines. With the 1916 Jones Act, America attempted to give the Philippines partial self-rule. The law conferred Filipino citizenship on former Spanish subjects, provided for male suffrage, established an elected senate, and vested authority in a governor general appointed by the U.S. president.

The Trials of Neutrality

The world plunged into "an abyss of blood and darkness," Henry James said, after a Serbian nationalist assassinated Archduke Franz Ferdinand, heir to the throne of Austria-Hungary, in the Bosnian town of Sarajevo on June 28, 1914. For decades Europeans had engaged in an arms race; alliances ensured that any war would spread. The late nineteenth and early twentieth centuries were fervently nationalistic. Ethnic groups yearned to become nations. Major nations competed to become dominant economic and military powers, acquiring colonies or seeking to preserve empires. The chief rivals were the British and French on one hand and Germany on the other. The decrepit empire of the czars in Russia was allied with the smaller Slavic nations, portions of their territory ruled by the Habsburg monarchy (Austria). Now those developments moved to a rendezvous with the apocalypse.

In the wake of the archduke's assassination by Gavrilo Princip, who wanted to unite the Serbian enclaves of the Habsburg Empire in an independent state, Germany gave a "blank check" to Austria. Kaiser Wilhelm offered to support any steps Vienna took to crush Serbia, including war with Serbia's Slavic protector, Russia. The Serbs complied partially to a stiff ultimatum from Austria, apologizing for the slaying but denying Austria a role in the investigation. Austria mobilized. Russia mobilized against Austria-Hungary, followed by mobilizations of the French and German armies. On August 1 Russia and the Habsburg monarchy declared war, drawing their respective allies, France and Germany, into combat. The Germans, seeking to outflank French defenses, invaded via neutral Belgium. Britain, bound to Belgium by treaty and hoping to protect France, declared war on Germany. World War I, then called the "Great War," commenced.

Since the time of George Washington, America's tradition had been to avoid European intrigues and wars, limiting interventions to the Western Hemisphere. In adhering to this precedent, on August 4, 1914, Wilson proclaimed neutrality. Most Americans sympathized with the Triple Entente powers—Britain, France, and Russia, bound by ties of language, culture, and trade—over the autocratic Central Powers, Germany and Austria-Hungary. Wilson hoped the United States could serve as a model of principled neutrality. But he also wanted a British victory due to his lifelong admiration of Britain.

The British blockade of German ports disrupted American trade, which annoyed Wilson, but German submarine warfare threatened lives, not merely cargoes. Submarines, the strength of the German Navy, could not fight by the existing rules of war. These required the searching and unloading of passengers before a nonmilitary ship could be sunk. Yet these rules assumed warships operated on the surface, as they had in previous wars. Now technology made the rules outdated. A surfaced submarine was too vulnerable to fire to be an ineffective weapon. Something had to give. It would not be Woodrow Wilson, who considered submarines immoral.

In February 1915 Germany said that its submarines would sink, without warning, ships entering a war zone around Britain. Wilson warned that he would hold Berlin to "strict accountability" for American losses. His resolve was tested on May 7, when a U-boat sank the British passenger liner *Lusitania*, killing 1,198, including 128 Americans. Wilson wrote three sharply worded notes to Germany implying that more sinkings would mean war. Bryan objected to the second, refused to sign it, and resigned. Bryan's pro-British successor, Robert Lansing, urged the president to stand firm against Germany. Outside the government, some of Wilson's critics, notably Theodore Roosevelt, demanded tougher measures.

On August 19, 1915, the Germans sank the British passenger ship *Arabic*. Forty-four, including two Americans, died. Privately, Wilson threatened to break diplomatic ties, hinting that Washington would go to war if Germany continued its sinkings. Berlin agreed not to sink liners without warning, yet on March 24, 1916, a U-boat torpedoed a foreign steamer, *Sussex*, injuring Americans. This time Wilson threatened to sever relations. Germany pledged to observe the rule mandating warning and evacuation of ships, provided Britain honor it as well. The president accepted the *Sussex* pledge and ignored the condition. He knew London could not comply because it would nullify the advantages of the British blockade. The American people were distraught about the sinkings, yet divided over whether to go to war. Business favored stability; it could make money by selling to the belligerents without war. Ethnic groups supported their mother country. Yet most Americans believed a German victory would be hostile to their interests.

Meanwhile, the president sent his adviser, Colonel Edward House, as an emissary to Europe in early 1916. House and his friend, British Foreign Secretary Sir Edward Grey hammered out an agreement to end the war on London's terms. If Germany would not accept an American offer to mediate a settlement, the United States "probably" would enter the war on the Allied side. The British cabinet rejected the deal. Wilson rewrote the House-Grey memorandum into a general statement that did not commit America to war. Henry Ford attempted to mediate, sending pacifists to Europe aboard a "peace ship." If he could manufacture cars, Ford said, he could make people stop killing each other.

★ EDWARD M. HOUSE:
THE QUIET CAMPAIGNER ★

My ambition has been so great that it has never
seemed to me worthwhile to strive to satisfy it.

—EDWARD M. HOUSE

A DIMINUTIVE, soft-spoken man who refused appointment to high office, Colonel Edward M. House (1858–1938) came to wield more authority than most of the highest officials in the United States. As Woodrow Wilson's chief adviser, especially in foreign policy, House preferred to work outside the channels of government as the president's representative.

Born in Houston, Texas, to the southern aristocracy and educated in elite schools, House held ambitions for political office but fragile health and a weak voice forced him to be content with the role of adviser. Aligned with the reform wing of the Democratic Party, he was awarded the title of "colonel" by the governor of Texas.

In 1912, House met Wilson as the New Jersey governor campaigned for president, and found a soul mate. "We found ourselves in such complete sympathy, in so many ways, that we soon learned to know what each was thinking without either having expressed himself," House wrote. After Wilson's election, House became a behind-the-scenes mover in the administration. An enigmatic figure with a fertile imagination, he penned a novel about a private citizen who imposed world peace in 1912. House's influence waxed during the Great War.

Distrusting the judgment of his secretary of state, William Jennings Bryan, Wilson increasingly relied on House's discretion. House's friendship with the British Foreign Secretary, Sir Edward Grey, facilitated negotiations with the British, who regarded him highly.

After the United States declared war on Germany in 1917, House served as the president's confidant in negotiations with the Allies. He helped Wilson draft the Fourteen Points and accompanied the president to the peace conference at Versailles in 1919, acting in Wilson's place when the president was ill. House disappointed his mentor by his willingness to compromise with the harsher terms demanded by Great Britain and France. Now Wilson came to distrust House, believing that his old friend betrayed their ideals. After Versailles, Wilson never spoke to House again. Once one of America's most powerful men, House returned from France with no political position or importance. He worked on Franklin D. Roosevelt's presidential campaign in 1932, but never exercised any influence over his administration.

Sources: For the relationship between House and Wilson, see Alexander L. George and Juliette L. George, *Woodrow Wilson and Colonel House* (1956). For House and Grey's negotiations, see Joyce Grigsby Williams, *Colonel House and Sir Edward Grey* (1984).

Wilson faced a formidable Republican challenger in the 1916 presidential campaign, Charles Evans Hughes, former progressive governor of New York and U.S. Supreme Court justice. The Democrats campaigned as the peace party. Wilson reluctantly accepted the slogan "He kept us out of war," although he feared war was imminent. International tensions overshadowed Wilson's accomplishments in domestic policy. The incumbent trailed most of the night until late wins in Ohio and California reelected him, one of the closest elections of the century. Wilson won 49 percent of the popular vote to 46 percent for Hughes. Wilson's margin in the Electoral College was 277 to 254. The congressional vote showed a decline in the progressive movement. Conservatives prepared to take up the reins of government and to limit Wilson's leadership. Outside government, debates over government's role in regulation waned, superseded by issues related to the war, business, consumerism, and cultural rebellion. Although these developments would be postponed by the necessities of war and temporary government involvement, their seeds were planted in the last election before American boys embarked for the battlefields of Europe.

"A Message of Death"

Late in 1916 Wilson sought once more to broker a peace. He described his proposals in a speech to the Senate on January 22, 1917. He wanted "peace without victory" and an international organization where nations would resolve differences. Proud idealism led him to think he could impose these provisions for the peace settlement without entering the war. His goal of peace could not be pursued while he defended neutral rights.

Early in 1917 German military leaders concluded that the British blockade would strangle their nation if they did not mount a massive offensive to win. A ground assault and resumption of submarine warfare, they realized, would draw the United States into the war, but they believed combat would end before America could make a difference. Germany gambled it could win by sinking all ships bound for Britain. On January 31, Berlin informed the United States that Germany would proclaim a war zone around Britain, France, and Italy, and that the *Sussex* pledge would no longer be observed. Wilson broke relations with Germany.

War grew imminent in February, when the British intercepted and decoded a telegram from German Foreign Secretary Arthur Zimmermann to the German Embassy in Mexico. Zimmermann instructed his envoy to negotiate an alliance with Mexico in the event of war with America. Mexico was to try to persuade Japan to switch sides and declare war on the United States. In return, Germany would give Mexico territory lost

★ Jeannette Rankin: Warrior for Peace ★

This woman has more courage and packs a harder punch
than a regiment of regular-line politicians.
—FIORELLO LA GUARDIA, WHO SERVED IN CONGRESS WITH RANKIN

FIRST WOMAN IN CONGRESS
Jeannette Rankin opposed the war.
(Library of Congress)

JEANNETTE RANKIN served just two terms in the House of Representatives, more than twenty years apart. But she made a lasting impact as a feminist, as the first woman ever elected to Congress—and as the only member of Congress to vote against American involvement in both world wars.

Elected from Montana in 1916, Rankin found herself tested by her first vote, cast on April 6, 1917. She felt intense pressure to vote for war; the majority of her supporters in the women's suffrage movement urged her to do so. Striving to keep an open mind, she listened to the debate and waited until the second roll call. When her name was finally called, the chamber grew silent and every eye fixed on her. Slowly Rankin half rose, clutching a chair, and whispered, "I want to stand by my country, but I cannot vote for war." The "no" vote that followed was nearly lost in the muttering of colleagues and a smattering of applause from the galleries. She had cast a stunning vote and defied tradition by commenting on a roll call.

For the rest of her term, Rankin supported the war effort and championed reforms affecting women and children. None of her work, however, quelled the clamor against her antiwar vote. She never regretted the vote, although she was warned that it would cost her reelection. "I'm not interested in that," she said. "All I'm interested in is what they'll say fifty years from now." Gerrymandered into a predominantly Democratic district, Rankin ran instead for a U.S. Senate seat, and lost.

In the 1920s and 1930s, Rankin worked as a lobbyist for peace groups. "You can no more win a war than win an earthquake," she said. In 1940, fearing the United States would be pulled into World War II, Rankin ran again for the House from Montana and won. After Japan attacked Pearl Harbor on December 7, 1941, she once more defied public opinion by opposing the declaration of war—the only vote in Congress against war on the Japanese. Once more, Rankin's subsequent support of the war effort did not deter the public backlash against her vote. She retired from

Congress when her term expired. Her colleagues praised her courage, yet considered her vote folly.

During the next quarter century, Rankin traveled around the world—including India, where she became a disciple of Mahatma Gandhi—but lived reclusively. Then in 1968 she lent her name to the Jeannette Rankin Brigade, an organization of women opposing the Vietnam War, and led several thousand women in a protest march to the national Capitol. "We have to get it into our heads once and for all that we cannot settle disputes by eliminating human beings," Rankin said. Later, one congressman called her "the original dove in Congress" and told her, "Look at the record now. We're voting your way, Jeannette." She spoke publicly for peace and government reform until a few months before her death in 1973 at the age of ninety-two.

In Rankin's long lifetime of activity, she remembered one act above the rest. "The most important accomplishment, I believe, was my voting against the First World War."

Sources: The most useful short treatment of Jeannette Rankin is Glen Jeansonne, "The Lone Dissenting Voice," *American History*, Vol. XXXIV (April 1999), pp. 46–54. Also see Kevin S. Giles, *Flight of the Dove: The Story of Jeannette Rankin* (1980).

in the Mexican-American War of 1846–1848, including Texas, Arizona, and New Mexico. Britain gave the telegram to the U.S. government, and reports of the document in the press increased the clamor for hostilities. Wilson still opposed war. Instead, he asked Congress to authorize the arming of merchant ships. The bill passed the House but was killed by a Senate filibuster by a handful of isolationists. "A little group of willful men, representing no opinion but their own, have rendered the great government of the United States helpless and contemptible," Wilson complained. Later, the president found legal grounds to justify arming the vessels by executive order.

Overseas, the Russian Revolution overthrew the czar and momentarily ushered in a democratic government under the liberal Alexander Kerensky, who pledged to continue the war. To Wilson, the mission of the Great War now seemed clear-cut: democracy must defeat autocracy. By joining the war, America could gain a voice at the peacemaking and ensure a permanent peace. On April 2, 1917, Wilson stood before a joint session of Congress to urge America to wage war.

Wilson addressed the lawmakers with majestic rhetoric but a sad heart. American entry, he knew, would postpone reform and inspire intolerance. Nevertheless, the world had to be made safe for democracy. "It is a fearful

thing to lead this great peaceful people into war, the most terrible and disastrous of all wars, civilization itself seeming to be in the balance. But the
right is more precious than the peace . . . the day has come when America
is privileged to spend her blood and her might for the principles that gave
her birth and happiness and the peace which she has treasured. God helping her, she can do no other."

At his conclusion, the lawmakers stood and applauded. "Think what
it was they were applauding," Wilson told his secretary, Joseph Tumulty.
"My message today was a message of death for our young men. How
strange it seems to applaud that." In the next four days, both houses of
Congress supported the commander in chief's call for war against Germany.
The United States would devote its energies, its souls, its young men, to
Europe's most awesome catastrophe since the Black Death killed one-third
of the population in the 1340s.

CHAPTER SIX

From World War to Lost Peace

THE PARADOXES of Woodrow Wilson's presidency closed the Era of Awakening. A renowned academic, successful governor, and reform president, he emerged in his second term as a great war president, an eloquent statesman for world peace, and, ultimately, a failed peacemaker. He is often considered a tragic figure, abandoned by all but history. Yet out of his one magnificent failure grew lessons and an appreciation of the enormity of the task he had undertaken. "Show me a hero and I will write you a tragedy," the novelist F. Scott Fitzgerald wrote.

Home Front Management

Even before running as the peace candidate in 1916, Woodrow Wilson prepared for war. The army had just one hundred thousand soldiers, the fewest of any major nation. The navy ranked third in battleships behind Britain and Germany and had an antiquated command structure and supply system. Wilson's preparedness program met with opposition from Secretary of State William Jenning Bryan's dovish followers in Congress. Wilson compromised, dropping its most controversial feature, a reserve force to be known as the Continental Army. War Secretary Lindley Garrison, the architect of the plan, resigned in protest, so it was up to his replacement, Newton D. Baker, to push the scaled-down proposal through Congress.

Two weeks after declaring war in April 1917, Congress gave Wilson authority to draft men between twenty-one and thirty-five into the Army. Around 10 million registered, 2.7 million were drafted, and 1.5 million volunteered. Some 520,000 volunteered for the Navy and Marines, neither of which held a draft. Many draftees were disqualified because of ill health. Some conscientious objectors on religious grounds were assigned

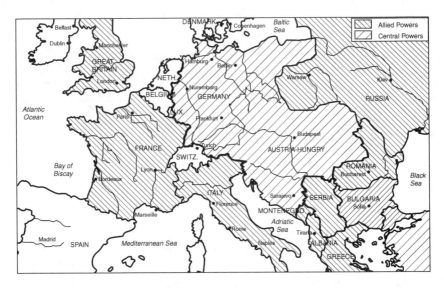

WWI IN EUROPE
Allied and Central Powers

to noncombatant military jobs in the United States. A few changed their minds and fought overseas, including the greatest Army hero, Sergeant Alvin C. York. A reluctant soldier owing to his religion (Christian Union), he had learned marksmanship by hunting in his mountainous Tennessee home, a talent he used to kill 25 Germans with 25 shots and capture 132 prisoners and 35 machine guns.

To finance the war, the Revenue Acts of 1917 and 1918 raised income taxes to their highest rates, peaking at 79 percent. Taxes, however, supplied only part of the money required. The rest came from large-denomination Treasury bonds and smaller Liberty Bonds. The return on Liberty Bonds was low, so the government made profits tax-exempt and urged their purchase as a patriotic contribution. Federal borrowing redirected capital from open markets, and government spending and economic expansion almost doubled the amount of money in circulation between 1916 and 1920. The size of the federal government doubled during the war, as the budget grew from $712,967,000 in 1916 to $18 billion in 1919. The national debt rose from $1 billion in 1916 to $24 billion in 1920.

Academics and businessmen advised economic planning, the latter receiving a dollar per year in pay from the government and the rest of their salaries from their companies. Business received waivers from antitrust prosecutions, government contracts, and permissions to merge. To spur production, the government guaranteed profits. Wall Street speculator Bernard

Baruch, head of the War Industries Board, applied coercion. When the automobile industry resisted converting to military production, he threatened to deny it steel. When railroads failed to provide efficient transportation, the government took them over. The government also fixed commodity prices and supervised the production of coal, oil, and food.

Herbert Hoover won accolades by furnishing food for Belgium, pinched between German occupation and a British blockade. After America entered the war, Hoover became Wilson's food administrator. Through a combination of conservation, small gardens, and scientific methods, he enabled farmers to provide enough food and fiber to supply the American armed forces, the civilian population, the Allies, and, after the war, much of Europe and the Soviet Union. Hoover relied on voluntarism, and appeals to patriotism, and limited regulation.

While Hoover fed bellies, George Creel, who headed the Committee on Public Information, the chief propaganda agency, sought to feed minds.

ALCOHOL DOWN THE DRAIN
Prohibition agents pouring liquor into the sewer, circa 1920.
(Library of Congress)

His army of writers, cartoonists, and speakers stuffed Americans with facts, figures, and patriotic speeches. Celebrities were recruited to deliver speeches, sometimes in theaters before films were shown. Historians wrote pamphlets justifying America's fight. Some of Creel's messages amounted to unnecessary hyperbole that incited hatred.

In wartime, alcohol consumption seemed wasteful. Prohibitionists finally achieved their goal, first in temporary legislation to conserve grain and prevent drinking near military bases in 1917. In December of that year, Congress passed the Eighteenth Amendment prohibiting the manufacture, transportation, and sale of alcohol. By January 1919 the amendment had been ratified. The Volstead Act, passed over Wilson's veto, defined an alcoholic beverage as one containing at least 0.5 percent alcohol by volume and allocated enforcement to the Bureau of Internal Revenue. The Prohibition Era had begun.

Women, too, achieved goals. One and a half million went to work, mainly in war industries, earning higher wages than previously. Though not all the work was permanent, it helped demonstrate the competence of women in a variety of occupations. The biggest gain, however, was suffrage, approved by Congress in 1919 and ratified by a sufficient number of states in August 1920. Women voted for the first time nationally three months later and joined men in the Warren G. Harding landslide.

"Over There"

Americans marched to war to the tune of George M. Cohan's "Over There" and vowed "We won't be back until it's over, over there." When the blare of the horns stilled, the doughboys (infantrymen) fought one of the most grisly wars in history. Their involvement was short, but violent and victorious. Their impact lay less in their victories than in their timing. With an endless caravan of fresh troops stretching across the Atlantic, Germany had to win quickly or lose. The American contribution was both small and potentially infinite; Europe was exhausted; America was rested and ready. The American commander, General John J. Pershing, a West Point graduate, had fought in Cuba, the Philippines, and Mexico. The American Expeditionary Force, which eventually reached 2 million, of whom 1.8 million engaged in combat, for the most part fought under an independent identity, at Pershing's insistence. He believed if Americans were integrated into Allied units their contribution would be less visible, and less impressive at the peace table.

The Rainbow Division, commanded by the army's youngest general, Douglas MacArthur, established a high standard for heroism and esprit de corps. Comprised of the star soldiers selected nationally from National

WINNING THE RIGHT TO VOTE
Women demonstrate for suffrage, 1917.
(Library of Congress)

Guard units, they emulated the dash of their commander. Americans had few military planes, yet built more than thirty thousand engines used by British planes. The United States contributed eleven thousand pilots, half assigned to France. The most famous was Captain Eddie Rickenbacker, who shot down twenty-six German planes.

The armed services treatment of its African American soldiers and sailors tarnished the nation's commitment to democracy. Blacks were barred from the Marines and could serve in the navy but only as cooks or in menial capacities. Tensions erupted occasionally. Taunted by white civilians, black soldiers rioted in Houston in August 1917, killing seventeen white people. After a summary trial, thirteen black soldiers were hanged for mutiny and murder and forty were sentenced to prison. Still, given the opportunity, African Americans served with distinction. The all-black 369th Infantry Regiment, integrated into the French Army because of emergency needs for replacements, was the first Allied unit to reach the Rhine. It served the longest of any American regiment attached to a foreign army; the 369th never lost territory or a man through capture. American Indians also felt the paradox of fighting for a democracy whose benefits they did not entirely share. Indians, unlike African Americans, did not fight in segregated units. Pershing used Apaches chiefly as scouts and, after two Choctaws used their native language, as a radio code.

Theodore Roosevelt yearned to duplicate his heroism in the Spanish-American War by leading a volunteer regiment. Wilson refused, stating

AFRICAN AMERICANS AT WAR
A segregated unit at attention.
(Library of Congress)

times had changed. The army needed professionals trained in the technology of modern warfare. To invite the aged, partially blind Rough Rider
would politicalize the conflict, and perhaps cost Roosevelt his life. Sadly,
TR's youngest son, Quentin, a pilot, was shot down behind German lines
and killed in July 1918.

Roosevelt's romantic view of war denied reality. Technology killed
more efficiently than medicine could cure. Lacking antibiotics, amputation
was the chief method to prevent infection from spreading. Machine guns,
barbed war, and primitive tanks made massed charges suicidal. Most
heinous was poison gas, which could kill its users if the wind changed direction. It proved so ghastly it was outlawed for future wars. Soldiers fought
in the stench and human waste of trenches, drenched by rain, baked by the
sun, paralyzed by the cold. French troops mutinied, refused to charge, and
were court-martialed. Perhaps only because America's involvement was
short was it spared the massive casualties and some of the deadening mental pain that poisoned morale.

Germany was sinking beneath the onslaught of infinite numbers of enemy troops, diminishing supplies, and the threat of mutiny. In 1918 the generals decided to gamble on a spring offensive that would win the war on the Western Front or lose it. Then, like a bolt from Heaven, their eastern enemy, Russia, dropped out. A second revolution, following the overthrow of the czar, overthrew the Alexander Kerensky democratic government. The Bolshevik victors, facing a civil war at home, surrendered to Germany on draconian terms, giving up Latvia, Lithuania, Russia, Poland, and the Ukraine. The new communist government, by the Treaty of Brest-Litovsk, yielded 386,000 square miles of territory, 40 percent of Russia's iron and steel production, and 75 percent of its coal deposits. Some Americans romanticized the new regime under V. I. Lenin, believing the Bolshevik humanitarians would reform the nation oppressed by the czars. Wilson, on the other hand, refused to recognize the new regime.

Shortly before Russia withdrew, Wilson delivered a speech specifying Fourteen Points. He hoped to outflank the appeal of communism with his idealism and generous peace terms. The president's recommendations included freedom of the seas, free trade, restoration of Belgian independence and Russian territory, and adjustment of colonial claims with consideration for subjects. The program was embraced by the masses, but European heads of states were dubious. Russia, its people, and its new leaders, were exhausted and not inclined to trust the president's promise.

Japan, too, received Wilson's attention. An ally of the Entente, the Japanese seized German zones in China, extending its domination to the Shantung Peninsula. Wilson wanted to retain Japan as an ally, yet preserve China's territorial integrity. In the Lansing-Ishii agreement of November 2, 1917, the United States sanctioned Japanese economic domination of China, yet the Chinese interpreted it to imply military and political domination as well.

America sent troops to Russia, along with Japan, France, and Britain, to observe the civil war that followed the Bolshevik Revolution. London and Paris hoped to encourage the victory of the noncommunist White Army, and Tokyo aspired to seize concessions in the Far East. Although he favored the White Army, Wilson believed intervention unwise and impractical. There was no way to dictate the outcome without a massive investment of military resources that would be unacceptable to the American public. Wilson, however, wanted to remain on good terms with the Allies, protect American property, and counter Japanese influence. Wilson also hoped to enable anti-German Czech forces in Russia to reach the United States via Siberia and the Pacific, then cross the Atlantic to fight Germany. By the time this unrealistic plan materialized, the war was over. The only tangible result of the Western occupation, which lasted until 1920, was to foster communist resentment.

On the Western Front in March 1918, the Allies faced a German offensive strengthened by the release of thousands of troops from the East after the Russian surrender. But inexperienced American soldiers helped repel Germany at Cantigny in May and at Chateau-Thierry and Belleau Wood in June. The initiative shifted to the Allies after their victory in the Battle of the Marne in July. Having exhausted themselves in the offensive, the Germans fell back, now confronting an adversary with virtually unlimited manpower. In a war of attrition, they could not win.

The Allied commander, French General Ferdinand Foch, gave the Americans a central role in the counteroffensive of September 1918. They were, first, to reduce the German salient behind the village of St. Mihiel, and, second, to attack the main German lines to the northwest of Verdun through fortified terrain bounded by the Meuse River on the west and the Argonne Forest on the east. The main objective was to sever the railroad connection at Sedan. Some 550,000 American troops were committed to St. Mihiel and 1.2 million to the Meuse-Argonne offensive. Although the St. Mihiel campaign caught the Germans evacuating and drove them out easily, the Meuse-Argonne offensive found a deeply entrenched foe difficult to dislodge. Still, the progress of the Americans, who could replace casualties as Germany could not, was inexorable, and they won their objective.

Foch planned to use almost 2 million American troops for an offensive in early 1919 that would cross the Rhine and take the war to German soil. This action proved unnecessary because Germany's army and civilians were spent; to continue the war, their military leaders felt, would mean humiliation. Desiring to salvage their armed forces, officials asked Wilson to arrange an armistice based on the Fourteen Points. A new government headed by Prince Max of Baden conveyed the request through the Swiss in early October. Wilson declined to deal with the Kaiser, who abdicated and escaped Germany on November 9 after a naval mutiny at Kiel and the outbreak of a revolution in Bavaria. By this time Austria had surrendered. France and Britain, however, did not favor the Fourteen Points as a basis for negotiations.

Wilson turned the final negotiations over to Foch. Germany agreed to evacuate the Western Front immediately, release prisoners of war, and accept the British blockade until a treaty was signed. A republican government under socialist Friedrich Ebert, signed a truce on November 11, 1918. The United States won a seat at the peace negotiations without suffering the staggering casualties of the other warriors. America lost 53,000 killed and 204,000 wounded in battle; another 63,000 died from disease, most in the 1918–1919 influenza epidemic. Germany lost the most to battle, 1.8 million, followed by Russia, 1.7 million, France, 1.4 million (one-third of its combat-age men) and Britain, 900,000. In proportion to population, the French suffered the most deaths and maimings.

The "war to end all wars," as Wilson called it, proved a misnomer. Yet, the Era of Awakening ended as it had begun, with victory in a military conflict, this time a major one. Arguably the greatest economic power at the turn of the century, the United States was now the most potent military power, certainly the one with the most potential. Yet if the war provided an explosion of America's military might, the aftermath produced a dud. A short period of intolerance was capped by a generation of withdrawal.

Intolerance and the Red Scare

While America fought for liberty abroad, the government cracked down on civil liberties. The degree should not be exaggerated and must be placed in the context of the time. All wars limit freedoms until victory is in sight, and in comparison with the other democracies, the United States was not the worst. Still, America was, and should be held to high standards. The nation's prestige was tarnished by its excesses, and hatred is never justified, not even in wartime.

To stifle dissent, the government enacted the Espionage Act, which prohibited sabotage and criticism of the war effort. A second law, the Trading with the Enemy Act, barred trade with enemy nations and authorized censorship of foreign language publications. In 1918 two additional laws were passed. The Alien Act permitted the deportation of noncitizens considered a threat; the Sedition Act outlawed criticism of the Allied cause. Leftists were stigmatized. Anarchists Emma Goldman and Alexander Berkman were convicted of inciting draft resistance, fined, sentenced to jail, and deported. Socialist Roger Baldwin defied the draft and was sent to prison. Victor Berger, a Wisconsin socialist who had won a congressional election, was sentenced to jail for publishing antiwar articles. However, Berger's conviction was overturned by the Supreme Court. Eugene V. Debs was sentenced to ten years for disputing Wilson's claim that the war was waged to uphold democracy. Some 160 members of the Industrial Workers of the World, including William Haywood and Elizabeth Gurley Flynn, were sentenced to long terms for violating the Sedition Act.

The Supreme Court reluctantly upheld most convictions, although it overturned some. In *Schenck v. United States* Justice Oliver Wendell Holmes wrote, in upholding the conviction of Debs, that the right of free speech was not absolute. Context was a key. Falsely shouting "Fire!" in a theater, for example, was unacceptable. Holmes helped establish the precedent that talk constituting a "clear-and-present danger" was illegal.

The public was intolerant of Germany. German food was taken off restaurant menus and German books were removed from library shelves. At a time when the military needed translators, some schools ceased teaching German. The fear and prejudice culminated in the Red Scare of 1919. The catalysts were a large number of high-profile strikes in 1919, the Bolshevik Revolution of 1917, and militant speech and some violent action by homegrown radicals. Most concern was directed at the American Communist Party, the Communist Labor Party, and the Socialist Party. More action-oriented, a few anarchists mailed bombs to federal officials in New York, Pittsburgh, Boston, and Washington. Postal officials defused most, yet a bomb exploded on the front porch of Attorney General A. Mitchell Palmer, who became the Red Scare leader. Uninjured, Palmer ordered raids to round up and deport aliens suspected of radicalism. In November 1919, 250 aliens were netted in a twelve-city sweep, followed by 249 rounded up in December. Among those sent to the Soviet Union were Goldman and her lover, Berkman. The raids peaked on January 2, 1920, when 4,000 radicals were arrested and 550 deported.

The Red Scare was based on fear, not a realistic threat. To some degree, it expanded beyond fear of the overthrow of the government to fear of those who were different. Some of the fear was generated by the idea that determined minorities had power beyond their numbers. The Bolsheviks, for example, had been a tiny minority when they overthrew the Russian government. Of course, America was not Russia, although some Americans advocated tactics similar to the Russian regime. Some states banned Communist flags. The New York State Legislature expelled five duly elected Socialists. Palmer predicted a communist takeover attempt on May 1, 1920, a coup that did not transpire. In a last burst of terrorist activity, anarchists detonated a bomb on Wall Street on September 16, killing thirty-eight and injuring two hundred.

Fear of radicalism ebbed after Palmer's false prediction, and the country turned to other matters. On the uplift of war the economy soared, particularly infant industries such as radio and aviation. A key economic indicator, the gross national product (GNP), the value of all goods and services produced in the country, swelled from $48.3 billion in 1916 to $84.0 billion in 1919. The largest debtor in the world, the United States became the largest creditor, and the dollar replaced the British pound as the foundation for international trade. Still, reconversion to a peacetime economy on a massive scale had no precedent. Wilson's task was vexing. When he removed curbs on wages and prices, inflation climbed, increasing the cost of living and motivating labor to demand higher wages. The wartime experiments in government economic planning, called "wartime socialism," were terminated. Although many believed the railroads had been better operated in government hands than in private ones, they were returned to their owners under the Esch-Cummings Transportation Act of 1920.

The difficulty of reconversion was only one of a host of problems the United States confronted near the end of the Era of Awakening. In the last years of the decade the anxieties included not only the Red Scare and the labor unrest and extremist agitation that precipitated it, but also racial unrest; Wilson's illness; and a global influenza epidemic that claimed some 686,000 American lives in 1918 and 1919, far exceeding the U.S. toll from the war.

The Peace Conference

If the war seemed comparable to the Battle of Armageddon, the peace conference that convened in Paris represented the Day of Judgment. To this day came Wilson, deciding to attend the conclave because he trusted only himself to shape its outcome. The world's most respected statesman in 1919, he was showered by the European masses with cheers, flowers, and honors. He headed an American delegation that included Robert Lansing; Colonel Edward M. House; Tasker Bliss, the general who had represented America on the Allies' Supreme War Council; Henry White, a diplomat and the only registered Republican in the delegation; and a group of thirteen hundred experts called the Inquiry. Wilson, however, consulted just a few men he trusted.

The major decisions were made by the Council of Four: Wilson, British Prime Minister David Lloyd George, French President Georges Clemenceau, and Italian Prime Minister Vittorio Orlando (Japan was represented in some sessions). Each had different priorities. Wilson wanted lasting peace policed by a League of Nations. Clemenceau wanted to disarm and weaken Germany. Lloyd George wanted to maintain Britain's supremacy at sea and preserve its empire. Italy coveted territory the Allies promised it in the secret 1915 Treaty of London. Japan desired to expand its domination of China and to include language recognizing racial equality. The cynical nationalist Clemenceau complained that the idealistic Wilson "thought himself another Jesus Christ come upon the Earth to reform men." Wilson's self-righteousness, Clemenceau predicted, would wear thin. "God has given man Ten Commandments. He broke every one. Wilson has his Fourteen Points. We shall see."

Battling Clemenceau and others tried Wilson's patience, and strained his frail health. At the end of March he suffered from what might have been a viral infection or a series of minor strokes. Still Wilson persisted, and the conference worked out the treaty that Germany signed in the Palace of Versailles on June 28, 1919. The reconfiguration of Europe marked the greatest changes since the Congress of Vienna ended the Napoleonic era. Poland reappeared on the map, with a route to the sea carved from German territory. Yugoslavia and Czechoslovakia were created to provide ethnic self-determination—Wilson's principle that political units should reflect the will of the ethnic groups within them. France received a demilitarized buffer zone between itself and the Germans taken from the Rhineland, in addition to a temporary right to occupy the Saar Basin coal region in Germany.

Italy's boundary was moved north to annex the Brenner Pass, but Wilson refused to concede the port city of Fiume because it was not populated by Italians and because Yugoslavia needed a port. Nor did the Japanese receive everything they sought, for the conference did not adopt a statement promising racial equality. Wilson, whose pledge for self-determination did not include nonwhite races, realized that the British and the French, each possessing colonies, would not tolerate such a statement, which would embarrass Americans as well. Yet the conference offered the Japanese something they wanted more: control over the Shandong Peninsula.

Although the terms were less harsh than those that a victorious Germany might have imposed, the Germans were furious. They were judged guilty of causing the war, shorn of their colonies, disarmed, and ordered to pay $56 billion in reparations to the Allies. Their country lost 6.5 million people and one-eighth of its territory. Any German government that signed such a document was certain to be vilified by its people. The Germans haggled over the terms for six weeks before representatives of a new republic created at Weimar signed the treaty.

In an absolute sense, the treaty was unduly punitive toward Germany. In a relative sense, it was fairer than most treaties of such magnitude. Much of the world had assumed that Wilson, despite being only one player at the peace table, held the cards and could deal the hand he chose. It was unrealistic to assume the Americans, who intervened late and shed less blood than the British and the French, could unilaterally dictate the terms. Wilson, nonetheless, had substantial influence. Without his contributions, the pact would have been worse. What was surprising was that he incorporated as many of the Fourteen Points as he did, not that he was thwarted on many issues, British statesman Winston Churchill observed. The recognition of independence for Poland and Baltic states, the formation of Czechoslovakia and Yugoslavia, the system providing for Allied trusteeship of the former German and Turkish colonies as a theoretical prelude to self-government—all these reflected Wilson's beliefs in democracy and self-determination. And, of course, the treaty included the League of Nations.

"Dare We Reject It?"

The narrow straits of European diplomacy, churned by centuries of ethnic, religious, and national turmoil, were less perilous than the treacherous currents of politics in the United States. Wilson had an opportunity to name Republicans to the American delegation at Paris, but included only White. Then, during the 1918 election campaign in the closing weeks of the war, he urged voters to return a Democratic majority to Congress to support his plans. This partisanship misfired. Republicans gained control of both houses. Returning home in February 1919, the president received a petition from Massachusetts Republican Henry Cabot Lodge, chair of the Senate Foreign Relations Committee, stating that thirty-nine GOP senators or senators-elect—enough to prevent ratification—opposed the League Covenant. Upon his return to Paris, Wilson had to negotiate changes. He satisfied the Republicans by having the covenant amended to exclude tariff and immigration issues and regional security arrangements, such as the Monroe Doctrine.

When Wilson brought home the completed treaty in July 1919, he believed the Senate would ratify it quickly. "Dare we reject it and break the heart of the world?" he asked. Probably a majority of the Senate, and a majority of the people, favored ratification, although there was no consensus on the nature of treaty they wanted. In the Senate a two-thirds majority was required. Moreover, Lodge, the Senate majority leader and the president's political and intellectual foil, hated Wilson and was dubious of the League. He delayed consideration by reading the entire treaty into the *Congressional Record*, which took two weeks. Then he held six weeks of hearings and drafted a series of amendments, or reservations. Of the reservations, the most important mandated congressional approval before the United States could dispatch armed forces under the League's peacekeeping obligations.

To build support, Wilson embarked upon a speaking tour in which he covered eight thousand miles in three weeks and delivered thirty-six speeches. He ridiculed the argument of some that the League would order soldiers from the United States to distant lands to keep the peace, insisting that Americans would be involved only near their borders, where their interests were at stake. "If you want to put out a fire in Utah, you do not send to Oklahoma for a fire engine. If you want to put out a fire in the Balkans

. . . you do not send to the United States for troops." Wilson's speeches stirred the masses, yet did not gain votes in the Senate. After an address at Pueblo, Colorado, on September 26, 1919, he collapsed and was rushed to Washington. On October 2 the president suffered a stroke that paralyzed his left side, slurred his speech, and disturbed his emotional stability.

For a few days Wilson lingered between life and death; for the next six weeks he did little work. With no chief, Edith Wilson and her husband's doctors concealed his infirmity from the public, limited his contacts, and protected him from stress. Some of his strength returned, yet Wilson remained in bed or in a wheelchair. Prone to outbursts, he fired Lansing, accusing him of disloyalty. The president refused to compromise to win Senate approval.

Wilson believed Lodge's reservations would "cut the heart" from the treaty. Accordingly, he ordered pro-League Democrats to vote against the treaty with reservations. On November 19, 1919, they obliged, joining the "Irreconcilables," senators who would not support any form of

BLOCKING THE TREATY
Henry Cabot Lodge defeats
Wilson's plan for world peace.
(Library of Congress)

League, to defeat the treaty with the reservations, 39 votes in favor and 55 opposed. The treaty also failed without the reservations, 38 to 53.

Shocked by the rejections, moderates pleaded for compromise. Instead, Wilson insisted that the issue be placed before Americans as a "solemn referendum" in the 1920 presidential election, in which he would be the Democratic candidate. Practically, this scheme was impossible because of the two-term tradition and his poor health. Lodge agreed to hold another vote, on March 19, 1920, and it was closer, as 21 Democrats ignored their president to support the treaty with reservations. It passed, 49 to 35—seven votes short of a two-thirds majority. The League would have to keep peace without the United States.

Wilson ended his public career a tragic figure, much like Roosevelt who had died on January 6, 1919. For a time Wilson was blamed for arrogance and pride that led to the defeat of the Treaty. Yet after World War II his reputation rose, his idealism and inspiration were revived again, and some speculated that a League, such as Wilson envisioned, might have stifled Nazism. A retrospective look, however, does not comfort the observer with the thought that the League might have contained Adolf Hitler and other aggressors. It offered a way to do so, but not the will, which was not strong enough in the world between the wars. Not until after World War II would Wilsonian ideas of an international peacekeeping body and collective security have their day.

Having dreams of greatness for humanity, Wilson would have been foolish not to pursue them. Yet, if there is nothing so powerful as an idea whose time has come, there is nothing so futile as an idea that is premature. Wilson appreciated this in the twilight of his life, when he said to his eldest daughter: "I think it was best after all that the United States did not join the League of Nations. Now when the American people join the League, it will be because they are convinced it is the right thing to do, and then will be the *only right* time for them to do it." He smiled and added, "Perhaps God knew better than I did after all."

Bibliographic Essay

BECAUSE OF space constraints, the compilations of supplementary readings in this book emphasize general and more recent studies (although older, seminal works receive their due).

The 1890s

On the populists, see John D. Hicks, *The Populist Revolt* (1931), dated but essential; Lawrence Goodwyn, *The Populist Moment: A Short History of the Agrarian Rebels in America* (1978); O. Michael Kazin, *The Populist Persuasion: An American History* (1995); and Robert C. McMath, *American Populism: A Social History, 1877–1898* (1993). Other works on politics include three books by Richard Hofstadter, *The Age of Reform: From Bryan to F.D.R.* (1955), *The American Political Tradition and the Men Who Made It* (1948), and *The Paranoid Style in American Politics and Other Essays* (1964); C. Vann Woodward; *The Strange Career of Jim Crow* (1974), another seminal work; Michael E. McGerr, *The Decline of Popular Politics: The American North, 1865–1928* (1986); Joel Williamson, *A Rage for Order: Black–White Relations in the American South since Emancipation* (1986); and Nancy Cohen, *The Reconstruction of American Liberalism, 1865–1914* (2002). For foreign policy, see Ernest R. May, *Imperial Democracy: The Emergence of America as a Great Power* (1961); Walter LaFeber, *The New Empire: An Interpretation of American Expansion, 1860–1898* (1963); David F. Healy, *U.S. Expansionism: The Imperialist Urge in the 1890s* (1970); Robert L. Beisner, *Twelve against Empire: The Anti-Imperialists, 1898–1900* (1985); and *From the Old Diplomacy to the New, 1865–1900* (1986), both excellent; and the revisionist William Appleman Williams, *The Tragedy of American Diplomacy* (rev. ed., 1989).

Useful business, labor, and technology studies include Melvin Dubofsky, *Industrialism and the American Worker, 1865–1920* (1975); James Tobin,

To Conquer the Air: The Wright Brothers and the Great Race for Flight (2003); Leon Fink, *Workingmen's Democracy: The Knights of Labor and American Politics* (1983); and Paul Krause, *The Battle for Homestead, 1880–1892: Politics, Culture, and Steel* (1992).

1900–1920

Valuable works include H. Wiebe, *The Search for Order: 1877–1920* (1967); a study of social modernization; Eric F. Goldman, *Rendezvous with Destiny* (1952); Otis L. Graham, *The Great Campaigns: Reforms and War in America, 1900–1928* (1978); James MacGregor Burns, *The Workshop of Democracy* (1985), beautifully written; Lewis L. Gould, *Reform and Regulation: American Politics from Roosevelt to Wilson* (2nd ed., 1986); Nell Irvin Painter, *Standing at Armageddon: The United States, 1877–1919* (1987), strong on women, African Americans, and labor; and John M. Cooper Jr., *Pivotal Decades: The United States, 1900–1920* (1990).

The worst natural disaster of the century's first decade is described in Philip L. Fradkin, *The Great Earthquake and Firestorms of 1906: How San Francisco Nearly Destroyed Itself* (2005).

Progressivism

On progressivism, start with Eldon J. Eisenbach, *The Lost Promise of Progressivism* (1983); William L. O'Neill, *The Progressive Years: America Comes of Age* (1975); John Whiteclay Chambers II, *The Tyranny of Change: America in the Progressive Era, 1900–1917* (2000); Steven J. Diner, *A Very Different Age: Americans of the Progressive Era* (1998); Louis L. Gould, *America in the Progressive Era* (2000); Michael E. McGerr, *A Fierce Discontent: The Rise and Fall of the Progressive Movement in America, 1870–1920* (2003); and Alan Dawley, *Changing the World: American Progressivism in War and Revolution* (2003). For unconventional interpretations, see Gabriel Kolko, *The Triumph of Conservatism* (1963) and *Railroads and Regulation, 1877–1916* (1965); and James Weinstein, *The Corporate Ideal in the Liberal State* (1968). Among the best regional studies of Progressivism are C. Vann Woodward, *Origins of the New South, 1877–1913* (1951); Russell B. Nye, *Midwestern Progressive Politics* (1951); George B. Tindall, *The Emergence of the New South* (1967); Jack Temple Kirby, *Darkness at the Dawning: Race and Reform in the Progressive South* (1972); Monroe Lee Billington, *The Political South in the Twentieth Century* (1975); David P. Thelen, *The New Citizenship: Origins of*

Progressivism in Wisconsin, 1885–1900 (1972); Herbert F. Margulies, *The Decline of Progressivism in Wisconsin* (1968); Spencer W. Olin Jr., *California's Prodigal Sons: Hiram Johnson and the Progressives* (1968); James Wright, *The Progressive Yankees: Republican Reformers in New Hampshire, 1900–1916* (1987); Dewey W. Grantham Jr., *Southern Progressivism: The Reconciliation of Progress and Tradition* (1983); and Lewis L. Gould, *Progressives and Prohibitionists: Texas Democrats in the Wilson Era* (1973).

Major Political Leaders

The literature on the major political leaders of the era is rich. On Theodore Roosevelt, Edmund Morris, *The Rise of Theodore Roosevelt* (1979), and David McCullough, *Mornings on Horseback* (1981) are important for his early life. Edmond Morris, *Theodore Rex* (2001), describes Roosevelt's life during the presidential years. Perhaps the best complete biographies are H. W. Brands, *T.R.: The Last Romantic* (1997), and William H. Harbaugh, *The Life and Times of Theodore Roosevelt* (rev. ed., 1975). Also good are Lewis L. Gould, *The Presidency of Theodore Roosevelt* (1991), an administrative history. George E. Mowry, *Theodore Roosevelt and the Progressive Movement* (1946) and *The Era of Theodore Roosevelt and the Birth of Modern America* (1958), and John Morton Blum, *The Republican Roosevelt* (1954), are important studies of his political career. Roosevelt's foreign policy is described in Raymond A. Esthus, *Theodore Roosevelt and the International Rivalries* (1970), and Frederick W. Marks III, *Velvet on Iron: The Diplomacy of Theodore Roosevelt* (1979). On the Panama Canal see David McCullough, *The Path between the Seas* (1977).

The essential works on William Howard Taft include Henry F. Pringle, *The Life and Times of William Howard Taft* (2 vols., 1939), and James R. Anderson, *William Howard Taft: A Conservative's Conception of the Presidency* (1973). Taft's foreign policies are the subject of Walter Scholes and Marie Scholes, *The Foreign Policies of the Taft Administration* (1970).

Woodrow Wilson has inspired numerous studies. The most comprehensive biography is Arthur S. Link, *Wilson* (5 vols., 1947–1965). Kendrick A. Clements, *Woodrow Wilson* (1987), is a reliable portrait. John Cooper, *The Warrior and the Priest: Woodrow Wilson and Theodore Roosevelt* (1983), is an outstanding dual biography. Also important are Arthur S. Link, *Woodrow Wilson and the Progressive Era, 1910–1917* (1954); John Morton Blum, *Woodrow Wilson and the Politics of Morality* (1956); and Edwin A. Weinstein, *Woodrow Wilson: A Medical and Psychological Biography* (1981).

Other Political Figures

Works on other politicians include Horace S. Merrill and Marian C. Merrill, *The Republican Command, 1897–1913* (1971); David Sarasohn, *The Party of Reform: The Democrats in the Progressive Era* (1989); Paolo E. Coletta, *William Jennings Bryan* (3 vols., 1964–1969); Lawrence W. Levine, *Defender of the Faith: Bryan, the Last Decade, 1915–1925* (1965); Kendrick A. Clements, *William Jennings Bryan, Missionary Isolationist* (1983); Le Roy Ashby, *William Jennings Bryan* (1987); Robert W. Cherny, *A Righteous Cause: The Life of William Jennings Bryan* (1994); David P. Thelen, *Robert M. La Follette and the Insurgent Spirit* (1976); Nancy C. Unger, *Fighting Bob La Follette: The Righteous Reformer* (2000); and Stephen Kantrowitz, *Ben Tillman and the Reconstruction of White Supremacy* (2000).

Racial Issues, Sound Reform, Business, and Labor

Aspects of racial issues, social reform, business, and labor are treated in Robert M. Crunden, *Ministers of Reform: The Progressives' Achievement in American Civilization, 1889–1920* (1982); Robert H. Wiebe, *Businessmen and Reform* (1962); Nick Salvatore, *Eugene Victor Debs, Citizen and Socialist* (1982); James Weinstein, *The Decline of Socialism in America, 1912–1925* (1967); Philip Taft, *The A.F.L. in the Time of Gompers* (1957); Melvin Dubofsky, *We Shall Be All: A History of the Industrial Workers of the World* (1969); W. Elliott Brownlee, *The Dynamics of Ascent* (1974), which traces the rise of business and the economy, as does Alfred D. Chandler, *Strategy and Structure* (1982), and *The Visible Hand: The Managerial Revolution in American Business* (1977). Paul S. Boyer, *Urban Masses and Moral Order in America, 1820–1920* (1978); George Chauncey, *Gay New York: Gender, Urban Culture, and the Making of the Gay Male World, 1890–1940* (1994); and John D'Emilio and Estelle Freedman, *Intimate Matters: A History of Sexuality in America* (1988), describe aspects of the sexual revolution.

Some excellent works on African Americans include Mary Frances Berry and John W. Blassingame, *Long Memory: The Black Experience in America* (1982); Herbert G. Gutman, *The Black Family in Struggle and Freedom, 1750–1925* (1976); August Meier, *Negro Thought in America: Racial Ideologies in the Age of Booker T. Washington, 1880–1915* (1963); Louis R. Harlan, *Booker T. Washington* (2 vols., 1972–1983); Manning Marable, *W.E.B. Du Bois* (1986); and David Levering Lewis, *W.E.B. Du Bois* (2 vols., 1994, 2000).

On women, see Aileen Kraditor, *The Ideas of the Woman Suffrage Movement, 1890–1920* (1965); William L. O'Neill, *Everyone Was Brave: The Rise and Fall of Feminism in America* (1969); Mari Jo Buhle, *Women and American Socialism, 1870–1920* (1981); Nancy Woloch, *Women and the American Experience* (1984); Carl Degler, *At Odds: Women and the Family from the Revolution to the Present* (1980); Nancy F. Cott, *The Grounding of Modern Feminism* (1987); and Eric Rauchway, *The Refuge of Affections: Family and American Reform Politics, 1900–1920* (2001).

Immigration history is covered in Oscar Handlin, *The Uprooted* (rev. ed. 1973); John Higham, *Strangers in the Land: Patterns of American Nativism, 1865–1925* (1955); John Bodnar, *The Transplanted: A History of Immigrants in Urban America* (1985); Thomas Archdeacon, *Becoming American* (1983); Alan M. Kraut, *The Huddled Masses: The Immigrant in American Society, 1880–1921* (1982); Victor Greene, *The Slavic Community on Strike: Immigrant Labor in Pennsylvania Anthracite* (1968); James S. Olson, *Catholic Immigrants in America* (1987); Irving Howe and Kenneth Libo, *World of Our Fathers: The Journey of East European Jews to America and the Life They Found and Made* (1976); and H. L. Kitano and Roger Daniels, *Asian Americans: Emerging Minorities* (2nd ed., 1988).

On intellectual and cultural history, consult Richard Hofstadter, *Anti-Intellectualism in American Life* (1962); Christopher Lasch, *The New Radicalism in America* (1965); Lawrence N. Levine, *Highbrow/Lowbrow: The Emergence of a Cultural Hierarchy in America* (1988); Daniel J. Singal, *Modernist Culture in America* (1991), extremely useful; Henry F. May, *The End of American Innocence: A Study of the First Years of Our Own Time, 1912–1917* (1959); and Christine Stansell, *American Moderns: Bohemian New York and the Creation of a New Century* (2000).

Diplomacy and War

The best overview of the era's foreign policy is Warren Zimmerman, *First Great Triumph: How Five Americans Made Their Country a World Power* (2002), which examines Theodore Roosevelt, Alfred Thayer Mahan, Henry Cabot Lodge, John Hay, and Elihu Root. Also see Walter LaFeber, *The American Search for Opportunity, 1865–1913* (1993); Akira Iriye, *The Globalizing of America, 1913–1945* (1993); George F. Kennan, *American Diplomacy, 1900–1950* (1951); and Robert E. Osgood, *Ideals and Self-Interest in America's Foreign Relations* (1953). On prewar diplomacy and World War I, begin with John Cooper, ed., *The Causes and Consequences of World War I* (1971). On Wilson's foreign policy see Arthur S. Link, *Woodrow Wilson: Revolution, War, and Peace* (1979); and Link, ed., *Woodrow*

Wilson and a Revolutionary World, 1913–1921 (1982); N. Gordon Levin Jr., *Woodrow Wilson and World Politics: America's Response to War and Revolution* (1967); Patrick Devlin, *Too Proud to Fight: Woodrow Wilson's Neutrality* (1975); Gnonel Kolko, *Century of War: Politics, Conflict and Society Since 1914* (1994); Lloyd C. Gardner, *Safe for Democracy: The Anglo-American Response to Revolution, 1913–1923* (1984); Robert H. Ferrell, *Woodrow Wilson and World War I, 1917–1921* (1985); Thomas J. Knock, *To End All Wars: Woodrow Wilson and the Quest for a New World Order* (1992); and David Steigerwald, *Wilsonian Idealism in America* (1994).

On the military history of the war, Edward M. Coffman, *The War to End All Wars: The American Military Experience in World War* (1968), is the best work, but see also John S. D. Eisenhower, *Yanks* (2001); and Jennifer D. Keene, *Doughboys, the Great War, and the Remaking of America* (2001). For other topics, consult William J. Breen, *Uncle Sam at Home Civilian Mobilization, Wartime Federalism and the Committee for National Defense* (1984), and Stephen L. Vaughn, *Holding Fast the Inner Lines: Democracy, Nationalism, and the Committee on Public Information* (1980). On the peace negotiations, the best work is Margaret MacMillan, *Paris 1919* (2002). Also see Arthur Walworth, *Woodrow Wilson and His Peacemakers* (1983). On Wilson's efforts for the League of Nations, see John Cooper, *Breaking the Heart of the World: Woodrow Wilson and the Fight for the League of Nations* (2001); and Lloyd G. Ambrosius, *Woodrow Wilson and the American Diplomatic Tradition: The Treaty Fight in Perspective* (1988).

For the effects of the war on the United States, see John Cooper, *The Vanity of Power: American Isolationism and the First World War* (1969); David Kennedy, *Over Here: The First World War and American Society* (1980); Maureen W. Greenwald, *Women, War, and Work: The Impact of World War I on Women Workers in the United States* (1980); Robert K. Murray, *Red Scare: A Study in American Hysteria*; Norman H. Clark, *Deliver Us from Evil: An Interpretation of American Prohibition* (1976); Paul Murphy, *World War I and the Origins of Civil Liberties in the United States* (1979); Gina Kolata, *Flu: The Story of the Great Influenza Pandemic of 1918 and the Search for the Virus That Caused It* (1999); John M. Barry, *The Great Influenza: The Epic Story of the Deadliest Plague in History* (2005); Stuart D. Rochester, *American Liberal Disillusionment in the Wake of World War I* (1977); and David Burner, *The Politics of Provincialism: The Democratic Party in Transition* (1986).

An Era of
Trial and Triumph,
1920–1945

Prologue

A DECADE of prosperity, political conservatism, and cultural bohemianism, the 1920s were followed by a mirror image, a decade of depression, political change, and cultural retrenchment, and then by World War II, the greatest transforming event of the century. The Era of Trial and Triumph ushered in more change than many periods twice or three times as long. Mature Americans in 1900, who might have been comfortable in 1921, would have found themselves in a different world by 1945. The generation that came of age during this era, literary historian Malcolm Cowley wrote, "belonged to a period of transition from values already fixed to values that had to be created. Its members were seceding from the old and yet could adhere to nothing new; they groped their way toward another scheme of life, as yet undefined; in the midst of their doubts and uneasy gestures of defiance they felt homesick for the certainties of their childhood."

Hopes and dreams were realized, crushed, reborn. It seemed that the nation repeatedly was poised on a precipice above a canyon of despair, made a leap of faith, and landed on the other side. No roller-coaster ride could have been more dizzying. Still, one takes only a small risk in riding a roller-coaster. People who bet on the stock market, moved from Mississippi to Massachusetts, or landed at Normandy took risks that defined, or ended, their lives. Anyone who lived through the era should have emerged exhausted. Instead, most people were grateful, subdued, and optimistic. These years constituted neither a steady march toward greater democracy nor a story of inexorable oppression. "Never did bitterer disappointment follow high hopes," historian James Harvey Robinson wrote. Whatever the chagrin, though, the age was ultimately one of affirmation; far more people subscribed to capitalism and democracy than rejected them. Answering grave challenges to these systems when many considered their country in decline, Americans made their nation wiser and richer.

Throughout the era, change, whether cultural or political, was met with resistance and consequently occurred in spurts, with lapses and regressions. A society in dynamic tension between change and resistance characterized the period (such tension is present to some degree in all periods but its impact in this era is unrivaled). The former happened despite the latter, although the resistance partly shaped the nature and pace of change. Not all of the change was positive; to win both an economic war and a military war, the United States had to pay dearly in dollars and lives, and the victories were not guaranteed to last. Perhaps more environmental pollution occurred during the war than over the next thirty years, yet this facet of the war is rarely mentioned. Moreover, the end of World War II unveiled new perils, making the planet more dangerous than at the opening of the era in 1921.

The most important change was an explosive increase in knowledge, precipitating modernization, the adaptation of institutions to knowledge. Previously such increases had occurred incrementally over hundreds, even thousands, of years. Yet World War II, requiring reorganization of politics, centralization of government, and rationalization of industry and transportation, accelerated the pace of modernization. The greatest pushes were the rapid advance of scientific knowledge and the speed with which scientific discoveries made an impact upon jobs, lifestyles, and beliefs. Race and gender issues gathered momentum, accompanied by rising expectations. The federal government grew enormously, first during the depression, then during the war. After Republican political domination during the 1920s, the Democrats seized control with the election of Franklin D. Roosevelt, who became one of the most powerful presidents in history.

As knowledge grew, the basis of belief in traditional verities was shaken. Changing more swiftly than religion or politics, science introduced ideas and standards by which to judge old verities; truth became relative or contextual, not eternal or absolute. Institutions were judged by utility, not by abstract criteria. Those who sided with only custom or science were apt to be ostracized or ridiculed by the other side. Those who tried to adhere to both were pulled in different directions: they could no longer believe things they wanted to believe, and they began to believe some things that shattered their serenity. It was widely debated whether science was a tyrant or a liberator, whether the future was radiant with promise or dark with foreboding.

Modernization was related to, but differed from, a movement in the arts known as modernism. Modernism arose partly in reaction to modernization. Modernists applauded scientific knowledge but criticized the dehumanizing aspects of the machine civilization and government bureaucracy. Modernists argued that the prevailing Victorian culture and the conventional in the fine and literary arts stifled self-expression by suppressing the emotional side of human nature. With modernism, the aim was integration of the emotional and the rational. In the short run it rejuvenated the emotional aspects of humankind, expressed through abstract art, Freudian psychiatry, rejection of materialism, and sexual experimentation. To traditionalists, modernism was a fad; to modernists, traditionalists were archaic. Their struggle, waged in literary journals, art galleries, and intellectual discussions, raged over the period, the modernists appealing to the avant garde, the traditionalists to the masses.

Sexuality, which aggravated generational and religious conflicts, opened one rift between traditionalists and modernists. Habits such as smoking and drinking were linked to sexuality. Conservatives deplored women who were openly sexual, used cosmetics, bobbed their hair, and shortened their skirts. Birth control, more technologically feasible than before, led to moral and social dilemmas. Yet the age was not so libertine as the movies and magazines might have us believe. There were clear boundaries, and the predominant practice among singles was sexuality without intercourse, except among engaged couples.

Cultural sterility and materialism were attacked before the Great Depression by writers who insisted that a prosperous society meant neither cultural sophistication nor economic equality. H. L. Mencken satirized materialism, and Sinclair Lewis depicted the hypocrisy and banality of small town life. Ironically, the people they ridiculed bought and read their books.

In no sphere were hypocrisy, inequality, and neglect more poignant than in race relations. The prosperity of the 1920s largely eluded minorities, particularly African Americans, most of whom lived in the rural South, mired in poverty and lacking in educational opportunities. They would later make economic progress during the era, but not political progress, and despite their accomplishments, many failed to share the nation's bounty. So did the millions of other Americans who lived in poverty and crowded into city tenements or farm shacks without running water or electricity. Millions more, many of them children, toiled in unhealthy factories for subsistence wages; women were underpaid and confined to gender-segregated jobs; and ethnic and religious groups felt the sting of discrimination.

In foreign relations, there were tensions between crusades for peace and the stark reality of a violent world. The public was nationalistic and cautious throughout much of the period. Isolationists and internationalists clashed in the late 1930s until a world in turmoil overwhelmed them all.

Nevertheless, during the 1920s social stresses and weaknesses were an undercurrent, not the mainstream. Republican Presidents Warren Harding and Calvin Coolidge presided over an economy of abundance with limited intervention. Business was ascendant. Literature and art flourished. Henry Ford put the nation on wheels. New forms of entertainment, including radio and the movies, helped change the morals of a newly urban nation. Puritanism was in retreat. Bootleg liquor was abundant.

Then a way of life crashed with the stock market in 1929, and easy money vanished. After living in a fool's paradise, the United States, led by the once-vaunted progressive Republican Herbert Hoover, grimly tried to cope with privation. Hoover, a transitional figure, was more inventive than previous chief executives. He struggled valiantly and rationally to combat conditions largely beyond his control, failing because he lacked precedents to learn from. There had never been such a severe, long-lasting depression in our history. Hoover's successor, Franklin Roosevelt, would be bolder, yet he would not end the Depression either. World War II would.

Roosevelt evinced initial reluctance to change, but reacted to circumstances, aided by overwhelming Democratic majorities in Congress. Winning four elections, he fundamentally altered the presidency, the government, politics, and the economy. Under his New Deal, a domestic revolution, government provided the spark that restarted the economic engine and restored hope, if not prosperity. Labor realized significant gains, and the government acted as an employer of last resort. With the United States' entrance into World War II, the government focused on winning the war and the New Deal retreated into the background. Roosevelt proved a great war leader as well as an innovative domestic president. Although the war ended the Depression, the New Deal brought long-overdue reforms, swelling the size and power of the government, which grew further during the war. The conflict ended in a flash over Hiroshima that brought a new weapon of unlimited destruction into the arsenal of warfare. Eventually human beings would rush to build bombs that could destroy one another many times over. One could hardly imagine an era more tense than the Era of Trial and Triumph. Yet in the decades that followed, the Era of Uncertainty, an arms race and domestic divisions would make stress unrelenting. We had leaped out of the fire of war and into the cauldron of a potential atomic apocalypse that made life more uncertain than ever.

Time Line

An Era of Trial and Triumph, 1920–1945

August 26, 1920 Nineteenth Amendment, women's suffrage, ratified.

November 2, 1920 Warren G. Harding elected president.

November 2, 1920 KDKA, Pittsburgh, first radio station, broadcast presidential returns.

April 7, 1922 Lease granted for Teapot Dome oil field.

August 2, 1923 President Warren G. Harding dies; Vice President Calvin Coolidge succeeds him.

July 10, 1925 Scopes "Monkey trial" opens in Tennessee; concerns teaching of evolution.

May 20 and 21, 1927 Charles A. Lindbergh becomes first person to make solo, non-stop flight across Atlantic.

October 6, 1927 "The Jazz Singer," first "talkie" motion picture, is released.

October 29, 1929 Stock market crashes.

November 8, 1932 Franklin D. Roosevelt elected president.

January 23, 1933 Twentieth Amendment which moves presidential inauguration to January 20 from March 4 ratified.

December 5, 1933 Twenty-First Amendment repealing Prohibition ratified.

July 5, 1935 National Labor Relations Act passed.

August 14, 1935 Social Security Act passed.

December 7, 1941 Japan bombs Pearl Harbor.

June 6, 1944 Allies launch D-Day invasion of France.

April 12, 1945 Roosevelt dies and Vice President Harry S Truman succeeds him.

May 7, 1945 Germany surrenders.

August 6 and 9, 1945 United States drops atomic bombs on Hiroshima and Nagasaki, Japan.

September 2, 1945 Japan surrenders.

October 25–26, 1945 United Nations established.

CHAPTER SEVEN

The 1920s: Decade of Fear, Decade of Excess

A PERIOD OF hedonism and materialism, the 1920s elicited from songwriter Hoagy Carmichael the observation that "The postwar world came in with a bang of bad booze, flappers with bare legs, jangled morals and wild weekends." The time was dubbed the Jazz Age, although the Elastic Age might have been more appropriate, for in the tug-of-war between permissiveness and restraint, the country's institutions and patience were stretched nearly to the breaking point. Some people clung to the past and lashed out against new people and new ideas, a loss of tolerance felt in many nations after the Great War. Both the forces of the change and the forces of reaction were strong in this decade, with the paradox of progress amidst intolerance reflected in the era's trials and triumphs.

Intolerance and Discrimination

Of the forces of reaction, the strongest was the Ku Klux Klan. The Klan practiced intimidation and violence against minorities; allied with fundamentalist Protestant churches, it was a potent reactionary influence. The Klan of this decade represented a powerful social current. The growth of its membership, from five thousand in 1920 to five million in 1924, and its virtual demise just a few years later, epitomize the ascendancy and defeat of ultraconservatism.

Created to promote white supremacy in the Reconstruction South, the original Klan became discredited because of its violence against former slaves and faded by the mid-1870s. In 1915 a former minister, William J. Simmons, revived the organization, inspired by the popularity of fraternal groups, not only white supremacy. He devised an elaborate ritual and costume based partly on those of the Reconstruction Klan. He added the

CROSSES BURNING IN THE NIGHT
Ku Klux Klan spreads terror in Swainsboro, Georgia.
(Library of Congress)

burning cross, an emblem the first Klan had not used, borrowed from the
movie *Birth of a Nation*. Under Simmons the Klan was a small organization until 1920, when he hired public relations experts Edward Y. Clarke
and Elizabeth Tyler to increase membership. Hiram Evans replaced
Simmons as Klan "Imperial Wizard" in 1922, but the changes set in
motion through Clarke and Tyler persisted. Their techniques included
advertising, the use of recruiters who received commissions for selling
memberships, and an appeal based on self-righteous morality. Clarke and
Tyler created possibilities for growth outside the South by expanding Klan
enemies to include Catholics, Jews, Bolsheviks, and foreigners. Animosity
toward these groups soon eclipsed hostility toward African Americans. At its
peak, the Klan had more members in New Jersey than in Alabama, more
in Oregon than in Louisiana, and more than 40 percent of the membership was in the midwestern states of Illinois, Indiana, and Ohio.

Paradoxically, the Klan had a positive program as well as a negative mission: Klansmen were expected to attend a Protestant church, abstain from
alcohol, support their families, and practice patriotism. When Klansmen

felt their values threatened, they became bigoted, reckless, and criminal, particularly when opposing Catholics. The typical Catholic was loyal to the pope rather than the United States, the Klan argued. As church-required celibacy of priests and nuns was unnatural, said the Klan, they must be engaging in illicit sex; if children resulted from these liaisons, they must have been aborted or buried alive. Catholic schools should be abolished because they trained children to undermine American democracy and prepare the country for a takeover by the pope, who would invade by tunneling under the Atlantic Ocean. Jews, too, were seen as a danger. The Jew personified vices Klansmen identified with modernity, among them chain stores, large banks, motion pictures, and sensuous music. Jews supposedly refused to assimilate, planned wars to slaughter gentiles, lured young girls into prostitution, and spearheaded communism and racial equality for black people.

Women joined Klan auxiliaries, the Kamelias, the Queens of the Golden Mask, and the Women of the Ku Klux Klan, the last becoming the largest, with about five hundred thousand members. Some women considered the Klan a protector from abusive husbands. Klansmen tried to shield the virtue of Nordic women by driving prostitutes out of town, searching country roads for teen couples in parked cars, and thwarting interracial marriages.

The Klan's fall was partly a product of its gratuitous violence, a divisive battle over the leadership of the organization, and the moral lapses of its Indiana "Grand Dragon," David C. Stephenson. Stephenson kidnapped a young woman and raped her; an overdose of sleeping pills took her life. When he was sent to prison, he exposed the illegal deeds of his political cronies. The Klan evaporated in his state, losing 335,000 members within a year, but part of the Klan's demise was due to its successes. Accomplishing its objectives of restricting immigration and muffling radicalism in a time of political conservatism, the organization was shorn of its purpose. The Klan worked to defeat the presidential candidacy of Catholic Al Smith in 1928, then lingered until 1944, when it became bankrupt.

Minorities continued their struggle for respect and fairness. The administration of Warren G. Harding proved less biased against African Americans than had the administration of Woodrow Wilson, and Harding appointed some black people to minor positions in the federal bureaucracy and diplomatic corps. In October 1921 he became the first chief executive since the Civil War to deliver a speech in a southern city, Birmingham, Alabama, urging amicable race relations. Belying his words, though, he would not denounce the Klan and was woefully ignorant about black culture and achievements; he had never heard of Booker T. Washington, for example.

Harding's successor, Calvin Coolidge, urged Congress to make lynching a federal crime, yet he was not much interested in race relations. Democratic nominating primaries barred blacks from voting in a region where Republicans were too weak to meaningfully contest elections. The labor movement also resisted black participation, but A. Philip Randolph persisted in seeking a voice for his constituents. The only African American leader of his generation to fuse the economic uplift message of Washington and the civil rights emphasis of W.E.B. Du Bois, he became head of the first major black union, the Brotherhood of Sleeping Car Porters. His unionization of the porters set a precedent for organizing black workers when many AFL unions discouraged them from joining. After Randolph won a decade-long fight for AFL recognition, he became a major force for African Americans in the labor movement.

Like African Americans, Hispanics knew poverty and discrimination. The promise of prosperity brought millions of Hispanics, mostly Mexicans, to the United States, many of them migrant workers on Western farms and ranches. About 728,203 Mexicans crossed the border between 1901 and 1930, and demand for Mexican labor rose as European immigration ebbed. Hispanic workers were unorganized, and their living conditions were primitive—shacks without running water or an indoor toilet. Wages were meager. Entire families had to work in the fields, meaning that children seldom received an education. Most Mexicans settled in California and Texas, and some started businesses that lifted them from poverty. The flow reversed during the 1930s. Mexicans returned to their native land because the Great Depression ended the Western labor shortage. Some were forcibly repatriated under Hoover administration policy. Native Americans were made citizens by virtue of federal policy, but continued to endure the most hardships of any minority.

Protests of injustice were at the heart of the Sacco-Vanzetti case. Two Italian anarchists, Nicola Sacco and Bartolomeo Vanzetti, were tried and sentenced to death for robbing a shoe company payroll and murdering a paymaster and his guard in 1920 in South Braintree, Massachusetts. They were armed when arrested, and ballistics tests suggested the gun found on Sacco had been taken from the guard and used to slay him; it also had a nick in the handle, matching a witness's description of the guard's firearm. Several witnesses identified Sacco and Vanzetti as the culprits. Such eminent intellectuals as H. L. Mencken and John Dewey argued that the two were found guilty because of their atheistic and anticapitalist views. Communists seized on the case as proof that capitalism was immoral. However, thorough reviews of the court record failed to reveal any procedural errors, the only basis for appeal.

Several men convicted of other crimes confessed to the robbery and murders, yet their versions of the crime did not equate with the known facts, and appeals were denied. After the Massachusetts Supreme Court affirmed the conviction and the U.S. Supreme Court decided it had no jurisdiction, Governor Alvan T. Fuller appointed a commission to review the case. The commission concluded that the two were guilty, and they were executed on August 22, 1927, martyrs to radicals. Novels, a play, and poems were written to denounce the legal system. Belief in the innocence of Sacco and Vanzetti became a dogma vindicated sixty years afterward when Governor Michael Dukakis expunged their guilt from the record.

Ballistics tests conducted in 1961, employing more precise scientific instruments than were available in the 1920s, indicated that the gun found on Sacco was the murder weapon. The significance of the case, though, does not lie in the guilt or innocence of Sacco and Vanzetti. Its importance is twofold: it was exploited to become a trial of America, of traditional values and unconventional ideas; and despite the duo's probable guilt, the controversy demonstrated the persistence of the paradox that in the land of equality, some were more equal than others.

Prosperity and Poverty

The 1920s are known as prosperous, but two sectors of the economy, labor and agriculture, floundered. Government and the media favored industry; bankers and business titans were the idols of the time. The stock market was portrayed as the way to make a fortune in a hurry. Workers and farmers were hurt by decline in demand for the products they supplied; wartime demand for labor and food was temporary, and export markets contracted. Technology, paradoxically, was both boon and bane. It increased productivity and wages, but it stole jobs, and wages failed to keep pace with profits. Greater productivity was especially ruinous for farmers, who overproduced. In retrospect, the decade was less stable than it appeared. Beneath the glitter of Wall Street was an undercurrent of anguish by those who were excluded from the carnival of wealth.

One of the most heated fights of the decade pitted unions in an unequal contest against employers for a greater share of profits and control of the workplace. During the 1920s the proportion of nonagricultural workers holding union cards plunged from 19.4 percent to 10.2 percent. AFL membership reached a high of 4.079 million in 1920, only to fall to 2.926 million in only three years. Organized labor was concentrated in a handful of industries—coal, construction, railroads, garment, manufacturing, longshoremen—and had no presence among clerical workers, unskilled and semiskilled

LONG HOURS, DANGEROUS CONDITIONS
A child laborer in a South Carolina textile mill photographed by Lewis Hine, 1908.
(National Archives)

factory workers, white-collar workers, and domestic servants. Several factors were responsible for the limited reach of unions. Productivity was high because of new technology; yearly wages increased 10.8 percent between 1923 and 1928. Credit buying raised the purchasing power of workers higher than their incomes; more married women workers enhanced family incomes; and the variety of inexpensive items for sale left laborers relatively content. The migration of African Americans northward between 1915 and 1928 provided cheap competition to white union workers. Labor leaders, such as William Green, Gompers's successor as AFL president in 1924 were less aggressive than Gompers. Green's reticence earned him a reputation as the "Calvin Coolidge of the labor movement."

The Republicans in the White House in the 1920s were no friends of labor, although Harding, encouraged by Hoover, helped negotiate a voluntary eight-hour day to replace the twelve-hour day in the steel industry and tried to stay neutral in labor disputes. His attorney general, Harry Daugherty, had no qualms about breaking strikes, however. When railroad workers struck in 1922 after two wage cuts, he obtained the most sweeping injunction in labor history to crush the strike. Unrest among railroad laborers led to the creation in 1926 of a presidentially appointed mediation board that sought to persuade parties to submit to arbitration. (Not until the Railway Labor Act of 1934 and the elimination of company unions during the New Deal did genuine progress occur in negotiating railroad labor peace.) John L. Lewis's United Mine Workers (UMW), likewise made little headway. Its national strike over wage reductions in 1922 became violent, resurrecting the Red Scare; public opinion turned against the strikers, who settled for preserving wage levels. UMW membership, largest in the nation among unions in 1920, declined steadily because of overproduction and the availability of cheap, nonunion southern miners.

Industrialists sought to forestall worker radicalism by allowing profit sharing, retirement plans, health insurance, and labor-management committees, all under the aegis of company unions, which helped make workplaces safer but lacked bargaining power. Commerce Secretary Herbert Hoover spearheaded the effort to make labor and capital partners, a philosophy that appealed to capitalist chieftains because they held the upper hand. Another supporter, the Supreme Court, favored business and voided more prolabor laws than it had in decades. The justices limited picketing outside factories, ruled boycotts illegal under most conditions, and nullified laws prohibiting injunctions against unions and setting minimum wages for women. It interpreted the Clayton Antitrust Act in a way that allowed labor few rights. Further, the tribunal and other federal courts upheld employers' use of "yellow-dog" contracts requiring that workers agree not to join a union.

Violent strikes ignited in 1929, precursors of the labor unrest of the 1930s. These were concentrated in the largely unorganized southern textile industry, which faced excess capacity and competition from synthetic fabrics. The mills paid workers, many of them women and children, lower wages and required longer hours than any factories. Strikes left demonstrators and police dead and caused extensive property damage. A strike in Gastonia, North Carolina, won notoriety because of the role of communists in trying to organize the mills and because seven strikers convicted of killing a police officer jumped bail and escaped to the Soviet Union.

Business was poised to dominate the decade because the world war that had ravaged Europe left the United States untouched—except to stimulate industry, consolidate banking, and hasten scientific discoveries. American industry became the most efficient on the planet, owing to mass production, technical wizardry, higher productivity per worker, and use of the movable assembly line that Henry Ford adapted to the automobile industry. New products appeared—the automobile, radios, rayon, cosmetics, telephones, and electric appliances—many sold in chain stores such as

Sears, Roebuck and Company, and J. C. Penney, and through catalogues. Mass advertising, making up 80 percent of all mail and 60 percent of newspaper space, stimulated demand for the goods and services and fed the economic boom. Ads beckoned buyers with themes of sex, eternal youth, and envy. One told of a man whose "faulty elimination" blocked him from climbing the ladder of executive success until he began eating Post Bran Flakes. Charles Atlas advocated "dynamic tension," or isometric exercise, which transformed him from a "ninety-eight-pound weakling" into "the world's most perfectly developed man."

Incomes rose consistently, even though richer Americans reaped the most and many did not share in the plenty. Because wage increases lagged behind business profits, eventually purchasing power would be limited and business would decline. Even during the boom, the coal, textile, shipbuilding, shoes, leather, and farm sectors languished. Understandably, none of this troubled middle-class Americans while they prospered and admired the wealthy. Business leaders were believed to have judgment superior to that of artists or intellectuals and experience that was valuable in government. Hoover, who had made unprofitable mines lucrative, had the chance to reorganize on a larger scale once he became secretary of commerce, prompting a contemporary to say, "He is engineering our material civilization as a whole." The pursuit of fortune was deemed character-building. One's worth was determined by one's wealth.

The acquisitive ethos was derived not from Mammon, the god of lucre, but from the Christian God who ordained the capitalist system and bestowed favor upon businessmen in the form of riches. Metaphors linking riches with holiness proliferated. A wildcatter who struck oil nearly every time he drilled linked his results to tithing. "I couldn't miss because I was in partnership with the Big Fellow and He made geology," he observed. Salesmen could follow the example of Moses, portrayed in an insurance company tract as the first successful realtor. Jesus "spent more time in marketplaces than in synagogues," one writer pointed out. The Last Supper was interpreted as the first Rotary Club luncheon, and a minister called Christ "the first president of Lions International. I quote you from the Bible: He was "Lion of the tribe of Judah." God's son, in fact, was the greatest businessman of all time, according to Bruce Barton, an advertising executive and politician whose biography of Jesus, *The Man Nobody Knows* (1924), was the number one best seller two successive years. The "proof" that he was a businessman was his reply to the doctors in the temple, "Wist ye not that I must be about my father's business?"

Business captains could take credit for substantial accomplishments, yet in their zeal, irresponsible elements among them grew greedy, sought too much, and, in the ultimate irony, wrecked themselves with rampant stock speculation. A force for modernization at the start of the decade, business hardened into defense of the status quo at the end of the 1920s, a paradoxical switch from progress to reaction.

Lindbergh and Ford: Heroes in the Air, on the Road

Although businessmen were heroes in the 1920s, no hero soared as high or as far as Charles A. Lindbergh, the first person to make a solo flight across the Atlantic Ocean. His flight from New York to Paris in May 1927 set off a celebration greater than the one that greeted the armistice ending World War I. Americans hungered for heroes and were anxious to replenish their idealism in the wake of the Great War and failed peace. Conqueror of one of the last frontiers, Lindbergh filled these needs, his flight commanding more newspaper space than any event in the decade.

A stunt flier and airmail pilot, Lindbergh was intrigued when Frenchman Raymond Orteig offered $25,000 to anyone who would fly nonstop from New York to Paris. With financing from businessmen in his base of St. Louis, Lindbergh designed and built a single-engine monoplane, *The Spirit of St. Louis*, with abundant fuel reserves. Because each pound he saved meant an extra quart of gasoline, he eliminated all excess weight, flying without a navigator or radio operator, eschewing a radio, carrying no parachute, and even tearing extra pages from his notebook. Unable to sleep the night before, Lindbergh faced more than thirty hours in the air with no sleep, confronting hazardous weather. But on the morning of May 20 he took off in the rain, barely clearing the runway in his gasoline-laden plane. Lindbergh remained on course despite crude navigation devices. Then he was over Ireland, over England, over the French coast. Thirty three hours and twenty-nine minutes after takeoff, Lindbergh landed in Paris, where one hundred thousand people welcomed him. The journey for the man who had "flown like a poem into the heart of America," as the *New York Post* stated, was just beginning.

Lindbergh met the kings of Belgium and England. President Coolidge sent a cruiser to bring him to Washington, where the elite of the political and social worlds waited. Lawmakers pinned medal after medal on him. He was offered millions to star in movies and endorse products, yet modestly refused. Lindbergh did write a book, *We*, about himself and his plane, for which he received $200,000. Initially enjoying the publicity, he soon resented his loss of privacy and the public's expectations intimidated him. When one is on top of the world at twenty-five, there is no where to go but down.

In 1929 Lindbergh married Anne Morrow, who became his copilot and navigator and wrote books about their flights to Latin America, Africa, and China. In 1930 she gave birth to a son, Charles, at their country estate in New Jersey. Nineteen months later the infant was kidnapped from his bedroom and murdered despite a ransom. Evidence incriminated a German American, Bruno Richard Hauptmann, who was tried, convicted, and executed for the crime, although there were doubts about his guilt. Before the execution the Lindberghs fled to England to escape the press and to build a home for their growing family. America did not forget them, however, and Charles Lindbergh returned in 1939, urging Americans to avoid war with Germany, a war he said the United States could not win because of the might of the Luftwaffe.

Yet another hero of the 1920s was Ford, whose autos freed Americans from barriers of time and geography. Cars had been on the scene since early in the century, although it was not until this decade that Americans started their love-hate relationship with the automobile. Auto registration jumped from eight thousand in 1900 to 8 million in 1920 and close to 23 million in 1930. By 1925, there were 20 percent more cars than telephones, and 60 percent of farm families had a car, whereas just 12 percent had running water. A farm wife explained her family's decision to own a car but not a bathtub, saying, "You can't go to town in a bathtub." But technology that offers to liberate individuals from restraints also inspires the state to regulate. Thus, the noisy contraptions that clanked along dusty roads and frightened horses prompted requests to lawmakers to curb their use. Tennessee adopted a law requiring a motorist to advertise his plan to drive one week in advance. In Illinois, a proposed statute stated that when approaching a corner that allowed no view of the road ahead, "the automobilist must stop not less than one hundred yards from the turn, toot his horn, fire a revolver, halloo, and send up three bombs at intervals of five minutes."

Some uses of the automobile especially concerned ministers and parents. A juvenile court judge called the vehicle a "house of prostitution on wheels" because one-third of the girls appearing before him on sex charges had committed their offenses in cars. Technology once more battled tradition and facilitated sexuality. The automobile made dates chaperon-free and encouraged the advent of motels, which were "little more than camouflaged brothels," Federal Bureau of Investigation (FBI) Director J. Edgar Hoover said. Sociologists found that three-quarters of the patrons of Dallas tourist camps were local couples, not tourists, and that one cabin had been rented sixteen times in a single night.

Serious crime—bank robbery, bootlegging, kidnapping, insurance fraud, car theft, and drunken driving—also became easier because of the car. On the other hand, automobiles aided law enforcement by allowing police to cover more territory, particularly when dispatched by radio, and ambulances could speed the ill or injured to hospitals.

Both city and farm were transformed. Previously compact cities could sprawl, encouraging the growth of suburbs, branch offices of businesses, and shopping centers. School buses helped eliminate the one-room school in favor of consolidated schools. Wasteland became prime real estate when a major highway traversed it. Rural life was reinvigorated as automobiles eased isolation and loneliness, and gasoline-powered threshers, tractors, and reapers made arduous hand labor unnecessary. Millions began to vacation via automobile. Tourists traveled to once isolated destinations such as Florida and California. Already fluid, the pace of society quickened.

The automotive industry paid some of the highest wages in the United States and stimulated the economy. By 1928 it was the nation's largest industry, and by 1929 it employed one of every ten workers. It consumed 85 percent of the rubber imported, 19 percent of the iron and steel manufactured, 67 percent of the plate glass, 27 percent of the lead—and practically all the gasoline. Ford, the high priest of the industry, was the first to conceive of his car as a product for the masses rather than the elite and, by the early 1920s, had captured 60 percent of the market. He made just one model in one color, black, but it was dependable and cheap, because Ford cut the price yearly to outsell competitors: in 1924 the Model T sold for a mere $290, down from $450 ten years before. Forward-looking in technology but backward-looking in politics, Ford was voted the third-greatest figure in world history in a poll of college students (Jesus was first and Napoleon second). Nevertheless, he fell behind the times, so much that by 1927 General Motors Chevrolet was outselling the Model T. Ford's answer was to halt production while he designed the Model A, in part to satisfy women's demands that cars be stylish and comfortable. When it appeared on December 2, 1927, he overtook General Motors and regained his luster. Ford even received a fan letter from bank robber Clyde Barrow, who was proud to write that he drove Fords exclusively whenever he could get away with one.

New Manners and Morals

Victorian morality, a code stressing restraint, silence about sex, prim and proper women, and starkly delineated gender roles, yielded to a morality that was less disciplined and more tolerant, an environment that considered love erotic and sex enjoyable. Young people were in the forefront of this revolution, which emerged from the temporary couplings of World

War I, the exposure of troops and nurses to looser European lifestyles, and a live-for-the-moment mentality. Rebellion began among an elite, college students on urban campuses, and spread to rural areas and high schoolers, although it was less apparent on farms and in small villages. By the end of the decade, however, the rebels, their free spirits disseminated by the mass media, had won the cultural battle. The sexual revolution that surfaced most prominently in the 1920s (and again in the 1960s) was, arguably, the most significant revolution of the twentieth century.

A woman who flaunted her sexuality, the flapper, personified the young insurgent. The word "flapper" came from the fad of college women wearing open galoshes that flapped when they walked. Ignoring petticoats, corsets, and girdles, the flapper wore short skirts and short-sleeved dresses, bobbed her hair, and applied cosmetics. She accentuated her sexuality by appearing provocative and naughty.

Sexual rebels had a supporter in Sigmund Freud, whose writings spread to the United States in popularized form after the war and were embraced by Americans. His emphasis on sex and his thesis that sexual repression was unhealthy and caused mental illness fascinated and titillated. From Freud, sexual experimentation attained the imprimatur of science, and people spoke more frankly about sex, except for homosexual relationships, for the mainstream rejected them.

Contributing to the new sexuality in a different way, Margaret Sanger crusaded for birth control. She devoted a magazine and several books to her cause, established the American Birth Control League, forerunner of the Planned Parenthood Federation of America, and started three hundred clinics. Fought by traditionalists, Sanger was incarcerated for "maintaining a public menace," but by 1930, allied with physicians, she was gaining support. Meanwhile, with condoms, spermicides, and diaphragms available, increasing numbers of couples practiced birth control.

The new practice of dating abetted the sexual revolution. In Victorian times, ladies invited men to their homes, where they would spend an evening in the parlor or on the front porch with chaperons. Dating shifted the initiative to men, who invited women to a restaurant or a movie or for a drive. It was assumed the man worked and the woman did not, hence he paid. Dates became acts of consumption in which a woman sold her company; the higher the price she commanded and the more dates she had, the more popular she was considered. There was an element of competition—of women getting invited on numerous dates and of men striving to be seen with attractive females. Couples were expected to neck and pet. In the slang of the time, necking involved caresses above the neck and petting involved caresses below the neck, including genital stimulation short of intercourse. Men expected to pet in exchange for spending money on a date.

Movies and magazines encouraged sexual libertines. Watching stars such as the voluptuous Greta Garbo taught women how to kiss and to hold a cigarette and a drink. Mass magazines were accused of inciting lust. *True Story* had three hundred thousand readers by 1923, four years after it started, and almost 2 million by 1926. It published articles titled "Indolent Kisses" and "What I Told My Daughter the Night before Her Marriage." Promiscuity, nonetheless, was not so widespread as the magazines might suggest. A survey in the early 1930s found that around one-fourth of the women and one-half of the men had sex before marrying, and that three-fourths of the women limited it to sex with their fiancés. Attitudes about sexuality changed more than practices. Virginity was no longer an ideal.

Grace Coolidge became the first president's wife to light a cigarette in the White House. From 1911 to 1928 yearly cigarette sales doubled, largely because of women. Advertisements showed pretty women asking men to blow smoke their way. The American Tobacco Company, aiming at women determined to win gender equality, labeled cigarettes "torches of freedom" and staged a march of women smokers at the 1928 New York Easter parade. Smoking became an emblem of sexuality, as was drinking, which women began doing more often in the company of men. Nice girls, who would not have sipped gin before, liked to get drunk. Hip flasks were evident at school dances and football games, and women carried dainty versions in their purses. "In order to be collegiate, one must drink," the University of Chicago handbook announced. Drinking was illegal under Prohibition, of course, yet this only made it a more powerful weapon in the arsenal of youthful rebellion.

Many watched the relaxing of standards with dismay. The rate of divorces to marriages climbed from about 1 in 10 to 1 in 6 during the 1920s. Women initiated two-thirds of the divorces. Divorce, attributed in part to promiscuity, lost some of its stigma, and people were unwilling to endure unhappy unions, even for the sake of children. Traditionalists tried to clamp down on sexuality with legislation. A Utah lawmaker wanted to imprison women caught wearing skirts higher than three inches above the ankle; Virginia thought of banning dresses that exposed more than three inches of a woman's throat; and Ohio considered a bill to outlaw "any garment which unduly displays or accentuates the lines of the female figure." Colleges banned women from smoking or confined it to off-campus areas, penalizing violators by withholding their degrees or expelling them. Universities imposed curfews or forbade students from owning cars and women from riding in them, rules designed to make sex logistically difficult.

Women, paradoxically, held a central place in the culture wars on both sides, as advocates of transformation and as disciples of tradition: they grew less passive in all aspects of life. They were liberated not only from sexual taboos but also from laborious housework because of advances in food preparation, electrical appliances, and smaller houses. They worked more outside the home. By the close of the decade, 10.6 million women did such work, up from 8.3 million ten years previously. Some 11 percent of white married women and 31 percent of African American married women were employed as domestics, clerical workers, and factory laborers. Some fields opened for women, yet most jobs remained segregated by gender. In the professions women fared poorly, losing ground numerically or proportionally among physicians, architects, chemists, lawyers, college students, and holders of doctorates.

Women's incentive for taking jobs was usually financial exigency instead of personal fulfillment. For single women, work was believed to be a stop-gap, something to do until they married and raised families. The main goal of the flapper, for all her rebelliousness, was to get a man, wed him, and raise children. Hard-pressed to meet the demands on their time, women were expected to keep themselves attractive if they were to hold on to their husbands and to bring up their youngsters properly, despite the confusing advice that child-rearing experts dispensed. Mothers were told that too much attention would hinder a child's development but that too little was also harmful. John B. Watson, the most famous child psychologist, counseled women to prepare to send children into the world as independent persons as soon as the age of two. "Never hug and kiss them, never let them sit in your lap," he wrote.

Religion: Beacon of Hope; Ally of Prejudice

After 1900 most immigrants to the United States were Catholics, and by the 1920s, 23 million lived in the country, making Catholicism the largest denomination in the nation. No other large religious group inspired such a wave of nativism and ethnocentricity. As with Protestants and Jews, disputes between traditionalists and modernists divided Catholics. Many American priests and bishops were more liberal on theological and social issues than their European counterparts. In the 1920s most American Catholics practiced birth control (although opposing it in theory), and there was an increase in divorce among them. Joining Catholics as a persecuted minority, Jews faced prejudice common among wealthy Americans such as Ford, who lent the prestige of his industrial empire to the publication of anti-Semitic articles in his newspaper, the *Dearborn Independent*.

Most Jewish immigrants were impoverished, but Jews prospered faster than any minority group and became prominent philanthropists, intellectuals, and civil libertarians.

Protestants, polarized between liberal and conservative factions, debated issues such as the literal truth of the Bible, tithing, prayer, and church attendance. The majority of churchgoers showed up only on Sundays, and churches devised gimmicks to fill pews. A midwestern minister held an "auto Sunday" at which he awarded a prize to the person who could squeeze the most people in a car and bring them to church. The next Sunday he promised a prize to the church member with the biggest feet (the minister himself won). One New York congregation, tying itself to the prestige of business, gave an engraved certificate of stock in the kingdom of God to anyone who donated $100 to the church building fund.

One of the most puzzling religious phenomena of the decade, as far as liberals were concerned, was the persistence of fundamentalism. "Heave an egg out of a Pullman and you will hit a fundamentalist almost everywhere in the United States," said Mencken, who, like other secular commentators,

RELIGION FOR THE MASSES
Aimee Semple McPherson, circa 1931.
(Used by permission of the Heritage Department of the
International Church of the Foursquare Gospel)

did not respect or understand fundamentalists. In fact, it was quite easy to learn where fundamentalists stood: belief in the literal truth of the Bible, in the virgin birth and deity of Jesus, in his literal resurrection and atonement for the world's sins, and in his second coming in bodily form. The leading fundamentalist of the period was Billy Sunday, one of the first evangelists to apply modern business and organizational techniques to his crusades. Renowned more for emotional enthusiasm than for theological sophistication—"I don't know any more about theology than a jack-rabbit knows about Ping Pong," he said, "but I'm on my way to glory"—he converted listeners by the hundreds.

The flamboyant Aimee Semple McPherson settled in Los Angeles, where she preached to huge crowds, held faith-healing sessions, and constructed a five-thousand-seat, $1.5 million temple. In May 1926 she vanished while swimming in the Pacific Ocean and was believed to have drowned, stunning the world thirty-two days later by emerging in a Mexican village and claiming she had been abducted. The "disappearance," one of the major news stories of the decade, was exposed as a hoax when neither the kidnappers nor the cabin where they allegedly held her was found. Actually, McPherson was having an affair with the married man who operated her radio station, and they fled Los Angeles together. Returning to her temple, she continued to draw larger crowds with dramatic sermons. McPherson created mission churches and planned to establish a "Salvation Navy." Although membership in her denomination, the Four-Square Gospel, increased, the Salvation Navy never sailed. Her personal life grew more unstable, and McPherson died in 1944 of a barbiturate overdose, possibly a suicide.

McPherson, Sunday, and their fellow believers were alarmed because they lived in a time of transition in which their views became minority ones. They became counterrevolutionaries, buffers against modernization. "This is not a battle, it is a war from which there is no discharge," said W. B. Riley, a leading fundamentalist minister. The clash culminated in a debate over whether Charles Darwin's theory of evolution should be taught in schools. Fundamentalists argued that the theory undercut belief in the biblical story of creation and, by implication, the credibility of the Bible. Modernists retorted that academic freedom protected teachers from censorship. Further, they considered the Bible an unreliable source for science. By 1925 Oklahoma and Tennessee passed laws banning the teaching of evolution in public schools, and almost half the states were considering such measures. Looking for courts to declare the laws unconstitutional, the American Civil Liberties Union offered to finance the defense of any teacher who would violate an antievolution statute. High school teacher John T. Scopes volunteered after business leaders in his farm community of Dayton, Tennessee, asked him to raise the issue so the town could attract tourists.

More than one hundred newspapers sent reporters, including Mencken, to cover the trial, the first broadcast on radio. Revivalists flocked to Dayton to preach on street corners, bookstores marketed volumes on theology, and hot dog vendors set up stands. Obviously it was naive to presume that the issue of biblical vs. scientific truth would be resolved in a brief trial in a small Tennessee town before a county judge; the real battle was for public opinion. To compete for that opinion, the prosecution welcomed William Jennings Bryan, the famous orator, secretary of state, and three-time presidential nominee. The defense boasted Clarence Darrow, one of the most brilliant trial lawyers in America. With each unwilling to concede that the other might be acting on good faith or had a right to his beliefs, their debate was irreconcilable.

Frustrated when Judge John T. Raulston would not allow scientific experts to testify for the defense in the presence of jurors, Darrow asked to put Bryan on the stand as a biblical authority. Accepting, Bryan testified that the world was created in 4004 B.C., that Eve was literally created from Adam's rib, that the world's languages originated at the Tower of Babel— responses that offended modernists, who believed the Bible should be interpreted metaphorically. For the judge and jury, however, the case did not concern the validity of the Bible, only whether Scopes flouted the law. He was convicted, and Raulston fined him $100. Inadvertently, Raulston violated the law, which specified that juries, not judges, should set the fine, an error that the Tennessee Supreme Court cited a year later to nullify the sentence and avoid the issue of the statute's constitutionality. There the case ended, for the ruling meant that opponents of the law could not appeal it to federal courts.

Mencken and other journalists decided that fundamentalism had been exposed as a fraud because of Bryan's testimony. Bryan, who did not regret his role in Dayton, died in his sleep five days after the trial ended, his reputation in decline. Some believed that Darrow's renown, too, was wounded, as the attorney had showed a mean-spirited, vindictive streak. In fact, neither made many converts, and for all the ridicule heaped on it, fundamentalism never disappeared. By the end of the century, it remained a vital force in the United States, its churches adding members more rapidly than mainstream Protestant denominations. The Tennessee law remained in force until 1967, yet was not enforced to avoid another test.

Prohibition in Triumph and Trial

Prohibition has become one of the best-remembered symbols of the 1920s. The authors of the Eighteenth Amendment did not expect to stop all drinking, but they hoped people would respect the Constitution. Aiming to punish only makers and sellers of booze, not ordinary people, they did not criminalize possession. Initially their ideas appeared plausible, for consumption declined, yet by the late 1920s the sale of alcohol had become a profitable paradox, and enforcement became impractical. There were simply too many ways that someone determined to drink could get an alcoholic beverage. Alcohol could be smuggled across 18,700 miles of borders and coastline, overwhelming security. Underpaid enforcement officials accepted bribes, and local judges and juries set bootleggers free with small fines.

If one could not afford costly smuggled liquor, alcohol could be obtained with a doctor's prescription or it could be made. All the equipment needed to construct a still was sold in hardware stores, and the U.S. Agriculture Department helpfully published a pamphlet on how to manufacture home brew. Near-beer with little or no alcohol was available, and many people bought wort, a mixture that could be converted to beer by adding yeast. Also, speakeasies served drinks almost openly in big cities. A Treasury agent found one just thirty-five seconds after arriving in New Orleans. Bootleggers sold dangerous concoctions such as Jamaica Jake, 90 percent alcohol, that paralyzed people, and Jackass Brandy, which caused internal bleeding. Alcoholics resorted to antifreeze, wood alcohol, hair tonic, and patent medicines containing alcohol. Midwestern farmhands drank fluids from the bottoms of silos, where silage had rotted and fermented. Moonshiners were so busy making money they rarely stopped to wash their tubs and vats, where agents discovered cats, mice, rats, and cockroaches that were attracted by the odor, fell in, and drowned.

Prohibition became a bonanza for organized crime. By intimidating or murdering competitors, a gang could secure a monopoly on the alcohol trade and a share of the $2 billion yearly that bootleggers earned in the United States, at a time when the federal budget was $3 billion to $6 billion. Al Capone, the most notorious bootlegger, dominated Chicago and suburban Cicero, grossing $60 million from beer and distilled liquor, as well as his take from gambling, prostitution, and the "protection" racket. Paradoxically, he thrived because he served a need, albeit illegal. To embellish his image, he gave away food and coal to the poor, donated money to charity, and invested in legitimate businesses (he shunned stocks, though, claiming that Wall Street was crooked). Yet few could admire Capone or dismiss him after St. Valentine's Day in 1929, when his men massacred six members of a rival gang. In 1931 he was imprisoned for federal income tax evasion.

Herbert Hoover was the only president to exert a sincere effort to enforce Prohibition, increasing penalties, transferring jurisdiction from the Treasury Department to the Justice Department, and placing enforcement agents under civil service rules for salaries and professional advancement. In addition, he appointed a commission led by former Attorney General George Wickersham to study federal law enforcement, particularly the alcohol ban. The commission reported that Prohibition violators were straining the federal prison system. As early as 1924 half of all federal prisoners were incarcerated because of Prohibition offenses, even though they represented just a fraction of those who disobeyed the law. Eventually most reformers concluded that the ban was unenforceable. The clinching argument, during the Great Depression, was that the return of the legitimate industry would create jobs, furnish revenue for the government, and aid recovery.

By 1932 the Republican and Democratic platforms called for repeal or alteration of the Eighteenth Amendment. After Democrat Franklin D. Roosevelt unseated Hoover that year, the lame-duck Congress that met before his inauguration enacted the Twenty-First Amendment, repealing the Eighteenth. Ratified in December 1933, it closed the Prohibition Era. Still, eight states and several counties remained dry, and Prohibition was not universally branded a failure. Defenders reminded people that alcohol consumption, auto accidents, and diseases such as cirrhosis of the liver declined under the alcohol ban; nor could illicit drinking be held responsible by itself for organized crime, when urbanization, the auto, the availability of guns, and greater criminal sophistication contributed. Alcoholism exacted a heavy toll on individuals, persuading Prohibition supporters to help found Alcoholics Anonymous in 1935. Repeal did not solve problems any more than did Prohibition. Compulsive drinkers resorted to the bottle to escape anxiety, and in no decade did they seek escape so desperately, and so unsuccessfully, as in "the Roaring Twenties."

CHAPTER EIGHT

Republicanism from Prosperity to the Great Depression

THE 1920S WERE paradoxical in that they resembled a second Gilded Age (1877–1900), an era that appeared golden on the surface, yet in fact was only gilded. The glitter of society was fascinating, yet the reality beneath lacked substance. The Republican presidents were popular in their time and have some significant accomplishments to their credit, yet their reputations, and the economy, floated on thin ice.

The 1920 Election

Its luster fading with Woodrow Wilson, the Democratic Party's star was in decline by 1919, and the Republicans' was ascendant. There had been just two Democratic chief executives since the Civil War. The second, Wilson, won in 1912 only because of a GOP split, and he barely defeated his Republican foe in 1916. By 1920 Wilson was infirm and unpopular, his party discredited, because he could not secure approval of the Versailles Treaty, and because he neglected to plan adequately for conversion to a peacetime economy. Registered Republicans outnumbered Democrats.

The chief problem for the Republicans in 1920 was to find a suitable candidate after Theodore Roosevelt's death on January 6, 1919. General Leonard Wood, who had commanded the Rough Riders and considered himself Roosevelt's heir, Illinois Governor Frank Lowden and U.S. Senator Hiram Johnson of California led the field. Both parties made overtures to Herbert Hoover, a fabulously successful mining engineer and humanitarian, yet Hoover would not campaign for the job.

IN A PLAYFUL MOOD
Warren G. Harding with his dog at the White House.
(Library of Congress)

Ohio Senator Warren G. Harding, who had announced his candidacy in 1919, ran a low-key campaign. Harding had nominated William Howard Taft for president in 1912 and had delivered his party's keynote address in 1916, in his first term in the U.S. Senate. In 1918 and 1919 Harding delivered speeches nationwide, positioning himself as a potential nominee. His campaign strategist, Harry Daugherty, devised the tactic of collecting pledges to Harding as a second choice should the leading candidates deadlock. A newspaper publisher, Harding was a friendly unifier who understood intuitively the mood of the nation. Shaken by a victorious war followed by a lost peace and a declining economy, America wanted what Harding termed "normalcy." Not a profound orator by present standards, Harding's patriotic, alliterative speeches were effective because of their delivery, though lacking in intellectual content. A Democratic opponent labeled them "an army of pompous phrases moving over the landscape in search of an idea."

As the convention approached, Harding's campaign gained momentum. Wood was injured by an investigation into his campaign finances; as was Johnson, when it was learned he had helped inspire the investigation to discredit Wood. The leading candidates were destroying one another. This fratricide made Harding's superficial calm attractive. Florence Harding, the candidate's wife, played a major role. Initially, she did not want him to run. She knew, as the public did not, that Harding had entered a Michigan hospital on several occasions for treatment of stress. Yet once Harding entered, she would not let him quit. After her husband was trounced in the Indiana primary, she insisted he remain a candidate. But Florence had premonitions. She had a reading with a Washington psychic, Madame Marcia, who predicted that a deadlock would develop at Chicago leading to Harding's nomination and election. However, he would die before his term ended.

The deadlock predicted by the psychic and hoped for by Daugherty materialized. Wood led the first ballot but could not expand beyond his core of delegates. Neither could Lowden or Johnson. They disliked each other, and neither would release their delegates to another front runner. Yet this animosity did not extend to Harding.

When the convention adjourned temporarily to sort out the mess, Daugherty's second-choice pledges began to cash in their chips. Many believed Harding could win the election. Although not a party leader, neither was he a novice. He had served in the Ohio senate, as lieutenant governor of Ohio, and as a U.S. senator. He was likeable and a reliable party regular. He came from an elector-rich, closely contested state.

Harding was nominated after the leading candidates released their delegates. The nominee grasped Lowden's hand and said, "I am not sure that I would be happier, Frank, if I were congratulating you." Daugherty, once exiled to a cameo role by the political heavyweights, was now grudgingly respected as Machiavelli reborn. Harding left the selection of a vice presidential running mate to the convention, which chose the diminutive governor of Massachusetts, Calvin Coolidge. Coolidge had become a symbol for law and order when he dispatched a blunt telegram to labor leader Samuel Gompers during the Boston police strike of 1919: "There is no right to strike against the public safety by anybody, anywhere, any time."

Not everyone considered Harding a model leader. *The Nation* wrote: "In truth he is a dummy, an animated automaton, a marionette that moves when the strings are pulled." And Florence Harding, having witnessed the fulfillment of the first installment of Madame Marcia's prophecy, now feared fulfillment of the latter, telling reporters, "I can see but one word written over the head of my husband if he is elected and that word is 'tragedy'."

Two weeks after Harding's nomination, the Democratic convention in San Francisco also bogged down. Wilson wanted a third term to make the election a referendum on his treaty, but his physical condition prevented it. The leading candidates were William G. McAdoo, Wilson's treasury secretary, and A. Mitchell Palmer, the attorney general and Red Scare leader. It took eight days and forty-four ballots before the party nominated a compromise choice, Ohio Governor James M. Cox. The vice presidential nominee was another surprise: Franklin D. Roosevelt, selected because delegates thought his name might appeal to Republican voters who remembered his distant cousin, Theodore. He was well liked in both parties, but many leading politicians did not consider him a serious person.

Harding paced his campaign deliberately. Initially he remained home, speaking to delegations who hiked to his front yard. The press appreciated his candor and affability. Neither party found the public responsive to the League of Nations issue. A racist professor wrote a book and compiled a fake genealogy purporting that Harding was part black. Cox and Roosevelt refused to exploit it. In early August, Harding took to the campaign trail delivering 112 speeches before November 2. Coolidge did little campaigning. The Democratic ticket campaigned energetically, yet could not escape the clouds of Wilson's turbulent presidency.

Florence Harding voted for her husband, thanks to the Twentieth Amendment, one of a tidal wave of voters who swept Harding into the White House. The Republican won 404 electoral votes, the greatest total up to that time, and 16.2 million popular votes, or 60.4 percent, one of the highest percentages in American history. Cox carried just eleven states, 127 electoral votes, and 9.1 million popular votes. The GOP controlled both houses of Congress. The main protest candidate, Eugene V. Debs of the American Socialist Party, was serving a federal prison sentence for subversion, having delivered a speech against the war. Debs, whose campaign literature featured his prison number, received almost 920,000 votes, the most ever for a Socialist candidate.

Harding's Presidency

Always modest, some said with good reason, Harding asserted: "I should not be fit to hold the high office of President if I did not frankly say that it is a task which I have no intention of undertaking alone." He planned to tap "the best minds in the United States" as cabinet members, and with a few exceptions succeeded. Most of Harding's cabinet members were generalists rather than specialists. The most important were Herbert Hoover, young, assertive, and imaginative, as secretary of commerce; and Andrew Mellon, the second-richest man in the world, who, financial journals predicted, would become the greatest secretary of the treasury since Alexander Hamilton. Harding nominated Charles Evans Hughes, a man with a brilliant legal mind, as secretary of state. Albert Fall, who sat next to Harding in the Senate, became his secretary of the interior. The most controversial nominee was Harding's friend Daugherty for attorney general. The *New York Times* wrote of rumors of Daugherty's appointment: "It would be universally regarded as the payment of a political debt. But it would be worse than that. It would be the naming of a man not believed to be competent to do the important work to be placed in his hands." The cabinet, for the most part, had good minds, indeed. But the advice it gave him was hydra-headed rather than uniform or consistent. Harding despaired of his own indecisiveness.

At the time Harding entered office, the nation had been drifting under the declining health of President Wilson, unable to provide a rudder for the Ship of State. The presidency was listing, foreign policy was in chaos, domestic policy was unattended. The postwar economy was a shambles. Nonfarm unemployment grew from 2.3 percent in 1919 to 4.0 percent in 1920 to 11.9 percent in 1921. Harding made uprighting the economy and restoring domestic calm his primary objectives.

Excelling at public relations, and gregarious, Harding kept the White House gate open and the curtain drawn, and every day during the lunch hour he greeted anyone who wished to meet him, shaking hands with a quarter of a million people in three years. His generosity was expressed through pardons of Debs and other political prisoners shortly before Christmas 1921. Wanting to be successful, Harding worked hard, arriving at the Oval Office by 7:00 A.M. and often remaining until midnight.

Harding's first message to Congress stated his priorities: negotiate a separate peace with Germany, Austria, and Hungary; cut government expenditures by creating a Bureau of the Budget; enact an emergency tariff followed by a permanent tariff and aid farmers. He wanted Congress to limit immigration; regulate new technology such as aviation, radio, and automobiles; create a department of public welfare; and enact antilynching legislation. This was not a reactionary agenda, and some of it was progressive. Harding was responding to public demands in some areas; in others, such as the Bureau of the Budget, a department of public welfare, and antilynching legislation, he was moving ahead of public opinion, demonstrating a degree of leadership.

Congress quickly passed and Harding signed the Emergency Immigration Act of 1921. Workers feared loss of jobs to immigrants, and racial and ethnic bias determined the apportionment. The act, which Harding signed on May 19, 1921, reduced immigration quotas to 3 percent of a country's nationals residing in the United States in 1910. Not until after Harding's death, in 1924, did Congress pass a more permanent, more restrictive statute. About a week after authorizing the measure, Harding signed his second major measure, an emergency tariff law. Expected to help protect farmers from foreign competition, it did little to relieve their plight. Farmers overproduced for American markets and retaliatory tariffs shut down foreign sales. They would have to produce less or sell on world markets. A second, more lasting act, the Fordney-McCumber Tariff, signed in 1922, raised tariffs and provided favors to special interest groups.

The administration's greatest domestic accomplishment was the Budget and Accounting Act of June 10, 1921. The Bureau of the Budget organized and balanced expenditures with income, helped cut taxes, and eliminated waste and duplication. Charles G. Dawes, a Chicago banker, became the first director. Harding asked Dawes to slice $1 billion from the federal budget; Dawes did better.

Veterans began agitating for a bonus for their service in World War I during Harding's tenure, and he vetoed the first measure to pass Congress in 1922. As farmers continued to languish and tariffs did not prove their salvation, the administration enacted ameliorative measures. These included the Capper-Volstead Act (1922) to exempt farm cooperatives from antitrust prosecution (sometimes called agriculture's "Magna Carta"), appointment of a farm representative to the Federal Reserve Board, the Grain Futures Acts of 1921 and 1922, restricting speculation, and the Packers and Stockyard Act (1921) to regulate prices charged by livestock processors.

Harding found it difficult to work with the lawmakers, because he rarely provided the leadership needed to overcome opposition. Only when there was broad agreement did he publicly campaign for bills. With the nation in a recession in 1921, both parties favored a tax cut to stimulate the economy. Mellon believed that tax cuts for the wealthy would make capital available for investment, and progressives preferred broader reductions. Ultimately Harding endorsed Mellon's proposal, yet the law that emerged was a compromise. General tax rates were unchanged, exemptions were raised, and the excess profits levy was abolished. The maximum surtax on incomes greater than $1 million was dropped from 65 to 50 percent, the corporate tax was raised from 10 to 12 percent, and the first-ever capital gains tax, 12.5 percent, was imposed. This was hardly a "soak-the-poor" law; under it most working-class Americans paid nothing. For the other half of his financial formula, Mellon, with the aid of Harding and Dawes reduced spending and helped retire the federal debt, which fell from $23.1 billion in 1921, to $21.8 billion in 1923, and to $16.5 billion in 1929. Hoover organized a national conference on unemployment, collected and distributed economic statistics, helped manufacturers eliminate waste and duplication, and encouraged industry to cooperate through trade associations.

Harding's Supreme Court appointments were one of his most enduring accomplishments. His first appointee, former President William Howard Taft, had a fine legal mind and led a strict constructionist court. In addition, Harding appointed George Sutherland (1922), Pierce Butler (1923), and Edward T. Sanford (1923), the latter three upon the recommendation of Taft.

Scandal and History's Verdict

On December 8, 1922, Harding delivered his second State of the Union address. The economy had pulled out of its slump and was growing. Harding moved in a progressive direction, calling for internal improvements, conservation, federal development of waterpower and electricity, and an end to child labor.

Yet Harding's health waned even as his oratory waxed. He appeared calm and in command, but the stress of the presidency was straining his already damaged heart. Harding enjoyed the ceremonial and interpersonal aspects of the presidency, although he was a poor administrator, meticulous to a fault. Not until late in his short term did he learn to delegate or set priorities. Although it has been written that Harding was lazy, just the opposite was true. He was a perfectionist in human relations because he did not like to hurt people. Harding's chief problem was that he could not relax amid undone work. "I never find myself done," he said. "I never find myself with my work complete. I don't believe there is a human being who can do all the work there is to be done in the President's office." His various attempts at recreation—golf, poker, and heavy drinking—were in part efforts to escape tension and depression. Like other men who sought the presidency, the power ceased to become an honor and grew into a burden. The White House became a prison he had to pretend he liked. Like presidents before and after him, the public image was at odds with reality.

Harding kept working despite a severe case of influenza contracted in early 1923. Some doctors believe the flu was accompanied by an undiagnosed heart attack. The president's morale began to sag when he learned of rumors of scandals in his administration. Inklings came that Charles R. Forbes was looting Veterans Administration hospitals. Forbes took kickbacks for giving lucrative government contracts to friends and selling hospital supplies below cost, while buying expensive new supplies. Forbes traveled to Europe, where he resigned, but was belatedly brought to justice after Harding's death. His confederate, Charles F. Cramer, committed suicide during a Senate investigation. A friend of Attorney General Daugherty, Jesse Smith, accused of selling pardons and alien property seized during the war, committed suicide when his crimes were uncovered. Meanwhile, Secretary of Interior Fall, the culprit in the most famous scandal, resigned from the cabinet on January 2, 1923, to become effective on March 4.

Of the brewing scandals, Harding knew most about Forbes. He probably suspected others. The president planned a cross-country railroad tour to lift his spirits and revive his health. Before departing, he altered his will and sold the *Marion Star*. The vacation only aggravated his angst. He played bridge compulsively. He asked Hoover, aboard for the trip, what he would do if he learned of a scandal in the administration. After Hoover advised him to reveal it, Harding refused to elaborate. Harding ended the journey in Alaska, Washington, Oregon, and California. After a series of strokes he succumbed to pneumonia in California.

Harding's death on August 2, 1923, had the impact of a comet crashing into earth. His body was borne on a train back to Washington as tens of thousands lined the tracks and sang his favorite hymn, "Nearer My God to Thee." To them, he was a man with an average mind but a generous nature, calm, patient, patriotic, whose kind voice was silenced.

History has not treated Harding as generously as his contemporaries. Journalists, congressional committees, and enemies began to drive silver stakes through his reputation. Within months of the president's death a pall of scandal that has not lifted to this day had enveloped Harding's administration. The best known, probably because of its catchy name, was the Teapot Dome scandal, so named because of a teapot-shaped rock formation that dominated the landscape at a government oil reserve in Wyoming. Another oilfield at Elk Hills, California, was equally involved but is less remembered.

Believing World War I's ultimate weapon, the battleship, would need fuel to patrol the seas, the government bought oil lands and placed them under the Department of the Navy. Navy transferred them to Interior at the request of Secretary of the Interior Fall. Fall, in turn, leased them to two oilmen, Harry Sinclair and Edward Doheny, without competitive bids. The oilmen promised to build pipelines and storage tanks to deliver the oil to the fleet, including a base at Pearl Harbor. The arrangement made logistical sense and might have been acceptable had not Fall accepted bribes for the leases. Fall, eventually convicted of bribery, became the first member or former member of the cabinet to serve time, though only nine months. Tried by separate juries, Sinclair and Doheny were acquitted of bribing Fall, though Sinclair was convicted of contempt. The cases, handled by a special prosecutor, dragged on into the Coolidge administration.

Harding's reputation slid rapidly downward after Nan Britton, who claimed to be his mistress, published her memoirs in 1927. She described trysts in the Oval Office and the birth of a baby girl fathered by Harding.

Later, it was learned that Harding had a second affair, this one with Carrie Phillips, the wife of his best friend in Marion. Their romance cooled after Harding refused to leave his wife to marry her. Neither affair was known to the public during the president's lifetime. The sexual revolution had reached the White House.

What the public of the 1920s knew of Harding's administration, we now know, was the tip of the iceberg. The scandals repeated in history books through generations made Harding seem one of the most corrupt presidents in history. Yet it is more accurate to say that the Harding administration was corrupt than to label Harding himself financially corrupt. He was responsible for the deeds of those he appointed, of course, and if he did not know of their misdeeds, he should have. Still, Harding's greatest failure was neither personal corruption nor lack of intelligence. A unifier, a man who made friends easily, who won a huge popular victory in 1920, he failed as a politician. His loose-reined approach could not harness the wild horses he unloosed upon the national treasury.

"Silent Cal"

When Harding died, most politicians issued respectful condolences. However, Henry Cabot Lodge's first reaction was "My God, that means Coolidge is president!" Asked later what his first thought was, the new chief executive said, "I thought I could swing it." Lacking a dynamic personality and leadership qualities, Calvin Coolidge might not have been considered presidential timber, yet he possessed assets that politicians covet. Shrewd, cautious, lucky, and opportunistic, he gauged voters' attitudes as perceptively as any politician of his era. Nor was Coolidge lazy; his long afternoon naps were due to poor health, particularly stomach disorders, not lassitude. Known as "Silent Cal," he was reticent because of depression. The fear of death haunted his family. His mother died when he was twelve, his sister when he was fifteen; his stepmother died in 1920; and he lost his father and younger son while president. Coolidge was not as silent as some observers portrayed him, but he was shy and laconic. Unlike his immediate predecessor, it was impossible to suspect him of dishonesty; he was so frugal he quibbled about nickels.

An archetypical New Englander, Coolidge never truly felt that he left the green hills and stony soil of his native Vermont. Born in 1872 in the hamlet of Plymouth Notch, Coolidge worked on his father's farm and, after outgrowing the local school, went to a Ludlow boarding school and then Amherst College in Massachusetts, where he earned a Phi Beta Kappa key. He had few close friends and rarely participated in extracurricular activities. When Coolidge filled out a questionnaire asking seniors what they expected to do after graduation, he wrote, "Nothing, I reckon." Instead he settled in nearby Northampton and studied law. In the early 1890s he entered politics at the local level and became adept at winning elections, with an approach that included few promises. In 1905 he married the gregarious and witty Grace Goodhue, an unlikely pairing, as Grace was as spontaneous as her husband was reserved.

The public confidence he inspired enabled Coolidge to serve as mayor of Northampton, a member of the Massachusetts legislature, and lieutenant governor before becoming governor. As vice president, though, Coolidge became known as a quaint nonentity who spent much of his time attending banquets and delivering speeches. Asked why he attended so many dinners when he clearly did not enjoy socializing, he answered, "Got to eat somewhere." Grace Coolidge enjoyed telling stories about her spouse's reputation for silence, which the press reported in an effort to make him interesting. A reporter who sat with the Coolidges through a baseball game said that Coolidge spoke only once during nine innings, when he asked Grace, "What time is it?"

When Coolidge rose to the presidency, his surface calm charmed the country and reassured business. He rarely intervened in congressional affairs unless a crisis arose, and during his presidency there were few crises. So relatively tranquil was his tenure that near its end, when a woman asked Coolidge what had worried him most, he said, "The White House hams," explaining that he never found out what happened to the leftovers. Typically he followed a dictum he had laid down as governor: "A great many times if you let a situation alone, it takes care of itself." His program, was of limited governmental activity, in consonance with the times. Coolidge's liabilities, nevertheless, were substantial. He lacked vision, procrastinated, and ignored advice. Confronted with problems, he diverted conversations to irrelevancies. The chief executive did not understand the complexities of government, economics, or human relations, and he read superficially. He did not fathom the modern world and was largely ignorant of the vast, pluralistic nation over which he presided.

Philosophically, Coolidge was more conservative than Harding. To Coolidge, economy in government was a sacred principle; to Harding, it was expedient. In his first message to Congress after Harding died, Coolidge called for more cuts in taxes and spending, better race relations, aid for African American education, a constitutional amendment to restrict child labor, and a minimum wage for women. Like Harding, Coolidge did not lobby Congress to pass legislation, so only the tax and budget cuts were enacted. His first budget was just $3.3 billion, the lowest since World War I.

The Revenue Act of 1924 reduced income taxes to 2 percent on the first $4,000, from 4 percent; to 4 percent on the next $4,000, from 8 percent; and to 6 percent on the rest, from 8 percent. The maximum surtax was sliced from 50 to 40 percent and applied only to incomes greater than $500,000, up from $200,000. Despite the tax reductions, federal revenue increased, and Mellon continued retiring the national debt.

In his standpat posture and his disposal of the Harding scandals, Coolidge became a formidable candidate for a full term. No one mounted a serious challenge for the 1924 GOP nomination, and the president was selected on the first ballot. Coolidge did not choose a running mate, so delegates nominated Lowden, who declined, then chose Dawes, who accepted. In sharp contrast with the Republican conclave, the raucous Democratic convention, fittingly, took place in New York's Madison Square Garden, the site of many prizefights. The party was split between an urban, liberal wing that opposed Prohibition and a rural, conservative faction that favored it. Another polarizing issue was the Ku Klux Klan; a motion to condemn it in the platform failed narrowly. On the choice of a presidential nominee, the convention could not decide between New York Governor Al Smith and McAdoo, somewhat tainted because he was Doheny's attorney in the Teapot Dome scandal. Needing a two-thirds majority to nominate a candidate, the Democrats exhausted themselves by balloting endlessly. "This thing has got to come to an end," humorist Will Rogers wrote in his newspaper column. "New York invited you people here as guests, not to live." McAdoo offered to release his delegates to support his friend from Indiana, Senator Samuel Ralston, who declined because of poor health. Finally, on the 103rd ballot, the party nominated a compromise candidate, John W. Davis, a corporate lawyer from West Virginia who had served as a congressman and ambassador to Britain. His running mate was Nebraska Governor Charles W. Bryan, the younger brother of William Jennings Bryan.

Finding little reason to back Davis or Coolidge, some liberals supported Senator Robert M. La Follette, the Progressive Party candidate, who called for federal ownership of railroads and hydroelectric power and a constitutional amendment permitting Congress to override Supreme Court decisions. Most of La Follette's support came at Davis's expense; without his candidacy the Democrats would have posed a stronger threat to Coolidge. The Republicans' chief strengths were prosperity and that theirs was the majority party. Henry Ford expressed the views of many voters when he said: "The country is perfectly safe with Coolidge. Why change?"

Polls showed Coolidge leading throughout the campaign, helped by Republican spending that topped Democrats' almost 5 to 2. The result: the Coolidge-Dawes ticket won 382 electoral votes and 15.7 million popular votes, to 136 and 8.4 million for the Democrats, who carried only the South, and to 13 electoral votes for the Progressives. Further, the GOP won safe majorities in Congress.

The Economy According to Coolidge

Coolidge and Mellon continued to cut taxes and spending. The Revenue Act of 1926 reduced maximum inheritance and surtax rates to 20 percent (from 40 percent), repealed the gift tax, and raised personal exemptions. The income tax was lowered to 1.5 percent on the first $4,000 (from 4 percent) and to 5 percent on the rest (from 6 percent). The corporate income tax rose to 12.5 percent in 1926, up 0.5 of a percent, and to 13.5 percent the next year. The tax reductions were hailed, although farmers, who continued to languish, resented Coolidge for twice vetoing bills that would have provided agricultural price supports. Known as the McNary-Haugen plan, the legislation had been under consideration since the Harding administration. It would have set a high domestic price for agricultural products; the federal government would have bought surpluses and sold them abroad at a loss, to be compensated with a tax on food processing. Coolidge, however, was correct in pointing out that the plan would encourage farmers to produce more when overproduction was the reason prices were low. Production limits might have helped, but neither the government nor farmers were willing to require them. Farm unrest persisted, one reason the Republicans lost seats in the 1926 congressional elections.

Coolidge signed a bill providing $165 million to construct federal buildings despite curtailing most spending. He even pared a flood control appropriation to $500 million, from the $1.4 billion that Congress wanted, after a flood in the Ohio and Mississippi valley left two hundred people dead and 1.5 million homeless and caused millions of dollars in damages. Business expanded, with new products such as automobiles and electrical appliances flowing off assembly lines, prompting investment in stocks that seemed destined to rise. The paradox of such plenty was that the economy was overheating.

Almost all groups that benefited from Coolidge prosperity voted Republican in the 1920s. Women, who voted nationally for the first time in 1920, seem to have voted for Harding and Coolidge in about the same percentages as men. They voted much less than did men in the decade—about 74 percent of eligible males cast ballots, compared with only about 46 percent of eligible women—but steadily increased their political involvement as delegates to national party conventions. In 1920, ninety-six women were Democratic delegates (9 percent of the delegate total) and twenty-six were Republican delegates (2 percent); in 1928 the numbers had risen to 156 Democrats (14 percent) and seventy Republicans (6 percent), and the national committees of each party included women, including a vice chair. Women's officeholding for the decade peaked in 1928, when there were seven women in Congress, 131 in state legislatures, two heading state treasuries, and one woman serving as a state Supreme Court justice. Two women succeeded their husbands as governors.

Women were active in political clubs and pressure groups, including the League of Women Voters, the General Federation of Women's Clubs, the Women's Trade Union League, and the mostly female National Consumer's League. The smallest and most militant, the National Woman's Party led by Alice Paul, had eight thousand members. The party made its sole objective enactment of an Equal Rights Amendment to the Constitution, that would eliminate all discrimination against women as well as nullify laws giving them special protection. Many women's groups opposed the amendment, believing they would lose more from the abolition of protective laws than they would gain from an end to discrimination. Introduced in each session from 1923 through 1970, the amendment was never adopted. An amendment outlawing child labor, which the Women's Joint Congressional Committee and the National Child Labor Committee promoted, passed Congress, only to win ratification in just four states.

It was assumed that women would join men in reelecting Coolidge in 1928. The president, though, had grown ill in the White House, with an ailing stomach and heart, and his spirits waned after Calvin Jr.'s death from an infection in 1924. "When he went, the power and the glory of the presidency went with him," Coolidge said. The office had become a painful paradox for him, much as it had been for Harding. On vacation in August 1927, Coolidge issued a statement that was enigmatic in its brevity: "I do not choose to run for President in 1928," he said, without elaboration. Enjoying inscrutability, he had consulted no one about his decision, not even his wife, who learned of it from a senator.

Coolidge has been maligned for inaction while the economy hurtled toward the stock market crash in 1929. Many of what appeared his virtues in the 1920s were viewed as vices in the 1930s, yet it must be remembered that in the 1920s there was no demand for a New Deal—and that after 1929 there was no demand for a lackadaisical president. Coolidge was fortunate to have retired from presidential politics when he did, for if he had won in 1928, he, and not his successor, Hoover, would have been blamed for the Great Depression.

Coolidge retired to Northampton, never again to participate actively in politics. His health failing, he sometimes sat on his front porch and watched motorists drive by to look at a former president in his rocking chair. Asked if he was pleased to see so many cars, he answered: "Not as many as yesterday. Yesterday there were 163 of them."

Hoover from Triumph to Tragedy

With Coolidge's withdrawal, Hoover became the leading Republican candidate and won the 1928 nomination on the first ballot; delegates chose Kansas Senator Charles Curtis as his running mate. Using words that would be ironic in depression America, Hoover said in his acceptance speech: "We in America today are nearer to the final triumph over poverty than ever before in the history of the land. The poorhouse is vanishing from among us. We shall soon with the help of God be in sight of the day when poverty is banished from this nation." Of course, at the time, such optimism was widely shared. The GOP claimed credit for prosperity, and Hoover's background inspired faith that the nominee would preside over good times.

A native of West Branch, Iowa, Hoover was the first president from west of the Mississippi River. Only Abraham Lincoln's birthplace was more humble than his. Orphaned in childhood and raised by relatives in Oregon, Hoover did not regularly attend high school, but enrolled in the first class of Stanford University. There, he was an outstanding student because of his ability to organize, raise money, and serve others. Graduating with a degree in geological engineering in 1895, he eventually joined an English mining firm that sent him to Australia, then to China. With a reputation for good judgment and dealing effectively with difficult people, Hoover managed international mining operations for thirteen years, becoming a millionaire by forty.

Hoover's wife, Lou Henry, was Stanford's first female graduate in geological engineering. After marriage, Lou devoted herself to her husband, two sons, volunteer work, outdoor activities, and writing. Never a political activist, she did not work outside the home, except for volunteer activities such as the Girl Scouts of America.

When World War I broke out, Hoover, in London, aided Americans stranded in Europe, helping some pay passage to the United States with his own money. In one of the great humanitarian endeavors in history, he fed Belgium, trapped between German occupation and the British blockade. Once the United States entered the war, Hoover, as food administrator under Wilson, fed America and Europe. Following the armistice, he spent eight years as commerce secretary, among the most creative cabinet tenures in memory. Hoover distinguished himself in alleviating the great Mississippi flood of 1927, supervising rescue work, refugee care, and rehabilitation, and helping enact the Mississippi Flood Control Act of 1928.

HOOVER AND HOLLYWOOD
Actress Mary Pickford gives President Hoover a ticket for a film industry benefit for the unemployed, 1931. (Herbert Hoover Presidential Library)

Hoover's Democratic foe in 1928, Al Smith, was another rags-to-riches story. Smith was born in the shadow of the Brooklyn Bridge, as quintessentially urban as Hoover was rural—so provincially eastern that he thought Wisconsin was east of Lake Michigan and asked, while traveling through the prairies, "What do people do out here?" His East Side accent and his nervous fidgeting made him ineffective on radio, although he was witty in person. Unlike Hoover, Smith was a seasoned politician who rose through the ranks of Tammany Hall as state assemblyman, sheriff of New York, and president of the Board of Aldermen. He championed equal pay for women teachers, better health care for the disabled, and adequate appropriations for public education; he reorganized and consolidated state government and revamped welfare. Paradoxically, Smith later opposed programs on the national level similar to his innovations on the state level, and his closest ally in the 1928 campaign, Franklin D. Roosevelt, became his most bitter rival. As paradoxical a figure as Hoover, Smith reflected the complexities of changing times.

The first major party Catholic presidential nominee, Smith found religious prejudice an obstacle. "If this man Smith is elected, the pope is going to come over here with all his wives and concubines and live in the White

House and run the country," a Delaware man said. What hindered Smith most, however, was Republican prosperity. Almost any GOP candidate would have defeated Smith. Hoover polled 21.4 million popular votes and 444 electoral votes to Smith's 15 million and 87; Republicans also increased their majorities in the House by 30 seats, to a margin of 100, and in the Senate by 7, to a margin of 17.

The new chief executive planned to provide stronger leadership than Coolidge, yet he cautioned admirers that he was no magician. In terms that ring ironic, Hoover said, "If some unprecedented calamity should come upon the nation I would be sacrificed to the unreasoning disappointment of a people who expected too much." Hoover did expect much of himself, working seven days a week without diversion, becoming the first president to have a telephone on his desk, mothballing the White House yacht, and closing the White House stables.

On the activist side of his ledger, Hoover supported civil rights, entertained an African American in the White House, addressed Congress on lynching, appointed more African Americans to middle-level jobs than did Harding and Coolidge combined, launched a program to reduce black illiteracy, and devised a plan to give sharecroppers money to purchase land. Also, he undertook prison reform, designed plans for child care and protection, upgraded the condition of Indians, and restricted oil drilling on public lands. A conservationist who spent much of his early life in the outdoors, the president increased the National Park Service budget 46 percent in two years and added 2 million acres to national forests. He planned inland waterways and the St. Lawrence Seaway. His appointments to the Supreme Court were distinguished—Charles Evans Hughes, Benjamin Cardozo, and Owen Roberts. On the debit side, Hoover failed to publicize his achievements. He was not adept at getting bills enacted, and achieved his most significant accomplishments through executive order instead of legislation. A better administrator than a politician, he expected lawmakers to accept his proposals because they were logical, not politically expedient. The president misfired with one of his high court nominees, John J. Parker, whom the Senate rejected after unions and African Americans opposed him. In ordinary times he might have been an above average chief executive, but after the first six months of his term, times were no longer ordinary.

The Stock Market Crash and Onset of the Great Depression

A speculative land boom in Florida in 1925 and 1926 preceded the bull market that gave way to the 1929 stock market crash. Land values soared far above the worth of the properties, only to collapse after the market grew saturated. From the episode, investors learned little. During the decade too much money was borrowed for stock speculation, and share prices were pushed artificially high. Imprudently, bankers entered the market, speculating with depositors' money; corporations lent money to brokers, discovering that lending was more profitable than investment in productivity. Brokers, the agents for stock buyers and sellers, lent money to people to purchase shares, a practice that worked well only when stocks went up, facilitating repayment. Nationwide there were probably not even 1 million speculators, although they wielded a consequence beyond their numbers, soaking up capital, dominating the news and culture, and feeding the notion of easy riches for grab.

Booms, obviously, always end, whether from a deliberate decline at an early point or from a cataclysmic crash later. Hoover said he considered values inflated and speculation risky, disposed of some of his stocks, and asked newspapers and magazines to tone down statements that encouraged market players. But no one in authority appreciated the dimensions of the danger, signaled in a stock market that trickled, then gushed downhill in September. Next month came the deluge. On the morning of "Black Thursday," October 24, prices staggered on the New York Stock Exchange, a slide halted only when bankers tried to soothe investors' nerves and bought millions in major stocks. The plunge could not be arrested for long, and on "Black Tuesday," October 29, an unprecedented 16.4 million shares were traded at shockingly low prices, summarized the next day in a *Variety* headline, "WALL STREET LAYS AN EGG." In a few weeks the market lost $30 billion, equal to the U.S. expenditures in World War I and almost twice the national debt. By the end of November the market saw $100 billion vanish.

The crash would not have led inexorably to a depression if consumers had been able to keep buying the products pouring forth from factories and farms. Yet given an overproducing economy, depression would have arrived sometime, even without the crash. Backlogs of merchandise accumulated, and as orders slowed manufacturers cut production and laid off workers. International trade could not alleviate the surplus, for when the 1930 Hawley-Smoot Tariff raised rates, foreign nations erected walls against American imports. The conditions that led to the depression evolved from World War I, which undermined European economies, saddled them with huge debt, and created a large temporary demand for American goods. In Europe, democracy shuddered. The German dictator Adolf Hitler spellbound his nation behind programs of nationalism, racism, and militarism, like Benito Mussolini in Italy. Paradox carved a canyon through the Era of Trial and Triumph: world war helped trigger a depression that led to another world war that ultimately ended the depression.

Back home, merchants desperately cut prices, accelerating deflation, which was problematic for those who owed money, particularly farmers, because they had to repay debts in dollars more valuable than those they had borrowed. Businesses and banks toppled. That people could not consume all that industry and agriculture produced was in part a result of an inequitable distribution of wealth. Almost everyone enjoyed a rising standard of living in the 1920's, but the rich had grown richer faster than the poor had become less poor. During the decade real wages increased 13 percent, whereas returns to industry grew 70 percent; in 1926, 1 percent of the people owned 60 percent of the wealth; and one year later, two hundred of the largest corporations controlled more than 44 percent of all business assets. Companies gobbled up others with impunity, creating monopolies, fixing prices, and cowing labor. Trade associations contributed to vast oligopolies, stifling competition and fixing prices. Banks incorporated investment affiliates that made irresponsible investments with depositors' money. Trusts and holding companies were created to exploit investors. Such concentrated wealth diminished consuming power, made the economy dependent upon the sale of luxuries, and encouraged speculation. Money that might have gone into wages and salaries was invested in stocks and bonds, bloating the market. Employee productivity, spurred by technological advances, outpaced the rate of pay increases, so producing power exceeded consuming power. The wage scale was lowered further, and unemployment was swelled, when farmers who had failed at agriculture, sought industrial jobs. Credit purchases mitigated some of the disparity, yet loans had to be repaid, requiring saving that necessitated a decline in consumption. High taxes on imports provoked retaliation against American imports, hobbling international trade.

As the economy spiraled downward, so did Americans' faith in capitalism, in democracy, in themselves. Unprecedented because of the magnitude of the depression, the panic ushered in an atmosphere in which industrialists were afraid to invest and consumers were afraid to buy. Money was hoarded and demand kept plunging. The federal government, whose policies had done much to bring on the economic peril and, hence, low morale, might have helped prevent depression via stricter business regulation, higher taxes on the wealthy, and encouragement of labor organization. It would have taken remarkable political will and vision to adopt the necessary actions, however, and no presidential aspirant or Congress was likely to advocate them. Production controls and price supports that might have assisted farmers, for example, had been proposed, and not enacted, because farmers opposed them.

Misery was pervasive. Unemployment, the most conspicuous sign of the depression, rose from about 2 million in 1929 to a range of 13 to 14 million in 1932; from 1930 to 1940, the average jobless rate only once dipped

★ SAMUEL INSULL: NAPOLEON ABDICATES ★

> With him—to the top and then to the bottom—went hundreds of thousands
> of stockholders who shared his faith in his own invulnerability.
> —FORREST MCDONALD, INSULL'S BIOGRAPHER

EMPIRE OF ELECTRICITY
Utility magnate Samuel Insull.
(Library of Congress)

AT HIS PINNACLE in 1929, Samuel Insull reigned over a $2.5 billion Midwest-based utility empire that encompassed six thousand power plants in thirty-nine states. The magnate's companies furnished nearly one-eighth of the electric power in the country and had 1 million investors; his securities, people swore, were safer than government bonds. His personal fortune was $150 million, and he lived in a mansion that had gold-plated bathroom fixtures. His estate had the nation's only post office on private property. The most powerful man in his home area of Chicago, he was once told that he was practically as powerful as Napoleon. Insull sneered, "Napoleon was only a soldier." Insull's wife had a different view: "Sam, you should learn about that man and what happened to him. If you don't, that's what's going to happen to you." Her warning was prescient, for her husband, like the French emperor, brought about his downfall because he extended his empire beyond his resources to control it.

Insull came to the United States from England at twenty-one to become private secretary to Thomas Edison. An organizational wizard, he took over the Chicago Edison Company, then absorbed competitors and created holding companies to build five corporate systems with more than 150 subsidiaries. The financing defied comprehension—ultimately perhaps even Insull's. Acquiring properties for inflated prices, he issued overvalued stocks against them and siphoned profits from operating companies into holding companies.

Unfortunately, after the 1929 stock market crash, the profits dried up, and Insull, like a juggler juggling too many balls, could not control his vast corporate structure. In a dramatic illustration of depression tragedy, his companies collapsed—the largest business failure in history. His investors lost $750 million. Insull retreated, quit every one of his corporate offices, and became "too broke to be bankrupt." Later, he recouped enough to live on. A conquering hero during the apogee of business in the 1920s, he became a villain, a betrayer, because his stockholders went down with him.

Vilified by politicians who held him up as an archetype of business corruption, pursued by creditors and the law, Insull fled to Europe in 1932, prepared to remain abroad until the American mood mellowed enough to allow him a fair trial. "Why am I not more popular in the United States?" he wondered. "What have I done that every banker and business magnate has not done in the course of business?" Proposing to answer him, the government extradited Insull from Turkey in 1934 to face charges of fraud and embezzlement. Three times he stood trial in Chicago; three times he won acquittal. But the American public never forgave Insull, and he spent most of his remaining life in Paris. He did leave America a legacy, however, by provoking an outcry that resulted in New Deal financial reforms, the Tennessee Valley Authority, and the Rural Electrification Association.

Insull was found on a Paris subway platform on July 16, 1938, killed by a heart attack at age seventy-nine, with only eighty-five cents. Like others of the Era of Trial and Triumph, Insull found that money purchased notoriety and power, yet the long-term price was stress and humiliation. The Great Depression did not play favorites.

Sources: Samuel Insull's biography is Forrest McDonald, *Insull* (1962). Edward Robb Ellis, *A Nation in Torment* (1970), contains a useful, shorter treatment of his career. Arthur M. Schlesinger Jr., *The Age of Roosevelt*, vol. 1, *The Crisis of the Old Order, 1919–1933* (1957), is also helpful.

below 8 million, in 1937. At times, 25 percent of the workforce was without employment. Labor income declined from $50 billion in 1929 to $29 billion in 1933, gross farm income from $12 billion in 1929 to 5.3 billion in 1932, corporate income from an $8.7 billion profit in 1929 to a $5.6 billion deficit in 1932, and national income from $81.1 billion to $40 billion. Farm income dived 20 percent in 1930 and 30 percent the next year. People wandered among breadlines and soup kitchens. Men lived in sewer pipes in Oakland, California, in shacks in Central Park in New York, and in squalid shantytowns called "Hoovervilles." The president's name was seized for other grim symbols: "Hoover hogs" were rabbits that farmers shot for food; "Hoover flags" were empty pockets turned inside out. Weddings were postponed, husbands deserted families, and evictions multiplied. The home of a Chicago municipal worker was auctioned off because he was $34 in arrears in city taxes; meanwhile, the city owed him $850 in unpaid salary. Schoolchildren were undernourished and fatigued, in no condition to learn.

With surpluses on their hands, northwestern farmers gave apples on credit to unemployed men, who tried to sell them for a nickel apiece with the slogan, "Buy an apple a day and eat the depression away"; in 1930, there were six thousand apple peddlers on New York streets. "Apple sellers crouched at the street corners like half-remembered sins sitting upon the conscience of the town," a Manhattan reporter wrote. While millions hungered in cities or wore ragged clothes, crops that could not be sold rotted in the countryside. Compounding the despair, in 1930 the worst drought in history parched the Missouri Valley. As animals died from the lack of fodder, Hoover provided feed, provoking the caustic criticism that he fed cattle, not people. The rich, too, felt the depression—the Rockefeller fortune shrank to one-fifth its precrash size—but some of the privileged did not comprehend the anguish of the poor. One of the Du Ponts, asked to advertise his products on Sunday afternoon radio, objected, "At three o'clock on Sunday afternoons everybody is playing polo."

Marshaling the financial and moral resources of the nation, Hoover displayed unprecedented activism. Unlike previous chief executives, he was unwilling to trust the economic cycle alone to bring recovery. He tried to persuade those who could afford it to open their pocketbooks. He obtained pledges from industrialists not to cut wages or dismiss workers and promises from union leaders not to strike. Hoover hoped that private charity, supplemented by local action, could provide effective, decentralized relief, but he believed that states and the federal government should intervene if necessary. "I insisted that the first obligation of direct relief rested on local communities, and that they should not call upon the state and federal governments until the load overtaxed their capacities." Hoover urged the Red Cross to feed the hungry, yet the charity rejected federal aid, as did forty-seven governors, including Franklin D. Roosevelt of New York. As the depression deepened, Hoover, government, and charities began to change their minds about government involvement. But after privation appeared intractable, politicians and the public turned on Hoover for clinging to views they had shared earlier.

As the depression deepened, Hoover moved more slowly than the public desired, yet he was far from inactive. At the president's request, Congress appropriated $800 million and reduced taxes by $160 million to stimulate spending and investment. Hoover also created a pool of money contributed by bankers to provide loans to businesses, yet the $500 million fund was insufficient. Then he submitted a bill, enacted, creating the Reconstruction Finance Corporation (RFC) to aid exports, stimulate employment, and lend money to agricultural cooperatives, banks, railroads, and manufacturers. The RFC became a mainstay of the New Deal under Hoover's successor, Roosevelt. Hoover and Congress additionally established Home Loan Discount Banks to enable banks to borrow from the federal government, using mortgages they held as collateral. With such resources available, banks could avoid foreclosures. As for farmers, the Agriculture Marketing Act of 1929, enacted before the stock market crash, provided for the Federal Farm Board, which promoted voluntary acreage controls and lent money to

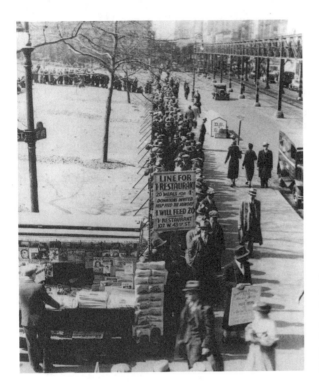

WAITING FOR
THE DEPRESSION
TO END
A breadline in New
York City, 1932.
(Franklin D. Roosevelt
Presidential Library)

cooperatives. Stabilization corporations were set up to buy grain, cotton, and other commodities to sustain prices. Failing to generate farm prosperity, the board at least preserved price levels until 1931, and without it the prices of 1932 would have been lower.

To boost business morale, Hoover believed he must protect the gold standard. Gold was flowing abroad because creditors redeemed securities for gold, considering gold safer than paper money. It appeared that the Treasury might exhaust its gold supply, creating more panic. Yet certain kinds of "eligible" paper, besides gold, backed dollars, and by increasing the eligible paper, the gold drain might be stemmed and the gold standard preserved. Legislation containing such provisions was enacted as the Glass-Steagall Act of 1932. The act liberalized Federal Reserve requirements for collateral, making more member banks eligible for loans and, thus, making more credit available to business. Seeking to boost the economy, Hoover also planned more public works than any of his predecessors. By the end of his term, 360 public structures had been completed and 460 were under construction. His administration began or completed buildings for the city of Washington: the Supreme Court; the Commerce, Labor, and Justice departments; the Post Office; the Interstate Commerce Commission; and the National Archives, as well as additions to the House and Senate buildings. Hoover's program was plausible, and his opponents offered no feasible alternative. Raymond Moley and Rexford Tugwell, advisers to FDR, wrote in their memoirs that many of the New Deal programs were borrowed from Hoover's ideas. Under Hoover, the United States weathered the early years of the depression more successfully than much of the Western world, and the nation's institutions remained intact.

Hoover's greatest failure lay in public relations. He could not inspire, lacked communication skills, and could be stubborn and self-righteous. He was accustomed to getting his way. Persuasive before small groups, Hoover was less effective with the masses and with Congress. His approach seemed inflexible and uncaring. Hoover reinforced this image by refusing to show his empathy, which was real, deep, and intellectually honest. The opposition caricatured him as stubborn and hard-hearted, and Hoover, the "fighting Quaker," did not strike back. Hoover was imaginative and a skilled administrator, yet what he needed was the magic of an alchemist. A tragedy for millions, the Great Depression was a personal humiliation for Hoover. Sandwiched between Coolidge prosperity and the frenetic pace of the New Deal, the Hoover administration is sometimes dismissed as a time when nothing happened, or when only bad things happened. Such was not the case.

"I Pledge . . . A New Deal"

Believing that the economy was improving in 1932, Hoover felt he had to run to vindicate his administration. The Republicans, who had reaped the harvest of prosperity, now were trapped in the whirlwind that swept it away. Regardless, the Hoover-Curtis team was renominated because the GOP was not prepared to repudiate incumbents. Democratic hopefuls knew Hoover was vulnerable, and competition for their presidential nomination was avid. The candidates included Al Smith and House Speaker John Nance Garner, yet the front-runner was New York Governor Franklin D. Roosevelt. Garner helped break a log jam, giving Roosevelt the nomination, and was named his running mate. Breaking tradition by flying to the Chicago convention to accept the nomination, FDR said, "I pledge you, I pledge myself, to a new deal for the American people." A cartoonist highlighted the phrase "new deal" the next day, establishing the term for Roosevelt's program.

Like Hoover, Roosevelt was a millionaire, a protégé of Woodrow Wilson's, an opponent of federal relief, and an advocate of a balanced budget. In temperament the candidates were a striking contrast, for FDR was more gregarious, eloquent, and optimistic. If Roosevelt appeared too eager to please, indecisive, and superficial, "all clay and no granite," as Felix Frankfurter said, he had courage that at least matched Hoover's and had overcome polio as the Republican had overcome poverty. People had overestimated Hoover's potential for the presidency in 1928, and they underestimated Roosevelt's four years afterward.

In the deepest irony, neither presidential nominee made the Depression the chief issue of the campaign. Rather, they talked more about peripheral issues, such as Prohibition, with Roosevelt considered somewhat stronger for repeal. Still, there was a drama that enlivened the campaign, outraged the public, and damaged the Republican. In the summer of 1932, some twenty-two thousand impoverished World War I veterans, dubbed the "Bonus Expeditionary Force" or the "Bonus Army," descended on Washington to seek payment of a bonus for their service. The veterans were paid $1 a day during the war, while shipyard workers' earned $90 per week, an inequity that Congress redressed by enacting over Coolidge's veto in 1925 a bill to credit each veteran with additional money, cashable in twenty years. Thirteen years ahead of the payoff, the veterans assembled to lobby for a measure that would provide it immediately.

Showing some care for the Bonus Army, Hoover supplied the Washington police chief, Pelham Glassford, with food, eating utensils, and tents for the veterans, many of whom camped in Anacostia Flats, on the outskirts of the District of Columbia. Many Washingtonians, though, were alarmed over the veterans' presence, and Hoover refused to meet with the protest leaders, fearing that such a course would encourage disorder. Confounding his apprehensions for the moment, the men assembled peaceably to learn that the repayment bill failed in the Senate, sang "God Bless America," then returned to their camps. But Glassford was ordered to evict veterans who had occupied abandoned federal buildings scheduled for demolition. Ironically, new public buildings, designed to stimulate employment, were to be built on the site. Glassford warned there might be violence during the eviction, and there was. Two veterans died.

Fearing a combustible situation, Hoover ordered the army to drive the veterans out of town while leaving their camps intact and persuaded Congress to appropriate $100,000 to pay for train fare home. General Douglas MacArthur directed troops in dispersing the veterans over the objections of a junior officer, Dwight D. Eisenhower; in the resulting tumult, a brick struck another of MacArthur's subordinates, George S. Patton. Preceded by tanks and tear gas, soldiers with fixed bayonets evicted the Bonus Army from the city. MacArthur then directed his charges to defy Hoover's orders and cross the Anacostia Bridge to destroy the veterans'

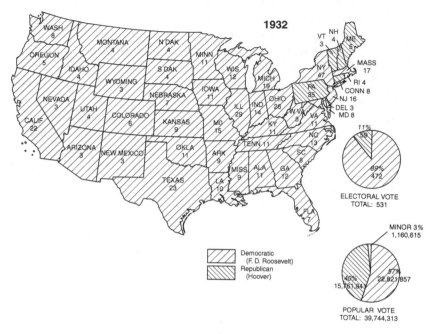

Election of 1932

Camp Anacostia, which was burned; a few veterans resisted, most fled. Hoover worsened the situation by not reprimanding MacArthur.

The electorate chose Roosevelt, even though it did not know exactly what to expect from the Democrat, who polled 22.8 million popular votes and 472 electoral votes to 15.8 million and 59 for Hoover. Socialist Norman Thomas led the minor candidates with more than 872,000 popular votes. Uncertainty grew between the election and the inauguration in March 1933. The depression reached its nadir as banks failed and businesses closed, declines that Hoover blamed on Roosevelt, reasoning that the country had more to fear from an incoming president than an outgoing one. Already some people detested Roosevelt. On February 15 in Miami, Giuseppe Zangara, who hated the privileged and who had tried to assassinate the Italian king, fired a pistol at FDR. Zangara's aim was deflected, but he killed Chicago Mayor Anton Cermak, who was accompanying Roosevelt.

It was left to Roosevelt to do what Hoover could not. If he succeeded, a friend told him, he would go down in history as the greatest American president, and if he failed, he would be known as the worst. Roosevelt turned grim. "If I fail," he said, "I shall be the last one."

Franklin D. Roosevelt and the New Deal

FRANKLIN D. ROOSEVELT seemed as much a paradox as the New Deal he inspired. Born wealthy, he became a champion of the underdog. Handicapped by polio, he became the greatest politician of the twentieth century. He dominated the last half of the Era of Trial and Triumph as few Americans have dominated an epoch, before or since. In Roosevelt's era, it was the government, not rebellious, bootleg-guzzling flappers, that made the noise.

A Presidential Temperament

Descended from the old Dutch aristocracy of New York State, Franklin Delano Roosevelt was the only child of James Roosevelt, a railroad executive and businessman, and Sara Delano, also of an aristocratic family. Young Franklin met some of the nation's most famous people, including President Grover Cleveland, who made a wish for him: that the boy would never suffer the ordeal of becoming president. Roosevelt's first presidential vote, in 1904, was for his distant cousin, Theodore Roosevelt. Theodore's niece, Eleanor Roosevelt, was Franklin's fifth cousin and fiancée. Uncle Theodore gave away the bride when the couple wed in 1905.

After compiling mediocre academic records at Groton prep school and Harvard, Roosevelt enrolled at the Columbia University law school, but failed two courses and did not graduate. He learned enough to pass the New York State bar exam and through family influence was hired for a position with a Wall Street firm. His political allegiance wavered until a Democratic delegation, intending to take advantage of his name, asked him to run for the state legislature. The novice politician won an upset victory

THE FIRST LADY SPEAKS OUT
Eleanor Roosevelt at a WPA site in Des Moines, Iowa, in 1936.
(Franklin D. Roosevelt Presidential Library)

in a Republican district in 1910. In the assembly, Roosevelt achieved a reputation as a reformer. He soon moved from Albany to Washington. Roosevelt supported Woodrow Wilson for the 1912 Democratic presidential nomination and then became his assistant navy secretary. Franklin's career survived his affair with Lucy Page Mercer, Eleanor's social secretary. The Roosevelts did not divorce, but their marriage became one of respect without physical intimacy. Politically, Eleanor was more interested in racial justice and feminism than was her husband.

In 1920, FDR lost as Democratic vice presidential nominee to the Harding ticket. Soon afterward, Roosevelt caught polio, was paralyzed from the waist down, and never walked unaided again. Physical adversity strengthened him, teaching him patience, perseverance, and empathy. Retiring from political candidacy while striving to regain use of his legs, Roosevelt nominated his mentor, Al Smith, for president in 1924. Four years later Smith won the Democratic nomination, yet lost the election to a world-famous figure, Herbert Hoover. Roosevelt was elected governor of New York. After the stock market crashed in 1929, FDR practiced retrenchment and rejected federal aid. As the economy spiraled downward, however, Roosevelt developed a program that made New York one of the first states to provide public relief.

Following his election to the presidency in 1932, Roosevelt visited former Supreme Court Justice Oliver Wendell Holmes to celebrate the famed jurist's ninety-second birthday. "A second-class intellect. But a first-class temperament," Holmes declared of FDR. The assessment hit the mark. Roosevelt was not a deep thinker, although he had an above average mind, good judgment, and common sense. Although he had attended elite schools, he never immersed himself in government theory, preferring as president to surround himself with intellectuals and borrow ideas from them. Neither religious nor inquisitive about theological or philosophical questions, he possessed a sense of command that enabled him to deal on even terms with the world's best minds and most powerful leaders. He was confident, tough, and inspirational, eloquent in person and via radio. Roosevelt assembled a gallery of gifted speechwriters. The new president perceived the depression as a problem of morale, politics, and economics.

FDR had faced adversity before. "If you had spent two years in bed trying to wiggle your big toe, after that anything else would seem easy." His optimism inspired Winston Churchill to remark, "Meeting him is like opening a bottle of champagne." Roosevelt was an innovator and a pragmatist who relied on trial-and-error. He could boldly gamble, lose, and raise the stakes for the next hand. A man who had risen above a crippling disease was not easily intimidated; he only half-joked that if he was a pure guesser he would be right half the time. And the president was a man of action who enjoyed political battles and had huge Democratic majorities in Congress to work with.

Although he was born to an elitist family, had never experienced poverty and had no poor friends, Roosevelt connected with the indigent. In the Denver freight yards, a hobo scrawled in chalk, "Roosevelt is my friend." From his own class, the social stratum that produced plutocrats, Roosevelt elicited a different reaction, in which he was considered a dictator who was browbeating the country to ruin. He was no dictator, but a resourceful politician. His cabinet reflected all political views and regions and Roosevelt dominated it. Labor Secretary Frances Perkins became the first woman cabinet member. Outside the cabinet, FDR relied upon a group of intellectuals called the "Brains Trust."

THE SECRET
LIFE OF FDR
A rare photo of
Franklin D. Roosevelt
in a wheelchair.
(Franklin D. Roosevelt
Presidential Library)

The Hundred Days and the First New Deal

In his inaugural speech, FDR echoed Hoover's belief that the chief problem was psychological, predicting, "The only thing we have to fear is fear itself." He said he would not hesitate to use executive power to fight poverty—as if it were a military enemy. That evening, the new administration, with the aid of officials from Hoover's cabinet, worked late to address the banking crisis. Across the nation banks were shutting down while depositors lost their money. Hoover had sought from Roosevelt a joint resolution closing the banks but the incoming chief executive had declined. Now he had no choice. Twenty-two states had closed their banks. FDR declared a temporary banking holiday, during which Americans resorted to barter and credit. Instead of panic, there was relief.

To pass banking legislation, FDR summoned a special session of Congress. Roosevelt cracked the whip and Congress snapped to attention. Bills roared forth. The Emergency Banking Act passed the first day. Many of those who voted for it did not have the time to read it. The bill allowed for a federal audit of banks, classified them according to their stability, and permitted them to reopen on a phased-in basis; 75 percent were cleared to open on the first day. No one knew whether there would be a run on the banks when they reopened, yet before the reopening, Roosevelt delivered his first radio address, termed an informal "fireside chat," to persuade depositors the banks were safe. When the banks opened, $10 million more was deposited than withdrawn.

Roosevelt's next proposal, the Economy Bill, intended to help balance the federal budget by cutting government salaries by $100 million and veterans' pensions by $400 million, was unpopular. Later the president would be pushed, reluctantly, into deficit spending, which he considered a tool to be used only during economic decline. During his first term, however, he wanted to save money. Despite the opposition of most Democrats, who criticized the plan as deflationary, it passed because House Republicans favored it. Roosevelt also introduced a popular bill permitting the sale of beer and wine. Adopted swiftly, the Beer and Wine Revenue Act was an interim measure to legalize light alcohol while the states were ratifying the Twenty-First Amendment, approved by the previous Congress, to repeal the Eighteenth.

Roosevelt decided to use the momentum from his successes to keep legislators in Washington to deal with the depression. Lawmakers remained three months, a span known as the Hundred Days, the most productive New Deal session. With no program ready, FDR improvised. Asked to define his plans, he compared himself to a quarterback in a football game: the quarterback knows what the next play will be, yet beyond that, he cannot plan too rigidly because future plays will depend on how the next one works.

The New Deal orchestra sounded like a cacophony of contradictions. Indeed, it evolved without a grand design, precipitated by political necessity. Some programs were undermined by others. The ideological jumble did not bother Roosevelt. Congress complied, giving extraordinary authority on the chief executive and shifting the balance of power from the states to the federal government. Democratic majorities, coupled with divided Republicans who had no alternatives to FDR's bills, eased passage of the measures. Nevertheless, Congress shaped the president's program. Most bills did not emerge exactly as the administration drafted them, and some ideas originated in Congress.

One of the first bills Congress enacted addressed unemployment, the Civilian Conservation Corps (CCC), created to employ young men in semimilitary camps located in national forests and parks to plant trees, control erosion, and construct recreational facilities. By 1936 the CCC had employed some 1.6 million men. They planted more trees than had been planted in the entire previous history of the United States. Embraced by the public, the corps lasted until World War II. Also aimed at unemployment, the Federal Emergency Relief Administration (FERA) distributed money to cities and states to provide work.

Harry Hopkins, the FERA leader, helped persuade Roosevelt to implement a more ambitious policy to help the destitute through the harsh winter of 1933–1934. The New Deal created the Civil Works Administration (CWA), the first all-federal program focusing on job relief. Hopkins spent nearly $1 billion to employ 4 million workers before the CWA was terminated in the spring of 1934. The jobs included building and repairing roads, developing parks, digging sewers, and refurbishing neighborhoods. Given Hopkins's emphases on putting people to work and pumping spending power into the economy, some of the jobs amounted to no more than raking leaves, yet they provided income to those who performed them.

Whereas Hopkins's efforts were aimed at furnishing wages, the Home Owners Loan Act was intended to save homes from foreclosures. Commercial banks were allowed to use mortgages as collateral for government loans, effectively making the government the holder of the mortgages. The government had superior resources to individual banks and less urgency to foreclose. Banks and other businesses benefited from a revitalized Reconstruction Finance Corporation that distributed as much money as all of the work-relief programs.

Addressing the meager income of farmers—a primary cause of the depression, the Agricultural Adjustment Act (AAA) tried to adjust production to consumption. The AAA paid farmers to limit production in order to eliminate their surplus. Induced scarcity would raise prices. Money to pay farmers came from a tax on food processing. Because the agency was not organized until May 1933, after spring planting, about one-fourth of the cotton crop was plowed under and 6 million pigs were slaughtered before reaching maturity. A limited success, the AAA helped reduce deflation, yet it did not eliminate overproduction. Gross farm income rose from $4 billion in 1932 to $6 billion in 1936, but not until 1941 did income reach the 1929 level. Also, more cotton was produced in 1933 than in 1932, despite destruction of part of the crop; and higher domestic prices for cotton and wheat diminished the export market. Surpluses would have been greater if not for a severe drought in the South and West from 1932 to 1936, which dried out fields. The "Dust Bowl" destroyed crops and animals from Texas to the Dakotas. Thousands of farmers abandoned their land to seek work elsewhere, many in California. "Noon was like night," a train conductor said of the Dust Bowl. "There was no sun, and at times, it was impossible to see a yard." Dust blew as far east as the White House.

The AAA, which the Supreme Court declared unconstitutional in 1936, hurt sharecroppers and tenants because they saw nothing of the government checks that went to farmers who owned the land. Higher prices for crops pinched consumers, particularly those on fixed incomes. Because most farmers were in debt and had to borrow money to live until the next harvest, some hoped inflated dollars might relieve their hardship. Oklahoma Senator Elmer Thomas introduced an amendment to the AAA giving the president authority to provide inflation by coining silver, issuing paper currency, and devaluing the dollar. Roosevelt supported the amendment to avert more radical inflationary schemes, then used his authority to take the country off the gold standard.

The New Deal also helped rural people by creation of the Tennessee Valley Authority (TVA), an experiment to develop the Tennessee River basin in Tennessee, Alabama, Kentucky, and other states. Federal agencies implemented programs of flood control, soil conservation, tree planting, production of fertilizer and explosives, development of recreational facilities, and generation of electric power. The agency encountered opposition from businessmen, because the TVA competed with private utilities and used its cost of generating electricity as a yardstick to determine whether independent companies charged fair rates.

A plan to invigorate industry under the National Industrial Recovery Act (NIRA), the most complex legislation ever submitted, involved a government-business partnership. Again FDR embraced the scheme to avert a more radical remedy. Alabama Senator Hugo Black, for example, wanted to revive the economy by limiting the workweek to thirty hours without decreasing wages.

Based on the idea that ruthless competition was destructive, the law established a National Recovery Administration (NRA). Each industry drafted codes of fair competition, including maximum hours and minimum wages, elimination of duplication, and, in some cases, price fixing (the president could exempt industries from antitrust prosecution). Section 7(a) of the law ensured unions the right of collective bargaining but made no distinction between company unions and independent unions. Because the law provided no means of enforcing codes, the NRA director, General Hugh S. Johnson, resorted to social pressure, employing parades and mass rallies, publicizing the motto "We do our part" and featuring a blue eagle emblem for cooperating businesses. Patriotic consumers were supposed to patronize only businesses displaying the blue eagle. The reliance on voluntary compliance for the major New Deal program for business regulation was ironic, because Democrats (and, later, historians) criticized Hoover for relying on voluntarism.

The NRA had serious flaws. Small businesses had little voice in drafting codes, consumers had virtually no influence in determining prices, and micromanagement in the form of central planning was cumbersome. The NRA was a disappointment: production and employment increased at first, then declined, and national income for 1934 was down $10 billion from the previous year. The NRA was outlawed by the Supreme Court in 1936. Still, the NRA contributed to reform. It banned child labor, required collective bargaining, and established maximum hours and minimum wages.

The National Industrial Recovery Act created the Public Works Administration (PWA). With an initial appropriation of $3.3 billion, it was placed under the direction of Interior Secretary Harold Ickes, who was determined to prevent waste. Ickes's program employed skilled workers hired by private contractors and erected durable and colossal projects, including the Triborough Bridge in New York and the Grand Coulee Dam in Colorado. From 1933 to 1939 the PWA built 70 percent of the public schools, 65 percent of the courthouses and city halls, 35 percent of the hospitals, and two aircraft carriers. Fraud was absent.

Fearing public works did not infuse money into the economy rapidly enough, some of Roosevelt's advisers felt that manipulating the currency might achieve immediate results. By inflating the currency to produce cheaper dollars, they argued, the government could raise domestic prices and ease debts, and a weaker dollar would make American goods competitive abroad. One way to inject dollars into circulation was to pay more for gold than the market price. Thus, the government increased what it paid for gold daily, raising the price by random amounts to confuse speculators. Gold buying yielded neither recovery nor ruin, and in January 1934, Roosevelt ended it. Some New Dealers advocated the remonetization of silver over-valued it to stimulate inflation. Farmers, miners, and other inflationists rallied behind silver, and the administration agreed to test the idea. In December 1933, the government agreed to buy the entire domestic production of silver at 21 cents per ounce above the market value. In the next fifteen years the government spent $1.5 billion on silver, more than it spent to support farm prices. The program was lucrative for the silver industry, which employed fewer than five thousand people, yet silver inflation proved no panacea for the economy.

Recognizing the Great Depression as an international problem, businessmen looked to London's world economic conference in June and July 1933 for solutions. Roosevelt sent a delegation divided along ideological lines. Brains Truster Raymond Moley arranged a compromise on international currency stabilization, but FDR rejected the compromise. After wavering between the advice of nationalists and internationalists, Roosevelt sided with the nationalists. He feared international currency stabilization might jeopardize his efforts to raise domestic prices. Unwisely, he rejected a global approach to the worldwide depression.

In another search for answers, the Senate Banking and Currency Committee investigated abuses in banking and businesses that led to the crash. The inquiry led to reforms in banking and the sale of stocks and securities, including a second Glass-Steagall Banking Act in 1933. Separating investment from commercial banking to prevent bankers from speculating with depositors' money, the law also created the Federal Deposit Insurance Corporation (FDIC) to guarantee deposits of less than $5,000. Under the measure, fewer banks failed than in any year of the prosperous 1920s. Securities were the focus of a 1933 law, the Truth in Securities Act, requiring publication of data relevant to the sale of stocks and securities, and a 1934 measure, the Securities Exchange Act. The latter established the Securities and Exchange Commission to license stock exchanges and brokers.

Pressure for inflation resumed in 1934. In March, Congress restored the salary and pension cuts made in the Economy Act, overriding Roosevelt's veto. Three months later, lawmakers passed the Silver Purchase Act, ordering the Treasury to increase the silver supply until it reached one-third the value of the gold it held and to issue certificates redeemable in silver.

Despite its inconsistencies Americans approved of the New Deal in the 1934 congressional elections. For only the second time in history, the president's party increased its congressional majority in an off-year vote. More demoralizing to conservative Republicans, GOP members who backed the New Deal fared better than Republicans who opposed it. Still, the acceptance of the early New Deal owed more to Roosevelt's leadership than to its success in easing privation. The program realized its most critical short-term approval by energizing politics and raising morale. In the long term, the New Deal suggested new possibilities that touched every citizen.

The Second New Deal

By late 1934 it was apparent that neither the NRA nor the AAA had produced recovery, and that Roosevelt's program had lost momentum. Concluding that he had to reevaluate his approach, FDR reacted with a shift to the left that preempted radical critics. The importance of the bills passed in the spring and summer of 1935 led some historians to label the period "the Second New Deal." Resembling the First New Deal, it was based less on ideology than expedience. However, it veered from the centralizing aspects of the NRA to a more fragmented economy in which smaller businesses competed. Roosevelt declared war on monopoly and ear-marked aid to organized labor and farmers. Additionally, New Dealers recognized that unemployment was a long-range problem. The government should create additional jobs. Putting money into the hands of consumers was the most effective means of stimulating recovery. Unemployment insurance, retirement benefits, and support for collective bargaining, they argued, might mitigate the hardships of capitalism. Slum dwellers should be given the opportunity to reside in open spaces with clean air; farms should receive electricity.

In January 1935, Roosevelt asked Congress for $4 billion for work relief, the largest peacetime appropriation. With part of the money he created the Works Progress Administration (WPA), the centerpiece of job creation. Employment became a federal responsibility. Under Hopkins's direction, the WPA became the longest-lived New Deal agency. It lasted more than eight years; employed 8.5 million, chiefly unskilled workers—one-fifth of the workforce—paying wages higher than relief and lower than private wages. The WPA constructed 500,000 miles of highways, 100,000 public buildings, 8,000 parks, and thousands of irrigation ditches. It subsidized art, planted trees, strung rural electric lines, and prevented floods and erosion. Only a partial success despite these achievements, the WPA fell short of FDR's goal to provide every able-bodied unemployed person with a job. Still, it helped the economy grow and lifted gloom. Because the WPA did not use men and women under twenty-four, Eleanor Roosevelt advocated a program to keep young people in school and to teach them skills. Following her lead, Congress established the National Youth Administration (NYA), which hired 4.7 million part-time employees, increasing college enrollment, and keeping youths from competing with adults for jobs.

The WPA broke precedent by employing artists and humanists. Congress appropriated $27 million in 1935 to finance jobs in writing, music, the theater, and the visual arts. The Federal Writers Project employed about 6,500 at its peak in 1936 and aided promising novelists such as Conrad Aiken, Richard Wright, John Cheever, and Ralph Ellison. Fiction was too subjective and too controversial to subsidize, so the project used writers for tasks such as preparing guidebooks, taping oral histories, indexing newspapers, compiling inventories of historical records, and interviewing former slaves. This work bored creative writers, yet supported them while they wrote novels, poems, and plays during their free hours.

More than fifty thousand musicians were jobless. The Federal Music Project employed about fifteen thousand of them to perform and teach; they played in orchestras and bands and sang in choral groups in parks and schools, free of charge. By the time the project expired in 1939, 150 million Americans had heard 225,000 performances and 500,000 children had received free music lessons.

The most controversial venture was the Federal Theatre Project (FTP), under the direction of Hallie Flanagan, a Marxist playwright. Some performances were experimental; the Living Newspaper dramatized news stories, and Orson Welles produced *Macbeth* with an African American cast. The most ambitious production was a production of Sinclair Lewis's *It Can't Happen Here*, a story of fascism arising in America. Not all plays were ideological; the project staged *Cinderella*, Mark Twain stories, puppet shows, and Gilbert and Sullivan comic operas. Future stars such as Orson Welles, Burt Lancaster, and Arlene Francis appeared in FTP shows, aimed primarily at blue-collar audiences, staged in schools, public buildings, and CCC camps. By 1935, 12.5 million people had seen 924 government-sponsored plays, cheaply or free.

Some painters and sculptors, who could not earn a living because of a decline in demand for art, were hired by the Federal Arts Project. Among the 5,300 employed were easel painters and muralists. Artists painted 4,500 murals, more than 450,000 paintings, and made 19,000 sculptures. Like the FTP dramas, some art was critical of capitalism.

Federal subsidies had an impact on photography. Photographers documented the depression for the Farm Security Administration; they produced provocative work. Celebrated photographers, including Margaret Bourke-White, Dorothea Lange, Walker Evans, and Ben Shahn, photographed breadlines and Hoovervilles. Their work stood above the overall quality of WPA-financed art, which was mediocre. Employment, rather than quality, was the priority. Nevertheless, the WPA set a precedent for government aid to the arts.

Work for the Workers

Concern for workers led to the most enduring New Deal legacy: the Social Security Act of 1935, which established unemployment compensation, retirement pensions, and survivors' benefits. These were financed with taxes on employers and money withheld from employees' pay. Social Security laid a foundation for a federal social welfare system that would come after the New Deal.

The Resettlement Administration tried to transplant city dwellers and marginal farmers to suburban communities that blended the rural and urban lifestyles. Settlers were given tools, equipment, and training in subsistence agriculture. But the government resettled only 4,400 families.

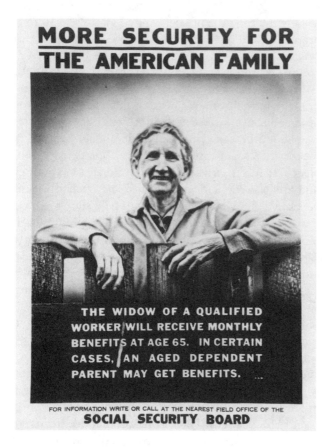

MORE SECURITY FOR THE AMERICAN FAMILY

THE WIDOW OF A QUALIFIED WORKER WILL RECEIVE MONTHLY BENEFITS AT AGE 65. IN CERTAIN CASES, AN AGED DEPENDENT PARENT MAY GET BENEFITS. ...

FOR INFORMATION WRITE OR CALL AT THE NEAREST FIELD OFFICE OF THE
SOCIAL SECURITY BOARD

A SAFETY NET FOR EVERYONE Americans learn about Social Security. (Franklin D. Roosevelt Presidential library)

"Greenbelt" towns proved so expensive that only three were built—near Washington, Milwaukee, and Cincinnati. In 1937 the Bankhead-Jones Farm Tenancy Act replaced the Resettlement Administration (FSA) with the Farm Security Administration, a source for low-interest loans that enabled tenants to purchase farmland.

Farmers also benefited from the Soil Conservation Service (SCS) and the Rural Electrification Administration (REA), both created in 1935. The former helped tame the dust storms by teaching farmers to control wind and water erosion. Commitment to soil conservation was strengthened in 1936 with the Soil Conservation and Domestic Allotment Act, adopted to replace the AAA after the Supreme Court nullified it. Under this law, farmers were paid to curb production of crops that depleted soil and to plant grasses and legumes that enriched land. Filling another need, the REA extended power lines to farmhouses where industry found it unprofitable.

When the program started in 1935, 90 percent of such families lacked electricity; by 1950, 90 percent had current.

The Public Utility Holding Company bill addressed the problem of monopolies. In 1932 the thirteen largest utility holding companies controlled 75 percent of the industry. The measure included a "death sentence" providing that any company that could not prove its usefulness to the public within five years would be dissolved. FDR's proposal aroused more antagonism from business than any previous New Deal measure.

The rich were angered by the Wealth Tax Act of 1935 that raised income, inheritance, and gift levies. Rates were increased on personal incomes above $50,000, peaking at 75 percent on incomes of more than $5 million, as well as on corporate incomes. Opponents condemned the statute as a scheme to win votes for Roosevelt from the envious masses. The legislation, paradoxically, raised little revenue and represented a deflationary strategy during economic contraction. Its chief impact was symbolic, allowing the president to portray himself as a champion of the poor and an enemy of the wealthy.

Roosevelt won political plaudits with the Banking Act and the Wagner Act. The first centralized the banking system and provided more government control, permitting the Federal Reserve Board to set discount rates and to determine the size of loans from federal banks. The Wagner Act encouraged labor's attempts to organize, outlawing some management practices, including company unions. It required employers to bargain with workers in good faith and created a strong National Labor Relations Board (NLRB) to oversee plant elections of bargaining agents and enforce labor laws. The Wagner Act was the most important pro-labor bill enacted.

Unionized labor increased its membership and organized new industries in the 1930s. A series of strikes erupted in 1934 by independent labor leaders demanding the right to represent workers. During the spring and summer strikes occurred among auto parts workers in Toledo, truck drivers in Minnesota, maritime laborers in San Francisco (escalating into a general strike), and textile workers in the South and New England. All but the textile workers won victories. The most significant transformation in organized labor, however, involved the American Federation of Labor (AFL), presumably outdated after the assembly line increased the demand for unskilled labor. Failure to organize the unskilled into unions that included all workers in a single industry ignited a rebellion against the AFL, led by John L. Lewis of the United Mine Workers (UMW). The AFL Council opposed industrial unions because organizing across work lines created jurisdictional disputes and dual unions. If workers in automobile plants, for example, were given the choice of joining a craft union or a union that included all auto workers, the competition might splinter the labor movement. Lewis countered that industrial unions were the only type practical in industries that made products such as autos, steel, and rubber. Industrial unions that combined under the Committee for Industrial Organization (CIO), which Lewis and his allies founded, would affiliate with the AFL, he promised. The council, claiming that the CIO violated the AFL constitution, ordered it to disband. After the CIO refused, the council expelled the ten CIO unions affiliated with the AFL in 1935. Three years later the CIO made the break final by transforming itself from a temporary committee into the Congress of Industrial Organizations.

The preeminent labor leader of the 1930s, Lewis began his organizing by forming the Steel Workers Organizing Committee, led by Philip Murray, the UMW vice president. In 1937 the Committee won a contract from the United States Steel Corporation that recognized it as the exclusive bargaining agent and provided a 10 percent wage increase, an easy victory over Big Steel. The smaller corporations, known collectively as Little Steel, resisted and the union struck, followed by months of industrial warfare. Roosevelt split with Lewis over tactics in the strike and condemned labor and management, calling for "a plague on both your houses." Eventually Little Steel capitulated after the NLRB ruled in favor of the union.

Automobile manufacturing was the largest unorganized industry. The CIO employed sit-down strikes for the first time to organize General Motors (GM). In sit-down strikes, the workers, instead of walking off the job, sat down at machines and refused to move, a tactic that prevented management from hiring strikebreakers—and provoked violent confrontations. Government officials, even those who sympathized with labor, doubted the legality of sit-down strikes because they might violate the right of private property. Sit-down strikers could halt production nationwide by seizing a key plant in an integrated industry. The United Automobile Workers (UAW), which shifted its affiliation from the AFL to the CIO in 1936, paralyzed the industry with a sit-down strike against GM at the Fisher Body plant in Flint, Michigan. Staying in the plant six weeks despite violence, the strikers helped win, in February 1937, concessions that gave the UAW an organizing monopoly for six months preceding an election (which the union won), and a 5 percent pay raise. The UAW also organized Chrysler after a sit-down strike. The Ford Motor Company proved more stubborn. Only after Henry Ford's wife threatened to leave him did Ford yield, approving a union contract that guaranteed the most generous terms in his industry. By the time of Pearl Harbor, the auto industry was unionized.

For all the gains labor made during the decade, there were setbacks. Organizing lagged in the South. The Supreme Court deprived unions of a weapon by ruling sit-down strikes illegal in 1939. The CIO, apparently dominant in the labor movement, had 71 percent of its membership in only six unions, and the largest pool of unorganized workers was among white-collar professionals, which favored the AFL. Some considered the CIO tainted because of its militant tactics and because communists had gained positions in the organization. Lewis was a villain to much of the public. In 1940 he vowed to destroy Roosevelt by endorsing his Republican foe, Wendell Willkie, pledging to resign as CIO president if FDR were reelected. When Roosevelt won, Lewis was forced out and Philip Murray succeeded him.

The Paradox of Minorities: Economic Help, Political Neglect

The New Deal ignited a revolution in the voting preferences of African Americans. Most of them backed the party of Abraham Lincoln until 1936, when they began to support Democrats. This trend continued for the rest of the century. For economic reasons, African Americans and other minorities became important allies of the New Deal. Not only did black people receive better jobs and housing through federal agencies than before, but they had advocates within the administration, including Harold Ickes, the interior secretary. A network of African Americans in government organized into a "Black Cabinet" under Mary McLeod Bethune, head of the NYA Division of Negro Affairs. Ickes had a firm ally in the first lady, teaming with her to arrange for the black singer Marian Anderson to perform at the Lincoln Memorial after she was barred from other Washington facilities. Eleanor Roosevelt made African Americans a priority, addressing interracial audiences, and inviting black entertainers to the White House.

Unlike his wife, FDR lacked African American friends and was not knowledgeable about their culture. Cautious, he paid little attention to the problems of black southerners because he feared alienating white southerners, especially members of Congress. The president appointed some advisers who were segregationists. In theory, the New Deal barred discrimination in its agencies, although it was practiced in some places. A bill to make lynching (murder by a mob, not limited to hanging) a federal crime, was introduced in the House and the Senate, only to be killed. FDR rejected his wife's pleas to back the legislation. Still, working-class African Americans, helped by jobs and relief, supported FDR despite his indifference to civil rights.

The legal system offered African Americans little hope, however, particularly in the South. A blatant injustice occurred after eight young black men were arrested in 1931 near Scottsboro, Alabama. Accused of raping

★ FATHER DIVINE:
"GOD, HARLEM, U.S.A." ★

Father Divine has not simply made God black; he has made a black man God—and
a humble American lynchable black man at that. [Marcus] Garvey had black devotees
to worship his black God; Divine has white men to bow to his deified Black Man.

—WILLIAM PICKENS, NAACP

HEAVEN'S GATE
Father Divine's Peace Mission, New York City.
(Library of Congress)

ARGUABLY THE most charismatic mass black leader of the Era of Trial and Triumph was George Baker, a minister who called himself Father Divine and who said he was God. Little is known about his early life, although it is clear that he was a sharecropper's son who grew up in the rural South during the last quarter of the nineteenth century. The early 1900s found him in Baltimore, where he preached part time in a Baptist church and joined another preacher in a church, which broke up after a few years. Back in the South, he gained adherents of his own, only to run afoul of the law in Valdosta, Georgia, over his divine claims. Accused of causing a public nuisance, Baker was named in a lawsuit as "John Doe, alias God," and was ordered to leave the state or go to a mental hospital.

Northward he went again, finally settling in Sayville, New York, around 1918, calling himself the Reverend Major J. Devine and, later, simply Father Divine (as his followers referred to him). He became leader of what became known as the Peace Mission movement. His religious communes attracted disciples of all colors who rejected government aid and often gave all their possessions to the movement. They abstained from alcohol, tobacco, and sex. The movement offered religious guidance, help in finding jobs, and meals free of charge to anyone. The Missions provided nourishment for the body and soul that was welcomed during the Great Depression. "Because your god would not feed the people, I came and am feeding them," Divine told a skeptical mission guest. "Because your god kept such as you segregated and discriminated, I came and am unifying all nations together. That is why I came, because I did not believe in your god." The crowds Divine attracted so disturbed authorities that he was once more accused of being a public disturbance, convicted, and sentenced to a brief jail term. Days after the sentencing in 1932, the judge died of a heart attack, which Divine's flock took as further evidence of their God's power. "I hated to do it," he said.

One year later, Divine moved the Peace Mission to Harlem, and the movement began to grow rapidly, ultimately encompassing almost two hundred major centers, or "Heavens," mainly in New York City and Philadelphia. A letter arrived at Divine's door addressed to "God, Harlem, U.S.A." Membership statistics were not kept, yet the rolls likely numbered thousands, among them many well-off, educated whites in addition to poor blacks, brought together to banish the prejudice that kept people apart. The effort earned praise from no less than W. E. B. Du Bois, who observed that the movement was "interracial among people of the laboring and middle-class." In a more dramatic defiance of racial convention, as well as a contradiction of his own pronouncements against marriage and sex, Divine wed a white woman who was fifty years younger than he, Edna Rose Ritchings, in 1946, after the death of his first wife, Pininnah. Ritchings, or "Sweet Angel," became Mother Divine, who would inherit the leadership of the movement. Their marriage was a spiritual union and a means for Peninnah to live on in a new body, Father Divine assured his flock.

Divine's public voice was largely silent late in his life, as he remained secluded on his estate in suburban Philadelphia. His commitment to racial harmony, nonetheless, remained unshakable. A few months before his death in his eighties, in 1965, he commended President Lyndon Johnson for a speech urging passage of the Voting Rights Act, writing to Johnson, "It is with profound gratitude that I have witnessed this great ship of state being steered into a new world of unity and dignity for all mankind." The ship has yet to dock in that world, though Divine did much to point the vessel toward it. A national reform leader courted by politicians, "he had greater success in lifting followers from poverty and in breaking down the color line, in white suburbs and black ghettoes, than any other religious leader of the day," historian Robert Weisbrot wrote.

Divine's life was an example of the work of the hereafter accomplished in the present. "I would not give five cents for a God who could not help me here on the Earth, for such a God is not a God at hand. He is only an imagination," Divine said. "It is a false delusion—trying to make you think you had just as well go ahead and suffer and be enslaved and be lynched and everything else here, and after a while you are going to Heaven someplace. If God cannot prepare Heaven here for you, you are not going anywhere."

Sources: Robert Weisbrot's biography is *Father Divine* (1983). Also see Kenneth E. Burnham, *God Comes to America: Father Divine and the Peace Mission Movement* (1979).

SENATOR HUEY LONG
Shown here addressing the students of Louisiana State University
in New Orleans on November 12, 1934.
(AP/Wide World Photos)

two white women on a freight train, though there was no physical evidence
of rape, an all-white jury convicted the "Scottsboro boys," and all but one
were sentenced to die. The Supreme Court overturned the verdicts and a
series of proceedings consumed eleven years and three more trials. The prejudice against the youths made their case notorious. The Communist Party
exploited the injustice to promote anticapitalist propaganda. Ultimately,
five defendants were convicted and sentenced to long terms. Charges
against the others were dropped.

Communists worked diligently during the 1930s to recruit southern
blacks, vowing to carve a black republic in the South. They did not gain
many converts, but added martyrs to their cause. Angelo Herndon, a young
black who became a recruiter for black labor unions in Birmingham,
Alabama, was arrested in Atlanta for his ties to the Communist Party. While
incarcerated, he was charged with inciting an insurrection. Convicted in
1933 and sentenced to twenty years of hard labor, Herndon failed at several
appeals until the Supreme Court overturned the verdict in 1937. Communists'
attempts to use the Herndon and Scottsboro injustices were reprimanded

by W.E.B. Du Bois, who wrote of the Scottsboro tragedy, "American Negroes do not propose to be the shock troops of the Communist Revolution, driven out in front to death, cruelty and humiliation in order to win victories for white workers." Du Bois became alienated and controversial in the 1930s, resigning as editor of *Crisis* after quarreling with NAACP Executive Secretary Walter White, who advocated racial equality through integration. Du Bois himself argued for cultural and economic segregation. Late in the decade Du Bois became an apologist for Soviet and Japanese aggression, approving of the Hitler-Stalin Pact of 1939.

American Indians suffered during the depression as much as any minority group, but the Roosevelt administration produced an Indian New Deal led by John Collier, who had worked for improved conditions for Indians as commissioner of Indian affairs. Collier pumped federal funds into reservations to build schools, hospitals, and irrigation systems, improving tribal life and offering employment. The reforms also included the Indian Reorganization Act of 1934, intended to stop the sale of tribal lands to individuals and to return to Indians some control over their lives. Seventy-five percent of tribes voted to organize self-governing councils under the law, which slowed forced assimilation into white society. The measure also made the interior secretary the final authority over Indian affairs, a stipulation that harmed Indian interests when the sympathetic Ickes retired.

The prominence of Jews among New Dealers angered anti-Semites, whose hatred peaked during the 1930s. Gerald L. K. Smith, Elizabeth Dilling, Father Charles E. Coughlin, and other bigots blamed Jews for the depression, claimed Roosevelt was a Jew, denounced the "Jew Deal," and spread rumors of Jewish plots to control the world. Henry Ford lent his credibility to anti-Semitism, publishing anti-Jewish articles in his weekly newspaper, the Dearborn Independent. Organizations such as the Ku Klux Klan and pro-German groups proposed a solution to the "Jewish problem" in the United States that involved deporting or exterminating Jews. Jewish organizations, meanwhile, contributed to philanthropy, worked for racial justice, and for a foreign policy that would punish dictators.

Among Hispanics, immigration declined because of the depression; in fact, during the 1930s more Mexican Americans returned to Mexico than entered the United States. Most left for economic reasons. Hispanics learned that their language was a barrier to finding work, and most were limited to menial labor in city barrios or as migrant fruit and vegetable pickers. Hispanics rarely voted, so politicians ignored their interests.

The condition of the Japanese in America deteriorated in the 1930s. Those native to Japan clung to traditional ways, although their offspring, the Nisei, were inclined to adopt American culture. Many educated Japanese

Americans experienced job discrimination, as Japanese militarism rose in the Far East. Chinese Americans, too, suffered from economic hardship. Yet white Americans viewed them as intelligent and admired their ability to survive destitution, to save, and to refuse government relief. They perceived the Chinese as victims of Japanese aggression and as potential allies in hostilities against Japan. Still, the Chinese could not become naturalized citizens until 1943.

In the workforce, the proportion of women increased marginally, from 24.3 percent in 1930 to 25.4 percent in 1940. Thirteen to 19 percent of WPA employees were women, most engaged in sewing, and eight thousand women worked in CCC camps, compared with 2.5 million men. Twenty percent of white women and 40 percent of black women worked outside the home, most due to economic necessity. Many African Americans were domestic servants; others were agricultural laborers. Some men resented the competition of women for scarce jobs, and 82 percent of men and women in a 1936 Gallup poll believed that wives should not work if their husbands had a job. Of professional women, three-quarters were teachers or nurses. Positions for female teachers, musicians, and doctors declined. Law and medical schools imposed quotas that restricted female students.

Women were prominent in the fight for racial equality. Lillian Smith and Paula Snelling, editors of literary journals, urged fellow southerners to cease using derogatory terms for blacks. Likewise, women admired Eleanor Roosevelt and played an active role in New Deal politics. Under the New Deal, more women were appointed to political jobs than in any previous administration, including the first woman cabinet member, ambassador, and appeals judge.

Opponents of the New Deal

As an advocate of gradual transformation, Roosevelt sought change to defend American values and institutions. "Reform if you would preserve," counseled FDR. Those who wanted radical change, and those who wanted no change at all, condemned him. Alone, none of these dissenters were formidable; in a disciplined coalition they might have posed a threat. Because they rejected the New Deal for different reasons, however, a coalition was unlikely. Foes on the Far Right believed that Roosevelt was part of a conspiracy of Jews, blacks, communists, and unions whose aim was to make the president world dictator, eradicate Christianity, and enshrine communism. The wealthy considered him a traitor to his class. On the Left, leaders such as the socialist Norman Thomas accused FDR of being a fascist.

Some of the opposition was personal. Roosevelt was accused of insanity, alcoholism, and of having contracted syphilis. Rumors circulated that

Idaho Senator William Borah found the president cutting out paper dolls in the White House study. It was also rumored that maniacal laughter could be heard in the mansion and that Roosevelt's friends kept him in a straitjacket and put bars on the windows to prevent him from leaping out. Some argued that because his legs were disabled, the president's mind must be diabolical, a punishment from God. FDR was even accused of kidnapping the Lindbergh baby.

The main foe of the New Deal, the Republican Party, remained weak. The GOP was blamed for the depression and lacked competitive candidates to challenge Roosevelt. But foes of FDR found kindred minds in organizations created to battle the New Deal. The best known of these groups, the American Liberty League, included conservative businessmen but also former Democratic presidential nominees John W. Davis and Al Smith. Its membership peaked at 125,000 in 1936.

Communism, romanticized by a number of intellectuals as the wave of the future, should have grown in the United States during the depression, seemingly the fulfillment of Karl Marx's prophecy of the collapse of capitalism. Yet Communist Party membership grew slowly; not until 1938 did it surpass 60,000, its level in 1919. Communists denounced New Dealers as social fascists whose policies of limited reform would postpone a workers' revolution. This idea changed in 1935, however, at the direction of the Soviet Union. Deciding that fascism posed a greater danger than liberalism, the Soviet Party ordered its satellites to cooperate with liberal reformers in popular fronts. American communists worked to reelect Roosevelt in 1936. Under popular fronts, the Communist Party grew to almost 100,000 members in 1939. Then the Soviets twice ordered their parties in other countries to change course—in favor of an alliance with Germany in 1939, when the U.S.S.R. signed a treaty with Adolf Hitler, and against it in 1941, when the Fuhrer invaded the Soviet Union. The revelation that the party in the United States was a Kremlin puppet destroyed its credibility, and after 1939 it was never a mass movement.

Demagogues who promoted prescriptions for the economy represented the most serious challenge to the New Deal, none bigger than Louisiana senator Huey P. Long, the sole dissenter who was a professional politician with popular appeal. "There is no rule so sure as the one that the same mill that grinds out fortunes above a certain size at the top grinds out paupers at the bottom," said Long. His solution was to confiscate millionaires' property and redistribute it. Long wanted the government to take all yearly income above $1 million and all wealth in excess of $5 million, then use it to give every family a home, car, and radio, valuables worth at least $5,000. The Louisiana senator, known as "the Kingfish," would guarantee a yearly income of at least

$2,500, old age pensions, a veterans bonus, public works, and free college educations. Though unworkable, the plan appealed to the poor. In 1934 Long organized a Share-Our-Wealth Society to publicize the scheme and hired Gerald L. K. Smith to promote the group nationwide. A more bombastic orator than Long, the minister was so successful that the organization had two hundred thousand adherents within a month, 3 million by the end of 1934, and 7.5 million by February 1935. Long hoped to launch a third-party candidacy for president in 1936, with the potential to win 11 percent of the vote, according to a poll Roosevelt commissioned. The Louisianan might decoy enough liberals' votes from FDR to elect a Republican, setting the stage for the Kingfish to win in 1940. Long was charismatic, had a genius-level IQ, and was a mesmerizing orator who spoke in the idiom of the common man. Possibly bipolar, he was gifted with enormous energy, a disarming sense of humor, and confidence verging on megalomania. He was single-minded, imaginative, and his energy fueled limitless ambition.

Yet Long and his Louisiana machine were vulnerable. Federal investigations discovered graft and tax evasion. Before federal officials could get to Long, an assassin's bullet beat them. Wounded by a gunman on September 8, 1935, the Kingfish died two days later, due in part to bungled surgery. On the state level, Long is remembered as one of the most powerful political bosses ever to dominate an American state. At the national level, the Kingfish is the subject of speculation about what he might have become.

Before Long's death, some journalists warned that he might consummate an alliance with Father Charles E. Coughlin, a Catholic priest in suburban Detroit who broadcast radio sermons about religion and politics. Coughlin became so popular that by 1932 he was addressing the largest audience in the world and receiving $500,000 per year in donations via mail. Turning from theology to politics, Coughlin supported Roosevelt in 1932, broke with him by late 1934, and founded a weekly newspaper. Less effective in advancing practical solutions than scapegoating, the priest identified an alleged conspiracy of Jews, bankers, FDR, and communists who had plotted the depression, as a prelude to world takeover. His feud with FDR intensified when the administration revealed that Coughlin had used listeners' donations to speculate in silver.

An unlikely ally of the demagogues of the depression, retired California physician Francis E. Townsend proposed a plan to give people over sixty a pension of $200 a month, on the conditions that they retire and spend each check before receiving the next one. In 1934 he and a friend founded a national organization that enlisted 10 million members within a year. The Townsend plan was introduced in Congress, where it was bluntly dismissed. Still, Townsend attracted the attention of Smith, who had left Louisiana after Long's death in search of another cause. Smith elbowed his way into the Townsend movement, trying to merge it with the Long and Coughlin organizations, and used his oratory to captivate Townsend's older audiences.

Trial and Triumph for Roosevelt

Roosevelt declared war on big business during the 1936 campaign, blaming greedy capitalists, in tandem with Hoover, for the economic calamity. He launched the first antitrust prosecution of his administration. Congress passed a windfall profits tax and a law to protect small businesses from chain store competition.

At the Democratic convention in Philadelphia, after Roosevelt and John Nance Garner were renominated by acclamation, Roosevelt summed up his crusade and contrasted his humane experimentation with the alleged indifferences of Hoover's administration. "Governments can err. Presidents do make mistakes, but the immortal Dante tells us that divine justice weighs the sins of the cold blooded and the sins of the warm-hearted in different scales." FDR challenged the nation to meet the tests that it faced, referring to the depression, but, ironically, more appropriate to a war he did not know was coming. "There is a mysterious cycle in human events. To some generations much is given. Of other generations much is expected. This generation has a rendezvous with destiny."

The Republicans nominated Kansas Governor Alfred M. Landon for president and Chicago newspaper publisher Frank Knox for vice president. Simple, homespun, Landon was a moderate who favored New Deal relief and public works but denounced the bureaucracy, deficit spending, and Roosevelt's domination of Congress. Landon was barely known outside the Midwest, faced a popular incumbent who controlled patronage, and lacked an attractive alternative to the New Deal. An ineffectual campaigner, Landon gave speeches that included trivialities such as, "Everywhere I have gone in this country, I have found Americans."

The Communists nominated Earl Browder, who knew he had no chance of winning and wanted Roosevelt reelected. Calling other minority candidates stooges for Landon, Browder asked Communists to vote for FDR in states where the Communist ticket was not on the ballot. The Socialists nominated Norman Thomas, who assailed both the Communists and the president. Coughlin, Townsend, and Gerald L. K. Smith formed the Union Party and picked North Dakota Congressman William Lemke as its standard-bearer. The three demagogues, though, were more interested in their own programs than in electing Lemke. Coughlin seldom mentioned Lemke in his speeches. Townsend told his followers to vote for Landon where Lemke was not on the ballot. Lemke and Townsend condemned Gerald Smith as a fascist and broke with him a few weeks before the election.

In the most one-sided voting since 1820, the Democratic ticket won 60.7 percent of the popular vote, a share that would stand as a record for twenty-eight years, and 523 electoral votes to eight for the GOP. (Lemke polled 882,000 votes, Thomas 190,000, and Browder 80,000.) Roosevelt's party devastated the Republicans in congressional races, winding up with three-quarters of the House and almost four-fifths of the Senate. Economic issues dominated and the Democrats became the majority party.

The Supreme Court proved a more difficult obstacle for Roosevelt. Divided ideologically, with four conservatives, three liberals, and two moderates, the Court had knocked the props from under the New Deal in 1935 and 1936, nullifying the NIRA, the AAA, and a New York State minimum wage law. New Deal legislation, the justices ruled, granted excessive power to the chief executive, preempted states' rights by extension of the interstate commerce clause, and intruded in areas in which it had no regulatory authorization. Fearing that the Wagner Act and the Social Security Act would be overturned for similar reasons, Roosevelt condemned the Court for ruling on the wisdom of reform legislation rather than its constitutionality.

Without consulting Congress or his cabinet, FDR—who did not have the chance to appoint a justice in his first term—drew up a bill that would enable him to appoint enough justices to ensure a liberal majority. Introduced in February 1937, the measure authorized the president to appoint a justice whenever any justice with at least ten years of service did not retire within six months after turning seventy. Roosevelt said his objective was to inject youthful vigor into the legal system and allow it to dispose of cases promptly. His real purpose, as everyone knew, was to transform the Court, six of whose nine members were older than seventy, into a rubber stamp for the administration.

A firestorm of opposition ignited. Liberals and conservatives worried that Roosevelt's proposal would endanger the balance of power in the federal government. Even those who agreed with Roosevelt's goals disagreed with his methods and ridiculed the hypocrisy behind his public aim of making the judiciary more efficient. The Court counterattacked. Chief Justice Charles Evans Hughes predicted that more justices would require more conferences and discussions, prolonging hearings. Then the Court upheld a Washington State minimum wage law, the Wagner Act, and the Social Security Act—decisions called "the switch in time that saved nine." Also, conservative Justice Willis Van Devanter announced his retirement, convincing members of Congress that court-packing was unnecessary. Six months after his proposal was introduced, Roosevelt settled on a compromise that streamlined the judiciary without giving him additional appointments. And in the end he got his liberal court; vacancies permitted him to appoint seven justices in five years. The appointees included Hugo Black and William O. Douglas, who had long, distinguished tenures.

Roosevelt liked to say that he won the battle of wills with the court, if not with Congress, by intimidating the justices into sanctioning the constitutionality of the Second New Deal. If so, it came at the price of FDR acting like the village bully. Probably it was Roosevelt's awesome victory in the 1936 election, not the court-packing bill, that prodded the court to change direction. The defeat of his plan was the sharpest congressional rebuke Roosevelt suffered.

Economic decline followed the setback on court–packing. Concerned about the deficit, particularly the costs of the WPA and the PWA, Roosevelt slashed spending in the summer of 1937. He cut WPA employment by 59 percent and ordered Ickes to phase out the PWA. The economy slowed by August, unemployment rose by nearly 2 million people from September to December, and another 1 million people lost their jobs by Christmas. National income began to fall at nearly $800 million per month, steel production declined by three-fourths, and factory production sank to 1933 levels. By 1938 there were nearly as many unemployed as there were under Hoover—one of the great paradoxes of the New Deal, largely overlooked.

Roosevelt summoned a special session of Congress in November 1937, but it adjourned without enacting his recommendations. Ickes, Hopkins, and Perkins urged the administration to resume spending, and Roosevelt consulted with the British economist John Maynard Keynes, a leading advocate of deficit spending, who remarked afterward, "I don't think your president knows anything about economics." Roosevelt was unwilling to spend at the levels that Keynes proposed, yet in April 1938 he proposed a $3 billion package that Congress approved. The economy recovered by the summer of 1939.

Roosevelt never accepted a defeat without retaliating, a trait that belied his genial public persona. Livid when some senators deserted him during the court-packing debate, he stopped the flow of patronage to several conservatives, reasoned that only liberals would be faithful allies, and decided to transform the Democrats into the party of liberalism. In 1938 primary elections he campaigned against some conservative candidates of his own party in a fruitless effort. In November, Republicans made their first gains of the New Deal era, winning seventy-five House seats, seven Senate seats, and thirteen governorships. Democrats retained comfortable majorities in Congress, however, and even though conservatives could be effective in opposition, they could not enact a program. The result was a standoff that practically ended the New Deal.

Congress, nevertheless, approved a few important economic measures during Roosevelt's second term. In addition to the Bankhead-Jones Farm

Tenancy Act in 1937, there was the National Housing Act, which provided $500 million for public housing projects and clearing urban slums. The next year produced a more limited AAA and a Fair Labor Standards Act. The agriculture law, directed toward the continued farm surpluses and low prices, created procedures for curbing production of basic crops and allowed the government to extend loans to farmers and store their surpluses in warehouses until they could repay the loans and market their crops profitably. The labor act required a minimum hourly wage, a forty-hour workweek, and prohibition of child labor.

An Assessment of the New Deal

Debate over the New Deal long outlived Roosevelt. Leftists argued that it was too cautious and did not reach out to minorities. From the Right, writers criticized it for aggrandizing federal power and for introducing welfare dependency, a monstrous bureaucracy, and bloated deficits. To be sure, the New Deal failed to end the depression: it would take wartime spending to finish the job of recovery. More reasonably, the New Deal battled the Great Depression to a standstill.

Still, the quantity and quality of New Deal legislation are impressive, and it arrested the decline and brought hope to the masses. Roosevelt, by his activism, his oratory, and his optimistic personality, lifted the spirits of a nation whose problems were both economic and psychological. The president tapped the imaginations of brilliant academicians and intellectuals. Following his uncannily accurate intuition, he became perhaps the greatest party leader in American history. His New Deal was an improvement over the single-interest presidencies of the 1920s, paying attention to underrepresented groups and guaranteeing Americans a minimum of sustenance; and when recovery finally arrived, it can be argued, it was better based because of Roosevelt's contributions in the 1930s. Except for his affliction with polio, he led a charmed life, bold, fearless, nearly invulnerable in politics.

Roosevelt built a potent Democratic coalition of groups that supported the party though the end of the century. He established a clear ideological division between Democrats and Republicans, making his party the advocate of the "forgotten man." He and Eleanor Roosevelt, who set standards for activism by a first lady, were a synergism. During the Era of Trial and Triumph, the United States was fortunate to have them at the helm. Historians and public opinion polls of the twenty-first century continue to rank Franklin D. Roosevelt among the nation's three greatest presidents, in the company of George Washington and Abraham Lincoln.

CHAPTER TEN

Culture: Revolt and Retreat

PARADOXICALLY, THE culture between the wars complemented the sizzle of prosperity and vented depression angst. Whether dancing to an upbeat tempo or soothing the beast of adversity, in the Era of Trial and Triumph the arts carried a message—a critical one, necessary for the nation's equilibrium. In the 1920s the arts dazzled; in the 1930s they helped provide a psychological safety net; in the 1940s they praised ammunition, the Almighty, and peace.

The 1920s and the 1930s

A nation of affluence and abundant leisure, the United States became the entertainment capital of the world in the 1920s. Industrial jobs aggravated nervousness, created a demand for amusements to fill time, and made Americans willing to pay billions to avoid boredom. The resulting popular culture homogenized a people once sharply defined by regional traits. Now, Americans listened to the same songs and news, danced the same dances, watched the same stars in movies and sports, read the same books, and practiced the same fads.

The 1920s, moreover, were a time of American adolescence, of cultural testing and innovation. When the decade ended, the United States and the rebels of the decade had grown up, sober and resigned. Like everyone who looks back at adolescence, the revolutionaries did so with regret, because the period had its wasted opportunities and dissipated energies; but they also looked back wistfully, as the decade had been enjoyable and they could not have matured without it. Part of the magic of youth is paradoxical— the failure to recognize its joys before they pass into memory.

In the depression—burdened 1930s, writers, artists, musicians, and actors—many of them unemployed—were in a struggle to survive amid adversity. Having fought for individualism in the 1920s, they changed course, experimenting with collectivism. Disillusionment with capitalism and sympathy with Marxism permeated their community. Once neglected, common people were portrayed as heroes. As the economy rebounded, the popularity of Marxism waned.

"The Lost Generation"

In the 1920s the insatiable curiosity about Charles Lindbergh illustrated to the public's craving for heroes. Mass-market writing provided an escape from urbanization and industrialization. Few people read serious books. The best-selling writers were Geneva "Gene" Stratton-Porter, Harold Bell Wright, Zane Grey, and Edgar Rice Burroughs. Stratton-Porter emphasized optimism, love of nature, victory over adversity, and nostalgia. Rivaling her as a dispenser of optimism, Wright sold an average of 750,000 copies of each of his first twelve books. Grey, author of more than fifty Western novels that glorified self-reliance, sold 20 million books during the decade. Burroughs wrote more than forty novels, most about Tarzan's African adventures, reviving the frontier spirit.

The masses devoured periodicals such as newspapers, whose ownership was concentrated in chains, the largest belonging to William Randolph Hearst. Daily newspapers declined from 16,944 in 1914 to 10,176 in 1929, but total circulation increased. Tabloids that sensationalized news multiplied and passed older, traditional dailies in sales. Magazine reading increased, with publications that appealed to families having large circulations, among them the *Saturday Evening Post, Ladies' Home Journal,* and *Literary Digest.* Magazine advertising was so lucrative that an issue of the *Post* included one hundred pages of ads. Short-story magazines specialized in sports, romance, mysteries, and "true confessions." The prolific and acerbic journalist H. L. Mencken was an elitist and a conservative in politics, if not culture. The American people, he wrote, "constitute the most timorous, sniveling, poltroonish, ignominious mob of serfs and goosesteppers ever gathered under one flag since the end of the Middle Ages." Asked to explain why he lived in a country he criticized and satirized, he replied, "Why do men go to zoos?"

In the 1930s and 1940s, a generation in a hurry read more magazines than books, especially family-oriented periodicals with fiction that reinforced traditional values. Magazines and newspapers reflected the growing importance of political stories. The Washington press corps doubled, and foreign correspondents reported on the rise of European dictators. Political columnists Walter Lippmann, Arthur Krock, and Mark Sullivan were widely read, but so were humor writer Will Rogers, etiquette specialist Emily Post, and gossip columnist Walter Winchell.

In one of the paradoxes of the century, American literature and art in the 1920s enjoyed their greatest flowering since the mid-nineteenth century. The blooming was unexpected, as if someone intending to compose a grocery list ended up writing the great American novel. Americans who were ashamed of their literature at the decade's dawn could boast of it after 1929.

The artistic geniuses of this decade enlisted on the side of modernism against Victorian values. Because Victorian self-control was repressive, they strived to liberate spontaneity; modernists sought to inject passion into art. The best writers of the 1920s, called "the Lost Generation," rebelled against American society, against Puritanism, and against small towns. Historically original, members of the Lost Generation were frank, experimental, and daring. Seeking self-fulfillment, living for the moment, many of these marvelously naughty and incredibly witty authors were obsessed with sex. Some were unhappy, growing cynical before ceasing to be naive, drowning in drink or escaping in suicide. They fled the Midwest, seemingly a bland region that produced great writers, for Greenwich Village, Paris, Italy, and England, only to discover in their native land the themes they sought.

The representative figure of the decade and of the Lost Generation was F. Scott Fitzgerald, who amused, tantalized, and taunted with the brilliance of an exploding star. He broke through with *This Side of Paradise* (1920), an autobiographical book that described the collegiate experience in terms that appalled moralists and delighted young people. No mere chronicler of youthful rebellion, Fitzgerald and his wife, Zelda Sayre, lived it. Once Sayre called in a false fire alarm at a swank hotel; when firefighters arrived and asked about the source of the blaze, she pointed to her breasts and said, "Here!" Her spouse wrote one of the most enduring novels of American literature, *The Great Gatsby* (1925), the story of a poor man who lost a rich woman, became a wealthy bootlegger, and tried to win her again. Fame, however, did not bring contentment to Fitzgerald and Sayre. They burned themselves out in an endless round of parties. He became an alcoholic, and his productivity waned, while she suffered a nervous breakdown. Fitzgerald became a Hollywood screenwriter and died of a heart attack in 1940, at forty-four.

The most emulated writer was Ernest Hemingway, who joined the colony of expatriate American writers in Paris, the setting for his first novel, noteworthy, *The Sun also Rises* (1926). He developed a lean, spare style, used few adjectives, and let the dialogue carry the story. Tough and realistic, Hemingway dealt with love, death, and stoicism in the face of tragedy. He was less productive after the 1920s, but *To Have and Have Not* (1937)

F. SCOTT FITZGERALD
1937. Photograph by
Carl Van Vechten.
(Library of Congress)

sold briskly, and *For Whom the Bell Tolls* (1940), set amid the Spanish Civil War, was an artistic success. Bipolar, he won the Nobel Prize for literature in 1954, seven years before taking his life.

Sinclair Lewis wrote merciless satires about the village (*Main Street*, 1920), the businessman (*Babbitt*, 1922), medical science (*Arrowsmith*, 1925), religious fundamentalism (*Elmer Gantry*, 1927), and politics (*The Man Who Knew Coolidge*, 1928). In 1930, the Nobel Prize committee made him the first American to win their honor for literature. Following his productive period in the 1920s, Lewis grew concerned by European fascists and American demagogues such as Huey Long and Father Charles E. Coughlin, anxiety that shaped the plot of *It Can't Happen Here* (1935). The title is ironic because in the novel fascism comes to the United States, under a totalitarian president who is toppled in a coup. By the conclusion, America is fighting a second civil war.

John Dos Passos, another social critic, established his reputation with *Three Soldiers* (1921) and *Manhattan Transfer* (1925), disdaining conventional capitalization and punctuation. Dos Passos raged against materialism in the 1930s and fed the revolutionary fervor of the depression era, until his faith in Marxism waned and he turned to conservative themes. Aspiring to write an autobiography of the United States in the twentieth century, he produced the most ambitious literary project of his generation, *U.S.A.*, a trilogy collected in 1938 after publication of the separate books *The 42nd Parallel* (1930), *1919* (1932), and *The Big Money* (1936).

Thomas Wolfe won fame with publication of *Look Homeward, Angel* in 1929. Perfecting the genre of autobiographical fiction, he sparkled briefly but brightly, writing three more novels, two issued posthumously. William Faulkner ranked Wolfe first among the writers of his generation. Some critics disagreed, placing Faulkner at the top. Setting his best fiction in Mississippi, his birthplace, Faulkner employed the stream-of-consciousness technique better than any American writer, shifting perspectives, mixing chronology, weaving bewilderingly complicated plots. Faulkner won the Nobel Prize in 1950, but his most productive period ran from the mid-1920s to the mid-1930s, during which he wrote *The Sound and the Fury* (1929), *As I Lay Dying* (1930), and *Absalom, Absalom!* (1936).

Although not comparable with Faulkner individually, southern writers known as the Fugitives, or the Agrarians, collectively exerted important influence. As students and teachers at Vanderbilt University, they founded a poetry magazine, *The Fugitive*, which published complex poems characterized by precise language. Later they addressed regional themes, publishing essays, novels, short stories, critical studies, and epic poems. In 1930 their group inspired *I'll Take My Stand*, a defense of southern agrarian culture. Another southerner, Ellen Glasgow, reached her apogee in the 1920s. In Dorinda Oakley, the protagonist of *Barren Ground* (1925), Glasgow created the most sharply crafted female character of the decade. Other women writers, including Willa Cather and Edith Wharton continued to write prolifically in the 1920s, having launched their careers in the previous decade.

Just as literature flourished among white southerners, it prospered in Harlem. The 1920s saw the Harlem Renaissance, when African American writers developed African themes. Protest and alienation inspired this renaissance. A participant in this ferment, critic Alain Locke, called the movement "a spiritual coming of age" that allowed the "New Negro" to change "social disillusionment to race pride." Versatile, the renaissance fostered jazz and blues, particularly at the Cotton Club, where musician Duke Ellington performed and Ethel Waters sang. James Weldon Johnson, successful as a high school principal, civil rights activist, consular official, and Tin Pan Alley songwriter, published a novel, a book of poetry, and a social history. Langston Hughes wrote poems, plays, fiction and nonfiction. African American culture blossomed in the works of Claude McKay,

Countee Cullen, W.E.B. Du Bois, Zora Neale Hunston, and Jean Toomer. In Harlem, where cafes, speakeasies, lounges, rib joints, and supper clubs catered to a largely white clientele, white and black people mingled. On Broadway, more than twenty black musicals opened from 1922 to 1929, singer Paul Robeson thrilled audiences, and Eugene O'Neill wrote plays about black themes.

Considered the greatest American dramatist, O'Neill won four Pulitzers and a Nobel Prize. From 1919 to 1934, he wrote twenty-five plays, almost two per year, opening four in 1924. Among his 1920s plays were *Anna Christie* (1921); *All God's Chillun Got Wings* (1924), about interracial marriage; and *Desire under the Elms* (1924). O'Neill's explorations of the dark side of the human psyche contrasted with the majority of popular plays, light musical comedies.

American poetry attracted serious attention between the wars. T. S. Eliot and Ezra Pound, still living in Europe, wrote intricate, pessimistic poetry that became staples of college anthologies and drew admiration from the elite. Hart Crane wrote the greatest epic poem with an American theme, *The Bridge* (1930), which used the Brooklyn Bridge as a metaphor for the United States. Edna St. Vincent Millay wrote the most-quoted verse of the decade, a stanza from the first poem in *A Few Figs from Thistles* (1920):

> *My candle burns at both ends,*
> *It will not last the night;*
> *But ah, my foes, and oh, my friends—*
> *It gives a lovely light.*

Millay won the Pulitzer in 1923 for her collection *The Harp-Weaver and Other Poems*. Another important poet, Marianne Moore, wrote of commonplace topics such as animals, baseball, and art objects in descriptive verse that incorporated quotations. Her poems were overlooked in her, but she contributed to contemporary directions in American literature as a key critic and editor of the literary magazine *Dial*.

The Proletariat as Protagonist

The proletarian novel, concerned with the struggles of the laborer, developed during the 1930s. Tough-minded realism characterized the works, with profanity, violence, and sex animating the plots. Most of these novels were ephemeral because they were morals with stories rather than stories with morals, although some were great, lasting efforts. The most influen-

FLEEING THE DUST BOWL
Dust storm in Cimarron County, Oklahoma, 1936. Scenes like these
served as the inspiration for John Steinbeck's *Grapes of Wrath*.
(Franklin D. Roosevelt Presidential Library)

tial proletarian writer, John Steinbeck, set his best novels in the West, depicting migrant workers, ranch hands, and union organizers. Steinbeck's greatest work, *The Grapes of Wrath* (1939), described the migration of an Oklahoma farm family from the Dust Bowl to the fields of California. Other writers produced just a handful of works apiece, yet proved popular and enduring. Among them were Katherine Anne Porter, known for her exquisitely crafted short stories, and Nobel Prize winning Pearl Buck, whose novel *The Good Earth* (1931), set in China, was a best seller. Margaret Mitchell published her only novel, *Gone with the Wind*, in 1936 after ten years of writing. This epic of the Civil War and Reconstruction in Georgia sold 1 million copies in six months and became the most successful motion picture of the time.

Dramatists shared some of the sociopolitical tendencies of novelists, seeing the masses as prey of capitalist oppression. Most in tune with the radical tenor of the times, Clifford Odets wrote *Waiting for Lefty* (1935), the biggest hit of the decade. Audiences responded enthusiastically to the drama, based on a New York taxicab strike. Lillian Hellman was also a political leftist, but her plays did not reflect proletarian themes. Her first hit, *The Children's Hour* (1934), concerned false allegations of a lesbian relationship between two teachers at a boarding school; her second, *The Little Foxes* (1939), depicted a turn-of-the-century Southern family weakened by greed. Robert Sherwood, a speechwriter for President Franklin D. Roosevelt as well as a successful playwright, was another exception to the proletarian influence. He won Pulitzer Prizes for his plays, including *Abe Lincoln in Illinois* (1938) and the book *Roosevelt and Hopkins: An Intimate Story* (1948). Other hits included George Gershwin's *Porgy and Bess* (1935), Moss Hart's and George S. Kaufman's *You Can't Take It with You* (1936), and Thornton Wilder's *Our Town* (1938).

During World War II, authors profited from the largest mass market for books in U.S. history. The number of volumes published nearly doubled, and book sales increased more than 20 percent yearly. Bibles and dictionaries were in such demand that they had to be rationed. Writers were less alienated than in the 1920s and 1930s and more willing to explore themes of sentimentality, nostalgia, and religion. A dissenter was Richard Wright, who joined the Communist Party and established himself as the major black writer of the period with *Native Son* (1940), the story of a Chicago black man who accidentally killed his white employer's daughter. In 1945 Wright published the autobiographical *Black Boy*, expressing his rage at racism. Coming to believe that Communists exploited blacks for political purposes, he broke with the party in 1944.

Contrasting with Wright's passion, nonfiction grew more conservative. In 1943 Ayn Rand published *The Fountainhead*, which praised individualism over collectivism, sold steadily during and after the war, including millions of paperbacks. The favorite book of conservatives was *The Road to Serfdom* (1944), by an expatriate Austrian economist, Friedrich Hayek, who argued that modern liberalism was the path to tyranny. National planning would fail in the Soviet Union and the United States, he predicted.

Wartime produced few remarkable plays, although Arthur Miller and Tennessee Williams established themselves as top dramatists. Williams's *The Glass Menagerie* was produced on Broadway in 1944. Several successful musicals debuted during the war. Irving Berlin wrote the score for the popular *This Is the Army* (1942), and Richard Rodgers and Oscar Hammerstein II wrote *Oklahoma!* (1943), which played for more than 2,200 performances.

A BREAKTHROUGH ARTIST AND ENTERTAINER
Jazz musician Louis Armstrong.
(Library of Congress)

"All That Jazz"

Some of the most memorable popular music in U.S. history was first heard in the 1920s. The most important, jazz, was America's original contribution to music. Rooted in the blues, a genre that working-class African Americans created, jazz was born in New Orleans among black musicians who entertained in the opulent houses of prostitution. When the United States entered World War I, the War Department closed the district because New Orleans was a port of debarkation for troops. The musicians migrated to St. Louis, Chicago, New York, and the West Coast, where they played a music that was cathartic, a rebuttal to conformity and convention. Originally unwritten and improvised, yet intricate and sophisticated, emphasizing beat and accent rather than melody, jazz was designed to be listened and danced to, an urban art that thrived in crowded places. It was, a journalist wrote, "a perfect expression of the American city, with its restless bustle and motion, its multitude of unrelated details, and its underlying rhythmic progress toward a vague somewhere."

Early pioneers included Joe "King" Oliver, Ferdinand "Jelly Roll" Morton, and two men who became the leading jazz artists, Louis Armstrong and Duke Ellington. A pianist, bandleader, and prolific composer whose popularity soared in the 1920s, Ellington ranked as one of the greatest American musical geniuses. Another key figure, Paul Whiteman, was not Ellington's equal musically, but his more structured big-band music helped ensure the popularity of jazz among white people.

Because jazz was the "tom-tom of revolt," in Langston Hughes's term, traditionalists disliked it. Of the genre that a writer scorned as "music in the nude," one professor argued, "If we permit our boys and girls to be exposed indefinitely to this pernicious influence, the harm that will result may tear to pieces our whole social fabric." Perhaps the nation was beyond hope. One clergyman claimed that "in 1921–1922 jazz had caused the downfall of 1,000 girls in Chicago alone." Another foe complained that jazz had corrupted 70 percent of the women who became prostitutes in New York.

Popular melodic music concentrated in Tin Pan Alley, dominated by Irving Berlin. Among other talented composers were George Gershwin, whose "Rhapsody in Blue" was the most celebrated song of the 1920s, and Cole Porter. Bringing the composers' works to life was the job of singers including Rudy Vallee, whose soft crooning was the antithesis of jazz, and Al Jolson, whose life paralleled the role he played in the movie *The Jazz Singer* (1927). His father, a rabbi, wanted him to become a cantor, but Jolson turned to popular music and made more hit records than any singer of his time, popularizing "My Mammy," "April Showers," and "California Here I Come."

The 1920s were a boom time for Broadway musicals, giving rise to more than four hundred, twice as many as would open in the next decade. Jerome Kern was an accomplished composer and a pioneer in modernizing the musical theater. In addition to writing ten complete musicals, he scored *Show Boat*, the first musical in which music, dialogue, and dance were integral to the plot—previously a simplistic device used to introduce songs. Kern's lyricist was Oscar Hammerstein, one of the greatest songwriters of his era, who later collaborated with Richard Rodgers. The writer of fifteen scores for Broadway and London shows from 1925 to 1930, Rodgers worked with Lorenz Hart before joining Hammerstein. Musical comedies yielded hit songs, as did musical revues such as the *Ziegfeld Follies*.

When Americans were not watching musicals, whistling Tin Pan Alley tunes, or listening to jazz, they were likely to be dancing, performing steps as frenetic and uninhibited as the music of the 1920s. The first dance craze, which the voluptuous actress Mae West popularized, was the shimmy. The dancer stood in one place and, with little movement of the feet, shook the shoulders, torso, and pelvis. The shimmy gave way to the Charleston, a creation of black stevedores who worked in the harbor of Charleston, South Carolina, and moved north to take industrial jobs during World War I. Featuring rapid foot movements and relying on the hit song of the same name for its popularity, the Charleston receded in favor of the Black Bottom. The title referred to the muddy bottom of the Suwannee River because the dance suggested the dragging of feet through mud. More sedate, ballroom remained popular, and Arthur Murray earned millions teaching couples to dance.

Like jazz, dance critics warned of its effects on the social order. Clergy deplored the exhibitionism of the Charleston, saying it was sending people to hell. Some cities passed laws to inhibit dancers. A Cleveland ordinance stated, "Don't dance from the waist up; dance from the waist down." A law in Oshkosh, Wisconsin, must have been difficult to enforce, as it prohibited partners from "looking into each other's eyes while dancing." Some did carry dancing too far, participating in dance marathons, exhausting themselves and risking their health to win small prizes.

The marathons were one of the fads of the era. A classic paradox, a fad was an activity that began as a statement of noncomformity and became something that many people did. In 1923 the Chinese game of Mah-Jongg became a national craze, only to be supplanted one year later by a craze for crossword puzzles. The most exotic fad began in 1925, when Alvin "Shipwreck" Kelly became famous for flagpole sitting. On his perch, he slept with his thumbs anchored into a wooden seat and, during a sleet storm, used a hatchet to chip ice from his body. A young woman who became enamored of Kelly was hoisted up to meet him, and when he descended, they were married. In the depression decade of the 1930s, the times favored Monopoly, a board game that encouraged players to drive their rivals into bankruptcy, parodying the 1920s monopolies that facilitated the crash.

The 1930s music benefited from improvements in recording technology; sound movies, which made musicals possible, and the dissemination of songs via jukeboxes, and radio. Popular music never had a larger audience, a boon to leading composers, among them Irving Berlin, George and Ira Gershwin, Jerome Kern, Cole Porter, and Hoagy Carmichael, who extended their repertoire by writing Hollywood scores. When it came to performing, swing was king during the big band era. Although swing was rooted in black jazz styles, white bandleaders such as Tommy Dorsey, Artie Shaw, and Glenn Miller came to dominate it. Meanwhile, Bing Crosby, Frank Sinatra, and Billie Holiday crooned in a conversational manner.

During wartime, songs reflected the national mood about America's enemies. Some were bellicose or racist, including "You're a Sap, Mr. Jap," "We're Gonna Find a Feller Who is Yeller and Beat Him Red, White, and Blue,"

DANCE TO THE MUSIC
Dancing in a Harlem nightclub, late 1930s.
(Bettmann/Corbis)

"In the Fuehrer's Face," and "Praise the Lord and Pass the Ammunition."
Country music, too, began to boom, encouraged by feelings of nostalgia
for less complicated times and the mass migration of rural southerners to
the industrial centers of the North and the West.

The Radio

Without radio, jazz might not have spread beyond New Orleans, and the
denizens of Tin Pan Alley might have been limited to selling sheet music.
Initial broadcasts were confined to ships and the military, and people bought
radios as a novelty. The industry, consisting of one commercial radio station
in 1921, grew to thirty the next year, and exploded to 556 in 1923. The
Radio Corporation of America, which built the first station to promote the
sale of radios, organized the first network, the National Broadcasting
Company (NBC), in 1926. The Columbia Broadcasting System (CBS) followed in 1927, the Mutual Broadcasting System in 1934, and the American
Broadcasting Company (ABC) in 1943. Music dominated the airwaves,
although programs began to vary. In 1920 presidential election returns were

broadcast, and eight years later, candidates used radio to campaign. In 1921 the World Series was broadcast, pioneering coverage of sports. Soon there were comedy shows starring such performers as comedians Jack Benny and Fred Allen, dramatic programs such as *Buck Rogers* and *The Lone Ranger*, variety shows, soap operas, and quiz contests.

Sales of radios increased from $12.2 million in 1921 to $168.2 million in 1925 and $366 million in 1929. Almost half of American families owned radios by 1930, and there were more receiving sets in the United States than in all other countries combined. Advertisers recognized the potential of the medium, and by 1928 Henry Ford was paying $1,000 a minute for a chain of stations to advertise his cars. At first stations were so few they could broadcast ads at any frequency without overlapping. But as stations multiplied, Commerce Secretary Herbert Hoover negotiated voluntary agreements for transmission at different frequencies. In 1927 the Radio Act formalized federal oversight over broadcasting and created the Federal Radio Commission to license stations. The Federal Communications Commission assumed regulatory responsibilities in 1934.

Radio became pervasive in the 1930s. In 1929 there were 10,250,000 household radios in the United States, whereas by 1940 there were 28,040,000, and about 80 percent of all Americans had access to a radio. Technical aspects of broadcasting improved; radios became smaller; radios were installed in cars; and stations proliferated. Music dominated radio's menu. Politicians relied on broadcasts to promote themselves, most conspicuously President Franklin D. Roosevelt with his fireside chats. The volume of news programs doubled between 1932 and 1939.

Radio occupied a central role in family life. Daytime shows included soap operas, cooking shows, and programs on raising children. The evening offered heroes such as *Superman* and *Tarzan*; and quiz shows such as *Information Please*. Comedy fare included George Burns and Gracie Allen, and ventriloquist Edgar Bergen and his dummy, Charlie McCarthy. The most popular show was *Amos 'n' Andy*, on the air from 1928 to 1960. It was the creation of white comedians Freeman Gosden, who played Amos, and Charles Correll, who played Andy. First set in Chicago, then in Harlem, the show derived its humor from the misadventures of the owners of a taxi company with one cab.

Radio's credibility and power were so great that when Orson Welles broadcast H. G. Wells's "War of the Worlds" on Halloween eve in 1938, thousands fled their homes, thinking that stations were reporting an actual Martian invasion of Earth. A Pittsburgh man found his wife in their bathroom holding a bottle of poison and screaming, "I'd rather die this way than like that!"

Silence to Sound on Screen

For most of the 1920s, movie actors lacked the voices of their radio counterparts. When film producers realized there was a market for longer films, the silent industry expanded. There were twenty thousand theaters in the United States in 1920, when movies were the fifth-largest business, and some twenty-eight thousand in 1928. Among them were palaces such as the Roxy in New York, which seated 6,200, had 125 ushers, and boasted a 110-member orchestra. Attending the theater involved a full evening, beginning with a newsreel, followed by a short comedy, previews, an episode in a serial, and the feature presentation. By the mid-1920s major studios, notably Metro-Goldwyn-Mayer, Warner Brothers, Columbia, RKO, and United Artists, were churning out enough films to enable theater owners to change their offerings every other day.

If the early industry excelled in one genre, it was comedy, whose craftsmen raised pantomime to a level that has not been matched. Producer Mack Sennett assembled the finest stable of comedic talent in Hollywood history, and his Keystone Kops films elevated slapstick to an art. Other leading comedians were Harold Lloyd, Buster Keaton, W. C. Fields, and the team of Stan Laurel and Oliver Hardy. With brilliant producers and directors including D. W. Griffith and Cecil B. DeMille, the young industry continued to explore the genres of Westerns, love stories, and biblical epics. Early in the 1920s producers discovered that sex sold tickets, and roles went to sex symbols. Movies were given suggestive titles: *Married Flirts, Sinners in Silk, Rouged Lips,* and *The Queen of Sin.* The advertisement for *Flaming Youth* beckoned people to see "neckers, petters, white kisses, red kisses, pleasure-mad daughters, sensation-craving mothers, by an author who didn't dare sign his name; the truth, bold, naked, sensational." Worried about its image and fearing censorship, the industry hired Will Hays, President Warren G. Harding's postmaster general, to create and enforce a code assuring that movies had a moral ending and that on-screen sex and violence were limited.

The silent screen era started to ebb in 1926, when Warner Brothers introduced sound, first in several short films, then in *The Jazz Singer.* The first commercially successful movie with sound, it was more a "singie" than a "talkie," having six songs that Jolson lip-synched, only about five hundred spoken words, and subtitles for most of the dialogue. Despite its modest advances, *The Jazz Singer* inaugurated a trend, and before the decade was over, the silent picture was an anachronism.

Furnishing escape from the depression, movies became so important that families skimped on necessities to attend; seeing films was the most frequent dating activity. After a decline in movie attendance starting in 1929, theaters began cutting prices, and by 1933 attendance revived and stayed high the rest of the decade. Hollywood met the demand by turning out a large volume of cheap films, including gangster movies in the early 1930s. Gangsters were shown as financial successes, but morality required that they be killed at the end.

Among comedians, the greatest were the Marx brothers, who combined slapstick with puns. The brothers made five films from 1929 to 1933, including *Animal Crackers*, Paramount's most lucrative motion picture of 1930. W. C. Fields's persona was a braggart who drank excessively and hated children. Sometimes he was paired with the funny and seductive Mae West, who launched a genre of films about sexually aggressive women, one of which had her say, "When a girl goes wrong, men go right after her." West advanced the century's sexual revolution. Inspiring laughter, Frank Capra directed "screwball" comedies from 1931 to 1941. The most famous was *It Happened One Night* (1934), a romance starring Clark Gable and Claudette Colbert. Gable was one of the leading box-office attractions of the 1930s, thanks to his role in *Gone with the Wind* (1939). Following the movie, Gable was asked how it felt to be considered the world's greatest lover. "It's a living," he replied. Besides Gable, the motion picture industry was enriched by Walt Disney, who made the animated cartoon a fine art. Child star Shirley Temple was the top box office draw from 1935 to 1938 and the model for a line of dolls, clothes, and books. The era included musicals whose quality has never been surpassed, many of them starring Fred Astaire and Ginger Rogers.

During World War II, musicals, war films, spy films, and movies about resistance to Nazism were popular. Several classic movies appeared early in the 1940s: *The Grapes of Wrath* and *The Great Dictator* (both 1940), the latter an antifascist comedy in which Charlie Chaplin parodied Adolf Hitler. Other important films included the influential *Citizen Kane* (1941), featuring Welles as director and lead character, a newspaper publisher based on William Randolph Hearst; and *Casablanca* (1942) starring Humphrey Bogart. Alfred Hitchcock, the wizard of suspense and macabre humor, became the best-known director in the United States.

Visions of America

Visual art held up mirrors to the nation. During the decade of plenty a galaxy of art museums opened, among them the Museum of Modern Art in New York in 1929. Artists demanded high prices for their work, which was experimental and increasingly concerned with urban life. Joseph Stella found New York a rich environment, painting *Brooklyn Bridge* (1922) and a series entitled *New York Interpreted* that featured innovative use of light and shadow. Edward Hopper specialized in bleak city images—a lonely diner in an all-night restaurant, a tired usher in an empty movie theater—that elaborated on ideas the Ash Can school explored. Many realists, though, focused on the nation's rural and small town heritage and were dubbed Regionalists. Thomas Hart Benton, Grant Wood, and John Stuart Curry received popular and critical applause for painting the Midwest. The most enduring Regionalist image, Wood's *American Gothic* (1930), portrays a stern, pious farm couple symbolizing the stark Midwest.

Representative art remained popular with the public, but the avant garde was dominated by abstract styles pioneered in Europe. Modernist painters distorted reality, sometimes breaking it into cubes and triangles creating visual dissonance. Even artists who retained a regional emphasis began to revolt against the representational tradition. Georgia O'Keeffe, for instance, interpreted Western deserts by enlarging details so that objects lost their recognizable quality. Modernism in art existed during the 1920s in a symbiotic yet angry relationship with industrialization. The style was a paradox: progressive in an artistic sense, it was reactionary in its resistance to technological advancement, depicting machines that the artists considered dehumanizing. Modernist techniques and nonrepresentational experiments also influenced sculpture, but the public continued to prefer conventional forms. Gutzon Borglum carved busts into the sides of mountains in Georgia and South Dakota, Confederate army heroes in the former and presidents George Washington, Abraham Lincoln, Thomas Jefferson, and Theodore Roosevelt in the latter, at Mount Rushmore.

Like literature, painting was critical of capitalism in the 1930s. A furor arose when Diego Rivera, whom Nelson Rockefeller had paid $14,000 to paint a mural in Rockefeller Center, depicted V. I. Lenin scowling as American police beat strikers. Rockefeller fired Rivera and had the scene painted over. Other muralists depicted proletarian themes, and abstract art was enlisted in the struggle against capitalism. Then, in the World War II era, prosperity came to artists, whose sales soared, never to reach 1945 levels until 1960. Europeans driven from their native lands by the war, among them Marc Chagall, Salvador Dali, and Max Ernst, enriched American painting.

Photography continued its progress as a new art form in the 1930s and 1940s, finding markets in mass-circulation magazines. Architects found that work was plentiful in the 1940s, entire cities springing up around war plants. Walter Gropius and Ludwig Mies van der Rohe brought formal, structured, coherent theories of architecture to America after fleeing Europe. Frank Lloyd Wright, enjoying a revival in popularity, claimed that the box was the shape of fascism and disliked the coldness of much modern architecture. He endowed simple structures with warmth.

Education and the Intellectuals

The new art had a large audience of educated Americans. High school enrollment increased from 2.4 million to 4.2 million in the 1920s. When the decade started, there were more illiterates than college graduates, but the illiteracy rate dropped from 6 percent to 4.3 percent by 1930—from 23 percent to 16 percent among African Americans. Small schools were consolidated, allowing teachers to specialize, and they taught more vocational subjects and less Latin and Greek. Over the decade, college enrollment rose from 598,000 (4.7 percent of the college-age population) to 1,101,000 (7.2 percent, of which 43.7 percent were women), and the number of Ph.D.s awarded increased from 560 in 1920 to 2,071 in 1930. Many college students were preoccupied with extracurricular activities and were poorly informed; some freshmen at the University of Maine thought Martin Luther was the son of Moses, whom they described as a Roman emperor. College teaching became more professionalized, and the pressure to publish increased.

Veterans of academe, Frederick Jackson Turner and Charles A. Beard, remained among the outstanding historians in the decade, joined by Vernon Parrington, Carl Becker, and Arthur M. Schlesinger. Parrington was an obscure scholar until the first two volumes of his three-volume work *Main Currents in American Thought* appeared in 1927. He described the development of the idea of democracy in the lives and work of intellectuals from 1620 to the late nineteenth century. Becker challenged the belief that historians could write objectively about the past when present-day values shaped their assessments. Objectivity was an ideal for writers such as Schlesinger, whose chief contribution was to coedit the thirteen-volume *History of American Life*.

Beard became interested in historical relativism in the 1930s and concluded that objectivity was an illusion, arguing that a historian must begin research with a viewpoint. Most of his writing was devoted to keeping the United States out of war. Historians' social visions were not entirely liberal; William A. Dunning, Ulrich B. Phillips, William Dodd, and Frank Owsley focused on slavery, the Civil War, and Reconstruction from a prosouthern perspective. Professional historians and their debates, however, mattered little to lay readers, who were a market for popular history. Frederick Lewis Allen sold more than 1 million copies of his chronicle of the 1920s, *Only Yesterday* (1931). Douglas Southall Freeman and Allan Nevins, meticulous researchers and eloquent writers, captured broad audiences. Public attention was drawn to historic preservation.

In anthropology, Margaret Mead began fieldwork in the South Pacific in 1925 and published *Coming of Age in Samoa,* a milestone in the comparative study of cultures, three years later. Also pathbreaking, Robert and Helen Lynd produced the sociological study *Middletown* (1929), an examination of Muncie, Indiana, that provided a wealth of information on attitudes and lifestyles.

Refuge in Religion

Millions of Americans looked to religion for comfort during the depression. Attendance at fundamentalist churches rose fifty percent, whereas attendance at mainline Protestant churches declined 11 percent. Overall, religion lost ground to secularism during the Era of Trial and Triumph and did not regain it until World War II.

Catholics were enthusiastic about the New Deal, about 80 percent of them supporting the Roosevelt administration. Some thought the New Deal implemented the program that Pope Pius XI outlined in *Quadragesimo Anno* (1931), an encyclical that condemned laissez-faire capitalism, rejected unregulated competition, and insisted upon a living wage for workers and a new partnership between labor and capital. FDR appointed more Catholics than any previous president.

Many Protestant ministers were reformers; the most prominent was Reinhold Niebuhr, who revived interest in theology by making it relevant to contemporary life. Critical of both capitalism and Marxism, he argued that humanity could never achieve utopia because solutions to earthly problems were ephemeral. Still, people were obliged to strive for social justice. More optimistic, Norman Vincent Peale, the leading Protestant popularizer, promoted positive thinking, advising "You can if you think you can." Jews joined Protestants and Catholics in backing the New Deal, whose circle included young Jews such as Treasury Secretary Henry Morgenthau and Supreme Court Justice Felix Frankfurter.

The depression made it economically difficult for couples to marry. Weddings were postponed, and the average age at marriage was the oldest since before the turn of the century (26.7 years for men, 23.3 for women). Birth control was increasingly practiced. Women who married and had children compensated for declining family income by canning, baking, laundering, and sewing at home.

Sports: Cheering and Playing

Families could enjoy spectator sports, which basked in a golden age in the 1920s. Urban Americans no longer had the opportunity to participate in many sports, but they had the time to watch. Sports benefited from better equipment and places to play, radio broadcasts, and the demand for heroes. Sports appealed to fans largely because it was one of the last refuges of individualism and pure competition in an automated society.

Baseball was the most popular professional sport. By 1924, 27 million people were watching games, and attendance doubled from 1921 to 1930. Great players lured fans, none more than George Herman "Babe" Ruth. He specialized in the home run, which appeared more frequently in the 1920s, due to a livelier ball and rule changes. Ruth had excessive appetites for food, drink, sex, and gambling and, at 6 feet 2 inches and 215 pounds with a beer belly and spindly legs, did not look like an athlete. Still, he was good enough to break in as a pitcher with the Boston Red Sox and was moved to the outfield so he could bat daily. In 1920 the cash-strapped Red Sox sold Ruth to the New York Yankees, whom he helped set an attendance record in his first season. "The Sultan of Swat" and the Yankees enjoyed a spectacular season in 1927, when Ruth hit sixty home runs, a mark that would stand for thirty-four years, and led a powerful "Murderer's Row" lineup to the World Series championship.

The Yankees continued their dominance in the 1930s. Their first baseman and captain, Lou Gehrig, set a record by playing in 2,130 consecutive games and faced death with courage after contracting a fatal muscular disease. Late in the decade, Yankees centerfielder Joe DiMaggio, a star at the plate, in the field, and on the bases, started a memorable career. World War II sent more than four thousand players into the armed services, including Red Sox slugger Ted Williams. Women tried to fill the wartime void, and carve out a larger place for themselves in sports, by playing in their own professional baseball league.

Challenging baseball for fan loyalty, football was the centerpiece of college social life and attracted alumni donations and national name recognition. Yale, Stanford, Michigan, and Illinois built huge stadiums. Illinois had the best attraction, halfback Harold "Red" Grange, the "Galloping Ghost." In the first game in the new Illinois stadium in 1924, he returned "the opening kickoff ninety-five yards for a touchdown. Grange ran for four other touchdowns—three in the first quarter—completed several long passes, and gained 402 yards in total offense. On the sidelines, Knute Rockne of Notre Dame was a legendary coach. Unselfishness, teamwork, and dedication—values that Americans sensed were fading—characterized Rockne's teams, which won with speed, deception, cleverness, and finesse instead of brute force. Rockne was among the first coaches to use the forward pass and the single-wing formation, which made football more offense oriented.

Wartime brought fears of a Japanese attack, so the Rose Bowl was moved east from Pasadena, California, to Durham, North Carolina, for 1942. Professional football continued on a reduced scale; players who were not drafted worked in defense plants and played on weekends. College basketball lost fewer players because many were too tall for the military. An influx of tall centers early in the 1940s led to rules to limit the dominance of big players.

Perhaps the single greatest professional sporting event of the Era of Trial and Triumph was the rematch between boxers Jack Dempsey and Gene Tunney in 1927. Their first fight in 1926, in which Dempsey lost his heavyweight title, grossed $1.9 million. The next grossed $2.5 million, the two largest purses ever. Some 60 million people listened to the rematch on radio, the biggest radio audience for any event. In the seventh round Dempsey knocked Tunney down, but the referee delayed the count until Dempsey moved to a neutral corner, giving Tunney time to recover. Tunney knocked Dempsey down in the next round and, as his adversary tired, battered Dempsey and won a unanimous decision. In ath-

HEAVYWEIGHT CHAMPION
Boxer Joe Louis wins respect for African Americans. Photograph by Carl Van Vechten. (Library of Congress)

letics as in technology, raw power was yielding to technique, and future champions would emulate the faster, more sophisticated Tunney.

In golf, amateur Bobby Jones was the biggest star. Jones won the U.S. Amateur championship five times, the U.S. Open four times, and the British Open three times in the 1920s. Tennis was dominated by William "Big Bill" Tilden, who won the U.S. title in 1920 and went unbeaten from 1921 to 1928. Among women, Helen Wills, won three U.S. singles championships and eight Wimbledon singles titles. Swimming had stars in Johnny Weismuller, who set world records, then played Tarzan in the movies, and Gertrude Ederle. A gold medal winner in the 1924 Olympics at seventeen, Ederle became the first woman to swim the English Channel, beating the times of five men who had managed the feat, in 1926, when she held eighteen world records.

Sports was an avenue of achievement for minorities. African Americans, shut out of major league baseball late in the 1880s, formed Negro Leagues that remained popular through World War II and featured players whose greatness was recognized decades later. Rarely admitted into other professional sports, African Americans made strides, particularly in boxing, in which Joe Louis had a long reign as heavyweight champion. They starred in football, basketball, and track and field. In the 1932 Los Angeles Summer Olympic Games, Eddie Tolan and Ralph Metcalfe finished first and second, respectively, in the 100-meter dash; Tolan also won the 200-meter dash, making the sprints a sweep for the United States. Four years later at the Berlin Summer Games, Jesse Owens won the 100- and 200-meter dashes and the long jump, and anchored the winning 400-meter relay team.

Women's athletics was dominated by Mildred "Babe" Didrikson Zaharias, the greatest female athlete of all time and the most versatile athlete of either sex. In the 1932 Amateur Athletic Union national track meet, she won five events, tied for first in a sixth, and finished fourth in a seventh, single-handedly winning the team championship. In the 1936 Olympics, she won gold medals in the javelin and high hurdles and the silver medal in the high jump. Turning professional, Zaharias pitched for a women's baseball team; taking up golf, she was the top women's player in the 1940s. Not only did she run and jump, but she swam, shot at targets, rode horses, boxed, and excelled at tennis, basketball, polo, and billiards. Asked whether there was anything she did not play, she replied, "Yeah, dolls."

Riven with paradox, cultural transformation coexisted with prosperity, depression, and war. The land that produced unemployed millions, also produced millions who persevered. There burst forth from a seedbed of geniuses a blossoming of Americans who entertained, inspired, and awed with their passion, imagination, agility, and intellectual virtuosity.

CHAPTER ELEVEN

Interwar Diplomacy

T HE INTERWAR era represented more trials than triumphs for American diplomacy and culminated in the greatest military conflagration of the century. Disillusioned after World War I and the failed Versailles peacemaking, Americans viewed European affairs like a child burned by touching a hot pan. They did not want to touch it again. Paradoxically, it touched them.

Nonintervention and Internationalism

The 1920s and 1930s have been termed a period of isolationism, or, more accurately, noninterventionism for American diplomacy. Americans conducted more world trade than ever, consummated a significant naval reduction treaty, and traveled abroad. American culture was influential worldwide, as were missionaries for Christianity. Some Americans were proud of their country's relative military isolation, or nonintervention, and determined to preserve it. Among them were such notables as William E. Borah of Idaho, chair of the Senate Foreign Relations Committee; William Randolph Hearst, the leading newspaper publisher; Robert McCormick, publisher of the *Chicago Tribune*, the largest midwestern daily; and Henry Ford.

The key to the American mind-set, however, was nationalism, as it was to many European countries and Japan. Ethnic minorities struggled to form nations and took pride in their heritage. In some European nations, nationalism was coupled with colonialism. Others, such as Germany and Italy, envied the greater colonial holdings of the British and the French. In the Soviet Union Stalin formally theoretically eschewed nationalism in his effort to build a classless world order, yet proved no different than the other colonial powers when his interests were at stake. Washington's international emphasis was on stability rather than democracy or economic equality worldwide.

The chief goal of American internationalists, like their counterparts, the isolationists, was to preserve world peace, a goal they shared with pacifists. They differed over how to achieve this goal. Internationalists believed collective solutions to wars could preempt them. Noninterventionists held that if wars erupted, the United States should remain above the fray. Pacifists did not believe in fighting, period. Yet Americans were major players on the world scene. By 1919, a debtor nation just five years before, the United States was a creditor. American technology in consumer products seized world leadership. Still, many Americans believed that Europeans constantly connived to involve them in another war. Presidents and secretaries of states reacted to events. President Warren Harding, ignorant of world affairs, told journalist Theodore Draper, "I don't know anything about European stuff." He delegated authority to Secretary of State Charles Evans Hughes. President Calvin Coolidge was not interested in foreign policy. President Herbert Hoover, in his career as a mining engineer, had lived and traveled abroad more than any twentieth-century president.

The United States technically remained at war with Germany, a consequence of not approving the Versailles Treaty, until Congress adopted a joint resolution ending hostilities and Harding signed it on July 2, 1921. Membership in the League of Nations continued unrealized, as Harding, Coolidge, and Hoover never advocated it. They favored American membership in the World Court, yet the 1926 congressional vote endorsing membership had reservations that were unacceptable to the other members, and Coolidge dropped the matter. The presidents continued Woodrow Wilson's policy of refusing to recognize the Soviet Union. Trade was not restrained, however. By 1928, one-fourth of all foreign investment there was American; one-third of all Ford-exported tractors went to the Soviets. In 1929 Ford agreed to help Soviets build cars and trucks. As commerce secretary, Hoover coordinated public and private relief efforts that sent $78 million worth of food to the famine-stricken Soviets and saved 10 million from starvation.

Postwar Payback: Debts and Reparations

During and after World War I the United States, with money from war bond sales at home, lent about $10.5 billion to the Allies and other European nations. Europeans argued that Washington should erase their debts because America had suffered neither the casualties nor the property damage they incurred. The United States from 1923 to 1930 renegotiated interest rates from an average of 5 percent to 1.6 percent, eliminating more than half the debt. Cancellation of the debts was unacceptable to Americans because it would have made the debts the responsibility of U.S. taxpayers who had bought war bonds. The United Sates also pointed out that the Allies were receiving reparations from Germany. An Allied commission had set reparations at $33 billion plus interest, payable in annual installments, but Germany fell behind and defaulted in December 1922. French and Belgian troops occupied the industrialized Ruhr Valley to compel payment; Germans resorted to passive resistance, and their economy collapsed. Whereas before the war one American dollar was worth 4.2 German Marks, by 1924 it took 4 trillion Marks to equal a dollar. Inflation destroyed the savings of the German middle class, inciting resentment and provoking demands for an authoritarian regime to exact revenge.

In 1924 a League of Nations commission under Charles G. Dawes, formerly Harding's budget director, developed a plan that pared reparations and provided Germany with a $200 million loan, half from the United States, to stabilize its currency. After the Germans accepted the proposal, the Ruhr occupation ended, payments resumed, and Dawes won the Nobel Peace Prize. Germany fell behind, and in 1929 another commission reduced reparations to $8.8 billion plus 5.5 percent interest yearly. It set a graduated scale of payments over fifty-nine years, an agreement that shipwrecked on the rocks of the Great Depression. In 1932 President Hoover called for a one-year moratorium on all intergovernmental debt, hoping the move would enable private creditors to collect obligations and save American banks that had invested in European securities. That June, Germany's creditors agreed to forgive nine-tenths of reparations owed them if the United States would cancel the war debts. Washington declined, but after 1932 few reparations or debts were paid.

Campaigns for World Peace

During the 1920s a movement for peace and disarmament flourished in the United States. Ernest Hemingway, John Dos Passos, and William Faulkner wrote antiwar novels. With their recently won right to vote, women devoted themselves to the peace crusade, constituting two-thirds of the activists. They formed groups such as the Women's International League for Peace and Freedom, led by Jane Addams, whose work brought her the 1931 Nobel Peace Prize. The Women's Peace Union tried but failed to get a constitutional amendment to outlaw war passed in each Congress from 1926 to 1939. Still, the women's peace movement was a factor behind a naval disarmament conference that met from late 1921 to early 1922 in Washington. Money also was a motive. The cost of constructing a battleship increased from $5 million in 1900 to $40 million in

1920. Britain had an aging fleet that would be expensive to replace; and Japan knew that it could not compete with American wealth in an arms race. Limiting naval competition required settlement of issues in the Far East, a crucial area of competition. At London's suggestion, Hughes invited nations with an interest in the region to participate.

Three complementary covenants emerged. The Four Power Treaty bound the United States, Britain, France, and Japan to respect each other's Pacific possessions and to consult if disputes arose. The Nine Power Treaty sought to curb competition among foreign powers in China and opened all of China to international trade. Under the Five Power Treaty, the parties agreed not to fortify their Pacific colonies as well as to scrap some battleships and to construct none for ten years. Tonnage ceilings were established, with each nation given a ratio. For every 5 ships allowed to the United States and Britain, Japan could have 3 and France and Italy 1.67 each. Aircraft carriers were included in the ceilings, but no bounds were set on planes, submarines, destroyers, or cruisers. This provision proved a major shortcoming, as was the failure to invite Germany and the Soviet Union. The agreements were the most significant diplomatic achievements between the world wars. The Five Power Treaty was the first major arms limitation accord in the history of the modern world.

Later attempts to curb arms were less successful. In 1927 Coolidge initiated a conference in Geneva to limit smaller warships, yet France and Italy refused to take part. After the conference adjourned without an agreement, American peace leaders refocused on a project long under consideration, to make war illegal. Even in the absence of sanctions, peace activists thought, the stigma of world opinion would deter potential aggressors. Also, they could be tried in an international court for waging offensive wars. Borah had introduced such a resolution in the Senate in 1923, with no result. Then, in 1927, James T. Shotwell, an official with the Carnegie Endowment for International Peace, asked French Foreign Minister Aristide Briand to propose a treaty outlawing war between the United States and France. Secretary of State Frank Kellogg resisted because it would effectively ally the two nations. He countered with a proposal asking all countries to adhere. Outmaneuvered, Briand agreed, and sixty-four nations, among them future war makers, signed the Pact of Paris, or the Kellogg-Briand Treaty, in August 1928. Kellogg won the Nobel Peace Prize. Some dismissed the treaty as hopelessly idealistic because there was no way of enforcing it. One senator mocked the pact as an "international kiss."

Hoover tried to limit arms at conferences in 1930 at London and in 1932 at Geneva. At London, the United States, Britain, and Japan promised to apply the 5:5:3 ratio to smaller ships. In addition, the Japanese were granted parity in submarines, the moratorium on capital ship construction was extended to 1936, and rules for submarine warfare were codified. The Geneva meeting was a failure. Hoover proposed the elimination of offensive weapons, reduction of total weaponry by 30 percent, and limitation of armies. His plans were doomed when, during a recess, Adolf Hitler's militaristic Nazi Party won a plurality in German's parliamentary election.

Japanese Aggression

The major foreign crisis of Hoover's administration began with Japanese aggression against China in Manchuria. Japan, whose army defied its civilian government and intimidated its prime minister, expanded into Manchuria after World War I to exploit timber, coal, and iron. The move triggered competition with the Soviet Union and China, in which Tokyo gained the upper hand by wresting control of key railroads. By the early 1930s, nearly 90 percent of Japanese foreign investment was in Manchuria; however, rising Chinese nationalism jeopardized control of the colony. China had been in turmoil since the overthrow of the Manchu dynasty in 1911. Subsequent civil wars broke out between Sun Yat-sen and regional warlords, but Sun's successor, Jiang Jieshe (Chiang Kai-Shek), leader of the Nationalist Guomindang (Kuomintang) Party, appeared on the brink of adding Manchuria to his conquests. To justify its dominance of the province, the Japanese army staged an incident on September 18, 1931, setting off an explosion on the South Manchurian Railway near Mukden and blaming the Chinese for sabotage. Retaliating, Japan seized Mukden and surrounding territory, violating international law. The Japanese compounded their aggression by bombing civilians in Shanghai. The League of Nations, despite the obligation to defend Chinese territory, only investigated the affair.

As the Hoover cabinet debated options, Secretary of State Henry L. Stimson and the president stalled for nearly four months. Hoover was no pacifist; his philosophy reflected the nickname of the football team in his hometown of West Branch, Iowa, "the Fighting Quakers." But no American official advocated military intervention because U.S. forces were too weak and American interests were not directly at stake. "The American people don't give a hoot in a rain barrel who controls North China," the *Philadelphia Record* declared. Stimson favored economic sanctions against Japan, yet Hoover disagreed, fearing they might lead to war. Early in 1932, the Stimson Doctrine was announced, amounting to moral condemnation unaccompanied by sanctions. The secretary of state informed Japan and China that the United States would not recognize conquests that violated international law. Japan, undeterred, declared a puppet state, Manchukuo, independent of China. The United States and the League withheld recognition without taking additional action. Tokyo left the League, and aggressors in Europe scorned the weak reaction.

Possessor of the most powerful armed forces in the world at the conclusion of World War I, the United States permitted its army and navy to atrophy during the Great Depression. Under the Hoover administration, not a single warship was constructed, and the country did not build to the limits allowed under the Washington and London naval treaties. The army totaled only 136,000 troops and the air corps was impotent. Leader of army aviators in World War I, General Billy Mitchell advocated air power throughout the 1920s. He proved its potential when his planes sank obsolete battleships during practice runs. Because he stridently opposed his superiors' neglect of air power, Mitchell was court-martialed, and he quit the army. In 1942, the Pearl Harbor attack having vindicated his views, Congress removed the stigma of the court-martial and promoted Mitchell, posthumously.

The "Good Neighbor"

In dealing with Latin America, the United States faced dilemmas. Washington preferred friendly, democratic governments, yet stability was its main objective, partly to protect American business and American lives. If the United States refrained from intervening, dictators might proliferate throughout the Western Hemisphere. Yet intervening seemed like bullying, and it was easier to go in than to get out. When Harding took office, the United States had troops in Panama, Cuba, the Dominican Republic, Haiti, and Nicaragua, but by the end of the Hoover administration, nearly all of them had been removed. Harding, Coolidge, and Hoover made a transition from the interventionism of Theodore Roosevelt, William Howard Taft, and Woodrow Wilson to the disengagement of the New Deal.

Mexico presented the most urgent controversy. The 1917 Mexican constitution stated that natural resources belonged to Mexicans and that property owned by foreigners was subject to expropriation. This policy angered American businessmen, who by 1920 held 40 percent of Mexican land and almost 60 percent of oil reserves. Harding and Coolidge would not recognize the government of Alvaro Obregon, who enforced the constitution, seized Catholic Church property, and suppressed religious schools. Also, they demanded the repeal of laws banning foreign ownership. In 1923 the countries concluded the Bucareli Agreement, which exempted land developed before 1917 from confiscation and allowed land obtained after then to be expropriated, with compensation in Mexican bonds. Though American property owners remained unhappy, the United States recognized Obregon's rule and allowed loans to Mexico. However, Obregon's successor, Plutarco Elias Calles, repudiated the agreement, inflaming a crisis. Calles signed legislation limiting foreign ownership of property bought before 1917 to fifty years and specifying that foreigners who owned Mexican land could not appeal to their governments. To avert an American-Mexican war, in 1927 Coolidge sent banker Dwight Morrow to Mexico to arrange a compromise. Deferential to the Mexicans, Morrow negotiated a solution that saved face for both nations. Calles, in turn, persuaded the Mexican Supreme Court to invalidate the legislation.

Trouble emerged in Nicaragua in 1925, after Coolidge removed troops who had occupied the country since 1912. Civil war erupted, and four presidents were sworn in within thirteen months. Coolidge returned the soldiers in 1926 and sent Stimson to seek an accord the next year. Not all Nicaraguans accepted the deal, and the troops remained to supervise elections in 1928, 1930, and 1932. They withdrew shortly before Roosevelt took office. Indeed, the Good Neighbor policy in the region, usually associated with FDR, started during the Hoover administration. Hoover carried the policy of military disengagement further than did his predecessors. As president-elect, he toured Latin America and announced, "We have a desire to maintain not only the cordial relations of governments with each other but the relations of good neighbors." Later, Hoover said the United States would intervene militarily only if an outside power threatened to take over a hemispheric nation. He also refused to send soldiers during revolutions and began the phased withdrawal of troops that Roosevelt completed.

Franklin Roosevelt was a relatively cosmopolitan president, at least superficially. European governesses tutored him in German and French; he studied European history at Groton and Harvard. From 1900 to 1912 he toured Europe three times and the Caribbean twice. Still, he came to the White House with few principles to guide his foreign policy. So FDR improvised as the situation dictated. He made no speeches on foreign affairs during the 1932 campaign and, upon taking office, reduced appropriations for the small, underequipped army and used the money for domestic priorities.

In his first inaugural address, Roosevelt said, "In the field of foreign policy, I would dedicate this nation to the policy of the good neighbor." Reporters isolated "good neighbor" and applied it to his policy of nonintervention in the Western Hemisphere. If the term and the policy really originated with Hoover, however, FDR went further than the Republican by translating it into action. In 1934 Roosevelt negotiated a treaty abrogating the Platt Amendment, by which the United States asserted a right to intervene in Cuba. Before the year was over, all American troops had been withdrawn from Haiti. Two years later America concluded a treaty with Panama, relinquishing the right to intervene there.

The United States also loosened the reins on its major colony, the Philippines. In 1934 FDR signed into law the Tydings-McDuffie Act, providing for independence in 1946. In the interim the Philippines would have dominion status and would be given self-rule gradually. Roosevelt was one of the first Western leaders to recognize that the epoch of colonialism was ending, and the United States was one of the first nations to relinquish a colony voluntarily. His policies toward the Philippines and Latin America were meant to give America an anticolonial record, in contrast with the European dictatorships, and grip the hemisphere into an alliance against external threats, codified in the Declaration of Lima (1938) and the Act of Havana (1940). During World War II every nation in the hemisphere except Argentina cooperated with the Allies.

In Latin America Roosevelt neither rebuilt the economies nor reformed the politics of America's neighbors. Yet he proved more tolerant of their independence than were previous U.S. presidents. For example, in 1938, when Mexico nationalized foreign property, including oil, he accepted compensation to owners on terms favorable to Mexico. In another departure from previous chief executives, FDR extended diplomatic recognition to the Soviet Union in 1933, hoping closer relations would stimulate trade.

Hitler's Rise to Power

Depression and the sting of defeat in World War I paved Adolf Hitler's rise to power in Germany. A charismatic zealot, he believed in the triumph of will and violence. Hitler defined Germans, or Aryans, as a superior race destined to rule the world. Germany must conquer the inferior peoples of Eastern Europe and the Soviet Union, he said, liquidating the old, the ill, and Jews. Paranoid of Jews, Hitler said: "The heaviest blow ever struck humanity was the coming of Christianity. Bolshevism is Christianity's illegitimate child. Both are inventions of the Jews." Americans were a mongrel race incapable of thwarting him. At first they made no attempt to stop him, like the British and the French, and within six years of coming to power Hitler had overturned the European order. The United States, meanwhile, was grappling with the depression, and Britain was struggling to retain its empire. France was constructing the Maginot Line, concrete pillboxes, and artillery emplacements near the German border.

Hitler removed Germany from the League of Nations in 1933, began rearmament in 1934, and introduced conscription in 1935, defying the

Versailles Treaty. In March 1936 he violated the treaty again when his army marched into the Rhineland, a demilitarized zone. Hitler was bluffing; if the French Army resisted, his generals had orders to withdraw. Seven months later Hitler signed an alliance with Benito Mussolini, the ruler of Italy, who described the future of Europe as revolving around a Rome-Berlin axis, coining the term, "Axis alliance." Mussolini felt he needed colonies to brandish Italian might. The dictator attacked Ethiopia in 1935. Emperor Haile Selassie appealed to the League of Nations to save his country; but the League responded with no more than weak economic sanctions that did not include coal or oil. America took no tangible action at all.

Rather, noninterventionists prevailed. Some of the isolationists in Congress were to the Left of Roosevelt on economic issues. Among them were the Republicans William E. Borah, Gerald P. Nye, and Arthur H. Vandenberg; the progressives George W. Norris and Robert M. La Follette Jr.; and the Democrat Burton K. Wheeler, all in the Senate. Outside the Capitol the isolationists' Far-Right fringe groups were led by demagogues such as Father Charles E. Coughlin, Gerald L. K. Smith, and Elizabeth Dilling.

In 1934 the Johnson Act prohibited loans to any foreign government in default to the United States, a ban that applied to most of Europe. Around the same time, a Senate committee under Nye began an investigation into the role of arms manufacturers in seducing the country into involvement in World War I. The inquiry concluded in 1936 that the United States went to war as a result of a conspiracy of those manufacturers. Books about the arms industry added strength to the conspiracy theory. The isolationist impulse crested in January 1935, when Congress, intimidated by a coalition including Louisiana Senator Huey Long, Coughlin, and Hearst, defeated a proposal for American membership on the World Court. Lawmakers also stymied FDR's hope for an arms embargo against Italy in retaliation for its Ethiopian invasion. FDR wanted Congress to authorize him to distinguish aggressors from victims in implementing such embargoes. Instead, Congress passed an embargo against all belligerents. Worrying about the fate of New Deal measures if he resisted, the president reluctantly approved the embargo contained in the Neutrality Act. The law favored the well-armed Italians over the poorly armed Ethiopians.

European events hurtled out of control in 1936. In July, Spanish General Francisco Franco led a revolt against the republican, or Loyalist, government. Many Americans supported the Loyalists. Four thousand of them fought in a volunteer brigade. The Soviet Union backed the republic, but Germany and Italy favored Franco, supplying nearly 40 percent of his troops and almost all his arms. They helped him win a civil war that lasted three years and killed more than 1 million. Roosevelt's priority was to contain war, not save Spanish democracy. In keeping with that priority, Congress approved, in January 1937, a joint resolution applying the Neutrality Act to civil wars. On May 1, FDR signed a new, two-year Neutrality Act that gave the president discretion to certify whether a state of war existed; if he did, an arms embargo would be declared against both sides. Commodities other than weapons could be sold to belligerents only on a cash-and-carry basis.

Outbreak of War

In March 1938 German soldiers marched into Austria, and Hitler proclaimed the Anschluss, the union of Austria and Germany, claiming that it was the will of the Austrians. Britain and France protested mildly and the United States did nothing, although the Versailles Treaty barred the Anschluss. Next Hitler began making demands upon Czechoslovakia, insisting that the Sudetenland, a Czech region with a large German population, be annexed to Germany. Whenever the Czechs yielded to a German demand, the Fuhrer raised the ante. With war seeming imminent, Hitler, Mussolini, British Prime Minister Neville Chamberlain, and French Prime Minister Edouard Daladier met at Munich, Germany, to seek a compromise. The British and the French decided to appease Hitler by giving him the Sudetenland. Hitler declared, "This is the last territorial demand I have to make in Europe." Chamberlain announced that he had achieved "peace with honor . . . peace in our time," an assessment with which Winston Churchill, his chief political foe in Britain, disagreed. "Do not suppose that this is the end," Churchill warned. "This is only the beginning of the reckoning."

If Hitler's ambition had been limited to rectifying injustices, appeasement might have worked at the expense of neighbors bordering Germany. Yet he had an insatiable appetite for territory, and by refusing to commit themselves to containing him, the other European nations and the United States invited further aggression. The Fuhrer planned to bring other lands under his heel, and to exterminate Jews. There were only 500,000 Jews among the 85 million inhabitants of Germany, yet Hitler blamed them for all German afflictions, including the defeat in World War I. Jews' civil rights already had been restricted before a fateful incident in 1938. A young Polish Jew assassinated a minor German official in Paris, triggering Kristallnacht, or "the Night of Broken Glass." Nazi soldiers and civilians beat Jews, arrested them, burned their synagogues, destroyed their businesses, and compelled them to pay huge sums in damages to their own property. New regulations barred Jews from engaging in retail trade, attending college, using public libraries, and driving cars. Most ominous, twenty-five thousand Jews were sent to concentration camps, where many were murdered. Jews attempting to flee Germany, sadly, could find no country to accept them. The United States would not relax immigration laws, not even to allow twenty thousand Jewish children to be admitted outside quotas. A ship carrying 930 Jewish refugees en route from Hamburg to Cuba was not allowed to dock.

Hitler's intention to dominate all Europe became clear on March 15, 1939, when German troops invaded the rest of Czechoslovakia. He plotted to take Poland next, a move that necessitated neutralizing the Soviet Union. Joseph Stalin, eager for a slice of Poland, distrusting the British and the French, and naively trusting Hitler, obliged by negotiating a neutrality pact with Germany that made world war inevitable. Even as he completed the treaty, the Fuhrer planned to turn on the Soviets once he had extinguished his enemies in the West. Announcement of the treaty, signed on August 23, shocked the world, for communists and fascists were archenemies. Then Hitler made demands on Poland and escalated them beyond reason. Finally realizing the futility of appeasement, Britain declared that it would defend Poland. On September 1, Hitler invaded Poland, and two days later London and Paris declared war on Germany

Stalin emulated his cynical ally by seizing the eastern half of Poland, annexing the Baltic republics of Estonia, Latvia, and Lithuania, and demanding extravagant territorial concessions from neighboring Finland. When the Finns refused, he invaded, taking their country only after his Red Army suffered embarrassing casualties against a vastly smaller military. Albania, which Mussolini attacked in April 1939, also was under Axis control. At Roosevelt's suggestion, Congress repealed the arms embargo in November and adopted yet another Neutrality Act. This one allowed the Allies to buy arms and civilian goods from the United States on a cash-and-carry basis.

Hitler took Poland with a Blitzkrieg, or lightning war, featuring rapid penetration with tanks, planes, and personnel carriers. He did not attempt additional conquests during the winter of 1939-1940, inactivity that military experts called the Sitzkrieg, or phony war. But in April 1940 Hitler burst out of his defensive positions to seize Norway and Denmark, and in May he added Belgium, the Netherlands, and Luxembourg. Then, outflanking the Maginot Line to the north, he invaded France. His forces pushed the French and British armies toward the sea, where more than three hundred thousand troops were rescued in an evacuation at Dunkirk. Less than ten days later, German forces entered Paris. On June 22 the humiliated French signed a surrender in the railway car in the Compiegne forest in which Germany had surrendered in 1918. In the unoccupied south of France, General Henri Petain established the Vichy government that collaborated with the Nazis.

Only Britain, which no longer had an army on the continent, remained free, protected from invasion across the English Channel because its fleet still controlled the North Sea. Hoping to avoid an invasion, Hitler tried to bomb the British into submission with his Luftwaffe, but failed. The much smaller Royal Air Force, with the aid of radar and the incentive of self-preservation, won the Battle of Britain. Frustrated, the Fuhrer shifted his air attacks from air bases to cities and the bombing of civilian populations, only to fail again. Far from breaking the British spirit, the bombing stiffened their will to resist. Britain then bombed Berlin, making the conflict a total war in which civilians on both sides became targets.

FDR'S Third Term

In 1940, as France collapsed and Britain struggled to survive Hitler's attacks, Americans hoped the Allies would win the war and grappled with questions about their own country. If Britain fell, would the United States be next? Would the great moats—the Atlantic and Pacific oceans—insure immunity from attack? There was also a presidential election. The great riddle was whether Roosevelt would break the two-term tradition set by George Washington. FDR vacillated for months before the Chicago convention. Then he decided the Axis threat justified another term, a decision that alienated some of his close advisers. To overcome tradition, FDR felt he must appear to be drafted. Hence he publicly disavowed third-term ambitions and privately plotted a convention demonstration for himself that would look spontaneous. In addition, he stole some GOP thunder by appointing two prominent Republicans to his cabinet, Henry L. Stimson as war secretary and Frank Knox as navy secretary.

The Republicans at Philadelphia turned to an eleventh-hour entrant, Wendell Willkie, a utility executive and political novice. Handsome, an internationalist, and a supporter of many New Deal reforms, he became a Roosevelt foe when the Tennessee Valley Authority overwhelmed his company. To broaden the geographic and ideological appeal of their ticket, Republicans made progressive Oregon Senator Charles McNary Willkie's running mate. Roosevelt chose Henry Wallace, his controversial secretary of agriculture, having broken with Garner over the third term issue.

Willkie initially attacked the New Deal and Roosevelt for power-mongering. FDR said the war crisis mandated tested leadership. Though Willkie supported preparedness measures, late in the campaign, finding himself far behind in the polls, he began to brand the president a warmonger.

Roosevelt retorted: "I have said this before, but I shall say it again and again. Your boys are not going to be sent into any foreign wars." Willkie replied scathingly that if FDR's pledge "is no better than his promise to balance the budget, they're almost on the transports!" But every new danger in Europe or Asia enhanced Roosevelt's chances. FDR received 27 million popular votes and 449 electoral votes to 22 million and 82 for Willkie, the smallest plurality of any candidate since 1916.

Roosevelt had to overcome mounting opposition from anti-interventionists. With his encouragement, internationalists had created the Committee to Defend America by Aiding the Allies and a smaller, more militant group, Fight for Freedom Inc. Still, the isolationist organizations were more formidable and better financed. In July 1940 midwestern businessmen helped form the America First Committee, supported by leaders such as Hearst, Ford, Colonel Robert McCormick, and Charles Lindbergh. Boasting 850,000 members at its peak, the committee argued that the United States weakened its defenses by shipping to Britain weapons that American forces needed. Lindbergh was the most effective critic of Roosevelt's policies and the most influential isolationist. He traveled to Germany several times, mostly to inspect the Luftwaffe, was impressed by German might, and accepted and kept a top civilian medal that government gave him. Worse, he described Jews as a threat to America because of their alleged dominance over foreign policy, the radio, the press, and the motion picture industry. The anti-Semitic overtones of Lindbergh and others, including some German Americans and groups implicitly sympathetic to Hitler, embarrassed America First. Such elements constrained Roosevelt's ability to check aggression, due to their allying themselves with respectable anti-interventionists and pacifists.

"A Date Which Will Live in Infamy"

The British, rapidly depleting their financial resources by buying weapons and food abroad, faced a crisis. To overcome it, Roosevelt agreed in September 1940 to transfer fifty destroyers used in World War I to Britain in exchange for leases on British air and naval bases in the Western Hemisphere. He also signed a conscription bill. Then, in January 1941, FDR proposed the Lend-Lease Bill to let London purchase arms on credit or to borrow them for the remainder of the war. If the home of one's neighbor caught fire, one would not try to sell the neighbor a hose, but lend it to him and get it back after the fire was out, he said. The logic of Roosevelt's analogy did not impress isolationists. Elizabeth Dilling brought six hundred mothers to Washington to demonstrate against the measure.

Senator Robert A. Taft quipped: "Lending war equipment is a good deal like lending chewing gum. You don't want it back." Wheeler was more vicious in denouncing Lend-Lease as a perverse form of the Agricultural Adjustment Administration—the "New Deal's triple-A foreign policy" he said would "plow under every fourth American boy." Roosevelt replied, "That is really the rottenest thing that has ever been said in public life in my generation." To charges that the bill would inspire Hitler to attack the United States, FDR said: "Such aid is not an act of war. When the dictators are ready to make war on us, they will not wait for an act of war on our part. They did not wait for Norway or Belgium or the Netherlands to commit an act of war." Also, he had said that aiding Britain was the best way to protect the Western Hemisphere. "We must be the great arsenal of democracy," he announced. After heated debate, Congress passed Lend-Lease, and Roosevelt signed the legislation in March.

The British, however, needed an ally more desperately than supplies and received one from an unexpected quarter in the summer of 1941. On June 22 Hitler sent waves of troops into the Soviet Union, driving Stalin into the allied camp. Some Americans on the Far Right preferred a German triumph to a Soviet one. Others hoped the two great armies would grind each other down. Missouri Senator Harry S Truman suggested, "If we see that Germany is winning, we ought to help Russia, and if Russia is winning, we ought to help Germany." By contrast, Churchill, who had succeeded Chamberlain as prime minister, considered the Soviets expedient allies, "If Hitler invaded Hell, I would at least make a favorable reference to the Devil in the House of Commons," he said. American Communists, once foes of Hitler, then his friends, became enemies once again. With the world crisis peaking, the army was concerned that it would have to release one-year draftees. The administration wanted to extend the term of service for the duration of the war, but the Senate substituted an eighteen-month extension, which passed easily in that chamber but barely won a House vote, 203 to 202, evidence of the strength of isolationism.

London laid the grounds for a significant alliance in the secret Churchill-Roosevelt meeting on August 9, 1941, off the coast of Argentia, Newfoundland. The talks marked the start of a warm friendship between the prime minister and the president, Churchill told FDR, "It is fun to be in the same decade with you." Their chief objective, the stipulation of war aims, was expressed in the Atlantic Charter which upheld democracy. By fall, the American road to war reached another intersection. The United States, which had begun convoying British ships, was fighting an undeclared war in the Atlantic. On September 4 the destroyer *Greer* exchanged shots with a German submarine it had been stalking. Roosevelt called the incident an unprovoked German attack. On October 16, eleven crewmen died when a German torpedo struck the destroyer *Kearny*, and two weeks later 115 sailors went down with the destroyer *Reuben James*, the first American warship sunk by a U-boat. In November, Congress responded by revising the Neutrality Act to let merchant ships arm and to deliver cargoes to belligerent ports.

Yet for the United States, war did not break out in the Atlantic, where everyone anticipated it, but in the Pacific, from Japan, holder of a Far East empire seized while Americans were focused on Hitler. Japan lacked resources and sought to expand to become a great power in the Pacific by excluding the only potential competitor for regional dominance, the United States. In 1937, Tokyo expanded the fighting over China beyond Manchuria: Japan seized major Chinese cities. Jiang Jieshe retreated to the interior, and communists waged guerrilla combat against the invaders. Roosevelt did not proclaim a state of war, under the pretense that Japan had not declared war, and America rushed arms to China. His mind on the conflict, the president delivered his first major foreign policy speech on October 5, 1937. "War must be quarantined like an epidemic disease," the commander in chief said, although he offered no proposals and did not follow up. On December 12, Japanese planes sank the American gunboat *Panay* on the Yangtze River, killing three people and wounding seventy-four. Anti-interventionists questioned the stationing of a warship in such dangerous waters, and few Americans demanded war against Japan. The Japanese Empire apologized and paid an indemnity. A day after the sinking, a constitutional amendment requiring a national referendum before the United States could go to war (unless attacked) was brought to the House floor, where it was defeated, 209 to 188.

In September 1940, emboldened by the dazzling German victories, the Japanese formulating plans for an empire that included China, French Indochina, Thailand, British Malaya, British Borneo, the Dutch East Indies, Burma, Australia, New Zealand, and possibly India and the Philippines. That month, Japan occupied northern Indochina and signed the Tripartite Pact, an alliance with Germany and Italy. In response, the United States placed embargoes on aviation gasoline, lubricating oil, and scrap metal. The next spring Japan signed a nonaggression treaty with the Soviet Union. Stalin freed Tokyo to attack the United States. Then, in July 1941, Japan moved into southern Indochina despite warnings from Washington. FDR froze Japanese assets in America. Also, Roosevelt closed the Panama Canal to Japanese shipping and recalled General Douglas MacArthur from retirement to command American forces in the Far East. The State Department placed an embargo on oil, the most important commodity for Japan's navy.

THE PACIFIC FLEET IN FLAMES
Pearl Harbor, December 7, 1941.
(Franklin D. Roosevelt Presidential Library)

With the embargo tightening, Prime Minister Fumimaro Konoye proposed, in August, a summit to settle differences. Stalling for time while he dealt with Hitler, Roosevelt feared a conference would bring a showdown too quickly. Also, the Japanese might use a failed meeting as an excuse for war. FDR thus refused to meet Fumimaro Konoye, whose cabinet fell on October 18. His successor was the militarist war minister, Hideki Tojo. Throughout the fall, though, Japanese Ambassador Kichisaburo Nomura negotiated with Secretary of State Cordell Hull. China kept the two sides apart. Washington demanded that Japan withdraw, and Tokyo demanded that the United States stop sending arms to China.

Japan had a brief period in which an attack on the United States would be feasible. With no more than a six-month oil supply, it was close to losing its naval superiority to the American construction program (it did in 1942). Weather conditions and the supreme command favored an attack by early December 1941. Afterward, conditions would not be suitable until spring and the oil shortage would be crippling. The Japanese objective was an American base 3,900 miles from the home islands, Pearl Harbor in Hawaii. Contemplation of an attack on a nation so much larger, with more natural resources, seems mad, but Tokyo, realizing that it would be defeated in a protracted war, planned a knockout blow against the American Pacific fleet. The empire believed the United States would concede in the Pacific to focus resources against Hitler. Therefore, on November 25, 1941, a task force including six aircraft carriers, two battleships, and nine destroyers started for Hawaii on a route far to the north of usual shipping channels.

Since late 1940 American cryptanalysts had been able to read the most secure Japanese diplomatic code, called "Magic." On November 22, 1941, they decoded a message to Nomura and his associate ordering them to seek an agreement by November 29 because later "things are automatically going to happen." On November 26 navy experts decoded a long message that seemed to indicate an attack was being planned. Among the mass of messages intercepted, some pointed to Pearl Harbor, yet many appeared to suggest that the Philippines or Singapore would be targeted. Rumors abounded, one that a dog on an Oahu beach was "barking in Morse Code to [a] Japanese sub offshore." Roosevelt wrote to Emperor Hirohito on December 6, urging him to withdraw from Indochina. The note never reached him, for the Japanese war cabinet intercepted it.

That evening, FDR read the final message from Tokyo to its envoys in Washington and said, "This means war." He had expected war, but did not instigate it; his primary concern at the time was Germany. If there was no plot in the United States to provoke war, however, there was plenty of incompetence. The Pearl Harbor commander responded to a War Department warning by alerting his troops for sabotage, not for attack. Planes were parked wingtip to wingtip so they could be guarded from saboteurs; it would have taken four hours to launch them. Antiaircraft ammunition was stored and locked. No patrols were operating north of Oahu. Radar was in use only on an experimental basis. Reports of airplanes approaching were dismissed.

At daybreak on December 7, dive-bombers and torpedo planes roared in. By 10:00 A.M., battleship row was a smoldering ruin. The Japanese sank or damaged 8 battleships, 3 light cruisers, 3 destroyers, and 188 planes. The United States suffered 3,345 casualties, Japan less than one hundred. The defeat, paradoxically, was not so massive as it seemed: the battleship, the ultimate weapon in World War I, had been rendered obsolete by air power, and the American aircraft carriers were in port or at sea. Japan, nevertheless, had silenced the anti-interventionists, united Americans or war, and started a fight that it could not win. "I fear we have awakened a sleeping

WAR AGAINST JAPAN
Franklin Roosevelt
signs the Declaration
of War with Japan.
(Library of Congress)

giant," Admiral Isoroku Yamamoto, the planner of the attack, said soberly. The next day, Roosevelt appeared before Congress, and called December 7 "a date which will live in infamy." He requested a declaration of war that was swiftly adopted. On December 11 Germany and Italy declared war on the United States. Washington returned the compliment one day later. Hitler, who was not obliged to fight America because he was not consulted about the Pearl Harbor attack, thought victory was certain. Had he been imaginative, he might have declared war on Japan rather than on the United States, placing Americans in an untenable position.

Twenty-three years and twenty-six days after the armistice of 1918, America was at war again. The "rendezvous with destiny" which FDR predicted in his 1936 acceptance speech had arrived. Ironically, in 1936 Roosevelt was talking about the Great Depression.

CHAPTER TWELVE

World War II: Home Front and Battlefront, 1941–1945

I N THE Era of Trial and Triumph, World War II was the greatest trial and the greatest triumph. Paradoxically, it separated families, required sacrifice, and killed hundreds of thousands, yet it unified the nation, ended the Great Depression, and healed the nation. World War II is the story of people who marched out of 1941 and into 1942 bewildered by the planet exploding around them and were remade. War required the federal government to dominate Americans through massive spending and intervention in people's lives—a course that would be unpopular in peacetime. Changes on the domestic front in wartime surpassed those of any other period in the Time of Paradox.

Transformation

Facing their greatest challenge, Americans shared a purpose. Those who did not go abroad to fight wanted to contribute, donating blood, buying bonds, planting Victory Gardens, and collecting newspapers and tin cans for recycling. When the War Production Board asked for 4 million tons of scrap metal in two months, people responded with 5 million in three weeks; one town with 207 residents collected 225 tons. Women volunteered to work in hospitals, day care centers, and schools.

Sacrifices were required. Industrial accidents killed some three hundred thousand workers. More Americans relocated than at any time in history. To conserve resources, the country limited consumer access to new cars, tires, electrical appliances, and nylon stockings; ten major items were rationed, among them meat, shoes, sugar, and gasoline.

Military bases and war industries transformed communities and regions. The West Coast, once isolated, became the fastest growing part of the country, producing 20 percent of war goods despite having 10 percent of the population. Industrial growth, anticipated to take fifty years, occurred in four. People traveled less for pleasure, entertained in their homes, got to know their neighbors, and dressed informally. Circulation of library books increased. Parlor games, especially checkers, gained popularity, but hunting and fishing were banned. The government forbade the manufacture of tennis and golf balls to conserve raw materials.

Paradoxically, teen crime, delinquency, illegitimacy, prostitution, and venereal disease soared. Teenagers called "Victory Girls" crowded bus depots in cities, saying they wanted to meet soldiers for sex to help military morale. Overall crime declined, however, and medical and dental care improved. The army provided some people with the best diets they ever had. When the American Medical Association dropped its opposition to prepaid insurance, Blue Cross and Blue Shield enrolled tens of millions. Despite the war, the death rate dropped to a record low and life expectancy increased.

The United States became more of a middle-class nation. Personal income more than doubled, and it was more fairly distributed than ever: the share of the national income that the wealthiest 5 percent controlled declined from 23.7 percent in 1939 to 16.8 percent in 1944. The portion of national income going to interest and rent dropped 20 percent during the conflict. It took more than twenty years of postwar prosperity for income to increase comparably. "The more cheerful side of this tale is that the underprivileged third of America's population undoubtedly lived better during the war and for some time afterward than they had ever lived before," an economist wrote. Even the prosperity of the 1920s was eclipsed in terms of gross national product, retail sales, new investment, and national income. The war brought full employment. By 1945, in addition to the 11.4 million people in the armed forces, 52.8 million were employed at home, up from 45.7 million in 1939.

Mobilizing the Economy

The war was won as much on the assembly lines as on the front lines. Not only did the United States possess far more natural and human resources than the Axis powers, but it used them more efficiently. Six months after Pearl Harbor, American factory production exceeded the Axis nations combined, and before the end of the war, the United States was producing twice as much as the enemy. During the conflict, Americans built 88,410 tanks, 299,293 airplanes, 6,500,000 million rifles, 1,566 merchant vessels, and 5,777 merchant ships.

The war facilitated a reconciliation of government and big business. Honored throughout much of the 1920s and demonized during the depression, businessmen again were venerated. Some executives took leaves from their jobs to run government agencies. The government provided low-interest loans and tax deductions to enlarge plants and to retool factories for war production, relaxed enforcement of antitrust laws, and offered contracts that guaranteed a profit.

The auto industry ceased making new cars after January 31, 1942, and built planes and tanks. The most dramatic increase in productivity, though, was in shipbuilding, as merchant vessels were built more rapidly than anyone thought possible. Production was imperiled when the United States' supply of raw rubber from the Dutch East Indies was cut off, a problem addressed when industrialist Bernard Baruch devised a program of conservation and synthetic rubber production. The government spent $700 million to build fifty-one synthetic rubber plants and leased them to private companies, helping increase production one hundred times from 1941 to 1944.

To coordinate war production, Franklin D. Roosevelt created the War Production Board in 1942. Policies of war agencies were coordinated under James F. Byrnes, who resigned from the Supreme Court to lead the Office of Economic Stabilization and then the Office of War Mobilization in 1943. Coordination was also the goal of the Office of Defense Transportation (ODT), created in 1941, and the War Manpower Commission (WMC), formed in 1942. The ODT operated truck lines, buses, and railroads as an integrated system. Railroads remained privately held and doubled the amount of freight carried. The Big Inch pipeline was laid to transport oil from Texas to Pennsylvania, reducing the number of oil tankers sunk in coastal waters. By contrast, the WMC was charged with moving not goods but people, into jobs vital to the war effort.

For agriculture, the war was a bonanza. Farmers' income rose 250 percent from 1939 to 1945. Civilian food consumption was the highest in history, and one-quarter of agricultural goods went to feed the armed forces and the Allies. Although the farm population declined 20 percent and the number of tenant farmers and sharecroppers fell 33 percent, farm productivity increased 28 percent, thanks to mechanization, longer hours, fertilizers, hybrid crops, and pesticides. The federal government encouraged agriculture by exempting farm workers from the draft.

Overseas, the United States killed some 500,000 enemy troops at a cost of more than $360 billion and paid a high price for the property its military destroyed; metaphorically it would have cost less simply to buy the property. From 1940 to 1945 the country spent nearly twice as much as in the previous 150 years. The yearly budget was more than ten times that of prewar years, $100 billion in 1945 alone, and the national debt sky-rocketed from $43 billion in 1940 to $269 billion in 1946. Borrowing financed about 54 percent of the outlays; taxes paid the rest. Individual and corporate income taxes, which had provided 30 percent of government revenue in 1933, furnished 76 percent by 1944. The Revenue Act of 1942 raised income taxes to their highest rates ever, 81 percent in the top bracket, and reduced exemptions, so levies were made on lower-income groups for the first time. Forty-two million people paid income taxes in 1944, up from 17 million in 1942 and 4 million people in 1939. In 1943 another Revenue Act introduced payroll deductions for income taxes, and the next year Congress approved a tax increase, though less than Roosevelt had requested. Increased corporate and excise taxes took much of industry's profits, so few industrialists and investors grew rich from the war. Bonds, an additional source of money for the government, were sold not only to borrow funds but to soak up money available for consumer goods. This policy helped control inflation and gave people a sense of patriotic participation in the war. About $200 billion of war bonds were sold to 85 million people in eight loan drives. Schoolchildren bought $1 billion of bonds and war stamps.

Labor union membership rose from 9 million in 1942 to 15 million in 1945, and more Americans belonged to unions than worked on farms, a historic first. To handle labor disagreements, FDR created the National Defense Mediation Board in 1941; the next year the agency gave way to the National War Labor Board (NWLB), on which labor, business, and the public were represented equally. The NWLB applied "the Little Steel formula," so called because it had been worked out in a dispute concerning the smaller steel mills. Because the cost of living had increased 15 percent in 1942, the board permitted wages to go up as much as 15 percent excluding overtime, a move that helped check inflation. The NWLB handled 17,650 disputes involving 12 million workers, yet in forty cases Roosevelt seized plants to ensure production. When a nationwide railroad strike loomed in 1944, the government took over the railroads, only to return them in three weeks, after the president arbitrated the dispute. Work interruptions amounted to just one day per worker for the duration of the war. John L. Lewis, who returned as head of the United Mine Workers, became a villain for leading his members on strikes in 1941 and 1943 and gaining higher wages.

While they were winning labor peace, Americans were winning the war in laboratories. Scientists developed or perfected the bazooka, which could pierce a tank; the radio proximity fuse, which exploded according to nearness to the target; napalm flamethrowers; amphibious vehicles for landing on beaches; medical treatments for the wounded, including new drugs; insect repellents; improved navigational aids; and radar and sonar. Most consequential, revolutionary advances in physics made possible the atom bomb—presenting the deadliest paradoxes of the century. In 1939 several scientists aware of German progress in nuclear physics persuaded Albert Einstein to sign a letter to Roosevelt calling attention to the possibility of producing bombs from uranium. Little headway was made until the summer of 1941 when Vannevar Bush, FDR's top science adviser, told him a bomb appeared feasible, and in 1942 the first controlled nuclear reaction took place at the University of Chicago. One year later, a new unit of the Army Corps of Engineers, the Manhattan District, took over research, leading to a breakthrough in which scientists under J. Robert Oppenheimer at Los Alamos, New Mexico, brought together fissionable material to produce an explosion in July 1945. The entire project, costing about $2 billion, was unknown to most in Congress, even to Vice President Harry S Truman.

Defeating the enemy required the work of journalists and advertising executives as well. Poet and Librarian of Congress Archibald MacLeish and journalist Elmer Davis contributed by heading the Office of Facts and Figures and the Office of War Information, respectively. MacLeish's organization was charged with disseminating information about the war to the press and the public before Davis's agency took over the task. The Office of Censorship banned publication of weather forecasts that might aid enemy bombers and excised sensitive information from soldiers' letters home. Hollywood produced films to stimulate patriotism, some depicting individual Americans overcoming swarms of Germans and Japanese. Comic books, which reached millions, were sent abroad, showing superheroes single-handedly winning battles.

Civil Liberties and Racial Tension

Whatever the propagandists proclaimed, not all Americans welcomed the opportunity to inflict pain and death. Most conscientious objectors were allowed to fill noncombat roles in the military or to perform essential civilian work. But more than 5,500 were jailed for refusing to serve, more than three-fourths of them Jehovah's Witnesses who requested exemptions on the ground that all were ministers. They were denied status as conscientious objectors because they did not oppose all wars.

Prosecutions for sedition were rare, although in July 1942 a federal grand jury indicted twenty-eight native fascists on suspicion of undermining military morale. A mistrial was declared after the judge died, and the

JAPANESE CIVILIANS ARE SENT TO CAMPS
Newly arrived Japanese-Americans at an internment camp
in San Bruno, California, 1942. Photograph by Dorothea Lange.
(National Archives)

indictments were dropped after the war. The most serious breech of civil liberties was perpetrated upon 117,000 Japanese Americans, two-thirds of whom were U.S. citizens. They were rounded up, incarcerated in camps, forced to dispose of their property at a fraction of its value, and branded as disloyal. They were vulnerable because they belonged to a people who had inflicted a succession of defeats on the United States. They were easier to detain than German and Italian Americans, whose numbers were greater but were not as geographically concentrated. Attitudes changed over time. Early in 1943 the army began accepting recruits for a combat unit of Nisei, the American-born offspring of the Japanese. About twelve hundred fought in the 442nd Combat Team, which earned fame for bravery in the Italian campaign. By 1945 most of the Japanese Americans had been allowed to return home. The Supreme Court seemed of two minds about the episode, ruling in one case that the United States had the right to order the internment and in another that the government could not detain anyone whose loyalty had been established. Not until 1988 did

Congress apologize to Japanese Americans and agree to pay compensation to each surviving internee.

African Americans made significant economic progress because of the demand for labor. More than 1 million moved from the South to the North to take jobs in war industries; those who stayed in the South migrated from rural areas to cities for employment. More unions were open to them. The number of African Americans in manufacturing rose from .5 to 1.2 million and in government jobs from 50,000 to 200,000. After the war, 250,000 black veterans attended college with government benefits. Some white people resented competition from African Americans, who were not hired in war industries until the labor shortage became acute. Incensed when several war industries refused to hire African Americans, A. Philip Randolph threatened a massive protest march on Washington. Fearing racial violence, FDR agreed to declare an end to job discrimination in defense industries and government employment but refused to desegregate the armed forces. In June 1942 Roosevelt issued an executive order creating the Fair Employment Practices Committee to prevent discrimination in work, and Randolph canceled the march.

Recognizing the paradox of fighting for democracy outside the United States while denying it to black Americans, many white people felt that racial discrimination was immoral, a belief underscored by Gunnar Myrdal's findings in the comprehensive study *An American Dilemma* (1944). Eradicating it completely was not likely in a country where deadly race riots broke out in major cities. The worst started in June 1943 in Detroit, as fights erupted between black and white people at Belle Isle Park; looting and burning raged before federal troops quelled violence that left twenty-five African Americans and nine white Americans dead. Two months later Harlem erupted after a confrontation between a white police officer and a black soldier; six African Americans perished and three hundred people were injured. In meeting rooms and government halls, the struggle against segregation nonetheless made only modest gains, although it gathered momentum for postwar years. The NAACP grew from 50,000 members and 335 branches in 1940 to nearly 500,000 and 1,000 in 1945; the Congress of Racial Equality was founded in Chicago. Also, in 1944 the Supreme Court held in *Smith v. Allwright* that the Texas Democratic Party could not exclude black people from voting in primary elections.

Racial unrest was intense in California. Mexican American teens sporting ducktail haircuts and flashy, broad-shouldered zoot suits with thigh-length jackets allegedly attacked sailors who dated Hispanic women, triggering a wave of beatings by white soldiers and sailors in May and June 1943 in Oakland and Los Angeles. Indians in California sued the federal government for $100 million to pay for land that was taken from them in the 1850s. Roosevelt vetoed a compensation bill, saying the government had "a duty to the future, not the past." Litigation continued for thirty-five years until a deal was struck to pay tribes 47 cents per acre. Other changes for Native Americans were swifter: many left reservations to work in war plants, never to return. Those who did return brought the benefits of technology. Chinese Americans elicited sympathy because China was an ally of the United States. In 1943 Congress repealed the 1882 Chinese Exclusion Act. Four years later the War Brides Act allowed Chinese brides of American men to enter the country. Moreover, Congress granted all Chinese immigrants the long-denied right to become naturalized citizens.

The chief concern of American Jews was the rescue of their European kin from Adolf Hitler's Holocaust. Some 982 were admitted, but immigration quotas remained in place. FDR sought a haven for Jews outside the United States, only to encounter resistance. Even when information reached his administration about the Führer's gassing of Jews, Roosevelt found such

WOMEN AND THE WAR EFFORT
Building boats for the Marines, 1941.
(Franklin D. Roosevelt Presidential Library)

reports unbelievable. He rejected pleas to bomb gas chambers, crematoriums, and rail lines leading to death camps, arguing that doing so would divert air power from military targets and prolong the war. The administration pointed out that bombing death camps would kill inmates, and rail lines, a small target, could be quickly repaired. The public, although mainly ignorant of the Holocaust, did not consider stopping persecution of the Jews a priority. America did pluck some 200,000 Jews from harm's way by ransom, false passports, and other subterfuges under the War Refugee Board, established in January 1944. Millions could have been spared had the nation acted sooner.

As employment rose among racial and ethnic minorities due to the scarcity of workers, so it grew for women. The fictional "Rosie the Riveter" was a symbol. The female labor force increased 50 percent from 1940 to 1945. Employment rose in every field save domestic service, the most spectacular increases occurring in factory work, particularly defense industries. The federal government hired nearly 1 million, many as clerical workers in the nation's capital. Black women moved out of farm and domestic labor into service and manufacturing. Women's share of the labor movement climbed from 9.4 percent of union members to 21.8 percent in four years. Wages increased in absolute terms and in relation to men's, aided by a few state equal-wage laws and a NWLB decision ordering equal pay for women who did the same jobs as men. Advances for women were not limited to employment: their numbers also grew in college enrollment and political participation. At home there was revolution as well; a higher percentage of women married in the 1940s than ever before. Hasty marriages led to higher divorce rates and, starting in 1946, a baby boom that would prove one of the most important developments of the second half of the century. Many women used contraception, and abortions were common, if illegal; the rate of out-of-wedlock births increased nevertheless. More married women, mothers, and older women took jobs, and for the first time married women outnumbered single ones in the workforce. The government and some employers provided childcare, but most women used relatives. The war advanced the sexual revolution in ways that went beyond sexuality and included work and parenting roles, family structure, birth control, and a population explosion.

Integration came more slowly to the armed forces, than to civilian society. At the time of Pearl Harbor, only 5,000 soldiers in an army of 230,000 were African American. Many draft boards considered African Americans unfit for combat and were reluctant to conscript them; the Marines had no black personnel; the navy accepted blacks only as mess attendants and cooks. Attitudes changed when the government realized that discrimination wasted human resources. By September 1944, when the size of the armed forces peaked, 702,000 African Americans served in the army, 165,000 in the navy, 17,000 as Marines, and 5,000 in the Coast Guard. They were usually trained in segregated facilities and assigned to separate units under white officers for labor such as building roads and unloading ships. When assigned to combat units, African Americans fought capably. The 99 Pursuit Squadron, an Army Air Corps unit known as the Tuskegee Airmen, fought effectively in North Africa, Italy, and Germany.

There was less discrimination against Hispanics and Indians. Nearly 300,000 Spanish-speaking troops served in the military, and Mexican Americans were overrepresented, considering their share of the general population. They volunteered for dangerous missions, valor recognized with Congressional Medals of Honor for eleven Spanish speakers. Indians in large numbers sought military duty. Many were decorated for bravery. In communication units, they used codes based upon their languages to confuse enemy interpreters.

That warfare had grown increasingly technical, and that 10 percent of all armed forces personnel were administrative and technical, expedited the employment of women, who were hired for office, communications, and health care work. Around 140,000 women served in the Women's Army Corps (WAC), and 44,000 in the navy's Women Accepted for Voluntary Emergency Service (WAVES). Some 23,000 joined the Marine Women's Reserve, and 13,000 enlisted in the Coast Guard. Some performed risky tasks, such as test piloting, although they were not allowed in combat. Traditionalists feared that war would harden women and cost them their femininity or that female soldiers would encourage promiscuity in the armed forces—fears that were not realized. The rate of venereal disease was lower for servicewomen than for the general population. Some female soldiers served abroad. On most foreign bases they lived in barbed wire compounds and could leave only in groups under armed escort, believed necessary to protect them from sex-starved male troops.

The United States at War

Roosevelt inspired Americans and gave them confidence. No contingency plans were made for defeat or compromise. The president did not participate in tactical decisions, as did Winston Churchill, nor did he hire and fire generals, as had Abraham Lincoln. Complementing Roosevelt's skills was the dominant personality among top military leaders, General George C. Marshall, a statesman who selected able subordinates. The supreme Allied commander in Europe was General Dwight D. Eisenhower, who helped soothe difficulties between the Americans and the other Allies.

The Allies decided that defeating Hitler would take priority over subduing Japan because Germany appeared the more dangerous foe and because German scientists might develop weapons of mass destruction. Most of the army's forces and equipment were assigned to Europe, while most of the navy and almost all the Marines were concentrated in the Pacific. Control of the Atlantic, where the first American-German conflicts had taken place, was necessary for victory in Europe. In that ocean, the navy had to protect shipping, support amphibious landings, and shell invasion targets. The German surface fleet was never a major factor, despite some attacks on convoys to the Soviet Union, because it was no match for the British.

Germany's 150 submarines constituted their chief threat in the Battle of the Atlantic in 1941. The United States initially was ill equipped to combat submarines, which took a terrible toll, sinking 360 merchant ships in the first half of 1942. The U-boats operated in wolf packs in the mid-Atlantic, following convoys into nightfall before converging to attack. Allied technology and techniques improved and by May 1943 the battle was virtually won. Ships were grouped in convoys protected by planes and destroyers. Sonar was improved, and by 1943 miniature units were placed in planes and on small boats. Finally, the Americans' ability to build ships faster than the Germans could sink them was critical. The battle was costly on both sides. The Allies lost 2,828 merchant ships, 187 warships, and 40,000 men; the Germans lost two-thirds of their submarines and practically suspended naval warfare by late 1943, due to heavy losses.

Two weeks after Pearl Harbor, Churchill met Roosevelt in Washington for the Arcadia Conference and declared that American ground troops would be used first in North Africa. The decision angered Stalin, whose soldiers were fighting Germans alone on the Eastern Front and needed relief that only an invasion in Western Europe could bring. North Africa was of limited strategic importance, yet it was the only place where the British were fighting the Germans on land, and FDR was determined to give Americans a sense of participation. Britain had moved soldiers to the upper Mediterranean coast to defend Egypt and the Suez Canal, opposed at first by Italians, guarding their colonies. Vichy France was a presence, too, nominally in control of Morocco and Algeria. Eisenhower led the Allied invasion of North Africa, where the major questions were whether the French would resist, whether the campaign could be kept secret, and whether Germany might sink the invading fleet.

But the fleet approached undetected and, with air support from escort carriers and bombers based in England, landed at Casablanca, Oran, and Algiers on November 8, 1942. French resistance was light and ceased after the Germans occupied Vichy France on November 11. Almost simultaneously, the British launched an offensive from the East. General Bernard Montgomery defeated German General Erwin Rommel at El Alamein, Libya, in late October and early November, then began advancing westward to link with Eisenhower's forces. Germany rushed reinforcements to Tunisia, only slowing the Allies, and by May 11, 1943, Axis opposition in North Africa had been broken. Germany and Italy lost almost 1 million soldiers killed or taken prisoner.

At the Casablanca Conference in January 1943, Roosevelt and Churchill chose to follow the North African offensive with an invasion of Sicily. This offensive made the easiest logistical use of troops in North Africa and might divert some Axis troops from the Soviet front. Like the North African campaign, the effort in Sicily was not of great strategic impact, however, it postponed British-based troops from invading France. Early on July 10, 1943, the U.S. Seventh Army under General George S. Patton and the British Eighth Army under Montgomery landed in Sicily. Stormy weather and the lack of a preinvasion bombardment helped preserve the surprise. By the end of the second day, the Allies had put ashore eighty thousand men, in addition to support vehicles, landing craft, and tanks, many of which had bogged down in the beaches or were grounded on sandbars. Whatever their problems, their forces commanded air and sea and withstood furious counterattacks. Montgomery was to advance up the southeast coast to capture Messina, the city at the tip of Sicily separated from Italy by the Strait of Messina. Patton was to move from the southwest, offering support to Montgomery and preventing the Axis from blocking the capture of Messina, but he decided to take Messina himself, arriving there one day ahead of Montgomery. The Axis lost 164,000, killed or captured, although most escaped across the strait to Italy.

The conquest of Sicily precipitated the fall of Benito Mussolini and the collapse of the Italian war effort. Italians had grown disillusioned with the conflict, and their army had little incentive to fight. Adolf Hitler dominated the Axis, making Italians realize they had as much to fear from a German victory as from a German defeat. Two weeks after the Allied landing in Sicily, the fascist Grand Council voted no-confidence in Mussolini, and King Victor Emmanuel ordered his arrest. Italy negotiated a surrender and capitulated secretly to the Allies on September 3, 1944. Hitler rushed troops to Italy to disarm the army and rescue Mussolini from a mountain prison in a daring commando raid; then Der Führer installed Il Duce as ruler of a small German puppet state in northern Italy.

The invasion of Italy had started on September 9, 1943, when American soldiers landed at Salerno. Meeting little resistance at the beachhead, the troops, with air and naval support, repelled a strong German counterattack on September 12. On October 1, the Allies captured Naples and hoped to reach Rome by Christmas—an estimate that was too optimistic by a year. Few regions were less conducive to ground operations than the mountainous Italian peninsula, traversed by streams and rugged terrain that made tanks useless. Mountain fighting favored the defenders. Germans blocked the Allied advance at Monte Cassino, site of a fourteen-hundred-year-old Benedictine monastery, proving so formidable that the Allies decided to outflank it with an amphibious assault at Anzio. The landing surprised the Germans, and conditions were favorable for pushing in from the beach to the lightly defended countryside. Instead, the commander built up forces and supplies at the beachhead, awaiting a counterattack. When the counterattack came, it nearly drove the Americans into the sea. Anzio was the only amphibious invasion of the war in which U.S. forces failed to expand out of a beachhead.

Simultaneous with the Anzio invasion was an offensive at Monte Cassino, also a failure. Reluctantly, the Allies bombed the monastery. The war in Italy became a bloody impasse, with the longest-lasting static front in Europe. Finally French soldiers broke through German lines and opened the road to Rome. Allied forces captured Rome on June 4, 1944, two days before invading France.

Some American planners hoped that air power could crush Germany, without an invasion of France, yet military leaders differed over whether to use it to support ground operations or to wreck German industry and transportation. The British Royal Air Force, carrying the load early in the war, concluded that daylight raids cost too many bombers and resorted to night operations. By mid-1943, though, bombing was taking place around the clock, the British by night, the Americans by day. The chief American bombers, the B-17 Flying Fortress and the B-24 Liberator, were more heavily armed with defensive machine guns than the British planes and had accurate bombsights that made precision bombing during daylight feasible. Americans thought their operations were accurate enough to knock out specific targets such as airplane factories, in contrast to the British preference for saturation bombing. Allied research would conclude, however, that 65 percent of all bombs failed to come within five miles of their targets, and the United States grew skeptical of its ability to bomb accurately anything smaller than a city. By the end of the war, fire-bombing had replaced precision bombing.

Bombing raids set back the Nazi war effort. Germany was compelled to divert resources to combat the air offensive. By 1943, 1 million troops were assigned to antiaircraft duty, and it took a labor force of 1.5 million men to repair damage. Further, the air war disabled the Luftwaffe, depriving ground troops of tactical support. The Luftwaffe, the Allies initially discovered, was more lethal to bombers than antiaircraft fire. Bombers sustained costly losses when fighter escorts did not accompany them. By early 1944, the range of the P-51 Mustang and the P-47 Thunderbolt had been extended, and the Luftwaffe was ineffective in defending cities. Airpower did not destroy Germany, but it was instrumental in winning the war. It deterred an invasion of England, ensured the success of the Normandy invasion, and sank battleships and submarines in the Battle of the Atlantic.

As the war turned in favor of the Allies, Hitler invented new weapons. The first pilotless flying bombs, or V-1s, appeared over London in June 1944, a menace that killed 6,000 British civilians and wounded 17,000. Three months later, Germany launched the first V-2 supersonic rockets at London, leaving 3,000 dead and 6,500 hurt before the weapons' base was captured. Such arms heralded a new age in warfare and had a profound psychological effect on their victims, although fewer people died than from a single conventional air raid. Another German breakthrough, jet fighters, vastly superior to Allied planes, were used in July 1944, but there were not many and few pilots could fly them. The war ended before the impact of German science could be brought to bear, justifying the Allied decision to make Germany their first priority.

D-Day: The Great Invasion

In November 1943 Roosevelt met Churchill and Jiang Jieshe at two conferences in Cairo, Egypt, sandwiched around a parley with Joseph Stalin and Churchill at Tehran. Few strategic decisions were made at the Cairo meetings. At Tehran, the first gathering of the Big Three, one of the most important decisions of the war was made: the invasion of France was scheduled for the spring or summer of 1944. Stalin agreed to coordinate an offensive to complement the invasion. Since 1941 his armies had carried the burden of fighting on land, defeating Germany in the battles of Stalingrad and Leningrad in 1943 to check Hitler on the Eastern Front. Stalingrad, a turning point in the war, assured that the Soviets would survive and roll back the Nazis. By 1944 Hitler's armies were on the verge of being crushed between the jaws of a massive vise of two great armies advancing from the East and the West.

Elaborate efforts confused the Germans about the site for the Normandy invasion, the largest undertaking in the history of warfare. The Allies prevented Germany from conducting aerial surveillance of their control of the

ADDRESSING THE TROOPS
Dwight D. Eisenhower with paratroopers before D-Day.
(Library of Congress)

air. Planes dropped foil strips and the Allies launched barrage balloons to fool German radar into predicting that an invasion lay at the Pas-de-Calais, north of the objective. The allies broadcast simulated fake traffic and bombed more heavily near Calais than near Normandy. The English Channel was narrower and calmer at Calais, an obvious site for an invasion. Success in outmaneuvering the Germans came partly from the Allies' ability to read German codes. Hitler believed he had the most secure enciphering system ever developed, based on a machine known as Enigma. Confounding him, British cryptanalysts built their own Enigma and could decipher most messages within hours. The material that became known as Ultra was indispensable to the deception surrounding the Normandy invasion.

Other preparations proved effective. The air command bombed transportation facilities, and the French resistance sabotaged its rail system.

Practically every bridge west of the Seine was destroyed, making it impossible for the Germans to reinforce rapidly. Naval commandos landed by night to inspect German obstructions at the beaches. On the evening before the invasion, minesweepers began clearing the ocean. Tanks were designed to operate on soft, wet beaches and detonate land mines ahead of them. Because heavy equipment could not be loaded directly onto the beach, the Allies constructed two artificial harbors, which they towed across the channel, then sunk obsolete ships to create breakwaters.

Weather was critical. Ideal tidal conditions occurred on only three days per month. Surface winds could not exceed eighteen miles per hour, and paratroopers required moonlight for night landings. On the day the invasion was scheduled, Eisenhower's meteorologist predicted thunderstorms at Normandy, so Eisenhower postponed it until the next day. Conditions were not perfect then, either, but the rainy, windy weather added to the element of surprise. As dawn broke on June 6, Germans found the horizon filled with nearly three thousand ships, which launched an intense bombardment before the first of 155,000 troops landed at beaches, where 9,000 became casualties. Once the forces established a beachhead, their task was to break out into countryside that was not conducive to tank operations because of the thick hedges and mounds of earth that farmers used to fence livestock. Still, by the end of the month, the Allies had the Germans near collapse in Normandy and began to advance more swiftly than anyone expected. On August 25, French and American forces liberated Paris.

Some German generals, realizing the war was lost, tried to assassinate Der Führer. In the spring of 1943, a bomb placed on Hitler's plane had failed to explode. Then, motivated by the Normandy invasion, on July 20, 1944, a colonel planted a time bomb in his briefcase and carried it into a conference with Hitler; the blast killed four men, but Hitler escaped. Der Führer reacted by purging the army and government of everyone suspected of participating in the assassination scheme. He executed five thousand and sent ten thousand to concentration camps. Rommel, who knew of the plot, was given a choice: suicide or trial and execution. He chose death by cyanide.

Reeling from D-Day, the German military was exposed to a new threat when American and French forces invaded the French Riviera on August 15, 1944. Meeting little resistance, they captured fifty-seven thousand Nazi troops within two weeks. Preparing to strike another blow, Eisenhower directed Montgomery's army group to sweep northward toward the Ruhr as U.S. General Omar Bradley's moved east toward the Saar. They advanced so quickly that by late August they had outrun their supplies and competed for scarce gasoline. Each general claimed that if given all the gasoline, he could envelop the retreating Germans and bring the war in Europe to an end. Instead, Eisenhower settled on a slower offensive along a broad front, fearing that too swift of an advance by tanks would leave them without gasoline. Early in September, Montgomery proposed a daring move that Eisenhower accepted: airborne troops dropped behind German lines would take bridges over the Rhine in Holland intact, then Allied armor would close the gap. The operation, which began on September 10, marked the first daylight paratroop drop of the war but fell short of Montgomery's hopes and incurred heavy casualties. In December allied expectations were thwarted once more when Hitler's troops struck at the lightly defended line in the Ardennes Forest creating a bulge in Allies' lines. Hitler had ordered the audacious Panzer tank offensive, with the port of Antwerp in Belgium his objective. However, his army could not sustain an offensive, and the overly ambitious attack would, paradoxically, hastened his defeat.

With fog grounding the Allied aircraft, the Germans, striking in bitter cold and six inches of snow, penetrated sixty miles in the Battle of the Bulge. On December 22 they surrounded the crucial road-junction city of Bastogne and sent an ultimatum to the Allied commander to surrender. Brigadier General Anthony McAuliffe replied, "Nuts!" The skies cleared the next day, and fighter-bombers pounded German tank columns as the Panzers sputtered for lack of gasoline. Three days later, the Allies relieved Bastogne, then gradually pinched in the top and bottom of the bulge, squashing the offensive. The battle, the biggest ever fought on the ground by American arms, involved 600,000 U.S. troops and left 19,000 of them dead out of 70,000 casualties. The Germans, who could not replace their losses, had 100,000 casualties, contributing to the attrition of their army. The Battle of the Bulge delayed the Allied offensive in the west for a few weeks; the Soviets surged toward Berlin from the east.

1944: Wartime Election

During wartime the federal bureaucracy, which expanded by 60 percent under the New Deal, mushroomed by 300 percent; the president became more active, and Congress delegated immense authority to him. Nevertheless, the electorate seemed wary of Roosevelt. As prosperity returned, voters, who had more to conserve, became more conservative. In the 1942 congressional elections low turnout hurt the Democrats, whose majorities in both houses were pared. A combination of Republicans and conservative southern Democrats won the upper hand in Congress and terminated the Works Progress Administration, the Civilian Conservation Corps, and the National Youth Administration. With a war on FDR had no qualms about seeking the 1944 Democratic nomination, and no one challenged him. The chief suspense at the Chicago convention was about the vice presidential nomination, particularly because Roosevelt's health was failing. Willing to replace Vice President Henry Wallace, who was unpopular with conservatives, FDR privately endorsed a compromise choice, Missouri Senator Harry S Truman, chair of a committee that exposed incompetence and corruption in defense production. Delegates ratified his selection.

Wendell Willkie was a contender for the Republican nomination again, but after failing in the Wisconsin primary he withdrew, and New York District Attorney Thomas E. Dewey won the prize. Isolationist Ohio Governor John Bricker was tapped for the second spot. Dewey, whose only hope was for the war to end before election day, tried to make FDR's health an issue. He denounced Roosevelt for accepting the backing of the Congress of Industrial Organizations, and accused the administration of being influenced by communists and radicals. Roosevelt, who benefited from his role as commander in chief and American battle successes, condemned the GOP for isolationism and blamed it again for the Great Depression. Both parties endorsed membership in a postwar United Nations, a goal Willkie promoted in his book *One World*. The Senate would endorse the UN charter in late July 1945.

Roosevelt won 36 states and 432 electoral votes to Dewey's 12 and 99, gaining 53.4 percent of the popular vote (25.6 million ballots). Ominously FDR, sixty-two, had aged dramatically. He had grown frail and thin, his hands trembled, and he had dark circles under his eyes. Finding him suffering from heart disease and hypertension, and, without telling him how serious his condition was, his doctors told him to cut down on cigarettes and prescribed heart medications and at least ten hours of sleep nightly. "He has a great and terrible job to do, and he's got to do it even if it kills him," Labor Secretary Frances Perkins said.

End of the Third Reich

With combat in Europe raging in 1944 and 1945, the Allies held a series of diplomatic meetings to plan the postwar world. In July 1944 Treasury Secretary Henry Morgenthau led a conference at Bretton Woods, New Hampshire, to outline economic recovery; establishment of an International Monetary Fund and an International Bank for Reconstruction and Development were recommended. Two months afterward FDR and Churchill met in Quebec in an atmosphere of imminent victory and preliminarily approved a plan to dismember Germany, destroy its industrial

THE BIG THREE'S FINAL MEETING
Churchill, Roosevelt, and Stalin at Yalta, February 1945.
(Franklin D. Roosevelt Presidential Library)

base, and make it an agrarian nation. This scheme of Morgenthau's was scrapped. Meanwhile, representatives of the United States, Britain, China, and the Soviet Union gathered at Dumbarton Oaks, a Washington estate, to discuss the UN charter.

The Big Three met for the last time at Yalta, in the Russian Crimea, in February 1945. Roosevelt, though ill and frail, dominated the talks. The main issues were Poland, the UN, and the war against Japan. Churchill feared the Soviets would install puppet governments in Poland and other Eastern European countries the Red Army occupied. Stalin agreed to hold democratic elections in Poland, but argued that the country was in the Soviet sphere of influence and insisted on a friendly government. With his army occupying Poland, there was little the British or the Americans could do to stop Stalin from imposing a government. Such territorial conflicts, arising during the last months of European fighting, helped sow the seeds for a Cold War between the United States and the U.S.S.R.

In his other objectives, Roosevelt was more successful. Stalin assented to UN participation and to join the war on Japan within three months after the war in Europe ended. In return, the Soviet Union received three votes in the UN General Assembly and Far East territorial concessions. It was agreed that the Red Army would liberate Berlin, a controversial decision. Churchill wanted to beat the Soviets to the German capital, yet FDR deferred to Eisenhower, who did not consider it an important military objective.

First the Western armies had to cross the Rhine. Continuing to advance along a broad front, the Allies reached the Rhine at Dusseldorf, Germany, on March 2, 1945, to find bridges destroyed. On March 7 an American division took the bridge at Remagen intact, and the U.S. First Army, capitalizing on the breakthrough, sped eight thousand soldiers across the span in twenty-four hours. A German counterattack failed, as American troops poured in until the bridge collapsed on March 17. By that time pontoons spanned the Rhine. Patton's troops crossed the river on March 23, with Montgomery's following the next day. When April arrived, the Germans were near total defeat, losing two thousand prisoners daily to each Allied division. On April 4 Patton's men liberated the Ohrdruf-Nord concentration camp, confirming the most malignant side of Nazism: the slaughter of Jews, Gypsies, Soviets, and homosexuals. The battle-hardened Patton vomited when he saw the prisoners, and the mayor of Ohrdruf and his wife, after being forced to tour the camp, hanged themselves. At the liberation of another camp, an American sergeant observed, "It was like stepping into the Dark Ages."

The war was also coming to an end in Italy, where the Allies opened their final offensive April 9, 1945. On April 28 Italian partisans murdered Mussolini and his mistress, brought the bodies to Milan, and strung them up by their heels. German forces in the country surrendered on May 2, the day the Allies captured Berlin. Suited neither by temperament nor resources to fight a long war, Hitler could win campaigns but not a protracted war against the two mightiest powers on earth—the United States and the Soviet Union. Unable to face the ramifications of his malevolence, Hitler poisoned his wife and then himself. Fearing the poison might fail, he shot himself in his bunker underneath Berlin, two days after Mussolini died. On May 7, Germany surrendered and May 7 was Victory in Europe Day— an outcome that Roosevelt did not see.

Sitting for a portrait on April 12, 1945, at Warm Springs, Roosevelt suddenly raised his left hand to his temple, said, "I have a terrific headache," and slumped in his chair. He never regained consciousness and died of a stroke. Millions were shocked by the death of the only president they had ever known, a man who, according to many historians, was the greatest chief executive of the century. Roosevelt was by no means without flaws, but he helped free his office from the inhibitions of the past, his country from depression, and his world from tyranny.

The War Turns against Japan

In the Pacific, the decisive factor was naval airpower, in which ships and planes were closely coordinated. The Pacific fleet was organized into task forces centered on aircraft carriers, including the cruisers and destroyers that accompanied them. Battleships, too slow to keep up with the task forces, were more useful for shelling islands before an invasion. Submarines were used for scouting and preying on merchant and military vessels. Japanese aviators who had been fighting in Asia were more experienced than American pilots. Until the introduction of the F6F Hellcat, the navy had no plane as maneuverable as the Zero. But Japan could not replace lost pilots, planes, and ships as quickly as could the Americans.

American troops and their equipment had to be transported across thousands of ocean miles to land on hostile shores and face Japanese soldiers who fought tenaciously in the tropical jungles. Considering surrender a disgrace, the Japanese adopted suicidal tactics and had more casualties than their enemy in each island engagement. Their plan was to seize, fortify, and defend Pacific islands and archipelagos within thousands of miles of Japan, making the price to take them too costly for the Americans. Like the Germans, they did not consider Americans a match for them and believed they could hold a sphere of influence if they discouraged their foe from fighting a prolonged war. They misjudged the American intention, which was to fight the war to a conclusion, not a stalemate. Planners decided that they did not have to oust Japan from all islands, many of them small, sparsely populated, and relatively worthless except for their military value. Rather, they would frustrate the Japanese by leapfrogging—fighting to capture key islands, build airfields and naval bases and, with control of the air and sea assured, hop over strong defensive positions.

In the immediate aftermath of Pearl Harbor, the Japanese scored conquests comparable to the Blitzkrieg. As bombers were striking Pearl Harbor, air raids were mounted on Midway Island, Wake Island, Guam, Hong Kong, southern Thailand, northern Malaya, and the Philippines, all of which Tokyo claimed within six months. Rangoon and Singapore likewise fell. Worse, the Allies were beaten in the Battle of the Java Sea, the first noteworthy fleet action, in January 1942. On the other hand, the campaign for the Philippines was the longest and most arduous for Japan. After destroying the U.S. Air Force on the ground on December 7, 1941, the main Japanese force landed on Luzon on December 22. Under General Douglas MacArthur, the Americans retreated to the mountainous Bataan Peninsula jungle following two weeks of heavy fighting and, short of food and drugs, suffered more casualties from starvation and disease than combat. MacArthur set up command on the isle of Corregidor in Manila Harbor, but in February was ordered to go to Australia and fled through Japanese lines in a PT boat. Americans on Bataan surrendered on April 9, and the Japanese took Corregidor on May 6. Captured soldiers were forced to walk sixty-five miles in blistering heat without food or water—the infamous Bataan Death March that killed ten thousand American and Filipino troops (and, after the war, led to war-crimes trials for Japanese commanders). Survivors were taken to Japan as slave labor. On one ship, prisoners in a hold without air went mad with thirst and slashed each other's throats and wrists in an effort to suck blood. Many of the boats were sunk by American planes or submarines whose crews did not realize they were killing comrades.

In April 1942, a Japanese fleet set out to invade Port Moresby on New Guinea to put Japan within range to bomb Australia. The United States clashed with the Japanese in the Battle of the Coral Sea, sinking one carrier and losing one, a tactical draw that was a setback for Japan because it was compelled to cancel invasion plans. Fought entirely by carrier-based planes, it was the first naval battle in which surface fleets never made visual contact. That same month, American aviators, starved for a psychological victory, staged a daring raid on Tokyo. Sixteen B-25 bombers lifted off from the carrier *Hornet* some 650 miles offshore. Lacking sufficient gasoline to return, and unable to land bombers on an aircraft carrier, the planes were to fly on to friendly airfields in China. Most made it, yet eight fliers landed in enemy territory. Three were executed for bombing residential areas. The raid raised American morale, although it inflicted small damage.

With Japanese strategists seeking a decisive battle to smash the American fleet, Admiral Isoroku Yamamoto took most of his navy to attack Midway in June 1942, after a diversionary strike at the Aleutians. Aware of the scheme because of their ability to read Japanese codes, American planners set a trap, sending forces to await Yamamoto north of Midway. When Yamamoto's planes attacked, leaving their aircraft carriers unprotected, American pilots decimated his fleet, sinking four carriers to offset the loss of one carrier. Paradoxically, the decisive battle that Yamamoto sought was a devastating defeat. The Battle of Midway marked the end of Japanese expansion. American intelligence scored another coup that month. Cryptanalysts learned of Yamamoto's planned tour of the Solomons, allowing fighters to shoot down his plane, killing him and robbing Japan of its best admiral. The Solomons also figured in the first American offensive in the Pacific, at Guadalcanal in August. After Marines invaded, a series of naval engagements ensued while both sides attempted to reinforce troops. Ground fighting raged until the Japanese evacuated in February 1943. Guadalcanal marked another watershed in the war, for, henceforth, Japan was on the defensive and the United States did not lose a battle.

By the fall of 1943 the American offensive was proceeding rapidly, bolstered by six new Hellcat-stocked carriers for Pacific duty. Admiral Chester W. Nimitz was set to fight toward Japan through a line of islands including the Gilberts, the Marshalls, and the Marianas, as General Douglas MacArthur was to wage an offensive in the Southwest Pacific. On November 20 the navy attacked Tarawa in the Gilberts, preceding a landing of Marines, who subdued the island in three days. Nimitz next assaulted the Marshalls and took them by February 3, 1944, after stiff resistance. The next campaign, the most ambitious to date, focused in June 1944 on the Marianas, control of which was critical because B-29 bombers based there could attack the Japanese home islands. Saipan, the largest of the island group, was the scene of the bloodiest campaign and another serious defeat for Japan. The Americans lost 29 planes and 14,000 casualties. The Japanese lost 273 of the 373 planes that attacked the invading task force, 3 aircraft carriers, and 30,000 dead. About 50,000 Japanese were killed defending the Marianas. The United States constructed air bases there and a key harbor at Guam.

MacArthur, when forced to flee the Philippines, had vowed to return, a promise he insisted on redeeming. On October 20, 1944, as Marines landed on Leyte, MacArthur waded ashore to announce, "People of the Philippines, I have returned." The Marines seized the island, but not before the Battle of Leyte Gulf, the biggest naval engagement in the history of warfare and the last in World War II. For the first time the Japanese used kamikazes, planes loaded with explosives and flown into American ships by pilots on suicide missions, yet their navy was devastated, losing its four remaining carriers, three battleships, nine cruisers, and twelve destroyers. On January 9, 1945, Marines reached Luzon, the major Philippine island, and began fighting that took the lives of almost all the 260,000 Japanese defenders. In Manila, house-to-house fighting killed 100,000 civilians, but Americans captured the capital. Corregidor surrendered on March 2, and resistance ended by June 30, though fighting persisted in outlying islands.

The fighting for Iwo Jima, a small volcanic island, featured a moment that would be forever frozen in the American mind. Planes bombed the island for seventy-four days before 60,000 soldiers invaded on February 19, 1945, although the Japanese, who had constructed a maze of underground caves and tunnels, largely survived the bombardment and fought to the death. Mount Suribachi, dominating Iwo Jima, was honeycombed with caves, pillboxes, and bunkers that the Japanese defended ferociously, directing artillery fire from its peak toward the beaches. Nevertheless, Marines gradually fought their way up Suribachi, using flame throwers and explosives, and on the third day of combat three were photographed raising the American flag on the mountain, a photo that won the Pulitzer Prize and became the most famous picture of the war. Of the 23,000 defenders, 20,000 died; the United States lost nearly 6,000 dead.

The final American target before the planned invasion of the home islands was Okinawa, a sixty-mile-long island 350 miles southwest of Japan. Preliminary bombardment began on October 10, 1944, with the invasion getting under way on April 1, 1945. Seventy-seven thousand defended Okinawa against 183,000 American troops, the Japanese losing ten dead for each American killed and holding out more than eighty-three days, making planners in the United States fearful of the cost of invading Japan. There was apprehension despite faith in airpower. By early 1944 the Allies had the B-29 bomber, which flew at higher altitudes and had a longer range than the lighter, slower B-17, for an effort that wreaked havoc in Japan. At first, the director of the campaign, Major General Curtis LeMay, whose forces were based first in China and then in the Marianas, sought to cripple Japanese aircraft production. Soon, he shifted to area bombing, with incendiary bombs that ignited firestorms in cities built largely of wood and paper. A raid of 344 bombers on Tokyo on March 9, 1945, killed 84,000, wounded 41,000, and left more than 1 million homeless. Excluding nuclear bombs, the air raids destroyed 43 percent of sixty-three major Japanese cities, eliminated 42 percent of Japanese industrial capacity, and slew, injured, or left homeless 22 million.

If warfare in the Pacific turned from frustration to fruition for the Americans, it was unlike the war in China. The United States had few troops in China, yet a group of volunteers under retired Colonel Claire Chennault, the Flying Tigers, had been fighting in the air since 1940. Chennault's hopes that an air offensive against Japan by China-based planes would end the war proved unfounded. On the ground, aid from Washington was tangible in the person of Lieutenant General Joseph Stilwell, designated to represent Americans in China and to serve as chief of staff for Jiang Jieshe. Jiang's army was corrupt, demoralized, and ineffective, and Jiang was reluctant to fight. He wanted to conserve his army for the civil war against the communists that he knew would follow the defeat of Japan. His refusal to wage war aggressively, and the inability of his forces to recapture Burma, angered the irascible Stilwell, who quarreled constantly with the arrogant and secretive Generalissmo. In 1944 Roosevelt

★ PAUL TIBBETS: A FATEFUL FLIGHT ★

There is no morality in warfare. You kill children. You kill women. You kill old men. You don't seek them out, but they die. That's what happens in war.
—PAUL W. TIBBETS JR.

DEADLY CARGO
Paul Tibbets Jr. dropped
the first atom bomb.
(National Archives)

BOTH CARRIED a deadly cargo. In his coverall pocket, the pilot had a small box with twelve cyanide capsules; if their aircraft appeared to be in trouble, he and his eleven crewmen could choose suicide by poison or gun, to escape capture and torture by the enemy. In its bay, the plane bore the atomic bomb that was to be dropped on Hiroshima, Japan, on the morning of August 6, 1945.

Just before the runway ended near a cliff, Colonel Paul W. Tibbets Jr. lifted the *Enola Gay*, named for his mother, into the sky. He had led an 1,800-man force at Wendover, Utah, nearly a year in secret preparation. It was not until a few hours after takeoff that he told his crew the kind of bomb in the bay. Doubts about the righteousness of the mission did not trouble him. "Our crew did not do the bombing in anger," Tibbets said more than fifty years later. "We did it because we were determined to stop the killing, stop the war. I would have done anything to get to Japan and stop the killing."

Six hours and two thousand miles after takeoff, the moment came. Seventeen seconds past 8:15 A.M., the bomb bay opened and the weapon plummeted toward Hiroshima. Abruptly 9,700 pounds lighter, the plane bolted up ten feet and Tibbets pushed it into a sharp, diving right turn so it would not be directly above the blast. Forty-three seconds after it was dropped, the bomb detonated. Its flash blinded everyone aboard, and its rising shock wave battered the *Enola Gay* twice, jolting the crew. Then the air calmed, and the tail gunner saw flames and smoke on the ground, with a mushroom cloud billowing upward.

It was beyond compare, beyond comprehension. For the tape recording of the crew members' reactions, the thirty-year-old Tibbets confessed that he had expected to see a big explosion, but not of the magnitude he actually observed. Decades later, he recalled, "I looked at that city—and there was no city, there was nothing but the fringes of where the city used to be. There had been a city when we were making our approach, but now there was no humanity there."

The aftermath for Tibbets was often harsh, in the United States and overseas. Sent to a post in India in the 1960s, he was branded "the world's greatest killer" in procommunist newspapers and assigned a bodyguard. Eventually, the hostile press compelled the State Department to recall Tibbets and close the mission. Quitting the armed services following a distinguished thirty-year stint, he was sure that he was a victim of public opinion that blamed him for the bombing. He was, nevertheless, unapologetic. Asked whether he could sleep at night, Tibbets said in an interview published in 1999, "I sleep so well because I know how many people got to live full lives because of what we did."

And he added: "If you could fix me up so that I could do the same things in an airplane now that I could do in 1945? If you could do that and this country was in trouble, I would jump in there to beat hell."

Sources: For insight on Paul Tibbets and his mission, see Bob Greene's columns in the *Chicago Tribune* on January 10–13, 1999. Other good accounts of the mission are Gordon Thomas and Max Morgan Witts, *Enola Gay* (1977), and Peter Wyden, *Day One: Before Hiroshima and After* (1984).

sent a personal emissary, Major General Patrick J. Hurley, to resolve the Stilwell-Jiang dispute. After Hurley sided with Jiang, FDR recalled Stilwell and replaced him with Major General Albert C. Wedemeyer, who was no more successful in getting the Chinese to fight. Roosevelt's attempt to treat China as a great power was unrealistic, and to the Americans, the China campaign turned out to be one of the most vexing of the war. The main contribution of the Allied forces in China was to tie down Japanese troops.

The Atomic Age Begins

In the last seven weeks of the war, American planes, aircraft carriers, and surface vessels participated in the bombing of Japan, as the United States tightened a naval blockade of the islands. The deadliest bombs would be dropped last.

In July 1945, the Allies held their final wartime summit at Potsdam, Germany, at which Stalin alone remained of the Big Three. Truman had replaced the deceased Roosevelt as president, and during the conference Clement R. Attlee took over for Churchill, whom he had defeated in British elections. The conference settled few issues, and the Americans and the British were shocked when Stalin demanded huge reparations from Germany, a sign that the Grand Alliance was breaking up. At the gathering, Truman was informed of the first successful detonation of the atomic bomb on July 16, 1945, in a New Mexico desert. The United States, Britain, and China issued the Potsdam Declaration, urging Japan to surrender or face annihilation (although the bomb was not mentioned). Truman told Stalin of the powerful weapon, without revealing that it was an atomic bomb. Tokyo would not yield, so on August 6, three B-29s headed to drop a deadly payload on Hiroshima, chosen because it had been spared from heavy bombing and had no prisoner-of-war camps. The bomb caused 140,000 deaths and destroyed more than 80 percent of the cities. A few hours later, the White House announced the existence of the bomb and warned the Japanese that unless they surrendered, "they may expect a rain of ruin from the air, the like of which has never been seen on this earth."

Forecasts of bad weather advanced the date for use of the second atomic bomb, sparing the primary target, Kokura, and condemning Nagasaki to destruction. No presidential decision was involved in the timing of the second bomb; that was left to the military, which was instructed to delude the Japanese into thinking that the United States had a large arsenal of atomic bombs when there were only two. Ultimately, some 70,000 would die from the bomb dropped August 9 at Nagasaki. The Soviet Union declared war on Japan on August 10, helping convince the Japanese that their cause was doomed. Humanity had unlocked and unleashed the secret of the atom, a breakthrough fraught with paradox that held, and would fulfill, much promise for good, but also would leave the world in fear of nuclear destruction. Even after the Nagasaki bombing, though, Tokyo was slow to surrender. To Allied demands for unconditional surrender, Japan responded by asking for the right to retain Emperor Hirohito. The Allies agreed, provided that he was to be a figurehead subject to their command. Japanese dislike of the condition aside, Hirohito agreed and announced the surrender, after an unsuccessful military coup attempt, on August 15. The official treaty of surrender was signed in Tokyo Bay aboard the battleship *Missouri* on September 2, 1945.

In later years, use of the bomb incurred recriminations in the United States, with debate over whether the war could have been ended without resort to the weapon. Some scientists and historians argued that the bomb was unnecessary, inhumane, immoral, ill-timed, petty vengeance for Pearl Harbor, and even racist. But it is difficult to imagine Japan giving up without the effects of the atomic bombs supplemented by the Soviet declaration of war. The alternatives were worse. Continued nonatomic bombing would have cost more lives than atomic bombing, and an invasion would have meant terrible losses on both sides, including Japanese civilians. Destruction of the home islands in hand-to-hand combat, instead of swift, comparatively limited death from above, would likely have left more bitterness among the survivors. Moreover, there is no question that the atomic bomb would have been used against the Germans had it been ready, nor is

JAPAN SURRENDERS
Douglas MacArthur signs for the United States on Tokyo Bay, September 2, 1945.
(National Archives)

there any doubt that Germany and Japan, both of which had nuclear programs, would have used the weapon against their opponents. And in the long run, the destruction and revulsion from the bomb made future military use of nuclear weapons unlikely. The atomic genie was never again freed from its bottle in the twentieth century.

The war exacted a horrific price: 20 million dead from the Soviet Union; 10.45 million from China; 5.5 million from Germany; 5.8 million from Poland, most of them Holocaust victims; 1.9 million from Japan; 430,000 from Britain; and more than 400,000 from the United States. Among American servicemen, just one in ten was ever exposed to combat, and with an overall death rate of five per one thousand, the military was, paradoxically, safer than the industrial home front, where the death rate was twice as high. The American contribution to the war was essential, involving millions of troops over vast distances and massive amounts of supplies to allies. Still, it was the Soviets who made the most important contribution to defeating Hitler in Europe. While the United States relied primarily on technology to overcome the Germans far from its soil, the Red Army wore them down with brute force, incurring horrible losses on Soviet land.

World War II wreaked unprecedented destruction and environmental damage that would affect generations. It set colonialism on a course toward extinction, required massive spending, accelerated scientific development, helped discredit racism, precipitated substantial (if sometimes temporary) changes in women's roles, and effected major changes in the economy and society. It ended the Great Depression and was a greater factor in redistributing income than any social program in American history. Like the conflagration, the era from 1920 to 1945 was cathartic, shaping the United States to a degree matched in few periods of comparable length. The country showed bravery that most generations could not equal and, with victory over the Axis, reached the apogee of its influence as a global power—but it could not banish the many tensions that loomed. Never before or since did the future seem so promising, or so perilous, as it did in the summer of 1945.

The American Economy, 1929–1945

Percent of civilian Labor force[*1] (Unemployment rate)		Gross National Product in billions [*2]		Summary of the Federal Government Finances (as of 12/31 each year)[**] Total Gross Debt in Millions	
1929	3.2	1929	104.4	1929	16.9
1930	8.7	1930	95.1	1930	16.1
1931	15.9	1931	89.5	1931	16.8
1932	23.6	1932	76.4	1932	19.4
1933	24.9	1933	74.2	1933	22.5
1934	21.7	1934	80.8	1934	57.0
1935	20.1	1935	91.4	1935	28.7
1936	19.9	1936	100.9	1936	33.7
1937	14.3	1937	109.1	1937	36.4
1938	19.0	1938	103.2	1938	37.1
1939	17.2	1939	111.0	1939	40.4
1940	14.6	1940	121.0	1940	42.9
1941	9.9	1941	138.7	1941	48.9
1942	4.7	1942	154.7	1942	72.4
1943	1.9	1943	170.2	1943	136.6
1944	1.2	1944	183.6	1944	201.0
1945	1.9	1945	180.9	1945	258.6

[*]From the *Historical Statistics of the United States: Colonial Times to 1970 (Bicentennial Edition)*. September 1975. U.S. Department of Commerce, Bureau of the Census.

[2**]From the *Historical Statistics of the United States: Colonial Times to 1957 (A Statistical Abstract Supplement)*. 1961. U.S. Department of Commerce, Bureau of the Census.

Bibliographic Essay

General Works

General histories of the interwar period include Glen Jeansonne, *Transformation and Reaction: America, 1921–1945* (2004); David M. Kennedy, *Freedom from Fear: The American People in Depression and War, 1929–1945* (1999); Michael Parrish, *Anxious Decades: America in Prosperity and Depression, 1929–1941* (1992); Page Smith, *Redeeming the Time: A People's History of the 1920s and the New Deal* (1987), especially strong on the conflict between capital and labor; and Sean Dennis Cashman, *America in the Twenties and Thirties: The Olympian Age of Franklin D. Roosevelt* (1989).

Histories of the 1920s include Ellis W. Hawley, *The Great War and the Search for a Modern Order: A History of the American People and Their Institutions, 1917–1933* (1979); Goeffrey Perrett, *America in the Twenties: A History* (1982), detailed and well-written; David J. Goldberg, *Discounted America: The United States in the 1920s* (1999); Arthur M. Schlesinger Jr., *The Age of Roosevelt*, vol. 1, *The Crisis of the Old Order, 1919–1933* (1958), by an author noted for his erudite style; and Paul A. Carter's succinct *The Twenties in America* (1975), and *Another Part of the Twenties* (1977). For a general history of the 1930s, see Gerald D. Nash, *The Crucial Era: The Great Depression and World War II, 1929–1945* (1992).

On women, works include Glenna Matthews, *"Just a Housewife": The Rise and Fall of Domesticity in America* (1987); Alice Kessler-Harris, *Out to Work: A History of Wage-Earning Women in the United States* (1982); Lois Scharf and Joan M. Jensen, eds., *Decades of Discontent: The Women's Movement, 1920–1940* (1983); and Robin Muncy, *Creating a Female Dominion in American Reform, 1890–1935* (1991). On African Americans, Native Americans, and immigrants, Leonard Dinnerstein et al., *Natives and Strangers: Blacks, Indians, and Immigrants in America* (1990), is a sweeping survey. Among the better histories of African Americans are John Hope Franklin, *From Slavery to Freedom: A History of American Negroes* (1967); Herbert Aptheker, *Afro-American History: The Modern Era* (1971); and Nicholas Lemann, *The Promised Land: The Great Black Migration and How It Changed America* (1991). On Mexican Americans, see David Guitierrez, *Walls and Mirrors* (1995). On Asian Americans, see Roger Daniels, *Asian-Americans* (1988). On the Italians and the Sacco-Vanzetti case, see Louis Joughlin and Edmond Morgan, *Postmortem: New Evidence in the Case of Sacco and Vanzetti* (1985), and Paul Avrich, *Sacco and Vanzetti: The Anarchist Persuasion* (1991). The Ku Klux Klan is examined in Wyn Craig Wade, *The Fiery Cross: The Ku Klux Klan in America* (1987); Richard K. Tucker, *The Dragon and the Cross: The Rise and Fall of the Ku Klux Klan in Middle America* (1991); Kathleen M. Blee, *Women of the Klan: Racism and Gender in the 1920s* (1991); and Nancy MacLean, *Behind the Mask of Chivalry: The Making of the Second Ku Klux Klan* (1994). Regarding labor, the best study is Irving Bernstein, *The Lean Years: A History of the American Worker, 1920–1933* (1960). Also helpful are Robert H. Zieger, *American Workers, American Unions, 1920–1985* (1986); David Brody, *Workers in Industrial America* (1980); and James R. Green, *The World of the Worker: Labor in Twentieth-Century America* (1980). Among the many studies of business are James M. Cortada, *Before the Computer: IBM, NCR, Borroughs, Remington, and the Industry They Created, 1865–1956* (1993), a fine history that focuses on technology; and James W. Prothro, *Dollar Decade: Business Ideas in the 1920s* (1985). On the automobile, which transformed business and society, see James J. Fink, *The Automobile Age (1988)*; and Lois Scharf, *Taking the Wheel: Women and the Coming of the Motor Age* (1991).

Presidents, Prosperity, and Depression

On the Republican reign of the 1920s, see John D. Hicks, *Republican Ascendancy, 1921–1933* (1958), which is dated but remains a solid political history. On Warren G. Harding, the best biography is Francis Russell, *The Shadow of Blooming Grove* (1968); also useful are Eugene P. Trani and David L. Wilson, *The Presidency of Warren G. Harding* (1977); Robert K. Murray, *The Harding Era: Warren G. Harding and His Administration* (1969); the highly critical Andrew Sinclair, *The Available Man* (1975); and Robert H. Ferrell, *The Strange Deaths of President Harding* (1996). The most recent biography of Harding, John W. Dean, *Warren G. Harding* (2004), considers Harding an underrated politician. On Calvin Coolidge, the most balanced book by far is Robert H. Ferrell, *The Presidency of*

Calvin Coolidge (1998). Other biographies include Robert Sobel, *Coolidge: An American Enigma* (1998), and Claude M. Fuess, *Calvin Coolidge: The Man from Vermont* (1981). There are numerous biographies of Herbert Hoover and accounts of his administration. David Burner, *Herbert Hoover: A Public Life* (1979), finds Hoover's personality flawed but his presidential policies constructive; Albert U. Romasco argues in *The Poverty of Abundance: Hoover, the Nation, the Depression* (1965), that his policies were a failure; and Joan Hoff-Wilson, *Herbert Hoover: Forgotten Progressive* (1975), considers him a Progressive out of his element. The most detailed account of Hoover's policies is Martin Fausold, *The Presidency of Herbert Hoover* (1985).

The stock market is treated in Robert Sobel, *The Great Bull Market: Wall Street in the 1920s* (1968), and John Kenneth Galbraith, *The Great Crash, 1929* (1961). Accounts of the depression include John A. Garraty, *The Great Depression* (1986), which provides a worldwide perspective; Edward Robb Ellis, *A Nation in Torment: The Great American Depression, 1929–1939* (1970); Gerald D. Nash, *The Great Depression and World War II: Organizing America, 1933–1945* (1979), a general account; Robert S. McElvaine, *The Great Depression: America, 1929–1941* (1984); and T. H. Watkins, *Great Depression: America in the 1930s* (1993), and *Hungry Years: A Narrative History of the Great Depression in America* (1999).

Franklin D. Roosevelt and the New Deal have generated an enormous literature. The best synthesis of the New Deal era remains James MacGregor Burns, *Roosevelt: The Lion and the Fox* (1956). Frank Friedel has written a comprehensive study, *Franklin D. Roosevelt*, 4 vols. (1952–1973), and a one-volume study, *Franklin D. Roosevelt: A Rendezvous with Destiny* (1990). Other single-volume works include George McJimsey, *The Presidency of Franklin Delano Roosevelt* (2000). Blanche Wiesen Cook has written a virtually definitive biography of the best-known first lady, *Eleanor Roosevelt*, vols. 1 and 2 (1992, 1999). General histories of the New Deal include Arthur M. Schlesinger Jr.'s three-volume *Age of Roosevelt*; William E. Leuchtenburg, *Franklin D. Roosevelt and the New Deal, 1932–1940* (1963), and *The FDR Years: On Roosevelt and his Legacy* (1995); and Alan Brinkley, *The End of Reform: New Deal Liberalism in Recession and War* (1995).

On FDR's opponents, see Albert Fried, *FDR and His Enemies* (1999); T. Harry Williams, *Huey Long* (1969); William Ivy Hair, *The Kingfish and His Realm: The Life and Times of Huey P. Long* (1991); Glen Jeansonne, *Messiah of the Masses: Huey P. Long and the Great Depression* (1993), a critical interpretation; Alan Brinkley, *Voices of Protest: Huey Long, Father Coughlin, and the Great Depression* (1982), elegantly written; Glen Jeansonne, *Gerald L. K. Smith: Minister of Hate* (1997); and

Leo P. Ribuffo, *The Old Christian Right: The Protestant Far Right from the Great Depression to the Cold War* (1983). Communism in 1930s America is the subject of Harvey Klehr, *The Heyday of American Communism: The Depression Decade* (1984); see also Mark Naison, *Communists in Harlem during the Depression* (1983). More general studies include Donald R. McCoy, *Angry Voices: Left of Center Politics in the New Deal Era* (1958); Kate Weigand, *Red Feminism: American Communism and the Making of Women's Liberation* (2000); and Richard H. Pells, *Radical Visions and American Dreams: Culture and Social Thought in the Depression Years* (1998).

Culture

General works include Ethan Mordden, *That Jazz! An Idiosyncratic Social History of the American Twenties* (1978); Barbara H. Solomon, ed., *Ain't We Got Fun? Essays, Lyrics, and Stories of the Twenties* (1980); Paula S. Fass, *The Damned and the Beautiful: American Youth in the 1920s* (1972); Alice Goldfarb Marquis, *Hopes and Ashes: The Birth of Modern Times, 1929–1939* (1986); the classic sociological study by Robert S. and Helen M. Lynd, *Middletown: A Study in Contemporary American Culture* (1929), and the sequel, *Middletown in Transition* (1937). On the greatest popular hero of the age, the best study is A. Scott Berg, *Lindbergh* (1998); see also Von Hardesty, *Lindbergh: Flight's Enigmatic Hero* (2002). On literature, see Frederick Hoffman, *The Twenties: American Writing in the Postwar Decade* (1965); Daniel Joseph Singal, *The War within: From Victorian to Modernist Thought in the South, 1919–1945* (1988); Nathan I. Huggins, *Harlem Renaissance* (1971); and Addison Gayle Jr., *The Way of the New World: The Black Novel in America* (1976). On the visual arts and architecture, see William S. Lieberman, ed., *Art of the Twenties* (1979); Abraham A. Davidson, *Early American Modernist Painting, 1910–1935* (1981); and Brendan Gill, *Many Masks: A Life of Frank Lloyd Wright* (1987). New Deal contributions to the arts are covered in Richard D. McKinzie, *The New Deal for Artists* (1973); and Francis V. O'Connor, *Federal Art Patronage, 1933–1943* (1966). On music and dance, among the best studies are Arnold Shaw, *The Jazz Age: Popular Music in the 1920s* (1987); Burton W. Peretti, *The Creation of Jazz: Music, Race, and Culture in Urban America* (1994); and Tony Thomas, *That's Dancing* (1984). On radio, see Eric F. Barnouw, *A Tower in Babel: A History of Broadcasting in the United States*, vol. 1, *To 1933* (1966), and *The Golden Web: A History of Broadcasting in the United States*, vol. 2, *To 1948* (1968). For motion pictures, see Andrew

Bergman, *We're in the Money: Depression America and Its Films* (1971), and Edward Wagenknecht, *The Movies in the Age of Innocence* (1962).

The literature on religious history is rich. The standard work on fundamentalism is George N. Marsden, *Fundamentalism and American Culture: The Shaping of Twentieth-Century Evangelism, 1870–1925* (1980). On the Scopes trial, the best book is Edward J. Larson, *Summer for the Gods: The Scopes Trial and America's Continuing Debate over Science and Religion* (1997). Also see Bernard Weisberger, *They Gathered at the River: The Story of the Great Revivalists and Their Impact on Religion in America* (1958); Florence M. Szasz, *The Divided Mind of Protestant America, 1880–1939* (1982); Joseph L. Blau, *Judaism in America: From Curiosity to Third Faith* (1976); and William M. Halsey, *The Survival of American Innocence: Catholicism in a Era of Disillusionment, 1920–1940* (1980).

For sports, turn to Elliot J. Gorn and Warren Goldstein, *A Brief History of American Sports* (1993); Benjamin G. Rader, *American Sports: From the Age of Folk Games to the Age of Televised Sports* (1999); Donn Rogosin, *Invisible Men* (1995), about black baseball before integration; and John M. Carroll, *Red Grange and the Rise of Modern Football* (1999).

Diplomacy and War

Warren I. Cohen has written the best short account of foreign policy in the 1920s, *Empire without Tears: American Foreign Relations, 1921–1933* (1987). Foster Rhea Dulles, *America's Rise to World Power, 1894–1954* (1963), is a reliable survey. Akira Iriye, *After Imperialism: The Search for a New Order in the Far East, 1921–1931* (1965), examines policy in the Pacific. Peace movements between the world wars are covered in Charles DeBenedetti, *Origins of the Modern American Peace Movement, 1915–1929* (1978), and Harriet Hyman Alonso, *The Women's Peace Union and the Outlawry of War, 1921–1942* (1989).

FDR's diplomacy is discussed succinctly in Robert A. Divine, *Roosevelt and World War II* (1971), and in more detail in Robert Dallek, *Franklin D. Roosevelt and American Foreign Policy, 1932–1945* (1979). Attempts to aid the Allies are included in Warren F. Kimball, *The Most Unsordid Act: Lend-Lease, 1939–1941* (1969), and Waldo Heinrichs, *Threshold of War: Franklin D. Roosevelt and American Entry into World War II* (1988). Isolationists are covered in Wayne S. Cole, *Roosevelt and the Isolationists, 1932–1945* (1983), and *America First: The Battle against Intervention, 1940–1941* (1953), and Bill Kauffman, *America First! Its History, Culture, and Politics* (1995). Glen Jeansonne, *Women of the Far Right: The Mothers'*

Movement and World War II (1996), describes a movement that sympathized with Adolf Hitler and opposed the American war against fascism. On the coming of World War II, two of the best works, though dated and overly detailed, are William L. Langer and S. Everett Gleason, *The Challenge to Isolation, 1937–1940* (1952), and *The Undeclared War, 1940–1941* (1953). For a Pacific study, see Akira Iriye, *The Origins of the Second World War in Asia and the Pacific* (1987). On Pearl Harbor, see Gordon W. Prange, *At Dawn We Slept: The Untold Story of Pearl Harbor* (1981).

General works on the war and the American role include H. P. Willmott, *The Great Crusade: A New Complete History of the Second World War* (1989); John Keegan, *The Second World War* (1989); Gerhard Weinberg, *A World at Arms: A Global History of World War II* (1994); Geoffrey Perrett, *There's a War To Be Won: The United States Army in World War II* (1991); William L. O'Neill, *A Democracy at War: America's Fight at Home and Abroad in World War II* (1993); and Charles B. MacDonald, *The Mighty Endeavor: The American War in Europe* (1986). For other aspects of the war, see Samuel Eliot Morison, *The Two-Ocean War* (1963), a masterful account of naval warfare; Rick Atkinson, *An Army at Dawn: The War in Africa, 1942–1943* (2002), an acclaimed study of the first joint military operation conducted by the Allies; Dan Van Der Vat, *The Atlantic Campaign* (1988); Stephen E. Ambrose, *The Supreme Commander: The War Years of Dwight D. Eisenhower* (1970); Ronald H. Spector, *Eagle against the Sun: The American War with Japan* (1985); and two riveting biographies, William Manchester, *American Caesar: Douglas MacArthur, 1880–1964* (1973); and Barbara Tuchman, *Stilwell and the American Experience in China* (1975).

On Roosevelt's role, the best is James MacGregor Burns, *Roosevelt: Soldier of Freedom* (1970). Also consult Eric Larrabee, *Commander in Chief: Franklin Delano Roosevelt, His Lieutenants and Their War* (1987); Kenneth Davis, *FDR: The War President, 1940–1943* (2000), and Doris Kearns Goodwin, *Franklin and Eleanor Roosevelt: The Home Front in World War II* (1994). Michael Beschloss, *The Conquerors: Roosevelt, Truman, and the Destruction of Hitler's Germany* (2002) describes Roosevelt's and Truman's efforts to make certain that Germany would never threaten the world again. Accounts of genocide in Europe are included in Henry L. Feingold, *The Politics of Rescue: The Roosevelt Administration and the Holocaust, 1938–1945* (1970); David S. Wyman, *The Abandonment of the Jews: America and the Holocaust, 1941–1945* (1984); Richard Breitman and Alan Kraut, *American Refugee Policy and American Jewry, 1933–1945* (1987); and Richard Breitman, *Official Secrets: What the Nazis Planned, What the British and Americans Knew* (1998).

The development of the atomic bomb is well chronicled in Richard Rhodes, *The Making of the Atomic Bomb* (1986). Use of the bomb is studied in Martin J. Sherwin, *A World Destroyed: The Atomic Bomb and the Grand Alliance* (1975), and Gar Alperovitz, *The Decision To Use the Atomic Bomb and the Architecture of an American Myth* (1995).

On the war at home, the best general histories are Geoffrey Perrett, *Days of Sadness, Years of Triumph, 1939–1945* (1973), and John Morton Blum, *V Was for Victory: Politics and American Culture during World War II* (1976). Also see Lewis A. Erenberg and Susan E. Hirsch, *The War in American Culture: Society and Consciousness during World War II* (1998); Richard Polenberg, *War and Society: The United States, 1941–1945* (1972); Nelson Lichtenstein, *Labor's War at Home: The CIO in World War II* (1982); and Joel Seidman, *American Labor from Defense to Reconversion* (1982). For the internment of Japanese-Americans, see Roger Daniels, *Prisoners without Trial: Japanese Americans in World War II* (1993), and Tetsuden Kashima, *Judgment without Trial: Japanese-American Imprisonment during World War II* (2003). On the roles of women and blacks, see D'Ann Campbell, *Women at War with America* (1984); Margaret Paton-Walsh, *Our War Too: American Women against the Axis* (2002); Neil Wynn, *The Afro-American and the Second World War* (1976); and Richard N. Dalfiume, *Desegregation of the U.S. Armed Forces, 1939–1953* (1969).

An Era of Uncertainty, 1945–1968

Prologue

EVEN AFTER winning World War II, Americans lived with uncertainty. They seemed to be fighting constantly, waging wars abroad in Korea and Vietnam and waging wars at home—one against poverty and, ultimately, one among themselves. The Cold War permeated these struggles, affecting domestic politics, culture, and international relations.

President Harry S Truman promoted the Marshall Plan and the Truman Doctrine, sent the United States into the Korean War, promised civil rights to minorities, and espoused a Fair Deal. But much of his domestic program faltered or fell short of expectations, and Truman, an upset winner in 1948, was a lame duck by 1952. Dwight Eisenhower, the World War II hero who succeeded Truman, took office determined to ensure enduring peace but had to settle for an inconclusive end to the Korean conflict and a continuation of the Cold War.

In the Cold War, America experienced instant fortunes, instant celebrities, and the specter of instant death. Americans had believed themselves secure, unchallenged with the might of the atomic bomb, until the Soviets acquired the power. Subversives within the federal government were helping prepare the country for a communist takeover, warned demagogic Senator Joseph McCarthy, who became a victim of his own excesses. Bigger bombs, greater radioactive fallout, multiple warheads, and ballistic missiles were to come. Despite it all, most Americans lived normal lives. More important than world events, especially in rural areas and small towns, were families, friends, jobs, and schools. Socially and economically, there were a host of ways to enjoy life during these affluent decades. Instead of shrinking from the Cold War, some moviemakers parodied it. Although the times were uncertain, Americans were concerned, perhaps saddened, but not hysterical.

If the bomb did not explode, the population did. From the mid-1940s to the mid-1960s, a baby boom occurred that affected the United States economically and politically, particularly in the 1960s. The initial wave of baby boomers, born in the year after World War II ended, entered college in 1964, the year of the Gulf of Tonkin Resolution, the Mississippi Freedom Summer, the Berkeley free speech movement, and the beginning of the urban riots. Television was the companion of the baby boomers, whose generation was the first to come of age under its influence. In 1950 only 8 percent of American families had TV sets; a decade later, only 10 percent did not have one. People watched Ozzie and Harriet, Lucille Ball, Milton Berle, the Kefauver Committee hearings, and the Army-McCarthy hearings. Other shows featured preachers Billy Graham, Norman Vincent Peale, and Bishop Fulton J. Sheen, popularizers who offered religion as a tonic. Elvis Presley, on the other hand, shook everyone up. To adult dismay, the boomers gyrated with him and tuned in to rock 'n' roll music, introducing a culture much as their elders embraced jazz.

Unlike the 1950s—a golden age, if one were white, male, and middle class—the 1960s were inhospitable to moderation. Bob Dylan, troubadour of the young, warned the older generation about the impending deluge of change. Again it seemed that successive decades were virtual mirror images. Yet the 1950s were more complex than they appeared, and the 1960s, for all their ferment, closed with nostalgia for the more peaceful 1950s. Under presidents John F. Kennedy and Lyndon B. Johnson, practically every social conflict erupted into the streets, overloading the national circuits with challenges, including an intensified civil rights movement, a feminist revival, protests against the Vietnam War, an unfinished War on Poverty, and a campus revolt. The war in Vietnam cast a pall over the United States, enraged the young, and toppled Johnson. The country learned a lesson in humility in the jungles of a distant land, where the marvels of American technology lost a war to ill-armed guerrillas. The assassinations of John Kennedy, Martin Luther King Jr., and Robert Kennedy rent the nation. Finally, a backlash carried Richard Nixon to the White House in 1969. "If you liked the 1950s, you will love the 1970s," a graduate student predicted in 1970.

In the meantime, the era that had produced successes began to cruelly undermine the American dream. Vietnam would fall to communists. The economy, affluent in the 1950s and approaching overdrive in the 1960s, weakened. With an aging infrastructure and industrial base, the United States lost ground to international competitors. The nation entered a postindustrial era, when job growth would lag and be limited primarily to the service sector, and a posturban era, when the suburbs would swell and the cities would dwindle, apparently a permanent trend. The nation changed in ways unanticipated. Like all changes, some embraced them, others bemoaned them, and still others denied them. More problems, more paradoxes awaited.

Time Line

An Era of Uncertainty, 1945–1968

March 12, 1947 Truman announces Truman Doctrine.

April 15, 1947 Jackie Robinson breaks color barrier in major-league baseball.

June 5, 1947 Marshall Plan proposed.

June 25, 1950 Communist North Korea invades South Korea.

February 27, 1951 Twenty-Second Amendment which limits a president to two terms ratified.

November 4, 1952 Dwight D. Eisenhower elected president.

May 17, 1954 Supreme Court outlaws school segregation in *Brown v. Board of Education*.

December 1, 1955 Bus boycott in Montgomery, Alabama.

January 5, 1957 Eisenhower promulgates Eisenhower Doctrine.

April 17, 1961 Bay of Pigs invasion.

August 13, 1961 Construction begins on Berlin Wall

February 20, 1962 John Glenn becomes first American to orbit Earth.

October 22 to November 20, 1962 Cuban Missile Crisis.

November 22, 1963 President John F. Kennedy is assassinated; Vice President Lyndon B. Johnson takes presidential oath.

August 7, 1964 Gulf of Tonkin Resolution.

July 2, 1964 Johnson signs Civil Rights Act.

November 3, 1964 Johnson defeats Barry Goldwater in presidential election.

July 30, 1965 Johnson signs legislation creating Medicare and Medicaid.

August 6, 1965 Johnson approves Voting Rights Act.

January 30, 1968 Tet Offensive.

March 31, 1968 Johnson announces withdrawal from presidential race.

April 4, 1968 The Reverend Martin Luther King Jr. is assassinated.

June 5, 1968 New York Senator Robert F. Kennedy is assassinated.

November 5, 1968 Richard M. Nixon defeats Democrat Hubert Humphrey in presidential race.

CHAPTER THIRTEEN

The Fair Deal
and the Cold War,
1945–1952

T HE COLD War and an untested president brought open-ended dilemmas in foreign and domestic policy to the first administration of the Era of Uncertainty. Bluster and bluff were common on both sides of the canyon that divided communism and democratic capitalism. The wake of the war produced problems in the economy, in race relations, in gender roles, and in domestic politics. Paradoxically, the worst fears of Americans never materialized, but a host of smaller ones did.

Harry S Truman and the Postwar Economy

Throughout his White House years, Harry S Truman was haunted by the specter of Franklin D. Roosevelt. Roosevelt was imperial; Truman was ordinary. Roosevelt was eloquent, Truman was blunt. Roosevelt handled political problems with procrastination and finesse, whereas Truman carved up political opponents like a Thanksgiving turkey. Roosevelt battled for the top office four times. Truman did not want the presidency at all; it found him. He wanted to appear decisive, and to do so, he overcame self-doubt. He placed a sign on his desk that read: "The buck stops here."

Truman grew up in Independence, Missouri, where he graduated from high school yet never attended college. A World War I vet, he worked as a bank clerk, a farmer, and a clothing store proprietor. Entering politics late, he won an administrative post—county judge—with the assistance of the notorious Democratic Kansas City machine masterminded by Thomas J. Pendergast. He married his high school sweetheart, Bess Wallace, and settled in as a minor local official. In 1934, Truman was elected to the U.S.

Senate at Pendergast's initiative because the machine needed a veteran with a reputation for honesty. In 1944, after Vice President Henry A. Wallace was dropped for alienating conservatives, Truman was the compromise choice for second place on the ticket. The ticket won, Roosevelt died, and Truman became president.

World War II had unthrottled the economy and ended the depression. Postwar economic problems focused on shortages, reconversion to consumer production, readjustment of the labor force, and inflation. Despite fears of its resurrection, the depression was dead. Consumer demand, suppressed by the war, rushed to fill appetites for homes, automobiles, refrigerators, and other items. Congress enacted the G.I. Bill of Rights which furnished funds for former servicemen to go to college, obtain a technical education, or buy a house. Unemployment fell to 2 percent in 1945.

Still, the national debt had soared into the stratosphere, from $34 billion in 1940 to $248 billion in 1945. The nation spent more to defeat the Axis than in all the previous history of the republic. Inflation, held under control by the Office of Price Administration, leaped when the office was phased out. The Korean War, beginning in 1950, brought increased military spending, which stimulated the economy.

Inflation triggered demands from labor for higher wages. When these were unmet, unions struck, just as they had done in a similar situation in 1919. The strikes started with important industries such as steel and meatpacking in 1946, compounded by even more vexing strikes by railroad workers and coal miners in 1946. Truman ended the railroad strike by threatening to draft recalcitrant workers into the army. John L. Lewis, leader of the United Mine Workers, was the last holdout, but ultimately the strike was settled under government pressure.

Truman lost patience with some labor leaders, yet when Republicans sought to trim their sails via the Taft-Hartley Bill of 1947, he vetoed it, only to have his veto overridden. The Republican Congress elected in 1946, led by Ohio Senator Robert Taft, an arch-conservative, passed the bill over protests of the unions and the president. Designed to define unfair practices for labor as the Wagner Act of 1935 had outlawed certain practices for business, it outlawed the closed shop (requiring a worker to join a union as a condition of employment), and barred union contributions to political campaigns. Eighty-days notice must be given before major strikes, followed by negotiations. During the Korean War, strikes by telephone and telegraph workers and an imminent strike by steelworkers disrupted the war effort. After Truman threatened to seize facilities facing impending strikes, the Supreme Court declared such a seizure unconstitutional. A seven-week steel strike followed, costly to the country and Truman's reputation as an evenhanded chief executive.

Truman's first major address to Congress in 1945 produced a basket stuffed with liberal legislative proposals. Among them were national health insurance, a higher minimum wage, regional developments similar to the Tennessee Valley Authority, a permanent Fair Employment Practices Committee, and restrictions on business. His program was dead on arrival. The country was weary and wanted bounty, not social experimentation. Truman's popularity plummeted. People missed Roosevelt. The new president wanted to clamp a lid on economic expansion rather than let prosperity flourish. He lacked the ability to control inflation. He tried to bully unions. The Republican motto in the 1946 congressional campaigns summed up the nation's mood: "Had Enough?" The short answer was "yes." The GOP won control of both Houses of Congress for the first time since the Hoover administration.

Two significant acts were nonetheless passed regarding the presidency. The Presidential Succession Act placed the House Speaker and Senate president pro tem ahead of the cabinet in the line of succession after the vice president. Truman believed elected officials should be first in line. The Twenty-Second Amendment, ratified in 1951, limited the president to two terms. Meanwhile, Truman faced a divided country and party for his reelection bid in 1948. The cupboard was full of ambitious domestic proposals but practically barren of achievements. Truman proved more decisive internationally, but his foreign policy was not expected to help him much. At the time of the election Allied planes were airlifting sustenance to beleaguered West Berlin, blockaded by the communists.

Truman selected Kentucky Senator Alben Barkley as his running mate. The Republicans believed they had a winner by nominating New York Governor Thomas E. Dewey, pairing him with California Governor Earl Warren. Not only did this ticket provide ideological and regional balance; it coupled the two most populous states. Dewey had run before. In 1944 he had lost to Roosevelt, yet had done better than previous challengers. Moreover, Truman was no Roosevelt and the voters were restless.

So restless were the Democrats that their party cracked apart at their convention. The southerners defected over a prointegration civil rights plank, and created the States' Rights Democratic Party, dubbed the Dixiecrats. They nominated two southern governors: J. Strom Thurmond of South Carolina and Fielding Wright of Mississippi. Further splintering, Henry Wallace stole radicals and some liberals, running as the nominee of the Progressive Party. The Progressives received some support from communists, while the

Dixiecrats robbed the Democrats of some southern regional support. All that was left was the center, but that is where the votes were.

The Republicans wrote a liberal platform proposing a list of progressive reforms. Truman called their bluff by summoning Congress into special session and offering them the opportunity for the Republican-dominated branch to enact their program. When they failed to do so, he denounced them as hypocrites. Now the Missourian had his issue. He would run against the Republican Congress. Ignoring the fact that he was part of the government, he ran as an outsider. Moreover, he reached out to the common people, trekking cross-country by train to "Give 'em hell," as one supporter suggested. Dewey was overconfident. He remained dignified and avoided commitment on some issues in order to have a free hand when elected. All the polls said he would win.

But Dewey did not win. Nonetheless, the anti-Truman *Chicago Tribune,* which had gone to press before the late returns were in, ran a banner headline the next morning, "Dewey Defeats Truman." That morning a reporter snapped a photo of Truman brandishing the headline. Naturally he was grinning. The result was the presidential upset of the century. Truman won 24.1 million popular votes and 303 electoral votes to 21.9 million and 189

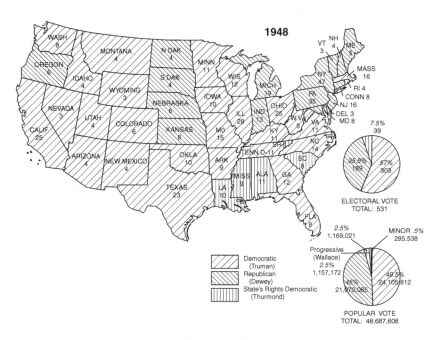

Election of 1948

for Dewey. Thurmond gained about 1 million popular votes and 39 electoral votes; Wallace also won about 1 million popular votes but no electoral votes. Dewey was decimated. What had gone wrong?

First, the polls stopped polling too early and used questionable methods, such as employing telephone books and automobile registrations to obtain lists of potential subjects to question. Many Truman voters were too poor to have either. The polls failed to account for the undecided vote, which shifted to Truman in the weeks after they ceased polling. Also, Truman was more down-to-earth and likeable than Dewey. Truman's aggressive campaign made Dewey resemble a stuffed shirt. Truman set a domestic agenda that attracted groups of Roosevelt's coalition, even though it did not pass. And his decisiveness in foreign policy did count. Finally, one cannot discount the factor that many of Truman's constituents identified with the underdog.

The Fair Deal

In his 1949 State of the Union address Truman used the term "Fair Deal" to describe his program. Truman wanted to expand social services, enact civil rights, and regulate business. In this session Congress agreed to his proposals for public housing, increased minimum wages, and extended Social Security coverage. Yet it remained opposed to national health insurance and the president's plan to wean farmers from price supports. Under plans developed by a commission led by former President Herbert Hoover, appointed by Truman, Congress reorganized the executive branch, consolidating departments and simplifying chains of command.

Truman was ahead of congressional and public opinion in seeking betterment for minorities. The first major presidential candidate to publicly solicit African American votes, he could not deliver major civil rights legislation. He did, however, take steps by executive orders. Truman continued the desegregation of the armed forces and sought an end to discrimination in interstate transportation, educational inequality, the poll tax, and lynching. Although progress occurred slowly or not at all in some areas, the president from Missouri set a liberal racial agenda that would, for the most part, reach fruition. There were symbolic and substantial gains for African Americans, such as Jackie Robinson's breaking of the color barrier with the Brooklyn Dodgers in 1947. Once the skill of black athletes was established, colleges and professional teams raced to recruit them.

The reality for most African Americans, in the rural South and in northern city ghettos, was grinding poverty, inadequate education, and public humiliation. They and other minorities made economic gains during the war, yet, they remained an underclass. In the South, racial segregation was

★ Jackie Robinson: Champion ★

His struggle predated the emergence of "the first black who"
in many areas of the American society.

—DAVE ANDERSON

CROSSING THE COLOR LINE
Integrating baseball as depicted
by Hollywood in *The Jackie
Robinson Story.*
(Library of Congress)

HE COULD HIT. He could vacuum up ground balls. He was the most daring base runner of his time. His skills alone merit his place in the Baseball Hall of Fame. Yet Jackie Robinson was much more than a baseball player. In the Era of Uncertainty he was a pioneer in race relations, a businessman, a fund-raiser for charities, and a civil rights activist. When his mentor, Branch Rickey, sounded the trumpet to sign Robinson to a Major League contract, the walls of segregation in professional baseball came tumbling down. Baseball lay at the heart of American culture, and Robinson's breakthrough was followed by a series of victories for African Americans, among them the 1954 Supreme Court decision ordering school desegregation and the sweeping 1964 Civil Rights Act.

In 1947, when Robinson joined the Brooklyn Dodgers, most white people believed that black athletes lacked the intelligence or skills to compete with white players. Desegregating the Major Leagues took someone who was more than a talented player. It took a person who was disciplined, who would not fight back when taunted, spiked, booed, or hit with a beanball. Asked at his first news conference what he would do if a white pitcher threw at his head, Robinson replied, diplomatically, that he would duck. But the restraint that he demonstrated in his early Major League years did not come easily for this angry man. "I had to fight hard against loneliness, abuse and the knowledge that any mistake I made would be magnified because I was the only black man out there," Robinson said. He chafed at being confined to segregated hotels and restaurants on the road and, once established, showed more of his fiercely competitive nature, arguing with umpires and tongue-lashing players who harassed him.

It is often overlooked that Robinson might have failed. If he had, it would have seriously jeopardized the ability of African Americans at that time to shatter the barrier of racial inferiority. He had to excel as a player before he could succeed as a racial trailblazer, and at both, he performed beyond expectations. "We were riding his shoulders right out from under the worst part of that white power lie," Roy Wilkins wrote. "Every time Jack got a hit, stole a base or made a great play in the field, he was telling them for all of us, 'It's a lie!'" Robinson was National League Rookie of the Year in 1947, when he led Brooklyn to the pennant. During his ten-year career, he was often among the league leaders in batting, stolen bases, and fielding. He was chosen the

Most Valuable Player in the league in 1949, when he led the circuit in batting average and base stealing. The most versatile Dodgers player, he started at first base, second base, third base, and in the outfield. With Robinson, the Dodgers dominated the National League, although they won only one World Series title, in 1955, his last season. He was elected to the Baseball Hall of Fame in 1962, his first year of eligibility.

Robinson retired before the 1957 season because age and injuries had eroded his skills. He then invested and worked in businesses, wrote a newspaper column, was a popular public speaker, and campaigned for politicians such as Nelson Rockefeller and Hubert Humphrey. He supported integration and quarreled with black nationalists. Robinson lived through profound changes in lifestyles. His son, Jackie, was wounded while serving in Vietnam, became addicted to drugs there, and died in a car accident the year before the elder Robinson died in 1972, at fifty-three. He had earned a place as one of the most respected men in the United States. But the paradox did not escape him that although he had opened the way for African Americans with superior skills, equal opportunity for ordinary African Americans remained incomplete. There was one more paradox: it was his sense of feeling alone that fired his will to achieve the feats that won him the hearts of millions. "You are Jackie Robinson, who is consumed by rage and pride," sports columnist Jimmy Cannon wrote. "You're a complicated man, persecuted by slanderous myths, using anger as a confederate. No athlete of any time has been assaulted by such an aching loneliness which created your personality and shaped your genuine greatness."

Sources: The best book on Robinson is Arnold Rampersad, *Jackie Robinson: A Biography* (1997). Also see Richard Scott, *Jackie Robinson* (1987), and Joseph Dorinson and Joram Warmund, *Jackie Robinson: Race, Sports, and the American Dream* (1998).

---

pervasive. African Americans could not attend white public schools, drink at segregated fountains, vote in most elections, attend most state colleges, or be considered for anything other than menial jobs. Health care was poor, and there was little opportunity for upward mobility, and the password was despair. Blacks in the North continued to vote Democrat, as they had since the 1936 election landslide for Franklin Roosevelt, but even the chance to vote could not ease despair.

Native Americans, too, were impoverished, underemployed, and largely ignored. Disease was endemic, including alcoholism. After John Collier resigned as federal Indian affairs commissioner in 1945, the government created a commission to compensate Indians for land seized. This action foreshadowed the policy of termination that became official in 1953, whereby the United States would sever its relations with tribes.

By 1950, when the Korean War broke out, the Fair Deal had run its course. Major legislation was lost; some minor measures passed. Truman was overly ambitious in announcing goals and lacked finesse in implementing them. Extensions of the New Deal were introduced in a climate less favorable than the Great Depression or the World War II, when public sacrifice for the common good seemed essential. There was no crisis but, rather prosperity. Many wanted to slim down the federal bureaucracy rather than expand it, to consolidate gains. Even Roosevelt had experienced a legislative roadblock to domestic reform by 1938. Truman could push proposals in one end of Congress but he could not pull them out the other. He lacked patience with politicians and even with music critics. When a journalist criticized Margaret's efforts at professional singing, Truman threatened to punch him in the eye. The president, like Margaret Truman, seemed out of tune with the times.

A host of minor furies nipped at the president's heels. His friend, military aide Harry Vaughn, accepted kickbacks for favors. Corruption emerged in the Reconstruction Finance Corporation and the Internal Revenue Service. Truman was usually loyal to his cronies, regardless of their dishonesty. Even his own party seemed bent on self-destruction. Tennessee Senator Estes Kefauver held televised hearings on organized crime and connected many of the criminal bosses to urban Democratic machines. The hearings were an early omen of the political potency of television and made a national reputation for Kefauver.

From World War to Cold War

Following World War II, War Crimes Trials were conducted in Nuremberg and Tokyo. Surprisingly, many were tried under provisions defined in the Kellogg-Briand Treaty, which meant something after all. The most grisly testimony related to the Holocaust in Europe and to Japanese treatment of prisoners of war. The testimony relating to the Holocaust, in particular, revealed an insidious underside of the Third Reich, the callous cruelty of its leaders. It also drove a nail into the coffin of the idea of racism, which would persist, but would never again be respectable. And sympathy for the chief victims of the Nazi atrocities, the Jews of Europe, helped survivors gain a foothold for a homeland in Israel.

Like Woodrow Wilson, FDR and his predecessors had cobbled together an international organization designed to confine war to the past. The United Nations, headquartered in New York, was much like the League of Nations. A major exception was that the United States, rather than remain aloof, would assume leadership. An eleven-member Security Council was charged with preserving the peace by collective action if necessary. The machinery was cumbrous, however. Each of the five permanent

READY
FOR WAR
U.S. Army tests
the atom bomb
in Nevada, 1952.
(National
Archives)

members: the United States, Britain, France, China, and the Soviet Union, could veto actions. The General Assembly, which included most of the world's countries, was a glorified debating society. Increasingly it engaged in rhetorical debate related to the protagonists in the Cold War.

The most uncertain facet of the Era of Uncertainty was the Cold War. Heaped on both sides were mountains of munitions, many of them nuclear bombs. Yet, paradoxically, it was not a war in the usual sense. It was characterized more by fear of war than actual war. There was fighting between proxies of the principals, limited wars, propaganda wars, and psychological wars. But, in a tribute to common sense on both sides, the big bombs were never launched or dropped. Never before had humanity possessed the opportunity to completely destroy itself. And humanity passed up the opportunity.

Some efforts were made to ensure international supervision of atomic weapons. Not surprisingly, since communists and capitalists distrusted each other and tried to stack proposals to favor their side, nothing substantial was accomplished. The arms race galloped out of the gates. In 1949 the Soviets detonated an atomic bomb, ending the American monopoly. There followed an American hydrogen bomb, far more powerful than atomic bombs, in 1952, and a Soviet hydrogen bomb in 1953. Bombs tested were so potent they had no practical value except to overawe the adversary.

Some factors in the Cold War were territorial and ideological. Communist ideology, as refined by V. I. Lenin and Joseph Stalin, was expansionist and driven to dominate. Its objective was, first, consolidation where it existed and, ultimately, world control. Highly motivated, it became the most messianic secular ideology of the twentieth century. Unlike fascism, it made converts as well as conquests. Based on the idea of loyalty to the working class rather than a nation, communism, in all its major manifestations, was in fact led by nationalists. It imposed a command economy, prohibited religion, banned free speech and free elections, and taught ferocious pride in competition with the West from fields as diverse as tractor production to the space race to the Olympic Games.

Capitalism was equally competitive and equally self-righteous. It, too, was expansionist; it needed trade to sustain prosperity. Yet it was not so regimented. Capitalism was compatible with democracy. A command economy, with its centralized government and productive plan, was incompatible with democracy. Capitalism boasted of the wonders of private property, which communism prohibited. And the West practiced, for the most part, freedom of religion and of the press and held competitive elections. Initially it appeared the discipline of communism gave it an advantage. A dictated economy could concentrate resources in one area, such as military might, or education, and excel, even while sacrificing other areas.

The Cold War made each side nervous because its outcome seemed uncertain. Soviets hoped to sustain moral superiority by pointing to industrial and military accomplishments. Americans, they said, wallowed in ease. Each side counted armies and courted Allies. Yet each side claimed, probably truthfully, that it wanted to win by peaceful competition.

When World War II ended Europe was already divided. Stalin's armies occupied the East, including Poland, with the dividing line drawn through Germany. Stalin could not and would not be ousted from these nations, which came to be called the Soviet bloc. Their economies were integrated and their governments were Soviet puppets. In a speech on February 9, 1946, Stalin declared capitalism and communism incompatible and vowed that communism would prevail. Winston Churchill also addressed the contest near its beginning, declaring memorably a month later that an "Iron Curtain" had descended across Europe.

Britain, America's most constant ally, was financially and emotionally exhausted after the war. It handed off its responsibilities in Greece and Turkey to the United States. In Greece, a civil war between monarchists and communists raged. In Turkey, the Soviets pressed for access to the Mediterranean Sea through Turkish-controlled straits. Truman requested $300 million to arm Greece and $100 million to aid Turkey, which Congress approved. More important, he issued a promise to spread the umbrella of American defense to protect any nation threatened internally or externally with communist takeover. This commitment, known as the Truman Doctrine, was a complement of the Marshall Plan, announced by Secretary of State George Marshall in June 1947, to give economic aid to rebuild Europe, making it less vulnerable to communist appeals. The Marshall Plan became the greatest success of the Truman administration. For a modest investment, the United States obtained trading partners and Allies. It was not entirely unselfish, yet it was mutually beneficial. Western Europe not only revived; it became an economic powerhouse.

Probing for a strategy to counter Stalin's, an American Russian expert, George Kennan, in a "long telegram" and in an article in *Foreign Affairs*, proposed the idea of "containment." The United States would meet force with counterforce and contain the Soviet bloc within its existing borders. Later applied to Asia as well as Europe, virtually every American president, whatever their rhetoric, practiced containment. The Cold War thus became a war of attrition.

Reforms helped improve the readiness of the military and intelligence organizations. The 1947 National Security Act combined the War and Navy departments in the Defense Department. The air force became independent of the army. The Central Intelligence Agency (CIA) centralized intelligence gathering, and the National Security Council (NSC) was created to advise the president on foreign policy. A memorandum issued by the National Security Council, NSC-68, called for a massive arms buildup. The memorandum was never approved, yet many of its recommendations were implemented with the outbreak of the Korean War. The United States was now prepared to confront communism on a variety of fronts.

Military challenges came with a flurry. In February 1948, a Soviet-instigated coup in Czechoslovakia enveloped another nation behind the Iron Curtain. America reauthorized the draft. Four months later, the Soviets blockaded access to West Berlin, a free outpost in the sea of East Germany.

After the war, Germany had been partitioned. The United States, France, and Britain occupied the western half, which became a capitalist democracy. East Germany, occupied by the Soviets, became a Soviet satellite. Berlin, the prewar German capital, was also partitioned into eastern and western sectors, though it was surrounded by East German territory. West Berlin was an avenue of escape to the West and a beacon of democracy, evidence of the productive power of capitalism.

Truman feared that forcing his way through the blockades on the ground might result in war with the Soviet Union. Therefore he ordered an airlift to send all necessary materials to West Berlin. The first shot, if one were to be fired, would come from the Soviet side.

The Berlin airlift strained the capacity of American cargo planes and the resources of West Berliners. Nonetheless, the communists were losing the struggle for world opinion. In May 1949, they lifted the blockade. The same year, two nations were carved out of prewar Germany: West Germany, with its capital in Bonn, and East Germany, with its capital in East Berlin. Significantly, the Berlin blockade inspired the North Atlantic Treaty Organization (NATO), binding American with Northern and Western Europe, Canada, and other anticommunist nations. Intended as a deterrent to communist aggression, NATO was the first permanent, peacetime alliance in American history. In response, the Soviets created the Warsaw Pact, a counteralliance of communist nations.

Containment in Asia, War in Korea

Some politicians and intellectuals argued that by focusing containment on Europe, the United States neglected a more populous, more dynamic, and more vulnerable part of the world—Asia. The "Asia First" group focused on China, Korea, and Indochina, all of which became Cold War battlegrounds. In China, where nationalists and communists competed for supremacy, Truman had dispatched Marshall in 1945 in a fruitless, yearlong quest to reconcile the foes. Washington continued to arm and equip the Nationalist leader, Jiang Jieshe, but the forces of communist chief Mao Zedong (Mao Tse-tung) drove the demoralized forces of Jiang's corrupt government off the mainland and onto the island of Taiwan (Formosa) in 1949. The United States refused to recognize communist China diplomatically, and Republicans charged Truman and Marshall with "losing" China. Mao's government proved no less repressive than Jiang's. He aligned it with the Soviet Union and made China a military state, but the newly cemented alliance began to crack before it dried, for both giants competed for leadership of the communist movement.

East of China, the Korean peninsula was divided at the 38th parallel. The North was a communist state under Dictator Kim Il Sung, who was anxious to conquer the South, led by Syngman Rhee. Rhee, on the other hand, was ambitious to take North Korea, so the United States denied him offensive weapons. Less inhibited, Moscow sent tanks to Kim, who was tempted further when the last American troops were withdrawn from the region in June 1949. Then, Secretary of State Dean Acheson excluded

Korea from the American defense perimeter in June 1950. After consulting with Stalin, Kim launched an invasion on June 25, 1950, that routed the South Koreans. Acheson persuaded the UN Security Council to brand North Korea an aggressor. The council voted to defend the South, thanks to a boycott by the Soviets who were protesting the council's refusal to seat communist China instead of Taiwan on the Security Council, and were thus unable to exercise their veto.

Truman authorized use of American naval and air forces in the conflict, then sent ground troops under General Douglas MacArthur. After stabilizing the minuscule perimeter around the southern port city of Pusan, MacArthur launched an audacious, amphibious attack at Inchon, a port near Seoul, the South Korean capital. North Korean troops were driven back above the 38th parallel, where they war had begun. Now Truman and the UN authorized MacArthur to cross the boundary and unite Korea under a noncommunist government. MacArthur drove almost to the Yalu River, the boundary between Korea and China. Undetected, Chinese troops massed at the border, and Chinese leaders had indirectly warned they might intervene if UN forces approached their border. The Chinese did intervene en masse, sending the surprised, outnumbered American troops into a retreat that ultimately stabilized at the 38th parallel.

So far, the war was a draw. The North could not conquer the South; the South could not capture the North. MacArthur found the stalemate humiliating. He proposed plans to threaten the use of atomic weapons, blockade the Chinese coast, and use Jiang's troops for a diversionary attack on the Chinese mainland. Like most good generals, MacArthur was assertive and desired total victory. Truman feared such a plan might precipitate a third world war, and ordered MacArthur to clear his statements with Washington. Instead, MacArthur offered to negotiate with Chinese generals personally and proclaimed, "There is no substitute for victory."

Whatever the merits of tactics, MacArthur had been insubordinate, he had violated the chain of command. Truman, who did not like MacArthur's imperious personality, fired him, with relish.

MacArthur returned to a hero's welcome in America, ticker tape parades and a moving address before a joint session of Congress. A gifted orator, he brought some to tears, especially when he concluded that "Old soldiers never die, they just fade away." Surprisingly, MacArthur did fade away, although he would have liked the Republican presidential nomination in 1952. The verdict of history has been less kind than his contemporary Americans to MacArthur's generalship in Korea. Active generals are supposed to carry out policy made by civilians, not make it themselves. Nonetheless, the general who succeeded Truman, Dwight Eisenhower, repeated MacArthur's threat to use nuclear weapons rather than tolerate indefinitely a static front. Possibly this was one factor in breaking the log-jam over truce negotiations at the village of Panmunjom.

While trying to extricate itself from a bloody war in Asia, the United States backed into another in Vietnam, a former French colony that Japan occupied in World War II. Ho Chi Minh, the leader of the communist-nationalist Vietminh, had been seeking the liberation of his country since the 1919 Versailles Peace Conference. On September 2, 1945, Vietnam pro-claimed its independence, but the French decided to reimpose colonial rule. Ho rebelled. The French refused to collaborate with American plans for defending Western Europe unless the United States supported them in Vietnam. Because the Vietminh were communists, Washington viewed the French presence in Vietnam as a deterrent to communism. In 1950 Congress approved $10 million to aid Bao Dai, the French-installed emperor.

Politics were interpreted through the Cold War lens in the volatile Middle East. The major issue in the region, a Jewish state, had simmered since the nineteenth century, when Zionists sought such a homeland, preferably in Palestine. Controlling Palestine under mandates from the League of Nations and the United Nations, the British limited Jewish immigration, but Jews smuggled in immigrants beyond the quotas; Arabs opposed the influx and violence raged. In mid-1947 Britain announced that it would relinquish its mandate. A UN commission recommended the partition of Palestine into Jewish and Arab states. On May 14, 1948, Jews in Palestine declared the independence of Israel, repelling attacks from five Arab nations. Seven hundred thousand Palestinians fled to the West Bank of the Jordan River and the Gaza Strip, a part of Egypt. Eleven minutes after independence was declared, Truman extended diplomatic recognition to Israel, beating the Soviets. The next year, the warring parties signed an armistice, yet a permanent peace remained elusive. The United States sup-ported Israel, while the Soviet Union armed the Arabs.

Iran also became a Cold War battleground. During the world war, Allied troops had occupied the nation to prevent a Nazi invasion, promis-ing to withdraw within six months after the end of the conflict. The United States and Britain evacuated their forces, but Soviet soldiers remained and began agitating a civil war between the Iranian government and separatist rebels. Only after Truman threatened to defend Iran with force did the Soviets pull out.

Pursuing friendship in Latin America, the United States signed the Inter-American Treaty of Reciprocal Assistance, a mutual defense pact, in 1947 and helped establish the Organization of American States in 1948. The United States set about dismantling its small empire. In 1946, the Philippines became independent and the United States gave Puerto Rico increased authority. The island would govern internal affairs, with Washington making foreign policy and providing defense. Two Puerto Ricans favoring independence tried to shoot their way into Blair House, Truman's temporary residence while the White House was being refurbished, to assassinate the president. One gunman was killed, and the other was wounded and captured.

The Cold War at Home

The Cold War not only dominated international affairs; it affected politics, culture, and the media in America. Free speech was compromised in the quest to silence communist sympathizers. The government grew in proportion to the perceived threat, yet some complained that large government constituted creeping communism. Tolerance of those who favored radical ideologies nosedived.

To be sure, there were real communists in America, and some spy rings. For the most part they were annoyances rather than threats. Moreover, to conclude that the nation was gripped by "hysteria" is rhetorical overkill. Most people led their daily lives as usual. Yet a few celebrated cases raised concern. In 1945, federal agents found secret government documents in the files of *Amerasia*, a magazine with a procommunist slant. In 1946, a Canadian spy ring was uncovered that had passed American military and nuclear information to the Soviets in World War II. The Truman administration imposed a background check on federal employees from 1947 to 1951 and established loyalty review procedures. Loyalty Boards fired three hundred, and three thousand resigned. Some cities, states, universities, and labor unions required loyalty oaths without considering whether anyone who was actually a spy would hesitate to lie about it.

In the courts, several cases captured the public's attention. During the 1948 presidential campaign, leaders of the Communist Party of the United States were convicted of advocating the violent overthrow of the government, a violation of the 1940 Smith Act. The Supreme Court upheld the convictions in *Dennis v. U.S.* (1951). The Alger Hiss case was even more polarizing. Hiss, a former State Department official, a polished Ivy Leaguer, and liberal intellectual, was accused by Whittaker Chambers, a former communist, of being part of his spy cell in the 1930s. Chambers alleged that Hiss had stolen diplomatic, not military or atomic secrets, for the Soviet Union. Hiss seemed the more credible of the two; he was better dressed and eloquent and had high-ranking friends in the Democratic Party. The affair degenerated into a morality play equating liberalism with communism and the Democratic Party with treason. Yet partisan motives did not mean that Hiss was innocent. Hiss and Chambers were questioned by the House Un-American Activities Committee (HUAC), then, in response to a challenge from Hiss, Chambers repeated the charges publicly. Hiss sued for slander; whichever man was lying was guilty of perjury. After the introduction of some convincing circumstantial evidence against Hiss, some of it produced by Congressman Richard Nixon, Hiss was convicted of perjury early in 1950 and sentenced to five years in prison. He never relented protesting his innocence.

More serious was the case of Julius and Ethel Rosenberg, a couple accused of stealing atomic secrets for the Soviets. The Rosenbergs were implicated by Klaus Fuchs, a German-born scientist living in Britain, who had worked on the Manhattan Project. Fuchs confessed to spying and identified four Americans, including the Rosenbergs, as collaborators. The Rosenbergs were convicted in March 1951, chiefly on testimony by their alleged collaborators, and sentenced to death. Protesting their innocence, the Rosenbergs claimed persecution because they were Jews and liberals. They refused offers of clemency if they would identify other spies and were executed on June 19, 1953.

The chief mischief-maker in the anticommunist crusade, because most of the communists he pursued were of his own invention, was Senator Joseph R. McCarthy of Wisconsin. More than any politician of his time, he gave some credibility to the impression that Americans were running from ghosts. Yet he never uncovered a real communist, although he garnered loads of publicity; initially, the publicity was mostly good. On February 9, 1950, McCarthy delivered a speech in which he claimed to possess a list of 205 communists working in the State Department. He never explained who had given him the list or showed it to anyone. Each time he was asked to pin down his accusations, he instead produced additional ones. He raced to stay ahead of the newspaper headlines, which piled up. A maestro at manipulating the press, he became one of the best-known politicians in the country.

McCarthy's shenanigans resulted in little tangible legislation. Not so with one of his political allies, Democratic Senator Patrick McCarran of Nevada, who helped steer through Congress the 1950 McCarran Internal Security Act. The act required that communists register with the attorney general and barred them from working for the government or in defense industries. The 1952 McCarran-Walter Immigration and Nationality Act prohibited communists from immigrating to the United States. McCarran's Senate Internal Security Committee held hearings in 1951 that blamed China experts, known as the "China hands" for the "loss" of China to communism. Some were discharged from their positions in the State Department.

DRIVING TO VICTORY
Dwight D. Eisenhower on the campaign trail, 1952.
(Dwight D. Eisenhower Presidential Library)

HUAC held hearings in 1947 on communist influence in Hollywood. Some suspected that Hollywood deliberately shaded movies to make communism appear attractive. The Hollywood Ten, a group of screenwriters, directors, and producers, refused to testify, citing the Fifth Amendment's protection against self-incrimination. They were fined, imprisoned briefly, and worse yet, denied employment.

"I Like Ike"

As the 1952 presidential campaign loomed, polls showed Truman to be one of the most unpopular incumbents in history. The Democrats therefore drafted Illinois Governor Adlai Stevenson, a respected liberal, an eloquent speaker, considered an intellectual by his supporters. For vice president the Democrats chose a segregationist, Alabama Senator John Sparkman. Candid and witty, Stevenson, told that he had the votes of all the thinking people in the country, replied that this was not enough; he needed a majority.

The Republican candidate was not an eloquent speaker, but neither did he talk down to the American people. Best, Dwight D. Eisenhower was a war hero, less controversial than MacArthur, who was waiting for a call from his party that never came. Eisenhower had common sense and an ingratiating grin as well as toughness, discipline, and a midas touch with the masses. He promised, if elected, to go to Korea, implying he would end the war. He did both. More important than his political principles was his temperamental stability; he was a harmonizer who inspired trust, and as he managed a vast bureaucracy during World War II, he was thought to be able to manage the Cold War. For his vice presidential running mate, Eisenhower tapped California Senator Richard M. Nixon, who had made a reputation as a member of HUAC by pursuing Alger Hiss. "Ike" never warmed to Nixon, yet Nixon was a professional politician with connections to his party's hierarchy. Eisenhower thought of asking Nixon to quit the ticket after newspapers reported that California businessmen had contributed a secret "slush fund" for him, but the senator saved himself with a televised speech that swayed viewers. The "Checkers" speech, so named because Nixon told of the cocker spaniel puppy his daughters had received as a gift from a supporter, marked a pioneering use of television to influence public opinion.

The Eisenhower-Nixon team won a comfortable victory, 33.9 million popular votes (55.1 percent) and 442 electoral votes to 27.3 million popular votes (44.4 percent) and 89 electoral votes for the Democrats. The GOP also won narrow control of Congress.

Although Truman's popularity lay at low tide when he left office, historians have judged him less harshly. In domestic affairs he proposed a progressive agenda, although he did not achieve it. In foreign affairs, his decisive actions might have saved Western Europe, Berlin, and Korea. After tumultuous times, though, Americans were ready for an aging former general who, they believed, would soothe the nation's nerves.

CHAPTER FOURTEEN

Peace and Peril, 1953–1960

I N THE Age of Uncertainty, the 1950s were an interlude of peace and prosperity. Paradoxically, the age was less stable, and more dangerous than it seemed. Prosperity was incomplete, and America feared for its security when the Soviet Union, a nuclear power, appeared to gain the lead in the space and missile race.

Dwight D. Eisenhower

The staid public image of the Eisenhower administration and the seeming colorlessness of its supporters prompted some to label the 1950s a period of "the bland leading the bland," a generalization that obscured the great paradox of the decade: calm at home and danger internationally from the Cold War. Nor were the politics and the generation bland; they were simply conservative in what was an ordinary period compared with the Great Depression and World War II. Befitting the time, Dwight D. Eisenhower was a man of paradox. He was raised in a pacifist family and became a man of war, commander of the Allied effort in Europe that helped end the greatest conflict to engulf the planet and, later, military leader of the North Atlantic Treaty Organization (NATO). His country looked to him to preserve peace. Despite his military background, he pared the defense establishment and warned the nation about the power of a military-industrial complex.

Born in Denison, Texas, Eisenhower grew up in Abilene, Kansas, and graduated from the United States Military Academy. He began in the Army in 1915, remaining stateside as a tank instructor during World War I and advancing slowly in the postwar Army, becoming a brigadier general in 1941. When World War II started in Europe, Eisenhower was assigned

WEATHERING THE COLD WAR
Eisenhower with Secretary of State John Foster Dulles.
(Dwight D. Eisenhower Presidential Library)

to work with General George C. Marshall, the Army chief of staff, who promoted him over senior officers to lead the invasions of North Africa, Sicily, Italy, and Normandy. A planner, not a bold field commander, Eisenhower kept peace among the fractious Allies and their temperamental generals. After the war, Eisenhower served as military governor of the American zone in Germany and wrote *Crusade in Europe* (1948), a book about the war that made him wealthy. He served briefly as president of Columbia University, and then was commander for NATO, a job he left to seek the GOP nomination.

To the public, "Ike" seemed friendly, yet he could be a hard, unsentimental man, thanks to his years in the military. He had never been religious, but he joined the Presbyterian Church to set an example for observance. Bright if not brilliant, a precise writer if a poor speaker, he delegated work so he could avoid details. The former general led by indirection, which spared him blame and denied him praise. With Mamie Eisenhower, he had a conventional marriage. Eisenhower's most influential cabinet member was an international lawyer, Secretary of State John Foster Dulles, a rigid anticommunist and moralist.

Eisenhower had his greatest domestic success in economic prosperity, sustained because of the baby boom, business expansion, and technology. He came to office promising to slow the growth of the federal government, although spending by state and local governments compensated. Welfare expenditures rose, and defense consumed more than half the U.S. budget each year during his term. The last was a source of concern, for Eisenhower believed that the country might spend itself into weakness with too much defense.

Among consumers, credit purchases soared. Most expensive items were bought on installment and prosperity was fueled by advertising, yearly automobile style changes, and cheap gasoline. Yet there were weaknesses. Poverty was endemic in city centers, the rural South, Appalachia, and declining New England mill towns. Recessions occurred in 1954 and 1958. During the first, the deficit grew to $12.1 billion, the largest since 1946, and unemployment rose to 6.4 percent, at which it stayed until the second. In the major downturn of 1958, corporate profits fell more than 25 percent and the government ran another deficit. The Achilles' heel of the economy was agriculture, as farmers overproduced and remained in business only with federal subsidies. The president planned to reduce but did not end the subsidies. He advocated a soil bank program to remove acreage from production and devote it to ungrazed grass, forest, or reservoirs. Thwarted when Democrats added amendments for higher payments to farmers, Eisenhower vetoed the bill. The economy faltered near the close of the decade.

The most significant domestic legislation enacted during Eisenhower's presidency was the Interstate Highway Act of 1956. A large undertaking, the bill was sold to Congress partly as a Cold War measure. The highways would enable cities to evacuate during a nuclear attack. New four-lane federal highways superseded the state-built two-lane roads that connected most cities. The interstate system changed society by expediting the transfer of traffic from railroads to highways. On water, transportation was upgraded when Congress passed legislation in 1954 allowing for construction of the St. Lawrence Seaway in cooperation with Canada. Connecting the Great Lakes with the St. Lawrence River, the seaway became a major transportation system upon completion in 1959.

Despite his antipathy to the growth of government, Eisenhower signed legislation expanding Social Security coverage to 7.5 million people, among them farmers, physicians, and clergy. He approved an increase in the minimum wage from 75 cents to $1 per hour and agreed to the Federal

Housing Act of 1954, which liberalized lending for home construction. But broad school construction bills foundered over inclusion of parochial schools and use of federal money as a wedge to accelerate school desegregation. Prospects for other significant Republican domestic measures were dampened in the 1954 elections, as the GOP lost control of Congress. Democrats retained a majority for the rest of the administration.

Senator Joe McCarthy continued his crusade against communism after winning a second term from Wisconsin voters in 1952. Eisenhower disliked McCarthy but did not want to criticize him openly. The administration had its own anticommunist agenda. In 1954, for instance, a security clearance was denied for atomic scientist J. Robert Oppenheimer, and the Communist Control Act stripped citizenship from those who sought the violent overthrow of the government. But McCarthy persisted. He excoriated the Voice of America, a radio network broadcasting U.S. views to communist countries in Eastern Europe, because it quoted from the works of controversial writers. And he agitated for the United States Information Agency to remove books by communists and their sympathizers from libraries abroad. The investigations that accompanied these crusades proved embarrassments.

If Eisenhower miscalculated his ability to deflect attention from McCarthy, he was right in one assessment: the senator's downfall would come at his own hand. In 1954, incensed that an Army dentist was promoted from captain to major despite failing to sign a loyalty oath, McCarthy charged that the army was soft on communism. McCarthy was vulnerable because his chief aide on his Senate investigations panel, Roy Cohn, had demanded that the Army grant special favors to draftee David Schine, who had parlayed a superficial knowledge of communism into an unpaid consultancy to the committee. The senator thought Cohn went too far, yet did not restrain him. Stung by McCarthy's allegations, the Army made public Cohn's threats. The Senate panel launched an inquiry into the matter. The televised Army-McCarthy hearings from April to June 1954 were the denouement of the communist hunter's career. Interrupting the proceedings and browbeating witnesses, McCarthy appeared a rude bully, short of credibility. The worst waited until Joseph Welch, the chief Army counsel, seized upon a miscue by his adversary. McCarthy had pledged not to mention that Fred Fisher, a young lawyer in Welch's firm who was not involved in the hearings, once belonged to a communist front organization. But when Welch baited Cohn, McCarthy lost his temper. The Wisconsin senator interrupted and disclosed the Fisher association. Welch accused McCarthy of cruelly smearing the young man, damaging his career. "Have you no sense of decency, sir, at long last? Have you no sense of decency?" Welch asked.

PEACE AND PERIL, 1953–1960 | **283**

The verdict of the investigating committee was split, faulting McCarthy and the Army. The public and the Senate were tiring of the senator's baseless accusations and publicity seeking. A recall effort against McCarthy in Wisconsin failed in 1954, but on December 2, 1954, the Senate condemned him for verbally abusing colleagues. (Condemnation was the least severe penalty, below expulsion or censure.) From that point he declined into depression and alcoholism, and three years after the rebuke, McCarthy died at age forty-eight of liver failure.

The Warren Court and the Judicial Revolution

Another paradox of the 1950s was that Eisenhower, who disliked federal activism, appointed the most activist chief justice of the century. In 1953, he nominated Earl Warren, a three-term governor of California and the GOP vice presidential nominee in 1948. Warren's career, too, revealed paradoxes: he championed civil rights and federally mandated reapportionment, yet as California attorney general he had advocated internment of Japanese Americans during World War II and opposed legislative reapportionment. Before ascending to the chief justiceship he had never been a judge, but he united and guided what had been a divided Supreme Court. His Court led public opinion and set more precedents than did the Court of the great John Marshall. The Court issued landmark pronouncements on civil rights, on procedural safeguards for those accused of crimes, on extension of the Bill of Rights to the states; and on freedom of speech, the press, and religion. Liberals applauded the Court's activism. Conservatives objected that the justices were making law, not interpreting it.

Arguably the most critical decision of the century was *Brown v. Board of Education* (1954), wherein Warren persuaded a unanimous court to repudiate the "separate but equal" doctrine accepted in the 1896 *Plessy v. Ferguson* case. "Separate educational facilities are inherently unequal," the court declared. Henceforth, America was not to be the land of opportunity for white people only. A constitutional logjam that had frustrated Congress was broken, yet it was simpler to change law than to alter attitudes.

Many white people, including Eisenhower, who criticized the court privately and refused to endorse the decision publicly, felt the justices were proceeding too quickly. White southerners dug in for "massive resistance," involving delay and intimidation of pro-integrationists, and demanded Warren's impeachment. Their legislators in Congress, denouncing northern attempts to implement a "Second Reconstruction," signed a "Southern Manifesto" designed to circumvent desegregation by legal yet devious methods. The Ku Klux Klan and other groups attracted militants who linked integration to communism, racial intermarriage, and the weakening of the white race. More respectable leaders, lawyers, and businessmen joined White Citizens Councils to oppose integration. White families fled public schools for suburban, private, and religious schools.

Except for law and graduate schools, higher education did not begin to desegregate until the 1960s in the Deep South, according to most histories. Yet the first Deep South University to desegregate was actually Southwestern Louisiana Institute (SLI), now known as the University of Louisiana, Lafayette (ULL). It is notable for several reasons: first, because it has been neglected by historians; second, because virtually no violence occurred; and third, because of the large number of black students involved. Although integration that occurred at such better-known universities as Alabama and Ole Miss involved only a handful of students, sometimes only one or two, eighty black students enrolled in 1954 at SLI. Possibly because the opposition was limited to verbal abuse, it might have seemed less newsworthy. Yet it might have been more typical than the massive resistance at Ole Miss.

The 1955 murder of Emmett Till, a black teen from Chicago visiting Mississippi, although it involved only one person, showed the charged racial atmosphere. Till flirted with a white woman, whose husband and half-brother killed him. The slayers, who later confessed to a journalist, were acquitted by an all-white jury.

Brown spurred the civil rights movement from the top down. At the grassroots level, the Montgomery bus boycott of 1955–1956 was a catalyst. African Americans mounted a successful protest against public buses after a seamstress, Rosa Parks, was convicted of violating a law requiring segregated seating. The Supreme Court struck down the statue. The boycott demonstrated the power of defiance against an unjust law and produced the major civil rights leader of the era, the Reverend Martin Luther King Jr. A Baptist pastor, he was selected to lead the boycott because he was new to the city and had few enemies. The ministry was one of the few professions open to educated African Americans who filled leadership roles in the fight against discrimination; their churches furnished networks for communicating resistance. Southern black people were willing to endure punishment to call attention to inequities. King borrowed his doctrine of civil disobedience from the teachings of Henry David Thoreau, Reinhold Niebuhr, and Mohandas Gandhi.

King instructed his followers to love their oppressors, emulating Jesus. The justice of his appeal and the long-suffering dignity of his followers brought widespread sympathy. King institutionalized his efforts by founding the Southern Christian Leadership Conference (SCLC) in 1957. In his brief lifetime the Nobel Peace Prize recognized his work; after his death, his birthday became a national holiday.

The accomplishments of King and his disciples did not occur in isolation, for the tides of history were flowing in their direction, part of a worldwide uprising of oppressed peoples that dismantled European colonialism in the 1950s and 1960s. Even the Eisenhower administration was swept up in the current. With White House backing, albeit lukewarm, Congress passed the first civil rights law since Reconstruction, the Civil Rights Act of 1957. Weaker than originally proposed, the measure created a Civil Rights Division in the Justice Department and empowered an assistant attorney general to investigate complaints regarding voting rights violations. In a test of the *Brown* ruling in 1957, Arkansas Governor Orval Faubus summoned the National Guard to block the integration of Little Rock's Central High School. Eisenhower federalized the Guard and dispatched one thousand paratroopers to maintain order and protect African American students. Presidential intervention came belatedly, yet demonstrated that *Brown* would be enforced.

CLAIMING THEIR RIGHTS
African Americans sit-in at a segregated lunch counter
in Greensboro, North Carolina.
(Bettman/Corbis)

Black students from North Carolina Agricultural and Technical University ignited the next confrontation, sitting down at a Woolworth's lunch counter in Greensboro in 1960 and refusing to leave until they were served. Complemented by boycotts and demonstrations, the sit-ins grew, and six months later, white businessmen integrated restaurants. Sit-ins spread throughout the South, a tactic favored by the Student Nonviolent Coordinating Committee (SNCC), more aggressive than King's passive resistance. Launched in the early 1950s, the movement's momentum was reflected in the Civil Rights Act of 1960. The law empowered federal courts to protect voting rights and made it a federal crime to obstruct court orders by intimidation. Considering where it started, the push for equal rights made important progress in the 1950s.

With other groups, the story was similar. Lives of Asian Americans slowly improved in the 1940s and 1950s. Native Americans were a virtually invisible minority, numbering just 343,000 in 1950 and 523,000 in 1960. Congress decided Indians were to succeed or fail on their own, subject to the same rights and responsibilities as other Americans. Federal termination policy let Indians assimilate into white society divorced from public aid, a policy that some Indians and white people said constituted neglect. Several tribes agreed to the plan in 1954, but by the middle of the decade, termination had lost momentum, although it remained in effect until 1969. Meanwhile, in 1954 responsibility for Indian health care was transferred from the Bureau of Indian Affairs to the Public Health Service, which served it better.

In mid-decade, the only developments detracting from an overall upbeat American mood were the fears of communism and Eisenhower's heart attack on September 24, 1955, in Denver. Luckily, no crisis arose while the president recovered and Vice President Nixon, Eisenhower's chief of staff, Sherman Adams, and the cabinet ran the country. Any doubts about Eisenhower seeking reelection in 1956 were dispelled when friends and advisers persuaded him that he was the only Republican who could win. His doctors cleared him medically. Ileitis, an inflammation of the small intestine, felled him in June 1956, but surgery brought him relief and Eisenhower remained a candidate.

For the Democratic nomination, the chief contenders were ex-Illinois Governor Adlai Stevenson and Estes Kefauver, who won the New Hampshire primary only to lose large, critical states. Nominated on the first ballot, Stevenson left the vice presidential nomination to the convention, and Kefauver won a close contest with Massachusetts Senator John F. Kennedy.

Campaigning less than he had in 1952, Eisenhower made enough speeches to assure the public of his fitness. His record of a booming economy and peace was formidable. Troubles abroad—the Soviets were suppressing a revolution in Hungary, and Israel, Britain, and France had invaded Egypt for seizing the Suez Canal—encouraged voters to trust in Eisenhower's steady hand. Eisenhower prevailed with almost 35.6 million popular votes and 457 electoral votes to Stevenson's 26 million and 73.

Peace—And a Tie—In Korea

Soon after his election in 1952, Eisenhower redeemed his campaign promise to go to Korea. During seventy-two hours on the peninsula, he traveled to the battlefield, met troops, visited wounded soldiers, conferred with South Korean leader Syngman Rhee, and decided that the United States could not incur more casualties along a static front. Since 1951 peace talks had stalled over the issue of prisoners of war. Many North Korean soldiers wished to remain in the South, rebelling against leader Kim Il Sung's insistence on repatriation. In 1953, however, North Korea agreed to American terms, following Eisenhower's threat to use nuclear weapons and expand the war. North Korea accepted voluntary repatriation, with the proviso that its officers be permitted to try to persuade prisoners to return. Rhee, who wanted to unify the Koreas on his terms, tried to sabotage the talks by releasing twenty-five thousand prisoners into the countryside. Eisenhower checked him by vowing to discontinue support for additional offensive maneuvers against the North. Rhee would be on his own if he attempted to resume the war. Yet if he cooperated in a settlement, the United States would sign a mutual security pact with South Korea. In July 1953 an armistice was signed at the village of Panmunjom, dividing Korea roughly at the 38th parallel, where the line had been drawn before the war. The truce (which fell short of a treaty) committed the two sides to negotiations leading to reunification, which never produced a united nation. The battles had cost the lives of thirty-three thousand Americans and of more than 1 million from the Koreas and China.

There were no victory celebrations, no cheering crowds to welcome American troops home. Like the War of 1812, the Korean conflict ended in a tie. The war, nevertheless, saved South Korea from communist conquest and led to a 1954 accord in which Washington extended protection to Taiwan. Notwithstanding the lack of enthusiasm at home, the Korean armistice was one of Eisenhower's main achievements. He stopped the fighting six months after taking office.

Fulfilling another 1952 campaign pledge about foreign policy was more difficult. The Republican administration, Dulles said, would take a more vigorous Cold War position than containment. If the United States fought to prevent communism from expanding without trying to uproot it, the best the Free World could hope for was a stalemate. Under Eisenhower, containment in Eastern Europe would be replaced with "liberation of these captive peoples," Dulles said. But when the Soviets crushed workers' demonstrations in East Germany in June 1953, protests fueled in part by American radio broadcasts in West Berlin, the administration failed to help them. Even a mere promise to liberate people from the yoke of communism might require a bigger military, confounding GOP promises to cut expenses and balance the budget. Defense spending, amounting to 60 percent of Truman's last budget, would have to be slashed, confronting Eisenhower and Dulles with the problem of providing more military muscle at less cost.

In 1954 Dulles announced a solution, the policy of massive retaliation. America would respond to any international threat with nuclear bombs that provided "more bang for the buck" because, relative to their destructive power, they were cheaper than a conventional army. Eisenhower would be able to pursue a "New Look" defense program relying primarily on the Strategic Air Command. A policy based on nuclear bombs, however, amounted to a one-dimensional defense incapable of fighting limited wars.

Into the breach stepped Dulles, arguing that the important factor was not whether a country used nuclear weapons but whether its antagonists took the threat seriously. The more credibility the American deterrent inspired, the less chance it would have to be used. To prevent war, the United States had to be willing to go to the brink of war. Brinkmanship, liberation, and massive retaliation made up the tripod of Eisenhower's defense program. Dulles claimed that he used brinkmanship to avert war in Indochina and over Quemoy and Matsu, islands claimed by Jiang and shelled by Mao. It is doubtful that the doctrine made a positive contribution. In practice, containment remained American policy, as reflected in Dulles's forging of mutual defense pacts with forty-three countries to encircle the USSR.

Another foreign policy challenge pitted the administration against fellow Republicans. Ohio Senator John Bricker thought the Constitution should prohibit executive agreements on diplomacy such as the "sellouts" that FDR had made at Yalta. In 1954, with strong GOP support in the Senate, he proposed an amendment providing that international agreements other than treaties could not become law in the United States unless Congress approved. Eisenhower opposed the plan, and in the upper house it failed by just one vote to gain the two-thirds needed to pass a constitutional amendment. Congress exhibited a paradoxical mind-set a few years later, practically giving Eisenhower carte blanche to mobilize military forces for intervention in crises over Quemoy, Matsu, and the Middle East.

Dominoes in Vietnam

American-Soviet relations thawed slightly after Joseph Stalin's death in 1953. Nikita Khrushchev emerged as leader after a period of collective rule. Taking command of an empire that was overextended and losing direction, Khrushchev had to impose Stalinist repression on Soviet satellites or relax his grip. In the spring of 1956 he seemed to choose the latter, delivering a speech to a secret Communist Party congress in which he attacked the brutality of Stalin's regime and promised that the Stalinist dictatorship was over. The Soviet Union could coexist with the United States. But the road to de-Stalinization was fraught with peril. Khrushchev wanted to allow more freedoms, although not to the point of losing his satellites. Once begun, de-Stalinization careened out of control. In June, riots erupted in Poland, where demonstrators demanded the removal of Stalinists, and Wladislaw Gomulka, who proclaimed that there were many roads to socialism, took power. Khrushchev threatened a crackdown, then retreated when Gomulka pledged to rally the Poles against it.

Rebellion went further in Hungary. Students marched on October 23, 1956, to demand that an anti-Stalinist, Imre Nagy, be returned to power. When secret police tried to crush the uprising, workers struck, Nagy seized power, and Hungary withdrew from the Warsaw Pact. Fearing that all of Eastern Europe might follow Hungary, Khrushchev sent in 200,000 troops and 4,000 tanks, killing 40,000 Hungarians and sending 150,000 fleeing. Violating a pledge of safe conduct to Nagy, the Soviets seized him, tried him covertly, and executed him. The repression of popular uprisings damaged the communists, who could maintain power only through force. Americans did not escape criticism, however, because after Radio Free Europe broadcast messages encouraging revolts, Washington did nothing to support them. "Liberation" was false hope.

With fallout from atomic tests intensifying global fear of the arms race, Eisenhower was more serious about nuclear arms control than about liberation. He proposed an "atoms for peace" program under which Washington and Moscow would contribute fissionable material to a United Nations agency for industrial use, as well as an "open skies" plan allowing the United States and the Soviet Union to inspect each other's defense installations from the air. Nothing came of these proposals, or of a 1955 Geneva summit that brought Eisenhower and Khrushchev face to face.

Three years later, without a formal agreement, both countries halted atmospheric nuclear tests for the rest of the Eisenhower administration.

The Cold War spilled over to Asia, where the superpowers battled through local proxies. Khrushchev vowed to wage "wars of national liberation" in Asia and Africa. Loath to have American forces wage a ground war in Asia, Eisenhower worried about an incremental communist takeover, starting in Vietnam. "You have a row of dominoes set up, and you knock over the first one, and what will happen to the last one is the certainty that it will go over very quickly." Therefore, the United States had to prevent the first domino from falling, even if it meant supporting a corrupt, unpopular government. The chief American objective focused on maintaining stability more than on encouraging democracy.

Seeking to reimpose colonialism, the French were frustrated by their inability to destroy Ho Chi Minh's Vietminh and to defeat the guerrillas' hit-and-run tactics. In 1954 they hoped to lure the Vietminh to Dien Bien Phu, a heavily fortified outpost along the Laotian border where they could trap the rebel army. But it was the French who were trapped. Twelve thousand troops discovered themselves surrounded by Vietminh and several Chinese divisions occupying high ground above the outpost. France erroneously believed that the Vietminh would never be able to get their artillery or enough ammunition to the isolated Dien Bien Phu. With the guerrillas encircling the area, though, the French were unable to rescue their soldiers without American intervention. The Pentagon devised a plan whereby bombers and carrier jets, possibly carrying nuclear weapons, would end the siege, but Eisenhower rejected it, unwilling to act without support from the British and the Congress. The French conceded that nuclear weapons would kill their troops as well as the Vietminh. Eisenhower disliked colonialism and urged France to grant Vietnam independence, but he needed support from Paris in the fight against communism in Europe, especially for German rearmament. He supported the French in Vietnam without giving them all they wanted.

On May 7, 1954, Dien Bien Phu fell. A new government committed to withdrawal took power in Paris. Meanwhile, a British- and Soviet-sponsored conference met at Geneva to consider Far Eastern problems, resulting in a treaty that the American delegation, participating as observers only, did not sign. A cease-fire was declared; the French were to withdraw; Vietnam was divided at the 17th parallel into a communist North under Ho and a capitalist South under former emperor Bao Dai. Reunification elections were to be held in 1956. With the settlement, the French passed the baton to the United States. America created the Southeast Asia Treaty Organization, binding Washington, France, Britain, Australia, New Zealand, the Philippines, Pakistan, and Thailand to consult in a crisis and to defend South Vietnam, Laos, and Cambodia. Washington could hardly have found a land less auspicious for nation building. The United States would be drawn in to defend a decrepit southern dictatorship against a brutal, militaristic northern one. Weapons and tactics adequate to defeat a determined jungle enemy, the Japanese, in World War II, would falter before an equally determined jungle foe, the communist Vietcong. In a contest of patience, nerve, and attrition, the Americans would fall short in all three.

Americans might have terminated their involvement by yielding an almost-certain victory to Ho's communists in the reunification elections, which they realized would probably mean the end of free votes. In the competitive context of the Cold War, this option was not seriously considered. The United States staked its hopes on Ngo Dinh Diem, who arrived from exile in America to defeat Bao Dai and become president of South Vietnam, with the help of the Americans and the Central Intelligence Agency (CIA), in 1955. A proud, principled nationalist who hated the French he formerly served, Diem was a devout Catholic who antagonized the largely Buddhist population. Defying world opinion, with backing from Washington, Diem set conditions for the reunification elections he hoped the North would not accept: it must permit international inspections of the polling. Ho was even less a democrat than Diem. Never elected, he had come to power through a series of coups. Then he liquidated political opponents to consolidate his dictatorship. The North was less corrupt, more purposeful, and more disciplined, but it was a regimented society which lacked religious freedom, censored the press and had a backward economy.

The United States proceeded to train a large South Vietnamese army and organized a force to assassinate Vietcong officials. Growing opposition to Diem in the South prompted the North to organize the National Liberation Front, composed of communist foes of Diem. Diem rejected American recommendations to implement reforms. Eisenhower's successor was to face the bleak choice of withdrawing or of expanding the American role.

Elsewhere in the region, Eisenhower had to avoid war between China and Taiwan over the offshore island chains of Quemoy and Matsu. The nationalists, who occupied the chains, and the communists both claimed the islands, considering them potential stepping-stones to invasion of the other side. In September 1954 the communists began shelling the islands. A mutual defense treaty that Dulles negotiated with Taiwan in December omitted Quemoy and Matsu. The next month, China attacked the Tachen Islands, also claimed by Taiwan, prompting Congress to pass the Formosa

Resolution which empowered the president to use force to prevent the conquest of Taiwan, the Pescadores, and other unspecified islands. This was the first time that Congress had given a president the advance authorization to engage in war at a time and place of his choosing. Eisenhower, who believed that the Soviets were behind all the trouble, and Dulles affirmed that if war broke out the United States would use nuclear weapons. In May 1955 the Chinese initiated talks aimed at resolving the crisis and stopped shelling.

Three years later, after the nationalists had increased their forces on the islands, China resumed bombardment of Quemoy and Matsu, then blockaded the islands. Eisenhower, who wanted neither appeasement nor war, sent Dulles to Taiwan to extract a pledge from Jiang Jieshe not to use his military to regain the mainland. China responded with a brief cease-fire, then an announcement that it would shell the islands only on odd-numbered days of the month, permitting resupply on even days. The crisis, Eisenhower said, had degenerated into a Gilbert and Sullivan comic opera. Subsequently, Jiang reduced his garrison and the communists ceased shelling. Eisenhower realized his objectives of avoiding war and preserving Taiwan's independence.

Uncertainty in the Middle East and Latin America

In the Era of Uncertainty, no region was as uncertain as the Middle East, where Cold War rivalries, Arab-Israeli enmity, and Western hunger for oil made a troublesome mix. One hot spot was President Gamal Abdel Nasser's Egypt, which illustrated the paradoxes of the Cold War. Eisenhower believed the nationalist Nasser was leaning toward alignment with the communist camp. The United States was firmly allied with Britain and France, yet their interests in the Middle East were not always compatible. Finally, in Egypt, America was asked to give financial support to a nation that was committed to the destruction of Israel, a country that counted on Washington's protection.

The United States agreed to finance the Aswan Dam on the upper Nile to produce hydroelectric power. Many Americans opposed the loan because Nasser recognized communist China, purchased arms from Czechoslovakia, and was stockpiling weapons to attack Israel. Eisenhower worried that Egypt would be unable to repay the money. Egypt countered with a repayment plan that was unacceptable to the administration. Eisenhower placed conditions on the loan that Egypt rejected, and the president canceled the financing. Nasser nationalized the Suez Canal, through which more than half the British and French oil supplies flowed, vowing he would pay for the dam with canal tolls. Israel, concerned that Nasser would acquire too much power, invaded Egypt in October 1956, and Britain and France did likewise in two days, ostensibly to protect the canal. In addition, the three nations also wanted to overthrow Nasser. Washington risked the loss of critical Arab nations if it sided with its traditional allies. Opposing nationalization of the canal but thinking his allies had overreacted, Eisenhower backed a UN withdrawal resolution. Ike organized an embargo of Latin American oil to Britain and France, and put American air forces on emergency alert to discourage Khrushchev from launching air strikes against the invaders. These actions led Israel, Britain, and France to announce early in November that they would leave Egypt.

In a matter of weeks, Eisenhower had weathered two international crises, over Egypt and Hungary, won reelection, and eased some global tensions. There were long-term effects to the Egyptian affair, however. Soviet influence grew in the region, with Khrushchev agreeing to finance the dam and send arms to Syria. The United States supplanted Britain and France as the leading Western power in the area, assuming responsibility for curbing communist influence in the Middle East and guaranteeing that the West would have access to oil. Following the crisis, in 1957 Congress adopted the Eisenhower Doctrine, a resolution authorizing the president to use force in the area to halt communist aggression. Twice in the next year Eisenhower invoked this power. First, he backed Britain, which sent troops to Jordan to protect King Hussein from pro-Nasser forces. Second, he dispatched fourteen thousand Marines to Lebanon to safeguard President Camille Chamoun from Muslim militias that the administration believed were communist inspired. No fighting resulted, but Eisenhower deterred the Soviets again.

An earlier Middle Eastern trouble spot, Iran, was the scene of a different type of American action: use of the CIA under director Allen Dulles, younger brother of the secretary of state. Eisenhower feared that Iran, containing vital oil deposits and bordering the Soviet Union, might fall into the Soviet orbit. Leftist Prime Minister Muhammad Mussadegh had nationalized the Anglo-Iranian oil company and accepted communist support. The administration found an alternative in Mohammad Reza Shah Pahlavi, who had ascended to the throne during World War II when the British deposed his father, a Nazi collaborator. If the Iranian people were forced to choose between the shah and Mussadegh, who shared power in a constitutional monarchy, they would side with royalty, Washington predicted. Learning that the shah planned to overthrow him, Mussadegh seized complete power in the summer of 1953. The shah fled to Rome. Then a pro-shah, American-hired mob filled the streets and backed the military when, with CIA assistance, it arrested Mussadegh. The shah returned and took control. Iran stayed in the Western camp under the shah, who grew arrogant and corrupt, as Americans would regret, painfully, two decades later. The United States masterminded, but to avoid alienating Egypt did not join, the Baghdad Pact, a defense treaty linking Iran, Britain, Turkey, Iraq, and Pakistan. Also, Washington negotiated a consortium of Western companies, in which Americans held a 40 percent stake, to develop Iranian oil.

Employment of the CIA cloaked American involvement in Iran; in Vietnam; in 1953 Philippine elections, as agency meddling led to the installation of a government favorable to Washington; and in 1954 in Guatemala. Another left-leaning leader, Guatemalan President Jacobo Arbenz Guzman, alarmed the administration by nationalizing land owned by the American United Fruit Company and by purchasing arms from Czechoslovakia. Further, the CIA claimed he was planning to establish a communist base in Central America from which to export revolution. The agency supplied and trained forces loyal to Carlos Enrique Castillo Armas to stage a military coup that drove Arbenz from power. Armas led a military dictatorship that returned the United Fruit property, yet became one of the most abusive Latin American dictators. Tyranny, though, seemed of less concern to the CIA than the downfall of leftist regimes that might destabilize the hemisphere. Apparent CIA successes prompted the United States to rely increasingly on the spy organization. In 1958 the agency unsuccessfully attempted to overthrow the Indonesian government; in 1959 it helped install a pro-Western regime in Laos. Eisenhower evidently did not know it, but the CIA also plotted to assassinate leaders Fidel Castro of Cuba and Patrice Lumumba of Congo.

Latin America harbored hostility toward the giant of the north, as evidenced in 1958, when Eisenhower sent Nixon on a tour there. In Peru and Venezuela crowds heckled, jeered, egged, and spat on him. Yet the spectacle paled before the threat of a communist outpost in Cuba, as Fidel Castro came to power in 1959, overthrowing the reactionary autocrat Fulgencio Batista. Castro nationalized American oil and sugar refineries without compensation, repressed religious expression, conducted show trials and executions of Batista's followers, and turned to the Soviets for a long-term trade pact. Refugees fled Cuba for south Florida, becoming an influential political faction and a potential exile army dedicated to ousting Castro. Before the end of Eisenhower's second term, the CIA was training such a force in Guatemala. In 1961 America severed diplomatic relations with Havana. The new communist outpost became a Cold War flash point where an error could trigger a nuclear exchange.

Anxiety from Above:
Satellites, Missiles, and Spy Planes

Long a dream of humanity, space exploration became a reality in the 1950s, although entwined with the nuclear nightmare. Rocket development became urgent, not because of the prospect of searching the heavens but because rockets could carry atomic warheads. Americans, therefore, were shocked when the Soviet Union launched a 184-pound satellite, *Sputnik*, on October 4, 1957. *Sputnik II* lifted off in November, weighing 1,100 pounds and bearing a live dog for medical monitoring. The United States had expected to launch the first satellite late in 1957 during observance of the International Geophysical Year, when scientific explorations of the Earth and space were emphasized. Yet it was not until January 31, 1958, that the Army, sandwiched between two failed navy projects, sent the eighteen-pound *Explorer I* into orbit. Even though American satellite launches soon became routine, Soviet satellites were heavier and boosted into orbit with rockets of greater thrust.

A major propaganda victory for Moscow in the Cold War, *Sputnik* shook the confidence of Americans, making them worry that Soviet technological prowess might prompt neutral nations to cast their lots with communists. Americans succumbed to self-doubt. The harshest complaints fell on the educational system, thought to lack some of the toughness and discipline of Soviet schooling. A book entitled *Why Johnny Can't Read* (1955) became a best seller. Eisenhower, too, was criticized. If he spent the same amount of time on the satellite program as on his golf game, detractors argued, the United States would be leading the space and missile race. In the interest of keeping defense spending down, Eisenhower tried to ignore the clamor for additional funds for missile research. He also rejected the report of a presidential panel that urged stronger defense and bomb shelters. Research and spending, nevertheless, were accelerated. Defense was cited to justify not only highway construction but also the 1958 National Defense Education Act, providing low-interest loans for college students who would teach math, science, and foreign languages in public schools, and for graduate students who would become college instructors. On July 29, the Congress created the National Aeronautics and Space Administration (NASA), and in 1959 the agency initiated Project Mercury, the manned space program. Accustomed to reaching for the stars, Americans aimed for the moon.

Communism prompted more than three hundred thousand East Germans every year to flee to the West via Berlin. The Berlin exodus depleted the East of skilled workers and embarrassed communism. In November 1958, Khrushchev warned that if the United States did not withdraw from Berlin in six months, he would turn over access to the city to the East German government, which was hostile to the American presence and which Washington did not recognize. Eisenhower said he was prepared to negotiate over Berlin only on the basis of German reunification.

As months elapsed and the Soviets did not act on their threats, tensions cooled. Eisenhower and Khrushchev scheduled a summit for May 1960 in Paris, to be preceded by an American tour by the Soviet leader. Eisenhower, in turn, would visit the USSR. Talks on Berlin were on the summit agenda, although the president hoped to achieve more: an arms control agreement that would be the big step toward ending the Cold War. The international climate was favorable. Both superpowers had declared voluntary moratoriums on nuclear testing in 1958. Khrushchev seemed ready to conclude a treaty, and during his American trip he and Eisenhower had promising discussions at Camp David, the presidential retreat in Maryland.

Even while the leaders chatted, American U-2 spy planes continued to overfly Soviet airspace and photograph military installations. Usually the U-2s flew too high for Soviet antiaircraft missiles, but Francis Gary Powers's plane had engine trouble, dropped to a lower altitude, and was shot down over Soviet territory in May 1960. Powers ejected, was captured, and confessed. When the Soviets announced the downing of the jet, on the eve of the Paris summit, the United States, assuming that Powers was dead and the wreckage dispersed, said the aircraft was a weather plane that strayed off course. Khrushchev next revealed that Powers had been captured, catching Washington in a lie and jeopardizing the summit. Khrushchev demanded that Eisenhower halt the flights, which the president did, and apologize, which Ike did not. The summit broke up without an arms deal and Eisenhower's trip to the Soviet Union was canceled. Still, it was doubtful that any political resolution could have been found to satisfy both sides. Future presidents negotiated deals but lacked sufficient determination or political clout to end the arms race.

1960: Running for TV Cameras

The aborted attempt to strike an arms control deal was the biggest in a number of disappointments and losses that, for Eisenhower, overshadowed his second term. In November 1957 he suffered a minor stroke from which he recovered, but it was clear to him and to his inner circle that the stress of the Oval Office was taking its toll. In each of the next two years, he lost

THE WORLD WATCHES A contemporary cartoon of the Kennedy-Nixon presidential debate. (Library of Congress)

an important member of his administration. A minor scandal led to Adams's resignation before the 1958 congressional elections. Adams had accepted a coat, a rug, and hotel expenses from a textile manufacturer under federal investigation, raising the question of influence peddling. The Adams scandal contributed to an election beating that made Eisenhower the first president to have to deal with three successive Congresses domi nated by the other party. Then in 1959, John Foster Dulles died of cancer, taking from Eisenhower his major partner in diplomacy. Under Dulles's successor, former Massachusetts Governor Christian Herter, Eisenhower's chief diplomatic activity was to make international trips to encourage peace.

Political setbacks at home seemed to weigh on Eisenhower. After the 1958 elections, he spent the rest of his term combating what he perceived as a spendthrift Congress eager to earmark more for defense, education, and social programs. Democrats had always been big, irresponsible spenders, he thought, but now, so, too, were members of his own party.

Looking to the 1960 presidential election, he was gloomy, worried that the GOP nominee would match his Democratic foe promise for promise, repudiating all that Eisenhower had done over two terms.

Nixon preempted his only strong rival for the nomination, New York Governor Nelson Rockefeller, by committing himself to a stronger national defense and more liberal positions on domestic issues. The promise discouraged the still-popular Eisenhower, who never warmed completely to Nixon and running mate Henry Cabot Lodge, from giving Nixon the rousing endorsement he sought, though he disliked the Democratic ticket of Kennedy and Texas Senator Lyndon Johnson. Perhaps the ambivalence of the Eisenhower-Nixon relationship damaged the vice president most when the president, asked about the administration decisions in which Nixon had participated, said: "If you give me a week, I might think of one."

Young, charismatic, handsome, and a World War II hero, Kennedy came from a wealthy family that lavishly financed his campaign. He faced potential liabilities in that he was in ill health and he was Catholic, a target of religious prejudice. But Kennedy and his well-oiled campaign machine deftly defused the religious issue and rolled into the general election to "get the nation moving again." Kennedy aimed to inspire Americans with the

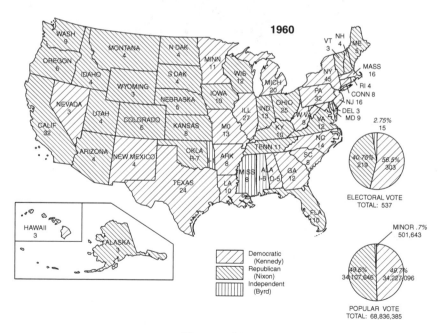

Election of 1960

noble purpose of winning the Cold War. Further symbolizing the dawning era of media-centered politics, Kennedy mastered television, outshining Nixon decisively in at least the first of three televised debates, based more on style than on substance. Kennedy won the closest popular election of the century, with only .01 of 1 percent more than Nixon, a margin of fewer than 120,000 votes, 34.2 million to 34.1 million, although the electoral margin was 303 to 219, and there were allegations of vote fraud in the key states of Illinois and Texas. The Democrat was the first Catholic elected president and, at age forty-three, the youngest man elected president.

Days before leaving office, Eisenhower delivered a nationally televised farewell address. Remembered most is the old general's admonition that "In the councils of government, we must guard against the acquisition of unwarranted influence, whether sought or unsought by the military-industrial complex." Even as he urged caution, his successor was planning the expansion of the military and an increase in defense spending. The changes sprang from a generation of leadership more aggressive than its predecessor.

In domestic and foreign affairs the president left the United States in only marginally better shape than he found it. On civil rights, progress was slow and Eisenhower provided little leadership; he was also reticent about confronting McCarthy. In diplomacy, the administration stuck to an outmoded China policy, failed to appreciate the urgency of nationalism, set dangerous examples of military and CIA involvement, showed poor judgment with the U-2 flights, and failed to curb the arms race.

Paradoxically, Eisenhower could take the most pride in what did not happen. He prevented major wars and limited defense spending. The Era of Uncertainty experienced a relatively stable decade while he was at the helm. If he did not inspire, neither did he panic. He kept the economy humming and treated his foreign adversaries with respect. After the Korean War, which he ended, not a gun was fired in anger on his watch. The next decade would not be so lucky.

CHAPTER FIFTEEN

The Affluent Society

MATERIAL RICHES were abundant in the Era of Uncertainty, yet peace of mind was elusive. Among the paradoxes was the mixture of rebellion, inertia, and spiritual seeking. Economic growth shaped American life in the quarter century following World War II, which ended the Great Depression. The 1950s were prosperous and stable. The following decade was turbulent yet even more prosperous, though inflation climbed toward the end and poverty persisted in spots. Minorities, farmers, and Appalachia lagged. At center stage in the Era of Uncertainty, under Dwight D. Eisenhower and Lyndon Baines Johnson, was a continuation of the debate over the size, power, and purpose of the federal government. Having begun under Theodore Roosevelt and waxed during the New Deal era, Americans asked of the Great Society: Was it an idea whose time had come?

The 1950s and 1960s

Scripture states: "The poor ye will always have with you." Americans set out to disprove that ancient adage, whether by prosperity wrought by free enterprise in the 1950s or by government action in the 1960s. Neglected groups, such as minorities and women, demanded to share the wealth. The baby boom generation, the most prosperous to date, raised its expectations more rapidly than they could be sated.

Americans were unified by the national purpose of winning the Cold War, and by the fear of losing it. In this materialistic period, interest in religion rose to new heights. In the 1950s religion was an ally of conformity; in the 1960s religious seekers made it an instrument of breaking away. Racial progress, too, advanced on the wheels of moral fervor, yet ultimately dissipated, another victim of unmet expectations. Science and medicine

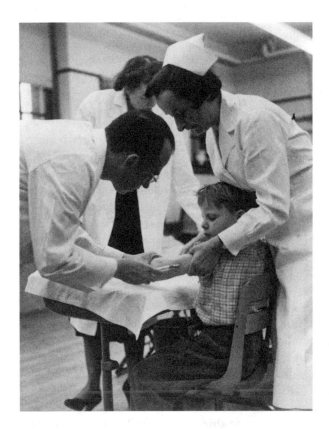

WIPING OUT
POLIO
Dr. Jonas Salk innoc-
ulates a child, 1954.
(Library of Congress)

produced marvels and medical miracles, lifted spirits, spurred the economy, and saved lives. The most irrepressible of revolutions, the sexual revolution, marched on.

The 1950s were politically conservative, yet politics does not dictate social mores. The 1960s seemed more adventurous. Conservatives and liberals argued throughout the era whether the government was doing too much too soon, or too little too late. In the end, the period reaffirmed that the only certain method of progress is trial and error. Remarkable changes occurred in politics, society, foreign policy, race and gender relations, and more. Yet change and progress are not synonymous, and the period included cataclysmic changes following assassinations. Like the 1920s, an effervescent decade punctured by the stock market crash, the 1950s had some qualities of a fool's paradise. As the 1960s closed, however, no one would have referred to the decade as a paradise, for fools or anyone else.

The Economy

America had the highest standard of living of any major nation during the Era of Uncertainty. Without realizing it, Americans were winning the Cold War with their mighty economy. Accounting for only 7 percent of the human population, America generated 40 percent of world income, nearly half the electricity and large shares of steel, copper, and coal on the globe, and more automobiles and domestic appliances than any other country. Farmers, too, outproduced their foreign counterparts, even though just 8 percent of Americans labored in agriculture by 1960, down from almost 63 percent a century earlier. Production boosts were rapid, without increases in labor, because of improved machinery, herbicides, and insecticides. Southern agriculture benefited from the development of a mechanical cotton picker, but this meant the loss of manual work, much of it performed by African Americans.

Women played a major role in prosperity; their number in the workforce jumped 44 percent from 1947 to 1962. The number of jobs traditionally held by women, such as nursing, clerical work, and teaching, grew because of the growth in the service sector of the economy. The consequences of increased numbers of working women affected families: parents were together less and divorced more, charities lacked volunteers, and office friends replaced neighborhood friends.

In the decades after World War II, many Americans realized their ambitions of home ownership. The proportion of families paying mortgages rose from 55 percent to 60 percent during the 1950s. Developers who employed thousands of construction workers could make fortunes in the crowded market of suburban housing. Notable were William Levitt, a skilled salesman, and his brother, Alfred, an architect, who teamed up to erect tracts of houses on Long Island, one of the first mass-produced subdivisions. The Levitts could complete a home every seventeen minutes and sell their houses immediately. Customers lined up for the homes the night before they went on sale. Each small, virtually identical house featured a bookcase, a fireplace, and a television. Eventually, seventeen thousand homes housed eighty thousand people. Air conditioning made homes more comfortable, especially in the South, which became a tourist mecca.

Tourists and others could drive to their destinations in more powerful, fancier automobiles. Cars, produced as new models annually, featured tail fins, chrome, radios, power steering and brakes, and automatic transmissions. General Motors, with its best-selling Chevrolet, became the world's largest corporation. Chain motels opened to serve motorists, beginning in the 1950s with the Holiday Inn. Kemmons Wilson, a Memphis builder, produced a simple, standardized design including a swimming pool, air conditioning, and television sets, which he franchised. By the end of the decade Wilson had fifteen hundred motels, with a new one going up every two and a half days. Mass-produced, standardized products that sold reasonably were applied to the food industry as well, notably with the McDonald's hamburger chain, which became ubiquitous. Dick and Maurice McDonald, who produced hamburgers by assembly line and limited the menu to that item, were bought out by Ray Kroc, who expanded nationwide, then worldwide. McDonald's helped initiate a mania for fast-food—the ten-minute lunch with no tipping.

The government contributed to the general prosperity with a strategic tax cut during the Kennedy administration, and increased spending during the Johnson administration. From 1963 to 1966 the gross national product increased at a virtually unprecedented 5 percent. Unemployment dropped from over 5 percent to around 3.5 percent. Still, the combined spending for the Vietnam War and the War on Poverty propelled the economy into overdrive and set the stage for the economic problems of the 1970s. The economy began to weaken in the late 1960s as many realized that American plenty was finite. Michael Harrington's *The Other America* (1962) inspired government programs to vanquish poverty, yet poverty persisted, though mitigated. The latecomers to the middle-class job market, especially minorities, women, and immigrants, continued to lag. A college education became a prerequisite for work previously requiring a high school or grade school education. The chain food, motel, and other service industries generated millions of jobs, but they were menial and low paying.

The origins of immigrants changed in the 1960s as immigration regulations placed more emphasis on uniting families than on job skills. Political refugees from communism were accepted from nations that had undergone revolutions, such as Cuba and Hungary. In 1965, the Immigration and Nationality Act changed immigration priorities, lifting some restrictions on Asian and African immigrants. Yet it capped immigration from the Western Hemisphere, at 120,000 annually, for the first time. New ethnic groups turned increasingly to religion, especially Catholicism, as a source of cultural identity. Ethnic and religious politics peaked in 1960 with the election of John F. Kennedy, an Irish Catholic. Kennedy received 80 percent of the Catholic and Jewish vote, but only 37 percent of the Protestant vote, in edging the Quaker Nixon.

Organized labor emerged from World War II bigger and stronger; the AFL at 10 million members and the CIO at 4.5 million. Workers rejected revolutionary schemes and supported mainstream unions. They won yearly cost-of-living increases and benefits such as medical care and vacations. Some leaders, notably Walter Reuther of the CIO, viewed political activity as embracing economic reform, civil rights, and equality for women. Labor remained liberal and a supporter of the Democratic Party, but there were rank-and-file defections to conservative George Wallace in the 1964 primaries and in the 1968 general election.

By the mid-1950s the AFL and CIO had evolved from rivals to confederates and in 1955 they merged as the AFL-CIO with 16 million members. Reuther and George Meany, the presidents of the combined union, believed that the future lay in the organization of white-collar workers, who by 1956 outnumbered blue-collar toilers. Union growth included the public sector, such as teachers and postal workers. Once more paradox was present: the percentage of union members in the workforce diminished in the 1950s. Labor was weakened by its failure to recruit African Americans and Hispanics aggressively. The decline in industrial jobs and increase in white-collar workers, many of them committed not to strike, restricted the pool of potential members. Prosperity also made workers reluctant to strike.

A catalyst to economic growth, science produced a wonderland of consumer products and millions of jobs. There were: electric clothes dryers, blenders, and frying pans; automatic garbage disposals; the Polaroid camera; and the long-playing record. Jet planes and rockets emerged from defense research, as did the computer. From early, slow, bulky computers developed during World War II, the computer went on to revolutionize transportation, industry, business, and education. Some consider it the most significant scientific development of the second half of the twentieth century.

Medicine developed in quantum leaps. Jonas Salk developed a vaccine for the crippling polio virus in 1955 and it was followed by an oral vaccine developed by Albert Sabin in 1962. There was a vaccine for measles, and there were hundreds of new drugs and antibiotics to combat rheumatoid arthritis and asthma; tranquilizers relieved some mental pain. An oral contraceptive, "the pill," appeared in 1960, a new weapon in the arsenal of the sexual revolution. In 1964, an ally in birth control, the intrauterine contraceptive device, reached the market. Gains were made against two killers: smoking and heart disease. In 1967 the first heart transplant was performed in South Africa.

Heart disease and lung cancer were linked to smoking in the 1960s, when 52 percent of men and one-third of women smoked. Ashtrays were ubiquitous. Athletes and physicians marketed cigarettes. Fraternities and sororities held "smokers" for pledges. But in 1966, two years after the surgeon general reported the health consequences of smoking, packages were required to carry warnings. In 1972 cigarette ads were banned from radio and television. Increasingly, people quit.

Suburbia, Migration, and the Baby Boomers

In the nineteenth and early twentieth centuries, Americans had moved from farms to cities, yet in the affluent decades, the migration was from cities to suburbs. Starting in 1950 and continuing for thirty years, eighteen of the twenty-five largest cities in the country lost population and the suburbs gained 60 million people. Urban critics disparaged suburbs as bland places of tasteless conformity in their dwellings and people. The criticism was overstated; suburban homes were no more alike than high-rise city apartments. The most basic motive for moving outward was that people wanted to own homes with lawns and gardens, as they could not in the crowded, expensive city. Suburbs offered excellent schools, wholesome places to raise children, dependable fire and police protection, and green, open space. The suburbs of the 1950s and 1960s were almost exclusively white. In some cases, developers refused to sell to minorities; in others, price was the chief barrier.

Although suburbs continue to be largely white and socially stratified, their diversity is increasing as they evolve, paradoxically, into small towns reminiscent of an earlier America. It would be a mistake to idealize either

THE SPREAD OF SUBURBIA
Tract housing and the postwar landscape.
(Library of Congress)

cities or suburbs, or to judge demographic trends in moral terms, as was done early in the twentieth century when rural Americans moved to cities. Places do not define individuals, nor do they dictate individual lifestyles, although they do influence them.

For better or worse, Americans by the twenty-first century are living in a post-urban society. Since 1950 more than 90 percent of metropolitan growth has taken place in suburbs. By January 2005 more than two out of three persons in the nation's urban areas lived in suburbs. Still, less densely populated cities, although experiencing problems, also offer opportunities to serve better the population that remains.

As the demographic landscape evolves, the pain that accompanies change cannot be denied. The rich are relocating into downtown condominiums paying a premium for access to cultural offerings. The poor cluster in inner cities, which lag in job opportunities as high-tech jobs follow skilled workers to the suburbs. Big-city education constitutes a failure in some respects. Schools that were virtually all-white in the 1950s have evolved into virtually all-minority, undermined by truancy, drugs, and low graduation rates. A sense of hopelessness, however, is offset by a determination to reform schools and inspire students. Some of the simplest reforms might be the most effective: reducing class size, and reading a daily newspaper at home, with parents, starting in elementary school. Newspapers, which are cheaper than television sets, should be read for enjoyment, outside of school. By college age these students might be literate, inquisitive, reasonably well-informed, and less bored.

Cities also continue to erode in stability because the downtown areas, appealing to rich, often childless couples, or older, highly successful executives, lack middle-class families with children. This is less a governmental problem than a demographic one. Most people did not flee cities because of bad government and good government will not necessarily bring them back.

Suburbs expanded from childbirths as well as flight from cities. From 1946 to 1964 some 75.9 million Americans were born, a "baby boom" that produced two-fifths of the national population. The baby boomers were the largest, richest, and best-educated generation in U.S. history and created a bulge in the population pipeline at each stage of their development. First they crowded into elementary school classrooms, leading to teacher shortages. Next they generated enormous growth in higher education, opposed the Vietnam War, led the sexual revolution, experimented with recreational drugs, and injected idealism into politics, only to retreat into disillusionment. In the 1980s many became young urban professionals, "yuppies." As the generation approached retirement questions arose over whether Social Security could sustain its numbers.

If there was a central paradox of baby boomers, it was their complexity, leading them in a variety of directions. Theirs was the most idealistic and altruistic generation—and the most selfish and narcissistic. Labeled bland as middle school students in the 1950s, they were called hedonists as college students in the 1960s, though they were often the same people. As they aged they became interested in jobs, families, and annuities, and many settled into conventional lifestyles they once ridiculed. The simplest explanation for the contradictions is that the generation changed its mind repeatedly as it evolved. The baby boomers stand out not because they were more fickle, but rather because there were so many of them and they thus had a wide impact. In fact, many of the changes sometimes attributed to politics and economics can probably be linked at least partly to demographics. For example, violent crime, frequently associated with the young, increased as the boomers reached their teens and beyond. By the time the boomers attained middle age, violent offenses decreased and white-collar transgressions increased.

Boomers and their families also moved southward and westward to the Sunbelt, seeking better jobs and climates. California was the prime destination. Its population increased by 5 million, 20 percent of national population growth, during the 1950s. California became the largest state in 1963. Low taxes and labor costs attracted industry and the region outgrew the North and East. In time the Republican Party dominated the Sunbelt. Though neglected by government studies and urban planners, small towns remained an alternative to cities and suburbs, offering a sense of history and community, self-sufficiency, cohesiveness, and the absence of traffic jams. Almost unnoticed, they were a "third way," hospitable, in particular, to retirees, extended families, and small businesses.

The Sexual Revolution

In the decades after World War II, sexuality exploded and sexual themes permeated popular culture. Sex became recreational as well as a means of producing families, an evolution that had begun a hundred years earlier. The war was a catalyst for change, introducing servicemen to cultures with more relaxed sexual standards and encouraging wartime dalliances, arising partly from loneliness, at home. Teenagers grew up more quickly and had sex at earlier ages. Babies were born to younger women, many of them unmarried. The sexual revolution was liberating, yet its dark side contributed to the paradox and uncertainty of the era: some perceived sex as gratification without cost, and such a view is seldom realistic. Although monogamy might or might not be natural, freer sex sometimes came at the cost of guilt or, at least, divided loyalties. The melting pot of popular culture encouraged the decoupling of sex from its traditional link to love. As one psychologist said, "Sometimes it's love and sometimes it's just sex." The profound power of sex, detached from moral strictures, made it difficult to determine whether lovers loved one another or merely loved having sex.

The sexual revolution had roots beyond the libido. The second feminist movement sprang largely from writers, marchers, and academicians, to whom sexual equality could be interpreted in terms that were physical, social, economic, psychological, and identity affirming. Most influential was Betty Friedan's 1963 book, *The Feminine Mystique*. Bright, highly educated, Friedan felt unfilled by motherhood alone. "The problem that has no name," as she called it, was essentially boredom. She wanted to be a writer and became one of the most significant ones of her time. Her book and activism helped stimulate creation of the National Organization for Women in 1966. In 1972 Gloria Steinem, ironically once a Playboy bunny, founded *Ms.* magazine, a major feminist periodical. The second feminist movement espoused the same sexual standards for women that society had taken for granted for men: women should be as free to take a variety of partners, families should not inhibit either gender sexually. Part of the sexual liberation that did not involve intercourse did involve fathers sharing in child care and housekeeping, freeing women to work, enjoy hobbies, and relax. Some feminists opposed pornography as an exploitation of women's bodies, but others considered it a matter of free speech. Some women "dressed" down, scorning heels, makeup, and other accoutrements that made them "objects" of men. Simultaneously, women had the right to take the initiative in calling a man, asking him for a date, approaching him in a bar, or proposing marriage. On the other hand, women who did not marry should be respected, not denigrated as "old maids." The thrust of the argument was that a woman did not have to find her self-value in a man. Feminists opened career opportunities for women and often considered women without careers inferior.

Feminists were a minority, yet a disproportionately influential one. Women who had careers in academia, publishing, government, or wrote in the new field of women's studies were rarely nonfeminists, but feminists, of course, did not represent all women. Some women chose to lead conventional lives as homemakers and enjoyed pursuing men by wearing the fashionable clothing feminists scorned. The debate also involved men. Some nonfeminists believed feminists were disrespectful of men, even those who were essentially well-meaning. No one dared ask the question openly, but at least in some male locker rooms men asked if they ought to have a

ONE MAN'S
SEXUAL
REVOLUTION
Publisher Hugh
Hefner with
Playmates of
the Month.
(Library of
Congress)

voice in whether their pregnant wife or lover had a baby or an abortion. Even by removing judgmentalism from the dialogue, it is clear that sexuality, in all of its manifestations from boardroom to bedroom, is perhaps the most complex paradox of the century and the most uncertain aspect of the Era of Uncertainty.

Sex was everywhere: movies, music, photo magazines, and celebrity lifestyles. Female Hollywood stars dressed provocatively and changed lovers and husbands like the weather, drawing more people to their films, perhaps to experience these lifestyles vicariously. Revealing dress percolated down to high school students and some college students. Drugs and alcohol loosened inhibitions, on the silver screen and small screen as well as at parties and on dates. If Americans had ever been prudes, they were prudes no more. The most popular genre was the romantic comedy, and many suggestive movies, rated PG-13, were considered acceptable for children. Because Hollywood movies were sexy did not necessarily mean that they were crude, artless, or unfit for consumption. Still, anyone who lived through the 1950s and 1960s cannot help but wonder at the rapid pace of sexual influence in everyday life. In 1953 Hugh Hefner launched the highly profitable *Playboy* featuring a seminude female centerfold. Next came the Playboy philosophy of sex for the moment, and Playboy clubs to serve rich white males, their drinks delivered by curvaceous female "bunnies."

Books such as Grace Metalious's *Peyton Place* (1956) depicted a small New Hampshire town as a hotbed of sexual intrigue, sold millions of copies, and spawned a radio and television series. Jacqueline Susann's *Valley of the Dolls* (1966), an account of a sexually active, unmarried professional woman, became one of the best-selling books of all times. The books appeared while the Supreme Court was creating a more permissive legal atmosphere. Spanning the 1950s and the 1960s, justices ruled on a series of cases that opened a window to obscenity. "A book cannot be persecuted unless it is found to be utterly without redeeming social value," the Court stated. Rock 'n' roll's premier pioneer, Elvis Presley, gyrated his hips suggestively while he strummed his guitar and sang. Presley had started as a gospel singer, and the mixture of sexuality and religion remained a staple of the musical industry, its performers, and its followers. In the 1980s the world-known evangelist Jimmy Swaggart, a piano pounding partisan of Christian music, was seen as a sexual libertine, and other examples followed. Sex, religion, motion pictures, and music had a common root in that they worked on the emotions and loosened inhibitions. The counterculture of the late 1960s produced musical festivals, such as Woodstock, famous for good music and good sex. The connection of music, sex, and dance was the intertwining of beat, rhythm, lyrics, and movement. The connection was historic, but the scope was revolutionary.

Science and academia to some degree supported liberalized sexual expression. Sigmund Freud had approved sex as an antidote to mental illness in the late nineteenth and early twentieth century. Anthropologist Margaret Mead concluded that Polynesian Island children were happier than American children, possibly because their lifestyle was less inhibited. Sex researcher Alfred Kinsey produced two pathbreaking books, *Sexual Behavior in the Human Male* (1948) and *Sexual Behavior in the Human Female* (1953). Kinsey began as a researcher of insects at the University of Indiana, then developed an interest in human sexuality, at that time almost a virgin discipline. Taking large samples of sexual histories, he interviewed his subjects in depth and filmed sexual activities. His research rocked the supposedly staid 1950s. Kinsey showed that a sexual revolution had long been underway, underground. Premarital sex, masturbation, adultery, and gay and lesbian sex were more frequent than most Americans realized. He tried to free sex from the inhibitions of dogma, and, more questionably, from love and emotion, trivializing it, some complained, as a mechanical act. On the one hand, Kinsey lit the fuse that ignited women's and gay and lesbian liberation movements in the 1960s. On the other hand, he had darker, more self-serving motives, advancing an agenda that at worst became another variety of dogma. As time passed, some researchers claimed that Kinsey's research was flawed because, although his sample was large, it was not representative of the general population, omitting, for example, highly religious individuals. Kinsey, nonetheless, helped legitimize human sexuality as a field of research.

Whatever the motives and influence of Kinsey, a gay and lesbian revolution burst forth in the late 1960s. The focal point was the "Stonewall riot" of 1969, in which gays and lesbians fought New York police who raided a gay bar. The theme of gay rights would have a major impact in succeeding decades as society became more tolerant in matters of sexual orientation. Yet criticism, some of it religious, surfaced again in the 1980s with the appearance of AIDS (acquired immunity deficiency syndrome), which appeared first in large numbers in the gay community. Eventually, such celebrities as the actor Rock Hudson and the basketball star "Magic" Johnson contracted the disease. By the time Johnson was infected the virus had moved into the heterosexual community and included drug users who shared contaminated needles.

The highest leaders of the land shared in the sexual revolution. Indeed, some were promiscuous. John Kennedy, Lyndon Johnson, Bill Clinton, and Martin Luther King had adulterous affairs. The great basketball center Wilt Chamberlain claimed he had slept with a thousand women. In Hollywood, on Broadway, among aspiring models and starlets, even in the news industry, sleeping with the boss was a way to get ahead. Powerful men and women, political leaders, and celebrities, were sought after as lovers. Henry Kissinger, Nixon's national security adviser and secretary of state, explained: "Power is the ultimate aphrodisiac." By the end of the baby boomer rein of the youth corps, the sexual revolution had gained the momentum of a locomotive roaring downhill. Like all-powerful impulses that move fast, it changed America, and the locomotive roars on.

A Spiritual Barometer

Religious interest in the 1950s often has been dismissed as superficial, and that of the 1960s has been described as waning. Always central to American life, religion had a prominent place in the affluent decades. In 1950 some 57 percent of Americans belonged to a church or synagogue; in 1959 that figure was 69 percent. No other Western culture equaled that of the United States in the percentage of population associated with a religious institution. Americans are seekers whose journey frequently involves religion, a trait that did not bypass the baby boomers, perhaps the biggest cohort of religious searchers ever.

In the context of the 1950s organized religion was prominent. Yet religion was something to do, rather than something to be. Usually it was found between the walls of religious institutions rather than in solitary reflection. Public prayer was more of a ritual than private prayer. Reflecting the sunny prosperity of the decade, religion offered an uplifting message that was largely responsible for the optimistic outlook of the era despite potential nuclear holocaust. The interest in religion was manifest by the popularity of such books as Henry Morton Robinson's *The Cardinal* (1950) and Catherine Marshall's *A Man Called Peter* (1951), both the basis of hit films. In 1956 *The Ten Commandments* became the top-grossing movie to that time, and children were released from school to see it.

In the Eisenhower years patriotism included an element of Christianity, sometimes called civil religion, but more appropriately, civic religion. The central idea, which had long been a part of the concept of American exceptionalism, was that America was God's chosen nation, set apart to be an example for the world. Yet the Soviets, whose official philosophy was atheism, also felt that destiny was moving in their direction, their victory inevitable. Just to make sure, both built bigger and better bombs.

Eisenhower rarely attended church before reaching the White House, but became a churchgoer to set an example for the nation. During Ike's administration Congress added "under God" to the Pledge of Allegiance in 1954 and "In God We Trust" to coins in 1956. Eisenhower was president during an age of religious popularizers and was friends with some of them. Protestant minister Norman Vincent Peale's 1952 book, *The Power of Positive Thinking*, sold millions of copies. Peale explained that faith in God and oneself were the keys to success. Modern psychiatry has used similar techniques to treat depression and other mental illnesses, with the caveat that if one has a happy outlook, success is not important. Evangelist Billy Graham, a North Carolina Baptist, filled stadiums to hear his sermons and made converts by the thousands. Later, his crusades, which he took worldwide, were a mainstay of television. Graham was no simpleton but his message was simple: faith in God was more important than rules. Salvation was a gift; it did not have to be earned. Graham became the friend of presidents, including some who exploited his friendship, as well as the civil rights leader and fellow Baptist Martin Luther King Jr.

RALLYING FOR RELIGION Evangelist Billy Graham preaches a sermon to 40,000 people attending the annual Reformation Day held in New York City, 1957. (AP/Wide World Photos)

King's role as a civil rights leader is the stuff of legend; his role as a religious leader is sometimes obscure. From the beginning, King and other civil right leaders used the black churches as a fulcrum of the movement. The churches provided a moral basis for direct action, furnished biblical foundations as the moral rationale for equality, and pointed out white hypocrisy. An interconnected network of dedicated believers, African Americans themselves found sustenance in biblical arguments for their crusade, at least in the early years. King learned from Gandhi and the Bible that love could overcome hate, though it would not be easy, and that those who rely on love must suffer and exercise patience. Like the conservative Graham, King's oratorical ability was a potent weapon in his arsenal. And he did overcome.

Popular religion overshadowed formal theology during the Age of Uncertainty, yet there were profound theologians who thought creatively and wrote inspiring prose. Reinhold Niebuhr was the best-known theologian, merging theology and activism, accepting imperfection, and striving for social justice. Yet his brother, Richard, might have been the most profound and systematic theologian of the era. Eschewing the popular journalism and lecture circuit in which Reinhold thrived, Richard led a comparatively quiet career, avoiding the increasing tendency to link secularism and religion. Emulating Richard Niebuhr, Paul Tillich, an inspiration to King, dismissed the connection between theology and nationalism.

For Catholics, the era produced a renaissance. Most important were the reforms of Pope John XXIII, especially those of Vatican II, a council convened by the pope from 1962 to 1965. For the first time the pope made an effort to embrace the ecumenical movement to unite all Christians. The council liberalized the Mass by approving the use of the vernacular and by giving the laity a greater role in the service.

Women, however, did not have much of a voice in Vatican II or in the other debates affecting religious institutions. At the grass roots they were active in denominations, attending services more often than men, dominating religious education, and doing most of the volunteer work. They seldom made policy and still were barred from entering the priesthood. Much the same could be said for gays and lesbians. They fought valiantly, with slow progress, to be ordained or even to have their lifestyle accepted. In the twenty-first century the issue continued to animate debates.

In the 1960s Americans turned inward. Some turned away from organized religion altogether or merged spirituality with meditation and a variety of philosophies, some of which, such as Marxism, excluded God. Religion motivated some to work to eradicate poverty, to volunteer for the Peace Corps, and to bring solid food as well as spiritual manna to the needy. Religion motivated some participants in the Vietnam antiwar movement, and elements of the counterculture crept into religious services, such as use of guitars, folk music, circling to hold hands and acknowledge the participants as spiritual partners, and criticism of materialism and the government.

The most important spinoff from the counterculture undercurrent was the rise of New Age philosophy and religion, which had no prescription for practice and for which any summary will oversimplify. Some turned to Eastern philosophies and religion such as Buddhism (including the Tibetan variety), Daoism, and Confucianism. Many took lessons in martial arts of the East; others were inspired by spiritual dance. A spate of books poured out, including self-help books exploring the connections between sex and spirituality and dismissing of the idea that God had a human form of the male gender. The seekers, who continued their quest in the twenty-first century, mixed astrology, alternative medicine, noncompetitive exercise, and the teaching of a spiritual lifestyle to their children. The New Age seekers continue to experiment with herbal medicine, acupuncture, and the Indian belief that energy centers called *chakras* influence one's physical and mental health. There was, and is among New Age practitioners, a strong strain of beliefs in psychic phenomena, including mind-body medicine and mental telepathy. Stress reduction techniques include massage, unblocking of energy, and communing with nature, surrounded by greenery, alone or in groups. Many believe in reincarnation, that humans have lessons to learn in every lifetime until they complete their journey and merge with the One Force. Some view God as a source of intelligent energy that dominates the universe, less like the Christian God than like the "Force" of the popular motion picture series *Star Wars*. In fact, notable movies of the period, especially those by George Lucas and Steven Spielberg, carry undertones with spiritual messages, and can be watched on several levels by adults and children. In some circles of young people, the departing words were not "Good-bye," but "May the Force be with you."

New Entitlements

Once upon a time in America, "rights," were protections for individuals against aggressions threatening personal safety or status. Most of the Constitution's amendments, most notably the first ten, protect individuals. This understanding began to change with the rise of group consciousness in the 1960s, particularly inspired by the civil rights movement and feminism. The list soon expanded to other groups defined by age, ethnicity, education, even neighborhood or region. Rights became something owed to a group by the government, and in part, Lyndon Johnson's Great Society and War on Poverty addressed these concerns. There was nothing inherently wrong with the concepts of group rights, or even their evolution into "entitlements"—benefits owed by the government. Yet there were practical problems. As opposed to most traditional rights, "entitlements" required resources, namely money. Once enacted, it was almost impossible to remove them from the federal budget, which rose automatically every year. Groups competed for entitlements, especially when there did not seem enough to go around. The concept polarized politics and political parties, which upped the ante to outpromise the opposition. Parties and politicians who refused to play the game were often defeated at the polls.

In the short run, especially while the Great Society was operating at full throttle, the concept did much good. But the idea of entitlements raised expectations and weakened economic incentives. LBJ did not deliberately encourage the notion; he believed in education and job training to enable people to better their lives. Yet over time this idea was translated into the idea that the government owed not opportunity but results. While many of the early antipoverty programs aimed to place trainees in jobs, over time the program came to imply the promise of a job and, eventually, a "decent job." Yet even if the government were to become the employer of last resort, there had to be something useful for the employees to do, they had to have the skills to do it, and there had to be money to pay them. When the resources could not be found to do all these things, the resentment contributed to the sour mood that closed the 1960s, producing, in the waning days of his term, the irony of poor people demonstrating on the Mall against Lyndon Johnson, of all people.

Though entitlements were not a hot subject of debate and there was much sympathy for groups that had suffered discrimination, who were denied an education, or whose job description stopped with "secretary," as demands increased and resources dwindled, a reaction set in. The backlash first arose among conservatives who believed the white middle-class and blue-collar workers had been demonized, patronized, and squeezed out in the scramble. They were expected to feel guilty for not being poor or for the possible sins of their forefathers. A good many were committed to social uplift, yet resented being scapegoats. If their complaints had not contained an element of truth, they would not have resonated. Some former liberals, termed neoconservatives, joined the march to the right. Journalists and scholars such as Daniel Patrick Moynihan, Nathan Glazer, Irving Kristol, and Norman Podhoretz took to the pages of *Commentary* and *The Public Interest* to challenge the prevailing liberal orthodoxy. Doubting the competence and compassion of big government, they wanted a government that served individuals, not groups. Although group identity had its place, in the long run, they believed, one's individual identity was the only thing no one could take away. If the government fed all the hungry with all the caviar they could gorge, it would not necessarily make them happy. White Christians joined neoconservatives in deploring the counterculture, drug use, lack of discipline, and a decline in self-reliance. They advocated sexual restraint, traditional families, and less glamorizing of unconventional lifestyles. By the late 1960s these conservatives were poised to take over politics.

The affluent decades were a failure only in the sense that they were not an absolute success. The 1960s ended not with a total rejection of the decade's values, nor of its predecessor's. The political dialogue was healthy, motivated less by mean spirits than by competing interests, and the best way to create a society that would not only be great, but good, moral, secure, and satisfying. A time of paradox indeed.

CHAPTER SIXTEEN

Cultural Dissent

THE ERA OF Uncertainty culminated in the youth rebellion of the 1960s, which destabilized the nation yet left a host of lessons. First, there is nothing wrong with uncertainty because progress means taking a chance. Second, if one wants space, he or she must allow others to have it. Finally, accept change, but do not try to force it. If it happens at all, it will happen at a pace influenced by historical circumstance, as an idea whose time has come.

Culture both shaped and reflected the times. The decade of the 1950s was mislabeled "placid," for the dissent and unconventional lifestyles of the 1960s could already be seen in the acting of Marlon Brando and James Dean, the rock 'n' roll of Elvis Presley, and the writing of the Beat authors Jack Kerouac and Allen Ginsberg.

Hollywood: A Star-Crossed City

Hollywood turned a dark face to the dilemmas of the 1950s, including the Cold War, the McCarthy era, and the nuclear nightmare. Films depicted labor corruption, prison violence, and racism. Nuclear testing prompted the genre of monster films that titillated and frightened young audiences, like an amusement park ride where the danger is illusional but the thrill is real. One film that achieved cult status later, partly because it resembled a caricature of the horror film genre, was *Invasion of the Body Snatchers* (1956), in which aliens took over human bodies.

Westerns were popular on the silver screen, as they were on television. John Wayne, the most popular actor, also played military heroes. Westerns helped satisfy the craving of Americans for a romantic view of the mythic past. The plots focused on the heroism of white male cowboys who were brave, pure, and deadeye gunslingers. Indians symbolized roadblocks to the advance of civilization. Nonetheless, as movies gained sophistication,

HOLLYWOOD'S IMAGE OF DESIRE
Movie Star Marilyn Monroe appearing with the
USO Camp Show, "Anything Goes," 1954.
(National Archives)

they grew more realistic in their depiction of cowboys and Indians alike. Delmer Dave's *Broken Arrow* (1950) was an early attempt to show the past from an Native American perspective. Fred Zimmerman's *High Noon* (1952) depicted a frontier town shadowed by fear and cowardice, with one man alone left to uphold its honor.

If the Western emphasized American triumphalism, *The Wild One* (1953) introduced a subculture of brawling bikers as the mouthpiece for criticism of the status quo, conveyed in a format that was physical as well as psychological. Marlon Brando represented a biker rebelling against the middle-class lifestyle others were trying to attain. Asked what he was rebelling against, Brando responded, "What've you got?" James Dean, too, was a rebel, though more nuanced, embodying the uncertainties of the first wave of baby boomers as they came of age.

Hollywood films became sexier and more daring, dealing with taboo subjects to outflank television. To do so, Hollywood had to circumvent its own code of self-censorship. Usually the public gets what it demands in the field of entertainment. What it wanted was actresses such as Marilyn Monroe, once a *Playboy* pinup, who combined sexuality, superficial innocence, and an undercurrent of sophistication. Her name on the marquee guaranteed an audience. The philosophy of the insatiability of the male libido was parodied in Billy Wilder's *The Apartment* (1960). Violence splattered the silver screen in Alfred Hitchcock's thriller *Psycho* (1960). A brilliant director, Hitchcock combined mystery, sexuality, humor, and plot with clever use of camera angles, a vivid imagination, special effects advanced for the era, and a deft touch.

In the 1960s Hollywood's self-censorship was stretched until broken. Stanley Kubrick's adaptation of Vladimir Nabokov's novel *Lolita* (1962) depicted a middle-aged professor's sexual encounter with a pubescent girl. Kubrick pushed Hollywood politically with *Dr. Strangelove; Or, How I Learned to Stop Worrying and Love the Bomb* (1964), a brutal satire about enthusiasm for nuclear war. Late in the decade Hollywood glamorized outlaws in *Bonnie and Clyde* (1967), a pair of depression-era bank robbers resurrected as beautiful people. *Easy Rider* (1969) harked back to the world of rebellious bikers in more complex terms than the 1950s films.

TV: Home Entertainment in a Box

Hollywood soon lost its near monopoly on the American imagination. Cinema entertainment lost ground rapidly following the war and fell behind the new medium of television. The small screen could be viewed with family, friends, or children in one's living room. Unlike the cinema, one could change channels if one did not like the show. Increasingly, there was more variety and higher quality. Let in as a friendly guest, television threatened to take over the home, eating up time for family meals, outdoor activities, parties, homework, and conversation. Teenagers seemed to flit between television and telephone. In the end, Americans became addicted, though this was not necessarily technological determinism. There was some truth in the idea that television inspired antisocial behavior, but this appraisal also carries an element of an alibi, or at least an evasion of individual responsibility. After all, one could simply turn it off. Early shows were largely all white and middle class. Though racism was a factor, marketing was a more important one. Television thrived on advertising and aimed at an audience that could buy Chevrolets and refrigerators, or, better yet, Cadillacs and mansions in Malibu.

Television was not all about actors and directors, prejudice and advertisers. As a technological catalyst for change in the Time of Paradox it ranks

★ CHARLES VAN DOREN: THE MAN FOR THE ROLE ★

I've learned a lot about good and evil.
They are not always what they appear to be.
—CHARLES VAN DOREN

QUIZ SHOW WITH A CHEAT SHEET
Contestant Charles Van Doren
on the quiz show *Twenty-one*.
(Library of Congress)

CHARLES VAN DOREN was perfect, decided the producers of *Twenty-One*, one of the quiz shows that had become a television fad in the 1950s. He was young, handsome, unassuming, and an English instructor studying for his Ph.D. at Columbia University. His father was a famous professor and writer at Columbia and his mother and uncle won acclaim as authors. The producers wanted to rig the show to make him their new champion. Initially Van Doren was reluctant, not seeking public glory. However, they persuaded him with the argument that his success would inspire teachers and students—and with the prospect of winning up to $100,000. And perhaps Van Doren thought it would be his chance to impress his family. "I've been acting a role for ten or fifteen years, maybe all my life," he admitted later. "It's a role of thinking that I've done far more than I've done, accomplished more than I've accomplished, produced more than I've produced." That *Twenty-One* was "fixed" to make the show dramatic and entertaining, that Van Doren would be coached and given the answers, did not matter.

So Van Doren said yes to the producers and became king of the NBC-TV show when the reigning champion, Herbert Stempel, "took a dive" by deliberately answering a question wrong. For weeks, from late 1956 into 1957, Van Doren kept winning, adding to his money total (which would reach $129,000), and receiving hundreds of letters daily from people thanking him for his contribution to intellectual life. Offers poured in to write, to lecture, to appear in movies. NBC promised him a job as a $50,000-a-year commentator on the *Today* show. He was a folk hero who magazines called "the new All-American boy." Still, Van Doren was tormented by guilt and begged the producers to be defeated. "I felt like a bullfighter in a bull ring with thousands and thousands of people cheering me on, and all I wanted to do was get out of there," he admitted. When he learned that he would finally lose to lawyer Vivienne Nearing, his reaction was, "Thank God!"

Van Doren went on to complete his doctorate and take a professorship at Columbia, in addition to his *Today* duties. His comfortable world, however, was shattered in 1958, when Stempel, angered that he missed out on the fame garnered by the more telegenic Van Doren, revealed publicly that *Twenty-One* was fixed. There were other reports of dishonest quiz shows, and a New York grand jury began investigating. Many who had been involved with the shows, Van Doren among them, said they knew nothing of wrongdoing, but the grand jury was skeptical, and a House of Representatives subcommittee held hearings. In the fall of 1959, Van Doren was subpoenaed, appeared before the lawmakers, and read a long statement of confession. "I would give almost anything I have to reverse the course of my life in the last three years," he said. "I was involved, deeply involved, in a deception. The fact that I, too, was very much deceived cannot keep me from being the principal victim of that deception, because I was its principal symbol. There may be a kind of justice in that." Cheap fame was expensive.

Soon after his statement, NBC fired Van Doren and Columbia accepted his resignation. His admission shocked a number of commentators, who wondered how such a bright man with so much to offer could have been involved in something so tawdry, and whether the quiz show scandals were symptoms of a sick society. Nevertheless, there was great sympathy for Van Doren. Letters to NBC protested his firing. Columbia students rallied in opposition to his dismissal from the university. Newspapers and magazines reported that a majority of people believed he had been punished enough and deserved another job. Several universities expressed interest in hiring him.

But Van Doren retreated from the public eye, moving from the East to Chicago, where he lived quietly, worked as an editor for *Encyclopedia Britannica*, and edited significant collections of literature. Having carved out considerable, genuine accomplishments on his own, he never again spoke openly of his part on *Twenty-One*. The paradox of what Van Doren seemed to be and the reality beneath the veneer, as well as the juxtaposition of his rapid rise and dramatic fall, make him an apt symbol for the Era of Uncertainty.

Sources: For book-length treatments of Charles Van Doren and the quiz show scandals, see Kent Anderson, *Television Fraud: The History and Implications of the Quiz Show Scandals* (1978), and Joseph Stone and Tim Yohn, *Prime Time and Misdemeanors: Investigating the 1950s TV Quiz Scandal—A D.A.'s Account* (1992). For useful and well-written short treatments, see Eric F. Goldman, *The Crucial Decade—and After: America, 1945–1960* (1960); Erik Barnouw, *Tube of Plenty: The Evolution of American Television* (rev. ed, 1990); and David Halberstam, *The Fifties* (1993).

with the automobile, the computer, antibiotics and vaccines, space exploration, and atomic energy. Few innovations made their impact so rapidly. In 1946 there were only six thousand TV sets in the country, more than half of them in New York City. By 1950, there were 12 million. By 1970 there were 70 million sets, 38 percent of them color. Among scholars, TV's negative effects seemed apparent. It pulled families apart or drew them together without communicating. They went out less, and the new diversion dulled minds and dimmed imaginations because the activity was passive. Yet television also brought news into homes as no previous medium. It shaped attitudes, generating emotional as well as intellectual reactions. It showed the graphic violence of the Vietnam War and the conflicts of the civil rights movement. Without television, Elvis Presley and the Beatles, who appeared on the *Ed Sullivan Show*, would not have become international celebrities.

Many of the formulas for television programs were borrowed from radio. These included soap operas, variety shows, police dramas, situation comedies, and, increasingly, athletic contests. Detective and police stories included *The Untouchables, Dragnet*, and *77 Sunset Strip*. Even more numerous were Westerns. In 1959 there were twenty-nine Westerns on the fall schedule of NBC, CBS, and ABC. Live dramas were a high point of television in the 1950s, yet live dramas were forced into extinction because of their cost and fear of making a mistake. Exposure of quiz show cheating in 1959 nearly destroyed the genre, discredited networks, and wrecked careers. The wages of network sin were public outrage, channel switching, and the virtual demise of the big-payoff quiz shows. Other formulas involved science fiction, sometimes combined with the mystique of the supernatural, as in Rod Serling's *Twilight Zone. Star Trek*, a science fiction adventure, had limited appeal in its first run, but it developed a cult following and was spun off into television sequels, books, and memorabilia.

Federal Communications Commission Chair Newton Minow in 1961 dismissed television as a "vast wasteland." Vast it was, and vaster it became. Yet viewers could be selective. Television brought news, sometimes live, into American homes with immediacy. Edward R. Murrow's CBS program *See It Now*, inspired hard-hitting documentaries in the 1950s. The middle 1960s were a golden age of national news anchors such as the trusted Walter Cronkite of CBS and the erudite David Brinkley and Chet Huntley of NBC. Their newscasts expanded from fifteen minutes at the dawn of the medium to thirty minutes in the 1960s. The trend culminated in *60 Minutes*, a CBS investigative news program that premiered in 1968. Television news also contributed to the decline of daily newspapers as many learned to take their information from sound bites. Television changed politics. Time for advertising was expensive. Candidates often paid more attention to the background and setting needed to attract news cameras than to their abbreviated message. People watched televised conventions but paid less attention to written platforms.

Rockin' to New Rhythms

If teenagers were addicted to television, to a large extent they dictated choices in popular music. If a single word could encapsulate popular music, it was "variety." As often in America, changes in taste were affected by technology. For the buying public, except performers, sheet music was of little concern. The period saw the growing popularity of durable vinyl sound recordings and high-fidelity record players. Amplifiers no larger than suitcases were stacked as high as buildings at the end of the 1960s. Radio broadcasted recorded, rather than live music. The electric guitar became more prominent, and tape began to change the way recordings were made.

SHAKING ALL OVER
The first rock star: Elvis Presley, 1956. (Library of Congress)

★ Janis Joplin: A Turbulent Life for Turbulent Times ★

Freedom's just another word for nothing left to lose.
—KRIS KRISTOFFERSON, "ME AND BOBBY MCGEE"

A PIECE OF HER HEART
Janis Joplin lived her songs.
(AP/Wide World Photos)

JANIS JOPLIN'S life was a paradox of artistic triumph and self-destructiveness. Like other musicians who came of age in the Era of Uncertainty, she was drawn into the deep end of rock, in which the volume level had become earsplitting and the electronic distortions were meant to simulate the sensory-bending experience of LSD. Also like her peers, she grounded her foray into the unknown on one of America's oldest forms of musical expression, the blues. Her hard-driving delivery reinvented the jubilance of such African American forebearers as Bessie Smith, called "the Empress of the Blues" in the 1920s.

By the time of Joplin's 1966 arrival in San Francisco, the mecca of music and the emergent counterculture, some white male vocalists had already immersed themselves in the blues. It was part of a search for authenticity in a culture that increasingly appeared artificial—plastic. Joplin was seen as a woman playing a man's game in the largely white, male-dominated rock scene of the 1960s.

Joplin waged a revolt against the conventional symbols of female beauty and celebrity. An ugly duckling by the standards of the previous generation, she was reincarnated as a swan on her own terms, with her frizzy hair and peacock frocks helping to broaden definitions of beauty and fashion. Her membership in and later leadership of a succession of all-male bands reinforced this image. With her first hit song, "Piece of My Heart" (1967), she set an image for herself of vulnerability beneath a swaggering exterior.

Joplin's performances and raw sexuality were an example of music's role in the sexual revolution of the 1960s. Symbolic of a hedonistic pursuit of pleasure, she was embraced by the counterculture for her refusal to submit to limits. It was this refusal to acknowledge limits that led to a succession of drug-related deaths among leading rock stars in the Era of Uncertainty, including Jim Morrison, Jimi Hendrix, and Joplin, killed by a heroin overdose in 1970 at twenty-seven. Joplin's biggest hit was posthumous, her recording of Kris Kristofferson's "Me and Bobby McGee," a low-key country ballad whose pensiveness stands at odds with earlier recordings and raises intriguing questions about the artist she might have become.

Equally intriguing, and more ironic, was the incorporation of the musical rebellion of the 1960s and its stars into the mainstream capitalism economy. "They're paying me $50,000 a year to be like me!" Joplin exclaimed. Fifty thousand dollars was big money in the 1960s, especially for a counterculture that prided itself on disdaining wealth. For an unpopular teen from Port Arthur, Texas, being encouraged to be herself might have seemed victory enough. To be paid handsomely for it struck Joplin as the most paradoxical turn of all.

Freedom means many things. To the rebels of the 1960s it often meant pushing the limits of conventional society, moving to a rock beat, flaunting sexuality, experimenting with drugs, taunting presidents, and living in communes. To Janis Joplin, freedom meant simply being her uninhibited self because she had "nothing left to lose."

Sources: Studies of Joplin include David Dalton, *Janis* (1971); Deborah Landau, *Janis Joplin: Her Life and Times* (1971); Dynise Balcavage, *Janis Joplin* (2000); Myra Friedman, *Janis Joplin and Buried Alive* (1999); and John Cooke, *Janis, Performance Diary, 1966–1970* (1997).

Electric guitarist and recording engineer Les Paul contributed the technique of "overdubbing," separately recorded layers of instruments and voices.

As the form of music changed, so did its content. African and European influences had cross-pollinated to create distinctly American music since the previous century, but black music acquired greater prominence after World War II. Frank Sinatra brought Tin Pan Alley to a pinnacle during the 1950s. Yet his old-style pop music was giving way to a defiant black sound that changed music worldwide. Jazz lost popularity, despite innovations. Saxophonist Charlie Parker and trumpeter Dizzy Gillespie pioneered a harmonically daring genre called bebop. Trumpeter Miles Davis inaugurated the emotionally restrained version, cool jazz. Popular audiences did not warm to these undanceable forms, and many of the popular dance bands disbanded. As for "serious music," it had grown entirely too serious for most audiences.

African Americans embraced a new music, rhythm and blues, which maintained the dance beat of big-band jazz in a small combo format featuring electric guitar. The sound was accepted in the South, where black and white people had always appreciated each other's music. Presley and other young southern whites enjoyed greater access to black popular culture than their northern peers, and they would take the lead during the

1950s in the mix of white and black music called rock 'n' roll. Even in country music, a traditional white genre, important artists such as Hank Williams and Bill Monroe acknowledged their black musical roots.

In the 1960s, rhythm and blues evolved into soul, derived partly from black gospel music. Berry Gordy founded Motown Records to promote the new sound and found buyers. Small recording companies nurtured rock, especially Sun Records, which released Presley's debut recording, "That's All Right (Mama)" in 1954. A year later Presley's music moved beyond the South when RCA signed him to a contract. Not until he appeared on television in 1956 did he become a national figure. The former Memphis gospel singer reeled off hits: "Hound Dog," "Jailhouse Rock," and "Heartbreak Hotel." At one point Presley recorded fourteen consecutive records selling more than a million copies each. Women found him seductive, although in private he was shy, and his chief loyalty was to his mother. Not even the payola scandals of 1959, in which disc jockeys admitted they had accepted bribes to promote records, retarded the rise of rock. It was already "All Shook Up."

Rock contributed to the generation gap that opened in the 1950s and yawned into a chasm during the late 1960s. Among the contributors to the youth musical rebellion were Chuck Berry, a black man nearing thirty when rock took hold, and Bob Dylan, a white man. Dylan began his career as a folk singer renowned for protest songs such as "Blowin' in the Wind," and "The Times They Are A-Changin'." He progressed from an acoustic to an electric guitar and a rock band. Across the Atlantic, British teenagers embraced rock. Like Presley, the Beatles achieved instant stardom after appearances on American television. A "British Invasion" followed that included the Rolling Stones.

As the antiestablishment counterculture developed, rock flirted with psychedelia, music that stimulated the experience of hallucinogenic drugs. Psychedelia brought in groups like the Doors, whose singer, Jim Morrison, drew from Near Eastern melodies and Brazilian rhythms. Eventually the mainstream turned from battling the counterculture to preempting it. A leading corporation advertised near the end of the decade, "The Revolution is on CBS."

History and Literature after the Guns of World War

Americans, proud of the victory in the world's greatest war, celebrated their heritage in a triumphalist spirit in the first years of the Era of Uncertainty. Magisterial narrative histories attempted to explain the American accomplishments and describe their heroic leaders. One of the first, and best, was

Arthur M. Schlesinger Jr.'s *The Age of Jackson* (1945). In fast-paced prose, the Harvard historian depicted the hero of New Orleans as a representative of American virtues such as adventure, ambition, rebelliousness, and gloves-off politics. In Schlesinger's mind, Jackson resembled a greater hero he was to chronicle, Franklin D. Roosevelt. Richard Hofstadter focused on themes such as interest group competition reflected in political leadership in *The American Political Tradition and the Men Who Made It* (1948). Hofstadter won Pulitzer Prizes for *The Age of Reform* (1956), a provocative look at populism, progressivism, and the New Deal, and for *Anti-Intellectualism in American Life* (1963). Another historian, who wrote chiefly about the South, C. Vann Woodward, a giant in the profession, wrote *Origins of the New South, 1877–1913* (1951) and *The Strange Career of Jim Crow* (1955).

As early as the 1950s, American intellectuals began to doubt whether their society worked as well as had been claimed. William H. Whyte Jr. criticized suburbia and large bureaucracies in *The Organization Man* (1956). C. Wright Mills's *White Collar* (1951) and *The Power Elite* (1956) portrayed the middle class as lacking purpose. In *The Lonely Crowd* (1950), David Riesman questioned whether middle-class Americans were as alienated as Mills believed and if it made sense to belittle the satisfaction many workers derived from rising into white-collar jobs.

Popular books helped energize social movements and inform debate in the Era of Uncertainty. Rachel Carson's *Silent Spring* (1962) drew attention to the pollution of natural resources and helped inspire the environmental movement. Ralph Nader's *Unsafe at Any Speed* (1965) questioned automobile safety and encouraged a consumer revolt. Penetrating analysis complemented the activism of the civil rights movement. Alex Haley assisted Nation of Islam leader Malcolm X in writing *The Autobiography of Malcolm X* (1965). James Baldwin's essays were arguably as influential as his novels; his *Notes of a Native Son* (1955) shared perceptive insights into the black community, its failures, and its relations with white America. Philosophy, considered esoteric by most Americans, soldiered on in academia, as Sidney Hook continued to unravel the implications of John Dewey's pragmatism in *The Quest for Being* (1961).

The most striking literary rebellion occurred among the Beats, who emphasized spontaneity, sexuality, illicit drug use, and spirituality. Allen Ginsberg's poem "Howl" (1956) and Jack Kerouac's novel *On the Road* (1957) invited young people to reject "square" society. Kerouac characterized it as "rows of well-to-do houses with lawns and television sets in each living room with everybody looking at the same thing and thinking the same thing at the same time." Critics countered that although the Beats fled convention, their destination was unclear. "We gotta go and never stop going till we get there," a character said in *On the Road*. When another character asked, "Where we going, man?" the answer was, "I don't know, but we gotta go."

Some authors who came of age after World War II grappled with the meaning of their place in society. Norman Mailer's *The Naked and the Dead* (1948) drawn from his service in the Pacific, and Kurt Vonnegut's *Mother Night* (1962) and *Slaughterhouse-Five* (1969) depicted World War II as a drama of the absurd. In *Catch-22* (1961), Joseph Heller went further, describing army policies as insane. If one were insane, he could be excused from flying missions. Yet if he asked to be excused, that would prove his sanity and he would have to fly them. Of course if he did not ask, he would have to fly them anyway. Another aspect of insanity was the subject of a 1962 classic, Ken Kesey's *One Flew over the Cuckoo's Nest*, which depicted a mental institution where the patients were saner than the doctors and nurses.

James Michener wrote historical novels on a grand scale. His best sellers included *The Bridges of Toko-ri* (1953) and *Hawaii* (1959). Michener's novels were long and intricately descriptive. Sloan Wilson's *The Man in the Gray Flannel Suit* (1955), a story of conformity among white-collar workers, was one of the few popular novels by a new writer to interpret the decade. In the 1960s Gore Vidal produced historical novels such as *Washington, D.C.* (1967) and a story of Hollywood transvestitism, *Myra Breckenridge* (1968). Like Mailer, Vidal became a highly publicized public personality, appearing on television and frequently quoted in newspapers and magazines.

As the center of the American publishing industry, New York remained a mecca for writers and a popular setting for fiction. *New Yorker* magazine nurtured the talents of writers whose short stories delighted in emotional nuance rather than conventional plots. One such writer, J. D. Salinger, reached an enormous audience with *The Catcher in the Rye* (1951), one of the handful of great American novels because it deftly appealed to shared human experiences. The protagonist, young Holden Caulfield, reflects on the hypocrisies and inconsistencies of the adult world and their betrayal of their own ideals. Ralph Ellison's intricately plotted *Invisible Man* (1952) also ranks as one of the great American novels. Like Caulfield, it involves a search for identity, in this case, a black youth coming of age in white America. Again like Caulfield, his journey ends with a mixture of disillusionment and acceptance. The nameless protagonist feels betrayed by white society and also by those who want to overturn that society.

Reflective, philosophical, and quintessentially southern, Walker Percy, in novels such as a *The Moviegoer* (1961) and *The Last Gentleman* (1966), wrote in a the cultural context of his native region. He depicted the South as becoming homogenized and estranged from its own history.

Poetry scattered in many directions after the war and produced no giants of the status of Robert Frost or Carl Sandburg. Social and political alienation were the themes of the Beat poets.

During the 1960s, many writers, such as Bob Dylan, who would probably have been poets in earlier times, turned to songwriting as a more effective way to reach a mass audience, due to the shrinking marketplace for poetry.

On Stage and Canvas

The end of the war ushered in a new generation of playwrights. Of the leaders of the post–World War I era, only Eugene O'Neill still enjoyed a fruitful career, with such psychological masterworks as *The Iceman Cometh* (1946) and *Long Day's Journey into Night* produced in 1956. The first major post–World War II playwrights, Tennessee Williams and Arthur Miller, like O'Neill, probed the unspoken feelings and recriminations of troubled families. Williams's *A Streetcar Named Desire* (1947) and *Cat on a Hot Tin Roof* (1955) visited sweaty southern settings, peopled by colorful characters, seething sexuality. Miller wrote one of the most important American plays, *Death of a Salesman* (1949), which featured an unforgettable character, Willy Loman, a traveling salesman ruined by capitalistic competition and his own ego, "never anything but a hard-working drummer who landed in the ash can like the rest of them!" exclaimed Loman's son, Biff.

The introduction of television and the growing popularity of home entertainment displaced Broadway from the center of culture. However, the theater remained an important training ground for actors, writers, and directors who moved on to Hollywood. Paddy Chayefsky's *Middle of the Night* (1956) was an adaptation of his well-received TV play, *Marty*, a story of lonely hearts who find each other in an insensitive world. *Marty* also became a successful movie. Neil Simon began as a writer for television comedian Jackie Gleason and went on to pen such Broadway comedy hits as *The Odd Couple* (1956), which was adapted into a movie and a popular TV series. Among the most popular and lucrative plays were Broadway musicals such as Frederick Lowe and Alan Jay Lerner's *Brigadoon* (1947), Richard Rodgers and Oscar Hammerstein's *South Pacific* (1949), and Frank Loesser's *Guys and Dolls* (1949). Departing from this upbeat tone, Stephen Sondheim and Leonard Bernstein's *West Side Story* (1958) was a contemporary tragedy about lovers and racial animosity modeled on *Romeo and Juliet.*

The stage took small steps in the direction of racial diversity, especially after the box office success of Lorraine Hansberry's *A Raisin in the Sun* (1959), about a black family whose mother's powerful love held them together against social deprivation. Yet most innovations in theater occurred "Off Broadway," districts in New York where performance spaces were cheaper and financial risks lower and where theater emulated the European avant garde more than Broadway. Off Broadway produced new plays on the cutting edge of culture. One such drama was *Hair* (1968), a musical popular for its then-shocking treatment of drugs, sex, and nudity.

New York also spawned a new movement in visual art, abstract expressionism, in which the object disappeared and only arrangements of color remained. Slinging paint onto canvases on the floor of his studio, Jackson Pollock became the most celebrated figure of abstract expressionism; Robert Rauschenberg assembled "combines" from objects he found on the streets of Manhattan, including mirrors, cardboard, postcards, and broken umbrellas. Rauschenberg's greatest influence was his idea that virtually anything is art if the artist says it is.

The rise of pop art in the 1950s delineated a change in intellectuals' attitude about culture. Modern art had been defined as avant garde, and as highbrow. Its supporters had felt threatened by the rise of popular culture. Pop art resulted from a generation of artists, many of working-class origins, who studied on the G.I. Bill and whose perceptions were shaped by popular culture. The most famous pop artist, Andy Warhol, adopted Rauschenberg's idea that the artist defines art. Beginning his career as a commercial artist, Warhol turned to commercial objects, such as his Campell's Soup can (1966). He and others attracted attention to genres such as rock music and comic strip art. The greatest paradox of pop art is that it never became truly popular; it circulated within a circuit of well-endowed museums, galleries, and private collectors. The irony was symptomatic of the state of visual arts after World War II, as painting and sculptures could no longer compete for attention with television.

Sports: Winning and Losing

During the Era of Uncertainty, no aspect of sports became more politicized than the Olympic Games. The Cold War competition between nations virtually dwarfed the competition among athletes. The United States and the Soviet Union each strived to win the most medals to prove the superiority of their system. The United States usually finished first or second to the Soviets in medal count. Individuals also tried to make political statements. In the 1968 Summer Games American sprinters Tommie Smith and John Carlos raised their arms in a clenched fist Black Power salute and were stripped of their medals for their protest. Still, Americans took pride in outstanding performances. Bob Matthias became the youngest decathlon winner in 1948. Wilma Rudolph, once disabled, won three gold medals in track in 1960; and Bob Hayes tied the world record in the 100-meter dash in 1964. America fielded strong teams in swimming, track and field, and basketball.

Football replaced baseball as America's favorite spectator sport. College football, broadcast on television, became a major spectacle. Universities with the best teams became better known than elite academic universities. Every year, colleges pursued the national championship and players competed for the Heisman Trophy, given to the best player. Among professionals, the National Football League expanded to the South and West. Its stars included quarterback Johnny Unitas of the Baltimore Colts and Cleveland Browns fullback Jim Brown. Yet the real star of the Era of Uncertainty was not a player but a coach, Vince Lombardi of the Green Bay Packers. When Lombardi took over the floundering Packers had great players who were playing out of position or sitting on the bench. Lombardi excelled as a strategist, a disciplinarian, and a motivator. The Packers, running a simple, bone-crushing offense and fielding an unyielding defense, developed a mystique, playing in the league's smallest town. Lombardi, emphasizing the team concept, coached the Packers to five world championships in nine years. Salaries soared after Alabama quarterback Joe Namath signed with the New York Jets of the upstart American Football League for $427,000 in 1965. Desperate to end the salary wars that ensued, the NFL and the AFL merged in 1970. After Namath predicted that his underdog Jets would defeat Unitas's Colts in the 1969 Superbowl, he helped fulfill the prophecy.

Baseball gave sports some of its most memorable moments. Don Larsen of the New York Yankees pitched a perfect game in the 1956 World Series. Yankees outfielder Roger Maris hit a record sixty-one home runs in 1961. A plethora of hard-hitting outfielders, including Ted Williams, Joe DiMaggio, Stan Musial, Willie Mays, Hank Aaron, and Mickey Mantle, thrilled spectators. The Yankees garnered a collection of championships that nearly equaled their dynasty of the 1920s. After Jackie Robinson broke the color barrier in 1947, teams rushed to recruit African American players. Baseball, more than football, planted teams in the West and the South, aided by jet travel. Curt Flood sued to invalidate the contract clause binding players to teams. He lost, but took a step toward free agency.

Basketball flourished. The Minneapolis Lakers, with the first great big man, George Mikan, dominated the late 1940s and early 1950s. The greatest dynasty of the Era of Uncertainty, perhaps in any sport, was the Boston Celtics, coached by Arnold "Red" Auerbach and featuring center Bill

Russell and guard Bob Cousy. Russell's chief competitor at center was the seven-foot Wilt Chamberlain, who scored a record one hundred points in one game while averaging over fifty points per game in a season. In college basketball, dynasties shined at the University of Kentucky in the late 1940s and 1950s and the University of California–Los Angeles in the 1960s. College basketball suffered point-shaving scandals in 1951 and 1961. Players on top teams accepted bribes to lose games or shave points to ensure gamblers won by the point spread.

Boxing existed in the shadows of brutality, organized crime, and fixed fights. Out of the shadows emerged Cassius Clay, an Olympic gold medal winner. He restored luster to boxing by defeating Sonny Liston for the world heavyweight championship in 1964. Clay converted to Islam, changed his name to Muhammad Ali, and denounced racism and the Vietnam War. Ali refused induction to the army in 1967, claiming he, and all Muslims, were ministers. Stripped of his title and imprisoned, he was later released and regained his title in 1971. At one point in time, Ali had the highest name recognition of any American in the world.

The Rise of the Counterculture

Asked to define the counterculture, one student in the 1960s, responded: "Look at what the mainstream culture is not. That's us." In clothing, music, lifestyle, and sexual standards, the counterculture was the counterpoint of their parents' culture. Like many cultural rebels against the mainstream, the students of the 1960s ultimately merged with it. Their fashions, philosophies, and practices, such as free love, likewise influenced the "straight" culture. The counterculture was about style, not politics. Its counterpart on the left, the New Left, was about politics.

The fashions included miniskirts for women and wide-lapeled coats and broad ties for men. Men sprouted beards, mustaches, and sideburns as well as long locks. Women often wore their hair straight. Both sexes went barefoot or wore sandals. Recreational drugs and profanity were part of the lifestyle. Hippies accused mainstream Americans of racism and narrow-mindedness, yet there were few black hippies and little tolerance of conventional lifestyles. Violence, and rough sports were scorned. There was tolerance for gays and lesbians. Having a variety of sexual partners was not considered disloyal, and partners frequently lived together before marriage. Love and peace were praised, but materialism and hard work were rejected. Like other protesters against capitalism, war, and poverty in the Era of Uncertainty, most hippies were not poor, or were poor by choice. They contributed an element of freedom and free thinking diversity to America, yet discouraged respect for standards.

A smaller number of students, constituting the New Left, were political activists, critical of the Right, the Center, and the Old Left. The best known organization was the Students for a Democratic Society (SDS), which was heavily influenced by anarchism and Marxism. SDS was critical of American democracy, capitalism, religion, technology, and bureaucracy. "We would replace power rooted in possession, privilege or circumstances, with power in love, reflectiveness, reason and creativity," SDS announced in its 1962 manifesto, the Port Huron Statement. The students found the large university bureaucracy repulsive. Mario Savio, a leader of the Free Speech movement at the University of California, Berkeley in 1964–1965, in a metaphor incorporating the students' ambivalence toward technology, told his followers: "You've got to put your bodies upon the gears, and upon the wheels, upon the apparatus, and you've got to make it stop."

The majority of students who demonstrated against the Vietnam War, for free speech, and for more individualized treatment by administrators were members of neither SDS nor the counterculture but a cross-section of the college community, vocal, though never a majority.

The lack of direction of the New Left—its indecisive, divided leadership and its vague goals—undermined its role in practical political change, though it contributed an element of idealism and self-sacrifice. However, its activities too often degenerated into senseless violence, attempts to provoke police, and rowdy demonstrations, sometimes directed at the wrong people. Perhaps its worst strategic mistake was the violent demonstration at the Democratic National Convention in Chicago in 1968, which helped defeat Democratic nominee Hubert Humphrey, generate a conservative backlash, and elect Republican Richard Nixon. Whatever the bravery and idealism of the New Left, what was most sadly lacking was good judgment and the temptation to demonize even potential allies, such as Humphrey.

Some of the New Left's criticism of materialism, militarism, hypocrisy, and the excessive influence of big business were justified. Yet the student's violent rhetoric and sometimes violent behavior belied their language of love, and their dogmatism was no more flexible than that of their adversaries. Communism and anarchism were no solutions to the shortcomings off capitalism and democracy. For most people, expressions of love were more appropriately expressed to other people or to deities than to ideologies or doctrines. On all sides as well, hate parading as love is the ultimate hypocrisy; it is the stuff of tyrants.

The Rainbow of Power

The Black Power movement inspired demands for power among groups such as Indians and Chicanos. In the mid- to late 1960s the civil rights movement shifted from the moderate desegregation objectives of Martin Luther King Jr. to the aggressive tactics and economic, cultural, and esteem issues promulgated by "Black Power." Malcolm X, an opponent of integration and nonviolence and an advocate of black pride and self-sufficiency, laid the groundwork for the doctrine. He was assassinated by rival Black Muslims in early 1965. Stokely Carmichael used the term "Black Power" at a march of the Student Nonviolent Coordinating Committee" (SNCC) in Mississippi and it caught on. H. "Rap" Brown, who succeeded Carmichael as SNCC head, translated "Black Power" into more threatening terms. Brown insisted that instead of trying to "love that honky [white man] to death," African Americans should shoot "shoot him to death." The Black Panthers, established in 1966, armed its members to guard black neighborhoods and clashed violently with police. The Panthers embraced black pride, wearing traditional African hairstyles and clothing and demanding black studies programs. They also sponsored community centers and school breakfast programs. Yet the "Black Power" slogan was incendiary. Few politicians asked openly, yet they knew that middle-class whites wondered how black people would feel if white people marched through their neighbors with upraised clenched fists chanting "White Power." Worse, the slogan was divisive among blacks and whites alike. It marked a turning away from integration just as it was making progress, and a return to a philosophy similar to the doctrine of white supremacy.

Young Hispanics challenged the social and economic status quo, led by Cesar Chavez of the United Farm Workers. Chavez struggled to obtain union recognition and better working conditions for migrant farm workers. Like Martin Luther King Jr., a believer in nonviolence, he organized a grape picker strike in 1965 and grape consumer boycott in 1968. In addition, the young, militant Hispanic activists who swelled the "Brown Power" movement sought bilingual education and Hispanic studies programs in schools and Hispanic-only organizations.

For Native Americans, who suffered acutely from poverty and substandard education and housing, there was "Red Power." They worked to get Indian studies in classrooms and secured more federal assistance from Lyndon Johnson's administration. Yet they remained at odds with the federal government over old treaties that ensured them rights to land that whites had taken.

The American Indian Movement (AIM) imitated the Black Panthers in starting armed patrols to protect Indians; it sometimes employed violent tactics.

Black, brown, or red, the militant power groups diminished after the 1960s. The Black Power idea did not die, yet won few new converts because most African Americans were integrationists. Certainly the issue of racial and youth groups contesting for power, battling at the end to near exhaustion, and ending with a resurrection of conservativism, added turmoil, tension, and uncertainty to the times. A few capitalized on ideas whose time had come. Others grew disillusioned supporting causes that could not prevail. There were partial victories and scapegoating. But most important in the long term were the dreams of the young, which is their prerogative.

CHAPTER SEVENTEEN

New Frontiers, New Anxieties at Home, 1961–1968

DURING THE Era of Uncertainty, no decade was more uncertain than the 1960s. At home, it was a turbulent time of social experimentation and youthful rebellion, led by two presidents who were mirror images: John Kennedy, an idea man whose strong suit was inspiration, and his action-oriented successor, Lyndon Johnson. Following a decade of relative stability under Dwight D. Eisenhower, the hallmark of the 1960s was change. Americans, unusually optimistic under the youngest elected president, mourned when he died. When the decade ended they were a different people—spent, confused, and disappointed. Their initial optimism had sown discord, their expectations, accomplishments, and disappointments a potpourri of paradox.

The Frontier of the 1960s

John F. Kennedy thrived on inspiring rhetoric. His inaugural address on January 21, 1961, evinced a sense of history and a call to sacrifice: "Let the word go forth from this time and place, to friend and foe alike, that the torch has been passed to a new generation of Americans—born in this century, tempered by war, disciplined by a hard and bitter peace, proud of our ancient heritage." Kennedy summoned Americans to a crusade to bring justice to the nation and the world: "And so, my fellow Americans: ask not what your country can do for you—ask what you can do for your country. . . ."

John Fitzgerald Kennedy was born to a large Boston-area Irish Catholic family whose wealth, privilege, and political influence resembled American royalty. Patriarch Joseph Kennedy, a millionaire from investments in shipping, liquor, and real estate, had been a New Deal official. His isolationism before World War II and his ethnic and religious background denied him his political and social aspirations. Thus he drove his sons to achieve, hoping one would become the first Irish Catholic president. He laid the groundwork for John's career by using his influence to generate favorable publicity and by engineering the publication of John's senior thesis at Harvard as *Why England Slept (1940)*, a book about why Britain was unprepared for World War II. In 1946, young Kennedy was elected to the House of Representatives from Massachusetts. Taking his legislative responsibilities lightly, he nonetheless kept winning reelection and, in 1952, upset Republican incumbent Henry Cabot Lodge in a Senate race. While serving in the upper chamber, he published a Pulitzer Prize–winning collective biography, *Profiles in Courage* (1956), researched mostly by his staff and ghostwritten by his speechwriter, Theodore Sorensen. He unsuccessfully sought the 1956 Democratic nomination for vice president. Kennedy's 1958 Senate reelection made him the front-runner for the top spot on the ticket two years later, however.

Promoted as a vigorous chief executive who sailed, swam, golfed, and played touch football, the fit and manly image was at odds with the truth. Kennedy, known as JFK, was in pain virtually every day. On four occasions, he received the last rites of his church. JFK suffered from a degenerative back problem that required a cloth brace, hot baths, and four operations— one almost killed him in 1954. Sometimes he used crutches to get around the White House, although never in public. JFK also suffered from Addison's disease, a once-fatal withering of the adrenal glands treatable by cortisone, injected or in the form of pills. Nor was he as energetic as he liked to pretend. To fight fatigue and depression, he and his wife, Jacqueline, took injections of amphetamines, now known as illegal "speed," from Max Jacobson, known as "Dr. Feel Good."

Jacqueline Kennedy was a political asset. Beautiful, sophisticated, and glamorous, she proved a popular first lady. An elitist who found politics boring, she preferred the company of artists and intellectuals to that of officeholders. Americans were proud of her fluency in foreign languages, her social grace, and her jet-set fashions. Again, though, reality belied the Kennedys' public image. Although an attractive couple with charming children, both were remote, private, and introverted, partners in a union of convenience with little love. Kennedy was too competitive for the first lady's tastes and did not regard women with the seriousness he reserved for men. JFK was emotionally blocked, which kept him from bonding, and was manipulative.

Of the dark halves of these paradoxes, the public knew nothing. Americans read, heard, and saw only that Kennedy and his men proposed

THE PHOTOGENIC PRESIDENCY
John F. Kennedy stands in his car waving to a crowd at the
conclusion of a speech in downtown Detroit in October 1962.
(AP/Wide World Photos)

to lead the United States to a "New Frontier." Highly educated advisers
displaying an unusually assertive esprit de corps were summoned to
Washington. Robert Francis Kennedy, known as RFK, a younger brother
of the president, became attorney general and a key confidant. Robert
McNamara, a Republican and efficiency expert, was recruited from the
presidency of General Motors to serve as defense secretary. Historian
Arthur M. Schlesinger Jr. was named a special assistant and became one of
the chroniclers of the administration, writing the best-selling *A Thousand
Days: John F. Kennedy in the White House* (1965), a Pulitzer Prize winner.
Sorensen, who wrote for Kennedy the memorable speeches of cadenced
rhythms and balanced phrases, was chief counsel with responsibilities for
domestic policy.

The New Frontier celebrated power, toughness, and decisiveness. John
Kennedy, whom many intellectuals regarded as one of them, did not enjoy
serious culture, but he was probably the best-read president since Woodrow

Wilson, articulate, witty, respectful of artistic accomplishment, and eager to honor poets and philosophers. JFK appreciated the subtle ironies of life, including the fear of dying young, and believed that he had to live in a hurry. He enjoyed *Camelot*, a Broadway musical, and his friends referred to the New Frontier as the second incarnation of Camelot, the legendary kingdom of Arthur. Young Americans, energized by the glamour of the administration, rallied around their Arthur, a thought that was heartening, if not nearly enough to convince a self-described "idealist without illusions" that his quest would be easy in the Era of Uncertainty.

The Economic Frontier

In his relations with Congress, Kennedy faced obstacles. One was his lackluster legislative skills. Despite fourteen years in Washington, he had few friends in Congress and lacked patience with the legislative process. Kennedy made little use of Johnson's legislative wizardry. The most critical hurdle, though, was that the president, elected by a razor-thin margin, lacked votes sufficient to overcome the conservative bloc of southern Democrats and Republicans. JFK was largely frustrated, getting just about one-third of his legislative proposals through Congress. The legislators defeated or deferred his bills to combat poverty, provide health insurance for the aged, and furnish federal aid for education.

There were some notable accomplishments. The 1962 Drug Industry Act tightened restrictions on the manufacture and sale of drugs after the births of deformed babies whose mothers had taken thalidomide, a sleeping aid. The 1963 Clean Air Act was a step to control pollution, a sign of an ecological awakening. Kennedy, who had a mentally ill sister, did more for mental patients than any previous president, and Congress appropriated $500 million to aid them. Turning from compassion to confrontation, the administration waged war on organized crime, led by RFK, whose pursuit of Teamsters Union boss James R. Hoffa led to Hoffa's conviction for jury tampering and pension fund fraud in August 1964.

Kennedy was successful in promoting economic growth. His first priority was to deal with a recession, and the administration secured adjustments. A small increase in the minimum wage was passed; the Area Redevelopment Act made grants and loans to communities and regions with persistent hardship; and $4.9 million was appropriated for housing. The economy rebounded in the spring of 1961, largely on its own.

The next year proved eventful. Kennedy gratified and angered big business. He achieved the former with a law that reduced business taxes by accelerating depreciation allowances and granting tax breaks for investment in new equipment. The latter was a product of Kennedy's showdown with United States Steel. Fearing inflation might blunt economic growth, he resorted to jawboning or implied threats to industry and labor to hold down wages and prices. Labor Secretary Arthur Goldberg persuaded the steel unions to accept a modest, noninflationary 2.5 percent wage increase, and because the steel industry had thus benefited from the federal intercession, it was expected to avoid an inflationary price rise. Yet on April 10, 1962, United States Steel President Roger Blough announced an increase of $6 per ton, or 3.5 percent. Kennedy felt betrayed and dismissed Blough's arguments, which had some validity, that profits were at a record low and that there had been no price raises since 1958. In a contest of wills the press likened to Theodore Roosevelt's dispute with J. P. Morgan, JFK criticized United States Steel and threatened it with antitrust lawsuits, the withdrawal of government contracts, and federal price-fixing investigations. Within seventy-two hours, the steel giant backed down, chastened because of meager demand for steel and Kennedy's actions. The press heralded Kennedy as a Robin Hood, but the affair shook business confidence, and the stock market plunged.

Reversing course after the stock slide, Kennedy spent the remainder of his administration attempting to reassure the business community, registering no complaints about two steel price increases in a year and making a tax cut the centerpiece of his program for 1963. His decision to seek reductions in personal and corporate taxes and to keep federal spending constant, while the government was running a deficit, a tool for stimulating growth, was paradoxical, for the recession had ended. Designed to promote long-term economic growth, the tax cut was languishing in Congress at Kennedy's death in November 1963. Still, the economy performed well on his watch. JFK's record on the agricultural economy was not as successful, as most farmers rejected mandatory acreage controls. The administration attacked the problems of overproduction and low farm income to limited effect, not surprising when one appreciates that Kennedy lacked empathy for rural America.

In the biggest New Frontier of all, space, a Soviet cosmonaut, Yuri Gagarin, was the first human to orbit the earth on April 12, 1961. Other Soviets followed. Almost a month and a half after Gagarin's feat, Kennedy said the United States should commit itself to landing the first man on the Moon and returning him safely to Earth during the 1960s. Over protests that these goals were too expensive or technologically impossible, scientists from the National Aeronautics and Space Administration (NASA) planned such a mission in the Apollo program. Meanwhile, the American manned space program, Project Mercury, began with Alan Shepard's suborbital flight in May 1961. A fellow astronaut, John Glenn, became the first American to circle the globe in 1962.

Civil Rights: Progress and Unmet Expectations

The frontier of human understanding on Earth might have seemed more distant than the frontier of the Moon. Kennedy's ascent to the White House held out hope to African Americans, but for much of his presidency, he took tiny, cautious steps. The chief executive feared large strides would alienate southern Democrats whose support he needed for legislation. His campaign promise to outlaw discrimination in federally funded housing by executive order went unredeemed for two years, until he issued a weak order that made barely a dent in segregation. Kennedy appointed a record number of African Americans to government posts, yet also picked white segregationists as federal judges.

The wave of agitation for civil rights in the South forced Kennedy's hand. Setting the stage, the Supreme Court in 1960 banned segregation in bus and train stations used for interstate travel, an edict that was ignored in the South. To expose this flouting of the law, the Congress of Racial Equality (CORE) sent "freedom riders" into the region, where violence awaited, in the spring of 1961. White mobs and Ku Klux Klansmen in Alabama assaulted the freedom riders in Anniston, Birmingham, and Montgomery before Kennedy deployed federal marshals to restore peace. Additional freedom rides and arrests of the riders led him to prod the Interstate Commerce Commission to enforce the law. JFK acted again in 1962. A federal court directed the University of Mississippi to enroll an African American student, James Meredith. Federal marshals escorted Meredith to the university, only to come under attack from mobs. Two were killed and scores were hurt before thousands of federal soldiers quelled the violence.

In 1963, Birmingham again became a focal point for civil rights. Rev. Martin Luther King Jr. launched nonviolent marches, sit-ins, and prayer demonstrations on Good Friday, April 12. Police Commissioner Eugene "Bull" Connor unleashed dogs, officers using electric cattle prods, and high-pressure fire hoses against the demonstrators. Some responded with stones and firebombs. King, jailed for instigating the march, penned the "Letter from Birmingham Jail," justifying civil disobedience to protest segregation. A federal Justice Department official helped negotiate an agreement whereby major city department stores agreed to desegregate and hire African Americans, and black leaders agreed to halt the demonstrations and cease boycotting of segregated businesses. On May 11, though, bombs exploded at King's brother's home and a motel that African American leaders used, triggering more rioting and violence in the Birmingham ghetto.

Newspaper and television scenes of the police brutality outraged Americans. Now Kennedy was convinced the government had to direct the pace of civil rights to improve the image of the United States abroad. Alabama Governor George Wallace, pledging "Segregation now! Segregation tomorrow! Segregation forever!" tried to keep two black students out of the University of Alabama in June 1963. Kennedy federalized the state National Guard to enforce a court desegregation order and forced Wallace to back down. Kennedy also delivered a televised speech, prodding the enactment of civil rights. Days later he introduced a civil rights bill that bogged down in Congress.

The movement responded with a March on Washington on August 28, attracting about 250,000 people, black and white, to the Lincoln Memorial.

MARCHING ON WASHINGTON Martin Luther King Jr. and supporters, 1963. (National Archives)

Kennedy opposed plans for the gathering, meant to show support for his bill, until he was assured the march would be peaceful. In fact, the event marked the apogee of the nonviolent, racially mixed phase of the crusade. The crowd heard speeches that King capped with a rousing address describing his vision of a just society. Promising that he and his allies would not rest until African Americans were free of discrimination, King said, "I have a dream" that the descendants of slaves and of slaveholders could unite in brotherhood. He envisioned his children judged "not on the color of their skin, but on the content of their character." Finally, he foresaw "that all of God's children, black men and white men, Jews and Gentiles, Protestants and Catholics, will be able to join hands and sing in the words of that old Negro spiritual: 'Free at last! Free at last! Thank God almighty we are free at last!'" The crowd, too, sang of freedom, including the hymn that became the anthem of the civil rights movement, "We Shall Overcome."

There was, regrettably, much to overcome. On the night of Kennedy's televised speech in June, a sniper killed NAACP field secretary Medgar Evers just outside his home in Jackson, Mississippi. The civil rights bill remained bottled up on Capitol Hill, notwithstanding the resolve of King and his marchers. And in September 1963, a bomb took the lives of four black girls in a Birmingham church. Murder took three civil rights workers in 1964 and six in 1965—four of them white—in the South, compounding the outrage. Blacks took notice of the promise of progress under Kennedy—and of the gap between promise and progress.

The Assassination of JFK

Even after Kennedy's early missteps, his star never shined as brightly as it did in the fall of 1963. Recent triumphs with the economy and diplomacy and signals of more victories helped give him high approval ratings. He was looking forward to reelection in 1964 over the likely Republican presidential nominee, Arizona Senator Barry Goldwater. But there was a feud between the liberal and conservative factions of the Texas Democratic Party. On November 22, Kennedy was in Dallas to close that breach and to make speeches.

Large, friendly crowds, bright skies and warm temperatures welcomed Kennedy's motorcade. Because the weather was pleasant, the president ordered the Secret Service to remove the bulletproof bubble top from his limousine. Shattering the scene, shots rang out, two of them striking the president in his neck and head. Jackie Kennedy, her pink suit splattered by her husband's blood and brain, climbed on the back of the car, only to be pushed back by bodyguards. The car pulled from the motorcade and sped to Parkland Memorial Hospital, where Kennedy was pronounced dead. Vice President Johnson was sworn in as chief executive aboard the presidential plane hours later at the Dallas airport.

Lee Harvey Oswald, twenty-four, an unstable former Marine and a communist sympathizer, probably fired the lethal shots from the Texas School Book Depository. His motives remain lost to history, for a few days later, nightclub owner Jack Ruby shot and killed Oswald, saying he wanted to punish the president's assassin. Johnson appointed a panel under Chief Justice Earl Warren to investigate the assassination, and in 1964 the Warren Commission concluded that Oswald, acting alone, killed Kennedy. Many of the commission's methods were flawed, making millions doubt the panel's conclusions and generating a minor industry of attempts to ferret out conspiracies behind the assassination. One theory had Cuba seeking vengeance on Kennedy for CIA attempts to kill Fidel Castro. Another said the underworld was retaliating for RFK's crusade against organized crime. Yet another implicated white southerners who considered JFK a threat to the racial status quo. No one, however, has convincingly refuted the commission's basic findings. A House committee later investigated the case and, in 1978, essentially agreed with the commission, but noted that acoustic evidence and witness testimony indicated the possibility of a second gunman on a grassy knoll ahead of the motorcade.

In the twenty-first century, many Americans could remember what they had been doing when they learned of Kennedy's assassination, just as many people could remember everything about the day Pearl Harbor was bombed. Millions watched television for the next three days, as all three networks halted programming to cover the funeral. The nation seemed to shift—instantaneously—from the sunshine of optimism to the darkness of despair. By the end of the decade uncertainty was ingrained as Americans had come to expect shock and trauma, despite notable domestic accomplishments by Kennedy's successor, including racial progress and an economy hitched to a locomotive. Still, the purpose and vision JFK had provided the nation vaporized, leaving the nation empty inside, like a flat balloon.

The Kennedy brothers often said that life is unfair, a notion that JFK's (and, later, RFK's) life made poignant. John Kennedy was the beneficiary of unearned wealth, was elected to the most powerful office in the world while young, was elevated to heroic status—and was borne to his grave at age forty-six. His slaying touched off a wave of adulation, myth-making, and nostalgia. The Treasury soon began minting 50 million Kennedy half-dollars and could not keep them in circulation because they were hoarded as souvenirs.

As for the verdict of history, it is mixed. Kennedy was regarded highly for his charisma, his power to inspire, his ability to master ideas and words, and his articulation of goals, but his administration was not effective at translating its ideals into deeds. JFK's intellect was not as great as his vice president's; his rugged, macho persona concealed physical weakness; his charm belied a calculating, ruthless mind and—for all his calls for sacrifice—a streak of selfishness. Kennedy made the early 1960s seem simple and heroic, an extension of the stable 1950s with the excitement of Camelot, even though his White House was no Camelot. His reign merely represented the calm before the storm.

Lyndon Baines Johnson

Lyndon Baines Johnson (LBJ) ranks as one of the most important political figures in American history, and as one of the most paradoxical. LBJ was intelligent but not book-smart, crude but crafty, serious but a teller of tall tales, naive but a wheeler-dealer supreme, idealistic but cruel—a man waging a battle to the death against himself. He spent most of his life running scared, superhuman energy yielding occasionally to crushing depression and self-doubt. Extremely ingratiating, Johnson insisted on being the center of attention, a quality that left him greatly loved and greatly hated.

Born in the Texas hill country, raised on a ranch and in small towns, Johnson loved his home yet felt a sense of inferiority because of it. He learned politics from his father, Sam, a tough, folksy man and state lawmaker, and identified with his mother's cultural pretensions. Trying to earn the love of two very different parents made Johnson insecure, taught him that compromise was a means to political achievements, and helped him treat politics as a means to earn love. His Disciples of Christ religion and his year of teaching poor Mexican American schoolchildren reinforced LBJ's desire to do good, compassion that clashed with the Texan's callous treatment of his wife Claudia, known as "Lady Bird." She laid the foundation of the Johnson fortune, owning radio and television stations, and stayed with her husband despite his temper and insistence on total domination.

Entering politics as a congressional aide, Johnson excelled and was ambitious. He became Texas director of the National Youth Administration (NYA), a New Deal post that led to his adoption of FDR as a political role model. He won election to the U.S. House of Representatives in 1937 and was narrowly elected to the Senate in 1948, on his second try. The

TAKING THE OATH OF OFFICE
Lyndon B. Johnson being sworn in as president aboard
Air Force One after Kennedy's assassination, November 22, 1963.
(Lyndon B. Johnson Presidential Library)

Senate was his habitat, in which he rocketed to power as Democratic whip
in 1951, minority leader in 1953, and majority leader in 1955. A master
legislator, persuasive in personal encounters, Johnson cooperated with the
Eisenhower administration to pass the 1957 Civil Rights Act, and sponsored the 1958 measure that created NASA.

Unhappy as vice president, Johnson thought that Kennedy was over-
rated, more style than substance. LBJ knew he was better prepared for the
Oval Office than Kennedy, who respected Johnson; but JFK's subordinates
disdained LBJ as a crude deal-maker and gave him almost no role in shaping policy. There was talk of replacing Johnson on the 1964 Democratic
ticket. When Kennedy's assassination tested LBJ's ability to soothe in a

moment of national anguish, he was superb, sensitive, and poised. Five days after Kennedy died, Johnson addressed a joint session of Congress, reminding his audience that in JFK's inaugural speech, Kennedy proclaimed, "Let us begin." Now, Johnson said, "Let us continue." Actually, LBJ wished not only to continue Kennedy's priorities but to expand them. Johnson wanted to exploit his predecessor's martyrdom and employ his own persuasive talents to enact a far-reaching program of civil rights and antipoverty measures that would mark him as a great and beloved president like FDR. Securing passage of Kennedy's civil rights and economic measures, especially the tax cut and the antipoverty legislation, Johnson reasoned, would give him a solid record on which to run in 1964. Thus he demanded that Congress pass them quickly, and lawmakers did, in 1964.

The tax cut ushered in the most prosperous period of the postwar era to that time. The gross national product increased 7, 8, and 9 percent in 1964, 1965, and 1966, respectively. Unemployment fell below 5 percent, amounting to "full employment," according to economists. By 1968, average family income would be twice that of ten years earlier. The 1964 Economic Opportunity Act, the most far-reaching federal effort to help the poor, followed his declaration of an "unconditional" War on Poverty and his vow to eliminate poverty in a decade. The law created the Office of Economic Opportunity, with a budget of $800 million, to oversee Project Head Start, which offered education for preschoolers from poor families; a Job Corps to train the young in employment skills; and the Volunteers in Service to America (VISTA) program that put youths to work in poor areas, a domestic version of the Peace Corps. Most daring was the Community Action Program, including local job training, legal aid, community health, welfare reform, and educational measures. The poor were to have the "maximum feasible participation" in deciding how local antipoverty funds were administered.

Another 1964 law, the Civil Rights Act, stands as one of the two greatest achievements of the liberal decade, the other being the Voting Rights Act of 1965. If Kennedy fired the hearts of African Americans, Johnson went further, cementing their claims to a stake in American life by pushing the two bills through Congress. He acted because of his political aspirations, because his passion for civil rights had grown during his vice presidency, and because of his need to feel loved. To pass the 1964 law, LBJ pried the stalled JFK bill from a House committee and, with the aid of Republicans, broke a fifty-seven-day Senate filibuster. The measure banned racial discrimination in public accommodations, prohibited discrimination on the basis of race, national origin, religion, and sex in employment, and denied federal funds to programs and institutions that practiced discrimination. "We can understand without rancor or hatred how this all happened," Johnson said. "But it cannot continue. Our Constitution, the foundation of our republic, forbids it. The principles of our freedom forbid it. Morality forbids it."

Then Johnson set out to personalize his program, which he called the "Great Society." There must be "an order of plenty for all our people" and "an end to poverty and racial injustice," he said. Nor was that all: LBJ's quest was "to advance the quality of our American civilization," to "create a place where the city of man serves not only the needs of the body and the demands of commerce but the desire for beauty and the hunger for community." First, however, he had to be president in his own right.

1964: Lyndon's Landslide

Within the Democratic Party, Johnson's chief challenger was George Wallace, who advocated small government, law and order, and segregation. Entering some 1964 presidential primaries without much money or organization, he stunned liberals by winning 34 percent of the vote in Wisconsin, 30 percent in Indiana, and 43 percent in Maryland. In June, Wallace announced that he would run for president on a third-party ticket, but withdrew before the November election, fearing that his candidacy would divide conservatives. Johnson also faced trouble from blacks at the Democratic convention in August in Atlantic City, New Jersey, where the Mississippi Freedom Democratic Party (MFDP) challenged the all-white delegation from the state and demanded to be seated. LBJ sympathized yet worried that southern whites would bolt the convention if the MFDP demands were met. With his backing, the convention seated the regulars and disappointed the African Americans by giving them only two at-large seats and a pledge to ban future discrimination by state delegations. The other significant development at the convention was Johnson's selection of Minnesota Senator Hubert Humphrey as his running mate. (Johnson initially served as president without a vice president. The Twenty-Fifth Amendment, which Congress passed and the states ratified in 1967, closed a gap in law by assuring continuity in the executive branch. It provided that the vice president could become acting president if the chief executive were incapacitated but not dead. Also, it provided for the appointment of a vice president upon the president's death, so the office would not have to remain vacant.)

After Wallace's withdrawal, right-leaning voters united behind the Republican nominee, Barry Goldwater, who distanced himself from moderates, announcing at the GOP convention in San Francisco that "extremism in the defense of liberty is no vice. . . moderation in the pursuit of justice is no virtue." His campaign slogan was "In your heart, you know

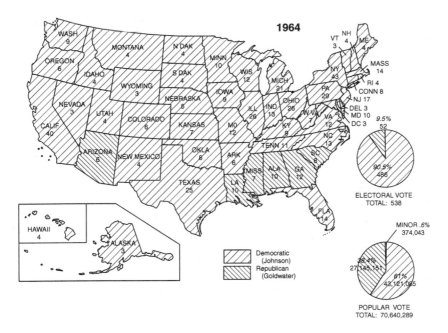

Election of 1964

he's right," and he vowed to offer "a choice, not an echo." Goldwater preached a sermon of personal responsibility, a stronger national defense, and limited government that would cease meddling in civil rights and social problems. Democrats exploited fears that he would eviscerate Social Security by making it voluntary and depicted him as a warmonger.

Johnson craved for a vote that would eclipse even FDR's margins. LBJ did not accept Goldwater's desire for a real debate on the issues or address directly the senator's attacks on his administration. He did not have to worry, as any Republican would have been unlikely to overcome the martyrdom of Kennedy and Johnson's legislative feats. LBJ won more than 43 million popular votes, 61 percent of the total—the greatest percentage that a presidential candidate ever received—and 486 electoral votes. Goldwater won 27 million popular votes and 52 electoral votes, carrying only his home state and five Deep South states. Democrats gained big majorities in Congress, giving liberals the margins they needed to pass Johnson's program.

In less than a year, Johnson seemed to have forged a magnificent coalition. Yet many people voted for him out of reverence for JFK and fear of Goldwater's ideas and personality rather than support for the incumbent. Johnson's base was broad but shallow, leaving him vulnerable to the backlash against liberalism in 1968 that helped drive him from the White House. Goldwater's candidacy was not the last gasp of an exhausted conservatism; it was the herald of a grassroots revival that would enable conservatives, mainly from the South and the West, to wrest control of the GOP from eastern moderates and realize future presidential triumphs. Goldwater was the ideological John the Baptist who presaged the coming of Ronald Reagan sixteen years later.

The Great Society

Moving swiftly to capitalize upon his election, Johnson directed a legislative assault for the Great Society, marching more than two hundred bills through Congress in 1964 and 1965, the pace rivaling that of 1933. His rhetoric gave an urgency to his commitments and raised hopes, contributing to one of the paradoxes of the postwar United States: no matter how great the nation's successes, expectations ran higher. Poverty was no worse than it had been earlier. Yet LBJ envisioned a government that could be kind and competent. Never seeking a major redistribution of income, he wanted a harmonious society that met the needs of all classes. To avoid conflict and decisions that defined winners and losers, Johnson, unlike FDR, refused to wage class war. By targeting specific groups for help, the Great Society made them conscious of their identities.

Congress built on the 1964 Great Society programs by approving a variety of measures. The Elementary and Secondary Education Act made more than $1 billion available for school textbooks, library materials, and special education programs; the Higher Education Act earmarked $650 million for scholarships and loans to college students and funds for libraries and research facilities. The Medical Care Act created Medicare, a federally financed program of health insurance for older Americans, and the Medicaid program provided money for states to give free health care to the poor. Other laws funded research on heart disease, cancer, and strokes and required cigarette packages to carry warnings that smoking is hazardous to health. The Omnibus Housing Act set aside $8 billion for housing for low- and middle-income families and rent aid for qualifying families. The Model Cities Act, the centerpiece of the new Department of Housing and Urban Development under Robert Weaver, the first black cabinet secretary, provided grants for redevelopment in slums. Environmental protection was the object of laws setting standards for auto emissions and air and water quality. Consumer safety motivated standards for cars and stricter rules for the labeling and packaging of food, drugs, and cosmetics. Cultural improvements included aid to museums, establishment of the Public Broadcasting System, and creation of

National Endowment for the Arts and Humanities. Other laws furnished $1 billion for development of depressed regions of Appalachia; and funds to enable cities to improve mass transportation, build sewers, and train police. Johnson's sweeping reforms created the Transportation Department; ended the national origins quota system for immigration; and promoted highway beautification, a project of the first lady's.

An Activist Supreme Court

Augmenting the liberal program, the Supreme Court under Earl Warren continued its activist agenda. Bolstered by two appointments each from Kennedy and Johnson—among them Solicitor General Thurgood Marshall, the first African American on the Court—the justices handed down major constitutional rulings. They ordered states to apportion legislatures on the principle of "one man, one vote," increasing the representation of urban minorities. They held that poor defendants in felony cases had a right to publicly financed legal counsel and struck down prayers and Bible readings in public schools. Melding the sexual revolution and technology, the court invalidated a law banning the sale of contraceptives. It also rejected prohibitions on interracial marriage and limited the impact of antipornography laws. Highly important, *Miranda v. Arizona* (1966) stated that police must advise suspects of their right to remain silent and to have counsel during questioning.

Liberals were disappointed when Warren announced his intention to retire near the end of Johnson's term. LBJ hoped to promote Justice Abe Fortas to replace Warren, but Fortas was forced to resign when it was disclosed that he had advised Johnson on political matters while a justice, a conflict of interest. When Johnson left the presidency and no successor to Warren had been designated, the next chief executive, Richard Nixon, appointed a conservative, Warren Burger.

Racial Rights and Wrongs

After 1964, the civil rights movement focused on voting rights. CORE and SNCC emphasized this goal through the Mississippi Freedom Summer Project of 1964, in which young volunteers went to that state to register blacks to vote, set up "Freedom Schools" that offered instruction in black pride, and established the MFDP. The volunteers found themselves harassed by law enforcement officers and Klan members, who firebombed churches and meeting places and threatened, beat, and even killed civil rights workers.

But shortly after King won the 1964 Nobel Peace Prize for his civil rights crusade, his Southern Christian Leadership Conference staged protests in Selma, Alabama, to dramatize the barriers that kept African Americans from voting. Sheriff Jim Clark had his men savagely attack the protesters, scenes that were shown on television and inflamed demands for federal action. Johnson spoke to Congress on March 15, 1965, pledging to end prejudice, urging lawmakers to pass a strong voting rights measure, and vowing, "We shall overcome." Nearly five months later, on August 6, he signed the Voting Rights Act. It allowed federal examiners to register qualified voters and to erase obstacles that were used to bar blacks, such as literacy tests. The law complemented the Twenty-Fourth Amendment (1964), which abolished the poll tax in federal elections. Across the South, the number of black voters skyrocketed, giving them clout to elect their candidates. During the 1960s African Americans won election to key offices, including seats in Congress.

Yet, paradoxically, the voting law and the 1964 civil rights law, however impressive, could not compete with rising expectations. Many African Americans remained members of an economic underclass and were losing patience with Johnson's leadership and with King's pace. Some became more militant, questioning the nonviolent tactics of the NAACP and the SCLC, espousing the slogan "Black Power." Only five days after Johnson signed the Voting Rights Act hostility erupted in the streets of Watts, a black ghetto in Los Angeles. White police and black youths clashed, triggering the largest race riot in twenty years. Fifty thousand blacks looted stores, bombed businesses, and fired at firefighters and law enforcement officers for six days and nights, a rampage that left thirty-four dead, almost four thousand arrested, and around $30 million in damages. African Americans in Chicago and Springfield, Massachusetts, soon rioted as well, a pattern that would intensify over the next three years. In 1966, more than twenty riots ripped northern cities. In 1967, more than forty riots tore at the nation, the worst in Detroit, set ablaze in a conflagration that claimed forty-three lives, injured more than one thousand people, and caused more than $50 million in property damage.

King denounced the violence, yet he understood blacks' frustration. He met with hostility when he and his followers tried to end housing segregation in inner-city Chicago. They rallied northern white support when targeting de jure legal segregation in the South, but failed to rally it by aiming at de facto segregation dictated by neighborhood patterns in the North. Once their movement headed north, public support waned. Another blow came when King announced opposition to the Vietnam War, angering

Johnson and turning some people away from the civil rights cause. Whatever the rifts, though, he was vital to the movement, which never truly recovered after a sniper, James Earl Ray, a white supremacist, killed him on April 4, 1968, in Memphis. King had flaws, but he was an example to millions. Like Gandhi, he turned to nonviolence to conquer a rage within himself and inspired the world with his patience, courage, and tolerance. "I may not get there with you, but I want you to know that we as a people will get to the promised land," King told supporters on the final night of his life.

Barely two months later, the unthinkable again occurred, and another young leader was cut down in his prime. Hours after winning the June 5 California Democratic presidential primary election on an antiwar platform, Robert Kennedy, forty-two, was shot in a Los Angeles ballroom, the victim of Sirhan Sirhan, a Palestinian who hated RFK's pro-Israel policies. A man of paradox, Kennedy was an investigator for Joseph McCarthy and an admirer of the communist-hunter, and a driven, ruthless campaign manager for his brother in 1960. A zealous attorney general, critics said he abused the law and suspects' rights in his pursuit of labor corruption and organized crime. A foreign policy hawk in the Kennedy administration, he was determined to have Fidel Castro removed. And since JFK's assassination, Robert Kennedy had become a senator from New York and an important advocate for the poor and minorities. Ironically, no longer a hawk during LBJ's presidency, he became the front-runner for the Democratic presidential nomination in 1968. When he became the third major leader to be slain in the 1960s, after John Kennedy and King, liberalism did not recover. As he said many times, in many parts of this nation, to those he touched and those who sought to touch him: "Some men see things as they are and say, 'Why?' I dream things that never were and say, 'Why not?'" eulogized his brother, Massachusetts Senator Edward Kennedy, the last Kennedy brother.

Contemplating the urban tumult that undermined RFK's, King's, and his own efforts, Johnson led the country in asking why rioting broke out despite so much social accomplishment. His National Advisory Commission on Civil Disorder blamed racism, saying that the United States was "moving toward two societies, one black, one white—separate and unequal," and calling for millions of new jobs and public housing units, a campaign against northern segregation, and money for national "income supplementation." Johnson knew such a prescription would not be accepted by white taxpayers, and personally, he complained of ingratitude. He passed one more important civil rights bill, the 1968 Open Housing Act. Yet, reflecting the dissonance of the times, it included amendments providing tough penalties for those who incited riots. The paradox of progress and pessimism ended Johnson's tenure on a note of uncertainty.

Assessment of the Great Society

The Great Society and the War on Poverty did much to ease suffering, and many of their programs outlasted 1960s liberalism. Besides the civil rights laws and Medicare, Head Start, for instance, proved so popular that it defied attempts to eviscerate it. But many of Johnson's measures, such as the local-level programs under Community Action, were poorly conceived and co-opted by local politicians. The War on Poverty did lift some people out of destitution, thanks in part to government programs. Johnson's backers cited statistics that apparently showed 8 million escaped poverty during his administration—but partly because domestic spending and Vietnam War outlays overheated the economy and elevated the poor with everyone else. Millions of poor Americans could not surmount poverty, though in five years, the federal government had doubled its regulatory role and the extent of its payments to poor people.

Significant wealth redistribution would have made a bigger impact upon poverty, yet Johnson believed that teaching job skills and education were preferable to direct distribution of money. Vietnam turned many liberals against Johnson, ending the momentum for domestic programs and contributing to the repudiation of liberalism by conservatives and the poor. At the end Johnson felt betrayed by the constituency he sought to help— the poor—because he could not keep up with their demands. Perhaps Johnson should not have tied the War on Poverty to a utopian pledge to eradicate poverty in one decade; a vow to mitigate poverty might have saved him from backlash. Further, poverty is a relative, not an absolute measurement, and in a free society some will always be poorer than others. In a period of emergency, such as the Great Depression, it might be possible to sustain the political and economic sacrifice necessary for such a program. But the decade of the 1960s was rich, not poor. People were inclined to ask, "Why now?"

Still, with the need for the Great Society and the opportunity to realize one, it would have been wrong not to pursue the vision. Individual programs were notable successes. In another context, without the Vietnam War (see chapter 18), for example, the Great Society might have done a great deal to uplift the nation. Conceived by Kennedy in a time of optimism, its fate was decided in a period of cynicism and uncertainty. Having the vision and the opportunity to uplift the poor, it seemed right to do so. Only by trying would we learn the possibilities, or whether it was an idea whose time had come.

The War on Poverty and the war in Vietnam taught Americans painful lessons in humility and paradox. They could lose wars like anyone else. Laws alone could not erase poverty. The optimism of the early 1960s was shattered by assassinations and violence. Yet the period was one of awakening as well as uncertainty. It was a time of fertility in politics, in the arts, and in technology. It was, doubtless, confusing. "We thought we knew society's rules," said a teacher who lived through the 1960s. "And every time we learned the rules, they changed them on us."

CHAPTER EIGHTEEN

Foreign Anxieties, 1961–1968

THE PARADOX of John F. Kennedy's New Frontier in foreign affairs lay in the president's charisma and glitter on one hand, and his inexperience and poor judgment on the other. In the Era of Uncertainty, his brief administration is both the most dazzling and the most uncertain.

His cabinet and advisers, like the president, were considered macho intellectuals, ironically termed "the best and the brightest" because their judgment on Vietnam proved unsound. The brightest star, Defense Secretary Robert McNamara, became disillusioned with his own Vietnam policies and issued a mea culpa near the end of the century. Kennedy died before the ramifications of his policies, and what he might have done, became apparent, adding to the uncertainties of the era.

Kennedy and Castro

Next to Ronald Reagan, Kennedy was the most ardent Cold Warrior of the Time of Paradox. His inaugural address concentrated solely on foreign policy; he did not intend to be a domestic president. Kennedy inspired the nation with purpose as few presidents have done. His objectives were to win the Cold War, extinguish communism, and beat the Soviets to the Moon before the end of the decade. Rejecting Dwight Eisenhower's dangerous doctrine of massive retaliation, he substituted flexible response, which would enable the nation to fight brushfire wars. To combat guerrillas, he created the Special Forces, or Green Berets, trained in counterinsurgency. As in most presidencies, the most important events in foreign policy were the unexpected ones.

Kennedy's first challenge came from the south. JFK feared Fidel Castro's communist Cuba might attempt to spread communism through-

THE ROAD TO VIETNAM
Vice President Lyndon B. Johnson inspecting a textile mill in Saigon.
(Library of Congress)

out the hemisphere. Attempts to kill him by use of a poisoned cigar, injection of poison through a hypodermic needle concealed in a ballpoint pen, and shooting him were devised. To implement the plots the CIA employed experts—the Mafia. Castro survived.

Next, the CIA planned an invasion of Cuba to topple the dictator, led by anti-Castro refugees, fleeing Cuba daily by the thousands bound for Florida. On April 15, 1961, the operation began. Disguised American planes tried, but failed, to destroy the six-plane Cuban air force on the ground, which doomed the invasion. Kennedy canceled two subsequent bombing missions, fearing American involvement might become known. He hoped to win a minor war without acknowledging American involvement; in fact, the *New York Times* had already published rumors of the plan. On April 17, fifteen hundred anti-Castro Cubans landed at the Bay of Pigs. They were strafed by Castro's planes, which sank a ship carrying supplies and communications equipment. Castro's much larger army enveloped the refugee army. Surrounded by swamps, they were trapped. Five hundred died and one thousand were captured, later ransomed by American food and medicine. Castro preempted an uprising by imprisoning thousands of political opponents. Ironically, the American people applauded the attempt, despite its failure, and Kennedy's approval rating in the Gallup poll rose to 83 percent, the highest of his presidency. Americans shared the president's anticommunism and his loathing of Castro and gave the president credit for trying, however ineptly.

Hotspots in Berlin and Indochina

In the 1960s, nuclear war appeared most likely to occur over Berlin. The divided city was the centerpiece of the war in Europe, a place where a war of wills and prestige was aggravated by the flight of thousands of refugees daily fleeing the East to West Berlin and freedom. The dingy, bleak Eastern sector, rebuilt by the Soviets, contrasted to the thriving, bustling capitalist city to the West. In military strength, however, the advantage lay with the East, whose huge army faced just fifteen thousand Western troops. At the Vienna summit in 1961, Soviet boss Nikita Khrushchev threatened to turn the city over to the East German government, committed to ejecting the West by force. Kennedy called for additional money for defense, doubled draft quotas, called up two hundred thousand reservists, and launched an accelerated fallout shelter program.

Khrushchev did not follow through with his threat to have a proxy expel the West. Rather, he constructed a wall around West Berlin, which halted the hemorrhage of refugees. With the refugee issue settled, the Soviets no longer had a reason to drive out the West. Kennedy was criticized for letting the wall stand, but this might have been deliberate, as it stabilized the crisis. Khrushchev was condemned roundly in the West. Democracies, Western leaders proclaimed, do not build walls to keep their own people in.

The Cold War began in Europe but migrated to Asia. Initially, the chief trouble spot appeared to be Laos, which was neutralized at a major power conference in Geneva in 1962. The problem in Vietnam was more serious. In the context of the Cold War, a communist takeover in the former French colony would be a setback. The South thrived economically under capitalism, yet it was also riddled with corruption and religious divisions. In the North, the communist economy struggled, yet the population was more disciplined and determined, and the North boasted of its leader the charismatic Ho Chi Minh. As in some other cases in Third World wars, the communists seemed tougher than their capitalist foes. Further, some South Vietnamese sided with communism and rebelled, becoming known as the Vietcong.

The war did not explode out of control on Kennedy's watch, yet it was about to. Although about 80 percent of South Vietnam's population was

SEEKING THE ENEMY
Marines patrol the Rice Fields, 1965.
(National Archives)

Buddhist, an elite of Catholics, led by Ngo Dien Diem, governed the country. Buddhists demonstrated against the autocratic Diem, and some even burned themselves to death in protest. By August 1963, the Americans had lost faith in Diem and implied they would not interfere if a military coup toppled him. The coup succeeded and Diem and his brother, the corrupt Ngo Dinh Nhu, were murdered in the process. Kennedy approved the overthrow yet felt remorse for the assassinations, which came just three weeks before his own. By Kennedy's death, there were 16,500 American advisers and Green Berets in South Vietnam to train the South Vietnamese Army in counterinsurgency.

Luckily for Kennedy, the war did not become an albatross on his watch. Had he lived, he probably would have followed about the same policies as his successor, Lyndon Johnson. Kennedy was a more militant Cold Warrior than Johnson, unwilling to lose. Both presidents were highly competitive and found it inconceivable that a primitive guerrilla army could defeat American technology. Yet they did not enter, and remain, simply for pride; they believed in their cause. Kennedy left the situation worse than he found it. Initially, Lyndon Johnson believed continuity required the fulfillment of Kennedy's policies. Neither believed that America could play a great power on the cheap. Yet even with great effort, the outcome was uncertain, a bitter irony in the Era of Uncertainty.

The Cuban Missile Crisis

If Vietnam posed uncertainties to Kennedy, the lands to the south in the Western Hemisphere were yet more uncertain. Here Kennedy enjoyed successes and failures, and in his biggest trial gambled and won. To assist Latin America, he created the Alliance for Progress, which he outlined in his inaugural address. The United States would invest $20 billion and Latin American nations $80 billion to revitalize their economies over the next decade. Raising hopes extravagantly, the alliance produced only marginal improvements and failed to transform the economies or democratize the governments of the countries involved. Several military coups took place during Kennedy's presidency, producing oligarchic governments that had little interest in uplifting their people.

More successful was a small-scale, people-to-people enterprise, the Peace Corps, created by Kennedy in 1961 to tap the idealism of Americans, young and old, and to utilize their talents. Peace Corps volunteers, working for meager pay, lived among the common people and taught them skills such as reading, agriculture, home building, sanitation, and disease control. Though the program's bottom-up approach did not solve large problems, the Peace Corps volunteers were goodwill ambassadors for America. Launched with a high profile, the Peace Corps received less prominence from later presidents and became marginal.

The emerging nations of Africa, freed from European colonialism, languished in turmoil during the 1960s, although Africa was less a Cold War battleground than Asia. Kennedy paid more attention to Africa than previous presidents. The Peace Corps was popular there, and he treated Africa with dignity, sending highly qualified ambassadors to represent America. Africa seethed in turmoil as new nations emerged from the ashes of colonialism. Power struggles broke out, including Marxist factions, yet the superpowers rarely confronted each other directly. However, covert operatives were active, including the CIA. The stakes were highest in the largest of new nations, the Congo, once a Belgian colony. In 1960 a civil war broke out. Moise Tshombe led mineral-rich Katanga and several other provinces in seceding from the central government under President Joseph Kasavubu and Prime Minister Patrice Lumumba. The Moscow-trained prime minister requested Soviet military aid, and the pro-Western Kasavubu repudiated him. Lumumba retired to plan a comeback with Soviet assistance, but Kasavubu's men captured him and turned him over to Tshombe's forces, who murdered him. Earlier, the CIA had plotted to kill Lumumba. In the end, United Nations peacekeepers crushed the secessionists and restored order, allowing the government to remain in pro-Western hands. Kennedy backed the UN and avoided sending troops.

In October 1962, Khrushchev took the biggest gamble of the Cold War by installing intermediate range ballistic missiles in Cuba. From Cuba, the missiles could strike targets in the southern and eastern United States in eight minutes, compared to twenty-five minutes for missiles based in the USSR. They could also strike targets in Central and South America with deadly speed, intimidating these nations from aligning with the United States in a crisis. They might even make Berlin a pawn in a game of nuclear blackmail.

The installations were photographed by high-flying American U-2 reconnaissance planes on October 15. Kennedy convened a committee of his major advisers, called Ex-Comm, largely influenced by Attorney General Robert Kennedy, to expeditiously consider alternatives. They considered an invasion, air strikes, or a blockade of Cuba, deciding on the latter. If the blockades failed, the riskier options could be reconsidered. Provocatively, Kennedy announced the blockade on national television on October 22, placing the prestige of the superpowers on the line. With the world watching, the side that backed down, if either, would suffer humiliation. Khrushchev conceded rather than start a nuclear war. When the Soviet missile-bearing ships approached the picket line of American war vessels, they stopped or turned back. The usually diffident Secretary of State Dean Rusk gloated, "We were eyeball to eyeball, and the other fellow just blinked."

There was still the question of the missiles already in Cuba. In fact, Khrushchev claimed all the missiles had landed and work on the installations continued. On October 26 Kennedy received a letter from Khrushchev offering to remove the missiles in exchange for an American pledge not to invade Cuba. The administration was ready to accept when a second, tougher letter arrived, perhaps inspired by Khrushchev's hard-line colleagues in the Kremlin. It added a condition: America must remove its missiles from Turkey. Superficially, the condition was not unreasonable. The American missiles in Turkey were about as close to the Soviet heartland as the Cuban missiles were to America. Kennedy, though, termed the condition "nuclear blackmail" and said he could not remove them without Turkey's consent. Trading missile withdrawals would set a bad precedent, leaving some allies undefended. Privately, however, he authorized his brother to tell the Soviet ambassador that the missiles in Turkey would be removed in a few months. The president was not willing to sacrifice his prestige to make a deal, yet had placed Soviet prestige in jeopardy by appearing on television to announce the missile installations and the American blockade. As usual, superpower diplomacy resembled a game of blind-man's bluff. Meanwhile, Robert Kennedy suggested a solution to the problem of the two letters: accept the first and avoid comment on the second. This solution worked.

The Cuban Missile Crisis was the greatest American propaganda victory in the Cold War, one of Kennedy's most notable accomplishments, and the closest the superpowers came to a nuclear holocaust. Kennedy's popularity soared, yet was lower in the polls than after the failed Bay of Pigs invasion. Khrushchev later was removed from office by Kremlin leaders who believed he lacked the toughness to win the Cold War. Few then, or even now, noted that by backing down, the Soviet leader took the more prudent, even statesmanlike, course. On the other hand, he had been responsible for placing the missiles in Cuba in the first place. Some believed Kennedy had grown in office since his indecisive behavior in the Bay of Pigs. Others remarked that sometimes it was better to be lucky than to be good.

After the crisis, there was a temporary lull in saber rattling. The leaders established a teletype linking them for instantaneous communication and translation. It was not, literally, a "red telephone." At American University in Washington in June 1963, Kennedy made the most conciliatory speech of his presidency directed at his Soviet adversaries. We share a common planet, a stake in our children's future, and all of us are mortal, he proclaimed. Later that year the superpowers consummated a treaty banning tests above the ground or under water. Yet Kennedy could not resist piling up propaganda points against the Soviets, with a presidential election looming in 1964. In one of his last major Cold War addresses, at the Berlin Wall, he compared Berlin, the most contested spot of the Cold War, to Rome, capital of the ancient world. Just as people had once been proud to call themselves Romans, all free men were, in a sense, Berliners. He concluded, "All free men, wherever they may live, are citizens of Berlin, and, therefore, as a free man, I take pride in the words, "Ich bin ein Berliner!" (I am a Berliner). Thus, near the end of his life, Kennedy remained a Cold Warrior, though a more vacillating one. He had sheathed the sword at American University only to draw it at the Berlin Wall. In the Free World, Kennedy was almost universally praised for his tough and eloquent speech, and the magic of the place and the timing. Later, President Ronald Reagan would travel to Berlin, stand before the brick and mortar that fenced in a city, and challenge the Soviets to tear down the wall. Ultimately East Berliners would tear it down themselves.

LBJ: The Benefactor and the Gunslinger

John Kennedy turned over to Lyndon Baines Johnson a more troubled world than the one he inherited from Eisenhower. This was not entirely Kennedy's doing. In fact, science was the chief culprit. The superpowers could now destroy not only each other, but the world. It would have taken cemeteries stacked like high-rise parking lots to accommodate the dead, assuming there was someone left to bury them.

LBJ was a man of peace who yearned to become a great president by building a Great Society and eliminating poverty. Like Woodrow Wilson before, fate, not the president, set the agenda. With little experience in foreign policy, and hoping to ride in the wake of Kennedy's martyrdom to win election in 1964, Johnson tried to follow Kennedy's policies, and to guess what Kennedy would have done. He embraced the Alliance for Progress and the Peace Corps. He kept Robert McNamara and Dean Rusk, both hawks in the Cold War, and other Kennedy advisers. He was impressed by their polish and academic credentials, though his own breadth and imagination equaled theirs, if shrouded by insecurity and inarticulateness. Publicly cruder than Kennedy, LBJ was better at dealing with people in small groups, at least Americans. Yet he had never been curious or well read about the wider world, and now he found himself leader of it. Troubles for Johnson began in 1964, in the Panama Canal Zone. Panamanian students wanted to fly the Panamanian flag next to the American banner at schools in the zone. American students wanted only the Stars and Stripes to fly. In a compromise, Washington ordered that no flags be flown. Defiant Americans raised their flag, and their Panamanian classmates rioted. Twenty people were killed, and buildings and cars were burned. Panama broke diplomatic relations with the United States and demanded a renegotiation of the 1903 Panama Canal Treaty. Johnson at first took a militant stand, then agreed to talks to gradually integrate the Canal Zone into Panama. Diplomatic ties were restored.

In the Dominican Republic, politics resembled a maze with factions of all stripes scurrying through the hedges. There was a military faction, a leftist faction, and a moderate faction. What Johnson wanted was what America wanted throughout the Cold War, not the most democratic faction but the most stable pro-Western one. Like other American presidents, if the country seemed unstable, he was willing to impose pro-American stability. America did not necessarily favor dictators, however. For example, in 1961 the CIA connived in the assassination of longtime dictator Rafael Trujillo. A civil war followed and a coup brought leftist Juan Bosch to power, but only briefly. Bosch was toppled by an army-led coup. Later, Bosch won an election as president, but violence continued. Fearing Bosch was tilting toward communism, in April 1965 Johnson dispatched fourteen thousand Marines to quell the turmoil. Troops from the Organization of American States (OAS) began to replace Americans in the middle of the year, and the moderate Joaquin Balaguer came to power. LBJ restored stability, yet liberals complained that Bosch was a reformer, not a communist, and the intervention piqued the nationalism of some Latin American nations.

Direct superpower confrontation took a sabbatical under Johnson and he held only one summit with a Soviet leader. While he was president the Soviets attained nuclear parity with America after lagging badly at the time of the Cuban Missile Crisis. When the Soviets crushed a democratization movement in Czechoslovakia, termed the "Prague Spring," in 1968, LBJ did not take a strong stand. Johnson made some progress on arms limitations. In 1967 the adversaries signed a treaty guaranteeing peaceful uses of outer space and in 1968 agreed to a nuclear nonproliferation accord. The same year negotiations opened on arms limitations that culminated in the Strategic Arms Limitations Treaty, or SALT I, four years later.

The Middle East brought a threat of a superpower confrontation that never materialized.

In 1967, Israel, America's closest ally in the region launched a preemptive attack on three of its Arab enemies—Egypt, Jordan, and Syria—that Israeli intelligence showed were plotting war. The Israelis destroyed the Egyptian Air Force on the ground, punished the armies of all three rivals, captured the West Bank of the Jordan River and eastern Jerusalem from Jordan, and seized the Golan Heights from Syria. Like his predecessors and most of his successors, Johnson had few solutions to the intractable hostility in the Middle East.

Further east, diplomacy proved frustrating. China, especially in rhetoric, was militantly anti-American. North Korea seized an American spy ship, the *Pueblo*, in 1968 and held the crew hostage almost a year before releasing them. Despite the provocation, Johnson did not act because he was facing more serious problems in Vietnam, where the Vietcong had launched the Tet offensive. If China and Korea frustrated Johnson, Vietnam destroyed him.

The Little War That Wouldn't Go Away

When Johnson inherited the Vietnam War, there were just two feasible options: withdraw or escalate. Both entailed risks, and Johnson was not a seer. He wanted to win the conflict, avoiding personal and national humiliation, yet not risk a nuclear war in the process. He escalated incrementally, without a grand design, because each decision depended on how the last one worked. Unfortunately, the decisions did not go well and more force was applied, requiring additional troops. Finally, the president and the American military found themselves trapped in a swirling river, in which it was as far to swim to one bank as it was to swim to the other bank. The imbroglio not only ruined Johnson politically; it worried him to death.

Johnson ran for president in 1964 against Barry Goldwater as the peace candidate, telling Americans that if they voted for Goldwater, the Republican, a dangerous warmonger, would escalate the Vietnam War. One voter later reminisced, "They told me if I voted for Goldwater the war would be escalated, so I voted for Goldwater and, sure enough, the war was escalated." The escalation began even before the election, with the Gulf of Tonkin incident in August 1964. Johnson had been hoping that an event would provide him the rationale for crushing the North. On a stormy night in the Gulf of Tonkin, the destroyer *C. Turner Joy* radioed it was under attack from enemy torpedo boats. No visual sighting was made, and there was no conclusive evidence that the destroyer was attacked. Still Johnson described the affair as an unprovoked assault by the North and used it to obtain the Gulf of Tonkin Resolution from Congress, passed by lopsided votes. It authorized him to use force to protect American armed forces in Southeast Asia and to preemptively thwart aggression. It was as close to a declaration of war as ever passed. The act was repealed in 1970.

Johnson launched a retaliatory air strike, then other air strikes in retaliation to specific enemy provocations. These evolved into Operation Rolling Thunder, the systematic bombing of the North. Air bases were constructed to accommodate the bombers. The first ground troops were landed in 1965 to protect the airstrips. Then their duties were expanded to "search and destroy" missions designed to wear down the enemy in a contest of attrition. Progress was slow, so more troops were sent, rising from 23,000 soldiers in Vietnam at the start of 1965; 184,000 a year later; 485,000 by 1967; and 536,000 at the start of 1968. Americans attempted to impose technological advantages in air strikes, artillery barrages, and helicopter attacks. When the enemy melted into the jungle, the United States used defoliants, such as Agent Orange, destructive to plants, animals, and people. Frustrating the

Americans, the communists refused to meet them head-to-head in a major set battle. As the battles shifted territory through the swamps and forests, there were no static lines and no easy ways of measuring gains. The army resorted to counting the number of enemy dead and reporting them, in often inaccurate "body counts," because the mathematically minded McNamara demanded statistical measurements of victories.

Statistically speaking, bombing the North was probably the least effective means of defeating the communists. The United States spent $9.60 for every $1 of damage inflicted and used an average of several tons of explosives for each soldier killed. America dropped eight hundred tons of bombs each day from 1965 to 1968, three times the daily amount dropped on Europe, Africa, and Asia during World War II. The best means of ending the war would have been a negotiated peace, but neither side was willing to negotiate on terms the other would accept. The North wanted a bombing halt as a precondition to talks, but every time Johnson agreed to a temporary stoppage, the communists exploited the opportunity to infiltrate troops and supplies into the South. The communists also insisted on the removal of President Nguyen Van Thieu, president after 1968, and the removal of all American troops, while northern troops remained in the South. To Johnson, this constituted not a compromise but a surrender. He wanted peace, particularly for political reasons, but was not willing to forsake the years of sacrifice and Americans carried home in body bags.

Johnson's dilemma was partly an inescapable by-product of the Cold War and partly of his own making. Ultimately the war he could not win was not in Vietnam but in the streets and on the campuses of America. The war polarized Americans as no event since the Civil War. As in 1861, Americans turned to fighting each other. The antiwar movement, which began small, on college campuses, never constituted a majority. Even after antiwar sentiment spread off campus via television into the living rooms of Americans, and a consensus emerged that it was necessary to end the war, there was no consensus over how to do so. Almost equally, Americans were divided over whether to stop the physical and psychological hemorrhaging by risking massive escalation to win a victory, or by simply giving up and pulling out.

Johnson lost his confidence and his public credibility. He lost Robert McNamara, consumed with guilt, who resigned to become president of the World Bank, a less stressful job. Walter Cronkite, the highly respected CBS news anchor, concluded that the war was unwinnable. In fact, that was precisely the problem for many moderates, not that the war was immoral or that South Vietnam would flourish under communism, or even that the war was unusually bloody. After all, almost as many Americans died on the highways every year in the decade as died in combat during the ten-year involvement in Southeast Asia. Surrender would of course stop the deaths, but that is true in any war.

The real war of attrition took place in America. The public's patience and Johnson's nerves were wearing thin. The military draft disrupted the lives of American men even when it did not kill them. The cause was not clearly defined. Many Americans believed that because Vietnam was far away it was irrelevant. Others thought that there was a plot on the part of America to plunder the resources of Vietnam. If so, the plot backfired for America, which lost far more economically than it gained. Some groups believed Marxism was a superior system, a belief most prominent among leftist students and intellectuals. But if America had been winning, and winning quickly, none of this would have mattered.

If morale was low on the home front, it was also low among American troops in Vietnam. There are atrocities on both sides in all wars, but no previous war had been scrutinized so intensely by television and journalism. Because most of the journalists in the field traveled with American troops, most of the atrocities they reported were committed by Americans. They were nothing to be proud of, and the actions could not be justified by the pressure of warfare. As they sat in their living rooms, Americans watched soldiers casually setting Vietnamese peasants' huts afire with cigarette lighters. Soldiers abused drugs and participated in "fragging," or killing, their commanding officers, often with grenades.

Vietnam and the Election of 1968

By late 1967 and early 1968 some American generals, including General William Westmoreland, the commander in Vietnam, believed an American victory was in sight. This was dashed by the Vietcong's Tet Offensive of January 30, 1968. Tet was the Lunar New Year, a time when both sides traditionally observed a truce. Communists attacked cities, towns, and provinces in the South, as well as American military bases and the U.S. Embassy in Saigon. Rallying after initial setbacks, American and South Vietnamese troops inflicted forty-seven thousand casualties on the Vietcong. The Americans lost 1,100 killed and wounded, the South Vietnamese Army 2,300. It would have been an ideal time to launch a counterattack, because the Vietcong were spent, no longer a major force in the war. Yet if Tet was a tactical victory for America, it was a Pyrrhic one. What Americans remembered was not the follow-up fighting in which the Vietcong were decimated, but the initial shock from their simultaneous attacks, temporarily successful, at cities and bases believed secure. If they could penetrate the walls of the U.S. Embassy, they could strike anywhere. The first, daring

FIGHTING IN THE STREETS
Violent protests outside the Democratic National Convention, 1968.
(Chicago Historical Society)

victories of the Vietcong were broadcast on television and radio, and drove a nail in the coffin of LBJ's war. The light at the end of the tunnel Westmoreland had claimed to see before Tet "was a locomotive headed in his direction," an observer quipped.

The importance of Tet lay as much in its timing as in its psychological wound.

It occurred at about the time of the nation's first presidential primary in New Hampshire. Johnson was not on the ballot, though his understudy won, albeit barely. Minnesota Senator Eugene McCarthy won 42 percent of the vote, running as an antiwar candidate. This outcome was considered to be a referendum against the war, yet, paradoxically, a poll taken later showed that many of the McCarthy voters believed they were voting for Senator Joseph McCarthy, the infamous communist hunter. The anti-Johnson vote convinced Robert Kennedy, now a senator from New York, that Johnson was vulnerable, and he entered the campaign. On March 31, Johnson announced on television that he was dropping out of the race and devoting his total attention to ending the war. Peace talks would begin in Paris.

McCarthy and Kennedy waged a primary war, Kennedy leading, which culminated in Kennedy's victory in California, sealing his nomination. Yet that evening he was assassinated by an Arab nationalist. Stepping into the vacuum left by Kennedy's death, Hubert Humphrey won the nomination without waging a major primary campaign.

Richard Nixon, the Republican nominee started with an initial lead in the polls. Slowly, Humphrey began to catch up as he distanced himself from Johnson's war policies. The campaign lacked precision. It was difficult to determine who was the peace candidate: Humphrey promised a negotiated peace; Nixon implied he would end the war. Although the war was a major issue, it was not the only one. Many Americans considered the Democrats lenient on drug use, overly tolerant of the counterculture, and unable to rein in crime in the streets. Nixon talked tougher than Humphrey on these issues, yet George Wallace, the Alabama governor, talked even tougher. Wallace campaigned as the candidate of his own third party, the American Independent Party, to the right of both major parties. His tart message of toughness on crime, vigorous prosecution of the war, and veiled racism drew support from middle working-class Americans who disliked antiwar and civil rights agitators and longed for simpler times. To Wallace, the bigger the liberal, the bigger the target. Ironically, he probably took more votes from Nixon than from Humphrey because their regional and ideological constituencies overlapped. Paradoxically, the radical Left hurt Humphrey more and the radical Right hurt Nixon more.

In one of the closest elections of the century, Nixon won. He took 31.8 million popular votes (43.4 percent) and 301 electoral votes to Humphrey's 31.3 million (42.7 percent) and 191 to Wallace's 9.9 million and 46 electoral votes. Few had expected Nixon to arise from his defeats in the 1960s, yet timing means as much in politics as in hitting a baseball. Nixon's elevator ride through American history included one of the closest losses for president, in 1960, a victory that was almost as close, in 1968, and one of the most lopsided victories, in 1972, culminating, in his becoming the first president to resign, in 1974.

If Nixon's political career seemed like a script written for a tragic hero, Johnson's career fit the script even better. Johnson was everything Nixon was not; he was more popular, less shy, and early in his presidency seemed destined to become a great president. Like Nixon, timing was important to Johnson's resting place in history. He came to office almost totally in sync with his times and left it virtually an anachronism. He wanted to do good and he wanted credit for it.

Johnson returned to his ranch, resumed smoking despite doctors' warnings, let his hair grow long, ruminated, and waited for death, never

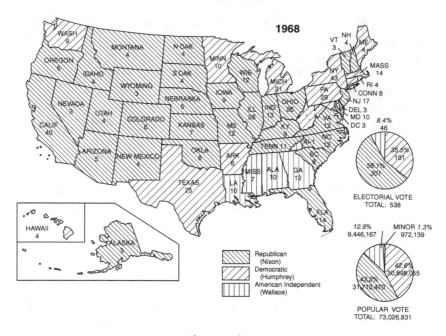

Election of 1968

to bask in the role of elder statesman. It must have seemed to Johnson that the harder he tried, the harder things got. Every group he had reached out to—blacks, students, the poor—seemed to have turned against him. American cities smoldered in riot-ravaged ruins that served as a metaphor for LBJ's reputation. Wanting to do the right thing, yet not knowing what the right thing was, he did not know whether he had come on too strongly or too weakly, whether the fault lay with him or with his critics. There is no monument in the nation's capital to the man who wanted to update and surpass Franklin Roosevelt's New Deal. Yet, to many, his memorial is a stone wall carved with the names of American servicemen who died in the war he did not start and could not end. The tall Texan's reputation had crested with the wave of public adulation in 1964 until it crashed upon the beach of Vietnam and rolled back in the other direction.

Lyndon Johnson, like Woodrow Wilson, wanted a world safe for democratic ideals as well as one that banished destitution. Like Wilson, Johnson was right in principle but wrong in degree. The aims of a Great Society and a world free for democracy were laudable, but as unachievable in 1968 as they had been in 1919.

Bibliographic Essay

Truman And Eisenhower

For general studies of the Era of Uncertainty, see James T. Patterson, *Grand Expectations: The United States, 1945–1974* (1997); Alonzo Hamby, *Liberalism and Its Challengers: FDR to Reagan* (1985); Eric Goldman, *The Crucial Decade—and After: America, 1945–1960* (1961); William L. O'Neill, *American High: The Years of Confidence, 1945–1960* (1986); and John Patrick Diggins, *The Proud Decades: America in War and Peace, 1941–1960* (1988).

Among the leading books on Harry S Truman are Alonzo Hamby, *Man of the People: A Life of Harry S Truman* (1995); William E. Pemberton, *Harry S Truman* (1989); David McCullough, *Truman* (1992), massively detailed and favorable to Truman; and Robert H. Ferrell, *Harry S Truman and the Modern American Presidency* (1983). On the Dixiecrats, see Kari Frederickson, *The Dixiecrat Revolt and the End of the Solid South, 1932–1968* (2001), practically definitive.

On domestic anticommunism, consult Richard Fried, *Nightmare in Red: The McCarthy Era in Perspective* (1990); Richard Gid Powers, *Not without Honor: The History of American Anticommunism* (1995); Ellen Schrecker, *Many Are the Crimes: McCarthyism in America* (1998); David Caute, *The Great Fear* (1978); and Harvey Klehr, John Earl Haynes, and Kyrill M. Anderson, *The Secret World of American Communism* (1998). The best biography of Joseph McCarthy is Thomas C. Reeves, *The Life and Times of Joe McCarthy* (1982), especially strong on McCarthy's rise to power. David M. Oshinsky, *A Conspiracy So Immense: The World of Joe McCarthy* (1983), does an excellent job of describing McCarthy's intellectual milieu. For the spy trials, see Allen Weinstein, *Perjury: The Hiss-Chambers Case* (1978). Ronald Radosh and Joyce Milton explore another famous trial in *The Rosenberg*

File (1983). For the Cold War, culture and politics, see Stephen J. Whitfield, *The Culture of the Cold War* (1991); Lary May, ed., *Recasting America: Culture and Politics in the Age of the Cold War* (1989); and Ellen Schrecker, *No Ivory Tower: McCarthyism and the Universities* (1986).

For diplomacy, see Wesley M. Bagby, *America's International Relations since World War I* (1999); Robert D. Schulzinger, *American Diplomacy in the Twentieth Century* (3rd ed., 1994); the succinct Ralph B. Levering, *The Cold War: A Post-Cold War History* (1994); Ronald E. Powaski, *The Cold War: The United States and the Soviet Union, 1917–1991* (1998); John Lewis Gaddis, *The United States and the Origins of the Cold War, 1941–1947* (1972), *Strategies of Containment* (1982), and *We Now Know: Rethinking Cold War History* (1997); Walter LaFeber, *America, Russia, and the Cold War, 1945–1988* (1990); Melvyn Leffler, *A Preponderance of Power: National Security, the Truman Administration, and the Cold War* (1992); Lloyd Gardner, *Architects of Illusion* (1970), *On Every Front: The Making of the Cold War* (1979), and *Meeting the Communist Threat* (1988); and Michael Hogan, *The Marshall Plan* (1987). On China, see June M. Grasso, *Truman's Two-China Policy: 1948–1950* (1987), and Warren I. Cohen, *America's Response to China* (rev. ed., 1980). For Vietnam in this era, see Gary R. Hess, *The United States' Emergence as a Southeast Asian Power, 1940–1950* (1988), and Lloyd Gardner, *Approaching Vietnam, 1950–1954* (1988). Among the histories of the Korean War are William Steck, *The Korean War: An International History* (1995); John Merrill, *Korea* (1989); and Paul M. Edwards, *The Korean War, 1950–1953* (1998).

On the 1950s, see David Halberstam, *The Fifties* (1993), a detailed popular history; J. Ronald Oakley, *God's Country: America in the Fifties* (1986), provocative, as is Paul A. Carter, *Another Part of the Fifties* (1983); also consult Tom Engelhardt, *The End of Victory Culture: Cold War America and the Disillusioning of a Generation* (1995), and Jeffrey Hart, *When the Going Was Good: American Life in the 1950s* (1982). The best biography of Dwight Eisenhower is Stephen E. Ambrose, *Eisenhower* (2 vols., 1983, 1984). Other valuable treatments are William B. Pickett, *Dwight D. Eisenhower and American Political Power* (1995); Alton Lee, *Dwight D. Eisenhower: Soldier and Statesman* (1981); Chester J. Pach Jr. and Elmo Richardson, *The Presidency of Dwight D. Eisenhower* (1979); John W. Sloan, *Eisenhower and the Management of Prosperity* (1991); Raymond Saulnier, *Constructive Years: The U.S. Economy under Eisenhower* (1991); and Jeff Broadwater, *Eisenhower and the Anti-Communist Crusade* (1992).

For an overview of Eisenhower's diplomacy, see Robert A. Divine, *Eisenhower and the Cold War* (1981); Richard A. Melanson and David Mayers, eds., *Reevaluating Eisenhower: American Foreign Policy in the*

1950s (1986); and H. W. Brands Jr., *Cold Warriors: Eisenhower's Generation and American Foreign Policy* (1988). Intervention abroad is chronicled in Richard W. Cottam, *Iran and the United States: A Cold War Case Study* (1988); Mark Gasiorowski, *U.S. Foreign Policy and the Shah: Building a Client State in Iran* (1991); and Piero Gleijeses, *The Guatemalan Revolution and the United States, 1944–1954* (1991). On covert operations, see Stephen E. Ambrose with Richard Immerman, *Ike's Spies: Eisenhower and the Espionage Establishment* (1981), and Blanche Wiesen Cook, *The Declassified Eisenhower* (1981).

Indochina is the subject of Melanie Billings Yun, *Decision against War: Eisenhower and Dien Bien Phu, 1954* (1988); Andrew Rotter, *The Path to Vietnam* (1987); David L. Anderson, *Trapped by Success: The Eisenhower Administration and Vietnam, 1953–1961* (1991); and James Arnold, *The First Domino: Eisenhower, the Military, and America's Intervention in Vietnam* (1991). For other aspects of policy, see Stephen G. Rabe, *Eisenhower and Latin America: The Foreign Policy of Anticommunism* (1988); Richard E. Welch Jr., *Response to Revolution: The United States and the Cuban Revolution, 1959–1961* (1985); H. W. Brands Jr., *The Specter of Neutralism: The United States and the Emergence of the Third World, 1947–1960* (1989); Isaac Alteras, *Eisenhower and Israel: U.S.-Israeli Relations, 1953–1960* (1993); Cole C. Kingseed, *Eisenhower and the Suez Crisis of 1956* (1995); Robert A. Divine, *Blowing in the Wind: The Nuclear Test Ban Debate, 1954–1960* (1978); and Michael R. Beschloss, *Mayday: Eisenhower, Khrushchev and the U-2 Affair* (1986).

Society and Culture

On civil rights, general studies include Steven F. Lawson, *Running for Freedom: Civil Rights and Black Politics in America since 1941* (1991); Harvard Sitkoff, *The Struggle for Black Equality, 1954–1992* (1993); Robert Weisbrot, *Freedom Bound: A History of America's Civil Rights Movement* (1990); Taylor Branch, *Parting the Waters: America in the King Years, 1954–1963* (1988); David J. Garrow, *Bearing the Cross: Martin Luther King Jr. and the Southern Christian Leadership Conference* (1986); and August Meier and Elliot Rudwick, *CORE: A Study in the Civil Rights Movement* (1975). White Southern opposition is discussed in Numan V. Bartley, *The Rise of Massive Resistance* (1966); Neil McMillen, *Citizens' Council* (1971), and Glen Jeansonne, *Leander Perez: Boss of the Delta* (2nd ed., 1995), the biography of a militant segregationist. The best book dealing with civil rights in the Eisenhower administration is Robert F. Burk, *The Eisenhower Administration and Black Civil Rights* (1984). Works on Martin Luther

King include Stephen B. Oates, *Let the Trumpet Sound: The Life of Martin Luther King Jr.* (1982), and David L. Lewis, *King: A Biography* (1978). Books on the civil rights movement in the 1960s include David J. Garrow, *Protest at Selma: Martin Luther King Jr. and the Voting Rights Act of 1965* (1978); Charles E. Fager, *Selma 1965* (1985); John Dittmer, *Local People: The Struggle for Civil Rights in Mississippi* (1994); Doug MacAdam, *Freedom Summer* (1988); Dennis C. Dickerson, *Militant Mediator: Whitney M. Young* (1998); David L. Chapell, *Inside Agitators: White Southerners in the Civil Rights Movement* (1996); Malcolm X (with Alex Haley), *The Autobiography of Malcolm X* (1965), a classic; William L. Van Deburg, *New Day in Babylon: The Black Power Movement and American Culture, 1965–1975* (1992); Mark Stern, *Calculating Visions: Kennedy, Johnson, and Civil Rights* (1992); and Hugh Davis Graham, *The Civil Rights Era: Origins and Development of National Policy, 1960–1972* (1990).

On the Earl Warren Supreme Court, see J. Harvie Wilkinson, *From Brown to Bakke: The Supreme Court and School Integration, 1954–1978* (1980); David J. Armor, *Forced Justice: School Desegregation and the Law* (1995); Richard Kluger, *Simple Justice: The History of Brown v. Board of Education and Black America's Struggle for Equality* (1975), the most complete account of the landmark decision; and James T. Patterson, *Brown v. Board of Education: A Civil Rights Milestone and Its Troubled Legacy* (2001).

Indians are discussed in Donald Fixico, *Termination and Relocation: Federal Indian Policy, 1945–1970* (1986); Ronald Dewing, *Wounded Knee: The Meaning and Significance of the Second Incident* (1985); and Charles F. Wilkinson, *American Indians, Time, and the Law* (1987). Among studies of other minorities, Ronald Takaki, *A Different Mirror: A History of Multicultural America* (1993), is a good general work. Also see David G. Guttierrez, *Walls and Mirrors: Mexican Americans, Mexican Immigrants, and the Politics of Ethnicity* (1995); David M. Reimers, *Still the Golden Door: The Third World Comes to America* (1985); and Ronald Takaki, *Strangers from a Distant Shore: A History of Asian Americans* (1989).

Women's history is covered in William Chafe, *The Paradox of Change: American Women in the Twentieth Century* (1991), especially strong on the 1960s; Sara Evans, *Personal Politics: The Roots of Women's Liberation in the Civil Rights Movements and the New Left* (1978); Cynthia Harrison, *On Account of Sex: The Politics of Women's Issues, 1945–1968* (1988); two classics by Gerda Lerner, *The Majority Finds Its Past: Placing Women in History* (1979), and *The Creation of Patriarchy* (1986); and Lillian Faderman, *Odd Girls and Twilight Lovers: A History of Lesbian Life in 20th Century America* (1991).

On television, see James L. Baughman, *The Republic of Mass Culture: Filmmaking and Broadcasting in America since 1941* (1992); Eric Barnouw, *Tube of Plenty: The Evolution of American Television* (1990); Lynn Spigel, *Make Room for TV: Television and the Family Ideal in Postwar America* (1992); and Mary Ann Watson, *Defining Visions: Television and the American Experience since 1945* (1998). On music, David Szatmary, *Rockin' in Time: A Social History of Rock and Roll* (1987, 1991), is informative; a recent account is Glenn C. Altschuler, *All Shook Up: How Rock 'n' Roll Changed America* (2003). Greil Marcus, *Mystery Train* (3rd rev. ed., 1990), is the best book on the place of folk, blues, country, and rock in culture. Works on motion pictures include Nora Sayre, *Running Time: Films of the Cold War* (1982), and Christopher Nicholas, *Somewhere in the Night: Film Noir and the American City* (1997), a penetrating study of social anxiety manifested in films. Robert Hughes, *Shock of the New* (1980), is a brilliant analysis of modernism and the arts. For literature, see Richard Ruland and Malcolm Bradbury, *From Puritanism to Postmodernism: A History of American Literature* (1991), and Ann Charters, *Beats and Company: Portrait of a Literary Generation* (1986), a fine introduction to the key Beats.

On religion, see Martin E. Marty, *Modern American Religion*, vol. 3, *Under God, Indivisible, 1941–1960* (1996), and Robert Wuthnow, *The Restructuring of American Religion: Society and Faith since World War II* (1988). On technology, see Alan I. Marcus and Howard P. Segal, *Technology in America: A Brief History* (2nd ed., 1999); Howard P. Segal, *Future Imperfect: The Mixed Blessings of Technology in America* (1994); Ruth Schwartz Cowan, *A Social History of American Technology* (1997); and Alfred D. Chandler Jr., and James W. Cortada, eds., *A Nation Transformed by Information* (2000).

The Sixties

William L. O'Neill, *Coming Apart: An Informal History of America in the 1960s* (3rd ed., 1975), is a lively account of politics and culture, especially strong on the counterculture. Other studies include W. J. Rorabaugh, *Kennedy and the Promise of the Sixties* (2002); Allen Matusow, *The Unraveling of America: A History of Liberalism in the 1960s* (1984), strong on the economic assumptions of the New Frontier architects; David Farber, *The Age of Great Dreams: America in the 1960s* (1994); John Morton Blum, *Years of Discord: American Politics and Society, 1961–1974* (1991); Dave Steigerwald, *The Sixties and the End of Modern America* (1995); Terry Anderson, *The Sixties* (1999); the balanced David Burner, *Making*

Peace with the '60s (1996); and Maurice Isserman and Michael Kazin, *America Divided: The Civil War of the 1960s* (1999). On the counterculture, see Terry Anderson, *The Movement and the Sixties: Protest in America from Greensboro to Wounded Knee* (1995); Timothy Miller, *The Hippies and American Values* (1991); Margaret Cruikshank, *The Gay and Lesbian Liberation Movement in America* (1992); and James Miller, *"Democracy Is in the Streets": From Port Huron to the Siege of Chicago* (1987). For the generation that entered college in the 1960s, see Landon Y. Jones, *Great Expectations: America and the Baby Boom Generation* (1980), and Helen Lefkowitz Horowitz, *Campus Life* (1987).

On John F. Kennedy, two massive accounts by insiders are still useful, although they conceal his flaws: Arthur M. Schlesinger Jr., *A Thousand Days: John F. Kennedy in the White House* (1965), and Theodore C. Sorensen, *Kennedy* (1965). Robert Dallek, *An Unfinished Life: John F. Kennedy, 1917–1963* (2003), is an excellent scholarly study. James N. Giglio, *The Presidency of John F. Kennedy* (1991), is a detailed administrative history. Herbert S. Parmet, *Jack: The Struggle of John F. Kennedy* (1980), and *JFK: The Presidency of John F. Kennedy* (1983), are balanced. Thomas C. Reeves, *A Question of Character: A Life of John F. Kennedy* (1991), is a devastating critique, as is Seymour Hersh, *The Dark Side of Camelot* (1997). For exhaustive books on JFK's assassination, see Sylvia Meagher, *Accessories after the Fact: The Warren Commission, the Authorities, and the Report* (1967), and Gerald Posner, *Case Closed: Lee Harvey Oswald and the Assassination of JFK* (1993). On Kennedy's domestic policy, consult Irving Bernstein, *Promises Kept: John F. Kennedy's New Frontier* (1990). For general works on JFK's foreign policy, see Michael R. Beschloss, *The Crisis Years: Kennedy and Khrushchev, 1960–1963* (1991). Crises regarding Cuba are chronicled in Peter Wyden, *The Bay of Pigs* (1979); Trumball Higgins, *The Perfect Failure: Kennedy, Eisenhower, and the CIA at the Bay of Pigs* (1987); William J. Medland, *The Cuban Missile Crisis of 1962: Needless or Necessary?* (1988); Raymond L. Garthoff, *Reflections on the Cuban Missile Crisis* (rev. ed., 1989); James G. Blight, *On the Brink: Americans and Soviets Reexamine the Cuban Missile Crisis* (2nd ed., 1990); Mark J. White, *The Cuban Missile Crisis* (1996); focusing on major participants, and the documentary history, Mark J. White, ed., *The Kennedys and Cuba* (2000). On other topics, see Norman Gelb, *The Berlin Wall: Kennedy, Khrushchev and a Showdown in the Heart of Europe* (1986); Bernard J. Firestone, *The Quest for Nuclear Stability: John F. Kennedy and the Soviet Union* (1982); Gerard T. Rice, *The Bold Experiment: JFK's Peace Corps* (1986); and Richard D. Mahoney, *JFK: Ordeal in Africa* (1983).

Among multivolume works on Lyndon Johnson, see Robert Dallek, *Lone Star Rising: Lyndon Johnson and His Times, 1908–1960* (1991), and

Flawed Giant: Lyndon B. Johnson, 1960–1973 (1998); Robert A. Divine, *The Johnson Years,* especially vol. 3, *LBJ at Home and Abroad* (1994); and Robert Caro, *The Years of Lyndon B. Johnson: The Path to Power (1982), Means of Ascent* (1990), detailed yet vastly overdrawn in their criticism, and *Master of the Senate* (2002). Paul K. Conkin, *Big Daddy from the Pedernales: Lyndon Baines Johnson* (1986), is balanced, with keen insights. Vaughn D. Bornet, *The Presidency of Lyndon Johnson* (1983), is a fine study. Michael R. Beschloss, ed., *Taking Charge: The Johnson White House Tapes* (1997), is gleaned from recordings LBJ made of his meetings. For efforts to combat poverty, see James T. Patterson, *America's Struggle against Poverty, 1900–1980* (1981), and Greg J. Duncan, *Years of Poverty, Years of Plenty* (1984). For the rise of conservatism, consult George H. Nash, *The Conservative Intellectual Movement in America since 1945* (1976); Michael W. Miles, *The Odyssey of the American Right* (1980); Paul Gottfried, *The Conservative Movement* (1993); John Ehrman, *The Rise of Neoconservatism: Intellectuals and Foreign Affairs, 1945–1994* (1995); and Kurt Schuparra, *Triumph of the Right: The Rise of the California Conservative Movement, 1945–1966* (1998).

On LBJ's foreign policy, start with H. W. Brands Jr., *The Wages of Globalism: Lyndon Johnson and the Limits of American Power* (1994). Of the voluminous Vietnam War literature, the best single-volume histories are George Herring, *America's Longest War* (2nd ed., 1986), and Robert D. Schulzinger, *A Time for War: The United States and Vietnam, 1941–1975* (1997). See also the government study of the war, *The Pentagon Papers, Senator Gravel Edition* (1975); David Kaiser, *American Tragedy: Kennedy, Johnson and the Origins of the Vietnam War* (2000); and David Halberstam, *The Best and the Brightest* (1972), a journalistic account of policy makers. General histories of the war include Stanley Karnow, *Vietnam: A History* (1991); Marilyn Young, *The Vietnam Wars, 1945–1990* (1991); George Donelson Moss, *Vietnam: An American Ordeal* (3rd ed., 1998); Gerard DeGroot, *A Noble Cause* (1999); and the brief but comprehensive Patrick J. Hearden, *The Tragedy of Vietnam* (1991). On the Johnson administration's role, see Brian VanDeMark, *Into the Quagmire* (1991); George Herring, *LBJ and Vietnam: A Different Kind of War* (1994); and Lloyd Gardner, *Pay Any Price: Lyndon Johnson and the Wars for Vietnam* (1995). On the antiwar movement, see Charles DeBenedetti with Charles Chatfield, *An American Ordeal: The American Antiwar Movement of the Vietnam War* (1990); Tom Wells, *The War within: America's Battle over Vietnam* (1994); and Melvin Small, *Johnson, Nixon, and the Doves* (1988). Milton J. Bates, *The Wars We Took to Vietnam* (1996), is an imaginative cultural study of the war and American stereotypes.

An Era of Diversity, since 1969

Prologue

DIVERSITY BY race, ethnicity, class, and gender was a major motif in the United States in the last third of the twentieth century. Yet the Age of Diversity also refers to the vast array of consumer products, new directions in science, religion, and philosophy, the end of the Cold War, and the challenges from international terrorism that followed. It involves regionalism, localism, revamped relations between the states and federal government, holistic health, and new priorities. The millennium and the century ended, old problems remained, past troubles were vanquished, new ones arose, and the world paused to give thought to what it all meant.

Group consciousness became a major factor in politics, consumerism, and labor organizing. Racial issues focused not on voting rights or public accommodations, but on busing to achieve school desegregation and affirmative action to give minorities a competitive edge. Blacks achieved political victories, electing mayors in many large cities, yet ordinary blacks struggled to enter the middle class.

Women entered the workforce in increasing numbers. They made political and legal gains as well, winning the right to abortion under the 1973 *Roe v. Wade* Supreme Court decision. Abortion opponents, many of them women, mounted a sustained attack on *Roe*, seeking to overturn the ruling or to restrict it. The Christian right, which became a cohesive political force, was instrumental in defeating ratification of the Equal Rights Amendment in state legislatures. Paradoxically, polls showed that men were slightly more supportive of "women's issues" such as abortion and the ERA than women.

The United States remained the most religious nation in the Western world, with a higher percentage of those attending a church, temple, or mosque than any developed country. By the 1980s Americans, especially conservatives, became more passionate and public about their religion,

which they applied to politics. A fault line developed between conservatives and liberals, with each attempting to define the cultural standards in
which families, sexuality, government programs, and education functioned.
Conservatives stood for tradition and continuity, conventional moral standards, and discipline. Liberals advocated change, tolerance, and flexible
standards. The vice of conservatives was self-righteousness; the vice of liberals was hypocrisy; and each side was vulnerable to the other's vices. Most
Americans, whether right-center or left-center, remained centrists, rejecting candidates such as Barry Goldwater and George McGovern whom they
deemed outside the centrist boundaries.

Some aspects of diversity might be more accurately called "variety,"
such as the broad range of products and services available to consumers.
Americans had more choices than before, which might have been a mixed
blessing. Cable television premiered in the 1970s and offered a virtual infin-
ity of choices, but there were times the average person could scan a hundred channels only to complain, "Nothing's on!" Computers, especially
personal computers, revolutionized communication, yet provided avenues
for fraud and the irony of falling in love with a person one had "met" on
the computer screen. There was computer dating, even "computer sex."
Jeeps and cars could climb mountains and exceed the speed limit by forty
miles per hour, but they polluted the environment, guzzled gasoline, and
contributed to injuries and deaths in traffic accidents. By comparison with
modern vans and sports utility vehicles, the chrome-plated, tailed-finned
gas-guzzlers of the 1950s seemed minuscule—and safer.

The sexual revolution accelerated. Men and women lived in coed college dormitories, with condom machines in the restrooms. Viagra, a pill
that could cure male impotence, removed obstacles to sexual intercourse.
Viagra was followed by a variety of competitors and sexual stimulants, some
prescription drugs, others sold over the counter, still others on sale at health
food stores. Meanwhile sexual harassment complaints proliferated. Adultery,
and lying under oath to cover it up, nearly brought the collapse of Bill
Clinton's presidency in the 1990s. The nuclear family disintegrated. Most
dangerous was AIDS, a fatal sexually transmitted disease that shut down
the victims' immune systems.

Purveyors of variety, or diversity, did not necessarily represent progress.
In the marketplace, huge stores such as Wal-Mart crushed smaller competitors by offering a vast amount of affordable goods, often of mediocre quality.
Service was often substandard. The slogan "The customer is always right"
became a relic. In politics and culture, some leaders of racial and ethnic
groups asserted that their followers were entitled to privileged positions not
by dint of work or ability but by virtue of group membership—ironically,

a claim that minorities had long resisted by the majority. Big cities were a major focus of life, and towns were often dismissed as dying. Yet small town values lived on and continued to be the molders of presidents.

Richard Nixon, who had sought the presidency his entire career, finally won it in 1968. During the first summer of his presidency, American astronauts walked on the Moon in the greatest voyage of discovery since the 1400s. On Earth, Nixon opened avenues to détente with the Soviet Union, traveled to Moscow and China, helped slow the arms race, and withdrew America from Vietnam. But the Watergate scandal, a tangle of deceit and ineptness, drove Nixon from office. The economy, affluent in the 1950s and 1960s, stumbled because of foreign competition, slow growth, and a loss of high-paying manufacturing jobs. Gerald Ford, Nixon's successor, pardoned the former president, ensuring he would not have to stand trial for Watergate. The pardon and the slumping economy contributed to Ford's loss to Jimmy Carter, a Washington outsider, peanut broker, and former Georgia governor. "All the legislation in the world can't fix what's wrong with America," the Georgian said. Carter had passion; he seethed integrity, yet he lacked the ability to inspire even as he called upon Americans to make sacrifices, especially in conserving energy, that would change their lifestyles. Carter's failure to cajole Congress into enacting major programs, the national humiliation in the Iran hostage crisis, and a failed effort to rescue the hostages doomed his performance to the lowest poll ratings in history. Yet Carter ventured boldly into the morass of Middle East politics and made major breakthroughs at the Camp David Summit. The economic mess of the 1970s was, however, enough to sink a battleship. Carter lost to former California Governor Ronald Reagan in 1980. He completed his life as possibly the most useful, most respected former president in history, arbitrating international disputes and monitoring elections, speaking out for human rights, building houses for the poor, writing numerous books on subjects from fishing to philosophy, winning a Nobel Peace Prize, and remaining the modest, religious man he had always been.

While Carter was too involved in the details of governing, Reagan was detached. He came to office with a handful of major objectives and accomplished most of them. Others, he delegated. He was neither an outstanding intellect nor a dunce. As a Hollywood actor he was famed for his memory; by the time he became president it was failing. The Iran-Contra scandal tainted his administration. Some considered him rigid and overly ideological. Yet if Reagan was not a great president, neither was he a mediocre one. He pushed the Soviets into an arms race they could not win, using a weapon no previous president had employed: the dollar. He was blunt in his assessment of Soviet communism, calling it an "Evil Empire." Many ordinary Americans had long believed this, but few politicians had dared say it publicly.

Having pilloried the Soviets in his first term, he bonded with their president, Mikhail Gorbachev, in his second, meeting with a Soviet leader at more summits than any previous president. He reached a major arms agreement on his terms. He set up the Soviets for the kill and lived to see the tumbling of the Berlin Wall and the implosion of the Soviet Union.

In domestic policy, Reagan slashed taxes, rebuilt the military, slowed the rate of the government bureaucracy, and produced nearly a decade of prosperity. Yet his tax cuts and defense increases produced a yawning deficit that saddled the nation with an albatross of debt. Still, Reagan's most important accomplishment was not in policy. He shifted the mainstream of politics rightward, inspired Americans, and lifted the malaise that had shrouded Jimmy Carter's America like a fog. He was a magnificent orator when reading from a script, the best of the Era of Diversity. His patriotic sentences were poetic in their simplicity and might have seemed corny, except that he really meant them.

Reagan's successor, his vice president, George Bush, emphasized foreign policy. He invaded Panama and deposed dictator Manuel Noriega, a onetime ally who had become a drug-corrupted pariah. Bush led an American-dominated coalition to victory over Iraq in the Persian Gulf War, rekindling national unity, and presided over triumph in the Cold War. Communism cracked first in Eastern Europe, where the Berlin Wall was torn down by Berliners. Next the Soviet Union, crushed by an unworkable economy and fragmented by ethnic demands for independence, dissolved. In the United States the end of the Cold War was not greeted with the euphoria that might have been expected. Americans, suffering a recession, groaning under deficits, elected Democrat Bill Clinton in 1992.

Clinton stumbled early in his first term: his proposal for national health insurance fizzled, and in 1994 Republicans won control of the House of Representatives for the first time in forty years. But Clinton outflanked the GOP with spending policies that led to budget surpluses and helped make the 1990s the most prosperous decade in American history. Reelected in 1996, he became the first two-term Democratic president since FDR and weathered accusations of marital infidelity, illegal campaign contributions, a questionable real estate deal—and Republicans' vote to impeach him. In diplomacy, Clinton attempted to broker peace in the Mideast and Northern Ireland, aid Russia to build a capitalist economy, and end ethnic violence in Bosnia and Kosovo. Public approval of Clinton's job performance (as opposed to approval of him personally) was high. Despite the satisfaction with administration policies, though, his vice president, Al Gore, lost a close decision to Bush's son, Texas Governor George W. Bush, in the 2000 election. Gore won the popular vote but lost the Electoral College, where Bush's victory in Florida was decisive.

Diversity means many things. Since the assassination of the century's first president in 1901 to the horror of September 11, 2001, technology had abetted killing, leaving human problems unsolved. In technical terms America had traveled light years, had become part of a diverse global community, emerging from an insular, provincial one. Yet many things, good and evil, remained remarkably unchanged. As Americans turned the page on the millennium, the next page read not "The End," but "Chapter Two."

Time Line

An Era of Diversity, 1969–Present

July 20, 1969 Neil Armstrong and Edwin "Buzz" Aldrin Jr. become first humans to walk on moon.

July 1, 1971 Twenty-Sixth Amendment lowering voting age from twenty-one to eighteen ratified.

June 17, 1972 Police arrest five burglars in Watergate break-in.

January 22, 1973 Supreme Court legalizes abortion in *Roe v. Wade*.

January 27, 1973 United States and North Vietnam approve Paris Peace Agreement, under which American forces withdraw from Vietnam War.

October 10, 1973 Vice President Spiro Agnew, facing charges of corruption, resigns.

August 8, 1974 Nixon resigns, taking effect the following day, and Vice President Gerald R. Ford becomes president.

September 8, 1974 Ford pardons Nixon for any offenses committed as president.

April 29, 1975 South Vietnam falls to North Vietnamese.

November 4, 1979 Iranian students take members of U.S. Embassy staff hostage.

June 5, 1981 Acquired immune deficiency syndrome (AIDS) is reported by the Centers for Disease Control.

January 28, 1986 Space shuttle *Challenger* explodes.

November 25, 1986 Iran-Contra scandal breaks.

January 16, 1991 Persian Gulf War begins.

April 19, 1995 Bombing of Oklahoma City federal building kills 168.

December 19, 1998 House of Representatives votes to impeach President Bill Clinton.

February 18, 1999 Senate acquits Clinton of charges.

December 12, 2000 George W. Bush named President by the Supreme Court.

September 11, 2001 More than three thousand die in terrorist attacks on United States; World Trade Towers destroyed.

January 29, 2002 Bush says United States will fight preemptive wars against countries that develop weapons of mass destruction.

January 28, 2003 Space shuttle *Columbia* explodes.

March 19, 2003 U.S.–led coalition goes to war against Iraq.

December 13, 2003 Saddam Hussein captured.

November 2, 2004 George Bush defeats John Kerry for president.

November 11, 2004 Palestine Liberation (PLO) leader Yasir Arafat dies.

January 9, 2005 Mahmoud Abbas elected new PLO leader.

January 30, 2005 Large number of Iraqis turn out for free elections for Parliament.

February 10, 2005 North Korea announces it has nuclear weapons.

April 2005 Syria withdraws its troops from Lebanon.

May 31, 2005 W. Mark Felt revealed as "Deep Throat" in Watergate scandal.

CHAPTER NINETEEN

The Nixon Years,
1969–1974

F EW PREDICTED that out of the ashes of the 1960s would arise Richard Nixon, whose political career included paradox in abundance. Admired and respected by millions, he had few personal friends and trusted barely a handful of people. Insecure and shy, he succeeded in a profession that rewards gregarious personalities. Detested by liberals, he was, relatively speaking, the most liberal Republican president of the twentieth century. An archetypal anticommunist, he became the architect of détente, a relaxation of tensions with the communist powers. He practiced the politics of division, but during his presidency, the race riots that had torn the nation ended and he accomplished much for civil rights—advances that were unintentional. He introduced humane and innovative domestic programs, yet is little remembered for them. Rather, Nixon is remembered for his bold opening to China and for his disgrace in Watergate, a tragedy that has the irony of a spider caught in his own web. Nixon's presidency bound together the strands of the age of diversity, metaphorically bundled in a time and man.

Richard Nixon

A native Californian, Nixon was born in Yorba Linda and grew up in Whittier, the son of Quaker parents who lived in near poverty and required him to work hard and be frugal. His mother, Hannah, was long-suffering yet rarely showed affection toward her children. Nixon's father, Frank, worked hard and had a violent temper. Losing two brothers to tuberculosis, Nixon grew up tough and determined, with a taste for the physical combat of football and the verbal sparring of debate in school, but deprived of love. After graduating from Whittier College, where he was a star student, he enrolled at Duke University Law School in Durham, North Carolina, impressed his peers by studying for long hours, and graduated third in his class. Briefly he searched for a Wall Street job, then returned to Whittier to practice law, met Thelma "Pat" Ryan, and married her.

In 1942, Nixon joined the Office of Price Administration, acquired a contempt for bureaucracy he never lost, resigned to enlist in the Navy, and served an uneventful tour of duty in the South Pacific. Then a group of Whittier businessmen asked him to run for the House of Representatives against the liberal incumbent, Jerry Voorhis. Nixon won a bitter 1946 campaign in which he accused Voorhis of being sympathetic to communism. He served two terms in the House, earning a reputation as an anticommunist by pursuing accused spy Alger Hiss, and on the strength of that renown, won an acrimonious campaign for the Senate in 1950. The Senate was a springboard to two terms as vice president under Eisenhower, from 1953 to 1961. But then came two successive difficult defeats, to John F. Kennedy for the presidency in 1960 and to Edmund G. "Pat" Brown for the California governorship in 1962. Nixon's heart was never truly in the latter campaign; he vowed he would not seek political office again. But he could not step away from politics for good, as he moved to New York, practiced law on Wall Street, and made his comeback in 1968.

In seniority, experience, and savvy, Nixon was the nation's senior politician, skilled at the craft he found unnatural and unenjoyable. From politics he had taken the bitter lessons that winning is all that matters and that he must destroy his enemies before they destroyed him. Since the 1952 campaign, when the alleged political slush fund that prompted his "Checkers speech" came to light, Nixon believed liberal newspapers were against him because he was a successful conservative. Consequently, he cultivated television, especially after his first 1960 debate with Kennedy, and ran slick TV campaigns in 1968 and 1972. Image matters more than substance in politics, Nixon and his aides sadly concluded.

In governance, too, Nixon's advisers reinforced the anger, paranoia, and the obsession with secrecy that marked the administration and helped defeat it. Chief of staff H. R. Haldeman ruthlessly limited access to Nixon and made enemies by insisting that the president's time could not be wasted. Vice President Spiro Agnew relished his public role of attacking young people, Democrats, and the press. Agnew's savage lyrics struck deep chords among the group that Nixon dubbed "the great silent majority," the white blue-collar workers and southerners who supported George Wallace in the 1968 election. They opposed affirmative action, school bus-

CULTURAL DIPLOMACY
Richard M. Nixon meets with Elvis Presley in December 1970.
(National Archives)

ing, abortion, recreational drug use, Vietnam War protesters, pornography, and "soft-on-crime" liberals.

Such inner workings of the administration belied an early theme of Nixon's presidency: his attempt to bring the country together after the tumult of the 1960s. "We cannot learn from each other until we stop shouting at one another," he told Americans in his first inaugural address. Aiding Nixon in his quest, astronauts walked on the Moon in the summer of 1969, fulfilling John Kennedy's wish that Americans reach Earth's satellite by the end of the decade. The lunar module *Eagle* from the *Apollo 11* rocket landed on the Sea of Tranquillity, and on July 20, Astronaut Neil Armstrong set foot on the lunar surface, informing an international television audience, "That's one small step for man, one giant leap for mankind." Armstrong and colleague Edwin E. Buzz Aldrin Jr. left an American flag and a plaque telling of their arrival "in peace for all mankind." Their feat foreshadowed other breakthroughs in space in the decades to come, among them longer Moon missions, rockets that brought back pictures from other planets, and space stations.

Fighting Inflation and Crime

Nixon served his tenure under the shadow of inflation, a holdover from the Johnson administration. The rate was 5 percent at the start of his presidency. At first he cut federal spending and prodded the Federal Reserve Board to raise interest rates. Unemployment rose and incubated a recession, yet inflation persisted. Now, wanting to end the recession more than curb inflation, Nixon reversed course on government expenditures in early 1971, proposing a Keynesian unbalanced budget. August brought more bad news, the first major trade deficit since 1890, which prompted another shift for Nixon. He imposed a 10 percent tariff on imports and said the value of the dollar would float, according to market conditions. In the most surprising change, Nixon imposed wage and price controls. These measures improved the economy, curtailing inflation and the trade deficit in time to help Nixon's 1972 reelection campaign. After he was inaugurated to a second term, Nixon changed directions. He ended the controls in favor of "voluntary" guidelines. Inflation rose to 9 percent.

Next, Nixon proposed a new approach to welfare reform. Aides drafted the most ambitious welfare proposal of the Era of Diversity, the Family Assistance Plan (FAP). Paradoxically devised by a conservative White House, it was more generous than anything offered by Lyndon Johnson. The Great Society's labyrinth of social programs would be replaced by direct cash payments. Whatever the causes of poverty, Nixon reasoned, the solution was to pay poor people a living. This was direct, simple, and actually less expensive. Each family of four would receive $1,600 plus $800 for food stamps. Able-bodied recipients except women with young children would be required to work or enroll in job training. The plan never passed Congress. Democrats, who controlled Congress, called it stingy and did not want credit to go to a Republican president. Many Republicans disliked the idea of paying people who did not work. Similarly, Nixon's plan for national health insurance faltered.

The Family Assistance Plan was part of a strategy Nixon called the "New Federalism." At its heart was "revenue sharing." Federal money was disbursed to the states and cities to use as they determined. Decision making would be decentralized. Nixon retained and even expanded some Great Society programs, including the Job Corps and housing subsidies. He supported a constitutional amendment lowering the voting age to eighteen. Nixon promoted the most progressive environmental program to that time. It included creation of the Environmental Protection Agency, the Clean Air Act of 1970, regulation of oil spill cleanups, and laws directed against pesticide contamination of water and noise pollution. The administration created the Occupational Safety and Health Administration (OSHA) to ensure job safety.

Nixon addressed middle-class concern about domestic crime and also targeted perceived domestic subversion. The FBI illegally wiretapped some leaders of the civil rights and antiwar movements. The CIA kept files on domestic radicals and infiltrated their organizations. Fearing leftist opposition to the government, Nixon established a group called "the Plumbers" to plug leaks. Among them were former FBI agent G. Gordon Liddy and former CIA operative E. Howard Hunt. An "enemies list" was compiled of persons to be harassed by federal agencies.

Nixon's ambition to impose "law and order" extended to his conservative nominees to the Supreme Court. His first two nominees, both southern conservatives, Clement Haynsworth and G. Harrold Carswell, were rejected. Northern liberals considered both men too far Right, and Carswell was said to have a second-rate mind. When he turned north for a conservative nominee, Nixon fared better, winning confirmation of federal Judge Harry Blackmun of Minnesota. In 1971 two more conservatives secured confirmation, Lewis F. Powell, of Virginia, a moderate, and William Rehnquist, a hard-liner who later became chief justice.

The Burger court proved moderate. It allowed the *New York Times* to publish the classified *Pentagon Papers*, accelerated school desegregation, and ordered Nixon to turn over Watergate-related presidential tapes to Special Prosecutor Leon Jaworski. Most important, in *Roe v. Wade* (1973) it legalized abortion in the months of pregnancy before a fetus could survive outside the womb.

Under Dwight Eisenhower, Vice President Nixon had been a leading advocate of civil rights. As the movement migrated leftward, he remained a supporter of civil rights, yet was less enthusiastic. Ironically, in a statistical sense, civil rights made great progress during his presidency. Nixon enforced court decisions and laws he personally opposed, such as school busing. At the beginning of his term, 68 percent of the African American children in the South attended segregated schools; by the end of his tenure only 8 percent did. To help blacks, Nixon created a program to lend money to start businesses. He became an early advocate of affirmative action, requiring contractors who worked for the government to design plans for hiring minorities. Neither did his Supreme Court roll back civil rights gains; in fact, it advanced them.

Emotionally, Nixon was most comfortable with white males, yet he adjusted to the changes that diversity brought to his times. He appointed more women to midlevel government positions than his predecessors. Yet there were none in the cabinet or the White House inner circle. Nixon

AMERICAN INDIAN
MILITANCY
The takeover of Wounded
Knee, a poster showing
Bobby Onco, a Kiowa,
and member of the
American Indian
Movement, holding
up a rifle.
(Library of Congress)

endorsed the proposed Equal Rights Amendment yet did not campaign for it. He opposed abortion as a means of birth control. The president enforced the law denying federal aid to schools and colleges practicing sex discrimination. Nixon insisted that the Civil Rights Commission enforce such requirements diligently and that child-care expenses become tax deductible when both parents worked.

The administration compiled a credible record in Indian affairs. Nixon broke with termination in favor of a program of enlightened self-determination and autonomy for tribes. The president appointed Louis R. Bruce, a Native American, as commissioner of Indian affairs and named Indians to the Bureau of Indian Affairs bureaucracy. The White House settled several claims against the government on terms that were generous to tribes, and the 1975 Indian Self-Determination and Educational Assistance Act was passed because of what the president had set in motion. Providing for direct negotiations between the tribes and the government to administer programs that the bureau formerly directed, the law was seen as the most important Indian-related law in more than forty years. Tribal fishing rights became contentious in the 1960s and 1970s. Sometimes whites staged violent protests, yet the courts usually favored the tribes. Native Americans grew assertive, emulating the militance of the Black Power movement. They occupied Alcatraz Island in San Francisco Bay, seized and trashed the offices of the Bureau of Indian Affairs and captured the village of Wounded Knee, site of the last major massacre of Native Americans. The White House responded calmly rather than punitively to the incidents.

Global Change: Détente and the Yom Kippur War

Nixon considered foreign affairs more important than domestic policy. The greatest presidents had drawn at least part of their reputation from international events. The president also had a freer hand in foreign policy; the security apparatus was less wieldly than Congress. Further, the minority party could initiate change, to some degree, without majority consensus, except for negotiating treaties. Nixon liked secrecy and surprises; he was skilled at intuiting what made foreign leaders tick; and he was a pragmatist. He wanted détente, especially with the Soviet Union and China, arms control, and an end to the Vietnam War. Henry Kissinger, his national security adviser, had a fine mind, a Harvard professorship, and like Nixon, an appreciation for intrigue. He exuded charm, talked tough, and got along with liberals. His colossal ego and desire for credit clashed with similar qualities in Nixon. The press debated whether Kissinger was the genius behind Nixon or Nixon the genius behind Kissinger. Although both men had fertile minds and were risk takers, Nixon devised the strategy, which Kissinger implemented.

Nixon was an anticommunist on principle, yet he believed in defeating the communists with finesse. Temporarily, he was content to lower tensions rather than overpower communism with force. Still, he prided himself on decisiveness, as did Kissinger. The president knew many communist rulers personally, they respected each other, and they had a common interest in survival. Nixon also believed he excelled at crisis management because of his experience under Eisenhower, his friendship with world leaders, and his extensive reading on foreign policy. For the most part, he did not intend to bully or be bullied. So long as he chained his temper and throttled the dark side of his personality, he might achieve this.

If creeping communism was anywhere apparent, it was in Cuba, the island ninety miles from American shores pointed like a dagger at Florida.

In 1962 John Kennedy had brought the world to the brink of nuclear war to keep missiles out of Cuba. In September 1970 American surveillance planes photographed a Soviet naval base being expanded to accommodate submarines carrying nuclear weapons. Nixon did not indulge in public brinkmanship, yet persuaded the Soviets to back down without losing face.

In Chile, the administration was more heavy-handed. In November 1970 Salvador Allende, a socialist allied with the Chilean Communist Party, came to power. Allende nationalized, with compensation, the property of major American companies such as Anaconda Copper and International Telephone and Telegraph. The United States suspended aid and loans to Chile and the CIA provided $10 million to forces opposing Allende. These actions helped the anti-Allende Chileans stage a coup that overthrew Allende in September 1973. Allende died in the coup, either by suicide or at the hand of revolutionaries. He was succeeded by General Augusto Pinochet, who established a repressive regime recognized by the United States.

Meanwhile, on the Asian subcontinent, Muslim Pakistan sparred with Hindu India over one-half of the nation of Pakistan. Pakistan was divided between eastern and western provinces, with India between. In 1972 East Pakistan seceded and proclaimed the nation of Bangladesh. Supported by India, it gained independence. The Nixon administration was divided, the State Department favoring India and the White House covertly tilting toward Pakistan, a Cold War ally. This split drove India into the arms of the Soviets, with whom India signed an alliance in 1972. The Soviet Union and India became major trade partners.

In the Era of Diversity, no nation was more diverse, and more mysterious to the West, than China, the world's most populous country. Nixon hoped the alliance between the communist superpowers might be pried apart by a determined finesse diplomat such as himself. China was an enormous potential trading partner, and Nixon saw trade and diplomatic avenues as the routes to cracking the cocoon that encased the communist giant. By normalizing relations with China while simultaneously practicing détente with the Soviet Union, the United States, as the uncommitted superpower, could wield the balance of power. This meant walking a diplomatic tightrope, which Nixon was willing to do. Détente would become a tripod, with the United States the base. Without the base, the other two sides would dangle.

Shortly after Nixon took office, the mating dance with China began. Nixon eased trade and travel restrictions. The Chinese invited, and thrashed, an American ping-pong team. Nixon erased the twenty-one year trade embargo. The UN expelled Taiwan and seated Mainland China on the Security Council. Then Nixon announced he would visit China in February 1972, an election year. He was the first president to go there since

DÉTENTE IN BEIJING
Nixon shakes hands with China's Mao Zedong in February 1972.
(National Archives)

Ulysses S. Grant in 1879. Nixon visited the Great Wall, talked with communist leader Mao Zedong and Prime Minister Zhou Enlai (Chou En-Lai), and conceded that the Chinese themselves must settle the fate of Taiwan. The two nations agreed to increase trade and normalize diplomatic relations. Formal diplomatic recognition did not come until 1979, under the administration of Jimmy Carter.

Détente with China enabled Nixon to negotiate from strength when he approached the Soviet Union. Like the Chinese, the Soviets were interested in trade and also in limitations of nuclear arms. For both sides, the weapons race had grown expensive and had reached the point of overkill. Nixon resumed talks on the Strategic Arms Limitation Treaty (SALT) that had begun under Lyndon Johnson and consummated the deal at a summit with Soviet President Leonid Brezhnev in Moscow in May 1972. The leaders also completed work on an Antiballistic Missile (ABM) Treaty. SALT set ceilings on the number of submarine-launched ballistic missiles and intercontinental ballistic missiles (ICBMs). The ABM pact limited each nation to protecting its capital. Nixon and Brezhnev also reached trade agreements: the Soviets committed to purchase $722 million of American grain for each of the next three years. Nixon hosted Brezhnev at Washington for a second summit in June 1973. At a third summit in Moscow during June 1974, the leaders discussed a SALT II treaty. By this time Nixon had been weakened by Watergate and lacked the credibility to make binding commitments.

At the first Moscow summit, Brezhnev warned of possible war in the Middle East, yet Nixon believed the Soviet leader overestimated the danger. Brezhnev said that Egypt and Syria were determined to retake territory seized by Israel in the Six-Day War of 1967. He suggested that the United States and the Soviet Union impose a settlement to preempt war. Brezhnev's intelligence reports were sound. On October 6, 1973, the Egyptians and Syrians struck. It was Yom Kippur, the Day of Atonement, the holiest day on the Jewish calendar. The Egyptians retook part of the Sinai Desert, and in the East, Syria drove Israel from the strategic Golan Heights. Well supplied with Soviet arms, the Arabs had never shown such military prowess nor such unity in their wars with Israel.

Israel had stockpiled weapons and ammunition for a three- or four-day war, yet this one seemed destined to last weeks. On October 13, the United States airlifted $2 billion worth of sophisticated weapons to Israel. Fortified, the Israelis counterattacked two days later, seizing all the territory they had lost and more. The Egyptian army was surrounded and in danger of annihilation when Washington and Moscow arranged a cease-fire. Meanwhile, on October 17, the Arab oil producers, united as the Organization of Petroleum Exporting Countries (OPEC), declared an embargo against the United States and its allies, leading to fuel shortages and inflated petroleum prices. Oil rose from $2.60 to $10 per barrel. To end the energy crisis and counter Soviet influence with Arabs, Nixon sent Kissinger on two years of "shuttle diplomacy," flying back and forth among Middle Eastern capitals, starting in November 1973. He helped arrange a cease-fire, Israeli withdrawal from lands captured in the recent war, and an end to the oil embargo, in May 1974. Nixon made a goodwill trip to Egypt, Saudi Arabia, and Syria in June 1974. A year earlier the Egyptians had ejected their Soviet military advisers and aligned with the Americans.

Withdrawal from Vietnam

North Vietnamese leader Ho Chi Minh died in 1969, yet the war in Vietnam went on. In America, the antiwar movement steamed ahead like a locomotive at full throttle. Nixon, having watched the war humiliate

Lyndon Johnson, realized he would be a one-term president unless he could defuse the issue. He decided to expand a policy begun late in LBJ's term: Vietnamization. American troops would be phased out and the fighting turned over to the South Vietnamese. The latter would be forged into an effective force with American training, weapons, and air and sea support. At home, Nixon dealt with the most divisive issue, the draft. First he devised a lottery, which provided some advance knowledge of the odds of being drafted. In 1972 he stopped sending draftees to Vietnam unless they volunteered. In 1973 the draft was abolished in favor of an all-volunteer army. These changes enabled Nixon to cut the number of American troops from more than five hundred thousand to less than thirty thousand.

To keep the pressure on, buying time for Vietnamization to work, American airpower pounded the North. The president secretly bombed supply routes in Cambodia and Laos. Early in 1970 North Vietnam infiltrated more soldiers into Cambodia to support the communist Khmer Rouge and make the country a staging ground for attacks on neighboring South Vietnam. Nixon reacted by ordering an American–South Vietnamese invasion of Cambodia in April, which killed two thousand North Vietnamese and destroyed several months' worth of enemy supplies but failed to locate North Vietnamese headquarters.

As American casualties declined, so did the antiwar movement. Yet each temporary escalation, such as the invasion of Cambodia, brought it roaring back to life, sometimes with tragic consequences. On May 2, 1970, Ohio National Guardsmen were sent to restore order at Kent State University after students burned down the Reserve Officer Training Corps building. On May 4, the troops panicked and shot into a crowd, killing four students and wounding nine. Ten days after the Ohio shootings, two died and twelve were hurt when state police fired into a dormitory at Jackson State College in Mississippi. Demonstrations erupted nationwide and seventy-five schools closed before the end of the academic year.

Escalations and protests continued in 1971. In January Congress repealed the Gulf of Tonkin Resolution. In February, American airpower supported South Vietnamese forces in an invasion of Laos to sever the Ho Chi Minh Trail, over which North Vietnam transported men and munitions. Initially the South Vietnamese fought well, yet when North Vietnam counterattacked, they fled in panic, some clinging to the skids of U.S. helicopters. Another blow struck the White House in June, when the *New York Times* began publishing the *Pentagon Papers*, a secret study of the Vietnam conflict that chronicled a record of government deception about American involvement. The papers, which former Pentagon analyst Daniel Ellsberg stole from the government and gave to the *Times*, revealed no information that discredited the Nixon administration; it ended before Nixon took office. Still, the president worried that other secrets might be published and that the papers' release weakened the security of government. The Justice Department obtained a court order against further publication. Appealing to the Supreme Court, the *Times* argued that the First Amendment prohibited prior restraints on the press, and the justices agreed, lifting the injunction. Infuriated, Nixon had the Justice Department indict Ellsberg for theft and spying and put "the Plumbers" on the case. Hunt and Liddy broke into the Los Angeles office of Ellsberg's psychiatrist in search of information that might prove him unstable. In 1973 a judge dismissed all charges against Ellsberg after it was disclosed that "the Plumbers" had burglarized the psychiatrist's office and had tried to bribe the trial judge by offering to name him FBI director.

By the election year of 1972 Nixon had achieved his objective of defusing Vietnam as an election issue. A settlement seemed possible because of his closer ties with the Soviet Union and China, which wanted American friendship and technical aid more than a communist South Vietnam. Best of all, while the two Vietnams battled, American casualties fell from three hundred weekly in 1968 to twenty-six weekly in 1971. In the last five months of 1972 casualties averaged only four per week. American troops in the field, aware that their efforts would soon be washed away, struggled merely to survive until their tour of duty ended. There were racial tensions, drug abuse, and "fragging"—the killing of officers by soldiers. Worse yet were massacres of civilians. As early as March 1968, army troops under the command of Lieutenant William Calley had murdered nearly three hundred and fifty women, children, and old men at the village of My Lai.

With the American presence in Vietnam declining and U.S. home front support weakening in 1972, the North Vietnamese launched their biggest offensive in Cambodia and South Vietnam, marshaling tanks and artillery. Nixon responded with bombing of the North and Cambodia and with the mining of North Vietnamese ports. Air and naval power stopped the advance and helped lead to a breakthrough in the Paris peace talks, which had been at a four-year impasse. Kissinger and North Vietnamese diplomat Le Duc Tho reached an agreement to withdraw all remaining U.S. troops, return American prisoners of war, and permit North Vietnamese soldiers to stay in the South. "Peace is at hand," Kissinger announced shortly before the 1972 election. But South Vietnamese President Nguyen Van Thieu balked over the communists' key demand, the provision letting North Vietnamese forces remain in the South. Concessions made to satisfy Thieu required offsetting concessions to satisfy the North. Kissinger broke off talks in hopes of bombing North Vietnam into agreement, and from

December 18 through 30, planes saturated the North in the most intense bombardment of the war. This "Christmas bombing" led the North Vietnamese to resume talks, and differences were worked out in a few days. Nixon promised Thieu that if he would sign the treaty, the United States would keep arming the South and employ airpower if the North violated the proposed cease-fire. If South Vietnam did not sign, Washington might terminate aid and sign the treaty alone. All parties signed the accord on January 27, 1973. Five days earlier Lyndon Johnson had died.

Some questioned whether a similar treaty could have been signed in 1969, averting four years of bloody war. The chief concession Nixon obtained during that time was North Vietnamese willingness to negotiate an agreement with Thieu still in power. Nixon believed he had given Thieu an opportunity to survive and had obtained an honorable peace. More realistic, Kissinger negotiated to provide a "decent interval" between the American withdrawal and a North Vietnamese conquest of the South. Nixon's promise to intervene if North Vietnam violated the terms proved worthless after his resignation. Congress curbed the power of future presidents by passing the 1973 War Powers Act. Presidents must notify Congress within forty-eight hours of troop deployment, and congressional approval is required to keep them in a war zone more than sixty days.

America's longest war ended in its most humiliating defeat. Although some believed the United States had no interest in the distant land, the war was fought in the context of the Cold War policy of containment. It was believed the Cold War was a zero sum game in which the superpower that accumulated and retained the most allies would triumph. Some 58,000 Americans died and 300,000 were wounded. In monetary terms it cost the nation $150 billion. Yet America's human losses paled in comparison to the other combatants. The South Vietnamese lost 184,000 killed and North Vietnam and the Vietcong a staggering 927,000. Ideologically driven, the North persevered despite these casualties. Yet the Vietnamese did not get the worker's paradise Ho Chi Minh had promised. What they got was "boat people"—desperate peasants and government officials fleeing communism, packed into flimsy boats which often sank, or were rejected by countries at which they sought asylum and reeducation camps in the south. Two dominos fell, Laos and Cambodia, the latter subject to massive genocide by the dictator Pol Pot. For the United States, the war was a lesson in humility. The military would be chained by the leash of public opinion for much of the remainder of the Cold War. Just as World War II had been the formative event of their fathers' coming of age, the baby boom generation was shaped by the failure in Vietnam. History, and historians, are more forgiving of winners than of losers.

Watergate

If ever there seemed a sure bet for reelection into a second term as president, it was Richard Nixon in 1972. He had neutralized the two most dangerous issues, Vietnam and the economy, although economic problems would return with a vengeance after the election. The Democrats nominated one of their weaker candidates, an antiwar senator from South Dakota, George McGovern. Liberal on economic and social issues, McGovern appeared indecisive after defending, then dismissing his choice for vice president, Senator Thomas Eagleton of Missouri. Learning that Eagleton had undergone electric shock therapy for stress, McGovern backed him to the hilt initially, then ordered him off the ticket. After several prominent Democrats refused second place, McGovern lined up former Peace Corps Director Sargent Shriver. George Wallace posed a threat on Nixon's right flank, yet was paralyzed in an assassination attempt and forced out of the race.

The only thing that could defeat Nixon was his own insecurity and in the long run it did. Long before polls revealed that Nixon had a lock on the White House, Nixon and his henchmen began a series of unethical and illegal acts that turned a magnificent victory at the polls into a devastating disgrace. Attorney General John Mitchell resigned to head the Committee to Re-Elect the President (CREEP): Democrats delighted in the acronym. The committee raised millions of dollars and poured some of the money into "dirty tricks" and domestic espionage on the Democrats. A bigger waste of money could hardly be imagined. Among various sordid ventures, the most historically significant one was an attempt to wiretap the Democratic National Committee headquarters at the Watergate office and apartment complex. Several attempts were made and bungled, especially the final one when the burglars were arrested. Some were traced to the White House, and they were paid hush money for their silence in court. Nixon professed ignorance, as did others at the White House. Nixon probably did not have prior knowledge of the break-in and was doubtless too savvy to authorize it. Yet almost from the beginning, he helped mastermind the cover-up and thereby broke the law. His main concern at the time was to contain the evidence of White House involvement until after the election.

The election was a Republican landslide. Nixon and Spiro Agnew were elected to a second term with almost 61 percent of the popular vote, second only to Johnson's percentage of the popular vote in 1964. They carried every state but Massachusetts and the District of Columbia. Nixon won 520 electoral votes to McGovern's 17, the greatest electoral rout since FDR's in 1936. Nixon was on top of the world; it was a long way down.

Nixon hoped Watergate would evaporate after the election, but his situation became grimmer. The Watergate scandal began to unravel when the five men who had broken into the Democrats' offices were caught, convicted after the election, and threatened with long prison terms. U.S. District Judge John J. Sirica said he would offer sentence reductions if the burglars informed on their superiors, and James McCord broke ranks to talk with prosecutors. Opening the floodgates on the administration, McCord admitted that top White House aides had known of plans for the break-in and said that the defendants, who claimed they had acted on their own, perjured themselves during the trial. McCord revealed the White House pressured him and other defendants to plead guilty and remain silent.

The Watergate investigation exploded onto the front pages of major dailies. *Washington Post* reporters Bob Woodward and Carl Bernstein published new revelations almost daily, relying on confidential informants. Their most important informant, known as "Deep Throat," remained secret until 2005, when he was revealed to be W. Mark Felt, second in charge at the FBI. In 1973 a Senate committee chaired by the folksy Sam Ervin of North Carolina opened hearings. Public pressure forced Nixon to allow Attorney General Elliott Richardson to appoint a special prosecutor. Richardson appointed his former law professor at Harvard, Archibald Cox, a Kennedy Democrat. Nixon hoped to head off the investigations by firing his chief counsel, John Dean, and accepting the resignations of his closest aides, Bob Haldeman and John Ehrlichman. Had anyone been willing to take the blame, the president might have been saved, but loyalty to Nixon proved thin. The Ervin committee, as it heard witnesses, uncovered skullduggery unrelated to Watergate, called the "White House Horrors," which cast doubt on the president's credibility. Still, there was no "smoking gun" pointing to the president. The committee's ranking minority member, Senator Howard Baker of Tennessee, summed up the issue they sought to resolve: "What did the president know and when did he know it?"

There was no direct eyewitness testimony, yet the committee stumbled across something better. White House aide Alexander Butterfield testified that the president had secretly taped almost every conversation in the Oval Office. Because the tapes were voice activated, the president soon forgot about them and talked normally, much to his later regret. When Cox subpoenaed the tapes Nixon refused to give them up on the grounds of executive privilege, and Nixon ordered Richardson to fire him. Richardson refused, as did his subordinate. Finally Solicitor General Robert Bork wielded the ax. The affair was called the "Saturday Night Massacre."

His credibility further strained, Nixon allowed the appointment of a new special prosecutor, Leon Jaworski, a distinguished Texas lawyer.

Jaworski proved as aggressive about getting the tapes as Cox. The House Judiciary Committee began hearings to impeach Nixon. Meanwhile, Vice President Agnew stepped from the shadows into the limelight. Agnew was indicted for accepting bribes and kickbacks while governor of Maryland and vice president. He pleaded "no contest," resigned the vice presidency and paid a $10,000 fine. For the first time, the provisions of the Twenty-Fifth Amendment, which allowed a president to appoint a vice president when the office was vacant, were invoked. Nixon, passing over controversial nominees, nominated the friendly, uncontroversial U.S. Representative Gerald R. Ford of Michigan, who was confirmed.

The issue of the presidential tapes continued to plague Nixon. Still refusing to turn over the originals, yet unwisely failing to destroy them, he issued edited transcripts. The transcripts were replete with omissions, typographical errors, and profanity described as "expletive deleted." The published transcripts became instant best sellers. Still, the Judiciary Committee and Jaworski appealed to the Supreme Court to order Nixon to provide the originals. In a 9-0 ruling in *United States v. Nixon*, the justices, many of them Nixon appointees, ruled that he must do so. Meanwhile, the Judiciary Committee voted three articles of impeachment: abuse of power by using the government to harass political enemies; contempt of Congress for refusing to honor a subpoena demanding the tapes; and obstruction of justice in trying to cover up the White House involvement in the Watergate break-in.

The tapes yielded the "smoking gun"—direct evidence of presidential involvement in the cover-up. Six days after the break-in, Nixon had ordered Haldeman to use the CIA to block the FBI's Watergate investigation on the grounds it might compromise national security. Even Nixon's own attorneys could not defend this breach of faith. On August 7, 1974, a group of respected Republican leaders informed Nixon that impeachment and conviction were certain unless he resigned. Nixon, who had prided himself on his perseverance, of never being a "quitter," now had to face the humiliation of resignation or the greater humiliation of conviction and removal from office. On August 8, the president announced his resignation, a one-sentence letter addressed to Secretary of State Henry Kissinger that became effective the next day. He became the first president to resign. "Our long national nightmare is over," declared Ford, who became the first unelected president.

Americans awakened from their nightmare to a world that was different than the one they had known. They were cynical about politics and politicians, about foreign adventures, and high-priced petroleum. For some time, the best qualifications for the White House were virtually no qualifications. Like Diogenes, Americans carried a lantern looking for an honest man.

Never before had a president soared to the pinnacle of success, then plunged into the abyss of repudiation as quickly as Nixon. The system worked, in a way: even the president was not above the law. But the price was high, the wound was deep, the ramifications were broad. Watergate and Vietnam were serious blows to presidential credibility. The media and the public imposed higher moral standards that proved difficult for some of Nixon's successors to meet. Congress gained power at the expense of the chief executive. The concept of a strong presidency was undermined.

History will probably be kinder to Nixon than his contemporaries, partly because he led a productive life as an ex-president. His legislative achievements were minor, yet he set an agenda that was ambitious, especially in foreign policy. Consistently overcoming adversity, except for his last political crisis, Nixon was the toughest man in politics in his generation, but toughness resulted in meanness; he was not generous in victory, a flaw that led to his downfall. Members of his White House staff wrote that Nixon's personality, deeply complex, had light and dark sides or, alternately, many layers, such as those of a cake. One biographer told the former president that he found Nixon too complex to get on paper. "Aha," Nixon replied, "now I know you are really getting somewhere."

CHAPTER TWENTY

Healing and Malaise:
The Ford and Carter
Administrations

IN THE Era of Diversity, politics demonstrated a striking range of diversity. There were elements of paradox as well, sometimes in parties and elections, sometimes wrapped up in individuals. Presidents are judged on their accomplishments and flaws. Richard Nixon had more of both than Gerald Ford. Nixon and Ford were both conservatives, yet they were better known for their differences, especially in temperament. Nixon was moody; Ford was even-tempered. Nixon was passionate; Ford lacked Nixon's win-at-all-costs mentality. Nixon was a loner; Ford liked people. Nixon was vindictive; Ford was forgiving. It was ironic that Nixon's landslide reelection was followed by the accession of the first unelected president.

The Tribulations of Gerald R. Ford

Both Nixon and Ford liked football, yet Ford was a better athlete, starring in high school and at the University of Michigan. He turned down professional offers in order to attend the Yale University law school, where he earned high grades. Ford worked his way through by coaching junior varsity football and boxing, learning boxing entirely from books. He returned to Grand Rapids, practiced law, and enlisted in the navy after Pearl Harbor. Ford served four years, two on an aircraft carrier, on which he saw combat. After the war, Ford starred in politics. He won a seat in the U.S. House of Representatives from Grand Rapids and remained there until he was confirmed as vice president in 1973. After eight months, he became president. Down-to-earth, humble, known for his integrity, Ford was a contrast to Nixon, and that was an asset.

Like her husband, First Lady Betty Ford was candid and forthcoming. She impressed the nation with her courage when she talked about her mastectomy for cancer in 1974. Even her flaws endeared her to the public because she shared them. Admitting to alcoholism after her White House years, she helped establish a clinic for alcohol and drug abusers. A feminist, she lobbied for ratification of the Equal Rights Amendment (ERA), supported *Roe v. Wade*, and pressed her husband, without much success, to appoint more women to office.

Ford was an instant president, barely briefed by Nixon. He mixed his own staff with Nixon's. The holdovers and newcomers clashed, and the White House, initially, was chaos. Trying to unite the liberal and conservative wings of his party, Ford nominated Nelson Rockefeller, a favorite of liberals, vice president. Ford promised Rockefeller he would coordinate domestic policy, yet the promise proved empty when Rockefeller was unable to overcome bureaucratic infighting.

The political bombshell of the administration, just thirty days after Ford took office, was his pardon of Richard Nixon for crimes he committed or might have committed. Ford's purpose was to end the bitterness over Watergate rather than prolonging it in a long trial of the former president. Nixon receded in the public mind, at least to a degree, as Ford hoped. Yet the pardon damaged Ford politically; some even said that he had agreed to the pardon when nominated for vice president, an agreement that is unlikely.

The nation did not forget Watergate sufficiently soon to avoid making the Republicans the underdogs in the 1974 congressional elections. To prevent disastrous losses, Ford embarked on a speaking tour to back Republican candidates. While on tour, there were two attempts to assassinate the president, both in California. First, Lynette "Squeaky" Fromme, a member of the "family" of young girls attracted to mass killer Charles Manson, aimed a handgun at Ford, but it did not discharge. Later, Sara Jane Moore, a former FBI informant, fired at Ford but missed, her aim deflected by a bystander. Neither brought much of a sympathy vote to Republicans, who lost the congressional races badly.

The economy brought equally bad news, spiraling downward. The condition was called stagflation, the rare occurrence of simultaneous recession and inflation. Interest rates were high, too high to buy or build homes. Many large cities, including New York, teetered on the brink of bankruptcy. New York begged for federal loan guarantees to survive the crisis. Initially, Ford refused, leading the New York *Daily News* to splash the headline: "FORD TO CITY: DROP DEAD." Ultimately, Ford changed his mind on the condition that New York begin operating on a balanced budget. Paradoxically, the federal budget remained sunk in red ink.

Ford's fiscal prudence induced him to call for tight money and tax increases, which were unpopular. His political prudence then led him to call for two tax cuts, which passed. The energy crisis was paradoxical. High prices were an incentive to conserve fuel, yet created inflation. Congress and the president worked out a bill that would temporarily roll back the price of domestically produced oil, yet would phase in price decontrol, a strategy that worked one way in the short run and just the opposite way in the long run. As for inflation, Ford said the solution was not to buy goods at stores that charged high prices. As encouragement he produced "WIN" buttons, standing for "Whip Inflation Now." Presumably most Americans had the common sense to buy cheaper goods anyway. Ford did not start inflation and did not end it; inflation soared into the stratosphere under his successor and beyond.

Another kind of strife surfaced in Boston, where a federal judge mandated a busing plan to mix students from an all-black high school with those from an all-white school. White parents boycotted the school system and violence broke out, in which a white student was stabbed and white adults threatened black students. Civil rights were not a priority for Ford, who believed that busing should be used to end deliberate segregation, not segregation that occurred as consequence of neighborhood patterns. He would not mobilize the National Guard, despite the tumult. Finally, in January 1975 Boston school officials produced a program for large-scale desegregation, and the plan was implemented with minimal violence that fall.

Less controversial was Ford's single nomination to the high court, federal Appeals Court Judge John Paul Stevens, unanimously confirmed in the Senate late in 1975. Modest, moderate, and scholarly, he replaced the longest-serving Justice William O. Douglas, who resigned after a debilitating stroke. Stevens frequently joined the liberal wing of the court in his opinions.

Overlapping domestic politics and foreign policy, the CIA was purged under Ford, and three investigations of the agency ensued, one internally, one under Vice President Rockefeller's Commission, and one under a Senate committee. The inquiries discovered serious abuses, including plots to assassinate foreign leaders. The Senate and the House established oversight panels.

The Fall of Saigon

If domestic affairs produced headaches for Ford, foreign policy brought migraines. Détente dissolved. Kissinger's star descended because of information implicating the Nixon administration in the fall and perhaps murder

FOREIGN POLICY HEADACHES
Henry Kissinger in decline.
(Gerald Ford Presidential Library)

of Salvador Allende in Chile. Ford was shackled by the War Powers Act and straitjacketed by public opinion and congressional suspicion. More than at most times during the Cold War, foreign policy became passionately partisan. Though Ford was a peacemaker by temperament, the only significant peacemaking on his watch came inadvertently in Vietnam, by surrender.

Crisis had erupted on Cyprus during the Nixon administration. Fifty miles off the coast of Turkey, the island was claimed by the Turks on the basis of proximity. Yet its population was four-fifths Greek, and on that basis Greece claimed the island. In 1974 the Cypriot National Guard, under Greek army officers, seized the government, prompting a Turkish invasion. After peace talks broke down, Ford sided with Turkey. His position was unpopular with Congress, which forced Ford to cut off military aid to Turkey. The Turks countered by closing American military bases on their territory. In 1975 Turkish Cypriots created a separate state in the area they controlled, on the northeast part of the island, and expelled Greeks.

The African nation of Angola ignited a further setback for Ford. When Portugal announced it would free its colony and withdraw in 1975, three factions competed for leadership of the new nation. Covertly, Washington aided factions opposed to the leading group, which had backing from the

Soviet Union and Cuba. When the pro-Soviet group gained the upper hand, Congress ended CIA aid to the other factions—the first time Congress had canceled a secret operation. Meanwhile, the United States and the Soviet Union continued to funnel money and weapons into other areas of Africa, intensifying civil wars and turning the continent into a bloody battleground of the Cold War.

Ford's record in dealing with Moscow and Beijing was mixed. He lacked Nixon's finesse and friendships with Soviet and Chinese leaders. The president talked with Mao about extending diplomatic recognition to China in Beijing, yet the discussions failed because Ford was unwilling to break relations with Taiwan. Ford was more successful with Leonard Brezhnev, signing a Strategic Arms Limitation Treaty negotiated by Nixon during a summit at the Soviet port of Vladivostok. In 1975 the Cold War adversaries met again at Helsinki, Finland, for a Conference on Security and Cooperation in Europe. The leaders agreed to peacefully settle conflicts over human rights, ratify the permanence of the boundaries of post–World War II Europe, and refrain from interfering in the affairs of other nations. The agreement was unpopular among many Americans, who claimed it legitimated the grip of communism on Eastern Europe.

In Southeast Asia, 1975 brought communist regimes to power in Vietnam and Cambodia. Saigon fell to a conventional invasion from the North, and the last Americans were evacuated by helicopter. Vietnamization had failed; the hard-fought American defense of South Vietnam had done no more than delay its conquest. Cambodia fell under the dictatorship of the communist zealot Pol Pot, who fanatically murdered his own people in order to impose his brutal version of communism. In terms of percentage of the population killed, he exceeded Hitler and Stalin. Pol Pot became a pariah even among other communist nations. Flexing their muscles, the Khmer Rouge seized an American freighter, the *Mayaguez*, headed from Hong Kong to Thailand. Wanting to prove the United States could be tough and decisive, Ford approved a rescue operation to free the crew of thirty-nine. It succeeded—although forty-one Americans died. To complaints that more men were lost than saved, Ford said his choice was a matter of principle. The nation rallied around him, raising his approval rating 11 percent in polls.

Patriotism, in need of replenishment, received a boost from the nation's bicentennial celebration on July 4, 1976. Tall sailing ships paraded in New York harbor, as millions watched and fireworks exploded. Hallowed public documents were displayed and exhibits of America's historic symbols toured the nation. It was a small step in restoring national unity in the wake of trauma, a mission of Ford's administration.

The Election of 1976

With the 1976 presidential primaries approaching, Ford faced difficult opposition from former California Governor Ronald Reagan. Ford won the early primaries, nearly eliminating the Californian. Then Reagan won a string of victories in the South and West that enabled him to pull nearly even. Taking a risk, hoping to attract the votes of liberal delegates before the convention, Reagan picked Pennsylvania Senator Richard Schweiker as his running mate. Ford edged Reagan for the nomination and chose Kansas Senator Robert Dole to complete the ticket. Reagan, once dismissed as an extremist, had come closer to taking the nomination from a sitting president of his own party than any candidate in the Time of Paradox.

Now Ford faced another outsider, ex-Georgia Governor Jimmy Carter, whose hard work and meticulous planning won the Democratic nomination. A complex mixture of virtue and ambition, an intense campaigner, Carter exploited Watergate by promising never to lie to the American people; however, he was also naive, inexperienced, and stubborn. Carter appeared at one of the rare moments in American history when a candidate lacking in Washington savvy and name recognition could lead a major party. (Carter's running mate, Minnesota Senator Walter Mondale, however, was a seasoned lawmaker with strong ties to liberals and organized labor.) The first campaign to be partly funded with public money, one of the Watergate-spawned election reforms, deprived the Republicans of their customary advantage of outspending Democrats. Ford chipped away nearly all of Carter's advantage in the polls, but the Democrat won narrowly, getting 50.1 percent of the popular vote and 297 electoral votes to Ford's 47.9 percent and 240. Among factors that contributed to Carter's victory were Ford's pardon of Nixon, a stagnant economy, and Reagan's divisive challenge to Ford. The president tripped in a debate with Carter by denying that the Soviet Union dominated Eastern Europe. Mondale outclassed Dole, who appeared shrill, in the vice presidential debate. Further, some wanted to punish the GOP for Watergate and elect a fresh face, someone with few connections to Washington.

Ford might have lost the presidency, but he helped restore respect for the institution and helped exorcize the demons of Vietnam and Watergate. He did not provide direction or vision. Then again, the switch from Nixon was so abrupt that few expected Ford to articulate goals; it was enough that he could pull the country from its morass of corruption. His transparent decency made Americans feel more confident. Ford gave the country an antidote of midwestern simplicity and humility, much needed after years of secrecy, arrogance, and self-destructiveness. "If I'm remembered," Ford said, "it will probably be for healing the land."

Jimmy Carter

The new president appeared a paragon of virtue and intelligence. A graduate of the Naval Academy, James Earl Carter Jr., who preferred to be called "Jimmy," had been a naval officer, a nuclear engineer, and a wealthy peanut warehouse broker from the hamlet of Plains, Georgia. A Southern Baptist evangelical, he expressed spirituality through service to humanity. He served two terms in the Georgia Senate and one term as governor, one of a new breed of southern chief executives who were conservative on fiscal issues and progressive on racial and social problems. Carter was nonetheless virtually unknown when he launched his race for the Oval Office. Even his mother, Lillian, had doubts. When he told her he was running for president, Lillian asked, "President of what?"

Striving to bring the presidency closer to the people not long after Nixon made it seem aloof, Carter walked instead of riding in a fancy car in his inaugural parade, dressed informally in a cardigan sweater for his first White House speech, and enrolled his daughter, Amy, in public school. He carried his own luggage, and discouraged the playing of "Hail to the Chief." Sleeping only six hours nightly, he was at the Oval Office by 6:00 A.M., ready to tackle part of a workweek that had grown to eighty hours, including thirty hours of paperwork. Initially there were no clearly defined organizational lines in the White House; cabinet secretaries had direct access to Carter, and no chief of staff limited the flow. Acting as his own staff chief, he read memos voraciously. Carter intended to run an open administration, in contrast to Nixon's. Overly conscientious, the president made himself a victim of a "tyranny of the trivial." He pushed his self-improvement to his limits—jogging until he collapsed, listening to classical music, reading a chapter of the Bible in Spanish each night, and still finding time to teach Sunday school. Some found him a humorless workaholic, and none of his assistants could keep pace.

First lady Rosalynn Carter was diligent and persevering as well. She had been eighteen when the couple married and they had four children. Rosalynn kept the books for the Carter Warehouse, handled family finances, made business decisions, and campaigned effectively in 1976. The Carters had a close, intimate marriage. Neither a social butterfly nor a policy wonk, Rosalynn concentrated her activities in a few areas: promoting ratification of the ERA and advocating equal pay for equal work, improving education, and improving care for the aged and the mentally ill.

At the outset of his administration, Carter stuffed the hoppers of Congress with an overload of bills. His proposals included tax reform and welfare reform, which were deferred and watered-down. He submitted a bill to create a federal Energy Department, which passed; an office of consumer affairs, which failed; and economic measures which languished. Straining his relations with Congress, lawmakers, Carter threatened to veto pork-barrel dam and irrigation projects, only to restore half of them under pressure. Impatient with interest-group politics, he appealed to national interests and angered traditional Democratic constituencies. Uncomfortable with the ego-stroking expected on Capitol Hill, the Georgian abstained from false flattery. Carter was neither capable of leading Congress in a collegial fashion nor inspiring the masses as a speaker. What he did was call for sacrifice, especially in conserving energy, which was necessary, yet unpopular.

The Economy and Malaise

Carter's campaign promise to hold down spending and balance the budget collided headlong with a recession. At first he attempted to combat the recession with corporate tax cuts, job programs, and a $50 rebate to each taxpayer. In April 1978, with the economy improving and inflation rising, Carter abandoned the rebate before it came to a vote. Worse, the specter of stagflation shadowed Carter's presidency. Seldom have the economic furies aligned against an administration been so powerful: trade deficits, a falling dollar, and a plummeting stock market. Carter's other measures—budgetary austerity, high interest rates to rein in expansion, and wage and price controls—proved ineffectual and unpopular. Democrats complained about his lack of spending on cities, education, and health care. Carter vacillated. However, even an experienced president might not have pushed through Congress a program that could address economic troubles without angering important groups. Inflation rose from 6.5 percent in 1977 to 7.6 percent in 1978, 11.3 percent in 1979, and 13.5 percent in 1980, when unemployment was 7.0 percent.

Energy was the chief culprit behind inflation. Since the Arab oil embargo of 1973, American dependence on imported energy had increased from $8.4 billion to nearly $40 billion in 1977. Referring to the crisis as "the moral equivalent of war," Carter presented comprehensive energy legislation. To encourage conservation and exploration, he sought measures such as punitive taxes on gas-guzzling cars, rebates for purchases of fuel-efficient vehicles, and taxes on crude oil and gasoline. The price of domestically produced oil would be allowed to rise to world levels, with rebates helping poor families pay the higher costs. Also, production of coal and nuclear power would increase. The House passed the complex bill nearly intact, yet the Senate Finance Committee dismembered the measure. Nearly a year and a half after

★ BARBARA JORDAN: A VOICE THAT COMMANDS RESPECT ★

Barbara Jordan was the first African-American elected
official to become an American hero.

—MARY BETH ROGERS

UNITY AND DIVERSITY
Barbara Jordan shares
her vision for America.
(Library of Congress)

IN THE Era of Diversity, Barbara Jordan was confident that unity could emerge from differences. Born to a lower-middle-class family in Houston, she excelled in school, graduating with honors from Texas Southern University and participating on the college debate team that defeated Yale and Brown and tied Harvard. In 1959 Jordan received a law degree from Boston University, passed the Texas bar examination, and entered politics by campaigning for John F. Kennedy for president. She then ran for the Texas Senate in 1962 and 1964, losing both times, but she then won a seat after redistricting in 1966. She became the first African American to serve in the body since 1883, and the first African American woman ever.

Six years later, once again aided by redistricting, Jordan was elected to the U.S. House of Representatives, the first black woman in Congress from a southern state. She became one of the stars of the House Judiciary Committee while it considered impeachment charges against President Richard Nixon for offenses during the Watergate scandal. "Now she had a message that matched her voice," biographer Mary Beth Rogers wrote.

Jordan worked even better outside the limelight. With a talent for getting along with people that rivaled her talent for public speaking, she became a consummate political insider, trading favors and dealing with the political structure on equal terms. "It is dangerous to enter the struggle to establish a civil society as a purist if, as a purist, you are unwilling to take in others and be flexible," Jordan wrote.

The breakdown in the nation's political order paralleled a decline in Jordan's health. In 1974 she was diagnosed with multiple sclerosis, a degenerative muscle disease. Jordan remained silent about her illness even after she began using a cane, then a walker, then a wheelchair. Still, she delivered keynote addresses at the Democratic National Conventions in 1976 and 1992, played a key role in renewing the Voting Rights Act of 1965, and led President Bill Clinton's commission on immigration reform.

In December 1977, Jordan announced her retirement from the House at forty-three. Her body was ravaged, and she wanted to pursue new interests: teaching, sitting on corporate boards, and speaking about national harmony. The policies of the Reagan and first Bush administrations, as well as new manifestations of black nationalism, disturbed Jordan, who warned, "A sense of harmony can only survive if each of us remembers that we share a common destiny."

In 1994 Clinton awarded Jordan the Presidential Medal of Freedom, the nation's highest civilian honor. Two years later, suffering from multiple sclerosis, diabetes, failed kidneys, heart problems, and leukemia, Jordan succumbed to blood cancer. A paradox of visible strength in a diseased body, she demonstrated the verities of the lyrics of the black spiritual "We Shall Overcome." She said, "The greatest motivation . . . has to come from inside you."

Sources: Studies on Barbara Jordan include Mary Beth Rogers, *American Hero* (1998); Barbara Jordan and Shelby Hearon, *Barbara Jordan: A Self-Portrait* (1979); Ira B. Bryant, *Barbara Charline Jordan: From the Ghetto to the Capitol* (1977); and James Haskins, *Barbara Jordan* (1977).

it was unveiled, in September 1978, the Senate approved a weaker version that removed most punitive taxes. By deregulating the price of natural gas and establishing a single price structure for intrastate and interstate gas, however, Congress and the administration had made an important contribution to ensuring consistent gas supplies nationwide.

Carter's energy proposals alienated environmentalists. Increased use of coal would cause pollution, and opening wilderness areas in Alaska to oil exploration would harm wildlife. Alarms over nuclear power multiplied after an accident in March 1979 at Three Mile Island near Harrisburg, Pennsylvania. A pump failure at the plant led to a breakdown in the reactor cooling system, the precursor to a possible meltdown of the reactor core. Fortunately, conditions stabilized and disaster was averted.

Carter's energy proposals, which included taxes on high energy uses, threatened to aggravate inflation and to anger taxpayers, just as the national mood had turned against high taxes. In California a tax revolt led by Howard Jarvis succeeded in placing limits on property taxes. So Carter decided to place his ideas about the energy crisis before the nation in a major televised speech and retreated to Camp David to write it. The Camp David plans expanded into a domestic summit at which Carter consulted national leaders. In his speech, Carter addressed problems beyond energy, a national crisis of spirit and morale. The press labeled it the "malaise" speech, although Carter never used the word. In the finale of the talk, Carter did address energy. Instead of calling for more sacrifice and higher taxes, he switched gears and emphasized new sources for fuels. His program included decontrol of oil prices to encourage exploration, complemented by a wind-fall profits tax to prevent price gouging. The government would subsidize the development of synthetic fuels for coal and oil shale. Also, an Energy Mobilization Board would cut red tape. The windfall profits tax and a scaled-down version of the synthetic fuel program passed Congress. The Energy Board was defeated because of concerns it would violate environ-mental regulations and states' rights. Following the speech, Carter asked cabinet members to resign and accepted five resignations. Early polls showed the speech was a success, but the cabinet shuffle backfired.

Interest Groups

Carter encountered political difficulties by alienating traditional Democratic interest groups. Black organizations, for example, believed he was penuri-ous with appropriations for programs that helped their constituents. Race riots flared in Boston; Wichita, Kansas; and Tampa, Florida. Still, most African Americans supported Carter rather than his Republican opponents. Befitting the Era of Diversity, he appointed more blacks to high positions, including the cabinet, than any prior president. A black women, Patricia Harris, served successively in two cabinet positions. Two black men, Andrew Young, followed by Donald McHenry, served as ambassador to the United Nations.

One of the remedies to discrimination, affirmative action, faced a test from Allan Bakke, a white man twice denied admission to medical school at the University of California-Davis, which reserved slots for minority students whose grades and test scores might not qualify them. Bakke sued, claiming the school was guilty of reverse discrimination by rejecting him even though his grades and scores were better than those of the minority applicants accepted. He prevailed in lower courts, and the case went to the Supreme Court. In the most important civil rights ruling since *Brown v. Board of Education*, the justices held 5-4 in *Regents of the University of California v. Bakke* (1978) that Bakke should be admitted but that affirmative action was acceptable if it did not employ rigid quotas. Race could be considered among a variety of factors in deciding whether to admit a student, the court said.

Feminists criticized facets of the Carter administration, yet, in princi-ple, the president tried to advance feminist aims. Besides his appointment of women to government posts, Carter joined his wife in supporting the ERA and favored an extension of the seven-year ratification deadline for the amendment. However, women criticized Carter on budgetary grounds, calling for more funding of projects such as day care. Although Carter, ideologically, was liberal, his fiscal austerity and strong belief in a balanced budget generated criticism among economic liberals, yet he won important objectives, including in 1980, a $1.6 billion "Superfund" to clean up areas contaminated with toxic waste, and a bill that more than doubled the size of the national parks and wildlife refuges. The amount of land designated wilderness almost tripled.

By 1980, with the domestic travails and the Iran hostage crisis (explained below), Carter's approval rating in the polls had fallen to 21 percent, lower than Nixon's 24 percent in the depths of Watergate, and Truman's low of 23 percent. Liberal Massachusetts Senator Edward M. "Ted" Kennedy was favored over Carter in a race for the Democratic presidential nomination, surveys indicated. Carter's identification of a deep-seated national crisis was unpopular, if well-founded. Americans did indeed lack faith—in Congress, in the business community, in the intellectual establishment, in the commitment of allies, and in the restraint of adversaries.

Cold Warrior and Peacemaker

Carter had even less experience in international affairs than in national politics. He failed to set a hierarchy of priorities and pitted a hawk national security adviser, Zbigniew Brezezinski, against a dovish secretary of state, Cyrus Vance. The arrangement muddied the administration's direction and made it unpredictable. Eventually, Vance resigned over a hostage rescue attempt in Iran. At the United Nations, Andrew Young also resigned after meeting secretly with Arab leader Yasir Arafat, who headed the Palestine Liberation Organization (PLO), which the United States did not recognize.

Just as Gerald Ford sought to banish the ghost of Watergate by pardoning Richard Nixon, Carter attempted to bury the memory of Vietnam by pardoning draft evaders. Both served their purpose in the long run, yet hurt each president politically. Idealistically, Carter sought to base his foreign policy on respect for human rights, applied not only to communist countries but also to nations that were our allies. Carter was critical of apartheid in South Africa and repression in Rhodesia and South America. He also publicized the plight of dissidents in the Soviet Union.

The Soviet Union considered Carter's policy meddling, and relations deteriorated. Still, the two nations had a common interest in arms control and negotiated SALT II in 1979. However, the treaty stalled in the Senate. To ameliorate misgivings, Carter authorized the development of the MX missile. Based on the principle of a shell game, these nuclear rockets would be placed on railroad tracks and shuffled among numerous shelters to mislead the Soviets about their location. Still, Carter rejected plans for other new weapons. He canceled the B-1 bomber as too expensive and the neutron bomb, which killed people with radiation yet left buildings intact.

With the communist superpowers, it was the best of times with China and the worst of times with the Soviet Union. After waiting since 1949, Mainland China received diplomatic recognition on December 15, 1978, requiring the United States to break relations with Taiwan. Yet when the Soviet Union invaded Afghanistan a year later to implant a communist dictator, Carter's vision of communism was transformed. The Soviets really did intend world conquest, he concluded, and now he would play hardball. The United States smuggled military aid to the Islamic rebels fighting the Soviets. Carter withdrew the SALT II treaty from Senate consideration and ceased high-technology exports to the Soviet Union. The president also declared an embargo on grain sales and ordered a boycott of the 1980 Moscow Summer Olympic games. According to the Carter Doctrine he proclaimed, the United States committed to defend the territorial integrity of the Persian Gulf region. Carter also abandoned fiscal austerity to begin a major arms buildup that continued through the Reagan years. Congress approved his request for a 5 percent increase in military spending, the largest arms program in thirty years. Young men were required to register for a potential draft. Promised military spending cuts were abandoned. Carter took credit for military technology developed during his administration—the cruise missile and the Stealth bomber that was virtually invisible to radar. The new password was "peace through strength."

In the late 1970s, after détente fell from favor, a new consensus began forming that America must take a tougher stand against communism. Ford had banned the word "détente" from his foreign policy vocabulary because of its unpopularity. More minds were changed by the invasion of Afghanistan, Soviet and Cuban soldiers in Africa, the leftist rebellion in Nicaragua, and the brutal regimes in Cambodia, Laos, and Vietnam.

Carter's attempt to forge a new relationship with Panama encountered pressure from the resurgence of nationalism in Central America. Carter believed the canal was a vestige of colonialism and could not be defended without Panamanian cooperation. Conservatives, most prominently Ronald Reagan, considered the canal a symbol of American achievement that should not be yielded. Nonetheless, Carter prevailed narrowly in winning Senate approval for his treaty with Panama that would incrementally turn over sovereignty in the Canal Zone to the people of Panama by 2000. The United States has priority passage and the right to defend the canal.

Carter's command performance came in the thicket of Middle Eastern politics. Since Egypt had broken with the Soviet Union, a window of opportunity had opened for peace with Israel. The initiative came from the leaders of the two nations. Egyptian President Anwar Sadat accepted an invitation from Israeli Prime Minister Menachem Begin to visit Jerusalem in 1977, followed by a Begin visit to Cairo. Never before had Arab and Israeli leaders talked face to face. Once the euphoria wore off, negotiations bogged down, and Carter invited Sadat and Begin to Camp David, where he acted as mediator. For Carter, the Camp David Summit was a huge risk, as failure would have been humiliating. The conference did not fail, however, partly because of Carter's persistence. After thirteen days of tough, sometimes acrimonious talks, he announced on September 17, 1978, that two accords had been reached. Israel and Egypt agreed to negotiate a peace treaty within three months, and Sadat and Begin decided that issues of Palestinian autonomy would be determined in long-range negotiations. When the postaccord discussions slowed and the rivals could not conclude a treaty by the deadline, Carter again intervened. After taxing negotiations

HANDING OVER THE WHITE HOUSE
President Jimmy Carter shaking hands with Egyptian President Anwar Sadat
and Israeli Prime Minister Menachem Begin at the signing
of the Egyptian-Israeli Peace Treaty, 1979.
(Library of Congress)

climaxing in a Middle East trip by Carter, an Israeli-Egyptian pact was signed on March 26, 1979, in Washington. Despite uncertainties and an evident inability to follow through on promises, the Camp David Accords laid a more pragmatic basis for future talks. Trying to settle long-held differences in a region that had resisted solutions, Carter enjoyed his finest hour as president.

In the Western Hemisphere, Marxist rebels, the Sandinistas, pressured the dictator, Anastasio Somoza, a longtime U.S. ally, to abdicate. The United States attempted to force Somoza to implement reforms, and when he did not, withdrew economic and military aid. Somoza fled Nicaragua, and the Sandinistas seized power. Carter courted the new Marxist regime, only to become disillusioned when it accepted Cuban military aid and encouraged Marxist revolutions elsewhere in Latin America. Moreover, the Sandinistas were no more willing to hold free elections than Somoza had been.

An ocean away in Africa, Carter and Young were sympathetic to black aspirations for majority rule. Like Kennedy, they believed the key battle-grounds of the Cold War were in the Third World. The administration helped ensure the transition from white minority rule to rule by the black majority in Rhodesia, employing sanctions against the repressive regime. Unfortunately, the new government, under Robert Mugabe, proved auto-cratic. In the horn of Africa, Somalia claimed Ethiopian land, and war ensued. The Soviets backed the Marxist Ethiopian government and Cuba sent troops. Ethiopia triumphed but the region remained unstable. The Cuban soldiers remained, a distraction for Washington.

Humiliation in Tehran

But the worst came in Iran. Shah Reza Pahlavi, an American ally who came to power in a CIA-backed coup in 1953, led a repressive regime that Islamic fundamentalists sought to overthrow. Agitation led by the Islamic religious leader, Ayatollah Ruhollah Khomeini, living in exile in Paris, cli-maxed in a general strike in 1979. The shah fled the country. Khomeini returned, and a new constitution was drafted, based on Islamic law, mak-ing Khomeini ruler for life. Such perceived Western vices as alcohol, rock music, and informal attire were banned. The new government labeled the United States "the Great Satan."

Carter admitted the exiled shah, dying of cancer, to America for med-ical treatment on humanitarian grounds. Outraged, Iranian fundamentalists vowed vengeance against the United States and demanded it return the shah to Iran to face "revolutionary justice." Finding a way to avenge them-selves, Islamic students seized more than fifty hostages at the U.S. Embassy in Tehran. Chanting in the streets, flaunting the impotence of America to free the hostages, the crisis slowly eroded Carter's political status. Carter resisted military intervention for months, fearing it might result in the deaths of the hostages. In April 1980 he severed diplomatic relations with Iran and imposed a trade embargo. Finally, he dispatched a complicated rescue attempt that ended in tragedy. Mechanical problems on three helicopters forced cancellation of the mission at the desert rendezvous. In the withdrawal, a helicopter and a transport plane collided, killing eight servicemen. Carter's hopes for a second term lay smoldering in the Iranian desert. If the daring plan had succeeded it is possible that Carter would have been reelected in 1980. If so, the subsequent history of the 1980s might have been quite different.

The 1980 Election

Carter's chief opponent in the Democratic primaries was the youngest, and only remaining Kennedy son, Edward M., "Ted." Ted shared the liberalism of John and Robert; in fact, he had moved to the left of John. Yet he did not share their intellects or abilities. In a television interview, he was unable to define why he wanted to be president. Troubling memories were resurrected: he had left a young woman to drown on Chappaquiddick Island in 1969; earlier, he had cheated in college. Southern Baptist Carter quipped that if Kennedy ran in the primaries, he would "whip his ass" and he did, winning so many primaries it embarrassed Kennedy.

The Republicans nominated ex-California Governor Ronald Reagan after he brushed aside George Bush, a former House member, CIA director, ambassador to China and the United Nations and chairman of the Republican National Committee. Reagan picked Bush as his running mate. Reagan focused his campaign on a few big objectives: he promised to cut taxes, increase defense spending, and balance the budget. The tone of the campaign was upbeat and optimistic, conveyed by Reagan's mastery of public speaking and the mystique of television. A third candidate, John Anderson, a liberal Republican, offered voters a choice. The U.S. Representative from Illinois, however, threatened to deprive Carter of liberal votes.

Carter had Achilles' heels on both feet: on one the poor performance of the economy, on the other the humiliation of the hostages. Reagan, like Carter, was a Washington outsider, yet he made the election a referendum on Carter's failures. "Are you better off than you were four years ago?" he asked Americans. Clearly, they were not. Americans warmed to Reagan's folksy style and tough talk against communism. The Republican ticket overwhelmed the Democrats with 43.9 million votes (50.7 percent),

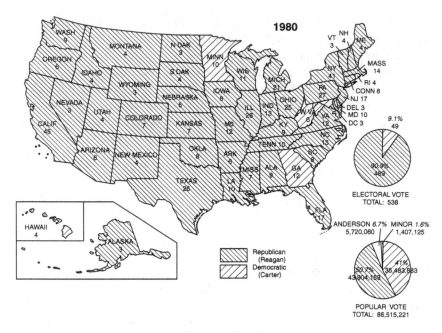

Election of 1980

to 35.5 million (41.0 percent) for Carter, and 5.7 million (8.3 percent) for Anderson. The totals were staggering in the Electoral College, Reagan receiving 489 votes, Carter 49, and Anderson none. Carter became the first president since Herbert Hoover to lose a bid for a second term. On January 20, 1981, just after Reagan completed his inaugural address, the Iranians released the hostages, having held them for 444 days.

In time Carter rebounded, answering the question, "Is there life after the presidency?" with "Absolutely!" He became a valuable elder statesman—the model of a successful former president, *Newsweek* magazine declared. He wrote major books, helped build homes for the needy through the Habitat for Humanity organization, and promoted social and political activism via the Carter Presidential Center in Atlanta. He advanced democracy by monitoring elections in Panama, Nicaragua, and Haiti, among a number of countries; traveled the globe speaking out for human rights, including Cuba, where in 2002 he became the highest-ranking American official to visit during Fidel Castro's regime; and won the 2002 Nobel Peace Prize for his efforts on behalf of international understanding.

Still, Carter's postpresidential activities did not redeem his performance in the White House; most historians rank Carter as a mediocre president. In both domestic and foreign affairs, his administration, like Ford's, was longer on good intentions and character than on accomplishments. Carter brought to government an engineer's intelligence, not a poet's vision, and the disturbing messages that sacrifice and restraint were necessary to meet national goals and that America did not have the resources to move simultaneously on all fronts at home and abroad. In fairness, it must be said that the country sought recovery and rest, not innovation and bold programs. Carter governed in the eye of the storm that still swirled around Watergate and Vietnam. Like Ford, he renewed respect in the presidency and gained grudging respect for his honesty, decency, adherence to principle, and peacemaking.

Carter knew his limitations. He enjoyed comparing himself to a man in a joke who was accused of getting drunk and setting his bed afire. "I admit that I was drunk," the man said. "But the bed was already on fire when I got in it."

CHAPTER TWENTY-ONE

The Reagan Rebellion

THE PARADOXES pile up for Ronald Reagan, a rebel of the right who vowed to change the status quo of conciliatory diplomacy, the welfare state, big government, and high taxes. He was, ironically, a greater advocate of change than any president since Franklin Roosevelt, and yet a conservative. In the Era of Diversity, purveyors of change came in all shades.

The liberalism that led to Barry Goldwater's burial under Lyndon Johnson's landslide in 1964 waned by 1968. Voters harkened to the conservative mantra that government had grown up too fast, was drunk on power, and needed to live within its means. With Richard Nixon, they elected a centrist who became the engine of his own destruction, followed by Gerald Ford, a right-center Republican, honest, but lacking charisma, and drowning in the muck of Watergate. Without Watergate there probably would not have been a Carter presidency, and perhaps not a Reagan one either.

Ronald Reagan

History is built on near misses. Republicans said they wanted a real conservative, like Goldwater, but without Goldwater's snap judgments. In Reagan they found one. Men who knew both said Dwight Eisenhower was calm on the surface, but Ronald Reagan was calm through and through. He took office wanting to accomplish a few big things and achieved most of them. He ended the country's drift and dispelled the fog of malaise that shrouded Jimmy Carter's America. Even people who were hurt by the former actor's economic or social policies sometimes voted for Reagan because he lifted their spirits. This paradox seems most perverse in the remark of a Milwaukee drug dealer who said he voted for the law-and-order Republican because Reagan made him feel good about himself.

Reagan, at sixty-nine, was the oldest man to assume the presidency. He delivered a polished performance when reading from a script, but faltered before extemporaneous questions. Once he nodded off at an audience with the pope. His spokesmen conceded that the president often forgot the names of those he worked with. He spoke to visitors to the Oval Office from note cards. Once, at a trade meeting with businessmen in the White House, he picked up the wrong note cards and delivered the wrong speech.

Reagan sympathized with poor people as individuals, yet he believed in personal responsibility. Ever since the New Deal, Americans had looked to the federal government to solve their problems. Once a New Dealer himself, Reagan warned that the federal government could not expand infinitely. Government was no longer the solution, he suggested; it was the problem. Reagan's detractors warned that the old man in the White House believed in a Hollywood version of reality where there were simple answers and a happy ending to every script. In the real world there were no simple answers. Reagan demurred: "There are simple answers," he said, "but there are not always easy ones."

Reagan remembered his hometown of Dixon, Illinois, as a place where neighbors and families cared for each other from a sense of Christian charity. "A Samaritan crossed over the road and helped the beaten pilgrim himself," he said. "He did not report the case to the nearest welfare agency." A lower middle-class boy known as "Dutch," Reagan was a churchgoer, a football star, and a lifeguard who saved seventy-seven people on the Rock River in seven summers. He starred in school and church plays and was class president, maintaining a low "B" average. His mother was a teetotaler and amateur playwright; his father was an alcoholic and a salesman.

Reagan continued to star in athletics and extracurricular activities at minuscule Eureka College, where he also earned a low "B" average. He was a mediocre football player but a fine swimmer and a star of the stage. He was also elected student body president. Reagan made the best of his assets: a pleasant, nonaggressive personality, a fit, athlete's body and handsome demeanor, a retentive memory, an eloquent voice, and a sense of humor. Many things came easy to him, but he rarely gave up when they did not.

Graduating in 1932, when the nation's cupboard was bare of jobs, Reagan visited Chicago radio stations, seeking work as an announcer. Advised to search in smaller towns, he was hired at WOC in Davenport, Iowa, to broadcast football games. In 1933 the station merged with the larger WHO in Des Moines, and Reagan gained fame as a sportscaster. In 1937, when Reagan covered the Chicago Cubs' training camp near Los Angeles, he took a screen test and signed a seven-year contract with Warner

Brothers. As an actor he made fifty-three films, including some hits, but never reached the pinnacle of the profession. *Knute Rockne: All American* (1940) and *Santa Fe Trail* (1940) established him as a promising star, and *King's Row* (1941) might have made him a top talent had not home front military service in World War II interrupted his career. Meanwhile, he met actress Jane Wyman on a film set, married her in 1940, and soon had two children. But the marriage and the movie career crashed about the same time: Wyman filed for divorce in 1948, when the postwar glut of younger talent made roles scarce for Reagan. Taking a different type of lead role, president of the Screen Actors Guild, he concluded that communists aspired to take over Hollywood, part of his conversion from liberal Democrat to conservative Republican. His ideological script was completed in 1952 when he wed another actress, Nancy Davis, who was from a solid GOP family.

Two years later, Reagan became host of the television's General *Electric Theater*, giving speeches for the company that extolled big business and small government. The talks made him a celebrity in the Republican Party. After the program left the air, Reagan became host of *Death Valley Days* in 1964 and devoted increasing time to politics. Effective speeches for Goldwater in 1964 led to an invitation from wealthy Californians to run for governor in 1966. Edmond G. "Pat" Brown, Reagan's Democrat opponent, attempted to label him an extremist yet could not make it stick because of Reagan's placid demeanor. Reagan defeated Brown, benefiting from a backlash against student antiwar demonstrators on California campuses. Turning the governor's responsibilities into a nine-to-five job, he reluctantly raised taxes. Despite this, the state deficit increased. After a lackluster second term, Reagan became a speaker, syndicated columnist, and radio commentator. He lost the Republican nomination for the second time in 1976, but in 1980 won the nomination and the election.

The Reagan Enigma

A politician, actor, and public speaker for much of his life, Reagan had many acquaintances, yet few close friends. The Republican Party championed family values, yet the chief executive's own family was dysfunctional. Reagan espoused religion yet rarely attended church and did not instill spiritual values in his children. Nearly all of Reagan's children, at one time or another, were estranged from their parents. Some felt the bond between the president and Nancy was so great it excluded them. Son Michael said his father "just finds it difficult to hug his own children." Nancy Reagan was criticized for extravagant spending on clothes, and, after an assassination attempt on her husband, for using an astrologer to help plan his trips. Registering the lowest public approval ratings of any modern first lady, she began to focus on her campaign against illegal drugs and her popularity improved. Yet, she influenced her husband, particularly in the hiring and firing of staff members and planning of the White House schedule. In that sense she was a powerful first lady. Nancy, for example, also persuaded her husband to take a softer line in the Cold War and use less threatening language.

In delegation of detail, Reagan was the opposite of Carter. He had little intellectual curiosity; rather, he waited for his staff to bring things to him. Despite his inclination to follow his staff's script, he did not inevitably do so. Reagan was an old-fashioned, people-oriented president who disliked cold, impersonal solutions to problems, and relied on intuition. The president was confused by computers and wrote everything longhand.

For his political confidants, Reagan relied mainly on Californians who were personal friends. They were not specialists but generalists who understood Reagan. They had common aims and were loyal. The first term was

MORNING IN AMERICA
Ronald Reagan minutes before being shot, 1981.
(Ronald Reagan Presidential Library)

managed by a triumvirate of Chief of Staff James A. Baker III, a friend of
Vice President George Bush; Edwin Meese III, who handled policy issues;
and Michael K. Deaver, who was close to Nancy Reagan. This trio controlled access to the president. Reagan's cabinet had only a few strong
members, such as Donald T. Regan, who served as treasury secretary and
later as White House chief of staff; Caspar Weinberger; and George Shultz,
defense secretary and secretary of state, in turn.

The troika of Baker, Meese, and Deaver was more important than the
cabinet because they understood Reagan and his priorities. Baker, a skilled
operative, played a key role in shepherding legislation through Congress.
He helped persuade Reagan at the outset of the administration to focus on
cutting domestic spending and upgrading the military rather than on divisive social issues

The Battleground of the Budget

The heart of Reagan's domestic program pulsated to the economy. He
planned to cut taxes 25 percent over 33 months, pare overall expenses, but
boost defense spending. Reagan was a convert to "supply-side" economics,
the theory that the existence of consumer goods would create customers for
the products, in contrast to the conventional idea that demand generated
supply. With lower taxes and fewer regulations, businesses would grow, create more products, and stimulate consumer demand for them. In turn, federal revenue from taxes would rise, even though tax rates were reduced.
Most economists and political theorists were skeptical of what some labeled
"Reaganomics." If the budget cuts were not deep enough, the loss of revenue from the tax cuts would lead to lopsided unbalanced budgets.
Politically, it was easier to cut taxes than to prune programs. Lawmakers
and interest groups rushed to defend their constituencies' funding.

Reagan made the package of tax and spending cuts his highest priority
in his program to shrink government, devoting virtually all his energies to
that objective. Then, as he was leaving a Washington hotel on March 30,
1981, he was wounded in an assassination attempt by a mentally disturbed
gunman, John Hinckley. A bullet lodged less than three inches from the
president's heart. Reagan's coolness and courage reaped respect. Wheeled
into an operating room, near death, he told his doctors, "I hope you're all
Republicans." The public rallied around Reagan and his programs.
Congress, too, came around, thanks to "boll weevil" Democrats, southern
conservatives who favored lighter taxes and fewer government programs. In
August, Reagan signed into law measures slashing $40 million from the
budget and cutting personal income taxes 25 percent over three years.

The economy slid into recession, largely because the Federal Reserve Board raised interest rates high to cool inflation. By 1983 the board's policy and lower world oil prices pushed inflation down to 4 percent. The recession, however, was worse than those in the 1970s. Factories operated below capacity, unemployment soared, and the underprivileged suffered because their income declined and because spending cuts reduced social programs. In January 1983 some twenty thousand people lined up in Milwaukee to apply for two hundred jobs at an auto frame factory. American products became more expensive overseas because the steep interest rates made the dollar more valuable than foreign currency. United States exports fell and imports increased, creating huge trade deficits. The slump in exports pinched farmers who depended on selling grain abroad, as well as businesses such as automakers, steel mills, and heavy equipment manufacturers in the Northeast and Midwest "Rustbelt."

Meanwhile, the highest budget deficits in history loomed. A harbinger of trouble would arise in the Social Security system as baby boomers retired and the number of workers paying into the system decreased. To address deficits, Reagan accepted a 1982 tax increase that restored one-third of the reductions he had sponsored the previous year. He also approved changes in Social Security that boosted payroll taxes, raised the retirement age to sixty-seven by 2027, and taxed benefits of high-income recipients. Finally, he scaled back the cuts in social spending and the increases in defense funding. Still the administration ultimately increased annual military spending by 7 percent above the 5 percent yearly boosts called for in Carter's last budget. Over Reagan's eight-year presidency, military spending rose 70 percent, and $1.5 trillion was spent by the Pentagon.

Congress tried to solve budget problems in 1985, enacting the Gramm-Rudman-Hollings Act to downscale the budget until it was balanced in 1991. Under the law, if federal forecasts predicted the budget would not meet its targets, they would trigger across-the-board cuts unless Congress acted to reduce the budget or raise taxes. In 1986 another tax reform act, which Ronald Reagan initiated, recouped more of the revenue the government lost as a result of the 1981 tax cuts. The last major domestic initiative of Reagan's second term, the law cut some rates and brackets and closed loopholes.

Despite deep deficits, 80 percent of Americans thought they were better off because of the measures enacted during Reagan's first term. In 1983, with inflation curbed, the Federal Reserve Board reduced interest rates and the money supply. By April, the economy began to recover and went on to record the longest period of sustained economic growth in modern twentieth-century America up to that time. People went on a buying binge. During the Reagan years, they purchased 105 million color television sets, 88 million cars and light trucks, 63 million videocassette recorders, 62 million microwave ovens, 57 million washers and dryers, 31 million cordless phones, and 30 million telephone answering machines. A bull market began in stocks, with the Dow Jones Industrial Average peaking at 2,722 in August 1987. Less than two months later, in October, the market plummeted 508 points, the largest one-day drop ever, yet because the economy was basically sound, the crash was not followed by a depression or even a recession.

Another component of Reagan's economic policy, deregulation, led to corporate destabilization. The program lifted regulations on business, relying on competition rather than rules. Billion-dollar business mergers and takeovers resulted. Sometimes floating high-risk, high-yield "junk bonds" to finance their ventures, a capitalist or a company would pay stockholders above market prices for their shares in a firm. If the takeover failed, it was costly to the company that prevented it. If the takeover was successful, the new owners were burdened by the huge debt they had just incurred. Often they found it necessary to gut their new companies by selling operations and cutting jobs to pay the debt.

Wall Street greed expanded on a staggering scale, as financiers began buying stock in companies that were takeover candidates. With corporate "raiders" and others trying to purchase control of the firms, the stock grew volatile, and many shareholders were glad to sell to avoid risk. Among this new breed of speculator, Ivan Boesky used his contacts to select companies that were susceptible to takeovers before that vulnerability became public information. He went to prison and paid the Securities and Exchange Commission $100 million, half as a fine for his insider trading and half as reimbursement of his illicit profits. He still had a fortune of $100 million when he left prison. To reduce the charges against him, Boesky told the SEC about his accomplices, including Michael Milken, a junk-bond specialist. Milken paid the commission $600 million in fines and served a prison term for securities fraud. Even after paying the fines, he was left with $1 billion.

The administration also relaxed restrictions on savings and loan associations, known as "thrifts." The government, which insured their deposits, allowed them to invest more aggressively. The tactic backfired when reckless investments and criminal activities forced many of the savings and loans into bankruptcy. By the time Reagan's successor, Bush, took action in 1989, the bankruptcy bailouts were costing the federal government $35 million a day. By 1996 the total cost had risen to $480.9 billion and was forecast to mount to seven times that amount before it was paid off, more than the cost of World War II.

The administration had tense relations with organized labor, especially after Reagan fired striking air traffic controllers in 1981. Subject to long hours and severe stress, the controllers felt they deserved better pay. But legally, they could not strike. When they walked out anyway, Reagan dismissed those who did not come back to work within forty-eight hours. Military controllers and returning employees directed landings and departures until new workers were hired. There were no major accidents, although controllers' conditions remained difficult. Also, Reagan's commitment to free trade angered some unions, who feared loss of jobs. Reagan signed a free trade agreement with Canada and worked for one with Mexico, to be concluded by his successors.

Reagan molded the federal judiciary to his conservative ideology, appointing more than four hundred judges, almost half the federal bench. The tactic of appointing young jurists assured they would still be shaping law long after his tenure expired. On the Supreme Court, some of his appointments were landmarks. His first Supreme Court appointee, in 1981, was federal Appeals Judge Sandra Day O'Connor, the first woman justice. When Chief Justice Warren Burger retired in 1986, Reagan elevated Associate Justice William Rehnquist, the most conservative justice. To replace him, the president appointed Antonin Scalia, another staunch conservative. Then Justice Lewis Powell retired in 1987, leaving Reagan the opportunity to nominate Robert Bork. Bork was controversial because of his conservative views expressed in a long paper trail of opinions and articles. Civil rights organizations and feminists helped liberal Senate Democrats defeat the nomination. Conservatives complained that Bork was rejected solely for his views, not for any blemish on his record. Moreover, Bork had a keen legal mind. In 1988 the Senate confirmed Reagan's choice of Anthony Kennedy, a more moderate conservative. Rehnquist and his colleagues shifted the Court to the right.

African Americans received little and contributed little to Reagan's political agenda. They voted for him in low percentages in 1980 and even lower in 1984. Not personally prejudiced, Reagan had little experience with blacks and was insensitive to their concerns. He never supported the use of federal power to advance civil rights, had opposed the 1965 Voting Rights Act, and inherited some of George Wallace's followers. His administration opposed affirmative action and busing to desegregate schools, and cut funds for legal services for the poor and minorities.

Reagan was unpopular among feminists because he opposed abortion and the ERA, because their concerns were not a priority, and because there were no feminist women in Reagan's inner circle. Women who dealt with

Reagan personally did not find him sexist, however, and he was popular with homemakers.

"Morning in America"

In the 1984 campaign, several Democrats sought their party's nomination to oppose Reagan, including former Vice President Walter Mondale and the Reverend Jesse Jackson, a civil rights activist. Mondale won and selected New York Representative Geraldine Ferraro as his running mate, the first woman nominated for vice president by a major party. Rejecting political expediency, Mondale said he would raise taxes. Reagan would raise them too, Mondale said, but would not admit it until after the election. Republicans depicted Mondale as a tax-and-spend liberal. Reagan ran a carefully scripted campaign that emphasized patriotic themes. The pall of the Carter years had receded, Reagan proclaimed, and it was "morning in America." Once more, one could be proud to be an American, enjoying prosperity and the protection of a strong military.

Because Reagan would be in his late seventies by the time he completed another term, his age and health became issues. In his second debate with Mondale, Reagan dismissed the question of his age with humor, saying: "I will not make age an issue of this campaign. I am not going to exploit, for political purposes, my opponent's youth and inexperience." Voters buried Mondale's aspirations. Reagan carried every state but his foe's home of Minnesota and the District of Columbia, polling 59 percent of the popular vote (54.4 million) and 525 electoral votes to 41 percent (37.5 million) and 13 for the Democrat. No gender gap materialized, for 56 percent of women voted for Reagan. He won just 9 percent of the African American vote and lost the Jewish vote, but took 63 percent of the white vote and 71 percent of the white Protestant vote. Polls showed people were more positive about Reagan than were negative about Mondale. The former vice president was frustrated by the outcome. "I tried to get specific and Reagan patted dogs," he complained.

In domestic policy, Reagan's second term was more difficult than his first. His major domestic goals had been achieved early. Most important, the triumvirate that planned his domestic agenda broke up. James Baker changed places with Donald Regan at Treasury, with Regan becoming chief of staff. Meese became attorney general, and Deaver became a political consultant. Regan, an egotistic, serious, austere personality, decided that the president should deemphasize public relations and focus more on substance. This was not playing to Reagan's strengths. Regan tried to push the president too fast. When Regan and his assistants spent weeks on a policy agenda for the second term, the president said simply, "OK" and did not read it. To the old actor, policy was not much different from "show business." It had worked during his first term when he was surrounded by nurturing aides. To make Reagan's administration succeed, one must understand him. For all his drive and wealth of administrative experience, Donald Regan did not know the president.

After the 1984 election, Reagan undertook few new initiatives except for tax reform and immigration reform. The Immigration Reform and Control Act of 1986 made it more difficult for illegal immigrants to enter America and obtain employment, yet offered an amnesty to those who had lived in America since January 1, 1982.

America's space program continued to soar, and, in one tragic accident, to crash. The Apollo program continued, yet near disaster struck *Apollo 13* in 1970, and the astronauts aborted their Moon mission and returned to Earth. In the 1980s, the reusable space shuttle became the major vehicle for manned space exploration. On January 28, 1986, the near tragedy of *Apollo 13* was eclipsed by the horror of the fourth space shuttle, *Challenger*, which exploded in the Florida sky seconds after liftoff. All seven astronauts were killed, and the shuttle program was grounded for thirty-two months.

On the ground, a new scourge surfaced, erecting roadblocks on the avenue to the sexual revolution. Acquired immune deficiency syndrome (AIDS), caused by a virus transmitted through unprotected sex with an infected person, the sharing of needles for drug injections, and transfusions of tainted blood, gave rise to a deadly pandemic. The human immunodeficiency virus destroyed the immune systems of patients, leaving them vulnerable to diseases. First diagnosed in 1981, the disease initially struck homosexuals and bisexuals who had unsafe sex, then moved into the population at large; 97,000 cases were reported by 1989, when 46,000 had died of AIDS. Medical experts, among them Reagan's surgeon general, C. Everett Koop, warned people to take precautions against AIDS, including the use of condoms during intercourse. New drugs were discovered to extend the lives of patients, but in the twenty-first century the stubborn virus defied efforts to find a cure, and emphasis continued on prevention.

Reagan and the "Evil Empire"

Whereas Nixon had ushered in détente and Carter focused on human rights, Reagan's initial foreign policies focused on combating communism. His objective was not continued stalemate or mere continuation of a fragile peace. His objective was to win the Cold War.

The scenario had surprises. The old warrior became a peacemaker, yet on his watch communism was set up for the kill. Few people, not even Reagan, foresaw the result, yet history proved again that surprise is its essence.

Early in the administration, prominent cabinet members such as Secretary of State Alexander Haig and Secretary of Defense Caspar Weinberger were bullish on America, skeptical of compromise with the Soviets. Reagan termed the Soviet bloc an "evil empire" destined for the "ash heap of history." His challenge invited ridicule, yet he was closer to the truth than anyone realized. Even Nancy Reagan cautioned her husband to temper his language.

Still, as Reagan entered the presidency, never had the Cold War seemed more wintry. As a series of Soviet leaders died in office, Reagan's first term lapsed without a single summit. Reagan complained that he could not meet Soviet leaders because they kept dying on him. Secretary Shultz, chastened for being a part of the first administration to go four years without a Soviet summit, retorted that he was not going to schedule a meeting merely to keep the record intact.

If Reagan was right about communism's destiny, he was wrong about the path it would travel to get there and about his role in the process. Yet he was determined to fight communism with all the tools available—military might, economic pressure, espionage, denial of technology, and withholding of credit and oil revenue, to squeeze the beleaguered economy. Whereas previous presidents had viewed trade as an avenue to understanding, Reagan viewed economic warfare as a weapon to add steam to the pressure cooker that was the Soviet economy. Meanwhile, the United States was armed to the teeth and extended aid to all nations resisting communism. Reagan rammed the MX missile program through Congress in 1987, and placed intermediate-range nuclear weapons in Europe to equal Soviet missiles there. The deployment inflamed the nuclear freeze movement in Europe and America.

As early as 1983 Reagan had added an untested new technology to the mix, proposing an intricate network of laser beams and missiles to destroy incoming missiles. Many American experts considered the Strategic Defense Initiative (SDI), nicknamed "Star Wars" after the popular science fiction movies, impractical. Star Wars was a dual threat to the Soviets: they could not match the technology and they could not afford the research. The new Soviet leader who came to power in 1985, Mikhail Gorbachev, realized that compromise and internal reform were essential for the communist system to survive, and he desired a more amicable relationship with the West. Gorbachev was ready to deal; Reagan, already holding the trump cards, was ready to play. In time, these two men bonded, and Reagan forged a closer relationship with Gorbachev than any president in history had established with a foreign foe.

Gorbachev embarked on policies of *perestroika*, or economic restructuring, and *glasnost*, or openness, and relaxed many of the restrictions on dissent in Soviet society. Fearful that the Cold War could consume his plans to build a viable consumer economy, he tried to reduce expenditures by relaxing tensions with the West at summits in Geneva, Reykjavik in Iceland, Washington, and Moscow. In 1986 at Reykjavik, the leaders struck the most sweeping arms agreement in history: to eliminate all nuclear weapons in ten years. But the accord never gelled because Gorbachev insisted that Reagan give up Star Wars. The Soviets took Reagan's missile defense plan seriously. Gorbachev believed Moscow would bankrupt itself trying to compete with SDI technology. For that reason, Reagan refused to give it up.

In 1987 Reagan traveled to Europe and, in a visit to West Berlin, stood at the Brandenburg Gate of the Berlin Wall, symbolic of the division of free

TAKING HIS MESSAGE TO THE HEART OF EUROPE
Ronald Reagan in Berlin, 1987.
(Ronald Reagan Presidential Library)

and captive worlds. "Mr. Gorbachev, open this gate! Mr. Gorbachev, tear down this wall!" Reagan said. Gorbachev did not then order the wall torn down, yet at a Washington summit later that year, the Soviets and the Americans signed the INF Treaty eliminating a whole class of weapons, intermediate-range nuclear weapons, and providing for on-site inspections to ensure compliance. Whereas previous treaties had limited growth of nuclear weapons, INF was the first to destroy weapons. Gorbachev and Reagan met once more, in 1988 in Moscow, cementing their relationship.

Meanwhile, Gorbachev was easing the Soviet grip on Europe. He cut the Soviet army by five hundred thousand soldiers and withdrew fifty thousand troops and five thousand tanks from Eastern Europe. Then he evacuated the last Soviet troops from Afghanistan, reduced aid to the Sandinistas, and asked Castro to remove Cuban troops from Africa. Gorbachev unleashed forces of liberation that he could not control, placing the Soviet Union on the brink of collapse. It needed only a nudge from nationalists in its republics, whom he would not crush with force. The denouement occurred under Bush, but Reagan was party to one of the greatest upheavals in world history. Historians differ over whether Reagan stage-managed the beginning of the end of the Soviet Union or whether he was mainly in the right place at the right time. They differ over whether he and Gorbachev rode the tides of history, beckoned them, or did a little of both. Regardless, they presided over momentous times and decreased the danger of nuclear war.

Other Foreign Challenges

Peace on a global scale, paradoxically, was easier to achieve than harmony in the Middle-East. Reagan, like his predecessors, found the region a place of problems with no solutions and crushed hopes. The Palestinians wanted a homeland, yet the Israelis considered that a threat to their security. Instead, Israeli leaders encouraged Jews to settle in the occupied territories to sustain their claim. Then in June 1982, the Israelis invaded Lebanon, a launching pad for terrorist raids by Yasir Arafat's Palestine Liberation Organization (PLO). The Palestinians evacuated Lebanon, leaving in their wake a civil war that pitted Christians against Muslims. Reagan sent two thousand Marines to Lebanon as part of an international peacekeeping force to supervise the PLO withdrawal, angering the Muslim militias. Violence struck the Americans on October 22, 1983, when a young Muslim detonated a truck-bomb that killed 239 Americans. Reagan tried to maintain the Lebanese mission, but in February 1984 the Lebanese government fell and the remaining Marines were withdrawn.

Jerusalem protested when Reagan sold tanks, missiles, and planes with sophisticated radar technology to Saudi Arabia, an American ally, yet an Israeli adversary. Washington opposed the Israeli bombing of Iraq's nuclear reactor in June 1981, yet benefited from the destruction later in its two wars against Iraq; otherwise, Iraq might have possessed nuclear weapons. Despite disagreements, Israel remained America's closest ally in the turbulent Middle East and the only democracy there. The administration promised not to have contact with Arafat and the PLO until it renounced terrorism and recognized Israel's right to exist. Not until Arafat satisfied the United States on these counts did Reagan's diplomats begin talking seriously to the Palestinians about a Middle-East accord. More intransigent, Libya became a target of a rare use of force by Reagan's administration. After U.S. naval maneuvers in the Gulf of Sidra, an area claimed by Dictator Muammar Qaddafi, Libyan jets harassed American forces, and U.S. planes shot down two of them. Washington later blamed Tripoli for the bombing of a German nightclub that claimed the life of an American serviceman. In retaliation, U.S. jets bombed Libyan military sites and Qaddafi's residence, killing one of his daughters.

Elsewhere, the administration had an easier time working its will. In 1982 the United States supported Britain against Argentina in the Falkland Islands War. Fighting broke out after Buenos Aires, backed by the Soviet Union and the Organization of American States, seized the islands off the South American coast, owned by Britain. A British naval expedition retook the islands, and Reagan won the gratitude of British Prime Minister Margaret Thatcher, his closest ally and ideological soul mate.

In 1983, shortly after the deaths of the Marines in Lebanon, the United States invaded the tiny Caribbean island of Grenada. Washington said it acted to rescue eight hundred American medical students. Also, it believed Soviet reconnaissance planes might use an airport under construction. In fact, the administration overthrew the Marxist government and installed leaders supportive of the United States. A force of American soldiers and small contingents from six Caribbean nations deposed the dictator, General Hudson Austin. The invasion was condemned internationally yet most Americans supported it.

Three years later, Washington helped oust two other dictators, Jean-Claude Duvalier of Haiti and Ferdinand Marcos of the Philippines. Duvalier had succeeded his father as ruler of his impoverished island and had continued the elder Duvalier's oppressive policies. Finally demonstrators drove him from power, after the United States warned Duvalier not to use force against them. Americans provided a plane to fly him to exile in France. Marcos, a longtime American ally, fell due to a declining economy and the

1983 murder of a popular opposition leader, which prompted a Marxist revolution. He surprised detractors by allowing elections in 1986 and won a rigged vote over Corazon Aquino, widow of the slain opposition leader. Popular demonstrations against Marcos followed, and part of the Philippine army defected to Aquino. Reagan withdrew his backing of Marcos and arranged for him to leave the country.

Central America drew much of Reagan's attention, and the United States became involved in two wars by proxy. It grew embroiled in battling Marxism, in one case supporting a government against guerrillas and in another case backing rebels against rulers. In El Salvador, leftists tried to overthrow the government, countered by death squads that assassinated leftists. Carter suspended aid to the Salvadoran government because of human rights violations, but Reagan restored it and sent CIA advisers. A reformer, Jose Napolean Duarte, elected president in 1984, implemented land reform, stopped the death squad killings, and opened negotiations with the rebels. Elections returned the right to power in 1988 after Duarte died. The war escalated, continuing after Reagan left the White House. In neighboring Nicaragua, the Sandinistas, who received aid from the Soviet Union and Cuba, tried to export revolution and vanquish the opposition Contras. Congress outlawed attempts to support the Contras or to overthrow the Sandinistas, yet Reagan continued aid.

The Iran-Contra Affair

Considering the Contras liberators, Reagan urged National Security Adviser Robert McFarlane to do whatever was needed to help them "keep body and soul together." A Marine officer on the National Security Council (NSC) staff, Lieutenant Colonel Oliver North, helped McFarlane secretly raise millions from third parties. North directed a covert operation that funneled supplies and information to the Contras. The actions defied the Reagan-approved Boland Amendments, which prohibited the government from furnishing support to the Contras. After journalists and members of Congress heard of the covert operations, McFarlane lied to House investigators in 1986, denying the NSC was involved.

Meanwhile, members of the Reagan administration hoped to establish links with Iranian moderates, selling them weapons and spare parts to use in their war against Iraq. In exchange, the Iranians were supposed to use their influence to free American hostages held by Islamic militants in Lebanon. The Iranians hoodwinked the Americans, led by North, stockpiling weapons but releasing few hostages. However, North also hoodwinked the Iranians by overcharging them for the arms he sold and giving the profits to the Nicaraguan

Contras. The transactions were illegal on both ends: law forbade trade with terrorist nations and Congress had cut off aid to the Contras. The subterfuge was exposed when the Sandinistas shot down a plane carrying weapons to Nicaragua in October 1986. The pilot, Eugene Hasenfus, confessed.

The United States denied knowing of Hasenfus's mission, but North, anticipating that Hasenfus would expose the operation, began to shred documents. Reagan admitted to the sales and to the aims of winning the freedom of American hostages and of courting Iranian moderates. Iranian-supported terrorism persisted despite the arms transfers, as groups took additional American hostages.

It was left to Attorney General Edwin Meese to scrutinize the affair and report to Reagan. North admitted to Meese that arms sales profits were diverted to finance the Contras, and when Meese informed the president of the discovery, Reagan seemed shocked. Someone in the administration had to take the blame, so North was removed from the NSC. Admiral John Poindexter, who replaced McFarlane as national security adviser—and who would reveal that he hid the fund diversion from Reagan to shield the president—resigned. Finally, a shaken Reagan and Meese revealed details about the Iran-Contra affair to the public and announced the creation of a board under former Texas Republican Senator John Tower to investigate. Reagan appeared before the country in a televised speech in March 1987, saying he accepted responsibility for what happened in his administration.

A House-Senate committee held televised hearings in the summer of 1987, in which North proclaimed that his actions, however illegal, were in the national interest, and appeared for a time as a heroic figure. The lawmakers did not conclude that Reagan personally knew of wrongdoing, yet assailed the administration for the flouting of the law and said that if Reagan did not know what his aides were doing, "he should have." Focusing on the illegalities, Lawrence Walsh, a court-appointed special prosecutor, indicted a number of Iran-Contra figures, including North and Poindexter, who were convicted. It took Walsh until 1994, five years after Reagan left office, to issue a final report in which he said that Reagan, although his actions fell short of criminal conduct, "created the conditions which made possible the crimes committed by others." Appeals courts overturned North's and Poindexter's convictions on technical grounds, though, and lesser figures received pardons from President George Bush.

Reagan's Legacy

Reagan was able to select his successor, Bush, who won the Republican nomination over a field that featured Kansas Senator Robert Dole, New

York Representative Jack Kemp, and televangelist Pat Robertson. Bush's running mate was the relatively obscure Indiana Senator Dan Quayle, who drew questions because he had used family connections to join the National Guard and avoid combat in the Vietnam War and because of doubts over his intelligence and experience. On the Democratic side, leading party members stayed out of the race, but there were plenty of contenders, among them Colorado Senator Gary Hart, who was the front-runner until it was learned that he apparently had extramarital affairs. The Reverend Jesse Jackson made the biggest impact of any African American candidate in American history. Massachusetts Governor Michael Dukakis won the nomination, largely because he revived his state's economy. He picked Texas Senator Lloyd Bentsen for the second place on the ticket.

WORKING FOR
A BETTER
FUTURE
Reagan and Soviet
leader Mikhail
Gorbachev in
Moscow, 1988.
(Ronald Reagan
Presidential
Library)

Dukakis emerged from the Democratic convention with a substantial lead in the polls over Bush, yet lacked the passion to inspire voters. Bush exploited the public's fear of crime by running advertisements blaming Dukakis for the release of murderer and rapist Willie Horton, who committed more crimes while out of prison. The ads were labeled racist because Horton was black. Bush also boasted of his experience in foreign policy and cited the prosperity under Reagan. He won comfortably, with 48.8 million popular votes and 426 electoral votes to 41.8 million and 111 for Dukakis. The election was, in effect, another referendum on Reagan, a reaffirmation that he was one of the most popular presidents of the post–World War II era, although Democrats retained control of Congress.

If Reagan was not a great president, neither was he a mediocre one. He defined the 1980s as no president had defined a decade since Franklin Roosevelt in the 1930s. His greatest contribution was psychological, like FDR's. Reagan, like Roosevelt, was a gifted communicator with a sunny disposition who made decisions intuitively. With Reagan setting the pace, the national mood was upbeat. Reagan made patriotism fashionable and dispelled the sense of inferiority that had infested the military since Vietnam. But his flaws were real. Race relations suffered; greed proliferated; cities continued to decline; and the military-industrial complex operated at full blast. The Iran-Contra scandal violated the law. Though Reagan's defense expenditures bankrupted the Soviet Union, they also nearly bankrupted the United States. Still, the ending of the Cold War on his successor's watch was a landmark event in the Time of Paradox, comparable to winning World War II. If the danger of war did not disappear, at least it decreased, and if Reagan appeared Janus-faced, a likeable grandfather, and a hard-hearted militarist, he was in fact more complicated than he seemed. His story is fraught with paradoxes and contradictions, as is America's—and full of surprises.

Reagan hoped to spend his retirement largely at his ranch, riding horses, watching old movies, and being with Nancy. However, late in 1994, he told the public he had been diagnosed with Alzheimer's disease, a fatal ailment that destroys the brain and central nervous system, causing senility and dementia in patients whose bodies appear otherwise healthy. Because the disease acts slowly, and because of his mental lapses, some wondered whether he had suffered from the condition while president. In a handwritten public statement he announced: "I now begin the journey that will lead me into the sunset of my life. I know that for America there will always be a bright dawn ahead." On June 5, 2004, Reagan slipped from the twilight of Alzheimer's to the darkness of death. At ninety-three, he was the oldest ex-president in history.

CHAPTER TWENTY-TWO

A Culture of Diversity

BY THE END of the twentieth century, popular culture was the oxygen of American life. Television shows and films gave more people a collective vision of themselves and reality than literature and painting. Even politics became a form of entertainment. American popular culture conquered the imagination of the world, integrating influences from other cultures and leaving its imprint. The arts addressed timeless human concerns, yet they lost their focus, as merchandising and marketing threatened to become the measure of success.

The Jaws of Hollywood

The 1970s were a golden age for Hollywood: artistry combined with box office success. But there was a descending spiral of violence, gratuitous sex, and graphic gore. Talented and untalented filmmakers felt free to extend the boundaries of decency. The 1970s brought a new generation of directors and landmark movies, among them Francis Ford Coppola with *The Godfather* (1972) and *Apocalypse Now* (1979), Martin Scorcese with *Taxi Driver* (1976), Steven Spielberg with *Jaws* (1975) and *Close Encounters of the Third Kind* (1977), and George Lucas with *American Graffiti* (1973) and *Star Wars* (1977). New actors became popular, notably Robert De Niro, Robert Duvall, and Harrison Ford. The best films of those years helped shape the culture of America and the world.

Millions of people imagined organized crime through *The Godfather*; *Apocalypse Now* helped Americans articulate their feelings about the Vietnam War; *Close Encounters* mirrored and magnified the growing belief that extraterrestrials were watching our world. *Star Wars* and its successors, the most popular science fiction ever, created a galactic mythology, embedded with moral and religious symbols.

Jaws, adapted from a novel about a killer shark that menaces a small resort town, had an enormous impact on Hollywood. It made so much money so rapidly that it invented the summer blockbuster and helped speed a reversal of the unprofitability of moviemaking (weekly admissions had reached an all-time low in 1971). *Jaws* inspired movies featuring bigger, louder, faster sensations rather than plot or character. The theme was spun off into toys, soundtrack albums, and, later, video games.

The blockbuster phenomenon rose to new levels with Spielberg's *Jurassic Park* (1993), a science fiction tale of dinosaurs resurrected. It grossed a record $50.2 million in its opening weekend, and, with video rentals, pay cable, and foreign markets, revenues surged to well over $1 billion. Spielberg made his mark as a serious filmmaker with *Schindler's List* (1993), a compelling exploration of good amid the evil of the Holocaust.

During the 1970s Hollywood discovered that films made for "niche" audiences, independently of the major studios could earn profits. Among the most successful "indie" producers were Spike Lee, *She's Gotta Have It* (1986) Quentin Tarantino, *Pulp Fiction* (1994), and Steven Soderbergh, *sex, lies, and videotape* (1989). These producers excelled at creativity rather than expensive special effects, often using handheld cameras. Lee gave a voice to the African American perspective and achieved a devoted following. Eventually, most of the successful "indies" were absorbed by the major studios. Another trend, often relying on special effects and thin plots, were movies based on comic book superheros of the 1950s and 1960s, such as Superman, Spiderman, and Batman.

When videocassette recorders became an appliance in most American homes in the early 1980s, doomsayers predicted the demise of movie cinemas. Instead, the 1990s marked a cinema building boom. Larger, multiscreen houses, often offering expensive customer amenities, rose at a furious pace. Video rentals and sales became a lucrative ancillary market, providing the studios with profits and even new outlets for distributing movies never shown on the big screen.

The Changing Sound of Music

Popular music continued its rapid development in the Era of Diversity, often in unexpected ways. Two of the biggest pop stars of the era, Michael Jackson and Madonna, represented the triumph of image and marketing made possible after 1980 by music videos, which revolutionized the way recordings and recording artists were sold to the public. Their fame was a facet of the cult of celebrity, raised to new levels because of the pervasiveness of television and the tabloid media. Neither Jackson nor Madonna was a musical innovator. By the 2000s Madonna's CD sales were in decline, though she seemed a fixture of tabloid journalism and celebrity television. Jackson's career plummeted as he was unable to stimulate public interest in his new recordings since 1990 and became embroiled in much-publicized charges of child molestation.

The sensibility of rock, grown mellow and theatrical in the 1970s, was shaken at the end of that decade by punk rock, an often abrasive but frequently ironic music born in New York. Punk rock inspired many younger musicians to follow less commercial paths, sometimes to great success, and spurred a number of developments, including the popularity of noncommercial college radio stations that promoted "alternative rock" (as much postpunk rock would be called).

POP ROYALTY
The Reagans and
Michael Jackson
at the White House
Ceremony to
launch the
Campaign against
Drunk Driving,
1984.
(Ronald Reagan
Presidential
Library)

Reggae, a Jamaican popular music drawing from American rhythm and blues, indigenous rhythms and postcolonial outrage, gained a following in America during the 1970s. It remained the most popular "non-American" music in the United States until a wave of Hispanic singers washed across the charts at the end of the century. Similarly, music called "rap" emerged to challenge rock as the idiom of youth culture. Originating among Jamaican immigrants in New York during the 1970s, rap began to displace rock from the music charts in the 1990s. Rap is essentially a rhythmic form of speaking in rhyme, rooted among Africans transported as slaves to the New World. Hip-hop, the music accompanying rap, created rhythm from turntables and by "sampling" a collage of excerpts from previous recordings. Although country music, long a staple of the working class, also enjoyed booming popularity during the years of rap's ascent, by 1998 rap for the first time outsold country. Like rock music before it, rap's lyrics became a source of concern among parents, politicians, and social activists. Many rappers described scenes of grotesque street violence; others appeared to glorify misogyny, violence, and unbridled materialism.

Sampling was the most radical development in music since the electric guitar. Electronic instruments called synthesizers became more accessible in the 1970s and turned up in everything from the most experimental rock to the biggest disco dance hits. Introduction of digital technology in the 1980s finally made the instrument widely affordable and easy to use. The dance music that young people enjoyed became an increasingly complex hybrid incorporating sampling, synthesized sounds, and the metronomic disco beat. But during the final decades of the twentieth century, upsurges of nostalgia accompanied innovation. In the 1990s younger audiences were fascinated with 1940s swing, 1950s rockabilly from the rural South, 1960s psychedelia, and 1970s disco. Jazz found a voice of neotraditionalism in trumpeter Wynton Marsalis, whose explorations of the music's prerock heritage led him to perform jazz in prestigious cultural centers, although the music's impact on record sales was meager.

Significant innovations in classical music occurred in the 1970s when modernist composers Philip Glass and Steve Reich responded to the hypnotic allure of Asian music and the forceful impact of rock. In the 1980s John Adams led postmodernists in a return to some of the tonality of an earlier age. Despite commissioning of new work, the core repertoire of American symphony orchestras was unchanged since the early twentieth century. The "early music movement," concerned with European compositions and instruments from pre-Mozart times, grew from a marginal subculture into an important influence on classical music in the 1990s.

★ MADONNA: MATERIAL GIRL IN A MATERIAL AGE ★

*I know I'm not the best singer and I know I'm not the best dancer.
But I'm not interested in that. I'm interested in pushing people's
buttons . . . in being political and provocative.*

—MADONNA

MATERIAL GIRL
1980s Pop Star Madonna poses at
the MTV Video Music Awards
in September 1984.
(AP/Wide World Photos)

THE AGE OF Diversity was epitomized by the political icon of the 1980s, President Ronald Reagan, and its cultural icon, the singer Madonna. Each represented one face of the decade, which featured political conservatism and cultural hedonism. Reagan was credited with bringing prosperity; Madonna flaunted her sexuality and touted herself as the "Material Girl." ("We are living in a material world, and I am a material girl," she sang.) Reagan made Americans feel good about themselves; he made patriotism and consumerism popular. Madonna freed Americans from their inhibitions and made them feel good about having fun. Although no Paul Revere of the sexual revolution, she plunged a dagger into the heart of conformity. Madonna dressed for shock value, championed her love of uninhibited sex, and became a celebrity superstar as much for her outrageous fashions and statements as for her modest talents as a singer and actress. "The arena I choose to express myself in is sexuality," she said.

Born Madonna Louise Ciccone in 1958 in Michigan, Madonna did not spend her formative years in the Hollywood entertainment industry in which she would make her career, but in the bohemian artistic and music culture of New York. There she absorbed the rhythms of contemporary dance music and was influenced by the gay subculture that spawned it. Her first big hit, "Lucky Star" (1983), was catapulted onto the charts because of MTV. The song launched a fashion fad, as millions of girls adopted the look Madonna had gleaned from New York street fashions.

Madonna continually reinvented her appearance, recycling the sexuality of such screen stars as Marilyn Monroe and surrounding herself with tuxedo-clad choruses of admiring men. Although First Lady Nancy Reagan urged young people to "just say no" to drugs and promiscuous sex, Madonna offered a countermessage. "Look, everybody has different needs and wants and preferences and desires and fantasies. And we should not damn somebody or judge somebody because it's different than yours," she said. Madonna attempted to portray just about every orientation imaginable in her music videos, stage performances, and her book *Sex* (1992).

Aside from her film debut, *Desperately Seeking Susan* (1985), Madonna's movies were usually greeted with critical hostility and public indifference. Although her high-profile marriage to actor Sean Penn ended in divorce, she continued to flirt with the cinema, picking up roles such as *Evita*, and marrying British director Guy Ritchie in 2000. Her recording career was not an unblemished record of success after 1990, but she remained almost ubiquitous in the media, which covered her interest in Jewish mysticism, her child-rearing, and her love of England.

Resolutely commercial and flaunting her ambitions, Madonna continued to update her image into the twenty-first century, assimilating new ideas in popular culture and reshaping them into commercial form. Her dominance in the spotlight prompts Americans to ponder whether she represents the light side or the dark side of their society.

Sources: Books containing useful sketches on Madonna include June Sochen, *From Mae to Madonna* (1999), and Tom McGrath, *MTV: The Making of a Revolution* (1996).

Enormous changes occurred within the recording industry in the 1990s and 2000s. Ownership was increasingly consolidated into the hands of a few corporate giants whose concerns had less to do with music than with short-term profitability. Classical music and jazz departments were gutted. Career development for rock and pop acts declined in an era when big, instant hits were expected. CD sales slumped because of widespread consumer dissatisfaction as well as the proliferation of file sharing technology, which allowed listeners to download music online. Being signed to a major record label was no longer the dream for many musicians, who began to manage their own careers by working through the internet or a network of small, independent labels whose owners were still concerned with quality.

Picturing and Wiring the World

By the 1990s the art business reached new heights of profitability, with powerful international auction houses setting records for sales of famous artists. Colleges conferred more master's degrees in visual and performing arts than in English, biology, and math. But the money that wealthy collectors spent at auction trickled into the pockets of relatively few contemporary artists, and the proliferation of art majors did not spur a new Renaissance. "All I see is art-school art," art historian Barbara Rose said.

"Basically it looks like homework, because what is homework but learning how to follow the teacher's rules?"

A gap remained between the general public and the visual arts, a problem since the birth of modernism. Public sculpture was seldom controversial until people no longer recognized the meaning of the abstractions being erected with their tax dollars. Even in New York, the art world's mecca, public complaints forced the federal government to remove Richard Serra's wall of curved steel, *Tilted Arc*, from the Federal Plaza in 1989. In the years that followed, cities and public agencies spent a larger amount of funds on public art, most of it decorative and whimsical rather than inspiring. An exception was Maya Lin's acclaimed Vietnam Veterans Memorial (1982) in Washington, a stark black wall bearing the name of every American killed in the Vietnam War.

In 1989 federal funding of the arts through the National Endowment for the Arts (NEA), established in 1965, became embroiled in a "culture war" between liberals and conservatives. The target was Andres Serrano's photograph *Piss Christ*, an image of a plastic crucifix submerged in amber-colored fluid. His work was a statement about the kitschy degradation of religious imagery. The Christian right and some members of Congress were outraged over a $15,000 grant Serrano received from a regional art center funded by the NEA. In 1990 similar fury erupted over an exhibition of Robert Mapplethorpe—photographs in Washington. Mapplethorpe's classically composed depictions of homosexuality and sado-masochism garnered accolades from the art world and denunciations from other quarters. Because federal money had funded the Corcoran Gallery, two prominent Republican senators—Jesse Helms of North Carolina and Alfonse D'Amato of New York—launched an attack that canceled the show.

Art of the 1990s often addressed sociopolitical topics such as AIDS, racism, and sexism. The most important political artworks—quilts memorializing AIDS victims—took their form from the oldest traditions of American folk art. By the end of the century, visual art had expanded to encompass video, performance art, and often room-size installations in addition to painting, printmaking, photography, and sculpture. Yet the ambitions of art seemed to have shrunk. Coherent ideologies engaged only a few artists, and there was neither a prevailing method nor a desire for one. Almost everything was acceptable, and nothing was particularly essential.

Postmodernism, the most popular catchall for cultural endeavors after the mid-1980s, found its most public and concrete expression in architecture. Philip Johnson moved architecture away from the rigid geometry of modernism to a style that honored, and often randomly appropriated, the past. The unadorned boxes of modernism became unfashionable, although the best postmodern architecture was witty, striking, and powerful. America nonetheless was soon covered with cheap, faceless buildings that aped postmodern styles.

Broadcasting underwent dramatic changes near the end of the twentieth century. Radio became an important national sounding board with the spread of call-in talk shows, many hosted by conservatives. The FM band, absent from many radio sets before 1970, was a growing industry. Programming became increasingly standardized, a dearth of variety that encouraged the popularity of noncommercial music stations. News-oriented National Public Radio, founded by the federal government in 1969, maintained high standards.

As radio evolved to satisfy the changing interests of its audience, television was transformed. A force for cultural uniformity in 1970, with millions of viewers glued to only three national networks (ABC, CBS, and NBC), TV became a vehicle for cultural diversity by 1999. New competitors brought the first changes. The corporation for Public Broadcasting established through federal law in 1969, won acclaim for its children's show *Sesame Street* and became an outlet for literate entertainment and documentaries. Other commercial networks, such as Fox and Warner Brothers, also gained reputations for creative programming in the 1990s.

Innovations sprang from technology. Hand-held remote controls allowed viewers to "surf" between programs. Cable TV, which became widely available in the 1980s, yielded hundreds of special interest channels. Viewers with satellite dishes could see still greater numbers of channels than cable provided. The global broadcasting market offered a variety of programming targeted at every conceivable audience, including sports, movies, fine arts, popular music, news, weather, comedy, and history. The introduction of videocassette recorders, a fixture in homes after the Supreme Court's 1984 ruling that home taping did not infringe on copyright laws, changed the way television was watched. It enabled viewers to record programs and watch them at their leisure.

The social changes and increased frankness stemming from the cultural upheavals of the 1960s had enormous impact on programs beginning in the 1970s. Among the groundbreaking series were *All in the Family*, which satirized middle-class prejudices; *M*A*S*H*, which satirized the military; *The Mary Tyler Moore Show*, which depicted an independent career woman; and *Saturday Night Live*, which pushed comedy to new levels of outrageousness. It introduced such stars as John Belushi, Eddie Murphy, Chevy Chase, Steve Martin, and Dan Aykroyd. Popular miniseries such as *Roots* influenced American perceptions of history. Sports, which had largely been

TV'S WORKING WOMAN
Actress Mary Tyler Moore holds two Emmy Awards that she won in 1974 for her role on the *Mary Tyler Moore Show*. (AP/Wide World Photos)

confined to Saturday and Sunday afternoon telecasts, began to spread into the rest of the week.

A significant addition to programming during the 1980s was the debut of the cable channel MTV, whose fast-paced aesthetic left a mark not only on the music industry but also on television, advertising, and movies. Meanwhile, network shows developed new sophistication with *Hill Street Blues*, a police story whose flawed heroes, gritty realism, and open-ended narrative paved the way for such popular realistic dramas as *NYPD Blue* and *Law and Order*. Epitomizing the response of many Americans to media saturation, comedian David Letterman presented an ironic talk, comedy and variety show. Jay Leno succeeded Johnny Carson as host of the *Tonight* show, featuring monologues based on current events. *The Oprah Winfrey Show* was serious and emotional. American television's first nationally prominent black talk show host, Winfrey dispensed hugs, shed tears, and contributed diversity to the culture that pervaded the United States at the close of the century.

The signature shows of the 1990s were noteworthy for dysfunctional families and cynicism about national institutions. *The Simpsons*, a witty, sarcastic animated show, appealed to children for its visual gags and to adults for its lampooning of middle-class life. *Seinfeld* saw humor in life's petty annoyances. Cable News Network (CNN) brought news into homes twenty-four hours a day. The Persian Gulf War received saturation coverage. Reporting of the murder trial of ex-football star O. J. Simpson also blurred the line between news and entertainment. Once the most reticent medium, television was sexualized in content to a degree difficult to imagine only a few years earlier. New social attitudes, competition from pay-per-view channels, and the no-holds-barred Internet brought sexuality to the small screen. Early in the 2000s, "reality shows" proliferated. Beautiful women and rugged men competed for dates, mates, and money, by surmounting a series of physical and mental challenges. These shows, too, were infused with sexuality. More changes loomed from the enhanced visual quality of high-definition television and hybrid digital technology that promised to diminish the distinction between TV and Internet, ultimately fusing electronic communication into one mega-medium.

The Internet, a global computer network that transcended geography, political barriers, and time zones, accelerated communications. At the start of the 1990s the Internet was an open frontier, yet by the end of the decade, civilization had begun to cultivate and control the medium. By 1999, 80 million Americans were online, sending e-mail, shopping, making investments, applying for mortgages, viewing pornography, and even consulting physicians.

Churning news and rumor with unsettling speed, the Internet gave traditional news media a run for their audiences. Some worried the Internet would supplant the older media. Ratings plummeted for nightly network news programs, and newspaper readership declined. Other problems accompanied the growth of the Internet. There were legal questions: how to protect intellectual property rights online, how to resolve competing claims to names for Web addresses. Shoppers' credit card numbers could be stolen if the online connection was not secure. Sex abusers employed the Internet to lure victims. "Hackers" introduced computer "viruses" into the network illegally to sabotage victims' machines. Researchers cautioned that habitual Internet users were susceptible to depression and loneliness. The Internet was no substitute for human contact.

Attempting to coexist with the Internet and broadcast news, print journalism was less of a presence than it had been earlier. Competition from television, changing demographics, and expenses reduced the number of daily newspapers. Meaningful newspaper competition vanished in most cities.

Local ownership waned, swallowed in a wave of mergers and acquisitions by larger companies such as Gannett and Knight-Ridder. Gannett hastened the process with *USA Today*, a national paper introduced in the 1980s that stressed bite-sized news stories and use of color photos and graphics.

Writing and Performing in an Electronic Age

Battles over books raged in academia during the 1980s and 1990s. One of the fiercest skirmishes concerned the study of "great books," the classics of literature and philosophy. By the end of the 1990s, only a few universities still maintained a core curriculum of great books, which usually began with Homer and ended in the early twentieth century. But given the fractious state of the humanities and the withering of consensus over Western civilization, it became harder for educators to agree on what to include in a core curriculum. Now it was expected to reflect diverse perspectives, including non-Western cultures and such previously marginalized groups as women and racial minorities.

Some of the most important nonfiction books related to the feminist movement. Kate Millett's *Sexual Politics* (1970) found a political dimension in even the most intimate aspects of male-female relations. Germaine Greer's *The Female Eunuch* (1970) argues that women have been robbed of productive energy by being confined to passive sexual roles. Jean Bethke Elshtain's *Women and War* (1987) urges more nuanced understandings of gender roles. Camille Paglia's *Sexual Personae* (1990) asserts that female sexuality is humanity's most powerful force. She criticized feminism as single-minded, saying it was preoccupied with victimhood.

The velocity of change was the subject of Alvin Toffler's best seller *Future Shock* (1970), whose title became shorthand for the anxiety caused by rapid technological growth. Other influential nonfiction works were ambitious attempts at reporting recent events. Published during the author's exile from the Soviet Union, Aleksandr Solzhenitsyn's *The Gulag Archipelago*, 3 vols. (1973–1975) alerted the world to the Soviet Union's systematic abuse of human rights. *Washington Post* reporters Bob Woodward and Carl Bernstein published *All the President's Men* (1974), an indictment of the Watergate scandal that stimulated investigative reporting. Radio interviewer Studs Terkel compiled such acclaimed volumes of twentieth-century oral history as *Working* (1974) and *The Good War* (1984). Introduction of novelists' tools into nonfiction writing reached a controversial height with Edmund Morris's *Dutch* (1999), in which the biographer inserted a fictionalized version of himself into a biography of Ronald Reagan.

The American scientist of the late twentieth century with the greatest public recognition, astronomer Carl Sagan, authored several best sellers, including *Dragons of Eden* (1977), but reached his greatest audience by arguments in favor of extraterrestrial life in his television series *Cosmos* and appearances on the *Tonight Show*. Other science writers found nonspecialist readers, notably British astronomer Stephen Hawking, who popularized theories about the nature of the cosmos in his best seller *A Brief History of Time: From the Big Bang to Black Holes* (1988). In 2004 Hawking conceded that his theory of black holes was flawed and it might be possible for energy to escape from a black hole. James Gleick's *Chaos* (1987) stimulated the pondering of "chaos theory." Paradoxically, if the universe is sheer chaos, then chaos becomes its organizational principle. The popularity of those books is evidence that questions about the meaning of life, and the search for ultimate answers, has not gone out of style.

Many American historians were troubled over a lack of dialogue between historians and the public, blaming the national amnesia in part on academics more concerned with impressing peers than informing average readers. Despite some historians' tendency to retreat to ivory towers, others were determined to engage the public in the meaning of their country's history. Notable among them was Howard Zinn, whose *People's History of the United States* (1980) placed such previously ignored groups as women, African Americans, American Indians, and the poor into mainstream American history. History started being taught in a broader context, shifting the emphasis from Western civilization to world civilization. John Hope Franklin pioneered in the writing and teaching of African American history. Some historians lamented that politics and diplomacy were neglected, but important books about major leaders rolled off the nation's printing presses, including Robert Dallek's *Flawed Giant: Lyndon Johnson and His Times* (1998), and James MacGregor Burns's influential study of FDR, *Roosevelt: Soldier of Freedom* (1970). Historians used newly opened archives, especially Soviet sources on the Cold War, and such domestic sources as the private conversations taped by presidents John F. Kennedy, Lyndon Johnson, and Richard Nixon. Yet it was television, not books, that provided history with its greatest audience, especially Judy Crichton's compelling PBS series *The American Experience* and Ken Burns's epic PBS production *The Civil War*.

The most influential new philosopher was a Frenchman, Michel Foucault, who was interested in the mechanisms of power that underlie societies and the ways by which knowledge is translated into power. Pop psychology became one of the most profitable genres of publishing, beginning with Thomas Anthony Harris's bestseller *I'm OK, You're OK* (1969) and continuing through uncounted self-help manuals. Writers and speakers, including Deepak Chopra and Wayne Dyer, merged Eastern and Western religious beliefs, asserted that the human purpose was to become one with the universe, and taught their readers to manifest their desires through meditation. Practices such as meditation, yoga, Chinese and Japanese martial arts, and alternative medicine, part of the 1960s counterculture and dismissed as narcissistic in the "Me Decade" of the 1970s, were in the mainstream by the 1990s. Mysticism and non-Western philosophies and religions found a new open-mindedness, and people increasingly tended to trust their intuition, as artists long had done. Far more Americans visited health clubs than saw doctors. Herbal remedies often were preferred over prescription drugs; they were preventive, cheaper, and had fewer side effects. Jogging, bicycling, and weight lifting were increasingly popular for health and recreation. Psychology itself underwent a revolution during the final decades of the century. Clinical experiments with drugs led to pharmaceutical treatments that virtually supplanted Freudian analysis.

With films and popular music replacing literature for many younger people, and with most middle-class Americans wired to television and the Internet, book lovers had reason for pessimism. But Americans gathered in growing numbers to read and discuss books in clubs, which often were used to preserve time for reading in a society pressed for it. National bookstore chains displaced local stores and offered such amenities as coffee bars and musical entertainment. One of the most discussed Internet businesses, Amazon.com, started by selling books.

Literature wrestled with doubt, as some writers worried that fiction could no longer grapple with the truth of life and that society was changing too rapidly to be captured in a realistic "great American novel." Tom Wolfe defied the trend against realism with best-selling novels that depicted the lifestyles of America. In the 1960s Wolfe had been among the originators of "New Journalism"; later, he wrote novels and reached a large readership with *Bonfire of the Vanities* (1987), a social chronicle. Joyce Carol Oates, among America's most versatile authors, wrote scholarly and critical essays, poetry, and novels that explored social and economic history through personal narratives. Joan Didion used popular culture to ironic effect in her novels *Play It as It Lays* (1970) and *A Book of Common Prayer* (1977). Maya Angelou's best-selling autobiography, *I Know Why the Caged Bird Sings* (1970), was a raw account of a black woman growing up in the pre-civil rights South.

Science fiction continued to examine the implications of technology and social change. By the time of his death in 1986, Frank Herbert had completed six novels in his *Dune* series, a sprawling saga of galactic empire, and ecological devastation. William Gibson's groundbreaking novel about a computerized future, *Necromancer* (1984), was credited with coining the term "cyberspace" and envisioning the ramifications of the Internet and virtual reality. Anne Rice and Stephen King sold millions of copies of their novels about the supernatural, which commented on social mores. Rice's and King's enormous popularity signaled that most readers were still concerned with primordial questions of love, life, and death.

In 1986 Robert Penn Warren, a Pulitzer Prize winner for both fiction and poetry, was named the first Poet Laureate of the United States, recognition that came at a low point in poetry's commercial viability and popular esteem. Many talented writers embraced the greater opportunities for gaining an audience in the rock arena. Jim Carroll was among the few writers who maintained respectable careers in rock (his 1980 album *Catholic Boy* was well regarded), memoirs (*The Basketball Diaries*, 1978), and poetry (*Living at the Movies*, 1973).

For playwrights, after World War II it was generally conceded that the most adventurous theater productions came from "Off Broadway," and places such as Steppenwolf Theatre in Chicago, which developed contemporary plays and actors who became Hollywood stars. After 1970 the most prolific and successful writers to originate Off Broadway were Sam Shepard and David Mamet. Shepard's *Buried Child* (1978) and *A Lie of the Mind* (1987) were acclaimed for tapping such American imagery as rock stars, gangsters, and cowboys. Mamet became known for eccentric sketches of American life and language such as *Glengarry Glen Ross* (1983). Both playwrights also realized success in Hollywood.

Musical spectacles thrived on Broadway during the 1980s and 1990s, many of them originating on the London stage, especially Andrew Lloyd Webber's *Cats* (1981) and *The Phantom of the Opera* (1986). Movies including *The Lion King* and *Footloose* also became popular stage productions in the 1990s. A shortage of tuneful new songwriting encouraged revivals of the great musicals of the 1940s and 1950s.

As the twentieth century ended, the theater community complained about the increasing cost of producing plays and the difficulty of maintaining a dedicated and discriminating audience. Despite some popular triumphs, many of which relied on technology and visual spectacle, it was not generally considered a great period for new plays. The discouragement aside, even pessimists conceded that the theater remained a powerful medium.

The Cost of Sports

Long an adult pastime, organized sports reached the level of children, who had previously played spontaneously, by their own rules. Some believed that structured play prepared the young for the grown-up world, yet others regretted the loss of joy of unorganized play and complained that children grew up too fast. Most popular was Little League Baseball, which staged a World Series in 1947 and expanded internationally in 1952. By 1990 there were some 16,000 leagues in forty countries with 2.5 million players. For girls, there were the Bobby Sox and American Girl Softball, with 500,000 participants by 1990. The football counterpart to Little League was the Pop Warner League, which grew to 185,000 players in thirty-nine states by the same year. In no sport was the pressure on the young more intense than tennis, in which Jennifer Capriati turned professional at age thirteen and signed product endorsement contracts for $1 million. Girl gymnasts, swimmers, and figure skaters likewise matured young at the Olympic level.

A nostalgic sport for the ever-young, professional baseball was popular with baby boomers, yet it underwent sweeping changes in the Era of Diversity. Major League baseball widened the strike zone to speed the game in the 1960s, then took steps over the next three decades to encourage offense and home runs. Roger Maris's season record of sixty-one home runs, set in 1961 with the New York Yankees, stood until St. Louis Cardinals first baseman Mark McGwire hit seventy in 1998; three years later, San Francisco Giants outfielder Barry Bonds passed McGwire, clubbing seventy-three. An influx of African American, Hispanic, and Asian talent gave the game more power, dazzling speed, and relief pitching. Big market teams grew less dominant because of expanded play-offs, free agency for players, and the amateur draft. Economic imbalances that continued to favor teams in large cities were addressed in a 2002 labor agreement that featured revenue sharing and a "luxury tax" intended to discourage teams from taking on huge player payrolls. There were no dynasties comparable to the Yankees and Dodgers of the 1945–1969 period, although the Yankees and the Atlanta Braves were leading teams in the American League and the National League, respectively.

Football eclipsed baseball as the most popular spectator sport, with its championship, the Super Bowl, becoming a cultural celebration. National Football League (NFL) Commissioner Pete Rozelle promoted the concept of splitting the league's television revenue among all teams, allowing small town franchises such as the Green Bay Packers to survive. Dominating the Era of Diversity, the San Francisco 49ers and Dallas Cowboys won five Super Bowls apiece, the Pittsburgh Steelers four. The "West Coast offense," stressing short, low-risk passes that allowed a team to move down the field efficiently, became the vogue in the 1980s and remained widely used. College football scaled new heights, in part because of television, and became a major source of money and prestige for universities. High school football became a virtual religion, especially in small towns in the South and the Midwest.

Basketball likewise thrived in high schools, colleges, and the professional circuit, probably outdrawing football and baseball in live audiences when all levels of the sport were combined. In college basketball, the greatest dynasty belonged to the University of California, Los Angeles, which won ten national championships, seven consecutively, under coach John Wooden from 1964 to 1975 and featured players such as Lew Alcindor (later Kareem Abdul-Jabbar) and Bill Walton, both of whom went on to stellar careers in the National Basketball Association (NBA). The National Collegiate Athletic Association tournament became one of the most-watched sporting events, so much that CBS-TV paid billions for the right to broadcast it. Other players who electrified fans—Michael Jordan, Larry Bird, and Earvin "Magic" Johnson—catapulted the NBA to global popularity in the 1980s and 1990s. Bird's Boston Celtics and Johnson's Los Angeles Lakers were perennial contenders, but it was Jordan who dominated the 1990s by leading the Chicago Bulls to six league titles. American basketball was humiliated in the 2004 Summer Olympics when the nation's team, composed mostly of NBA stars, was beaten by 19 points by the team representing Puerto Rico and then again by tiny Lithuania.

Professional hockey struggled to gain a wide following outside its limited fan base in the United States, yet the National Hockey League (NHL) benefited from a greater influx of American stars from the college ranks. At the 1980 Winter Olympics in Lake Placid, New York, an unheralded and young U.S. squad stunned the hockey world by upsetting the powerful Soviet Union en route to the gold medal. Another sport that originated outside the United States, soccer, found great popularity among youths, and some forecast that the game would become the most popular sport in the country. Professional soccer did not quite gain the foothold expected in America, though, and predictions of the game's growth as a spectator sport went unfulfilled.

Tennis became one of the fastest-growing games in the 1970s, thanks to stars such as Billie Jean King, Chris Evert, Arthur Ashe, and Jimmy Connors. The sport waned in the 1980s with failures of American men in international competition, then revived in the 1990s, when Pete Sampras, Andre Agassi, and the Williams sisters, Venus and Serena, seized the headlines. Few blacks other than Ashe had left an imprint on the professional game, but the Williamses soon dominated the women's circuit. Golf enjoyed even more growth and overcame its reputation as an exclusively upper-class sport, stimulated by television and players including Arnold Palmer, Jack Nicklaus, the greatest golfer of his generation, and

Tiger Woods, who threatened to shatter Nicklaus's records. Woods helped inspire black youths to take up the game, promising to diversify the sport.

African American participation in sports was pervasive, especially in professional football and basketball. Athletes such as Jordan and Woods reaped the benefits of fame and lucrative contracts, prize money, and endorsement deals. But there were few black head coaches in the NFL or managers in baseball. There were fewer professional opportunities for women, although they made great strides in sports in the Era of Diversity. Feminism was injected into sports as part of the social upheavals of the 1960s and 1970s. Billie Jean King struck a symbolic blow for feminism in 1973 when she defeated tennis hustler Bobby Riggs, who had boasted that he could beat any woman, in a nationally televised match. In 1972, Title IX of the Education Act put the federal government's weight behind this movement, stipulating that colleges or universities that discriminated on the bases of sex, age, or race would lose all their federal funding. Institutions hastened to establish varsity programs for women, paving the way for large increases in the number of women playing intercollegiate sports and in girls playing high school sports. But attendance at women's games lagged, and only a handful of women's sports generated sufficient revenue to sustain themselves; to support the programs, colleges often had to cut spending on men's sports.

The public's taste for sports soured in the 1980s and 1990s as player strikes troubled the major professional leagues, athletes' salaries soared, and fans blamed rising costs for skyrocketing ticket prices. Major league baseball, the NFL, the NBA, and the NHL sought to slow the growth in player wages, but the lure of a big payday enticed more athletes to quit college and turn professional. Rules implemented to curb abuses in college sports and reinforce the importance of academics proved ineffective. Taunting of opposing players increased, especially in the NFL and the NBA, and team-oriented play declined. Many Americans deplored the lack of sportsmanship and questioned whether sports heroes were proper models for the young.

Nor was that former redoubt of amateurism, the Olympics, immune. Permitted by rule changes, the United States sent a team of virtually all professionals to the 1992 Summer Games in Barcelona, Spain, that swept to the gold medal. The Olympic image, however, had become tragic and politicized earlier. Arab terrorists murdered nine Israeli athletes at the 1972 Summer Games in Munich, West Germany. The United States boycotted the 1980 Moscow Summer Games in response to the Soviet invasion of Afghanistan, and the Soviets reciprocated by shunning the 1984 Los

Angeles Summer Games. One tawdry incident involved not drugs but thuggery: figure skater Tonya Harding hired a "hit man" to disable rival Nancy Kerrigan before the 1994 Winter Games in Lillehammer, Norway. Kerrigan recovered and won a medal; Harding did not place.

Big-time sports captivated and entertained countless fans, even if they no longer had the innocence of child's play. Americans nonetheless continued to discover meaning and purpose in sports, which became a metaphor for life, an exercise, and a diversion. Sports was, like many things, a virtue in moderation, a vice in excess.

By 2000 the contours of the first truly global culture were clear, driven by American sports, movies, television, and music and powered by the convergence of media, with the Internet the nexus for TV, radio, films, literature, and most other facets of popular art. Music could be downloaded from the Web, athletic competition watched on television screens in homes. Nonetheless, young people flocked to dance clubs, and sports fans still gathered in arenas and around the electronic campfire of televisions at taverns. The importance of shared experience—part of what it means to be human—endures.

CHAPTER TWENTY-THREE

"Can We All Get Along?":
The Soul of the Nation

THE LAST decades of the twentieth century were times of swift growth in population and transition in moral standards. Paradoxically, the nation was more stable than it had been in many such periods. The population was more racially and ethnically diverse than ever, adding versatility in talents. Yet discord shattered peace at home and abroad, yielding, simultaneously, apprehension and a summons for tolerance.

Diversity and Change

Many Americans were proud of their nation's racial and ethnic diversity, yet others considered it a mixed blessing, a source of friction, at best a partial success. The hopes of the civil rights movement had expanded, then fallen short of expectations.

America's population shot upward: 205 million in 1970, 215 million in 1975, 227 million in 1980, 250 million in 1990, 261 million in 1996, and 281 million in 2000. The largest population growth came in the Sunbelt of the South and West; in the Northwest and Midwest growth was slow or stagnant. Offsetting a declining birth rate, life expectancy rose from 67.1 years to 71 for men, from 74.7 to 78.3 for women from 1970 to 1983. Baby boomers began to reach their thirties by the 1970s and middle age by the 1990s. The median age jumped from twenty-eight in 1970, to thirty-one in 1983, to thirty-three in 1992, and to thirty-five in 2000. By the 1990s the United States had one of the oldest populations in the world, and the fastest-growing segment of its population was those older than seventy-five. The rising tide of older Americans, whose political clout increased, stretched the finances of Medicare and Medicaid.

The sexual revolution continued. To some, born late in the century, it no longer seemed a revolution, simply a fact of life. As many people lived alone as lived in nuclear families of husband, wife, and children. The wife often worked; in some cases only the wife worked. Cohabitation was accepted. For many sex started in high school and continued through college, and did not necessarily become monogamous with marriage. Of those aged eighteen to twenty-four, some 90 percent of men and 80 percent of women acknowledged having premarital sex. Junior high and high school girls had unprotected sex and bore children, or aborted them. Sex became an expected part of dating. Affairs among politicians and ministers were common. Bill Clinton was impeached (but acquitted) for lying about sex. Such national leaders as John F. Kennedy, Martin Luther King, and Newt Gingrich had affairs. If Hollywood remained the sex capital of the nation, Washington, D.C., ran it a close second.

The strident rhetoric and noisy demonstrations of the 1960s diminished. In the 1970s some returned to pursuing material rewards, yet others turned inward to "New Age" philosophies. There was a new emphasis on finding meaning to life, dismissed by some at the time as narcissistic, yet in fact based less on selfishness than on the conviction that if the world could change, it would change one person at a time. Increasingly, self-improvement of body and soul became popular. Americans quit smoking, drank diet drinks, walked, and bicycled to keep in shape. Many played golf and tennis, sports increasingly taken up by the middle and lower middle classes. Perhaps most popular among all ages was swimming, which included lessons, leagues, and impromptu dips. The attention to personal health, once largely confined to children, was joined to new concerns with diet, vegetarianism, holistic medicine, and the kind of spirituality that went beyond the walls of churches and synagogues.

Many of the new lifestyles were connected with a bucolic craving for the grass and trees of suburbs and towns rather than the cement of cities. It was also part of the appeal of the Sunbelt, as was its climate. But the main stimulant in the push-pull dynamic that drained the cities was jobs. Just as people once moved to jobs, now jobs moved to people. By 1990 more than 60 percent of jobs were in the suburbs. In fact, many jobs could be done from the home, using computers. The type of jobs changed and with it their locations. Smokestack jobs were giving way to light manufacturing, such as electronics and service jobs. People did not stay in one place as long. Light industry needed workers who were highly educated and mobile. Industrial parks were built outside cities, where traffic and parking were not problems. Some cities outside the Sunbelt had severe financial crises, including

Cleveland, which declared bankruptcy. As whites fled to suburbs, blacks took over as mayors of a number of major cities, winning elections split along racial grounds. Many of the black mayors set about reforming their cities' police departments, which had been mostly white bastions and had mistreated the poor and minorities. Hispanics gained clout, winning elections in several cities in the Sunbelt. In the 1980s cities seemed to be making a comeback, as building surged in downtown areas, especially construction of convention centers and hotels. Many cities boomed despite cuts in their budgets and reductions in urban aid, yet cities never recouped the political and economic dominance they had once enjoyed..

Terrorism took a toll during the Era of Diversity. Sometimes terrorists were inspired by personal frustration, by religious fanaticism, or by grievances directed against the government or American institutions. America's material success and support of the state of Israel also made it a target. Moreover, America was an open society; it was difficult to protect buildings, airports, and other targets without restricting personal liberties. Islamic terrorists exploded a bomb at the World Trade Center in 1993, killing six and injuring one thousand. Radical Muslims bombed American installations abroad. In America, opponents of abortion attacked clinics and assassinated doctors. The site of the 1996 Atlanta Summer Olympics was bombed. Members of an armed cult, the Branch Davidians, perished in a 1993 fire at their compound in Waco, Texas, surrounded by the FBI. The blaze broke out because incendiary devices and ammunition stored inside the compound were ignited, but right-wing groups blamed the government. Vengeance for the Branch Davidians drove Army veteran Timothy McVeigh to bomb the Alfred P. Murrah Federal Building in Oklahoma City in April 1995, killing 168. McVeigh was executed and a coplotter was sentenced to a long prison term. Lashing out against a different target, technology and its allies, the so-called Unabomber, Theodore Kaczynski, mailed bomb packages to his victims from 1978 to 1986, killing three and wounding twenty-two. Not until 1996 did officials arrest Kaczynski, a brilliant math professor but an alienated loner. He pled guilty and was sentenced to life in prison.

In April 1999, a violent tragedy horrified the nation. At Columbine High School in Littleton, Colorado, two high school students shot to death twelve classmates and a teacher before killing themselves. Six years later, a high school student at a Chippewa Indian Reservation school at Red Lake, Minnesota, shot his grandparents to death, drove to his school, murdered seven students, and committed suicide without expressing a motive.

Alienation, perhaps a by-product of the velocity of change, seemed to disturb young people in particular. Some Americans called for gun control,

SCHOOL SHOOTINGS A participant at a memorial service for the victims of the Columbine High School shootings holds a "Save Our Kids" sign in Littleton, Colorado, in April 1999. (AP/Wide World Photos/Eric Gray)

yet others, such as the National Rifle Association, argued that the right to bear arms is embedded in the Constitution. Violence at Columbine, Red Lake, and other schools aroused principals and local police to tighten security. Metal detectors and the presence of policemen in the school hallways curtailed, but did not end violence. The social and psychological conditions that bred violent behavior, the saturation coverage by the media that inspired copycat crimes, and the longstanding American culture of homicide, reinforced by action movies, video games, and rock and rap lyrics, were also held responsible.

Booms and Busts

The United States experienced its greatest boom from 1940 to 1970, then slipped into stagflation, a decline of industrial jobs, and losses to foreign competition. Manufacturing began a long decline and was replaced by lower-paying service jobs. McDonald's and Wal-Mart became the nation's largest employers. Employers found it difficult to compete with nations such as Germany and Japan, which rebuilt their industrial plants with newer

★ CESAR CHAVEZ: ORGANIZING THE POOR ★

God writes in exceedingly crooked lines.
—CESAR CHAVEZ

GIVING VOICE TO MIGRANT WORKERS
Farm union leader Caesar Chavez.
(National Archives)

CESAR CHAVEZ was a labor leader, an advocate for the poor, a spokesman for Mexican Americans, and an inspiration for demoralized American liberals whose reform agenda faltered in the late 1960s. In the Era of Diversity, he espoused ethnic consciousness without rejecting the United States or capitalism and wedded an indomitable will to a commitment to nonviolence.

Chavez was born to a middle-class, Roman Catholic, Mexican American family in Arizona. After his father lost the family farm to back taxes, the Chavezes moved to California to become itinerant vegetable and fruit pickers. Educated sporadically, Chavez learned firsthand about the hard lives of the workers and found his mission—to alleviate their suffering. The growers had all the weapons on their side, the government, the law, and economic power. "We herd them like pigs," one grower said of the Mexican workers.

After briefly serving in the Navy, Chavez returned to California, married in 1948, and became an organizer for the Community Service Organization (CSO) in 1952. The CSO, which registered Mexican Americans to vote and provided rudimentary social services, was Chavez's steppingstone to labor organizing. In the 1960s Chavez became a national figure, the Chicano equivalent of Martin Luther King Jr. He founded the United Farm Workers (UFW) and led a series of successful strikes, especially against grape and wine producers. Even more important than work stoppages among Chavez's arsenal of tactics were boycotts and hunger strikes. "We have our own bodies and spirits and the justice of our cause as our weapons," he said. As the leader of a relatively weak group seeking to move the levers of power, Chavez recognized the paradoxes in his situation. He was an individualist, yet he knew his movement must be based on collective action. He witnessed pain and wanted to act to relieve it, yet he knew that success requires patience.

Chavez and his allies aroused the country; the UFW's grape boycott became a national cause in the 1960s. Still, victories were hard earned, and setbacks were numerous. The government, especially California Governor Ronald Reagan and President Richard Nixon, opposed the UFW strikes. But the biggest threat to the union's survival came from a competing union, the Teamsters, which offered easier terms to growers; sometimes growers covertly collaborated with the Teamsters in union elections. And there would be other fights. In the 1970s and 1980s Chavez and the UFW advocated strict enforcement of laws barring illegal immigrants who might compete with UFW workers and campaigned against use of environmentally unsafe pesticides. In the 1990s the UFW unsuccessfully sought to block Senate ratification of the North American Free Trade Agreement, fearing it would cost the union jobs.

By the time Chavez died on April 23, 1993, he had earned an international reputation. Tributes came from the Pope, the Mexican president, and President Bill Clinton. Militant yet mild-mannered, Chavez never lost his courage during more than thirty years of organizing. Most important, Chavez inspired the poor to try to seize control of their own destiny. "History will judge societies and governments—and their institutions—not by how big they are or how well they serve the rich and powerful, but by how effectively they respond to the needs of the poor and the helpless," he predicted.

Sources: Biographies of Chavez and accounts of his movement include Richard Griswold del Castillo and Richard A. Garcia, *Cesar Chavez: A Triumph of Spirit* (1995), and Susan Ferress and Ricardo Sanduval, *The Fight in the Fields: Cesar Chavez* (1997).

---

technology after World War II. They now produced efficiently such quality goods as electronic equipment and compact automobiles. Still, American cultural products permeated world markets. Perhaps the most memorable American ambassador to the world is Coca-Cola.

The economy began the Reagan years in a grim recession, recovered, and performed well for the remainder of the 1980s. Another decline set in which ended shortly before Bush's defeat in 1992, and thereafter, the 1990s were the most prosperous decade to that time. The stock market soared, and investors and entrepreneurs such as Bill Gates, the chair of the computer software giant Microsoft, became billionaires. Poverty and welfare rolls declined, yet the disparity between rich and poor increased; family income stagnated although hours worked increased. Some manufacturers outsourced work to lower-paying foreign companies or built factories abroad. Unions declined, as did their influence. From 31 percent of nonfarm workers organized in 1960, the percent fell to just 14 by the late 1990s. Unions were less militant about strikes because workers were easier to replace. Presidents of both parties worked to ratify the North American Free Trade Agreement (NAFTA), which won in Senate approval under President Bill Clinton. Union opposition notwithstanding, most economists put their faith in free trade.

The genie of prosperity was technology. It changed home, recreation, and work, making living more comfortable yet also making human beings more replaceable. Government-sponsored research in universities rolled back scientific barriers, yielding theoretical discoveries that were converted into practical applications. Much of the new technology had military and civilian uses. Lasers, powerful light beams, were first employed in the armed forces to direct missiles. By the end of the twentieth century they were being used in medicine to open clogged arteries, destroy tumors, seal capillaries, and cauterize ulcers. Laser eye surgery made it possible to see normally without glasses or contact lenses. Lasers also could sterilize wine without changing its taste and scan the prices of coded products at grocery store checkout counters.

The most important developments were the programmable computer chip and biotechnology. Programmable chips made possible pocket calculators, digital watches, and large, industrial computers. Along with smaller models for offices and homes, the computer revolution harnessed the Internet for worldwide communications. Biotechnology helped scientists understand the genetic basis of diseases, a critical step toward better cures. Biotechnology raised fear, in addition to promise, because of advances in cloning, the production of an individual with the exact genetic blueprint of its parent. Genetic engineering made it possible to create species and to exclude inherited diseases from offspring. Cloning could be used to make healthier or more productive animal species, such as cows who produced more milk, but species might be created that had no natural enemies and could multiply endlessly. Also, cloning of animals and human cells led many to fear that scientists would find a way to clone humans, a development that would pose ethical and religious problems. Embryonic stem cells offered the prospect of replacing diseased cells and generated impassioned debate over whether it was permissible to clone embryos merely to harvest the cells. To some, scientists were dangerously close to playing God. Theologians asked whether a human created by cloning would have a soul.

Almost as miraculous as cloning were advances in medicine. Prozac was developed to treat depression. New therapies alleviated heart disease and cancer. Diagnostic imaging machines eliminated much of the need for exploratory surgery and focused more precisely on the diseased portion of the body. Arthroscopic surgery on joints permitted rapid recovery. Households and hospitals changed because of new inventions and the refinement of older products. Use of microwave ovens soared after 1969, simplifying food preparation, and use of Teflon-coated pans made it easier to clean up after meals.

Moving toward the Right

The ascendance of the right starting in the late 1960s was one of the most significant developments of the era. Conservatives engineered the elections of a
host of Republican presidents mitigated only by Watergate: Richard Nixon,
Ronald Reagan, George H. W. Bush, and George W. Bush. Opposition to
communism, big government, and secularism united them. Some of their
books and essays were written by influential neoconservatives, or former
liberals. They believed in absolute morality, order in society, and personal
responsibility. For the most part, their appeals were directed at individuals
rather than groups. Thus they preferred individualism over collectivism,
and a marketplace relatively unfettered by government. They appealed to
numerous segments of the white middle and lower-middle class who were
weary of high taxes, affirmative action, welfare, and busing.

The Era of Diversity also gave birth to a resurgence of evangelicals.
Evangelicals and their religious cousins, Fundamentalists, were other
worldly. Evangelicalism is permeated by a "born again" experience in which
a person recognizes Jesus as Savior and commits to live for God. Their chief
mission is to make converts. Perhaps the best-known evangelical of the era
was President Jimmy Carter. Fundamentalists espoused the inerrancy of
Scripture, the miracles of the Bible, and the second coming of Jesus. Both
revered Judeo-Christian morality, yet Fundamentalists were somewhat
more militant. Since the Scopes Trial of the 1925, liberal theologians had
predicted that evangelicalism and fundamentalism would burn themselves
out because they were too passionate and outdated for the modern world.
Just the opposite happened. As mainline Protestant churches lost membership, and Catholicism lost vigor, the churches of the Right, such as the
Pentecostals and Assemblies of God, grew. Set back by the scandals of
the televangelists of the 1970s, they resumed their growth spurt during the
1980s. Relentless foes of abortion, they were joined by Orthodox Jews and
Mormons.

Two of the faster-growing evangelical sects were the Southern Baptists
and the Pentecostals. Practically all white, the Southern Baptists became
the largest Protestant denomination by the late 1980s. Starting from a
smaller base, Pentecostals grew even more swiftly in percentage terms.
Their largest branch, the Assemblies of God, rose from around a half-
million members in 1965 to more than two million by 1985. Pentecostals
were fundamentalists who talked of the gift of healing and who spoke
in unknown tongues, as had occurred on the day of Pentecost. With
Pentecostals, charismatics shared interest in healing and speaking in

LEADING THE MORAL MAJORITY Televangelist Jerry Falwell speaks at a rally on the steps of the Alabama Capitol in August 2003 in support of Alabama Chief Justice Roy Moore. Moore said that he would defy a federal court order to remove his Ten Commandments monument from public display in the State Judicial Building. (AP Wide World Photos/Dave Martin)

unknown tongues. Open to the supernatural, they reached Catholics as well as Protestants. Almost 30 million Americans identified themselves as charismatic Christians.

The Christian right was among the first to merge ideology with technology, allying with conservatives who obtained funds from the grassroots by means of computers, direct mail, television, and market research, as well as from big business. The Christian right's message came into millions of homes on Sunday mornings. With their TV programs, popular "televangelists" such as Oral Roberts, Pat Roberston, Jerry Falwell, Jim and Tammy Faye Bakker, and Jimmy Swaggart raised millions for their ministries. Falwell founded the Moral Majority, a movement that claimed a large share of credit for Reagan's election, and preached a conventional fundamentalism denouncing drug use, permissiveness, and sins of the flesh. He was a formidable political force from the 1980s onward. Swaggart, a skilled musician like his cousin, rock and roll pioneer Jerry Lee Lewis, periodically sat down to pound the piano and spoke emotionally, without notes, delivering fire-and-brimstone sermons. Robertson became the first televangelist to enter politics as a candidate, running in the 1988 Republican presidential primaries. He garnered about 10 percent of the vote in the early contests, but proved unable to expand on his base or break George Bush's hold on the party and eventually withdrew.

In the late 1980s scandals destroyed some televangelists' ministries. Roberts discredited himself by saying that he had received a message from God: if Roberts's followers did not contribute a large amount of money by a deadline, God would kill him. The prophecy failed to materialize. Jim Bakker admitted to having a tawdry affair with a church secretary and was imprisoned for defrauding his adherents. Swaggart, who had been highly critical of Bakker's improprieties, confessed that he had hired a prostitute on several occasions and was briefly suspended by his denomination, the Assemblies of God. Most of the televangelists subsequently retired from the airwaves or kept a lower profile during the rest of the era. Falwell and Robertson remained active, but lost some credibility by making anti-Semitic, anti-gay statements.

Conservative-versus-liberal clashes were not confined to Protestantism. Catholics in the era were still adjusting to the Second Vatican Council that lasted from 1962 to 1965. Now Masses were celebrated in English, not Latin, with the priest facing the congregation, which sang hymns and repeated prayers in English. More time was devoted to sermons that included a moral lesson. The practice of abstaining from eating red meat on Fridays waned. If the reforms of Vatican II brought the Catholic Church up to date, however, they did not restore enthusiasm among the faithful. Some disliked the less formal Masses and the change from Latin to English, finding them undignified. Fewer attended services regularly or went to confession. Many Catholics disagreed with their church. They wanted women ordained as priests; practiced birth control and divorced. Opposition to abortion and homosexuality weakened. Some Catholics considered liberation theology, a doctrine popular in Latin America that attempted to merge Christianity and Marxism to provide a rationale for social revolution. Liberal views were muted, however, after the 1978 papal election of John Paul II, a popular, anticommunist conservative who upheld church traditions.

The more liberal Protestant denominations and Reform Jews allowed women ministers and rabbis and gave women a larger role in services. Gender-inclusive language was introduced in Scriptures and hymns. Roles for gays and lesbians were controversial after a gay liberation movement emerged in the 1970s and 1980s. Because of Scripture and tradition, many Christians and Jews considered homosexuality a sin, but by the 1980s gays had gained some protections against discrimination.

As mainline churches wrestled with questions of diversity, new groups experimented with personal spirituality that borrowed from Eastern and Western religions as well as those of Native Americans. The key to the new spirituality was individual rather than institutional, connecting with the unity of all things through meditation and silence. Some meditators focused their minds by following their breath through their bodies; others chanted a mantra. For some, meditation was primarily a method of relaxation; for others it meant integrating with the universe. Asked the difference between meditation and prayer, one adherent explained: "When you pray, you talk to God; when you meditate, God talks to you. You have to listen closely because God's only voice is silence." Innovators such as Gregory Hoag of Colorado experimented with making meditation tools based on geometric forms, colors, angles and programmed energy which he visualized. Hoag combined a knowledge of ancient texts with engineering and intuition. Other Americans turned to the once-prominent healer and prophet Edgar Cayce, who could diagnose and heal patients thousands of miles away and left tens of thousands of pages of readings based on his observations while in trances. More than three hundred books have been written about Cayce, who died in 1945. Increasingly, Americans, especially young people, turned to mind-body medicine, Eastern rituals, and martial arts in the belief that God is energy or controls a force of energy, such as "the Force" in the *Star Wars* movies.

Other religions were more of the cult variety, frequently variations of Christianity that practiced fanatical commitment, intolerance, separation from society, and worship of an authoritarian leader. The best known was the Unification Church of the Reverend Sun Myung Moon, who believed he was a prophet of God who foretold a heavenly kingdom. Deadlier was the People's Temple under the Reverend Jim Jones, who moved his followers into isolation in Guyana in South America and led them in a mass suicide of nine hundred in November 1978, when he feared the authorities were poised to break up his movement.

Lessons in Education

The consensus of parents, academicians, and school officials in the Era of Diversity was that public schools were failing. Perhaps the schools were failing the students; perhaps the students were not trying; possibly both were true. After billions of dollars poured into city schools, and attempts were made to obtain and retain better-trained teachers, the schools, with some exceptions, were withering within the bureaucracy. The biggest problems seemed lack of discipline, high dropout rates, and lack of morale. The simplest and most effective reform—reducing class size—was often rejected in favor of new equipment and additional brick and mortar. Teacher and administrator burnout is rapid, partly because of low salaries. But most teachers knew salaries would be low when they entered the profession; it is their frustration with the educational process that disturbed them. From the 1950s, when the most serious problem cited by teachers was students chewing gum, the major problem in the 2000s is likely to be drugs or weapons in school, or, worse yet, students who do not think it is important to study.

Some educators and parents believed children might be better educated at private or parochial schools, where discipline was stricter and the learning environment was superior. Milwaukee, Cleveland, and other cities initiated "voucher" systems to pay for the education of some poor children at private schools. Public school officials feared the plans would drain them of money and students; when religious schools were included, they declared vouchers unconstitutional. The results of the programs were marginal; the chief variable in success seemed to be the students, not the schools, the teachers, or the money. Many African Americans began calling for a return to neighborhood schools. Parents would be involved and their children would be spared long trips on buses.

Parents, educators, and religious leaders also clashed over the teaching of evolution in public schools. Fundamentalists wanted to substitute "creation science" for Charles Darwin's theories of natural selection, pitting battles among plants and animals. At least, the religious educators wanted the Genesis account taught as an alternative and Darwin's account designated a theory. At stake was the fear that "secular humanism" was undermining Christianity because it excluded God and ridiculed religious values. Moreover, said fundamentalists, children would be confused if their Christian parents taught them one thing and their secular educators another. Teachers needed freedom of speech but they had no monopoly on truth. Moreover, parents deserved a voice in school curricula. The battle extended to high school textbooks, which temporized by publishing no accounts of creation, watered-down accounts, or both accounts.

In higher education, a vast complex of technical colleges, junior colleges, four-year colleges, and research universities served the nation by the last quarter of the twentieth century. The major universities, including the more prestigious ones, emphasized research, publication, and graduate education. Rarely did a research university reward or promote a professor solely on teaching; research was the key to advancement. On the other hand, many liberal arts schools and some four-year colleges rewarded teaching alone; at some liberal arts colleges, research was even discouraged. The junior colleges and technical schools were feeders to universities and colleges and also offered two-year degrees directed at learning a skill.

Student protests declined after the Vietnam War, although there were a few demonstrations against nuclear weapons, apartheid in South Africa, and the Persian Gulf War. For the most part, college students were pragmatic and materialistic, due to tight job markets. They wanted to earn graduate or business degrees and find well-paying jobs. When the baby boomers graduated from college, the glut in students became a glut of job seekers. From the late 1970s through the end of the century there was an oversupply of Ph.D.s in the humanities. Advertisements for assistant professors in American history, for example, often drew two or three hundred applicants. Some newly minted Ph.D.s found themselves on welfare, at least temporarily.

The racial problems that infected American society did not escape its colleges and universities. Prompted by federal incentives, universities recruited minorities, sometimes employing affirmative action, which included scholarships and favorable admissions standards for certain minorities in order to achieve racial balance. Some white people objected to affirmative action in education, as they did when it was used in the job market. The number of minorities in colleges grew, and those with degrees were highly likely to escape the trap of poverty. Still, ethnic and racial groups often were socially segregated within the college setting, by choice or because they felt unwelcome.

Technology, which permeated society, also grew on campus. Computers were used in libraries, in research, in writing, and in teaching. Colleges offered degrees in computer science, and initially graduates were in high demand. Schools began to teach courses via the Internet so students could take courses at home. There were abuses. Learning became impersonal, as contact with professors and peers was limited, and companies were created to sell term papers over the Internet.

Gender and Society

Feminism continued to evolve. Most disappointing to feminists was defeat of the Equal Rights Amendment three states short of ratification in 1982. Conservative women organized by Phyllis Schlafly and others played a large role in the defeat. Contention mounted over abortion. Women, paradoxically, were both the strongest defenders and the strongest critics of abortion; the voices of potential fathers of fetuses were virtually ignored. The Supreme Court did not overturn *Roe v. Wade* but ruled in *Webster v. Reproductive Health Services* (1989), that it was no longer permissible for tax-supported hospitals to perform abortions unless the woman's health was in danger. In *Planned Parenthood v. Casey* (1992), the Court tried to define what types of restrictions on abortions were acceptable. Militant abortion opponents picketed clinics and blocked the paths of women who wanted to enter them.

In the 1980s women began to take distinctive positions, different from the positions men took on some political issues. More than men, they opposed capital punishment, higher defense spending, military intervention overseas, and nuclear power, while they supported arms control. Ironically, there was little difference between the sexes on so-called women's issues. Men favored the Equal Rights Amendment in slightly higher percentages than women. The most prominent, and most controversial, woman in politics in the era was Hillary Rodham Clinton.

Feminism was not the only current in women's politics or lifestyles. In 1997 just one-quarter of women considered themselves feminists. Among black women, feminism had little appeal, as their problems and priorities differed from those of professional white women. Some women complained that feminism made child-rearing seem unimportant. Cultural feminists agreed that male domination of society was unjust, yet said it was unrealistic to deny the existence of differences between the sexes solely because such differences had been used to exploit women in the past. Instead, cultural feminists celebrated differences and urged women to take pride in talents learned from their experience as mothers. Differences did not imply inferiority, and it was time to use them rather than suppress them, argued Carol Gilligan, a leading advocate of cultural feminism.

Pornography and sexual harassment were battlegrounds in the cultural wars. Some feminists claimed pornography amounted to sexual harassment and should be outlawed. Others, however, believed it was a protected form of free speech. The end of sexual harassment on the job ranked higher on the feminist agenda, and the feminists demanded that damages be paid to women who suffered unwanted advances that created an uncomfortable environment. Several cases of sexual harassment disgraced the armed forces, although the military accepted new roles for women at least as well as society as a whole.

Feminists put a higher priority on education and job fulfillment than on motherhood. Women with graduate degrees married later or not at all. The surge in the divorce rate was striking. From 1960 to 1980 it more than doubled. By the late 1980s nearly one in two first marriages ended in divorce. By 1990 the divorce rate was triple that of 1970. Also striking was the increase in families headed by unmarried mothers. This fact was significant because two-thirds of woman-headed families received child welfare and because two-thirds of the long-term poor were women.

Pluralism and Polarization

For millions of African Americans, the Era of Diversity was a time of progress. Institutionalized racism declined, and many blacks became doctors, lawyers, professors, and businessmen. The condition of African Americans in inner-city ghettos worsened, however, with unemployment averaging 14 or 15 percent, more than double the rate among whites. Among black teens joblessness was as high as 40 or 50 percent. Drug use, crime, delinquency, high dropout rates, teenage pregnancies, and lack of stable families continued to plague the ghetto. By 1999 just 25 percent of black children lived in two-parent families, a statistic linked to the prevalence of poverty among African Americans. The arrival of crack cocaine devastated inner cities during the 1980s, turning them into war zones of feuding gangs and spawning a culture of violence.

At times the frustration boiled over. In 1991, in Los Angeles, police were videotaped beating a black motorist, Rodney King, whom they stopped on suspicion of a traffic violation. A white jury acquitted the four officers despite the videotape, touching off the worst riot of the century. Fifty-three people were killed, thousands were injured, some twelve hundred businesses were destroyed, and $1 billion in property was damaged. Choking back tears, King pleaded for calm on television, saying: "Can we all get along? Can we get along? We've just got to, just got to. We're all stuck here for a while. Let's try to work it out. Let's try to work it out." The four officers were subsequently tried on federal charges of violating King's civil rights, resulting in convictions and short prison terms for two of them.

Further polarizing the races, in 1995 a black former collegiate and professional football star, O. J. Simpson, was acquitted in the Los Angeles murders of his former wife, Nicole Brown Simpson, and her friend, Ronald Goldman, both slashed with a knife. The trial became the most celebrated courtroom drama of the century, attracting more attention than the Sacco-Vanzetti trial or the Scopes trial. Wealthy, Simpson was able to retain the best attorneys and won his case despite convincing circumstantial evidence, including the presence of his DNA at the crime scene. Most white people considered him guilty, but most blacks applauded the outcome, some calling it a payback to the white power structure. So disturbed were the Brown and Goldman families that they sued Simpson for the wrongful deaths of their children and won monetary damages.

Attempts to solve problems that were undermining race relations met with varying degrees of effectiveness. In 1995 Louis Farrakhan, leader of the Nation of Islam, staged a Million Man March in Washington to get black men to take control of their lives and be better husbands, fathers, and providers. The march drew hundreds of thousands, but far less than 1 million, and was controversial because Farrakhan was a notorious anti-Semite. Disturbed at the racial tension, and hoping to gain political capital, President Bill Clinton appointed a commission to study racial issues. Conservatives complained that their views were not represented on the panel. The chair, distinguished black historian John Hope Franklin, responded that conservatives were not included because they had nothing to contribute.

The commission and the controversy surrounding racism degenerated into an ideological skirmish that divided Americans. California banned affirmative action in public employment and college admissions in 1996 through a ballot initiative, and some federal courts prohibited universities from favoring minorities in admissions. Whites remained divided over whether the civil rights revolution had gone too far. The last years of the twentieth century featured more diversity, and probably more equal justice under law, than ever before in the United States. More white people seemed willing to accept laws that afforded equal opportunities, as opposed to laws that tried to guarantee equal outcome.

American Indians faced recurring problems, including alcoholism, diabetes, high rates of school dropouts, illiteracy, youth crime, prejudice, and cultural upheaval. During the latter years of the twentieth century, about half of Native Americans lived in cities and only one-quarter on reservations. Fewer spoke an Indian language as their first tongue, and more Indian children could not speak an Indian language at all.

Indian arts flourished, however. Powwows brought members of diverse tribes together. Novelists such as Louise Erdrich and Gerald Vizenor graced literature, exploring challenges and new dimensions of Indian life. Indian painters offered familiar, realistic works as well as experimental abstractions. By the late 1990s more than two hundred museums and centers of Indian exhibits had been created, many on reservations. Indians demanded the return of relics, such as bones, skulls, or skeletons held by museums or anthropologists, for reburial. Scientists claimed that the relics were too valuable to rebury and had cost them years of work, yet Indians persisted, often winning them back. Indians also found pride in athletic competition, especially basketball, rodeo, and lacrosse.

Another lifeline for Indians, casino gambling on reservations, stirred debate. Indians have the right to sponsor casinos on reservations, even when gambling is otherwise illegal in their states, because of their status as sovereign governments, according to the Supreme Court. The casinos brought economic development but were criticized for profiting from a vice on which Indians have a monopoly. Native Americans defended their prerogative on casinos. Indians also fought sports teams' use of Native American mascots and nicknames and frequently prevailed among colleges.

If Native Americans faced difficulties in the Era of Diversity, so did newcomers. The Immigration and Nationality Act of 1965 unleashed a new torrent of arrivals in the United States, in which women outnumbered men. Forty-five percent of immigrants, mostly Hispanic, came from the Western Hemisphere and 30 percent from Asia. Just 12 percent came from Europe. The Hispanic influx, about 25 percent of it illegal, was so large that Hispanics rose from 2 percent of the population in 1960 to 9 percent in 1990, to 12.5 percent in 2000. Demographers estimated that by 2013 Hispanics would surpass African Americans as the nation's largest minority. Hispanic families were stable, as were Asian families, many of which settled in California. Asian immigrants increased 40 percent in the 1980s. Japanese set a standard for economic achievement, with Japanese American income exceeding the national per capita income by the 1990s.

But because they concentrated in a few states, competed with other Americans for jobs, and required bilingual education and tax increases to support schools, welfare, and medical care, the new immigrants stirred resentment. The 1986 Immigration Reform and Control Act discouraged employers from hiring immigrants by punishing businesses that employed illegal immigrants. California went further: ballot measures halted most state aid to illegal immigrants in 1994 and called for an end to bilingual education in 1998. Nationally, the 1996 federal welfare overhaul cut off many benefits to illegal newcomers, although Clinton persuaded Congress to restore some. Illegal migration and efforts to control it frayed relations with Mexico and inflamed ethnic tension in the Southwest. Politicians from seven states in the region urged the construction of a wall along the border. Meanwhile, immigrants confronted the problems of finding adequate employment and of adjusting to society. Women immigrants were torn between the traditional, submissive roles of their native cultures and the assertiveness of American feminism. For immigrants, as well as for millions of other Americans, Rodney King's question would echo into the twenty-first century.

CHAPTER TWENTY-FOUR

From George Bush
to George W. Bush

THE ERA OF Diversity culminated with a conservative Republican president and a moderately liberal Democrat, further evidence of the diversity that characterized the nation's highest office after the end of the Second World War. They presided over a nation of technological virtuosity and ideological and racial complexity, one far more diverse than their ancestors had inherited at the dawn of the twentieth century. In 2001 George W. Bush took office, becoming the second half of the only father-and-son presidential tandem since John and John Quincy Adams in the formative years of the Republic. George W. Bush had a sense of adventure and preferred moderate change, not unlike the Republican who became president one hundred years earlier, Theodore Roosevelt. Yet, events, not men, rode the saddle during the tenures of both of these cowboy presidents.

George Bush

Before George W. Bush there was George Herbert Walker Bush. Born to wealth, Bush, who assumed office in 1989, was the son of Prescott Bush, a Wall Street investor and a Republican senator from Connecticut. Bush enlisted in the navy at eighteen, became the service's youngest pilot in World War II, flew fifty-eight combat missions, and was shot down twice. He returned to the United States to attend Yale University, where he was captain of the baseball team that finished second in the nation. Then he invested in the oil business in Texas and entered politics.

Bush ran for the Senate in 1964 as a Goldwater conservative and lost but later won two terms in the House of Representatives, starting in 1966.

After a second unsuccessful Senate race, in 1970, he was appointed ambassador to the United Nations in 1971, and national Republican chair in 1973. In 1974 Bush became envoy to China, then CIA director. His supporters, pointing to his impressive portfolio, plus his experience as Reagan's vice president, said he was the best-qualified politician to succeed the icon of the 1980s. Bush's wife, Barbara, also grew up in a wealthy family, and they had six children, two of whom became the chief executives of major Southern states (Jeb, governor of Florida, and George W., governor of Texas). As first lady, Barbara Bush made literacy her cause and promoted family values and volunteer work. Bush's vice president, Dan Quayle, was a favorite of conservatives.

In temperament, Bush, who led by quiet example, was unlike Reagan, who led by passion and inspiration. Also unlike Reagan, he was not an effective public speaker. In the Era of Diversity, Bush pleased neither political pole; he was neither a reformer nor an ideological conservative. Although he played first base in college, his position in politics was right-center field. He produced a meager domestic record, yet wielded his veto pen to keep liberal Democratic legislation off the books. Congress was a roadblock; Bush faced the largest opposing majorities of any twentieth-century president.

The battle of the budget was central. Deficits had soared under Reagan, yet Bush vowed to avoid new taxes during his campaign. The first budget, in 1989, was accomplished with relative ease. After an economic decline, the 1990 budget became difficult to negotiate. Bush had to back down from his "no new taxes" pledge to compromise with the Democrats. Economic necessity became political calamity, as violation of his pledge haunted Bush in his 1992 reelection campaign. The recession that began in 1990 ended during the campaign of 1992, too late to aid Bush but enough to help his successor's administration enjoy eight years of prosperity. Ironically, the decade of the 1980s, the most prosperous to that time, was followed by an even more prosperous decade.

Bush achieved a modest increase in the minimum wage, stimulated volunteer efforts through a program called "A Thousand Points of Light," encouraged education without significant new funding, and waged a war on drugs. Drug use declined in the 1980s and 1990s largely because 1960s lifestyles were declining as baby boomers aged. Calling for a "kinder, gentler America," the president's main contribution was the Americans with Disabilities Act of 1990. It prohibited employment discrimination against the handicapped and required that buildings and buses be wheelchair accessible. In addition, Bush provided funds for child care, and signed the Clean Air Act of 1990, which restricted emissions from factories and automobiles. An environmental disaster, the enormous oil spill caused by the grounding of the *Exxon Valdez* in Prince William Sound, off the Alaskan coast, on March 24, 1989, alarmed Americans and expedited passage of the bill.

Supreme Court appointments became increasingly politicized in the Era of Diversity, and attempts to obtain ideological and racial diversity often were the focus of the problem. Bush's first nominee, David Souter, an obscure justice of the New Hampshire Supreme Court, breezed through, largely because of a lack of information about Souter's record on controversial issues. In 1991, Thurgood Marshall, the only black Justice, retired. Bush nominated a black conservative, Clarence Thomas, to succeed him. Near the end of the hearings, Anita Hill, who had once worked for Thomas, testified that he had sexually harassed her, telling her dirty jokes and asking her for dates. Thomas was narrowly confirmed, but the affair polarized the country. Thomas went on to become one of the most conservative justices, and a virtual recluse in private life.

Delicate Diplomacy: Warmaking and Peacemaking

Bush will be known to history primarily as a foreign policy president. He preferred policies undergirded by caution and finesse, yet could act decisively. The president appointed an able foreign policy team and relied on world leaders he knew.

In Nicaragua, Bush obtained his objective of containing communism without war. The administration guaranteed $450 million in humanitarian aid, but no military aid, to the anticommunist Contras. With the civil war winding down, the Marxist Sandinistas permitted a free election, which they lost. Violetta Chamorro upset Sandinista President Daniel Ortega, ending Marxist rule.

Americans found a paradox in Panama. The Panamanian dictator, Manuel Noriega, once an American ally and an informer for the CIA, had degenerated into a drug lord. In 1987 American courts indicted Noriega; in 1988 Reagan imposed economic sanctions on Panama; and in 1989 Noriega allowed an election, which his candidate lost. In December 1989 Bush ordered the invasion of Panama and arrest of Noriega, who was captured, tried in the United States, and imprisoned.

Still, turbulence prevailed in many Latin American nations. An election in Haiti, long dominated by the malevolent Jean-Claude Duvalier, placed a reformer in power, Jean-Bertrand Aristide. Yet, reform was short-lived for Haiti. After seven months, the army toppled Aristide. Staying his hand for the time, Bush imposed economic sanctions. Thousands of Haitian refugees tried to reach the Florida coast, only to be turned back. Critics argued that they were rejected on racial grounds, pointing out that

Cuban refugees were accepted. The administration countered that the chief difference was that Cubans were fleeing a Communist regime.

Outside the hemisphere, Bush struggled with an array of problems. The Middle East, which had been the burial ground for many peace initiatives, continued to frustrate. Palestinians insisted that Israelis cease building Jewish settlements in the occupied territories, yet Prime Minister Yitzhak Shamir resisted. After a fruitless peace conference at Madrid in October 1991, Israel elected a more conciliatory prime minister, Shimon Peres. Peres advocated trading land for peace, but opinions were divided: How much land for how much peace?

In Africa, war and famine ravaged Somalia, and tribal battles threatened to destroy United Nations efforts to deliver food and supplies. During the last weeks of the Bush administration, America sent soldiers to protect the mission, hoping that later the U.N. could furnish security. Events had a better ending in South Africa, where years of international pressure against the apartheid regime paid off. In 1990 President F. W. de Klerk reversed the ban on the African National Congress, a leading anti-apartheid group, and black leader Nelson Mandela was freed after decades behind bars. Over the next three years, the country overturned laws that restricted blacks to "homelands," approved a constitution that gave blacks the vote for the first time, and elected Mandela as president.

The currents of history were also running against Soviet President Mikhail Gorbachev, who began contracting his overextended empire to preserve communism. Early in 1989, he began withdrawing tanks and troops from Eastern Europe. In June, he renounced the right to intervene, but events moved on their own momentum. Hungary was the first country to break with the Soviet Union in 1989; its Communist Party renounced Marxism and opened the nation's borders. The party agreed to free elections in 1990 and lost to noncommunists. Also, in 1989, the anticommunist Solidarity trade union, led by Lech Walesa helped draft a new constitution for Poland, won elections, and won control of a coalition government. In October, the new Ceausescu government announced that the country was converting to a market economy. Czechoslovakian lawmakers abolished the communist monopoly on power, and author Vaclav Havel won the presidency. Communism fell elsewhere in the Soviet bloc with little bloodshed, except in Romania, where Dictator Nicolae Ceaucescu tried to flee after nearly a quarter-century rule, only to be executed by revolutionaries on Christmas Day, 1989. And, in Yugoslavia, ethnic factions that had been held together under Josip Broz Tito descended into warfare.

In Germany communism's fall was most dramatic. Crowds demonstrated on both sides of the Berlin Wall, then surged over and through the Wall

TEARING DOWN THE WALL
Berliners demolish a symbol of oppression, November 11, 1989.
(AP/Wide World Photos/Lionel Cironneau)

while East German troops refused to fire on their own people. The crowds tore down the Wall with axes, shovels, and bare hands. In 1990, Germany reunified. The heartland of Europe, for one of the few times in its ancient history, was free. Later, Germany and many of the formerly communist Eastern European nations joined NATO.

Ironically, by the time these nations joined NATO, an American-led alliance created to deter communism, there was little communism to deter. Bush did not foresee the collapse of communism in its nerve center and worked with Gorbachev to preserve the Soviet state. Yet, time marched against communism. Not only could the Soviet state no longer compete economically or militarily with the West, but ethnic minorities demanded freedom. Gorbachev went further than any previous Soviet leader in reforming his state, and won a Nobel Peace Prize, yet he only accelerated its destruction. Glasnost and perestroika gave Gorbachev's people only a taste of freedom and Western consumerism without satisfying their pangs of hunger.

In June 1991 Moscow Mayor Boris Yeltsin, an advocate of Russian independence and rapid reform, became the first freely elected president of the Russian republic. Then, Soviet hard-liners staged a coup, placing

Gorbachev under arrest, moves that Bush opposed. Yeltsin climbed atop a hostile tank in Moscow and rallied the people. Much of the army remained loyal to Gorbachev and Yeltsin, and the coup failed. Gorbachev resigned as head of the Communist Party and disbanded its leadership. On December 7, Russia, Ukraine, and Belorussia declared the USSR defunct. Power flowed to Yeltsin, who broke with the party, denied it a role in the government, and confiscated Communist property. On December 25, Gorbachev resigned as president. The following day the members of the rump Parliament acknowledged the dissolution of the Soviet Union. Some of the newly independent states created a weak commonwealth. The Cold War ended suddenly, decisively, and peacefully. The danger of instantaneous nuclear annihilation receded, although terrorist threats remain. Bush shifted his allegiance from Gorbachev to Yeltsin. Yeltsin was unstable, lacked Gorbachev's polish and was unpredictable, but he was a champion of democracy.

Only one major communist power remained, China, though it moved rapidly toward a free market economy. Many Chinese, dissatisfied after seeing they had fewer freedoms and consumer items than people of Western nations, rebelled. In 1989 pro-democracy students gathered in Tiananmen Square, in the heart of Beijing, to protest. Prime Minister Li Peng imposed martial law and demanded that the protesters disperse. Refusing, they erected a "Goddess of Liberty" statue resembling the Statue of Liberty and defied troops. On June 4, troops and tanks moved in to expel the students, killing hundreds, perhaps thousands. Authorities imprisoned protest leaders, closed schools, and disbanded student and worker organizations. Washington imposed sanctions on Beijing, including an end to military sales.

Under Saddam Hussein, Iraq, too, was bottled up by repression. Hussein denied basic freedoms, sponsored terrorism, and threatened his neighbors. Hussein's invasion and conquest of tiny, oil-rich Kuwait in early August 1990, raised moral and geopolitical concerns. He was in position to threaten Israeli security and drive up world oil prices. Bush promised to punish Iraq for its aggression. After economic sanctions failed to persuade Hussein to withdraw, Bush assembled a coalition of forty-eight nations and sent half a million American troops to the Persian Gulf area. Many nations contributed soldiers, including some Arab governments, which also supplied financial aid. Congress authorized the use of force to expel Hussein from Kuwait. Soon afterward, the coalition bombed Iraq for forty-eight days, an unprecedented pounding. With Baghdad still ignoring Bush's ultimatum to withdraw from Kuwait, the president ordered an invasion. Hussein promised "the mother of all battles," but the ground war, like the air war, was so lopsided that the American commander, General H. Norman Schwarzkopf, ridiculed it as "the mother of all retreats" for Iraqi forces. In one hundred hours, the Iraqis were routed, Kuwait was liberated, and Bush terminated hostilities. Although Hussein was not at war with Israel, he attacked the Jewish state with missiles, killing two civilians. Overall, coalition casualties were light, including less than 150 battle deaths for the United States, compared with 300,000 for Iraq. Americans celebrated, yet because coalition forces stopped short of capturing and deposing Hussein, the triumph was incomplete.

From Victory in Iraq to Loss at the Polls

Bush's apparent invulnerability after the victory of Iraq discouraged prominent Democrats from entering the presidential race. New York Governor Mario Cuomo, the potential front-runner for the Democratic nomination, decided not to run, clearing the way for Arkansas Governor Bill Clinton, who was challenged by former Massachusetts Senator Paul Tsongas, Senator Bob Kerry of Nebraska, Virginia Governor Douglas Wilder, and former California Governor "Jerry" Brown. Tsongas upset Clinton in New Hampshire after newspapers reported that Clinton had conducted a twelve-year affair with Arkansas television reporter Jennifer Flowers. Clinton regained the initiative by winning eight primaries (mostly in the South) in

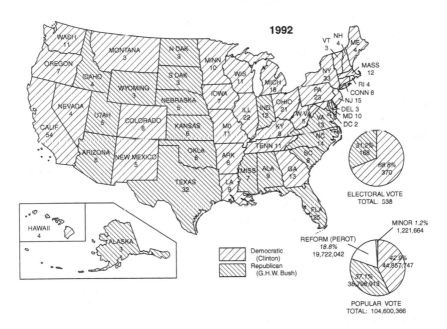

Election of 1992

a single day. Subsequent victories in Michigan, Illinois, and New York later ensured his nomination. Clinton selected a fellow southerner, Senator Al Gore of Tennessee, as his running mate.

Clinton ran as a New Democrat, taking a middle way between anti-government Reaganism and the Democratic tradition that government could solve most problems. He blended liberalism and conservatism, a center-left position similar to Eisenhower's center-right position in the Republican party. Just as Eisenhower had not attempted to roll back the New Deal when he became president in 1953, Clinton accepted some aspects of Reaganism. A fiscal conservative, he believed the government should act, but only when vital.

Clinton's candidacy grew out of the Democratic Leadership Council (DLC), an organization representing New Democratic views, organized in 1984, which gained increased influence after the defeat of Michael Dukakis in 1988. As governor of Arkansas, Clinton had become a leader of the group, which attributed Democratic losses in every presidential election since 1976 to the party straying too far from the political center. To regain the allegiance of the white middle class, necessary to win presidential elections, the DLC believed that Democrats must emphasize personal responsibility and limited government. Clinton's campaign was less ideological than those of previous Democratic candidates.

By the time of the general election, the decline of the economy had drained Bush's support. Clinton shifted the issue from social and foreign policy agenda to the faltering economy. A skilled speaker, highly intelligent, and opportunistic, Clinton attacked Bush's leadership. The president, he charged, lacked vision and neglected the economy while he obsessed over foreign policy.

Actually, Bush's caution at the end of the Cold War might have helped ensure the peaceful demise of the Soviet Union, and his leadership of the coalition that won the Persian Gulf War demonstrated sound leadership. After Reagan set up communism's fall, it collapsed on Bush's watch. Bush's solid record on foreign affairs, however, was not sufficient to dissuade Americans from voting on pocketbook issues, though, ironically, the recession actually ended before the election. In addition, breaking his promise not to raise taxes, although an economic necessity, damaged Bush politically.

A third candidate, Texas billionaire businessman Ross Perot, a conservative, siphoned votes from Bush, a fellow conservative, possibly costing him the election. Clinton won with 44.9 million popular votes (43 percent) and 370 electoral votes to Bush's 39.1 million (37.4 percent) and 168 electoral votes. Perot received 19.7 million popular votes (18.9 percent), the highest proportion ever for a third-party candidate. Democrats won control of Congress. Feminists called 1992 the Year of the Woman, as the

Congress elected in November included fifty-three women in the House and six in the Senate. California became the first state to elect two women to the Senate: Diane Feinstein and Barbara Boxer. Illinois sent the first black woman to the upper house, Carol Moseley Braun.

William "Bill" Jefferson Clinton

Clinton came from a background as humble as Bush's was patrician. Born in the village of Hope, the Arkansan was raised largely by his mother and grandfather, after his father died in a car accident. When he was four, his mother married Roger Clinton, an alcoholic. The family insecurity Clinton endured contributed to a tenacious drive and empathy. Charismatic, Clinton had strains of immaturity and self-destruction. Skilled at compromise, he preferred cutting a deal to standing on principle. Both eloquent and glib, critics termed him "Slick Willie."

An outstanding student, Clinton attended Georgetown University, then Oxford, and earned a law degree at Yale University, where he met his future

THE MAN FROM HOPE, ARKANSAS
Israeli Prime Minister Yitzhak Rabin, President Bill Clinton,
and Palestine Liberation Organization Chairman Yasir Arafat meet
for the signing of the Oslo Accords in September 1993.
(William Jefferson Clinton Presidential Library)

wife, Hillary Rodham. Born to a rich Republican family, she became a Eugene McCarthy Democrat and an antiwar activist in college. A feminist, she started a career before a family (the Clintons had one daughter, Chelsea) and was hard-edged and ambitious. Like her husband, highly intelligent, she possessed even more drive. Initially, Hillary and Al Gore were among the president's closest advisers. The cabinet included moderates and liberals, women and minorities. Two women, Janet Reno and Madeleine Albright, were the first of their sex to serve as attorney general and secretary of state, respectively. Another woman, liberal Ruth Bader Ginsburg, joined the liberal Stephen Breyer as Clinton's Supreme Court appointees.

Economic Laser Beam

Some successes in domestic politics mixed with defeats early in Clinton's first term. A bill Bush had vetoed, the Family and Medical Leave Act, received Clinton's signature in 1993; it permitted workers to take up to twelve weeks' unpaid leave from their jobs to care for a parent, spouse, or child. Clinton's attempt to remove the ban on known homosexuals in the armed forces misfired and he settled for a "don't ask, don't tell" policy. Gays and lesbians would not be asked about their sexual orientation by commanding officers. But, if they volunteered it, or practiced their sexuality openly, they would be dismissed.

Clinton fared even worse with a major initiative, comprehensive health insurance. Such proposals had been advocated by every Democratic president since Harry S Truman, yet Congress, or congressional committees, had been their graveyard. The plan had two objectives: universal coverage and cost control. These aims were difficult to synchronize. First, complete medical coverage was an item of infinite demand and limited supply. It involved competing interests, such as patients, insurance companies, doctors, hospitals, and drug companies. It also involved contrary objectives, such as maximum quality care of the greatest number at the least cost, allowing drug companies incentives to develop wonder drugs while simultaneously regulating drug prices. In addition to wonder drugs, there were wonder machines, that heroically kept patients alive, yet at a high cost. Government operation might create a mammoth bureaucracy vulnerable to political manipulation. Hillary Rodham Clinton headed a task force that worked in secret to shape a comprehensive plan. The president could hardly be objective, critics charged, about a plan developed by his wife. Unpopular even before it reached Congress, Democrats never brought it to a vote. Hillary Rodham Clinton lost status as a policy expert, and the complicated proposal added fuel to Republican charges that the administration was no less mired in a bureaucratic mind-set than previous Democratic presidencies. Clinton salvaged the 1996 Health Insurance and Portability Plan, which enabled workers to retain insurance when they lost jobs or changed work. In addition, the 1997 budget provided health coverage to uninsured children and extended Medicare.

The budget was Clinton's first priority. Vowing to focus "like a laser beam" on the economy, he proposed tax increases on the wealthy to bring down the federal deficit, spending to encourage economic growth and jobs, and retraining of workers whose jobs were threatened by the global economy. Pursuing deficit reduction, Clinton abandoned his campaign pledge to cut middle-class taxes and proposed a modest increase in the gasoline tax. Congress passed his program without the job stimulus, narrowly, in August 1993. The budget squeaked through by two votes in the House and Vice President Gore cast a tie-breaking vote in the Senate. The budget included an Earned Income Tax Credit to help the working poor. The economy gathered momentum. Unemployment plummeted to a four-year low. Inflation remained in check due to the Federal Reserve's high interest rates and tight money policies, and because oil prices stabilized.

By 1994, however, Clinton's approval ratings had slipped because of "character" issues and the public demand for tax cuts and leaner government. Georgia Representative Newt Gingrich proposed a "Contract with America," whereby Republicans pledged themselves to traditional values, balanced budgets, and term limits for Congress. Running on this platform, which resembled "Reaganism without Reagan," the GOP captured both Houses for the first time since 1954.

Electing Gingrich as Speaker, the House majority passed some elements of the "Contract." Clinton regained the momentum when the parties clashed over budgets in 1995 and 1996, causing two brief government shutdowns. The parties temporized by enacting continuing resolutions to keep the government running. Many Americans blamed the Republicans for the shutdowns and supported Clinton's vetoes of steep cuts in spending.

Politically, Clinton outflanked Republicans by borrowing issues from both the Left and Right. Although he professed a belief in personal responsibility, Clinton argued that the Republicans wanted to punish the poor. In 1996, after vetoing two Republican welfare reform measures, Clinton signed a third bill opposed by liberals in his party. The sweeping reform ended six decades of federal aid to indigent mothers and children and transferred major entitlement programs to the states. Recipients could not receive assistance for more than two successive years or five years over a lifetime.

Many whites considered welfare a race problem because of the high percentage of African Americans on welfare. Clinton's belief in a color-blind society clashed with his support for affirmative action, which he wanted to reform, not abolish. Clinton remained popular with blacks, even as he moved right, and a majority of blacks supported him in his election campaign and during his impeachment crisis.

Still, Clinton adopted policies designed to wean the white middle class from allegiance to presidential Republicanism. He supported the death penalty, backed a crime measure that put 100,000 additional policemen on the streets, and steered education measures through Congress, a tax credit for college study, and money to recruit teachers. The National Service Act (1993) provided educational grants in return for community service. Congress provided appropriations for vocational education and increased funds for college loans and scholarships. The Goals 2000 Act of March 1994 set targets for student achievement and teacher standards. Clinton achieved incremental reforms based on modest appropriations rather than blockbuster legislation comparable to the Great Society.

A Prosperous Yet Turbulent Second Term

Prosperity was the engine of Bill Clinton's reelection in 1996 and remains his chief legacy. With the economy performing well and Clinton taking moderate stands on many issues, the Republican nominee, Senator Robert Dole of Kansas, tried to make the campaign a contest of character and patriotism, to no avail. The incumbents defeated Dole, and Ross Perot, running once more. Dole and running mate Jack Kemp, a former House member and ex-Housing and Urban Development secretary, called for a 15 percent tax cut. Clinton countered that a cut this deep would jeopardize economic recovery by feeding the federal deficit, leading to inflation and higher interest rates. Clinton portrayed the Republicans as extremists while he appealed to Democratic core groups by pledging to defend Medicare, education, and the environment. A lackluster campaigner, Dole could not overcome "Clinton prosperity." Winning nearly all of the most populous states and key southern states, Clinton received 47.4 million votes, or 49.2 percent, and 379 electoral votes to Dole's 39.2 million, or 40.7 percent, and 159 electoral votes, the first Democrat since FDR to win two terms. Perot won a much smaller vote in 1996, yet again denied Clinton a majority. Perot received just over 8 million votes, or 8.4 percent, and no electoral votes. The Clinton-Gore ticket did not appreciably help other Democrats; the Republicans retained control of Congress.

In his second term, Clinton proposed relatively minor legislation to appeal to moderates, such as mandatory school uniforms. He moved to regulate tobacco products after the industry became the target of lawsuits by dying smokers and states seeking to regain money spent to care for them. In 1997 the industry approved a $368 billion settlement with states that included curbs on cigarette advertising to youths, but the industry mounted a lavishly-financed lobbying campaign and persuaded Congress to kill the bill. In 1998, cigarette companies reached a smaller court settlement with states, agreeing to pay $200 billion.

The economy continued to command Clinton's attention. In 1997 he signed a GOP measure including selective tax cuts and projecting a balanced budget by 2002, however, prosperity kept running ahead of projections. In his January 1998 State of the Union speech, the president announced the federal budget for 1999 would boast a surplus for the first time. Clinton wanted most of the surplus—which grew to a record $200 billion by the time he left office—devoted to paying off the federal debt and shoring up Social Security so baby-boomers would not bankrupt the system. The forecast of a surplus was just one indicator of how much the fiscal outlook and the economy had improved during the Clinton administration. By the end of his presidency, the United States had recorded its longest economic boom ever, 107 successive months. Wages, corporate profit, home ownership, and the gross national product increased; unemployment dropped below 4 percent for the first time in thirty years; poverty, too, declined. The stock market shot upward, fueled by high-technology firms. Not all was positive: the gap between rich and poor widened, as did the trade deficit; industrial workers' real wages, adjusted for inflation, increased only modestly. On the strength of the boom, large majorities in opinion polls rated Clinton's job performance high.

Although Clinton increasingly strayed beyond the bounds of conventional morality, the Republicans were less effective in exploiting those issues because some of their leaders suffered in moral lapses. Gingrich damaged himself by his arrogance and abrasiveness. After Clinton's reelection, the Speaker found himself investigated by the House Ethics Committee, which fined him $300,000 in 1997 for using a tax-exempt foundation for political aims. Then the Georgian, an exponent of "family values," admitted to an adulterous affair with an aide. Caught in the dual trap of political corruption and hypocrisy, he announced his resignation from Congress three days after the 1998 elections, in which Democrats gained five House seats. Gingrich's designated replacement as speaker, Louisiana Representative Bob Livingston, resigned in December, while the House was considering articles of impeachment against Clinton, after he acknowledged a sexual affair. (One of the paradoxes of the Era of Diversity is that a number of spokesmen of "family values" did not live up to those values in their personal lives.) Eventually, Illinois Representative Dennis Hastert took over as speaker.

A Dangerous World

Initially, Clinton seemed uninterested in foreign affairs, and tried to solve problems piecemeal. The Cold War won, some Americans argued that a large military was no longer necessary. Accordingly, Clinton reduced the armed forces, but the United States retained the world's largest military budget.

Because it affected the domestic scene, Clinton's first priority in foreign affairs was passage of the North American Free Trade Agreement (NAFTA) that Bush had negotiated. One of the Democrats' core constituencies, unions, opposed the agreement, arguing that it would encourage companies to move jobs to Mexico where workers were poorly paid and business regulations were lax. Since the 1970s, Democrats in Congress had become increasingly protectionist. Clinton argued that jobs would be gained by opening Mexican markets. Staking his prestige on ratifying the treaty, Clinton received support from Republicans for the pact, which cleared Congress in 1993.

Just after the 1994 elections, Congress ratified the Uruguay Round of the General Agreement on Tariffs and Trade (GATT), which approved formation of the World Trade Organization (WTO) and reduced tariffs worldwide. There was less opposition to this agreement than to NAFTA. But, the increasing globalization of the economy brought problems, as well as possibilities.

Some problems were more violent than trade. Clinton sent troops and food aid to war-torn Somalia, only to have American soldiers ambushed. Public opinion turned against the mission, yet it helped save some 250,000 Somalis from starvation.

China moved closer to America and free markets, yet, politically, remained totalitarian. Clinton and his successors believed that trade was preferable to isolation, and might in time open China to democratic ideas, as well as consumer goods. In 1999 the administration helped Beijing gain membership in the World Trade Organization. The following year, the United States granted permanent trade concessions to the Chinese. No longer walled off by an edifice of their own construction, the Chinese agreed to treaties that would limit nuclear and chemical weapons. Within and without, America found itself in a more diversifying world.

The newly diverse globe finds the American technological, sexual, and demographic revolutions superimposed upon economic and cultural revolutions that overshadow the vestiges of the Cold War. In fact, America's military prowess might prove less important than its growing status as the world's cultural superpower. Looking at the developing world, some entrepreneurs see an army of potential consumers whereas competition looms as well.

Nations such as China and Vietnam are becoming important trading partners with the United States, even while limiting the political freedoms of their people. Nonetheless, the more prosperous they become, the more they can buy from the United States, and nations whose economies become intertwined are less likely to go to war. What the Chinese most want to buy from the United States, for example, is not heavy machinery or nuclear weapons, but Hollywood films, DVDs, music videos, television sets, sports regalia, and autographed basketballs. Along with these, they embrace fast-food and motel chains as well as tourism in both directions.

Former arch-enemy Vietnam provides another example. After the collapse of the South Vietnamese government to the communists in 1975, the economy backslid, refugees fled, and the Vietnamese army fought wars with China and Cambodia. Yet three decades later Vietnam has adopted the Chinese model of "socialism with market orientation." Its 7.7 percent annual growth rate was second only to China among Asian countries in 2005. Ironically, the country's single largest private employer, with 130,000 workers, was the American firm Nike, which produced $700 million of footwear a year in 2005. Vietnamese who remained abroad after the communist revolution, an estimated 2 million, sent $3.8 billion back to relatives in 2004, fueling economic development. Although doubtless some jobs obtained by foreign workers came at the expense of American workers, what American capitalism needs most is global consumers, who cannot buy American products unless they can earn money. Otherwise, domestic overproduction will outpace domestic purchasing power as it did in the 1930s. In America, older, unskilled workers will suffer most from the changing global economy because the jobs created will be more numerous, but not in the same categories, as the jobs lost. As throughout the Time of Paradox, human dilemmas cannot be uncoupled from economic progress. The ambiguous relationship between Americans and the technology they innovate has been a principal thread in their history. Today, the ambiguity is global.

Yet there are opportunities as well. Many of the new jobs will be reasonably well-paying—airline pilots, cruise ship captains, tourism directors, construction workers, engineers, architects, and theme park designers. Within the coming years it is likely that major league baseball and basketball will expand to countries such as Mexico, Cuba, Japan, and China. The global economy will offer opportunities for Americans who master foreign languages, and for those who want to work and study abroad. In an aesthetic sense, Americans will have the opportunity to learn to appreciate foreign films, books, and music, just as there will be an unprecedented demand abroad for writers and teachers of American history. The information revolution will spill over with demands not simply for programmers and technicians but for researchers and inventors. The problems are real but the possibilities are limited only by the imagination.

Some nations, nonetheless, remain clouded in uncertainty. Clinton was cautious toward America's newly minted friend, Russia, as he watched the difficult transition from long years of communism to capitalism. He met with Yeltsin at a record ten summits and gave America's Cold War enemy billions of dollars in economic aid. Two agreements were signed to reduce nuclear weapons, and America helped supervise their destruction. Yeltsin, in poor health, announced he would not run for reelection in 2000. On December 31, 1999, he resigned and appointed his Prime Minister, Vladimir Putin, to replace him. Putin, a veteran of the Russian secret police, the KGB, won a full term as Yeltsin's successor. Tough and smart, he made no attempt to resocialize the economy, but ethnic tensions and consumer shortages continued.

Clinton's aspirations were high in the Middle East and Northern Ireland, where he hoped to broker lasting peace. With American assistance and Norwegian sponsorship, Israel and the Palestine Liberation Organization signed the Oslo Agreement, in September 1993, at the White House. The accord called for Israel to trade land it had occupied since the 1967 war, culminating in peace and a Palestinian state. Yasir Arafat renounced terror and recognized Israel's right to exist; Israeli Prime Minister Yitzhak Rabin granted self-rule to Palestinians in Jericho and the Gaza Strip. These promises, and other compacts involving Israel and its neighbors, encouraged administration hopes. Agreements in 1995 in Washington and in 1998 near the Wye River in Maryland advanced the land-for-peace formula. But the agreements failed because militant expansionists on both sides, often religious fundamentalists, opposed concessions by their leaders. Rabin paid for his peacemaking attempts with his life, murdered in 1995 by an Israeli opposed to compromise. After a summit called by Clinton at Camp David in 2000 failed to resolve issues, violence flared, leaving Clinton's ambitions as a peacemaker in tatters.

As in the Middle East, nationalism, religion, and history in Northern Ireland made peacemaking treacherous. Catholics, who wanted to affiliate with the Irish Republic, and Protestants, who wanted to retain an attachment to Britain, engaged in guerrilla war. A peace formula brokered by former Senate Majority Leader George Mitchell was announced on Good Friday in April of 1998. The Good Friday agreement provided for election of a provincial assembly representing both factions, yet its future appears dubious.

In Africa, civil wars initiated fratricide and famine. The most heinous occurred in Rwanda, where Hutus slaughtered eight hundred thousand Tutsis until the Tutsis gained the upper hand and killed Hutus. Clinton, still smarting from Somalia, did not send peacekeepers, nor could he devise a plan to end the conflict. Finally, in 1996, the president dispatched several hundred soldiers to protect United Nations relief efforts.

Genocide also tormented Bosnia, Herzegovina, and Kosovo, formerly members of the Yugoslav republic. Under Tito, and for a few years after his death, Yugoslavia managed to hold ethnic rivalries in check, but it broke apart in the wake of the implosion of communism. Hostilities erupted among Serbs, Croats, and Bosnians. In 1992 Bosnian Serbs declared independence and attacked the capital, Sarajevo. Under their leader, Yugoslav President Slobodan Milosevic, the Serbs carried out a campaign of "ethnic cleansing," including murder and torture, to drive Croats and Muslims from Serb areas. Although the Serb brutality sickened the world, President Clinton was unwilling to intervene. Former President Jimmy Carter arranged a December 1994 cease-fire, but it collapsed early the next year, and the White House decided to do more. Late in 1995 Clinton brought together Bosnians, Serbs, and Croats at Dayton, Ohio, and cobbled together a peace plan that preserved the unity of Bosnia-Herzegovina as a nation and divided the country into districts, one controlled by Serbs and one by Muslims and Croats. The United States also pledged to commit troops to help keep the peace.

Next, ethnic hostilities exploded in Kosovo, a Serb province where the Albanian majority demanded independence. In 1998 Serb police began to detain and murder Albanians, prompting Clinton and NATO to stiffen economic sanctions against Milosevic and Yugoslavia. Milosevic massed his army around the province and sent forces surging into Kosovo. NATO responded with eleven weeks of deadly bombing of Serbia. The Serbs surrendered in 1999. Milosevic lost the next election and was turned over to a UN tribunal, which convicted him of war crimes. Not satisfied with their victory, the Kosovars resorted to ethnic cleansing of Serbs in their territory. U.S. and NATO troops remained.

The Middle East continued to be the chief breeding ground for terrorism. Much of it was directed against the State of Israel, and its chief supporter, the United States. Iraq was one of the most anti-Semitic, anti-American hotspots. In 1993 Clinton authorized missile attacks after learning the Iraqi leader, Saddam Hussein, had plotted to assassinate George Bush. Hussein ejected arms inspectors, who wanted to determine whether Hussein was manufacturing chemical and biological weapons, and Clinton responded by placing economic sanctions on Iraq. In December 1998 Clinton ordered a brief bombing campaign against Iraq. Later, Clinton authorized air strikes on suspected terrorist sites in Afghanistan and Sudan, retaliating for bomb attacks against the American Embassies in Nairobi, Kenya, and Dar es Salaam, Tanzania. Sudan claimed a factory destroyed by American air strikes made only pharmaceutical products while the United States charged that it manufactured chemical weapons. In October 2000, a bomb planted by terrorists on a small boat damaged the destroyer *Cole* off Yemen, killing seventeen American sailors.

Earlier in 2000, a six-year-old boy drew Washington into an international dispute. Elian Gonzalez, plucked from the ocean in late 1999 after his mother drowned trying to flee Cuba in a small boat, went to live with relatives in Miami. His father, divorced from Elian's mother and still living in Cuba, demanded his son's return. Cuba's Fidel Castro accused America of kidnapping. Conservatives and anti-Castro Cubans in the United States fought to keep Elian in America. Clinton, Reno, and immigration officials thought Elian should be reunited with his father. Federal agents seized the boy early on April 22 and returned him to his father, who brought him back to Cuba. Castro won a propaganda victory.

Clinton's final two years in office focused increasingly on foreign policy, as the political climate at home deteriorated. The first president to travel to Africa in two decades, he journeyed to Europe and Asia as well.

Sex, Lies, and Impeachment

Paradoxically, a president so skilled at politics and some aspects of policy almost self-destructed. Virtually from the start of Clinton's tenure, the White House was on the defensive due to scandals. Numerous members of the administration became subjects of investigations, and some quit the government. Accusations of illegal political contributions resulted in penalties against a prominent donor and calls for campaign finance reform. Other scandals struck closer to the Clintons. In the "travelgate" affair, Hillary Rodham Clinton was accused of firing members of the travel office to replace them with political cronies. In the Whitewater scandal, a special prosecutor was appointed to investigate a land-development scheme harking back to Arkansas. The Clintons lost money on the deal and were never indicted for wrongdoing, yet there were appearances of influence-peddling and political favoritism. Several Arkansas friends of the Clintons were convicted of crimes.

Kenneth Starr, the special prosecutor with a bloodhound's nose for scandal, then found a salacious episode. A former White House intern, Monica Lewinsky, had a two-year affair with the president, including sex and dirty telephone talk. Worse, the president lied about the affair in a deposition taken by attorneys for an Arkansas woman, Paula Jones, who was suing the president for sexually harassing her while he was governor of Arkansas. Eventually, Lewinsky admitted the affair and Starr sought impeachment of Clinton for perjury and obstruction of justice. Clinton's critics believed the coverup might be grounds for impeachment, although adultery was not.

On December 19, 1998, the House voted along partisan lines to impeach Clinton on four counts. It was the first presidential impeachment (equivalent to indictment) since Andrew Johnson, Abraham Lincoln's successor. Public support for Clinton's economic successes, along with the belief that the gravity of the charges did not justify removal from office, helped save him. On February 12, 1999, the Senate voted to acquit. Clinton, however, suffered public humiliation. He apologized to the public, paid a $25,000 fine for lying in the Paula Jones lawsuit, settled with Jones for $850,000, and had his law license suspended for five years.

The events tarnished Clinton's reputation, though they did not negate his achievements. Many Americans felt ambivalent about Clinton as he left office. Despite the sexual revolution, and the fact that other public figures had strayed, the impeachment demonstrated that large numbers of Americans still took traditional morality seriously and expected potential role models to behave themselves. What most Americans sought in their political leaders was ability coupled with rectitude. Among the presidents of the Era of Diversity, none was more contradictory than Bill Clinton: gifted, human, weak. "He may come to be remembered as the most paradoxical president: an undisciplined man who reformed government and in so doing inspired trust in it, while inspiring none in himself," journalist Jacob Weisberg wrote.

As in the Watergate scandal, the First Family's dirty laundry was washed on national television. Power continued to corrupt. To many, the blood-sport of politics had become vindictive. The special counsel statute was terminated when it came due for renewal later in 1999. Democrats and Republicans agreed that investigations had become obsessively partisan. Every president since Richard Nixon had been investigated.

Since America had awakened to the world as the century dawned, it had made enormous strides economically. Fittingly, the last decade of the century was its most prosperous. Yet, as Clinton left office, his political failures lay in issues that had not been addressed satisfactorily since the time of Theodore Roosevelt and Woodrow Wilson. Is freedom free? Are we our brother's keeper? Both would be addressed by the presidents of the twenty-first century of the third millennium. Although America had won the Cold War on Bush's watch, his successor had failed to define a new role for his nation in the world. Caught between the expediencies of winning elections and holding party interest groups, the president, who had run as a New Democrat, had won tactical victories based on shifting coalitions but had not initiated a new set of priorities for his divided party. Clinton did not inspire idealism and partisanship embittered the nation at century's end. The paradox of opportunities seized and opportunities missed, of how far we had come and how far we still needed to go, reminded us not to take wealth, security, or freedom for granted.

The Era of Diversity provided infinite, chaotic choices. In the century's most prosperous decade, the enigma of poverty and abundance, sundered by class, racial, and gender differences, persisted. Prosperity failed to bring unity and at century's end, the place of the United States in the world was perhaps less clearly defined than it had been in the time of William McKinley. The twentieth century had awakened the nation, guided it through the perils of trials and triumphs, helped it weather uncertainty, and watched it emerge more diverse. The Time of Paradox was one of staggering accomplishments, and festering problems which defied solutions. The twenty-first century beckoned, eager to imprint an identity of its own, one in which the velocity of change would accelerate exponentially. Americans strained to stretch the limits of reality, to reconcile physics and theology, to produce and to conserve, to achieve peace of mind.

The Presidency of
George W. Bush

FOR THE ONLY time in their nation's short history, Americans living in 2000 witnessed the simultaneous turn of the century and turn of the millennium. The fireworks of January 1 were matched by the political fireworks of November as Americans wondered and fought for weeks over who they had elected president.

Vice President Al Gore defeated New Jersey Senator Bill Bradley to win the Democratic nomination and tapped Senator Joseph Lieberman of Connecticut, the first Jew nominated, as his running mate. The Democrats united behind Gore.

In 1997 and 1998 many Republicans had begun urging Texas Governor George W. Bush, the son of former President George H. W. Bush, to seek the Republican nomination. Bush wanted to run, yet he had reservations. With the economy prosperous and the nation at peace, Gore looked unbeatable. Moreover, Bush's wife Laura and his twin daughters valued privacy. Bush had been governor only four years and some Republicans believed he needed more seasoning. On the other hand, the Bush family had a network of political and business friends that could raise enormous sums and produce endorsements. If he entered the race, Bush would be the Republican frontrunner. By early 1999 some prominent Republicans were already in the race, including former Vice President Dan Quayle, Senator John McCain of Arizona, former Tennessee Governor Lamar Alexander, and Elizabeth Dole, ex-Transportation Secretary and wife of the 1996 Republican nominee. McCain won the nation's first primary in New Hampshire. In South Carolina, the next major primary, Bush overwhelmed McCain by waging a negative campaign. South Carolina ended McCain's momentum and Bush coasted to the nomination. Bush wanted an experienced politician for second place on the ticket, one without political ambitions of his own. At his father's suggestion, he appointed Richard Cheney, former Chief of Staff to President Ford, to head the search. Eventually, Bush picked Cheney himself. Bush defined his political philosophy as "compassionate conservatism," a kind of tough love. Two minor party candidates ran, liberal Ralph Nader, the candidate of the Green Party, and conservative Pat Buchanan, of Perot's Reform Party.

Gore won the popular vote yet on election night the electoral count remained close, to be determined by the state of Florida. Florida's popular count see-sawed, swinging initially to Bush, declared the winner by one thousand votes. Yet confusion reigned. A machine recount favored Bush. However, a hand count might favor Gore, some of whose supporters apparently were confused by the nature of the paper ballots. Further, different standards had been used in different counties to determine the counting of partially-detached paper ballots. The race would be decided by the courts. The Florida Supreme Court, with a Democratic majority, ruled for Gore. The climax came at the top. The U.S. Supreme Court, with a conservative majority, supported Bush's election by a 5-4 majority.

The final count showed Gore beating Bush by more than 500,000 ballots in the popular vote. This broke down to 50.9 million for Gore and 50.4 million for Bush, yet Bush narrowly carried the Electoral College, 271 to 266. Nader won 3.5 percent of the Florida vote, which Gore lost by less than 1 percent. Because Nader and Gore were both liberals, it is possible that Nader cost Gore Florida and with it the election. Bush was strong in the South, the Southwest, and the Great Plains while Gore scored well in the large industrial states. The Republicans retained control of Congress by narrow margins, with Vice President Cheney holding the tie-breaking vote in the Senate. One of the new Democratic Senators elected was Hillary Rodham Clinton.

The fourth man to win the presidency despite losing the popular vote, Bush, fifty-four, had graduated from Yale and received a degree in business administration from Harvard. Once a hard-drinking playboy, he changed his lifestyle after an arrest for drunken driving in 1976. George W., as he was known, turned to religion and married a schoolteacher, Laura Welch. He avoided the draft by joining the Air National Guard, and entered the oil supply industry in Texas. Later, he bought and then sold the Texas Rangers major-league baseball team.

Bush differed from his father. In policy, he was more conservative, closer in ideology to Reagan than to the senior Bush. In personality, he was more open and gregarious, more relaxed, with a better sense of humor. He identified with the West and the people of Texas and was less comfortable

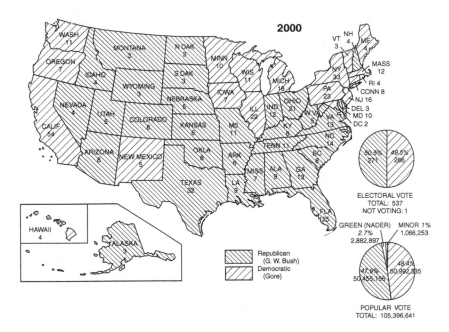

Election of 2000

with the Eastern elite. The father was more skilled at book learning, but the son was better at dealing with people.

Although the new president favored many of Reagan's policies, Bush was more positive about the role of government, although he felt it should be limited. He believed character and hard work, not simply wise economic policies, were necessary for prosperity. The younger Bush was open about his Christianity and the influence it had exerted on his life.

As president, Bush tried to avoid letting the media anger him as it had his father. He was less accessible to the press, preferring to ignore criticism than to confront it. The Washington social scene held less attraction for Bush than it had for his parents. The Bushes escaped Washington frequently for Camp David and their Crawford, Texas, ranch. Bush brought friends and members of the cabinet to Texas. He retired early and jogged daily, exercising to relax.

Bush appointed an experienced cabinet and relied heavily on Cheney. His foreign policy team included Secretary of State Colin Powell, Defense Secretary Donald Rumsfeld, and National Security Adviser Condoleeza Rice. The President's major domestic achievement was passage of a $1.35 trillion, ten-year tax cut in May 2001, a measure he hoped would stimulate the economy, which had dipped into recession. From the surpluses of the Clinton era, the Treasury now projected a sea of red ink. Unemployment rose and unions blamed Bush for allowing the loss of jobs to cheap foreign labor. Bush stayed the course and in 2004 the economy began to inch upward.

Terror from the Sky

Bush, unlike his father, did not intend to be a foreign policy president. Fate determined otherwise. Early on September 11, 2001, terrorists on suicide missions hijacked four passenger jets. Two crashed into the Twin Towers of the World Trade Center in New York, killing thousands and destroying the world's tallest buildings, symbols of American economic might. One smashed into the Pentagon, wrecking part of the massive building. The bravery of passengers on the fourth flight, who attacked the hijackers and forced them off course, saved the intended target, possibly the White House. Instead the jet crashed in rural Pennyslvania.

When the September 11 tragedy occurred most in the administration did not realize the attacks on the Twin Towers had been a deliberate act of terrorism until the second plane slammed into the buildings. Bush, who was talking to school children in Sarasota, Florida, tried to remain calm yet knew that his administration's priorities had been irrevocably altered. For better or worse, history will largely remember Bush as the president who launched a war on terrorism.

The end of the Cold War did not bring permanent peace and security, only a different type of war in which small, fanatical groups could wreak havoc on their larger, more powerful enemies. In this war military and political intelligence are as important as nuclear might. Rather than waging a defensive war, Bush introduced a controversial new tactic: preemptive strikes at nations believed to be harboring terrorists or preparing weapons of mass destruction. There was little hope of winning a clearcut victory; the best that could be expected was to defuse the threat. However, because terrorism worked undercover, some Americans considered it unwise to fight until it materialized, or feared combating it might jeopardize civil liberties.

Bush saw the issue of terrorism in distinct moral terms. Once he decided to wage war, he planned to do so with maximum force. Although diplomacy would be a tool, he was more willing than his father to initiate action without world approval. In the short run, the attacks on the World Trade Towers united Americans. As time wore on, and the war on terrorism appeared frustrating and interminable, opposition mounted.

The suspected mastermind of the attack was Osama bin Laden, operating from a base in Afghanistan. George Bush senior encouraged his son to rev up the American intelligence system. Instead of a massive assault on Afghanistan, the ex-president suggested a more limited, focused attack directed at overturning the fundamentalist Taliban government by collaborating with their opponents. Bush issued an ultimatum to the Taliban: turn over bin Laden or America would undertake military operations in Afghanistan. CIA operatives working with anti-Taliban forces combined with a precision air campaign to depose the Taliban, who continued limited resistance.

American intelligence believed the chief threat to security lay in chemical and biological weapons, especially the latter. Unlike nuclear weapons they did not require a sophisticated delivery system. Neither did they require years of research and the massive expense of constructing nuclear reactors. The programs could be carried out in small, remote areas, easy to conceal. During the first Persian Gulf War against Iraq Americans feared the Iraqi dictator, Saddam Hussein, possessed and might use chemical and biological weapons. When the war ended with Hussein defeated yet still in power, the Iraqi government was ordered to destroy its stockpiles and terminate its programs. Yet the American government and much of the international community feared Hussein had only concealed, not destroyed his weapons, and the Iraqi dictator contributed to the impression by not allowing international inspectors free access to sites throughout Iraq.

Bush considered Hussein a threat to global security. Moreover, there was personal animosity between the leaders; Hussein had planned to assassinate Bush's father. Bush's ambitions went beyond deposing Hussein. He wanted to plant democracy in the Middle East and ultimately transform the region. On March 6, 2003, Bush offered Hussein a final opportunity to give up power, leave the country, and avoid war. Hussein declined. The president, who believed his father had erred in the first Gulf War by not pushing on to Baghdad and removing Saddam from power, invaded Iraq. The force included some manpower from America's allies, but was less a coalition effort than his father's. The war was won with nearly the ease of the first Iraq war. Saddam, moving from village to village, sometimes living underground, was captured hiding in a hole near a ramshackle "safe house" on December 13, 2003. He was turned over to the new Iraqi government for trial.

Winning the war was the easy part. Saddam's partisans would not give up and directed suicide attacks against Americans, allied soldiers in Iraq, and Iraqi civilian and military officials who supported the United States. Even after the United States officially turned over the government to Iraqi officials in 2004, the attacks continued. Some Iraqis who once feared and detested Saddam and showered with flowers American soldiers who liberated Baghdad, now demanded that Americans leave their country. More important, as U.S. casualties mounted, some Americans turned against the mission, viewing it as a quagmire with no end in sight.

The Political War

The war in Iraq, along with the economy, became major issues in the presidential campaign of 2004. Forty years after Democrat Lyndon Johnson had won the presidency as the peace candidate, Bush found himself locked in rhetorical combat with Democrat Senator John Kerry, who pledged to wage war on war.

Kerry had defeated the early front-runner, ex-Vermont governor Howard Dean, in Iowa and New Hampshire, then vanquished Senator John Edwards of North Carolina, whom he subsequently chose as his running mate. A Vietnam veteran who had renounced the war after returning to America, Kerry offered a liberal critique of Bush's policies, claiming the president had misled the people, and was an inept leader. The election, newsmen agreed, offered a clear distinction between a liberal and conservative vision of America.

The campaign was bitter and intense. Kerry attacked Bush for going to war against Iraq when the real threat was Islamic militant Osama bin Laden and nuclear proliferation. Kerry charged he had a plan to free Americans from the grip of a second Vietnam: ask our allies to carry more of the burden; and train the Iraqis to defend themselves. He pointed out that after the conquest of Iraq, inspectors had found no evidence that Iraq possessed a program to produce weapons of mass destruction. Bush retorted that there was nothing in Kerry's plan that he had not already done. The president further charged that Kerry had supported in the Senate many of the policies he now opposed as a candidate.

The contest was close. The Democrats held the thickly-populated Northeast and the West, with Republican strongholds in the South and Great Plains. This made the Midwest the battleground. The campaign included three debates between the presidential candidates and one between their running mates. In the first, Kerry was assertive, placing the incumbent on the defensive. The others were almost a draw, although Kerry might have emerged with a slight edge. In the vice presidential debate, the exchanges revolved around Vice President Cheney's experience opposed to Edwards's youth and vigor. The campaign was polarizing; there were few voters in the middle, few undecided voters, and few who crossed party lines.

The outcome was determined by Ohio. Bush carried the state and with it the election, winning 286 electoral votes to 251 for Kerry. Bush won the popular vote by a margin of about 3.5 million votes. The turnout was the largest in history and Bush polled the most votes ever won by a presidential candidate. Third party candidate Ralph Nader polled 1 percent of the popular vote and no electoral votes.

Personality played a role in the voting, though the campaign was couched in terms of policy. Although Kerry scored points by his criticism of Bush, many Americans considered Kerry poor leadership timber because of inconsistency that seemed opportunistic. Kerry resonated with intellectuals, yet Bush connected emotionally with ordinary Americans because of his religiosity and open patriotism, even in his cowboy attire and prior part-ownership of a major league baseball team. In the aftermath of the campaign Democrats pondered whether they should turn to secure their left flank or move right to secure the center.

In his second term Bush would have the opportunity to make changes at home and abroad, including the opportunity to restructure the Supreme Court by appointment of a new Chief Justice and an Associate Justice. Although foreign policy continued to dominate the administration, domestic policies provoked debate. Bush's agenda included permanent tax cuts, reform of social security that permitted some of the system's funds to be invested in private accounts, reform of medical care, and protection of businesses and physicians from costly lawsuits. The first budget proposed by Bush in his second term, unveiled in 2005, emphasized tight domestic spending and increases for the military, but at a slower rate than in previous military budgets. Some funds were to be shifted, with an emphasis on domestic security and education reform. Some viewed immigration as a welcoming mat for the poor yet others feared it as an avenue for terrorists. Bush's cabinet was revamped. Rice succeeded Powell as secretary of state, becoming the first black woman to hold that position. The new administration enjoyed majorities in both houses, yet Democrats threatened to filibuster some sensitive issues, including conservative judicial nominees. As with many presidents, Bush's biggest challenges might come not from implementing his platform or keeping his promises but from events not yet on the horizon at the time of his reelection.

Foreign Policy in Bush's Second Term

Bush's second term began in a still dangerous world. On February 10, 2005, North Korea announced it possessed nuclear weapons and Iran moved toward nuclear weapons capability. Some 17,000 American troops remained in Afghanistan, yet casualties were smaller and the media focused on Iraq. Unfortunately, Afghanistan became the world's largest producer of opium. China and Taiwan squabbled, with Taiwan threatening to formally declare independence from the mainland and the People's Republic counterthreatening an invasion if it did.

The Middle East inched toward rapprochement between Israel and the Palestinians after the death of PLO leader Yasser Arafat and the election of Mahmoud Abbas as his successor. The new leader moved to relax tensions, including a crackdown on terrorists. Israel reciprocated by releasing some imprisoned Palestinians and returning some Jewish settlements in Palestinian areas to Palestinian control. Yet militants on both sides did not want peace. In Lebanon the assassination of a former prime minister in March 2005 provoked demonstrations against Syrian occupation of the country and counterdemonstrations by pro-Syrian groups. Syria reluctantly withdrew.

In Iraq, the situation was complex. Terrorist acts continued and American soldiers and larger numbers of Iraqis were killed. Yet Iraqis braved terrorist threats to vote in large numbers on January 30, 2005, and by March they had installed an interim government. Agreement was reached on a more permanent government, charged with writing a new constitution, in April, yet efforts to write a constitution that would satisfy all factions frustrated Iraqis and fueled the insurgency. Key issues included regionalism and the role of Islam. The Iraq war divided America from some of its European allies, yet most decided to deal with Bush in his second term. A few nations, most notably Britain, sent small numbers of troops or medical units to demonstrate support. Russia remained a nominal ally, yet Bush lectured President Vladimir Putin on the need for more democracy during his first trip abroad of the second term. Meanwhile, nations of the former Soviet Union hedged closer to democracy through bloodless revolutions, most notably Ukraine, which elected Viktor Yushchenko president. Many areas of the world seemed in transition to more open, pluralistic, and democratic societies, at least in a relative sense. Throughout what was formally known as the Third World (neither communist nor capitalist) economic growth offered jobs and opportunity, though a tragic tidal wave known as a tsunami killed hundreds of thousands on Pacific islands and on the mainland of Southeast Asia in March 2005 and destroyed cities, villages, livestock, farmland, and industry. Slow to respond, the United States government ultimately provided substantial aid, supplemented by additional donations from millions of individual Americans.

America did not escape national disasters. In late August and September, 2005, hurricane Katrina, followed by hurricane Rita, slammed into the Gulf

Coast. Katrina, the stronger, flooded the historic city of New Orleans and destroyed the Mississippi coastal communities of Gulfport and Biloxi. Before Louisiana had recovered from Katrina, Rita struck, devastating southwestern coastal communities in Louisiana, especially Lake Charles, and southeastern Texas, including Beaumont. The hurricanes temporarily disrupted oil supplies and sent gasoline prices soaring. The cleanup, rebuilding, and human costs ran into the hundreds of billions of dollars.

Earlier, a sad event transpired with the death of Pope John Paul II on April 2, 2005. One of the most influential Popes in the history of the Roman Catholic Church, John Paul's funeral was the largest in world history. He was succeeded by the German Cardinal Joseph Ratzinger, who became Benedict XVI. As has been the case since the end of the Cold War, the United States remains the sole superpower, though China is rapidly moving toward that status, as well as Japan, at least economically. World economic problems are complicated by nationalism and divisive religious wars, especially in Asia and Africa. Indeed with the focus on the Middle East, disease, famine, and war devastate Africa beneath the radar of world scrutiny. Internationally, America is viewed with a mixture of awe, respect, envy, hatred, and gratitude. Americans remained pregnant with hope yet feared the fickleness of fate. In the twenty-first century their world might scale new heights of achievements that had eluded previous generations, or it might topple into the abyss of a new dark age.

Bibliographic Essay

Nixon through Reagan

The best biography of Richard Nixon is Stephen E. Ambrose, *Nixon* (3 vols., 1987–1994). Also see Tom Wicker, *One of Us: Richard Nixon and the American Dream* (1991); Herbert S. Parmet, *Richard Nixon and His America* (1994); and Joan Hoff, *Nixon Reconsidered* (1994). Other sources include John R. Greene, *The Limits of Power: The Nixon and Ford Administrations* (1992), and Melvin Small, *The Presidency of Richard Nixon* (1999). David Greenberg, *Nixon's Shadow: The History of an Image* (2003) is an excellent survey of Nixon stereotypes. Studies on domestic affairs under Nixon include Allen Matusow, *Nixon's Economy: Booms, Busts, Dollars, and Voters* (1998); Robert M. Collins, *People of More: Economic Growth in Postwar America* (2000); and Walter I. Trattner, *From Poor Law to Welfare State: A History of Social Welfare in America* (1994), a thorough general account. The Cold War is discussed in Raymond L. Garthoff, *Detente and Confrontation: American-Soviet Relations from Nixon to Reagan*, rev. ed. (1995); Richard C. Thornton, *The Nixon-Kissinger Years: Reshaping America's Foreign Policy* (1989); and Diane B. Kunz, *Butter and Guns: America's Cold War Economic Diplomacy* (1997). The literature on Watergate is vast. See Stanley I. Kutler, *The Wars of Watergate* (1990), and *Abuse of Power: The New Nixon Tapes* (1997); Fred Emery, *Watergate: The Corruption of American Politics and the Fall of Richard Nixon* (1995); Bob Woodward and Carl Bernstein, *All the President's Men* (1974), and *The Final Days* (1976), journalistic exposes; and Theodore White, *Breach of Faith* (1975), an early yet worthwhile work.

   Studies of Nixon's successor include John Robert Greene, *The Presidency of Gerald R. Ford* (1995), the most comprehensive; James Cannon, *Time and Chance: Gerald Ford's Appointment with History* (1994); and Edward Schapsmeier and Frederick Schapsmeier, *Gerald Ford's Date with Destiny: A Political Biography* (1989). On Ford's role in the fall of South Vietnam see Alan Dawson, *55 Days: The Fall of South Vietnam* (1977), and P. Edward Haley, *Congress and the Fall of South Vietnam and Cambodia* (1983). On the *Mayaguez* incident, see Christopher Jon Lamb, *Belief Systems and Decision Making in the Mayaguez Crisis* (1988).

On Jimmy Carter's administration see Burton I. Kaufman, *The Presidency of James Earl Carter* (1993); Peter G. Bourne, *Jimmy Carter: A Comprehensive Biography from Plains to Postpresidency* (1997); Charles O. Jones, *The Trusteeship Presidency: Jimmy Carter and the United States Congress* (1988); and Haynes Johnson, *In the Absence of Power: Governing America* (1980), harshly critical. Aspects of Carter's domestic policies are covered in Anthony S. Campagna, *Economic Policy in the Carter Administration* (1995). More attention has been devoted to Carter's foreign policies than to his domestic policies. Significant studies of the former include Gaddis Smith, *Morality, Reason, and Power: American Diplomacy in the Carter Years* (1986); Alexander Moens, *Foreign Policy under Carter* (1990); Jerel A. Rosati, *The Carter Administration's Quest for Global Community* (1987); A. Glenn Mower Jr., *Human Rights and American Foreign Policy: The Carter and Reagan Experience* (1987); William M. LeoGrande, *Our Own Backyard: The United States in Central America, 1977–1992* (1998); and T. G. Fraser, *The USA and the Middle East since World War II* (1989). Carter's most significant accomplishment is described in William B. Quandt, *Camp David: Peacemaking and Politics* (1986). On Iran, see James A. Bill, *The Eagle and the Lion: The Tragedy of American-Iranian Relations* (1987), and Paul B. Ryan, *The Iranian Rescue Mission and Why It Failed* (1986).

On the ascendance of the right, see Sidney Blumenthal, *The Rise of the Counter-Establishment* (1986); J. David Hoeveler, *Watch on the Right: Conservative Intellectuals in the Reagan Era* (1991); Jerome L. Himmelstein, *To the Right: The Transformation of American Conservatism* (1990); John Ehrman, *The Rise of Neoconservatism: Intellectuals and Foreign Affairs* (1995); John K. White, *The New Politics of Old Values* (1988); Dan T. Carter, *The Politics of Rage: George Wallace, the Origins of the New Conservatism, and the Transformation of American Politics* (1995), critical of Wallace; Paul Gottfried, *The Conservative Movement*, rev. ed. (1993); and Melvin J. Thorne, *American Conservative Thought since World War II: The Core Ideas* (1990). For the New Christian right, see Robert L. Hilliard and Michael C. Keith, *Waves of Rancor: Tuning in the Radical Right*

(1999); Jeffrey K. Hadden and Anson Shupe, *Televangelism: Power and Politics on God's Frontier* (1988); Clyde Wilcox, *God's Warriors: The Christian Right in Twentieth-Century America* (1992); Steve Bruce, *The Rise and Fall of the New Christian Right: Conservative Protestant Politics in America, 1978–1988* (1988); and Michael Lienesch, *Redeeming America: Piety and Politics in the New Christian Right* (1993).

On Ronald Reagan, Edmund Morris had extraordinary access to the president in the White House and used it to help produce *Dutch: A Memoir of Ronald Reagan* (1999), richly detailed but flawed by Morris's insertion of himself as a fictional character who observes Reagan's life. Lou Cannon, *President Reagan: The Role of a Lifetime*, 2nd ed. (2000) is a thorough journalistic account as is Haynes Johnson, *Sleepwalking through History: America in the Reagan Years* (1991). William E. Pemberton, *Exit with Honor: The Life and Presidency of Ronald Reagan* (1997) is succinct, scholarly and fair. More recent is Gil Troy, *Morning in America: How Ronald Reagan Invented the 1980s* (2005).

Among works dealing with Reagan's domestic policy are Joseph J. Minarik, *Making America's Budget Policy: From the 1980s to the 1990s* (1990); David G. Savage, *Turning Right: The Making of the Rehnquist Supreme Court* (1992); and Nicholas Laham, *The Reagan Presidency and the Politics of Race: In Pursuit of Colorblind Justice and Limited Government* (1998). The literature on Reagan's foreign policies is extensive. See Coral Bell, *The Reagan Paradox: American Foreign Policy in the 1980s* (1989); Richard A. Melanson, *Reconstructing Consensus: American Foreign Policy since the Vietnam War* (1991); Warren I. Cohen, *America in the Age of Soviet Power, 1945–1991* (1993); Steve Crawshaw, *Goodbye to the USSR: The Collapse of Soviet Power* (1992); Richard Crockatt, *The Fifty Years War: The United States and the Soviet Union in World Politics, 1941–1991* (1995); John Lewis Gaddis, *The United States and the End of the Cold War: Implications, Reconsiderations, Provocations* (1992); Daniel Wirls, *Buildup: The Politics of Defense in the Reagan Era* (1992); Don Oberdorfer, *The Turn: From the Cold War to a New Era, the United States and the Soviet Union* (1991); and Thomas W. Simons Jr., *The End of the Cold War* (1990). Reagan and Central America are discussed in Roy Gutman, *Banana Diplomacy: The Making of American Policy in Nicaragua, 1981–1987* (1988). On the Iran-Contra scandal, see Don Lawson, *America Held Hostage: The Iran Hostage Crisis and the Iran-Contra Affair* (1991), and Theodore Draper, *A Very Thin Line: The Iran-Contra Affairs* (1991). On the Middle East, see Charles D. Smith, *Palestine and the Arab-Israeli Conflict*, 2nd ed. (1992).

Culture and Society

Norman F. Cantor, *The American Century: Varieties of Culture in Modern Times* (1997), is an excellent overview. Robert Hughes, *The Culture of Complaint: The Fraying of America* (1993), is a penetrating analysis of late twentieth-century art and its opponents. Also see James Davison Hunter, *Culture Wars: The Struggle to Define America* (1991). Although ostensibly a study of Bob Dylan, Greil Marcus, *Invisible Republic: Bob Dylan's Basement Tapes* (1997), is valuable for its analysis of themes in culture. Dylan's memoir, *Chronicles* (2004) is spellbinding, yet episodic. Gregor Ehrlich and Dmitri Ehrlich, *Crowd: Voices and Faces of the Hip-Hop Nation* (1999), is a study of hip-hop and rap music, complemented by Nelson George, *Hip Hop America* (1998). Ronald L. Davis, *Celluloid Mirrors: Hollywood and American Society since 1945* (1997), is a brief survey. Among studies of the media are David Halberstam, *The Powers That Be* (1979); Herbert J. Gans, *Deciding What's News: A Study of CBS Evening News, NBC Nightly News, Newsweek and Time* (1979); and Daniel J. Czitrom, *Media and the American Mind: From Morse to McLuhan* (1982).

General histories of the 1970s are Bruce J. Schulman, *The Seventies* (2001), and Peter Carroll, *It Seemed Like Nothing Happened* (1982). On the 1980s, see John Ehrman, *The Eighties: America in the Age of Reagan* (2005). On technology and business, see James Cortada, *Making the Information Society* (2002), an account of the computer revolution. For the 1990s, consult Alan Wolfe, *One Nation after All: What Middle-Class America Really Thinks About* (1998), and Michael Sandel, *Democracy's Discontent: America in Search of a Public Philosophy* (1996), which focuses on political ideas. Useful on economic change, are Haynes Johnson, *The Best of Times: The Boom and Bust Years of America before and after Everything Changed* (2002), and David Gordon, *Fat and Mean: The Corporate Squeezing of Working Americans* (1996).

Religion is examined in Thomas C. Reeves, *The Empty Church: Does Organized Religion Matter Anymore?* (1996); George Marsden, *Religion and American Culture* (1990); Robert Wuthnow, *The Restructuring of American Religion: Society and Faith Since World War II* (1988); and Howard M. Sachar, *A History of the Jews in America* (1992). Among the many books on abortion are Kristin Luker, *Abortion and the Politics of Motherhood* (1984), and Rosalind Petchesky, *Abortion and Women's Choice* (1984). A medical scourge that became an emotional issue in politics and religion is described in Randy Shilts, *And the Band Played On: Politics, People, and the AIDS Epidemic* (1987), and *AIDS: The Making of a Chronic Disease* (1992).

Books on race include William Julius Wilson, *When Work Disappears: The World of the New Urban Poor* (1996); Orlando Patterson, *The Ordeal of Integration: Progress and Resentment in America's "Racial" Crisis* (1997); Abigail Thernstrom and Stephan Thernstrom, *America in Black and White, Indivisible* (1996), an interpretation of race relations since the 1940s, Andrew Hacker, *Two Nations: Black and White, Separate, Hostile, Unequal* (1992), and Thomas Byrne Edsall and Mary D. Edsall, *Chain Reaction: The Impact of Race, Rights, and Taxes on American Politics* (1991). Debates over welfare, race, and class are discussed in Michael Katz, *The Undeserving Poor: From the War on Poverty to the War on Welfare* (1989). Valuable works on civil rights include Leon E. Panetta and Peter Gall, *"Bring Us Together": The Nixon Team and the Civil Rights Retreat* (1971), and Steven A. Shull, *A Kinder, Gentler Racism? The Reagan-Bush Civil Rights Legacy* (1993). On Chicanos, see Rodolfo Acuna, *Occupied America: A History of Chicanos*, 3rd ed. (1988), and Jorge Ramos, *The Other Face of America: Chronicles of Immigrants Shaping Our Future* (2002). On Indians, see Stephen Cornell, *The Return of the Native: Indian Political Resurgence* (1988); Wilcomb E. Washburn, *The Indian in America* (1975); and Vine Deloria Jr., *American Indian Policy in the Twentieth Century* (1985).

Books on ethnicity and immigration include David M. Reimers, *Still the Golden Door: The Third World Comes to America* (1985); John Crewdson, *The Tarnished Door: The New Immigrants and the Transformation of America* (1983); Patrick H. Buchanan, *The Death of the West: How Dying Populations and Immigrant Invasions Imperil Our Country and Civilization* (2001); Vernon Briggs, *Mass Immigration: The National Interest* (1994); James S. Olson, *The Ethnic Dimension in American History* (1994); Jose A. Hernandez, *Mutual Aid for Survival: The Case of the Mexican American* (1985); Henry Tsai Shi-shan, *The Chinese Experience in America* (1986); Gail P. Kelly, *From Vietnam to America: A Chronicle of the Vietnamese Immigration to the USA* (1977); and Paul Rutledge, *The Vietnamese Experience in America* (1992).

Women's history is the subject of Marian Faux, *Roe v. Wade* (1988); David Garrow, *Liberty and Sexuality: The Right to Privacy and the Making of Roe v. Wade* (1994); Winifred D. Wandersee, *On the Move: American Women in the 1970s* (1988); Susan M. Hartmann, *From Margin to Mainstream: Women in American Politics since 1960* (1989); Mary Francis Berry, *Why ERA Failed* (1986); and Nancy Caraway, *Segregated Sisterhood: Racism and the Politics of American Feminism* (1991). Jean Bethke Elshtain, *Women and War* (1987), is the best work on the subject.

The Bush and Clinton Presidencies

Studies of George H. W. Bush include John Robert Greene, *The Presidency of George Bush* (2000); Herbert S. Parmet, *George Bush: The Life of a Lone Star Yankee* (1997); and Michael Duffy, *Marching in Place: The Status Quo Presidency of George Bush* (1992). Among books dealing with politics and domestic policy are Haynes Johnson, *Divided We Fall: Gambling with History in the Nineties* (1994), and Kevin Phillips, *The Politics of Rich and Poor: Wealth and the American Electorate in the Reagan Aftermath* (1990). Much has been written about Bush's diplomacy and the end of the Cold War. David Halberstam, *War in a Time of Peace: Bush, Clinton and the Generals* (2002), is a good general work. For American relations with the Soviet Union, see Joseph G. Whelan, *Soviet Diplomacy and Negotiating Behavior, 1988–1990: Gorbachev-Reagan-Bush Meetings at the Summit* (1991). On the collapse of the Soviet empire, see Marshall Goldman, *What Went Wrong with Perestroika?* (1992), and Jack F. Matlock's massive but readable *Autopsy of an Empire* (1995). Also useful are Bernard Gwertzman and Michael T. Kaufman, eds., *The Collapse of Communism* (1990); Paul Kennedy, *The Rise and Fall of the Great Powers* (1987); and Robert Kuttner, *The End of Laissez-Faire: National Purpose and the Global Economy after the Cold War* (1991). Bush's chief foreign policy accomplishment is the subject of Alberto Bin, Richard Hill, and Archer Jones, *Desert Storm: A Forgotten War* (1998).

Bill Clinton has been the subject of several journalistic studies, including David Maraniss, *First in His Class: A Biography of Bill Clinton* (1995), which traces his prepresidential career; R. Emmett Tyrrell Jr., *Boy Clinton: The Political Biography* (1996), and Nigel Hamilton, *Bill Clinton: An American Journey* (2003). James MacGregor Burns and Georgia J. Sorenson, *Dead Center: Clinton-Gore Leadership and the Perils of Moderation* (1999) is more policy oriented. Alex Wadden, *Clinton's Legacy: A New Democrat in Governance*, is strong on Clinton's economic policies. Sidney Blumenthal, *The Clinton Wars* (2003), is an insider's dissection of the scandals that nearly ended the Clinton presidency. Richard A. Posner, *An Affair of State: The Investigation, Impeachment, and Trial of President Clinton* (1999), is a legal study. Roger Morris, *Partners in Power: The Clintons and Their America* (1996), a joint biography of the presidential couple, includes valuable insights. The Clintons published separate memoirs, Bill Clinton, *My Life* (2004), and Hillary Rodham Clinton, *Living History* (2003).

Studies involving politics and change include Theda Skocpol, *Boomerang: Clinton's Health Security Effort and the Turn against Government in U.S.*

Politics (1996); John F. Bibby, *Return of Divided Party Government* (1995); Felice D. Perlmutter, *From Welfare to Work: Corporate Initiatives and Welfare Reform* (1997); Robert M. Solow, *Work and Welfare* (1998), and Gwendolyn Mink, *Welfare's End* (1998). On terrorism in the 1990s, see Stephen Jones and Peter Israel, *Others Unknown: The Oklahoma City Bombing Case* (1998), an account by the defense attorneys in the case; David Thibodeau, *A Place Called Waco: A Survivor's Story of Life and Death at Mt. Carmel* (1999); and Michael D. Kelleher, *When Good Kids Kill* (1998). For treatments of foreign affairs, consult Robert J. Myers, *U.S. Foreign Policy in the Twenty-First Century* (1999); and Gerald B. Solomon, *The NATO Enlargment Debate, 1990–1997* (1998), are helpful.

Postlude

For developments after Clinton, see the Political Staff of the *Washington Post, Deadlock: The Inside Story of America's Closest Election* (2001), on the 2000 presidential election, and Bob Woodward, *Bush at War* (2002), which examines steps that President George W. Bush and the other major players in foreign policy took in the early months after the 2001 terror attacks. Steve Coll, *Ghost Wars: The Secret History of the CIA, Afghanistan, and Bin Laden from the Soviet Invasion to September 10, 2001* (2005), is useful.

Peter Schweizer and Rochele Schweizer, *The Bushes: Portrait of a Dynasty* (2004), is a favorable portrait of the family. Three books of essays also contribute to an early assessment of George W. Bush: Steven E. Schier, ed. *High Risk and Big Ambition: The Presidency of George W. Bush* (2004); Jon Kraus, Kevin J. McMahon, and David M. Rankin, eds. *Transformed by Crisis: The Presidency of George W. Bush and American Politics* (2004); and Bryan Hilliard, Tom Lansford, and Robert P. Watson, *George W. Bush: Evaluating the President at Midterm* (2004).

A Time of Paradox

There is a season for everything, a time for every occupation under heaven: A time for giving birth, a time for dying; a time for planting, a time for uprooting what has been planted. A time for killing, a time for healing; a time for knocking down, a time for building. A time for tears, a time for laughter; a time for mourning, a time for dancing. A time for throwing stones away, a time for gathering them up; a time for embracing, a time to refrain from embracing. A time for searching, a time for losing; a time for keeping, a time for throwing away. A time for tearing, a time for sewing; a time for keeping silent, a time for speaking. A time for loving, a time for hating; a time for war, a time for peace.

—Ecclesiastes 3:1–8

INTERPRETING the recent past is like hitting a baseball: it is easy to do, but almost impossible to do well. To me, dissecting the Time of Paradox is simple because I have lived through part of it and my memories are fresh, yet difficult, because my feelings are strong. A historian must call third strikes, but judging one's contemporaries might lead one to be hypocritical, mean-spirited, or judgmental. How is a historian to weigh a nation, a time? By Galileo's telescope, Napoleon's armies, the rebellions of Martin Luther and of Martin Luther King Jr.? Whatever one ventures will be challenged and revised. Generations view history differently. Girls at my daughter's high school wear sweatshirts with the peace symbol—but do not know what it meant to members of my generation during the Vietnam War. They wear the symbol because it is "cool," an attitude echoed by the girl who told me that her first high school dance was "terrible" because "The music was old." When I asked whether she meant that the music was from the 1950s or the 1960s, from Elvis or the Beatles, she replied, "No, last year!"

Sometimes I ask students in my twentieth-century history courses which decade they would select if they could choose any time in the century in which to reach maturity. More than 90 percent pick their own decade. When I ask them why, they mention technology, especially in medicine and entertainment; improved opportunities for women and minorities; sexual freedom; and computers. I grew up without many of these things, yet I would not trade my youth for theirs. It is no coincidence that people feel most secure in their own times and places, that we want to live in the present. History provides many avenues to knowledge, and through it, to wisdom, yet it is no recipe for perfection. My students, like my generation, appreciate who they are and who they might become. Whether historically, scientifically, philosophically, or theologically, things happen for a reason. Why certain things, good and bad, happen to certain people, is beyond the scope of this essay. It might be as simple as "some things happen so that other things can happen," in a universal rather than an individual perspective. Occasionally everyday personal experiences provide insights into the nature of change. A few years ago I walked into my favorite Chinese restaurant, declined a menu, and ordered sweet and sour chicken, as usual. The waiter brought my meal. I took the first bite.

"This isn't sweet and sour chicken. It's lemon chicken."

"I'm sorry sir. I'll take it back and bring you the meal you ordered."

"No, the lemon chicken is better."

Although such analogies do not verify how change takes place, they might dramatize the interaction between context, or accident, and human decision. Receiving the lemon chicken was an accident. But it was my choice to keep it rather than return it.

We cannot know the universe, but we can try to know ourselves. History is a story of how men and women embarked on their voyages of self-discovery, and sometimes found surprises. Whether a rock on the Moon or a continent blocking the route to the Indies, it is all related.

In my research and personal life I have conversed with Chinese scholars studying in America. Over dinner I discussed with one how the world had changed during our lifetimes. I told him that when I was a child, my mother urged me to eat every last morsel because "people are starving in China." I didn't quite get the point, but I ate the last scoop of my chicken gumbo.

I asked my Chinese friend what motivated Chinese people today. In a jocular compliment, he replied: "It's just like America. Greed."

"Well," I continued, "if one of your friends asked you a single question about America when you return to China, what would they want to know?"

He smiled facetiously, "What tastes better, Coke or Pepsi?"

If interpreting the past is difficult, using history to predict the future is risky. Predicting events based on the past is like forecasting the weather. On a day-to-day basis, "no noticeable change," would often be close, and common sense and the law of averages are the best guides. Sometimes meteorologists predict weather in generalities, such as "partly cloudy," yet how partly is "partly?" Is it safe to plan a trip to the beach or to hold an outdoor wedding? The most important types of weather predictions involve events that are least predictable, such as tornadoes.

Still, human nature rarely changes, and similar events evoke similar reactions. Paradox has been a steady theme in history, although it has been amplified in the period since 1890. Contradictions flourished, among them:

- the paradox of politics, which veers from reform to retrenchment and back again, so that the reformers of one age are the reactionaries of the next
- the paradox of the baby boomers, who got nearly everything they wanted, yet remain unfulfilled
- the paradox of accentuating multiculturalism when the United States is the chief force of global homogenization
- the paradox that Americans fear change, but are major innovators of change
- the paradox of a country that strived to save the world and risked losing its own soul to do so
- the paradox that the United States is flawed in an absolute sense, yet successful relative to other nations
- the paradox that the period is as significant for what did *not* happen as well as what did happen
- the paradox that America has long boasted scientists who can split the atom yet continues to deplore college students who split infinitives
- the paradox that throughout the world, the best-known Americans are not presidents and statesmen but sport and cultural icons such as Michael Jordan, Muhammad Ali, and Walt Disney
- the paradox that the sexual revolution and the cultural revolution affected more people, over a longer period of time, than any political or ideological revolution
- the paradox of technology, which has lifted our living standards to unprecedented heights, yet robbed us of jobs and rained terror from the sky
- the paradox that tiny microbes continue to defy medical science, mutating innumerably and unpredictably

- the paradox that we gloat about our superior wisdom over our predecessors, yet continue to make the same mistakes, and to borrow from their wisdom

In the twenty-first century of the third millennium, the paradoxes proliferate. Indeed, the new century was a baby when terrorism, limited wars, and computer viruses ravaged the globe. The Time of Paradox seems to have wrought a nervous world in which people are too tense to relax. Simple pleasures—the ability to park an unlocked bicycle at school or work, to have milk and ice cream brought to one's home each morning, to receive mail delivery twice daily—disappeared long ago. The worst anxiety, fear of the unknown, haunts Americans. Change clashes with religious and philosophic beliefs. Change can be disruptive as well as positive. Progress is mixed with insecurity.

The sexual revolution was the most powerful engine of change. Sex was a relatively private affair in the 1890s, but it and its public face, sexuality, has been liberated like a genie from a long-corked bottle. Today, sexuality saturates society, and the genie has brought self-destruction and pleasure. Avoiding the first will always be a challenge because sexual adventure is so stimulating that it can become obsessive. Perhaps the most significant question the sexual revolution poses is how it will alter the nuclear family, long the glue of American society. Some ask, when will it end? It won't end.

Racial issues, too, spanned the twentieth and twenty-first centuries, bearing out W.E.B. Du Bois's prediction at the start of the 1900s that the color line would be the critical question of the century. The legacy of slavery reached everywhere in America, tugged at the country's emotions, gratified the nation with major strides in civil rights, and disappointed those who believed the land of equality gleamed over the next hill. In part, trouble has persisted because minorities and white Americans differ over methods and goals. In this and other areas, it might be profitable to move on, to apply new ideas, and to let time heal. To wallow in guilt or self-pity is self-destructive. Mutual respect, not comfort, status, or a gilt-edged education, is what we have to offer. This is not a minority issue; it is a human issue.

One of the most persistent, if neglected, themes in the Time of Paradox is the unrelenting expansion and diversification of spiritual individualism, which commentators frequently overlook. The hardiness of fundamentalism should not surprise us; it is as solid as Plymouth Rock. In hamlets such as Herbert Hoover's West Branch, Iowa; Franklin D. Roosevelt's Hyde Park, New York; Dwight Eisenhower's Denison, Texas; Jimmy Carter's Plains, Georgia; Ronald Reagan's Dixon, Illinois; and Bill

Clinton's Hope, Arkansas, where the meek gather to inherit the earth and to send men to the White House, local residents find it curious that city dwellers consider religion irrelevant. Across the United States, in religious institutions, classrooms, and laboratories, theology, and philosophy join or jostle with physics, biology, astronomy, and medicine to resolve the nature and meaning of life.

The relationship people had with the technology they created was noteworthy for its ambivalence. For all the ways in which technology has improved life, it has not been an unqualified blessing, having ended jobs as well as created them, having caused pollution as well as cleaned the environment, and having increased stress while alleviating physical labor. Early in the twenty-first century, technology promised to make possible such a variety of entertainment and communications equipment that a user need never leave one's home—and that was the problem. People might become wedded more to machines than to each other, addicted to computer and television screens, unwilling to venture into the world unless it comes to them. Television invaded politics. Focus groups and polling told candidates what the people wanted to hear so candidates could tell it back to them. Electronic campaigning produced a more polished class of rascals.

Machines replaced people, not only in factories, but also in human spontaneity. People became annoyed when they called a business or a government office and could only talk to machines. If one is sitting at home typing a history book, the telephone rings, and the first three words are "Don't hang up": my advice is to hang up. Civility and service have declined, whether in huge grocery markets where there is no help to find food, or in clothing emporiums where two clerks are expected to patrol acres of merchandise. Once I rushed into the emergency room of a hospital run by my health maintenance organization, bleeding from glass cuts to my hands and arms, only to hear the receptionist ask, "Do you have an appointment?"

Most pernicious, technology such as nuclear, chemical, and biological weapons has made killing easier. Humans, countries, and religious sects—sometimes driven to eliminate enemies, even if that means dying alongside them—use sophisticated arms, making it difficult to deter desperate terrorists. Groups lacking large armies can inflict enormous casualties and property damage on powerful nations. Whether peace prevails on earth is a dubious proposition: based on humanity's record, improbable. People compete with each other for the sake of happiness, overlooking the endless energy of love. Some feel guilty so long as there is one starving child on the planet. Others consider material necessities the essence of happiness, and believe only government can provide them. Governments might provide physical sustenance—though never enough to meet demand, and only by taking it from someone else; they cannot provide spiritual nourishment or character. It is quite natural for everyone to demand more and more, but ultimately only individuals can achieve their goals and take pride in their achievements.

In the Time of Paradox Americans did not learn to live in love, secure world peace, ensure equality, cure cancer, or build gleaming white cities emulating the one at the 1893 World's Columbian Exposition in Chicago. Often they struggled to catch up with what they demanded of themselves. Tempered by humility, however, they could still conclude that most of their history contains more cause for pride than for shame. Many of the troubles the United States faced were problems that no society has ever solved. Human experience is bittersweet, oscillating between progress and peril, unable to reach the former without encountering the latter. At least it could be said that for most of the Time of Paradox, the nation endured, a little stronger, a little wiser, increasingly able to accept its imperfections. The United States reacted to crises courageously and often, but not always, wisely.

Americans need not despair over the legacy of the twentieth century or anguish over the portents of the twenty-first. Most societies improve as they evolve, and life in America will improve to some degree. The twenty-first century can be expected to bring vast scientific changes to cleanse the earth of disease, explore the universe and the human mind, and make possible quantum leaps in genetic engineering. With access to bountiful resources and a democratic tradition, people will find opportunities to open the door to self-actualization and purpose, enlightenment that will require effort and will reap great rewards. They can hope that their society is one in which dreams are realized but not given away, one that provides both a temporary respite from the world and a transition to it. They will continue to validate the entirety of Shakespeare's observation that "Some are born great; some achieve greatness; and some have greatness thrust upon 'em." Their country remains a source of inspiration to the rest of the world, not because its people are flawless, but because they are generous and humane. Answering the question that Benjamin Franklin posed more than two hundred years before, Americans could say that their democracy appeared to be a noonday sun.

Index

About the Author

GLEN JEANSONNE has taught twentieth-century American history at the University of Louisiana–Lafayette, Williams College, and the University of Wisconsin–Milwaukee. *A Time of Paradox* is his ninth book, which include *Leander Perez* (1977), *Gerald L. K. Smith* (1988), *Huey Long* (1993), *Transformation and Reaction* (1994), and *Women of the Far Right* (1997). Jeansonne received his B.A. in history from the University of Louisiana–Lafayette, where he graduated salutatorian in 1968, and his Ph.D. from Florida State University in 1973.

DAVID LUHRSSEN has lectured at Marquette University, Beloit College, and the Milwaukee Institute of Art and Design. He has written extensively on music, film, and culture.